Selected Readings on Information Technology and Business Systems Management

In Lee
Western Illinois University, USA

Information Science REFERENCE

INFORMATION SCIENCE REFERENCE
Hershey · New York

Director of Editorial Content: Kristin Klinger
Senior Managing Editor: Jennifer Neidig
Managing Editor: Jamie Snavely
Assistant Managing Editor: Carole Coulson
Typesetter: Michael Brehm
Cover Design: Lisa Tosheff
Printed at: Yurchak Printing Inc.

Published in the United States of America by
Information Science Reference (an imprint of IGI Global)
701 E. Chocolate Avenue, Suite 200
Hershey PA 17033
Tel: 717-533-8845
Fax: 717-533-8661
E-mail: cust@igi-global.com
Web site: http://www.igi-global.com

and in the United Kingdom by
Information Science Reference (an imprint of IGI Global)
3 Henrietta Street
Covent Garden
London WC2E 8LU
Tel: 44 20 7240 0856
Fax: 44 20 7379 0609
Web site: http://www.eurospanbookstore.com

Library of Congress Cataloging-in-Publication Data

Selected readings on information technology and business systems management / In Lee, editor.
p. cm.
Summary: "This book presents quality articles focused on key issues concerning technology in business"--Provided by publisher.
Includes bibliographical references and index.
ISBN 978-1-60566-086-8 (hbk.) -- ISBN 978-1-60566-087-5 (ebook)
1. Information technology--Management. 2. Management information systems. I. Lee, I. (In)
HD30.2.S454 2009
658.4'038--dc22

2008019466

British Cataloguing in Publication Data
A Cataloguing in Publication record for this book is available from the British Library.

Table of Contents

Detailed Table of Contents

The fundamental advantages of information technology in regard to efficiency and effectiveness assure that its diffusion in society and in most industries will continue. The constant and rapid development of Internet-related technologies in the accompanying net economy has inevitably had a significant influence on various possibilities for developing innovative online business concepts and realizing these by establishing entrepreneurial ventures. The term "e-entrepreneurship" respectively describes the act of founding new companies that generate revenue and profits independent from a physical value chain. With this in mind, this chapter focuses on the process of creating electronic customer value within the net economy as well as the success factors and development phases of electronic ventures.

This chapter provides an analysis of the role of government in e-business adoption with empirical evidence from Australia. It is shown that government influence is multifaceted. Governments champion e-business adoption for national economic gain; they provide the physical network on which much of e-business depends and increasingly provide e-government services to improve regulation and compliance effectiveness. E-government in particular can act as a strong driver of organizational adoption for some types of e-business processes. The authors hope that further research by IS professionals will guide future e-business project directions by improving the understanding of government's role in e-business adoption in practice, which in turn will improve theoretical understanding of how the benefits can best be maximized.

This chapter discusses the importance of business process simulation, illustrating the relationship between business process reengineering (BPR) and change management and focusing on both the role of simulation in supporting BPR and the effect of simulation on business environment related skills, business management related skills, leadership related skills, employees empowering level, process improvement, ethical issues, and stakeholders' management skills. This selection also discusses the value of simulation in implementing reengineering strategies, presents future challenges of business process simulation, and describes the limitations of simulation technology in reengineering business processes. Finally, it concludes with a discussion of the characteristics of successful simulation and simulation applications.

In front of traditional interpretations of the digital gap based on endogenous conditions of the firms, this chapter intends to emphasize the importance that some external pressures may have on the e-business strategy of small and medium enterprises (SMEs). The environmental factors analyzed here are market position, competitive intensity, and institutional pressures. SMEs have been grouped according to their level of e-business involvement, in relation to the number of e-business solutions adopted so far. A general conclusion is that different models seem to explain exclusion and involvement. Specifically, two factors among those analyzed reveal to be more suitable in explaining e-business exclusion. They are the size of a SME and a lack of institutional pressures to adopt. On the other hand, e-business involvement seems to be primarily prompted by a selective competitive environment and not by imitative behaviors, as in the previous case.

This chapter describes the architecture development process in an international ICT company, which is building a comprehensive e-business system for its customers. The implementation includes the integration of data and legacy systems from independent business units and the construction of a uniform Web-based customer interface. Research focuses on the creation of e-business architecture and observes that instead of guided by a prescribed method, the architecture emerges through somewhat non-deliberate actions obliged by the situation and its constraints, conflicts, compromises, and political decisions. Conclusions are drawn from the observations and possibilities and weaknesses of the support that UML and RUP provide for the process are pointed out.

This chapter presents the case study of the Nazar Group of Companies, which has been a leading producer and distributor of cookies, crackers, cakes, chocolate, and other products in Turkey for more than 40 years. This case describes the impact this group's management had in making the companies more consumer-focused using supply chain management as a strategic framework. Descriptions of supporting business systems are summarized and the challenges and problems facing managers are presented.

A critical success factor for information systems is their ability to evolve as their environment changes. There is compelling evidence that the management of change in business policy can have a profound effect on an information system's ability to evolve effectively and efficiently. For this to be successful, there is a need to represent business rules from the early requirements stage, expressed in user-understandable terms, to downstream system design components and maintain these throughout the lifecycle of the system. The BROOD approach, discussed in this chapter, aims to provide seamless traceability between requirements and system designs through the modeling of business rules and the successive transformations, using UML as the modeling framework.

This chapter describes a best practice model for standardization within companies, based on a process approach to the development of company standards. Per process, a best practice is developed based on an investigation within six multinational companies and a review of literature, if any. The findings are benchmarked against experiences in three comparable fields: IT management, quality management, and knowledge management. Though the number of company standards exceeds by far the number of external standards, they have been neglected in standardization research. The authors hope that standards practitioners will benefit from their study and that it will stimulate researchers to pay more attention to this topic.

Section III
Tools and Technologies

This chapter explains the best practice in implementing e-business technologies to achieve business cost reduction and business agility. Although the benefits of implementing e-business technologies are clear, enterprises struggle in integrating e-business technologies into supply-chain operations. Within this selection, the author illustrates the strategic and operational impact of e-business technologies on supply chains and explains the performance benefits and challenges firms should expect in implementing these technologies. Also, the author provides the best-practice framework in leveraging e-business applications to support process improvements in order to eliminate non-value-added activities and provide real-time visibility and velocity for the supply chain. Finally, this chapter presents the future trends of using e-business in transformation programs.

Business process management systems such as the workflow management system and the enterprise application integration system manage process flow on a minute-by-minute basis in various application domains. In the conventional approach, the business process must be predefined before it is implemented. However, involving business users in the early stage of the design phase is neither efficient nor realistic in the dynamic business world. This chapter proposes a framework to implement a dynamic business process in the P2P Semantic Web, which provides the flexibility to dynamically alter business process and to take semantic data into consideration.

Agents are rapidly emerging as a new paradigm for developing software applications. They are being used in an increasing variety of applications, ranging from relatively small systems such as assistants to large, open, mission-critical systems like electronic marketplaces. One of the most promising areas of applications for agent technology is e-business. This chapter describes a group of architectural patterns for agent-based e-business systems. These patterns relate to front-end e-business activities that involve interaction with the user, and delegation of user tasks to agents. Patterns capture well-proven, common solutions, and guide developers through the process of designing systems. This chapter should be of interest to designers of e-business systems using agent technology. The description of the patterns is followed by the case study of an online auction system to which the patterns have been applied.

Consumer decision support systems (CDSSs) help online users make purchasing decisions in e-commerce Web sites. To more effectively compare the usefulness of the various functionalities and interface features of such systems, the authors of this chapter have developed a simulation environment for decision tasks of any scale and structure. A set of experiments carried out in such simulation environments showed that most CDSSs employed in current e-commerce Web sites are suboptimal. On the other hand, a hybrid decision strategy based on four existing ones was found to be more effective. This result is consistent with earlier findings in that some advanced tools do produce more accurate decisions while requiring a comparable amount of user effort. However, the simulation environment will enable the efficient comparison of more advanced tools, and indicate further opportunities for functionality and interface improvements.

E-business processes are implemented through existing, as well as novel technologies. This chapter focuses on the field of electronic markets (e-markets), and studies the technologies and solutions that are applied and proposed in this field. In particular, the chapter reviews e-market literature in order to identify which are the technological trends that have appeared in the e-markets field during the last decade. A conceptual model that allows for the classification of e-market research literature according to a number of technical topics is first introduced. Then, e-market literature is reviewed, and the technologies that seem to be attracting more research attention are identified. Representative contributions are discussed, and directions for future research are indicated.

Section IV
Utilization and Application

Though Web services offer unique opportunities for the design of new business processes, the assessment of the potential impact of Web services is often reduced to technical aspects. This chapter proposes a four-phase methodology which facilitates the evaluation of the potential use of Web services in e-business systems both from a technical and from a strategic viewpoint. It is based on business process models, which are used to frame the adoption of Web services and to assess their impact on existing business processes. The application of this methodology is described using a procurement scenario.

This chapter highlights the importance of e-procurement and the barriers affecting its widespread adoption in the context of small and medium enterprises. The chapter takes a technical perspective and critically analyzes the importance of information systems in the procurement domain and the integration challenges faced by SMEs in today's digitally networked economy. Next, the role of XML-based Web services in solving the integration challenges faced by SMEs is discussed. Subsequently, a procurement transformation framework enabled by Web services which provides a clear methodology of the way in which information systems should be introduced in the procurement domain is discussed. The chapter concludes by a discussion of the measures that must be undertaken by various stakeholders like the government and universities in increasing the awareness levels of SMEs to the latest e-business mechanisms.

The lack of anticipated engagement in e-business by Small and Medium sized Enterprises (SMEs) is a rising concern to the UK government and service providers alike. This chapter uses the e-adoption model to examine the current practice of e-business technology adoption in SMEs and the driving forces for and against the adoption. Through interviews with 40 owner managers in the electronic components industry, the chapter reveals that most of the small firms in this industry are at the lower level of the "e-adoption ladder"—predominantly using the Internet and e-mail. The e-adoption ladder model is modified by incorporating the influential factors identified within this study. The findings have many implications for researchers, service providers, and policy makers.

Small businesses need Internet service to be competitive, and their spending on IT activities continues to grow. How can Internet Service Providers tap into this potentially lucrative market? This chapter attempts to identify Internet service features that are important to small businesses. Specifically, it used a survey method to explore the relationships between the importance of various features and organizational characteristics of small businesses, for example, size and type of business. The results show that the size of business affects the perceived importance placed on certain features, while the type of business does not. Implication of this finding for packaging Internet service is discussed.

large developing countries, China and India, in an attempt to understand their approaches to developing e-business. These approaches are based on a number of factors, including government initiatives and focus, infrastructure building, experience and understanding of business operations, and culture. China appears to be ahead of India in the mechanics and infrastructure, but India is ahead in e-readiness. While both countries are poised for rapidly increasing e-business, poverty and inequality between urban and rural connectivity must be resolved to really take advantage of e-business.

This chapter identifies various levels of governance followed by a focus on the role of information technology (IT) governance with reference to information security for today's electronic business (e-business) environment. It outlines levels of enterprise, corporate, and business governance in relation to IT governance before integrating the latter with e-business security management. The emergence of and dependence on new technologies, like the Internet, have increased exposure of businesses to technology-originated threats and have created new requirements for security management and governance. The proposed model achieves the necessary integration through risk management in which the tensions between threat reduction and value generation activities have to be balanced

This chapter develops a security blueprint for an e-business environment taking advantage of the three-tiered e-business architecture. This security blueprint suggests best practices in general. It involves (1) security control by layers — from physical access, to network communication, to operating systems, to applications, and (2) different stages of the management process, including planning, deployment, administration, and auditing. Also reported is a case study of the implementation of the proposed security blueprint in a Singapore multinational corporation. Such issues as security control analysis, management process analysis, and cost-benefits analysis are discussed in detail.

The emergence of e-business as a viable business model is unquestioned and global in its involvement and impact. Further, the value that intellectual property (IP) in the form of trademarks, copyrights, and patents plays in that medium of doing business impacts businesses, information technology (IT) profes-

Prologue

ABSTRACT

As attention to IT increases and society becomes more knowledge intensive, IT valuation will become a subject of great focus. New IT emerges rapidly as technological, societal, and competitive pressures push firms to transform and innovate themselves. New IT will shape our daily lives, jobs and firm structure, inter-firm relationships, and the industry in different ways from what it has been so far. Because of the potential benefits and costs created by IT, firms need to carefully assess every IT opportunity and threat to ensure that their resources are spent judiciously. This paper reviews the existing IT value research from IT justification, IT valuation, and business process perspectives. This paper also provides a basis for enhancing our understanding of IT value creation and measurement, and maximizing the value of IT-based business systems. A future research direction is also discussed.

INTRODUCTION

Increased competition, customer-centered market, and IT advances have rapidly changed the ways firms operate their businesses. These changes have driven firms to cut costs, enhance product/service quality, and redesign their business processes. Knowledge-intensive business organizations are utilizing IT to create new knowledge, store knowledge, share information, and facilitate inter- and intra-organizational collaboration. The timing and magnitude of new technology adoption and process redesign have become more critical than before as most firms strive to gain and sustain their competitive advantage.

In the past decade, e-commerce has revolutionized our society. E-commerce has created highly competitive market environments across all industries and contributed to the emergence of new business models and the demise of old business models. E-commerce pushed traditional firms to integrate e-commerce into the existing business models and to tightly digitize business processes. Leading click and mortar companies have tightly integrated front-end online order process systems with back-end support systems to minimize the discontinuity in the order fulfillment process. According to Jupiter Research (2006), the U.S. residents will increase their online spending for retail products and services at a 12% annual average through the end of 2010. Americans bought goods and services worth $81 billion from online retailers in 2005, and the online sales are expected to reach $144 billion in 2010.

Business systems management is a process of identifying IT, developing information systems, and managing information systems infrastructure to achieve business objectives. In this era of e-commerce and digital economy, business systems get more attention from senior management as a potential weapon for their sustainability and competitive advantage. As the business environment gets more dynamic, complex, and competitive, senior managers scrutinize the resource productivity more closely, and IT managers often compete with other functional managers to secure the required IT budget. As IT advances continue to open new opportunities and challenges for firms, the fundamental questions for IT managers to answer are whether IT can create a value that will justify its investment, and how the IT value can be measured.

Despite preponderant interests from industries, IT valuation methods have not been fully established, and measuring IT value has been elusive for IT researchers and managers. Traditionally, accounting and financial methods have been widely used to assess the value of projects. Return on investment, net present value, and payback period methods are classic in accounting and financial literature. However, the traditional accounting and financial methods have played a limited role in justifying the IT investment opportunities, because many of its benefits are non-quantifiable. Therefore, most studies have investigated ways of justifying and measuring IT business value beyond financial benefits (Lee, 2004).

In the early 90s, because of intensive global competition and a decline in the US industry's competitiveness, business process reengineering (BPR) drew manager's attention as a potential breakthrough for achieving competitiveness. The benefits obtained from BPR often cited in the literature include faster cycle time, reduced resource waste, improved productivity, enhanced customer service, and heightened competitive advantage.

Many studies reported that in managing business systems, BPR is one area where business strategy and IT have played a crucial role in generating potential value (Broadbent et al, 1999; Davenport, 1993; Hammer, 1990 & 2000; Ray et al., 2004). Some firms have reported significant productivity gains by integrating IT into their core business processes. Among successful examples of IT integration with BPR are Wal-Mart just-in-time inventory control systems with EDI and satellite network systems, Pfizer's web-based new product document management systems, Frito Lay's purchasing management systems with handheld scanning devices, and Dell Computer's supply chain management systems with web-based technologies. BPR has been further facilitated with ERP, CRM, and e-commerce applications (Ho, et al., 2004; Kotorov, 2003).

In light of the ongoing debate on the measurement methods and tools for IT valuation, this study will give an overview of existing studies and present a future direction for researchers and practitioners. Our paper proceeds with a literature review in Section 2 and a future direction for IT valuation and BPR research in Section 3.

LITERATURE REVIEW

Forrester research (Bartels, 2004) predicted that spending on IT goods, services, and staff will grow 7% in 2005 and continue at a similar pace through 2008, which is slightly faster than overall economic growth. According to IDC (2007), worldwide end users spent $1.16 trillion on IT in 2006 and will increase IT spending at a compound annual growth rate (CAGR) of 6.3% to reach $1.48 trillion in 2010. These statistics suggest that IT has become one of the most important cost drivers in business operations, thus IT investment deserves special attention from management. Large and small, many businesses have agreed that they should capitalize on business opportunities through the deployment of new IT such as e-business and m-commerce applications. On the other hand, another recent survey has sent alarming signals to IT professionals and researchers of a declining annual IT investment growth rate and a rapidly declining confidence of senior management in IT value (Martin, 2007).

The main purpose of IT value research is to develop theories and measurement tools that will help managers apply knowledge gained from the research to make an investment decision and to enhance the IT value. The term 'IT business value' is commonly used to measure the organizational performance of IT, which includes cycle time reduction, productivity improvement, profitability improvement, cost reduction, customer surplus, competitive advantage, sustained competitive advantage, inventory reduction, market share, and other metrics of performance (Hitt and Brynjolfsson 1996; Mata, et al., 1995; Melville et al., 2004).

Definition of IT

Information Technology Association of America (ITAA) defined IT as "the study, design, development, implementation, support or management of computer-based information systems, particularly software applications and computer hardware (wikipedia, 2008)." Researchers in information systems area have developed diverse views of IT, extending a widely accepted view of IT which includes hardware, software, supporting services, and infrastructure that are used to store, convert, process, retrieve, and securely transmit data and information. Observing that IT researchers have not engaged deeply in IT studies, Orlikowski and Iacono (2001) presented five conceptualizations of IT as a base for future theoretical research: (1) tool view, (2) proxy view, (3) ensemble view, (4) computational view, and (5) nominal view. The tool view regards IT as an engineered tool that does what its designers intended such as labor substitution, productivity, information processing, and social relations tools. In the proxy view, IT is conceptualized by one or a few key elements in common that are understood to represent the essential aspects or properties of IT which can be captured by individual perceptions of its usefulness or value, the diffusion rates, or dollars spent. The ensemble view focuses on the interaction of people and technology in both the development and use of IT. The research concerning this view regards IT as development project, development network, embedded systems, and structure. The computational view concentrates on the computational power of the IT and focuses on algorithm and systems development and testing as well as modeling and simulation. Finally, the nominal view invokes IT in name but not in fact. Examples of the nominal view include computer security and outsourcing practices. Understanding how IT has been conceptualized provides a firm foundation of IT business value research. The definition of IT sets the scope and granularity of IT valuation. IT value has been measured at different levels: individual, process, business unit, firm, network of firms, industry, and economy. Depending on the purpose and level of analysis, different metrics of IT value have been developed. In the following, two major IT valuation approaches are discussed: *ex ante IT justification* and *ex post IT valuation.*

IT Valuation: Ex Ante IT Justification Methods

While most studies have focused on the ex post evaluation of IT value, a number of studies have focused on ex ante IT project justification methods and specialized tools that can be used to predict and analyze IT investment benefits and costs. Most IT justification studies pointed out the limitations of traditional capital budgeting methods in measuring the true value of IT (Clemons, 1991; Kumar, 2004). Consequently, many IT investments are based upon "gut feelings" or "intuition," rather than quantifiable criteria (Dos Santos, 1991). However, given the financial impacts of IT investments and tight budgetary constraints, it is essential for IT managers to clearly understand whether their investments are financially justifiable, and likely to yield sufficient benefits or fail.

To investigate how organizations make IT investment decisions and how they should, Bacon (1992) conducted a survey of 80 major companies in four countries: the United States, Britain, Australia, and

New Zealand. He found that discounted cash flow (DCF) methods are the most widely used investment criteria for IT projects. The survey findings indicate that there exists a need to close a gap between practice and research, since many researchers do not recommend DCF methods, but practitioners prefer to use them most.

On the other hand, a recent study of 130 senior executives from large companies that spend an average of $230 million annually revealed a strikingly different picture of IT investment practices from the above-mentioned Bacon's study. This study reported that 51% of respondents have no process to evaluate IT investments against business strategy; 68% do not compare their IT projects' benefits to original targets; 74% do not track financial metrics after making an investment decision; and 80% lack the necessary financial skills (Chabrow, 2003). The lack of necessary measurement and analysis skills by the senior executives potentially leads to misalignment of IT and business strategies, over- or under-investment, inopportune investment, and eventually the lowered profit and productivity and decreased IT investments. The implications of this survey results are significant as the executives are the ultimate sponsor and champion of IT projects. In light of the significant lack of IT valuation knowledge by the senior executives, IT researchers and professionals urgently need to develop an education program to deliver executives the needed knowledge and skill sets.

Clemons (1991) suggested that managers take into account such factors as tangible and intangible benefits and costs of undertaking the program, the risks of proceeding with the program, expected competitive impact, and possible partnership with competitors. Business functions finance the IT projects, and the involvement of the relevant business functions in translating non-quantifiable benefits into monetary value was suggested by Tiernan and Peppard (2004). In addition to the above-mentioned IT justification approaches, more theoretical approaches based on option theory, game theory, and network effect have been proposed to gain insights into the elusive nature of the IT benefits.

Research on option theory-based investment emphasizes that companies must decide how to exploit various investment opportunities most effectively (Bardhan et al., 2004; Dixit and Pindyck, 1995; Dos Santos, 1991). These studies suggested that a company with an opportunity for project investment is holding something similar to a financial option: the company has the right, but not the obligation, to buy an asset before or at a future time of its choosing. The studies contended that the experience gained from initial investments could prove to be extremely valuable in the follow-on investments into other projects. However, appropriate option-based IT investment decisions require accurate estimation of key parameters, such as project risk and time to invest, which are still the most elusive part of the option theory.

Game theory has been also applied to capture behaviors mathematically in IT investment decisions, where an organization's success in making IT investments depends on the choices of others. Zhu and Weyant (2003) applied game theory to understand interdependencies of IT investment decisions among competing companies. They found decision dynamics more complicated, yet more interesting, when information asymmetry exists between firms. They also demonstrated that information asymmetry leads to different incentives and strategic behaviors in the IT adoption game.

Network effect suggests that as the number of IT adopters/organizations in a network gets larger, benefits to the network participation increase. Network effect becomes significant after a certain critical mass is achieved as shown in social networking. The side-effects such as utility and benefits arising from network effect are known as network externalities. Kauffman et al. (2000) suggested that due to the network effect, a company's technology adoption justification was influenced by the expected size of the shared network. Au and Kauffman (2003) showed the importance of expectations, as well as the network effect, on an IT investment decision.

A wide range of other IT pre-investment justification methodologies have been developed by researchers and practitioners including: index and ranking methods (Sethi et al., 1993), business process simulation

(Lee, 2004), analytical hierarchical process (AHP) (Goh, 1997), balanced scorecard (Kaplan and Norton, 1992), IT portfolio management (Bardhan et al., 2004; Jeffery and Leliveld, 2004), business case (Ross and Breath, 2002), technology road-mapping (Groenveld, 1997), Activity Based Costing method (Peacock and Tanniru, 2005), and total value of ownership (Luftman and Muller, 2005). The challenge for IT managers is that the success of the translation of non-quantifiable benefits into financial metrics often depends on the choice of justification methods and the validity of the assumptions made.

IT Valuation: Ex Post IT Valuation Methods

While ex ante IT justification studies suggested methodologies to predict IT value before investment occurs, most IT value research has focused on the ex post IT valuation theory building based on empirical data analysis. However, empirical studies show mixed results, and point to the measurement difficulties/errors as the sources of the inconsistent results (Brynjolfsson and Hitt, 1996; Floyd and Wooldridge, 1990; Harris and Katz, 1991). Researchers attributed inconclusive results to imprecise data, time lag, and mismeasurements (Barua et al., 1995; Brynjolfsson and Hitt, 1996). Barua and Mukhopadhyay (2000) pointed out that the tasks of obtaining granular data on IT investments, assessing changes in IT functionality, and isolating effects on a value-based variable are barriers to the attribution of IT value. Brynjolfsson and Hitt (1998) suggested that the value of IT should be measured not only by cost savings, but also by improvements in quality, customer service, and new product development. Other sources of firm productivity include organizational characteristics (Wade and Hulland, 2004), process redesign (Ho, et al., 2004), workplace practices (Bharadwaj, 2000; Black and Lynch, 2001), and environment (Dewan and Kraemer, 2000).

While many studies demonstrated the existence of positive returns on IT investment, their approaches provide limited insights into the value creating process of IT. Realizing the limitation of the traditional output-focused IT value measures, a number of studies focused on the development of IT valuation methods from process-oriented perspectives (Banker et al.1990; Barua et al., 1996; Kohli and Hoadley, 2006). Mooney et al. (1996) argued that a process focus should enhance the validity of the IT value assessment and the ability to explain the technological features, process characteristics, organizational settings, and competitive environments conducive to producing IT business value. Synthesizing previous studies, Melville et al. (2004) defined IT value as the organizational performance impacts of information technology at both the intermediate process level and the organization-wide level which comprises both efficiency impacts and competitive impacts. They suggested that the challenge of understanding IT value creation is addressed by the insights of multiple theoretical paradigms.

Most recently, Kohli and Grover (2008) summarized findings of the prior IT value research with seven concise statements: (1) IT does create value; (2) IT creates value under certain conditions; (3) IT-based value manifests itself in many ways; (4) IT-based value is not the same as IT-based competitive advantage; (5) IT-based value could be latent; (6) There are numerous factors mediating IT and value; (7) Causality for IT value is elusive. They further presented four major themes to understand how IT value is changing and what we must do to capture, measure, and demonstrate it: (1) IT-based co-creation of value, (2) IT embeddedness, (3) Information mindset, and (4) Value expansion.

Integration of BPR and IT

BPR is defined as the fundamental rethinking and radical redesign of business processes to achieve dramatic improvements in firm performance. Process is defined as a set of related tasks performed to achieve business objectives. IT enables firms to redesign business processes, strengthen their customer relationship management, integrate business functions, and develop a new business model (Hammer and Champy, 1993).

BPR drew manager's attention as a potential breakthrough for staving off competition and achieving strategic advantage in the early 90s. A recent study shows that about 87% of firms surveyed were either engaged in BPR projects or indicated their intention to embark on BPR projects in the next few years (Ranganathana and Dhaliwal, 2001). Realizing many BPR projects fell short of the expected payoffs, Attaran (2004) identified seven barriers to effective IT-enabled BPR implementations: (1) misunderstanding of the concept; (2) misapplication of the term; (3) lack of proper strategy; (4) unrealistic objectives; (5) management failure to change; (6) failing to recognize the importance of people; (7) IS failure to change.

BPR has received much attention from researchers as well (Davenport, 1993; Davern and Kauffman, 2000; Hammer, 1990; Markus and Benjamin, 1997; Venkatraman, 1994; Whitman, 1996). These researchers have argued that IT and BPR together can create more cost-effective, agile, collaborative, and communicative process capability than BPR or IT alone. Information-intensive business organizations are utilizing IT to create new knowledge, manage existing knowledge, distribute information, and facilitate inter- and intra-organizational collaboration. IT makes it possible to achieve coordination-intensive business processes in a way it was not possible before (Teng et al., 1994).

The performance evaluation of BPR and justification for BPR is a primary concern of senior management. Senior management expects a high payoff from BPR, since it requires significant financial investments, dramatic process change, risk management, and organizational change. IT can fundamentally change the ways in which business organizations interact with internal and external constituents, and therefore IT and BPR integration processes should take external business strategy and internal IT strategy into account. A few case studies attempted to identify metrics organizations use to measure the performance of IT-enabled BPR (Devaraj and Kohli, 2000; Kohli and Hoadley, 2006; Stiroh, 2001). However, drivers and inhibitors of IT integration of BPR have not still been well studied (Grovera et al, 1998) and reengineering projects have shown mixed results (Sarker and Lee, 1999). Thus, there is a need to develop a methodology that measures the degree of BPR and IT integration and evaluates the impacts of the integration on business value (Barua et al., 1996; Kohli and Hoadley, 2006).

More recently, BPR crossed the boundaries of the business organization to include suppliers, partners, and customers into the process redesign mix. Champy (2002) calls this approach X-engineering. Companies such as Cisco, Dell, Intel and Solectron are examples of successful X-engineering implementations. This new approach is a natural development as more companies begin to deploy the web-based inter-organization information systems, taking advantage of the web technology standards such as XML, web services, and Internet protocols.

FUTURE DIRECTION OF IT VALUATION RESEARCH

While a larger body of researchers has focused on the measurement issues of IT strategic value or firm-level productivity, senior managers have been consistently interested in the practical IT evaluation methodologies to financially justify IT investment. In time of economic downturns, they tend to be more conservative and risk-averse on IT spending. Recent surveys have sent alarming signals to IT professionals and researchers of a declining annual IT investment growth rate and diminishing roles of IT leaders (Martin, 2007). IT managers frustrated with the marginal benefits attempted to shift the responsibility of proving or securing value from IT investments to the internal business functions. It is time to critically review what we have learned and set a new direction for IT valuation research to turn around the declining IT status in organizations, to regain the confidence of senior management, and to jump-start the sagging IT value creation and productivity.

Our review reveals that a wide range of diverse views have been developing in the IT valuation and BPR studies. The existence of these diverse views strongly suggests that a single view is likely to provide only a limited understanding of how value is created. Most researchers agree that traditional budgeting and project evaluation methods are not enough to justify IT investments because these methods can not properly capture idiosyncratic IT values in novel contexts. Many studies indicate that operational, organizational, and strategic issues should be addressed when IT investments are justified. Since IT may fundamentally change the ways in which the business organization interacts with external constituents, we need to consider extended business processes in the evaluation process as well.

While numerous studies attempted to address the complex problem of linking IT to organizational performance, the absence of a unified theoretical framework has led to a fractured research stream with many simultaneous but non-overlapping studies (Chan, 2000), and there is still a debate on the nature of IT business value and whether IT is capable of creating value (Kohli and Grover, 2008). IT valuation research needs to deepen our understanding of the relationships between IT and value creations in many levels of organizations. Otherwise, the roles of our IT managers will continue to diminish and the significance of IS discipline will decrease further. To understand these relationships, we need to enrich our knowledge on what, when, where, how, and why these values are generated, and how we measure these values. More importantly, our research needs to move beyond the descriptive IT valuation studies to value maximizing IT prescription studies, the outcomes of which should be able to guide our IT professionals to plan on what IT we need to invest; how much we need to invest; when we need to invest; and how we can enhance the values. To do so, we need to develop a unified framework of IT valuation that links business strategies and processes with a multi-perspective valuation model derived from rich grounded theories and rigorous empirical validation.

REFERENCES

Attaran, M. (2004). Exploring the relationship between information technology and business process reengineering. *Information & Management.* 41(5), 585–596.

Au, Y.A., & Kauffman, R.J. (2003). What do you know? Rational expectations in information technology adoption and investment. *Journal of Management Information Systems*. 20(2), 49-76.

Bacon, C.J. (1992). The Use of Decision Criteria in selecting information systems/technology investments, *MIS Quarterly*. 16(3). 335-353.

Banker, R.D., Kauffman, R.J., & Morey, R.C. (1990). Measuring gains in operational efficiency from information technology: A study of the Positran deployment at Hardee's Inc. *Journal of Management Information Systems*, 7(2), 29-54.

Bardhan, I., Bagchi, S., & Sougstad, R. (2004). Prioritizing a portfolio of information technology investment projects. *Journal of Management Information Systems*. 21(2), 33-60.

Bartels, A. (2004). North American IT spending in 2005, *Forrester Research.* Web source:

http://www.forrester.com/Research/Document/Excerpt/0,7211,35137,00.html

Barua, A., Lee, C.H.S., & Whinston, A.B., (1996). The Calculus of Reengineering. *Information Systems Research*. 7(4), 409-428.

Barua, A., Kriebel, C. H., & Mukhopadhyay, T. (1995). Information technologies and business value: An analytic and empirical investigation. *Information Systems Research*, 6(1), 3-23.

Barua, A., & Mukhopadhyay, T. (2000). Information technology and business performance: past, present, and future," in: *Framing the Domains of IT research: Projecting the Future through the Past,* R.W. Zmud (ed.), Pinnaflex Educational Resources, Cincinnati, OH, 65-84.

Bharadwaj, A.S. (2000). A resource-based perspective on information technology capability and firm performance: An empirical investigation, *MIS Quarterly*, 24(1), 169-196.

Black, S.E., & Lynch, L.M. (2001). How to compete: The impact of workplace practices and information technology on productivity. *Review of Economics and Statistics*, 83(3), 434-445.

Broadbent, M., Weill, P., & St. Clair, D. (1999). The implications of information technology infrastructure for business process redesign. *MIS Quarterly*. 23(2), 159 – 182.

Brynjolfsson, E., & Hitt, L. (1996). Paradox lost? Firm-level evidence on the returns to information systems spending. *Management Science*. 42(4), 541-558.

Brynjolfsson, E., & Hitt, L. (1998). Beyond the productivity paradox. *Communications of ACM*. 41(8), 49-55.

Chabrow, E. (2003). IT staffs lack financial chops for project analysis. *InformationWeek*, 932, 20.

Champy J. (2002). *X-Engineering the Corporation: Reinventing Your Business in the Digital Age*, Warner Books, New York, 2002.

Chan, Y.E. (2000). IT Value: The great divide between qualitative and quantitative and individual and organizational measures. *Journal of Management Information Systems*. 16(4), 225-261.

Clemons, E.K. (1991). Evaluation of strategic investments in information technology. *Communications of the ACM*. 34(1), 22-36.

Davenport, T.H., (1993). *Process Innovation: Reengineering Work through Information Technology*, Ernst & Young, Center for Information Technology and Strategy, 1993.

Davern, M. J. and R. J. Kauffman, "Discovering Potential and Realizing Value From Information Technology Investments," *Journal of Management Information Systems*, Spring, 2000, pp. 121-143.

Devaraj, S., & Kohli, R. (2000). IT payoff in the healthcare industry: A longitudinal study. *Journal of Management Information Systems*. 16(4), 39-64.

Dewan, S., & Kraemer, K.L. (2000). Information technology and productivity: Evidence from country-level data, *Management Science*. 46(4), 548-562.

Dixit, A.K., & Pindyck, R.S. (1995). The options approach to capital investment. *Harvard Business Review,* May-June 105-115.

Dos Santos, B.L. (1991). Justifying investments in new information technologies. *Journal of Management Information Systems*, 7(4), 71-90.

Floyd, S.W., & Wooldridge, B. (1990). Path analysis of the relationship between competitive strategy, information technology, and financial performance. *Journal of Management Information Systems*, 7(1), 47-64.

Goh, C.H. (1997). Analytic hierarchy process for robot selection. *Journal of Manufacturing Systems*. 16(5), 381-396.

Groenveld, P. (1997). Roadmapping integrates business and technology. *Research Technology Management*, 40(5), 48-55.

Grover, V., James, T., Segarsb, A.H., & Fiedlera, K. (1998). The influence of information technology diffusion and business process change on perceived productivity: the IS executive's perspective. *Information & Management*. 34(3), 141–159.

Hammer, M., (1990). Reengineering work: Don't automate, obliterate. *Harvard Business Review*. 68(4), 104-122.

Hammer, M., (2000). Reengineering redux. *CIO*, 13(10), 143-156.

Hammer, M, & Champy, J. (1993). *Reengineering the Corporation*, Harper Collins, New York.

Harris, S.E., & Katz, J. L. (1991). Organizational performance and information technology investment intensity in the insurance industry. *Organization Sciences*. 2(3), 263-295.

Hitt L.M., & Brynjolfsson, E. (1996). Productivity, business profitability, and consumer surplus: three different measures of information technology value. *MIS Quarterly*. 20(2), 121-142.

Ho, C.F., Wu, W.H., & Tai, Y.M. (2004). Strategies for the adaptation of ERP systems. *Industrial Management & Data Systems*. 104(3), 234-251.

IDC. (2007). Worldwide spending on information technology will reach $1.48 trillion by 2010, Web source: http://www.idc.com/getdoc.jsp?containerId=prUS20514107

Jeffery, M., & Leliveld, I. (2004). Best practices in IT portfolio management. *MIT Sloan Management Review*. 45(3), 41 – 49.

Jupiter Research. (2007). Jupiter research forecasts online retail spending will reach $144 billion in 2010, a CAGR of 12% from 2005. Web source: http://www.jupitermedia.com/corporate/releases/06.02.06-newjupresearch.html

Kaplan, R., & Norton, D. (1992). The balanced scorecard: measures that drive performance. *Harvard Business Review*. (January/February), 71-79.

Kauffman, R.J., McAndrews, J., & Wang, Y. (2000). Opening the 'black box' of network externalities in network adoption. *Information Systems Research*. 11(1), 61-82.

Kohli, R., & Devaraj, S. (2003). Measuring information technology payoff: A meta-analysis of structural variables in firm-level empirical research. *Information Systems Research*. 14(2), 127-145.

Kohli, R., & Grover, V. (2008). Business value of IT: An essay on expanding research directions to keep up with the times. *Journal of the Association of Information Systems*. 9(1), 23-39,

Kohli, R., &; Hoadley, E. (2006). Towards developing a framework for measuring organizational impact of IT- enabled BPR: case studies of three firms. *ACM SIGMIS Database*. 37(1), 40- 58.

Kotorov R., (2003). Customer relationship management: strategic lessons and future directions. *Business Process Management Journal*, 9(5), 566-571.

Kumar, R.L. (2004). A framework for assessing the business value of information technology infrastructures. *Journal of Management Information Systems*. 21(2), 11-32.

Lee, I., (2004). Evaluating business-process integrated information technology investment. *Business Process Management Journal*. 10(2), 214-233.

Luftman, J., & Muller, H. (2005). Total value of ownership: A mew model. *Optimize*. 4(7), 51-54.

Markus, M.L. and Benjamin. R.I. (1997). The magic bullet theory in IT-enabled transformation. *MIT Sloan Management Review*, 38(2), 55-68.

Martin, R. (2007). The CIO dilemma. *InformationWeek*. 131(1), 38-44.

Mata, F.J., & Fuerst, W.L., &, Barney, J.B. (1995). Information technology and sustained competitive advantage: A resource-based analysis. *MIS Quarterly*. 19(4), 487-505.

Mooney J.G., Gurbaxani, V., & Kraemer, K.L. (1996). A process oriented framework for assessing the business value of information technology. *ACM SIGMIS Database*. 27(2), 68-81.

Mukhopadhyay, T., Kekre, S., & Kalathur, S. (1995). Business value of information technology: A study of Electronic Data Interchange. *MIS Quarterly*, 19(2), 137-156.

Orlikowski, W.J., & Iacono, C.S. (2001). Desperately seeking the 'IT' in IT research. A call to theorizing the IT artifact. *Information Systems Research*, 12(2), 121-134.

Peacock, E. & Tanniru, M. (2005). Activity-based justification of IT investments. *Information & Management*. 42(3), 415 – 424.

Ranganathana, C. & Dhaliwal, J.S., (2001). A survey of business process reengineering practices in Singapore. *Information & Management*. 39 (2), 125–134.

Ray G., Barney, J.B., & Muhanna, W.A. (2004). Capabilities, business processes, and competitive advantage: choosing the dependent variable in empirical tests of the resource-based view. *Strategic Management Journal*. 25(1), 23-37.

Ross, J.W., & Breath, C.M. (2002). Beyond the Business Case: New approaches to IT investment. *MIT Sloan Management Review*, 43(2), 51 –59.

Sarker, S., & Lee, A.S. (1999). IT-enabled organizational transformation: A case study of BPR failure at TELECO. *Journal of Strategic Information Systems*. 8(1), 83-103.

Sethi, V., Hwang, K.T., & Pegels, C. (1993). Information technology and organizational performance: A critical evaluation of Computerworld's index of information systems effectiveness**.** *Information & Management*. 25(4), 193-205.

Stiroh, K.J. (2001). Investing in information technology: Productivity payoffs for U.S. industries. *Current Issues in Economics and Finance*. 7(6), 1-5.

Teng, J., Grover, V., & Fiedler, K.D. (1994). Business process reengineering: Charting a strategic path for the information age. *California Management Review*. 36(3), 9-31.

Tiernan, C., & Peppard, J. (2004). Information technology: Of value or a vulture? *European Management Journal*. 22(6), 609-623.

Venkatraman, N., (2004). IT-enabled business transformation: from automation to business scope redefinition. *Sloan Management Review*, 35(2). 72-87.

Wade, M., & Hulland, J. (2004). Review: The resource-based view and information systems research: Review, extension, and suggestions for future research. *MIS Quarterly*. 28(1), 107-142.

Weill, P. (1992). The Relationship Between investment in information technology and firm performance: A study of the valve manufacturing sector. *Information Systems Research*. 3, (4), 307-331.

Whitman, M.E. (1996). IT divergence in reengineering support: performance expectations vs. perceptions. *Information & Management*. 30 (5), 239–250.

Wikipedia. (2008). Information Technology. Web source: http://en.wikipedia.org/wiki/Information_technology

Zhu, K., & Weyant, J.P. (2003). Strategic decisions of new technology adoption under asymmetric information: A game-theoretic model. *Decision Sciences*. 34(4), 643-675.

About the Editor

In Lee is an associate professor in the Department of Information Systems and Decision Sciences in the College of Business and Technology at Western Illinois University. He received his PhD from University of Illinois at Urbana-Champaign. He is a founding editor-in-chief of the *International Journal of E-Business Research*. He has published his research in such journals as *Communications of the ACM*, *IEEE Transactions on Systems, Man, and Cybernetics*, *IEEE Transactions on Engineering Management*, *International Journal of Production Research*, *Computers and Operations Research*, *Computers and Industrial Engineering*, *Knowledge and Process Management*, *Business Process Management Journal*, *Journal of E-Commerce in Organizations*, and *International Journal of Simulation and Process Modeling*. His current research interests include e-commerce technology development and management, investment strategies for computing technologies, and telecommunications planning and management.

Section I
Fundamental Concepts and Theories

Chapter I
E-Entrepreneurship: The Principles of Founding Electronic Ventures

Tobias Kollmann
University of Duisburg-Essen, Germany

ABSTRACT

The fundamental advantages of information technology in regard to efficiency and effectiveness assure that its diffusion in society and in most industries will continue. The constant and rapid development of Internet-related technologies in the accompanying net economy has inevitably had a significant influence on various possibilities for developing innovative online business concepts and realizing these by establishing entrepreneurial ventures. The term "e-entrepreneurship" respectively describes the act of founding new companies that generate revenue and profits independent from a physical value chain. With this in mind, this article focuses on the process of creating electronic customer value within the net economy as well as the success factors and development phases of electronic ventures. Elaborating on these points should help to clearly define the area of e-entrepreneurship and provide evidence that the establishment of electronic ventures is worthy of special consideration in the context of research on information technology entrepreneurship.

INTRODUCTION

With the dawn of the Internet in the last decade of the twentieth century, a structural change in both social and economic spheres was induced. Information technology has become an integral part of daily life and its influence on the transfer of information has become ubiquitous. The fundamental advantages of Internet-related technologies, especially in regard to their efficiency and effectiveness, assure that its diffusion in society and in most industries will continue. Above all, Internet-related technologies have produced new possibilities with respect to how enterprises create value for their customers. By offering physical and digital products and services via the World Wide Web, customer value may no longer be created on a physical level only, but also on an electronic level (Amit & Zott, 2001; Lumpkin & Dess, 2004; Weiber & Kollmann, 1998). In fact, an entirely new business dimension, which may be referred to as the net economy has emerged (Kollmann, 2006; Matlay, 2004). This has inevitably had a significant influence on various possibilities for developing innovative business concepts and realizing these by establishing entrepreneurial ventures that generate revenue and profits independent from a physical value chain. In this context, the term "e-entrepreneurship" describes the act of founding new companies specifically in the net economy. The expansion of the classical use of the term "entrepreneurship," however, raises several questions that will be answered in this chapter. In particular, the chapter will give answers to the following questions:

1. Which possibilities for innovative entrepreneurial activities does the net economy offer to create an electronic customer value?
2. What are the success factors for founding a company in the net economy?
3. What are the typical development phases that an electronic venture will undergo during its initial years of business?

This chapter will elaborate on these points in order to clearly define the area of e-entrepreneurship. Moreover, proof should be provided that the establishment of electronic ventures is worthy of special consideration in the context of research on information technology entrepreneurship.

BACKGROUND: THE NET ECONOMY

From a historical perspective, only the product characteristics (quality) and corresponding product conditions (e.g., price, discount) determined the success of a product (Kirzner, 1973; Porter, 1985). At that time, it was important to either offer products or services to the customer that were cheaper (cost leadership) or qualitatively superior (quality leadership) to the competitor's product. Later in history, speed and flexibility as two additional competitive factors joined the scene (Meyer, 2001; Stalk, 1988). On the one hand, it became increasingly important to offer products or services at a certain point in time at a certain place (availability leadership), while on the other hand, it became crucial to allow for customer-oriented product differentiation of important product characteristics (demand leadership).

Though these traditional competitive factors and the resulting strategies are still valid, one of the central characteristics of the post-industrial computer society is the systematic use of information technology as well as the acquisition and application of information that complements work-life and capital as an exclusive source of value, production, and profit. Consequently, the source of a competitive advantage will be rather determined by achieving knowledge and information superiority over competitors (information leadership). Those who possess better information about the market, potential customers, and customer expectations will be more successful than others. Whereas information previously held merely a supporting function for physical production processes, it has now become an independent factor for production and competitiveness in many industries (Porter & Millar, 1985; Weiber et al., 1998).

The growing relevance of electronic data networks such as the Internet has created a new business dimension. It is especially influenced by the area of electronic business processes that are concluded over digital data pathways (King, Lee, Warkentin, & Chung, 2002; Kollmann, 2001; Taylor & Murphy, 2004; Zwass, 2003). Due to the importance of information as a supporting and independent competitive factor, as well as the increase in digital data networks, it must be assumed that there will be two relevant trade levels on which the world will do business in the future. In addition to the level of real, physical products and services (real economy), an electronic trade level for digital products and services (net economy) is evolving. "The net economy refers to the commercial use of electronic data networks, that is to say, a digital network economy, which, via various electronic platforms, allows the conclusion of information, communication, and transaction processes" (Kollmann, 2006, p. 326).

The value chain of the real economy (Porter, 1985) divides a company into strategically relevant activities and identifies value activities that can be differentiated physically and technologically. The customer is prepared to pay for a valuable product that is based on these value activities. This product can then form the basis for establishing an enterprise in the real economy. In this model, the individual steps of a sequence of value generating or value increasing activities are analyzed in order to efficiently and effectively develop primary processes (for instance, in the areas of incoming logistics, operations, and outgoing logistics) and supporting processes (for instance, in the areas of technology development and procurement). Even here, information is extremely important when striving to be more successful than the competition. Information can be used to improve analysis and monitoring of existing processes. The crucial point is that information has previously been regarded as a supporting element only, but not as an independent source of customer value.

With the establishment of the net economy and the newly created dimension of information as an independent source of competitive advantage, value can be created through electronic business activities in digital data networks independent from a physical value chain as they are predominantly performed by the underlying information systems and do not include physical production machinery or personnel (Amit et al., 2001; Lumpkin et al., 2004; Weiber et al., 1998). These electronic value added activities are thus not comparable to the physical value creation activities presented by Porter (1985), as they are rather characterized by the way information is used. Such value activities might include, for example, the collection, systemization, selection, combination, and distribution of information. Through these specific activities of creating value

Figure 1. Value chain of the real economy vs. value chain of the net economy (Kollmann, 2006, p. 327)

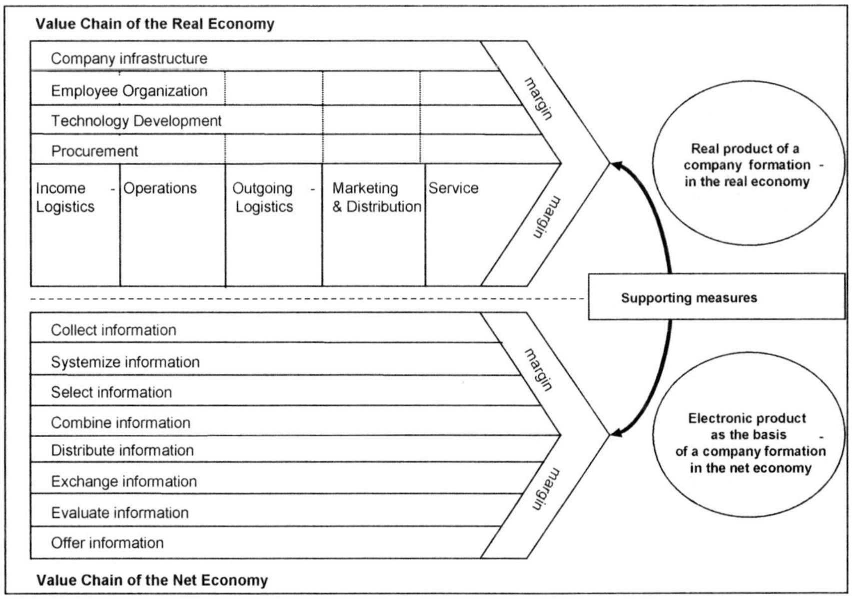

within digital data networks, an electronic value chain manifests itself (Figure 1). Based on this new value creation level, innovative business ideas evolve through the use of the various platforms and new digital products and Internet-based services are created. As customers are willing to pay for the value created by such an electronic product, it can form the basis for founding an electronic venture (e-venture) in the net economy (Kollmann, 2006).

FOUNDING ELECTRONIC VENTURES

In addition to having an electronic product when establishing an e-venture, it is also necessary to have a team of founders who have specific knowledge about the particularities of the net economy. Therefore, special emphasis needs to be placed on the combination of management and informatics to establish the company and guarantee the necessary technical processes. This is particularly important considering that information can change very quickly and with it the company's basis for the value creation activities in digital data networks. There is a further special characteristic trait of the net economy in addition to the electronic value chain – namely that this is a considerably new area of business and lacks the years of experience on which established business sectors can rely. Accordingly, e-ventures are oriented especially towards future innovations and developments. Furthermore, there is a high level of uncertainty on the customer side with respect to the amount and the timely presence regarding acceptance of innovative information technologies.

This risk is counteracted by the fact that the net economy and its underlying technologies represent a central growth sector and are therefore linked to numerous opportunities. This can be seen in the continuing, rapid expansion, and use of the Internet in the USA and Europe. Further, the level of investments in information technologies are still increasing, whereby, two aspects that are particularly pertinent for new companies become very clear. First, Internet-based platforms require a certain amount of capital or funding for the initial development and/or company, and, second, Internet-based technologies are subject to continuous change and constant development thus requiring subsequent investments. In addition to the need for capital to develop the technological platform, additional investments for the establishment of the new company in the net economy are necessary (such as personnel, organization, establishing a brand, sales, production, etc.).

This concludes the description of the basic conditions and requirements for establishing a company in the net economy. In particular, four central characteristic traits can be identified that clearly distinguish the process of establishing a business in the net economy from the "classical" company establishment in the real economy. First, an e-venture is often an independent, original, and innovative company. Second, an e-venture is characterized by enormous growth potential and, yet, is also marked by uncertainty of its future development concerning the true success of its technological platform (that, as a general rule, requires significant investments). Third, an e-venture is based on a business idea that can only be put into practice by the innovative use of information technologies. The idea itself focuses strongly on "information" as a competitive factor. Fourth and finally, an e-venture is based upon a business concept that involves the electronic creation of customer value offered on an electronic platform of the net economy. It requires continuous development and administration. In view of these characteristics of e-ventures, the following questions arise from the founder's point of view: What information do I need in order to create value for a customer? What type of platform should I use to present this information? How can I guarantee that my information product will remain attractive for the customer in future? How can my new firm grow independently? As a result of these questions, companies established in the net economy tend to be heterogeneous and more complex. They differ from companies established in the real economy in many aspects. This justifies an isolated and separate approach to researching how companies (i.e., e-ventures) are established in the net economy. In this context, e-entrepreneurship "refers to establishing a new company with an innovative business idea within the net economy, which, using an electronic platform in data networks, offers its products and/or services based upon a purely electronic creation of value. Essential is the fact that this value offer was only made possible through the development of information technology" (Kollmann, 2006, p. 333).

The Electronic Creation of Customer Value

Building upon the concept of creating information-based value in the net economy previously described, it must also be determined what kind of value is created in the eyes of the customer for which he would be prepared to pay (i.e., what makes an online offer attractive from the customer's point of view in the first place). In general, this might include the following six aspects:

- **Overview:** The aspect that an online offer provides an overview of a large amount of information that would otherwise involve the arduous gathering of information. The e-venture creates value through automatically structuring the information flood available.
- **Selection:** By submitting database queries, consumers can locate exactly the desired information/products/services more quickly with an online offer and, thus, more efficiently.
- **Mediation:** In this case, an online offer creates the possibility to bring together requests of suppliers and demanders more efficiently and effectively. By doing so, the e-venture creates a matching value.
- **Transaction:** This aspect refers to the possibility created by an online offer to design and structure business activities more efficiently and effectively (e.g., with regard to cost aspects or payment possibilities).
- **Cooperation:** This aspect deals with using an online offer to enable various vendors or companies to more efficiently and effectively interlink their service or product offers with each other.
- **Exchange:** In this case, an online offer allows different consumers to communicate more efficiently and effectively with each other. The e-venture creates a communication value.

Considering these aspects of customer value, it is certainly possible that an e-venture can create several different types of value and that both structuring value as well as selection and matching value are created. After the identification of the creation of value, the perspective changes to the entrepreneur's point of view. The question to be asked here is how the customer value can be created. To answer this question, the electronic value chain can once again be applied. The electronic value chain separates an e-venture into strategically relevant activities in order to better understand cost behavior and recognize present and potential sources of differentiation. Thus, the electronic value chain represents respectively those value activities, which, for example, involve collecting, systemizing, and distributing information. Through specific value activities within the Internet, an electronic information product is created that represents value for which the customer is hopefully willing to pay. The electronic value chain therefore embodies the total value that is generated by the individual electronic value activities plus the profit margin. In the following paragraph, the most important value activities within the electronic value chain will be identified. It is these value activities that form the basis of an electronic value creation process within a company (Figure 2).

Figure 2. The electronic creation of customer value

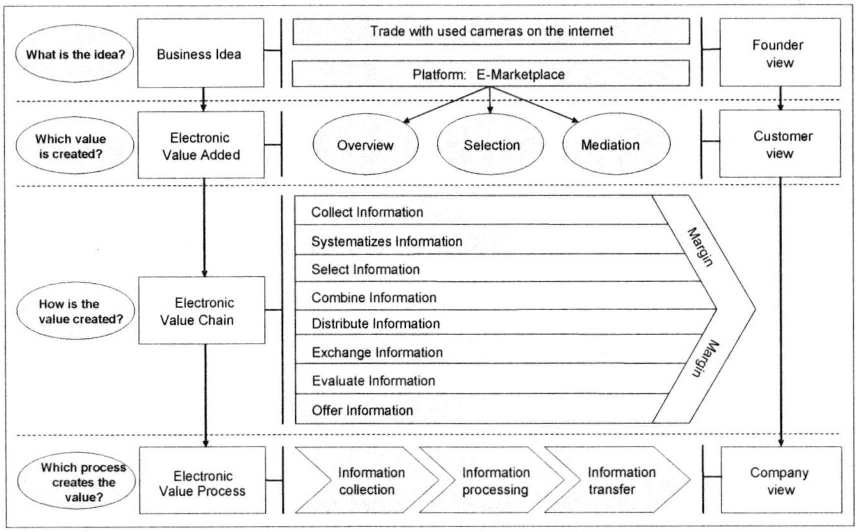

Should an idea be based upon, for example, dealing in used photo cameras in an e-marketplace in the Internet (founder's point of view), there is a typical way in which value can be electronically created. This value creation is directly reflected in the resulting added value for the user (customer view) and refers mainly to, in the example presented here, the overview, selection, and mediation functions. For instance, a supplier would be prepared to pay especially for the matching function, whereas a customer would be eventually willing to pay a fee for the overview function. In order to realize this creation of value, companies use the value chain to identify particularly those value activities that form the core of value creation. In order to do so, firstly, information on the object must be collected. Secondly, the location and the seller of the used camera must be determined, and, in a third step, systematically stored in a database. Using this database, information is then offered to the potential buyers who can formulate a query using appropriate search mechanisms. If a match is found through the query process, then the accompanying information pertinent to the request is exchanged. If all of this occurs, the final product is a transaction. The electronic value creation process from the company's point of view describes especially those information activities and/or the sequence of information activities, which in total create added value for the customer. This involves both the core and service processes. Core processes hold a true function in the creation of value, whereas service processes support the business processes along the value chain. As a general rule, the electronic value chain process begins with the input of information for the e-venture. In order to provide the targeted added value (e.g., overview function), the required information must first be gathered (e.g., who demands what at which level of quality and who offers it?). In the next step, the information is processed internally such that it can then be transferred on to the customer in the desired form as information output and in a way that specifically adds value for that customer. This process can be called the electronic value creation process and describes thus the core processes of most e-ventures. When considering e-ventures, it is then possible to formulate a representatively typical electronic value creation process (Kollmann, 1998):

- The first step is the acquisition of information, which involves gathering relevant data that serves as an input for the additional creation of value. This results in the collection of useful data. This step in the value creation process can also be called *information collection.*
- The second step involves the conversion of the collected data into an information product for the customer. This step of the value creation process can be called *information processing.*
- The third step involves implementing the newly acquired or confirmed knowledge obtained from collected, saved, processed and evaluated data for the benefit of the customer. The result is an output of information, which creates value. This step can be called *information transfer.*

It is important to recognize that it is not sufficient to go through the sequence of this electronic value creation process (which is here presented in its most ideal form) just once. Rather, a continual process of acquiring, processing, and transferring information is necessary. This is essential, as in many cases, the information underlying the process of electronic value creation is coming from many different sources (such as customers, partner firms, third-party Web sites and databases) and thus constantly subject to change. Some examples of electronic value creation processes in the net economy are presented in Figure 3.

Success Factors of Electronic Ventures

If one takes a closer look at the new companies in the net economy equipped with electronic value chains and electronic processes of value creation (such as *google.com* or *YouTube.com*), there are a

Figure 3. Examples for electronic value creation processes

	Information collection	Information processing	Information transfer	Value added
google.com	Information about web sites and search queries (=Input)	Matching of search strings and web content	List of appropriate web sites (=Output)	Overview Selection
webmiles.de	Information about products, customer and web offers (=Input)	Allocation of incentive points for the usage of web content	Information about points, options for exchange, customer information (=Output)	Transaction Cooperation
delticom.de	Information about tires and customer requests (=Input)	Matching of demand and supply	List of adequate offers and their possibility for online ordering (=Output)	Overview Selection Transaction
guenstiger.de	Information about product prices and customer requests (=Input)	Structuring of product prices, matching of demand and supply	Product information, price information, customer information (=Output)	Overview Selection Mediation
travelchannel.de	Facts about destinations, online booking and travel reports (=Input)	Matching of demands and supply, structuring of travel offers and travel reports	Travel offers, destination information, travel reports (=Output)	Overview Selection Transaction Exchange

number of noticeable, common traits with regard to the way the e-venture was established. Mostly, it is a so-called original company founding, meaning that a completely new company is established without relying on any previously existing or available company structures. Additionally, one observes that these cases were most often independently established companies initiated by company founders seeking full-time self-employment to secure their independent entrepreneurial existence. Finally, it can be seen that established e-ventures were most often innovative companies (i.e., not established to imitate an existing company). An innovative start-up presents a situation in which the initiating factors, in the classical sense proposed by Schumpeter (1911), are combined in a new way. This new combination can involve both tangible and intangible factors. The increasing importance of information as a significant factor in competitive advantage has recently increased the significance of the intangible factors, in particular knowledge and know-how. Due to this, a number of newly formed companies in the net economy are established consistently upon new knowledge-based and conceptually creative factors (the way in which information is dealt with and processed in the context of electronic value creation to form an electronic product).

At first view, success factors for establishing a company in the net economy do not particularly differ from those in the real economy. Nevertheless, one does find specific differences in the realization of and development of these success factors that are directly dependent upon the particular conditions in the net economy. In particular, these differences cover the areas of management, product, market access, process, and finance (Figure 4) that will be discussed in the following paragraphs.

The *management* building block places emphasis on the founders, who, through their personality, motivation, and creativity, strongly determine the activities of an e-venture. Studies on the influence of technical, social, and methodical skills and capabilities of business founders determined that these have a positive influence on the successful realization of the activities involved with establishing a company (Walter, Auer, & Gemünden, 2002). This also holds true with respect to the motivation of the founder or

Figure 4. Success factors of electronic ventures

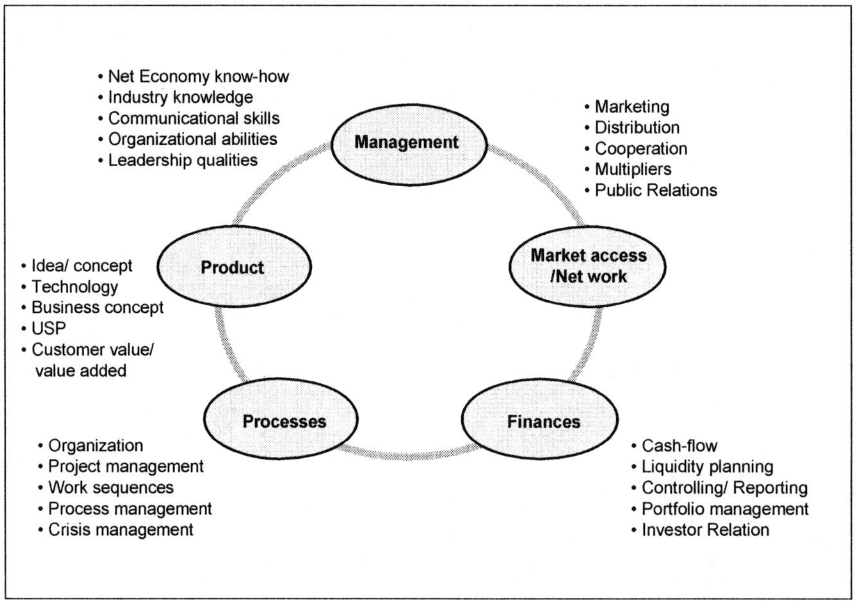

the team of founders. High stress limit, pressure to succeed, self-confidence, and awareness of risk characterize the actions during the sustainable phase of conception and thereafter in the realization phase. Whereas creativity on the one hand and analytical and conceptual thinking on the other dominate the first development phases of a new company, experience in the net industry, knowledge of the interrelated aspects of the net economy and real experience in operative management are significant points that matter when establishing an e-venture. In view of this, establishing a company in the net economy is very complex and the knowledge required to achieve this must be drawn similarly from the areas of informatics, information systems, and business administration. Accordingly, the founders must possess competence and know-how in all of these areas to a certain extent. However, an e-venture is often established by a team of founders due to the fact that seldom a single person possesses all of the following skills:

- **Informatics:** The technological aspect of the net economy makes it necessary to have a substantial understanding and knowledge of Internet-related standards and technologies, Internet architectures, databases, and software development.
- **Information systems:** The technological basis must be assessable with respect to its content and relevance for business issues. For this reason, it is important to have knowledge in areas such as IT security, data warehousing and data mining, e-business standards and electronic payment. It is just as important to understand the fundamental principles of the net economy, as it is to have sound overview of current existing business models and possibilities of creating electronic customer value.
- **Business administration:** At the business administration level, it is essential to have solid business knowledge. Topics, which should be especially emphasized here include marketing, business organization, management, as well as accounting and finance.

The *product* building block refers to the configuration of the services and offers of an e-venture. In this respect, the electronic product and/or service offer must be specified and communicated based upon its electronic added value. Thus, the essential question is, whether or not the customer needs the electronic offer/service provided by the e-ventures based on Information Technology and, if so, is the customer willing to pay for it? Further, it is the aim of the company to achieve added value for the customer through the realized output with electronically created value. Nevertheless, it is also the company's aim to assure its offer possesses a unique characteristic, which differentiates it from the other competitors. Furthermore, most e-ventures are dealing in new forms of business ideas and/or business models. From the customer side, initially it takes some time to get acquainted or acknowledge the effect provided as value added that results from such new ideas and models. For this reason, a regular reconnection with customers and users must take place, because in the end it is customer acceptance that determines if the electronic business idea is a success or not (Kollmann, 2006). Besides that, establishing a business in the net economy is singled out by the fact that an e-venture and its electronic business idea must not only satisfy a need, but also be superior compared to existing solutions in the real economy. For example, the need for books is already fulfilled through real bookshops. However, by offering overview, selection and transaction functions, Amazon.com creates an additional electronic value and was thus able to become one of the most successful players in the net economy.

The *processes* building block refers particularly to the need for a newly established company to quickly overcome that critical stage where its activities are informal and uncontrolled. This applies especially to work, finance, and organizational processes, which form a solid operative foundation in a newly established company. This essentially means that core processes must be firmly established and must also harmonize with the evolving company organization. Further, in this context it is also important that not too many activities are initiated simultaneously, because otherwise, there is an ensuing danger that some of these activities may not receive the full attention they require. Therefore, it is necessary to have a logical and effective project and process management. When dealing with an e-venture, sophisticated development and presentation of concrete workflows should be based on a model example of the value creation process that was previously determined. The company's business processes can then be conceptualized in parallel to the electronic process of value creation. These business processes should be understood as activity bundles necessary for realizing the value offer. They can be described as those targeted activities which are performed in a timely and logical sequence and their aim is directly determined by the company strategy (Hammer & Champy, 1993). Business processes thus describe the realization of the electronic process of creating value with the help of electronic resources within an e-venture. Particularly in the net economy, which is characterized by a high degree of virtualization, the knowledge of precise process flows is extremely important. Many business models in the net economy are based upon taking advantage of the effects of economies of scale. This is possible only when a large number of users can be serviced by either very few or with just one basic process (e.g., at online auction houses). The complexity of value creation, especially if the creation of this value involves the participation of multiple companies, requires a reduction of the process to the most essential steps. Weaknesses in core processes can then be more easily recognized. Especially with respect to electronic and thus automated process steps, mistakes can significantly impact the success of a company. Moreover, the process is externally visible to customers. Therefore, the quality of process flows has a direct influence on the customer's usage behavior. Supported by the virtual quality of information products, process flows become representatives of the quality image. The customer rates a company based upon the usability, functionality, and security of its processes.

The *market access* building block does not only mean to assure market entrance and establishing a product and/or brand, but also means reaching the customer via an electronic communication channel. The focus here is the question: How do I reach the customer with my information product? Hereby, it is possible to achieve market access through company-initiated marketing and sales activities. However this seems to pose a signification problem considering the lack of resources of start-up companies. Market entry in the net economy is, in most cases, characterized by the fact that most e-ventures are unknown, have limited capital, lack of range of resources, and do not have an established network. Particularly the lack of financial means often leads to deficits for a newly established company in the area of service or product performance, communication/sales and market positioning. In order to eliminate these deficits, especially when dealing with e-ventures, cooperation strategies play an elementary role in supporting the market entrance and positively steering the company's further development (Kollmann & Häsel, 2006). In view of the existing resource limitations, traditional marketing campaigns based on buyer-seller relationships are too cost-intensive and thus not feasible for many e-ventures. Affiliate programs, on the contrary, are predominantly understood as marketing and sales concepts that are directly based upon a partnership-like relationship and profit-scheme compensation. The e-venture (merchant) concludes an advertisement and/or sales agreement with a cooperation partner (affiliate), who in turn integrates the merchant's service/product offer on their internet presence or Web site. If this results in a successful transaction, the affiliate receives a commission on sales (Rayport & Jaworski, 2002). In this way, a newly established company can reach, from the very beginning, a wide range of customer segments and establish a comprehensive sales network.

The *finance* building block is tasked with guaranteeing the establishment and evolution of the firm from a liquidity point of view. There are two essential aspects, which are of importance here: On the one hand, there is a significant need for investing in technology and in establishing the company in the starting phase, whereby, on the other hand, the free-cash-flow cannot be too negatively influenced. The financing and cash planning is often a significant weak point for companies in the net economy. In particular, there often is a lack of realism, resulting in euphoric turnover forecasts or underestimated financial requirements. Hence, there should be a continually updated finance planning that can provide a realistic estimate of the financial situation of the company at any given point in time and also present the actual financing requirement. The financing of a company in this case becomes increasingly a mixture of equity (own capital) and various forms of participations. In situations such as these, risk capital should be strategically used for investments (e.g., sales), for example, for generating cash flow. The financing of the company furthermore requires a secure controlling, especially on the cost-side of the business. A further aspect concerns the communication with investors who want to be informed on a regular basis about the development of the company (Kollmann & Kuckertz, 2006).

Development Phases of Electronic Ventures

The future development of a company in the net economy can be outlined by just one simple question: What will happen to the idea in the course of time? At the very core, when a new company is to be founded, an idea for a possible business concept exists. This idea must first be discerned and then assessed for its potential for success (phase of idea finding). In a subsequent step, the idea must be transferred to a plausible and sustainable foundation, and a corresponding business plan for the idea must be prepared (phase of idea formulation). This must be done in order to actually realize the idea in the next step (phase of idea realization). Success of the e-venture is, however, not only dependent upon the initial realization of the business model, but also depends on the continual development and appropriate adjustment to market demands (phase of idea intensification). Finally, the idea must be capable of continually growing with the market and developing into a long-term business (phase of idea continuation). In each of these phases, it is essential that certain tasks along with the previously outlined building blocks for establishing a company are fulfilled. The individual phases (Ruhnka & Young, 1987) and specific questions which are of significant importance throughout the development of a company in the net economy are illustrated in Figure 5 and will be further discussed in the following paragraphs.

In the context of the financing of a new company or start-up, the phases of finding, formulating and realizing the idea are considered to be the *early stage*. Generally, this stage is divided into the pre-seed, seed and a start-up phase. In the pre-seed and seed-phase, the company has not been founded yet. These phases reflect more specifically the time in which the future founders of a company are searching for the idea and planning the realization of their business model. Even if no company and no marketable product exists in these phases, there is nevertheless a need for capital as, for instance, market studies or acceptance and feasibility studies must be performed (costs for preparation). If the company is to be established based upon a business plan (idea

Figure 5. Development phases of electronic ventures

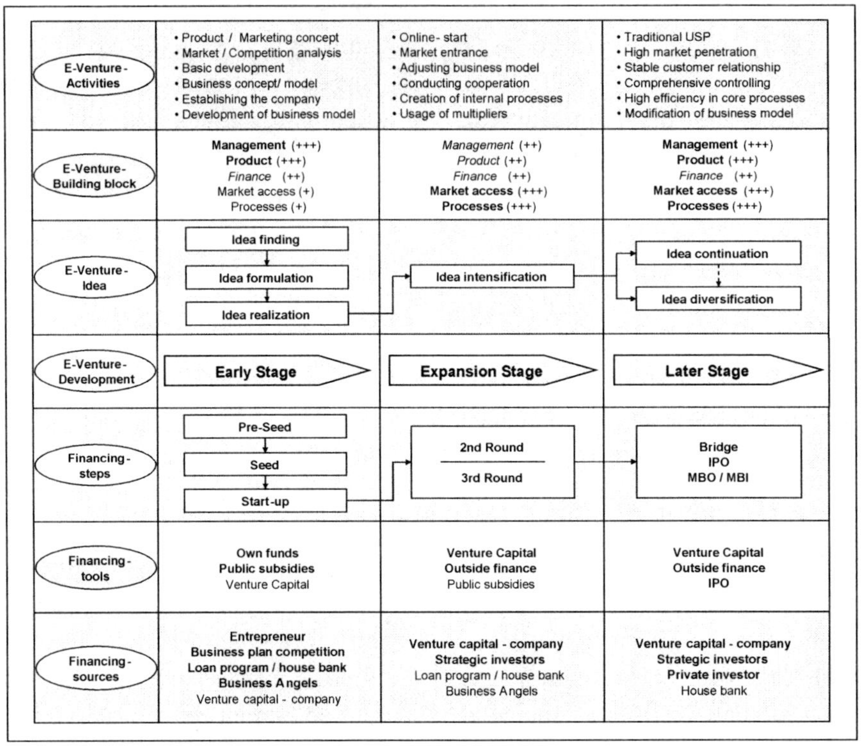

formulation), the start-up phase begins, in which production capacities are established, personnel is sought and the market entry is prepared. For an e-venture, this most often means the programming of the internet platform and its functionalities (development costs). When a successful online start can take place and the product or service offer is introduced into the market, the start-up phase ends. Especially during this early stage, the product and management building blocks play an essential role as there will definitely be no further progress without them.

The early stage is followed by the *expansion stage*, featuring the launch of the product or service and its introduction to the market. Beginning here, one of the central, strategic targets of the company is to expand the presence of its product/service on the market and achieve constant turnover growth. The newly formed company then enters the expansion stage and the first stable income is earned. In this phase, it is absolutely necessary to expand production and sales capacities. In order to achieve this, it is possible to form partnerships. As a general rule, the further expansion of the company cannot be solely financed through its cash-flow. The company is confronted with additional capital requirements. At this stage, potential investors can be offered far more security for their investment as compared to the early phase of the business development. Considering this, the management is nevertheless challenged by an entirely new problem of properly steering the growth of the company. This is the point where internal processes must be established. Within the expansion stage, the market access and processes building blocks are particularly important as, without them, further growth can most certainly not be achieved.

As soon as a company can rely upon an ever-increasing growth rate and guaranteed business income, the *later stage* of the company's development has been achieved. From a turnover perspective, the company is stable in its business development and there is eventually the opportunity to consider a diversification of the original idea. The company has established unique selling aspects for its product or service that separate it from the competitors and has achieved a significant market penetration. This means that even the future growth of the e-venture can be calculated and risks can be better defined than in the previous phases of the business development. When there is a significantly high level of growth potential, the break-even point can be achieved by bridge financing or the preparation of an initial public offering. Investors from the previous financing rounds also have the option of a trade sale to a strategic investor as well as selling their shares back to the founders or the management in a management buy-out, or respectively a management buy-in. During the later stage, all of the building blocks play a significant role due to the fact that, generally, growth can only be obtained when all of these elements are functioning seamlessly.

FUTURE TRENDS

The creation of new ventures plays a decisive role for the social and economic development of every country. This is due to the fact that with each new venture created, a market participant comes into existence, which potentially stimulates the competition and drives the economy further. The founding of electronic ventures within the net economy is therefore a key topic for every national industry. As the significance of Internet-based technologies has triggered a technological and societal development that is irresistible, e-entrepreneurship can be expected to gain further importance in the future. With the proliferation of digital television and third generation mobile technologies, novel and innovative ways of delivering electronic value can be expected to emerge. The boundaries between mobile services and the "stationary" Internet will increasingly become blurred. This will enable e-ventures to span multiple electronic channels and become a pervasive part of daily life. Moreover, the pervasiveness of digital technologies and changes in customer behavior are increasingly blurring the borders between electronic and physical trade levels. real economy and net economy are merging. Particularly in this context, the need for a complementary utilization of physical and electronic value creation activities can be expected, as customers will increasingly use online and off-line channels contemporaneously (Kollmann et al., 2006). Will customers in the future browse Web-based catalogs in order to create digital shopping lists that are then used in connection with a mobile phone to guide the customer through the physical retail store? Similarly, television has begun to turn into an interactive online channel incorporating distribution and service potentials going much beyond spot advertisements. For the combined management of physical and electronic value creation activities, a strategic cooperation between e-ventures and real economy firms can be expected to hold an outstanding potential, as this enables the partners to serve both online and off-line channels without extending themselves beyond their own means and competencies (Kollmann et al., 2006). Researchers will have to further elaborate the concepts presented in this chapter in order to explain the full range of commercial activities that future technologies will allow and future customers will ask for.

CONCLUSION

As this chapter has shown, the competent processing of information has to be the foundation of entrepreneurial attempts in the net economy. The chapter provided insight into how founders may conceptualize electronic value creation processes that create customer value, independent of a physical value chain. Thereby, the electronic value chain and the value-oriented collection, processing and transfer of information serve as a starting point for every e-venture. Once the business concept is in place, the general success factors for establishing a company in the net economy do not particularly differ from those in the real economy. However, studying the five building blocks of management, product, market access, processes and finance, the chapter suggests a range of specifics that must be borne in mind in order to succeed in the early, later, and expansion stage of an e-venture's life cycle. In addition, the importance of each of these building blocks has been found to be varying in the respective phases of development. The framework presented in this chapter may thus guide founders in setting priorities and assist them in adopting an analytical perspective on their current business activities. It should have become apparent that the net economy offers a wide range of opportunities to found electronic ventures. To fully exploit the potentials of Internet-related technologies, however, founders need to approach e-entrepreneurship in a systematic and precautious way that is backed by sound strategy, and never as an end in itself.

REFERENCES

Amit, R., & Zott, C. (2001). Value creation in e-business. *Strategic Management Journal, 22*(6/7), 493-520.

Hammer, M., & Champy, J. (1993). *Reengineering the corporation: A manifesto for business revolution.* New York: HarperBusiness.

King, D., Lee, J., Warkentin, M., & Chung, H. (2002). *Electronic commerce: A managerial perspective*. Upper Saddle River, NJ: Pearson Education International.

Kirzner, I. M. (1973). *Competition and entrepreneurship.* Chicago, IL: University of Chicago Press.

Kollmann, T. (2006). What is e-entrepreneurship?—fundamentals of company founding in the net economy. *International Journal of Technology Management, 33*(4), 322-340.

Kollmann, T. (2004). Attitude, adoption, or acceptance?—measuring the market success of telecommunication and multimedia technology. *International Journal of Business Performance Management, 6*(2), 133-52.

Kollmann, T. (2001). Measuring the acceptance of electronic marketplaces. *Journal of Computer Mediated Communication, 6*(2).

Kollmann, T. (1998). The information triple jump as the measure of success in electronic commerce. *Electronic Markets, 8*(4), 44-49.

Kollmann, T., & Häsel, M. (2006). *Cross-channel cooperation: The bundling of online and offline business models.* Wiesbaden: DUV.

Kollmann, T., & Kuckertz, A. (2006). Investor relations for start-ups: An analysis of venture capital investors' communicative needs. *International Journal of Technology Management, 34*(1/2), 47-62.

Lumpkin, G. T., & Dess, G. G. (2004). E-business strategies and internet business models: How the Internet adds value. *Organizational Dynamics, 33*(2), 161-173.

Matlay, H. (2004). E-entrepreneurship and small e-business development: Towards a comparative research agenda. *Journal of Small Business and Enterprise Development, 11*(3), 408-414.

Meyer, C. (2001). The second generation of speed. *Harvard Business Review, 79*(4), 24-26.

Porter, M. E. (1985). *Competitive Advantage.* New York: Free Press.

Porter, M. E., & Millar, V. E. (1985). How information gives you competitive advantage. *Harvard Business Review, 63*(4), 149-160.

Rayport, J. F., & Jaworski, B. J. (2002). *Introduction to e-commerce.* Boston: McGraw-Hill.

Ruhnka, J. C., & Young, J. E. (1987). A venture capital model of the development process for new ventures. *Journal of Business Venturing 2*(2), 167-184.

Schumpeter, J. A. (1911). *The theory of economic development: An inquiry into profits, capital, credit, interest and the business cycle.* 1934 translation. Cambridge, MA: Harvard University Press.

Stalk Jr., G. (1988). Time—The next source of competitive advantage. *Harvard Business Review, 66*(4), 28-60.

Taylor, M., & Murphy, A. (2004). SMEs and e-business. *Journal of Small Business and Enterprise Development, 11*(3), 280-289.

Walter, A., Auer, M., & Gemünden, H. G. (2002). The impact of personality, competence, and activities of academic entrepreneurs on technology transfer success. *International Journal of Entrepreneurship and Innovation Management, 2*(2/3), 268-289.

Weiber, R., & Kollmann, T. (1998). Competitive advantages in virtual markets—perspectives of "information-based-marketing" in cyberspace. *European Journal of Marketing, 32*(7/8), 603-615.

Zwass, V. (2003). Electronic commerce and organizational innovation: Aspects and opportunities. *International Journal of Electronic Commerce, 7*(3), 7-37.

KEY TERMS

Affiliate Program: Marketing and sales concept that is directly based upon a partnership-like relationship and profit-scheme compensation. The so-called merchant concludes an advertisement and/or sales agreement with a cooperation partner (affiliate), who in turn integrates the merchant's service/product offer on their Web site.

E-Entrepreneurship: Establishing a new company with an innovative business idea within the net economy, which, using an electronic platform in data networks, offers its products and/or services based upon a purely electronic creation of value.

Electronic Trade Level: A business dimension resulting from the proliferation of digital data networks and thus a new possibility of doing business in the so-called net economy, apart from the existing economy of physical products and services (real economy).

Electronic Value Creation: Refers to the creation of an added value by the means of a digital information product in the framework of the net economy. Electronic value is commonly created through value-adding activities such as the collection, processing, and transfer of information.

Electronic Venture (E-Venture): A recently founded and thus young e-business (startup). An e-venture results from a company foundation in the net economy.

Net Economy: Refers to the economically utilized part of digital data networks (such as the Internet) that allow carrying out information, communication and transaction processes, (and thus an electronic value creation) via different electronic platforms.

Real Economy: Refers to the real trade level of physical products and services (in contrast to the net economy, which refers to the electronic trade level of digital products and services).

This work was previously published in Information Technology Entrepreneurship and Innovation, edited by F. Zhao, pp. 141-155, copyright 2008 by Information Science Reference, formerly known as Idea Group Reference (an imprint of IGI Global).

Chapter II
The Role of Government in E-Business Adoption

Barbara Roberts
The University of Southern Queensland, Australia

Mark Toleman
The University of Southern Queensland, Australia

ABSTRACT

An analysis of the role of government in e-business adoption is provided in this chapter, with empirical evidence from Australia included. It is shown that government influence is multifaceted. Governments champion e-business adoption for national economic gain; they provide the physical network on which much of e-business depends and increasingly provide e-government services to improve regulation and compliance effectiveness. E-government in particular can act as a strong driver of organisational adoption for some types of e-business processes. Implications for theory from a DOI perspective are included. The authors hope that further research by IS professionals will guide future e-business project directions by improving the understanding of government's role in e-business adoption in practice, which in turn will improve theoretical understanding of how the benefits can best be maximized.

INTRODUCTION

Governments and big businesses are powerful stakeholders in driving and shaping economies and the communities in which those economies operate. In particular, governments are able to maintain a dominant position at the top of the stakeholder pecking order due to their regulatory and fiscal power. This powerful position allows governments to exert influence on e-business adoption patterns in a variety of ways. The discussion ranges from indirect pressures resulting from governments' strong championship of e-business benefits through to direct influences arising from the legislative controls introduced for the digital economy, the provision of the physical network infrastructure as a critical enabling adoption factor, and the effects of e-government activity on e-business adoption in general. Both theoretical explanations and empirical evidence, based largely on an Australian perspective, are provided to support the discussion on the role governments play in e-business adoption.

BACKGROUND

E-business is used for a wide range of purposes and types as the following definition illustrates: "the use of Internet technologies to link customers, suppliers, business partners, and employees using at least one of the following: (a) e-commerce Web sites that offer sales transactions, (b) customer-service Web sites, (c) intranets and enterprise information portals, (d) extranets and supply chains, and (e) IP electronic data interchange" (Wu, Mahajan, & Balasubramanian, 2003, p. 425). Also, it is often assumed that an explicit and close connection between e-business and competitive advantage exists, as the next definition illustrates: "As a way of doing business, e-business refers to the use of business processes that leverage technology—and especially the Internet and World Wide Web (the Web)—to maintain or create competitive advantage" (McKie, 2001, p. xvi). This automatic coupling of e-business with the delivery of some level of guaranteed benefit is one which appears regularly in the literature (Porter, 2001; Sawhney & Zabin, 2001). However the relationship between e-business and delivered benefit is unlikely to be consistent for all types of e-business processes, and does not necessarily exist for all stakeholders involved in its adoption and use. Despite this note of caution, many governments around the world are committed to providing e-government for their nation's citizens and organisations in the form of government information and services on the Web because of the expected benefits such as improved effectiveness and greater convenience of access (Gefen, Pavlou, Warkentin, & Rose, 2002; NOIE, 2003b; Turban, King, Lee, Warkentin, & Chung, 2002).

Internet-enabled e-business is credited with delivering a new type of Internet-based economy in which information flows are improved while associated costs are reduced (Dunt & Harper, 2002). Michael Porter's (2001) claim that "Internet technology provides better opportunities for companies to establish distinctive strategic positioning than did previous generations of information technology" (p. 65) supports the high confidence shown in e-business by government bodies and many business analysts (D. Anderson, 2000; NOIE, 2000; OIE, 2004a). Two major benefits of e-business adoption commonly identified are reduced costs and increased demand through increased services and new markets (Allen Consulting Group, 2002; OECD, 2002). These benefits directly flow from the Internet's intrinsic characteristics of providing low-cost and high-speed global communication, effectively reducing the limiting impact of geographic position and extending presence in the marketplace to 24 hours a day, 7 days a week.

Related benefits of e-business adoption promoted or marketed by Australia's National Office for the Information Economy (NOIE) include increased competitive advantage; provision of new ways of generating revenue; improved relationships with suppliers; improved services to clients; increased collaboration in the supply-chain; and improved business practices through the development of new business models built around the capability of networking (NOIE, 2002b). Thus e-business is closely associated with economic growth at both a national and organisational level in the minds of many, including economic and government analysts (Bakry & Bakry, 2001; Brown, 2002; Dunt & Harper, 2002; Porter, 2001). As a consequence, governments are not only keen to increase adoption rates by organisations, but are also keen to realize direct benefits by adopting e-business for the purpose of delivering government services more effectively, thus resulting in e-government.

Much of the empirical evidence and discussion included in this chapter are based on examples taken from Australia, and hence a brief background of the Australian government's efforts to promote and increase adoption within the Australian business community is examined next.

Government as Champion and Catalyst of E-Business Adoption: Australian Example

The Australian Government actively champions e-business adoption by Australian organisations in order to accelerate uptake and consequently improve the Australian economy. The Australian government's National Office for the Information Economy was restructured and renamed in April 2004, with the functions split between the new Australian Government Information Management Office (AGIMO), and the Office for the Information Economy (OIE). The research and strategic role setting function of NOIE has been taken on by OIE, with the government belief in e-business benefits clearly articulated: "Strengthening Australia's participation in the information economy will benefit all Australians by improving the efficiency of Australian firms, boosting the Australian economy and enhancing national wealth" (OIE, 2004a). The following statements of major objectives of OIE make their advocacy role clear: "identifying and promoting the business case for the adoption of e-business at the firm level, within supply chains and throughout industry sectors" and "to accelerate the uptake of electronic-business tools and practices that will lift the productivity and productive capacity of the Australian economy" (OIE, 2004a).

Thus, the Australian government explicitly promotes the adoption of e-business, particularly by small and medium sized enterprises (SMEs), because of the perceived benefit that e-business is expected to contribute to the future of the Australian economy (Brown, 2002). The case study methodology is frequently employed by government analysts, and case study reports are provided on government Web sites as examples of how organisations can derive benefit from adopting e-business practices (NOIE, 2001, 2002a, 2003a).

E-Government Adoption: Australian Example

The adoption of e-business technologies by governments for the purpose of providing better government services is a logical progression from simply acting as a champion for the technology. In 2003 NOIE produced a report, entitled "E-government Benefits Study" which detailed the Australian Government's aim to transform "traditional over-the-counter services to fully interactive online services" and that this transformation was driven by a "need to improve business processes, to engage citizens, and to provide services to yield better outcomes for government and citizens" (NOIE, 2003b). The report also claimed that increasingly it was Australians who were driving the demand for e-government in order to get easier access and save time (NOIE, 2003b). The push for increased e-government in Australia is mirrored in many other countries such as the U.S. (Cottrill, 2001; Gefen et al., 2002) and Singapore (Ke & Wei, 2004). Analysis of the successful e-government adoption in Singapore confirmed the finding that strong championship by government and clear articulation of the benefits to all stakeholders was an important factor in e-government success (Ke & Wei, 2004).

E-BUSINESS ADOPTION FACTORS: GOVERNMENT FACTOR IN CONTEXT

A review of literature examining adoption of e-business identifies government-related behaviour as just one of the many influential factors that have been identified from a wide range of sources. In order to better appreciate the level of impact coming from government related activity, it is worth quickly reviewing the range of other influential factors so that the role of government with regard to e-business adoption can be placed in context.

Diffusion of Innovation Theory

A major theory, first published in 1962, on the adoption of innovations and the rate at which subsequent usage diffuses through the population of potential users — the diffusion of innovations (DOI) theory by Rogers (1995) — has general application to e-business and is now briefly examined. DOI theory posits that the factors influencing adoption rates by organisations are drawn from two major sources: (1) characteristics of the innovation itself and (2) characteristics of the adopting organisation (see Figure 1).

Five innovation characteristics are singled out in DOI as independent variables influencing adoption rates, and these relate to perceptions of (1) relative advantage over alternatives, involving a range of social, technical, and economic benefits; (2) compatibility with existing values, experiences, and needs; (3) complexity; (4) trialability; and (5) observability of the innovation. As might be expected, the degree of perceived relative advantage, encompassing the full range of possible benefits, is found to be one of the best predictors of an innovation's rate of adoption by diffusion scholars (Rogers, 1995, p. 216). Interestingly, with regard to the characteristics of the adopting organisation, while many characteristics of the adopting organisation have been identified and studied (shown in Figure 1), Rogers claims that the results from several hundred studies show only low correlations between the identified factors and organisation innovativeness, with size/resource capacity the most significant (Rogers, 1995, p. 381).

In general, the degree of relative advantage an innovation delivers and the resource capacity/size of the adopting organisation emerge as the two most important of the identified factors (Rogers, 1995). The DOI theory also recognises that influence from managerial championship and opinion leaders acting as agents of change act as an accelerating force by affecting the potential adopters. Research by Fichman (2001) into the

Figure 1. Independent variables related to innovation adoption by organisations from Rogers' DOI theory (1995)

Innovation Characteristics

1) perception of relative advantage over alternatives; (+)
2) perception of compatibility with existing values, experiences and needs; (+)
3) perception of complexity; (-)
4) the degree to which the innovation can be tried on a limited and experimental basis; (+)
5) the degree to which the results of the innovation can be observed. (+)

+

Organisation characteristics

1) Attitude towards change of individual leader (+)
2) Internal characteristics of organisation's structure
   - Centralization (-)
   - Interconnectedness (+)
   - Complexity (+)
   - Organisational slack (+)
   - Formalization (-)
   - Size (+)
3) System openness – the degree to which members of the system are linked to others external to the system (+)

adoption of IT innovations specifically supports the DOI findings that the degree of perceived benefit and the size/resource capacity of the adopting organisation have significant explanatory power in understanding adoption and usage patterns.

TAM Related Theories

The technology acceptance model (TAM), a framework originally developed to explain the acceptance of information technology by individuals after the adoption and implementation stages have occurred (Davis, 1989) also identified perceived usefulness, which basically equates to perceived relative advantage or benefit, as the most significant construct in understanding acceptance and use of IT. Some variants of TAM have identified additional constructs which need to be taken into account in order to explain adoption of IT innovations by organisations. For example, work by Mathieson, Peacock, and Chin confirmed that the construct of perceived resources needed to be added to the simple TAM framework (Mathieson, Peacock, & Chin, 2001), while one of the latest variations to emerge, the unified theory of acceptance and use of technology (UTAUT), has also introduced additional broad brush constructs such as "social influence" to encompass managerial and opinion leader championship, and "facilitating conditions" to cover resource capacity and organisational conditions (Venkatesh, Morris, Davis, & Davis, 2003).

External Environment Factors

While external environment factors are not clearly identified in Rogers' DOI theory or the TAM variants discussed previously, the literature review confirmed the external environment to be an additional major source of influential factors on the adoption of complex information technologies such as e-business. This is particularly so for e-business due to high user interdependencies, potential to transform strategy and processes (Chau & Turner, 2001), and the potential to deliver organisation-wide business impact (Swanson, 1994). Environmental factors come from a wide range of sources and, for example, include characteristics related to industry, marketplace, culture, and government and industry regulatory conditions (Chengalur-Smith & Duchessi, 1999; Kwon & Zmud, 1987; Markus & Soh, 2002; Swanson, 1994; Yang, Yoo, Lyytinen, & Ahn, 2004). Factors related to national characteristics including culture, government policy initiatives, and legal regulations all appear to have strong explanatory power in improving understanding of e-business adoption and diffusion behaviours (Chen, 2003; Gibbs, Kraemer, & Dedrick, 2003; Palacios, 2003; Wong, 2003). Policy support and leadership from government are recognised as necessary and important enabling factors in providing an environment conducive for e-business adoption, while the provision of e-government services and online transaction options positively drive e-business adoption (Wong, 2003). Other critical enablers include pressure from multinational corporations; liberalisation of trade and telecommunications policies; improvement of telecommunications infrastructure; adequate legislation to manage risk; and the emergence of e-banking (Palacios, 2003).

For example, research into the initiation and adoption of client-server technology in organisations (Chengalur-Smith & Duchessi, 1999) identified three major sources of influence: (1) characteristics of the organisation itself, such as size, structure, and culture, including the selected migration strategy for the adoption of the technology; (2) characteristics of the technology itself, such as the complexity, scope, and cost of the system adopted; and (3) characteristics of the external environment, such as government regulation, the level of competition faced by the organisation, and the organisation's market position. Factors from all three areas were found to have a significant effect on the adoption process (Chengalur-Smith & Duchessi, 1999). As a second example, many factors from a range of sources were also identified as influencing diffusion of mobile broadband services in Korea (Yang et al., 2004). External environment features figure prominently, while software and telecommunication standards, the industry and government regulatory regime, marketplace forces, and internal skills and resources all contribute to usage levels. Complex relationships and interactions were found to occur between all influential factors, resulting in outcomes that are characterised by continual evolution and change (Yang et al., 2004).

Thus, it is reasonable to conclude that the factors influencing organisation adoption of e-business are many and drawn from numerous sources. In particular, an organisation's external environment is a rich potential source of influence on e-business behaviour at all levels: these include organisational, industrial, national, and global levels. It is clear from the previous discussion that government policy and activity does play a significant role in determining e-business adoption and usage by organisations, but it is not by any means the only key factor. To what extent government activity has the potential to influence e-business adoption, and the areas of e-business in which government influence is likely to have more impact than others is discussed in more detail after a brief discussion on implications related to the network externality characteristic of e-business.

NETWORK EXTERNALITY INFLUENCE ON E-BUSINESS ADOPTION

The reliance of many e-business ventures on attaining sufficient critical mass with regard to adoption in order to be successful is due to the *network externality effect* (Katz, 1986). Network externalities apply to information technologies which rely on corresponding usage by others to be effective, or when "one person's utility for a good depends on the *number* of other people who consume this good" (Varian, 1999, p. 606). Network externalities apply to many e-business processes such as e-mail and use of Web sites because the benefit of these technologies does indeed depend on the number of users, with benefit rising as numbers rise. For example, e-mail is not effective if only a few intended recipients are using it to access their correspondence.

Government Power Influencing Adoption Numbers

Given that e-business technologies are sensitive to the network externality characteristic, it follows that the success of many e-business systems, including e-government services and online transaction systems, is dependent on the number of citizens and organisations who consume these products. If the number of adopters remains low, then the perceived benefits to the system owners, including government in this context, of improving effectiveness and efficiency as well as lowering costs will not be delivered. Thus the success of e-business and e-government relies on having sufficient adopters. As a result, it is in the best interests of powerful stakeholders to encourage and enable adoption rates to rise. To what extent governments are able to influence adoption rates will now be explored in more detail by looking at an empirical study from Australia which involved investigation of e-business adoption rates by wineries, with government influence an identified factor under investigation.

EMPIRICAL STUDY: E-BUSINESS ADOPTION BY AUSTRALIAN WINERIES

The study described here was carried out in 2003 and 2004 in order to better understand the nature and extent of Internet-enabled e-business adoption by Australian organisations, taking into account the different types of e-business practiced within organisations. The research consisted of two major phases: a qualitative, exploratory stage using interviews designed to identify key issues of relevance to wineries which allowed significant industry feedback to inform the final selection of factors and issues most relevant to e-business adoption by wineries, and a quantitative survey stage, using a self administered questionnaire, designed to collect both statistical and descriptive information in order to gain a clearer understanding of e-business activity and test propositions. The research was conducted for a master's thesis, and for those readers wishing to follow up on more details of the study, the thesis is available online at http://adt.usq.edu.au/adt-QUSQ/public/adt-QUSQ20050113.103311/index.html.

Selection of Wineries as Unit of Analysis

Australian wineries were selected as the unit of analysis for research into e-business adoption within Australia for a number of reasons. One reason is that wineries are a rich subject for research because they have a very diverse range of business processes that span the agricultural (primary), manufacturing (secondary), and marketing (tertiary) sectors. Wineries usually have a high level of involvement in all three areas (ACIL, 2002). Further, wineries also have to comply with a wide range of legislative requirements and are required to interact and transact with numerous government bodies as well as industry organisations. The wine industry is also increasingly important to the Australian economy as the industry continues to expand, largely due to exponential growth in export sales for the last 15 plus years (K. Anderson, 2000; Anderson, 2001). This ensured that both domestic and export markets were included, thus covering a wide range of market types.

Wineries also vary greatly in size and resource capacity, which contributes to their richness as a research subject. In 2003 there were more than 1,600 wineries in Australia. Of these wineries, almost one third of them are in the microsize category processing less than 20 tonnes of grapes each year. At the other end of the size spectrum the top 22 wine companies account for about 90% of the annual national crush and for 96% of all sales of branded wine (Winetitles, 2003). And finally, while some wineries are close to urban centres, many are located in regional areas with limited access to network infrastructure: this provided scope to collect useful information on the impact of network access issues.

Phase 1: Interview Methodology

Interviews, recommended as a suitable technique for exploring issues and gathering rich empirical data (Sekaran, 2003; Yin, 1994; Zikmund, 2000), were conducted with representatives from nine different wineries in mid-2003. All nine respondents were volunteered by their company as knowledgeable informants, and all were confident in their ability to portray the e-business activities of their own winery with a high degree of accuracy. The nine wineries represented a broad range of company structure, size, and position within the industry with some ranking in the top five wine companies in Australia in terms of production and sales. All nine wineries were engaged in export of wine, and all were using the Internet in some capacity in the running of their business. Employee numbers ranged from 12 to over 2,000, illustrating a huge variance in size and internal capacity.

The interviews were conducted in a semi-structured way to make sure that each major e-business process domain was covered. General background questions were followed by more specific questions covering the winery's use of Internet technologies and related strategies. The extent of e-mail use was covered, as well as the range of Web sites, both external sites and sites belonging to the winery, that each winery used and for what purpose: in B2B — with suppliers, trading partners, and business customers such as distributors and retailers; in B2C — public Web sites and mailing lists; and in B2G — using government sites as an information source and for online compliance purposes. The respondents also provided information on the benefits and degree of relative advantage perceived to be delivered by the various e-business processes, and also on the factors that acted as facilitators or barriers to further adoption in each area. Cross-case analysis of the interview data helped to identify the major themes. Some themes appeared to be independent of the winery size, such as influence from e-government; while other themes appeared to be linked to size and market position.

Interview Finding: Government As E-Business Driver

While many factors of influence emerged during these interviews, this chapter focuses only on findings related to the perceived influence coming from government related activity. All interviewees identified the Australian government as one of the drivers of their winery's e-business behaviour. The types of e-business conducted with government ranged from e-mail to use of government Web sites for convenient access to government related information, and included several examples of online transaction processing and online submission of forms. Examples are now provided.

One winery respondent reported they use the Internet for access to government areas that are crucial in supporting their business processes:

We do actually do some compliance via the Internet such as Work Cover, and our tax. We do lodge our returns electronically, we do actually have occupation health and safety, and we have to keep abreast of the appropriate Australian standards on how things are done, and what plant materials you are supposed to use, so we do actually utilize that quite a bit to make sure we are meeting our requirements there so we do have people who are trained on the Internet constantly checking to see that what we are doing is correct.

Another respondent cited the following as an example of B2G communication within their business:

The EPA for example, or Environmental Protection Authority — legislation and reporting due to them is all electronic now. So that saves a lot of paperwork, postage and what not. You just update your records, your last results, and e-mail it, and the whole history is emailed together, and it is just a continuing spreadsheet type of format.

An example of online transaction processing is provided next. All wine exported from Australia must be approved as meeting a required level of quality before it is allowed to be exported. This quality control process is one example of the many legislative requirements facing Australian wineries, with compliance mandatory. Many wineries now process their Wine Export Approvals (WEAs) online. The option for gaining approvals using a Web-based process has been available for the last three to four years via the Australian Wine and Brandy Corporation Web site at http://www.awbc.com.au/.

The following comment from a small winery respondent illustrates the benefit of online WEAs and government sites in general:

wine export approvals — my brother now uses the Internet to do all that. There are all the application forms on the Internet, so he can do all of that via the net, so he doesn't have to talk to anybody and he gets the results back over the Internet or by email ... We are just about to put in some workplace agreements, so I have been to the Web-sites to check that out ... and we have to find the current wages for all the wages people, so we use those Web-sites to access that. We use the liquor licensing, we get all the permits and stuff for that ... that's really good — there are lots of government Web-sites that we use.

A second example of online transaction processing, one which applies to all Australian exporters and importers is examined next. At the time the interviews were conducted all Australian exporting companies were facing additional e-business process adoption for legislative compliance purposes due to the then impending roll out of the export component of a new system being developed by the Australian Customs Service (ACS). The Cargo Management Re-engineering project is Australia's largest ever public sector e-business project, and will consist of several subsystems to form the Integrated Cargo System (ICS). The ICS is designed to improve security and efficiency among other expected benefits. Visit http://www.customs.gov.au for details. The first system, the export component, went live in September 2004 after several delays from the initial scheduled cut-over period of late 2003. Use of the online interface to the ICS export system, while not actually mandatory, is strongly encouraged with a cost burden imposed for exporters choosing to use a manual process available through selected Australia Post Offices and customs offices.

Although the scheduled cut-over period to the new export component of the ICS was due soon after the time the interviews were conducted, awareness of the impending change to Customs' clearances among the interview respondents was variable, with only those from the larger companies raising it as an issue — respondents from the mid-size or small wineries seemed completely unaware of changes in this area. This indicates some flaws in communication by government in the initial stages of the project development.

The following excerpt from one respondent illustrates what, at the time of the interview, was thought to be the complete mandatory nature of the change:

Customs ... have brought in an edict that you will have to talk to them electronically by the end of September (2003) or you don't export ... To ship our goods overseas we have to talk to Customs, the Australian Customs Service electronically or we won't be able to ship. We have got to do that by the end of September.

Another respondent provided the following comment:

Australian Customs Service are putting in this new cargo tracking system which is why we have had to spend another $40,000 to work with this one, and we have to do it, it is compulsory, and we have to have it in by November this year. But part of this system is they have an online function of looking after a cargo status, so it is a cargo tracking system.

Yet another respondent's comment on the impending change in gaining Customs clearance follows:

We use a package called Trident — the Trident system interfaces directly with Customs in what is called an Exit One package. Now that's about to undergo a very, very significant change, and the actual way in which Customs handles the export of wines is about to undergo a fundamental change ... We came out of that with the instruction from Customs to apply for a digital certificate, so we need to get these processes in place.

Phase 2: Survey Methodology

A survey of all Australian wineries, excluding the microsize wineries processing less than 20 tons of grapes per year, was conducted in the latter part of 2004 using a self-administered questionnaire. The survey was designed to collect detailed information about the nature and extent of the wineries' e-business adoption, and among other things, to statistically test the proposition that some elements of e-business behaviour occur in response to government related activity on the Internet.

Responses were received from 198 of the 1,065 wineries, giving an overall response rate of 18.6%. The response rate varied by winery size, increasing significantly across the four size categories used in the analysis ($\chi^2(3) = 32.28$, $p < .001$). See Table 1 for winery size categories, population and response numbers. The survey collected basic background information on each winery, and included separate sections for each of the following types of e-business processes: e-mail; use of external Web sites; and three possible types of winery Web sites—public for B2C, extranet for B2B, and intranet for winery staff only. Feedback on the winery's overall use of e-business, along with identification of barriers to further (or any) adoption and general comments were also sought.

The survey included statements designed to test the proposition that government e-business activity was a factor of influence; respondents were provided with a 5-point Likert scale to show their level of agreement. The "Do not know" responses were treated as missing responses for the statistical calculations. The Likert scale, while strictly an ordinal scale, has been shown to have sufficient interval characteristics for the computation of means not to be invalid: "arithmetic means seem to closely reflect group attitudes towards the stimuli" (Hofacker, 1984). Therefore the response means illustrated differences in responses by winery size when the nonparametric tests for ordinal data showed a significant difference by size existed. Response differences by winery size for the factor statements were investigated using the Kruskal-Wallis K Independent Sample test. This test is appropriate for an ordinal scale and makes no assumptions about the underlying distribution of the data, which in this case was not normally distributed. Summary findings related to the role of government influence are now reported.

Survey Finding 1: Government Influences E-Mail and Use of Government Web Sites

The survey data analysis revealed that e-government activity influenced e-mail and external Web site use but had negligible direct impact on the operation or content of Web sites operated by the wineries. This is not particularly surprising when the purposes of the different e-business process types are considered, and is part of the wider finding that factors influencing e-business adoption do not impact in the same way across the various e-business process domains. Some specific government related results are detailed next.

With regard to e-mail use, three quarters of the wineries use e-mail to communicate with government agencies and departments, but

Table 1. Winery size categories, population, and response numbers

				Response		
Winery Size	Annual Tonnage Range	Population in 2003	Population %	Number	% of Population	% of Total Response
Small	20-249	801	75.7%	120	15.0%	60.6%
Medium	250-999	150	14.2%	35	23.3%	17.7%
Large	1000-9999	88	8.3%	31	35.2%	15.7%
Very Large	10000 and over	26	2.5%	12	46.2%	6.1%

small wineries, when compared with the larger wineries, find less convenience from using e-mail with government organisations. Turning to use of external Web sites, the most common type accessed by wineries are the specific wine industry Web sites, some of which are operated by Australian Government authorities (e.g., the Australian Wine and Brandy Corporation is the Australian government authority responsible for the promotion and regulation of Australian wine and brandy). Almost 90% of wineries, regardless of their size, use the Internet to access these sites. The next most common type of Web sites accessed by wineries is government sites connected with legislation and regulation compliance. In this case however, usage differs significantly by winery size: for example, 72% of small wineries compared with 100% of very large wineries ($\chi^2(3) = 11.88, p < .01$, N = 155). For exporting wineries, usage of online compliance processes differed significantly by winery size. For example, approximately 45% of the small and medium wineries used the online compliance process for wine export approvals compared with approximately 75% of the large and very large wineries, a significant difference in usage level ($\chi^2(3) = 15.92, p < .01$, N = 76). The same type of pattern was observed for wineries using the Web to process customs clearances, with only about 15% of small and medium wineries using this option, except that in this case the usage levels of very large wineries, at 64%, was markedly higher than that of the large wineries at 30%. The difference by winery size for online custom compliance is significant ($\chi^2(3) = 15.79, p < .01$, N = 31). Note: the uptake of online compliance for export customs declarations has changed considerably since the export component of Australia's Integrated Cargo System went live in late 2004. Online transaction processing for export declarations is now close to 100%; see Table 2 for details.

Analysis of survey responses indicated B2G related e-business is increasing, with clear evidence that most respondents are finding compliance with government regulations easier due to the functionality and utility of e-government Web sites. Respondents also anticipated that their e-business activities in the next 12 to 18 months

Table 2. Monthly export lodgment numbers by type for export component of ICS

	Lodgements of export declarations in Australia			
Month	Manual	Electronic	Total	% Manual of Total
Sep-04	250	8,961	9,211	2.71%
Oct-04	1,274	110,083	111,357	1.14%
Nov-04	827	111,486	112,313	0.74%
Dec-04	717	103,575	104,292	0.69%
Jan-05	600	85,558	86,158	0.70%
Feb-05	764	100,254	101,018	0.76%
Mar-05	677	110,308	110,985	0.61%
Apr-05	515	108,361	108,876	0.47%
May-05	502	111,894	112,396	0.45%
Jun-05	523	106,673	107,196	0.49%
Jul-05	331	78,458	78,789	0.42%
Totals	6,980	1,035,611	1,042,591	0.67%

will be dominated by increasing use in the areas of B2B and B2G rather than the area of B2C. Overall there was a perception that the role of e-government on e-business adoption by wineries in general is significant, and is in fact a stronger and more influential factor than that of the direct relative advantage delivered by e-business to the wineries themselves.

Survey Finding 2: Network Infrastructure Limitations Acts as Major Barrier

Empirical evidence from the census survey revealed that the limitations of available network speeds and network connection costs are two common barriers to further e-business adoption by Australian wineries, with close to 50% of respondents citing these two issues as barriers. These barriers apply to wineries regardless of organisation size. Telstra is the only network carrier with physical lines into all regional and remote sites. The quality of the lines away from major cities and regional centres provides only limited support for e-business activity. For example, ADSL broadband connections are only available within approximately three and a half kilometres of an ADSL enabled exchange (Telstra, 2004), and many wineries are located outside this range. As one interview respondent made clear, inferior Internet access in regional areas is also accompanied by higher costs: regional businesses pay more to get less.

The following example illustrates the problem in terms of e-commerce costs. A very large, privately owned winery with offices in all Australian states uses online processes for compliance where possible. However, the main production centre is located near a major regional town situated further than three kilometres from the nearest Telstra exchange, with broadband access not available. The standard Internet connection at their regional production site has an annual cost of $11,000 and is 130 times slower than the speed of a similar Internet connection at their city office which has an annual cost of $2,000. The winery spends an additional $90,000 a year to upgrade their Internet connection speed at the regional winery location to acceptable speeds, and Telstra has required up-front contributions of approximately $100,000 for infrastructure upgrades. The winery has little choice other than to make these investments in order to get sufficient speed for transaction processing across the Web.

The winery research confirmed that improvements in network infrastructure quality and lowering associated e-commerce costs are needed in order to reduce the most common barriers facing Australian organisations in the adoption of e-business processes. The current limited penetration of broadband access in Australia acts as a serious inhibitor for growth of e-business adoption, particularly for SMEs and many regional organisations who find the cost burden of upgrading their own telecommunication infrastructure to ensure an acceptable Internet access speed is too high for the resulting level of benefit. The various levels of government recognise their responsibility for improvements in network infrastructure. For example, the Australian Federal Government has developed a national strategy for improving broadband access across the country in partnership with state and territory governments. Objectives include the development of a coordinated approach to future network development in order to reduce price and location barriers, and in particular to provide affordable broadband services in regional Australia (OIE, 2004b). The Victorian State Government has gone further, by agreeing to combine with Telstra to establish a high-speed fibre optic network across Victoria to connect all schools, police offices, and government offices at a total cost of over $120 million (Barker, 2005). Once implemented, this high speed Internet access will advantage e-business operations in Victoria in comparison with the other states.

MANDATING ADOPTION ENSURES E-GOVERNMENT SUCCESS

An interesting point to note from the interview comments provided previously is the awareness of the lack of choice with regard to compliance with the changes stemming from the government's power to regulate and to control the means by which compliance with regulation occurs. The wineries were not *choosing* to adopt online transactions for export clearance compliance — they simply had no choice in the matter. Nor were the respondents anticipating much in the way of direct benefit for themselves — instead they were acting in response to a directive they could not ignore because the directive came from a stakeholder with a much higher degree of power than themselves. It is reasonable to assume that all Australian exporting organisations, not just wineries, will have been conscious of their lack of choice in deciding whether or not to adopt the online process for ICS.

So how successful has the Australian Government been in forcing Australian exporters to process their export declarations via online transaction processing using digital signatures as evidence of identity? The answer is they have been extremely successful. In a correspondence from the Federal Minister for Justice and Customs (C. Ellison, personal communication, August 1, 2005), less than 1% of all export declarations have been lodged since ICS went live in September 2004 using the alternative manual paper system. The manual system is designed with disincentives: extra costs are attached and it is only available at a limited number of locations. The monthly breakdown of export declarations processed between September 2004 and July 2005 between the electronic and manual alternatives is shown in Table 1.

The Australian government has gone to great lengths to support exporting clients during the rollout of ICS by conducting training sessions in capital cities and large regional centres; providing online guides; and by providing an electronic simulation of ICS for new clients in order to build familiarity with the system. Broadband access is not required for the Web-based system to operate with full functionality, and clients in remote regions of Australia have successfully adopted the online system.

The example of successful ICS adoption by Australian organisations illustrates the point that organisations sometimes adopt e-business processes because of stakeholder pressure. It is not relative advantage or ease of use driving the adoption decision. The decision to adopt is forced because a more powerful member of the stakeholder group, one with sufficient power to mandate change, dictates how the process will be managed. The role of relationship management between stakeholders in the context of e-government projects and uneven stakeholder power is examined further in work by Chan, Pan, and Tan (2003).

The development and adoption of the ICS by the Australian government is an example of e-government designed for the benefit of government and the nations' citizens as a whole, with a particular focus on increasing security levels. The Australian government has chosen to introduce online compliance with online evidence of identity (EOI) via digital certificates and provision of online security via public key infrastructure (PKI) in order to reap benefits of better government rather than for benefit to the exporters and importers. The need for online EOI has forced all participating users of the online system to purchase digital certificates. In turn many organisations will, for the very first time, have overcome any hurdle which the lack of online evidence of identity had previously presented. It is possible that the introduction of the ICS within Australia may pave the way for increased adoption of other online transaction processes which require digital certificates for EOI purposes, although at this stage, this is merely speculation.

FUTURE RESEARCH

There is much scope for future research in the role of governments with regard to e-business adoption and stakeholder relationships. The observations made in this chapter on the role of government in e-business adoption suggest that the theoretical framework from the DOI perspective needs modification when applied to e-business adoption. Figure 2 illustrates some suggested changes to the DOI theory by adding in an extra innovation characteristic related to the network externality effect when benefit depends on adopter numbers, while the stakeholder pressures from the external environment have also been included, with influence from e-government singled out because of its pivotal role in determining many e-business conditions and compliance processes within national boundaries.

E-government is still emerging and developing as a mechanism for reliable, secure, and effective government. As more e-government projects come online and experience grows, then analysis of the successes and failures will be vital to improving our understanding of how governments can best leverage benefit from e-business processes for their

Figure 2. Modified set of influential factors for e-business adoption, based on DOI theory (Source: Rogers, 1995), with additions shown in italics

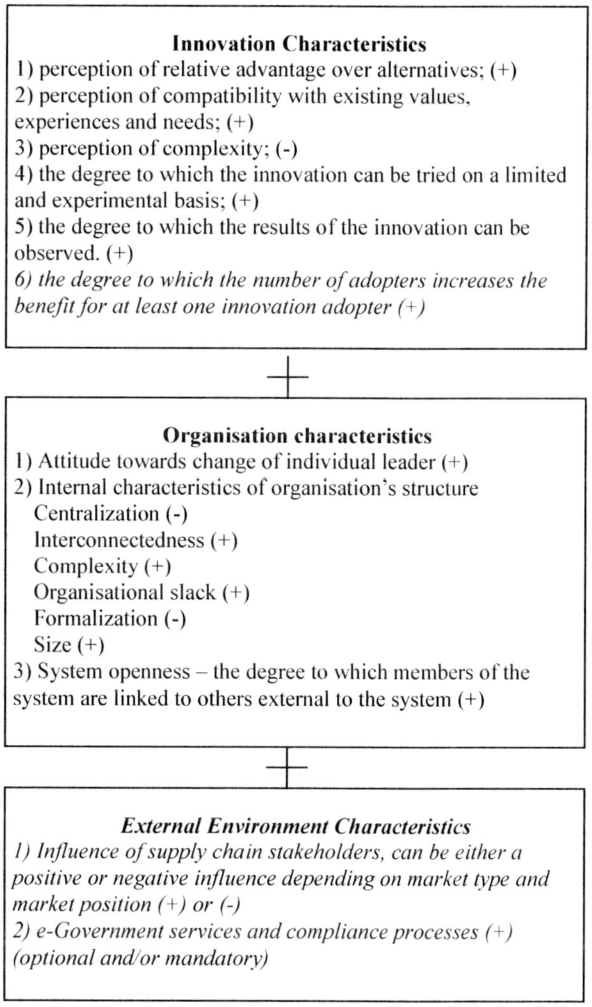

nation and citizens. Research by IS professionals will aid this analysis process and potentially guide future directions of both e-government projects and the provision of government controlled structuring conditions to allow e-business to flourish within the marketplace.

CONCLUSION

The role of government in e-business adoption has been shown to be multifaceted. First, governments play an important role as an e-business champion. The Australian government is committed to this role because of the strong belief that e-business will strengthen and improve the Australian economy. Second, governments are responsible for providing the physical network infrastructure that most of the nation's citizenry and organisations rely on for the conduct of their e-business practices. The quality, speed, and cost of this access are crucial elements in determining the effectiveness, depth, and extent of e-business adoption for many organisations. The example from Australia discussed earlier served to illustrate this point. Third, the development of e-government for the purpose of improving communication, flow of information, and online transaction processing to aid regulation awareness and compliance acts as a strong driver of e-business adoption in some, but not all, e-business process domains. There is evidence that governments can use their powerful stakeholder position to effectively force online adoption for compliance purposes when necessary, in order to maximise adopter numbers and thus increase the benefits for government and the nation to the level desired. A theoretical implication follows: all organisations with sufficient stakeholder power, whether private (big businesses) or government, have the potential to effectively mandate adoption of their own e-business processes which strongly depend on the number of adopters to achieve sufficient relative advantage.

REFERENCES

ACIL. (2002). *Pathways to profitability for small and medium wineries.* ACIL Consulting. Retrieved from http://www.aciltasman.com.au/images/pdf/wine_report_v2.pdf

Allen Consulting Group. (2002). *Australia's information economy: The big picture*. Melbourne: NOIE.

Anderson, D. (2000). Creating and nurturing a premier e-business. *Journal of Interactive Marketing, 14*(3), 67-73.

Anderson, K. (2000). *Export-led growth.* Retrieved April 29, 2006, from http://www.rirdc.gov.au/reports/GLC/00-52.pdf

Anderson, K. (2001, May). Prospects ahead for the wine industry. *The Australian Grapegrower and Winemaker, 448*, 67-74.

Bakry, S. H., & Bakry, F. H. (2001). A strategic view for the development of e-business. *International Journal of Network Management, 11*(2), 103-112.

Barker, G. (2005, June 8). High-fibre diet for regions. *The Age*.

Brown, E. (2002). *Accelerating the up-take of e-commerce by small and medium enterprises* (Report and Action Plan). Small Enterprise Telecommunications Centre (SETEL). Retrieved from http://www.setel.com/au.smeforum2002

Chan, C. M. L., Pan, S.-L., & Tan, C.-W. (2003). *Managing stakeholder relationships in an e-government project.* Paper presented at the 9th Americas Conference on Information Systems, Tampa, Florida.

Chau, S. B., & Turner, P. (2001, December 5-7). *A four phase model of EC business transformation amongst small to medium sized enterprises: Preliminary findings from 34 Australian case studies.* Paper presented at the 12th Australasian

Conference on Information Systems, Coffs Harbour, NSW, Australia.

Chen, T.-J. (2003). The diffusion and impacts of the Internet and e-commerce in Taiwan. *I-Ways, 26*(4), 185-193.

Chengalur-Smith, I., & Duchessi, P. (1999). The initiation and adoption of client-server technology in organizations. *Information & Management, 35*(2), 77-88.

Cottrill, K. (2001, March 5). E-government grows. *Traffic World, 265,* 19.

Davis, F. D. (1989). Perceived usefulness, perceived ease of use, and user acceptance of information technology. *MIS Quarterly, 13*(3), 318-340.

Dunt, E. S., & Harper, I. R. (2002). E-commerce and the Australian economy. *The Economic Record, 78*(242), 327-342.

Fichman, R. G. (2001). The role of aggregation in the measurement of IT-related organizational innovation. *MIS Quarterly, 25*(4), 427-455.

Gefen, D., Pavlou, P., Warkentin, M., & Rose, G. (2002). *EGovernment adoption.* Paper presented at the Eighth Americas Conference on Information Systems, Dallas, TX.

Gibbs, J., Kraemer, K. L., & Dedrick, J. (2003). Environment and policy factors shaping global e-commerce diffusion: A cross-country comparison. *Information Society, 19*(1), 5-18.

Hofacker, C. F. (1984). Categorical judgment scaling with ordinal assumptions. *Multivariate Behavioural Research, 19*(1), 91-106.

Katz, C. M. L. S. (1986). Technology adoption in the presence of network externalities. *Journal of Political Economy, 94*(4), 822-842.

Ke, W., & Wei, K. K. (2004). Successful e-government in Singapore. *Communications of the ACM, 47*(6), 95-99.

Kwon, T. H., & Zmud, R. W. (1987). Unifying the fragmented models of information systems implementation. In R. J. Boland & R. A. Hirschheim (Eds.), *Critical issues in information systems research* (pp. 227-251). New York: John Wiley & Sons.

Markus, M. L., & Soh, C. (2002). Structural influences on global e-commerce activity. *Journal of Global Information Management, 10*(1), 5-12.

Mathieson, K., Peacock, E., & Chin, W. W. (2001). Extending the technology acceptance model: The influence of perceived user resources. *The Database for Advances in Information Systems, 32*(3), 86-112.

McKie, S. (2001). *E-business best practices.* New York: John Wiley & Sons.

NOIE. (2000). *Taking the plunge 2000.* Canberra: National Office for the Information Economy.

NOIE. (2001). *Advancing with e-commerce: A summary of 34 case studies of small business e-commerce ventures.* Canberra: National Office for Information Economy.

NOIE. (2002a). *Advancing with e-business: Case studies.* Retrieved April 29, 2006, from http://www.dcita.gov.au/ie/publications/2002/november/advancing_with_e-business_case_studies

NOIE. (2002b). *The benefits of doing business electronically: E-business.* Retrieved April 29, 2006, from http://www.noie.gov.au/projects/ebusiness/Advancing/benefits/index.htm

NOIE. (2003a). *Advancing with e-business: Supply chain case studies.* Retrieved April 29, 2006, from http://www2.dcita.gov.au/ie/publications/2003/08/e-bus_supp_chain

NOIE. (2003b). *E-government benefits study.* Retrieved April 29, 2006, from http://www.noie.gov.au/publications/NOIE/egovt_benefits/index.htm

OECD. (2002). *Measuring the information economy 2002*. Retrieved April 29, 2006, from http://www.oecd.org/pdf/M00036000/M00036089.pdf

OIE. (2004a). *Information economy.* Retrieved April 29, 2006, from http://www.dcita.gov.au/ie

OIE. (2004b). *The national broadband strategy.* Retrieved April 29, 2006, from http://www2.dcita.gov.au/ie/framework/broadband

Palacios, J. J. (2003). Globalization and e-commerce: Diffusion and impacts in Mexico. *I-Ways, 26*(4), 195-205.

Porter, M. E. (2001). Strategy and the Internet. *Harvard Business Review, 79*(3), 63-78.

Rogers, E. M. (1995). *Diffusion of innovations* (4th ed.). New York: The Free Press.

Sawhney, M., & Zabin, J. (2001). *The seven steps to nirvana*. New York: McGraw-Hill.

Sekaran, U. (2003). *Research methods for business: A skill building approach* (4th ed.). New York: John Wiley & Sons.

Swanson, E. B. (1994). Information systems innovation among organizations. *Management Science, 40*(9), 1069-1092.

Telstra. (2004). *ADSL frequently asked questions.* Retrieved April 29, 2006, from http://www.telstra.com.au/demand/faq.htm

Turban, E., King, D., Lee, J., Warkentin, M., & Chung, H. M. (2002). *Electronic commerce 2002: A managerial perspective*. Upper Saddle River, NJ: Prentice Hall.

Varian, H. R. (1999). *Intermediate microeconomics*. New York: W.W. Norton & Company.

Venkatesh, V., Morris, M. G., Davis, G. B., & Davis, F. D. (2003). User acceptance of information technology: Toward a unified view. *MIS Quarterly, 27*(3), 425-478.

Winetitles. (2003). *Australian wine industry overview.* Retrieved April 29, 2006, from http://www.winetitles.com.au/awol/overview/wineries.asp

Wong, P.-K. (2003). Global and national factors affecting e-commerce diffusion in Singapore. *Information Society, 19*(1), 19-32.

Wu, F., Mahajan, V., & Balasubramanian, S. (2003). An analysis of e-business adoption and its impact on business performance. *Journal of the Academy of Marketing Science, 31*(4), 425-447.

Yang, H., Yoo, Y., Lyytinen, K., & Ahn, J.-H. (2004, February 25). *Diffusion of broadband mobile services in Korea: The role of standards and its impact on diffusion of complex technology system.* Paper presented at the e-Biz World Conference, Seoul, Korea.

Yin, R. K. (1994). *Case study research: Design and methods* (2nd ed.). Thousand Oaks: Sage Publications.

Zikmund, W. G. (2000). *Business research methods* (6th ed.). Orlando: The Dryden Press.

This work was previously published in Electronic Government: Concepts, Methodologies, Tools, and Applications, edited by A. Anttiroiko, copyright 2008 by Information Science Reference, formerly known as Idea Group Reference (an imprint of IGI Global).

Chapter III
The Role of Simulation in Business Process Reengineering

Firas M. Alkhaldi
Arab Academy for Banking and Financial Sciences, Jordan

Mohammad Olaimat
Arab Academy for Banking and Financial Sciences, Jordan

Abdullah Abdali Rashed
Saba University, Yemen

ABSTRACT

This chapter discusses the importance of business process simulation, while illustrating the relationship between business process reengineering (BPR) and change management, it focuses the discussion on the role of simulation in supporting BPR and the effect of simulation on business environment related skills, business management related skills, leadership related skills, employees empowering level, process improvement, ethical issues, and stakeholders' management skills. The chapter discusses the value of simulation in implementing reengineering strategies and argues the future challenges of business process simulation and describes the limitations of simulation technology in reengineering business processes. Finally, it concludes with a discussion of the characteristics of successful simulation and simulation applications.

INTRODUCTION

Business Process: Definitions and Concepts

The logic of business is to create an advantage and/or utilize an opportunity, given this context; it implies the necessity to identify driving forces in order to fully exploit this idea. In general, one or more of the following issue(s) has the tendency to drive any probable business improvement:

- **Customer:** His/her requirements, culture, expectations, consumerism and even his/her feedback on the final product/service may enforce an organization to change its policies in order to gain their satisfaction, since low satisfaction will negatively impact product promotion.

- **Cost:** Basic notion within business logic for both seller and buyer, and the complex side of this logic appears when this perception is related to quality sensitivity.
- **Competition:** Results from micro and macro business environment, that is, market status, legal issues, consumerism situations, and so forth.

The question here is how organizations can remain competitive and, protecting itself from increasing competition threats at the same time dealing with its revenue from costly operations, attract more customers? Surely the answer to this question is not easy; the question here links the company assets (resources) as inputs, how to treat these assets (processing) and the outcome of the business operations, where the acceptance of the product by customers echo its success. Therefore it can be noted that processing operations are stressed, since it determines the success or failure of any product. Accordingly organizations revise their processes so as to maintain their competitiveness.

Prior to carrying out the hows of redesign and improve organization processes, it is necessary to demonstrate some process definitions and the sagacity behind each one of them. There are many definitions of process; this is due to viewpoint, background and trends of the researcher as well as the market common strategies; that is, push/pull strategies, where the adopted strategies demand considering certain outlooks and neglecting others. Each definition considers one or more of the following perspectives: input (resources), activities, output (product/services), and customer and organization objectives. For example, Pall (1987) expressed process as arranging different organization resources (for example: people, materials, energy, equipment, and procedures) reasonably to accomplish work activities leading to specific work product. Correspondingly, Davenport & Short (1990) described it as a collection of sensibly interrelated tasks executed to attain a certain business product. Moreover, Harrington (1991) stated that business process is making use of the organization inputs by collection of judiciously interrelated tasks that facilitate achieving the organization's goals. Omrani (1992) argue that process is the result of cycle of activities that are collectively taken to attain business goals. Likewise, Talwar (1993) defined the process as a series of identified activities implemented to achieve a specified type of outcome. Hammer and Champy (1993) considered the customer perspective when they defined the process as a collection of activities that, all in all, generate a consequence of importance to a customer. The next definition stressed the process boundaries; this characterization was presented by Davenport (1993) who defines process as "an organizing work activities across the place, with a start, an end and obviously identified inputs and outputs." Earl (1994) characterized process as a lateral or horizontal form that sums up the interdependence of tasks, roles, people, departments and, functions required to supply a customer with a product or service. Ferrie (1995) defined processes as being a definable set of activities that form a known foundation. Finally, Saxena (1996) explains business process as a set of interrelated work activities characterized by specific inputs and value-added tasks that produce specific outputs.

Change Management Approaches: Comparative Study

There are many approaches to change management, in the following discussion the researchers will focus on total quality management (TQM), business process reengineering (BPR), and knowledge management.

Total Quality Management

Total quality management (TQM) can be seen as a non-ending process to achieve necessary quality improvement, which needs effort and time, furthermore leading to the emergence of these efforts properly, which means more degree of commitment and support from workers and management. It is necessary to note that TQM is a novel way to do business, acting as a map to guide organization working processes where TQM engages deeply in cultural change. Juran (1986) developed a quality management framework, in which customers' needs are the focus of TQM, for whom value is delivered through well known, appreciated and administered processes. According to Sink (1991) each process consists of five elements: providers, inputs, value-added processes, outputs and, customers. Processes must be distorted and different forms of information must be considered to support decision-making in the new environment (Olian & Rynes, 1991). In the context of the above process components, management is concerned with improving input, output, customer views, and process quality assertion, in addition to tending providers' management. Accordingly, TQM concepts are activated by controlling performance of the above components (Sink, 1991). To organize TQM efforts, a systematic methodology is necessary to deal with different problems and utilization of chances in a controlled approach, which binds all the efforts to the common target. The quality target ought to be converted into plans, specifications, and measurements, all of which are management's liability (Bonser, 1992). Quality information is a vital element of the TQM infrastructure (Godfrey, 1993). Providing the precise information is critical to support the comprehensive TQM efforts. In short, total quality should be managed based on facts rather than on instinct or feel (Garvin, 1991). Quality management requires data regarding such factors as consumer, product and service performance, operations, market, competitive comparisons, suppliers, internal processes, employees, and cost and finance. To deal with different TQM issues, decision-makers need quality information in which support his/her decision.

Therefore, in a TQM environment, effective processing and dissemination of quality information is a vital role in successful operations, especially if we know that decision quality cannot consistently rise above the quality of information upon which the decisions are based. To support TQM efforts, the organization's information base must be comprehensive and easy to find and use. Poor and inconsistent data will divert efforts by focusing on problems of data quality rather than on the quality of the organization's outcomes.

Business Process Reengineering

The concept of business process reengineering (BPR) was first introduced by Hammer in 1990. BPR has many definitions; Hammer (1990) defined BPR as making use of new information technology to fundamentally redesign business processes to attain remarkable progress in performance. Conversely, Goll (1992) describe it as the full transformation of a business; an unconstrained restructuring of all business processes, technologies, and management systems, as well as organizational structure and values, to improve performance throughout the business. Ahadi (2004) stated that from the practitioner point of view there are five building blocks that are obvious to shape the fundamental topics that characterize BPR: radical or at least considerable change; business process centered analysis; achieve major goals or dramatic performance improvements; information technology is a critical enabler; and organizational changes are a critical enabler. Several organizations have achieved success from their BPR attempts by controlling costs and achieving breakthrough performance in a variety of parameters, such as delivery times, customer service, and quality. However, not all companies that undertake BPR effort achieve their intended results. BPR has great potential for increasing productivity through reduced process time and cost, improved quality, and greater customer satisfaction, but to do so it must be implemented and managed in the best interest of customers, employees, and organizations.

Knowledge Management

Knowledge management (KM) is a process of elicitation, transformation, and diffusion of knowledge throughout enterprise so that it can be shared and thus reused (Turban et al., 2004). At the organizational level, knowledge value is limited if not shared. KM can also be seen as the process of generating value out of organization's intangible resources (Liebowitz, 1999, 2000; Liebowitz & Beckman, 1998). Grant (1996) argues that the ability to integrate and apply dedicated knowledge of organizational affiliates is essential to firm's ability to create and maintain competitive advantage. Therefore, the focus of knowledge management is how to share knowledge and how to create value added benefits to the organization. On the other hand, some organizations have an aged workforce and this may illustrate the necessity for sharing the skills of those experts. Knowledge management is a process of capturing, creation, codification, communication and capitalization of knowledge throughout an enterprise so that it can be utilized effectively and efficiently, where the authors refer to the above process as the KM 5Cs model. During the knowledge capture phase, searching for several sources of knowledge that are necessary and related for performing the work using analogy, metaphor, models, brainstorming, and similar mechanisms are conducted. Knowledge creation phase involve conducting research activities, verification and validation process consecutively to discover the knowledge in the organization, and utilizing experiences and routine procedures to prepare an appropriate culture and systems. Knowledge codification phase includes classification and categorization of existing knowledge in the organization according to its nature into categories, such as administrative, technical, financial, and so forth, knowledge of the organization to reflect what is actually known and done by the organization, and refining and filtering knowledge of the organization in order to access the most significant knowledge. On the other hand, the knowledge communication phase represents the process of considering sources, nature, and attributes of knowledge when transferring and sharing in the organization, encouraging and enhancing the culture of knowledge sharing among organizational members, anytime, anywhere, access when it is needed, and determining who can transfer knowledge. Finally, the knowledge capitalization phase is about investing and utilizing organizational knowledge in an innovative way, improving the existing methods of work practices leading to encouraging individual competitiveness and effectiveness. Enhancing the feeling of individual responsibility bring about changes in organizational culture. Knowledge capitalization is the process of finding new practices for performing organizational work to improve organization performance, balancing cost-benefits, enhancing creativity in decision-making process and problem solving, utilizing the embedded knowledge in order to direct the future behavior of organizational members, evolving organizational knowledge through the feedback, and evaluating the outcomes of organizational knowledge through the services that are offered by the organization.

Liebowitz (2001) discussed challenges that influence knowledge management scheme success in any organization. He argued that organization culture in reference to the required degree of knowledge sharing and how to build and enhance knowledge sharing is a vital role for successful knowledge management; furthermore, seeing knowledge management as part of the strategic vision of the firm. Maintaining knowledge repositories and security are among these challenges. He claimed that user-friendly design, trouble-free knowledge management programs are necessary; and finally, employees have to be motivated, that is through incentives, so that knowledge sharing will likely be accomplished.

WHY SIMULATION?

In the preceding sections, it was argued that the main benefit of BPR is to recognize and put into practice alternatives to the organization that desires to develop its activities and/or processes. This task might be easy when the processes that shape business cycles are static and trouble-free, but what is the solution when:

1. The processes are of dynamic nature (i.e., customer-based businesses).
2. The global market is the goal of the organization (i.e., competition conditions).
3. No time to conduct trial and error.
4. The company desires to manage customer expectations and outcome predictions that may result from radical change.
5. The direct execution of all alternatives will be unsafe.

The rate of failure in reengineering projects is over 50%: one of the major tribulations that has a say to the breakdown of BPR projects is the need for tools for evaluating the sound effects of a considered solution before execution (Hlupic & Vreede, 2005).

In the following section the authors will illustrate simulation definitions, the environs under which simulation is advised, the impact of new environments on simulation, the factors that shape the extra value of simulation, and finish with a discussion of the significance of simulation from a business viewpoint.

WHAT IS SIMULATION?

In the context of BPR, simulation can be regarded as a tool to aid the decision-maker to assess the on-hand alternatives, subsequently employing the most appropriate (not necessarily the appropriate) alternative as a tolerable solution for the problem under consideration. As BPR is changing approach, then there will be an as-is model which will brings to light the opportunities on hand, rewards that exist, the level of performance, well-built/frail processes, and so forth, and, on the other hand, a to-be model processing the challenging sides and infrequent potential. Finally, the judgment will exceed through the simulation panel to include, remove, or adjust any process that may guide to client approval. Following the simulation team observations, the client will appraise the model, which will be the portrait of the future according to his/her requirements. So simulation is the attempt to bridge the gap between the client requirements and the anticipated actual status from one side and bridging the gap between the decision-maker and his/her facilities before execution, when all alternatives may be costly. From the above argument, it may be concluded that simulation might result in information that could have different meanings according to the receiver, who may utilize it differently according to his/her requirements.

WHEN TO SIMULATE?

Simulation, as in any activity, may require time to be achieved, financial support is also a matter to bring the right outcome; moreover, specialists who need training and whose passable level of loyalty to the organization to work within the organization margins of benefit is needed. So the question arises as to when simulation is advised? To answer this question we must return to the process philosophy. Pressmen (2005) notes that each business system is composed of one or more business processes, and each business process is defined by a set of sub-processes. In the context of this notification about the hierarchical nature of business system, two related issues may be emphasized:

1. Complexity increases as we move descending in the hierarchy.
2. Risk increases as we move upward in the hierarchy.

Considering complexity, the combination between the business processes from one side and between the tasks that form these processes/sub-processes from another side play a major role to determine whether simulation is proper or not. As combination level increases, simulation has to be conducted. On the other hand, when it is difficult to divide the main processes (at the top of the hierarchy) and it is difficult to decide the appropriate alternative based upon the client requirements, simulation has to be conducted. Until now the business process/sub-process as a whole has been considered, but what about the process itself? During the introduction to this section, dynamism, globality, time factor, and expectations management were underlined, all of these factors drive the world toward process oriented adoption, which enable the client to be the controller of the market along with its changing requirements, where the process itself needs to be dynamic. As this dynamism increases, the need for simulation is increased. Simulation in general engaged in situations where the arbitrary content does matter and cannot be modeled by other methodical techniques. Cheng (1992) viewed simulation as a tool of final option to be engaged just once further methods are ruled out. He cited the high computational expenditure and time and effort required in constructing models as drawbacks of the simulation approach. On the other hand, Swain (1993) and Bhaskar (1994) recommended that the simplicity of model structure and price economies in computing originate simulation as a tool of selection for modeling complex systems and validating analytical models before going on to optimization. In the following section we will study the bond between new environment and simulation.

New Environment and Simulation

In the previous subsections it was distinguished that the business chain becomes process-oriented rather than production-oriented due to client enablement in the new economy, where the opportunities and advantages are disseminated among big as well as undersized organizations, as well as the risks affected both sides in the new economy. Enterprise resource planning (ERP) was a solution for many organizations, but this solution has a limited capacity to meet the repeated varying requirements that are the core success in the new economy. ERP may be a good proactive solution, but the new environment needs proactive and reactive or even rapid reactive solutions that sustain an accurate decision-making process as changes take place. It must be concerted that simulation is not substitute to ERP solutions, but hold and function with these solutions side by side to support decision-making.

Simulation Areas and Applications

Dynamism, frequent changes, Internet settings, and globalization are some of several issues that enforce using simulation in novel economy. One of the salient characters of the new economy is the diversity of applications that can be conducted within such huge environment. It can be said that simulation is a tool that can be used in most business applications; this is due to:

- Applications diversity: in the new economy companies found themselves enforced to conduct many profitable activities especially small to medium companies where the rivalry of large companies in a certain activity may bound their ability to survive or even to go on in the market.

- Unsafe environment: in conventional business world ethics, security, payment methods and similar issues can be managed to an accepted limit. In the new economy, these issues are hard to control to the same limit in traditional business world; besides, the frequently changing business surroundings formulate simulation as a preferred solution to control these matters.
- Complexity: complexity goes up rapidly due to the association of new relationships, new partners, new processes, supply chain improvement and so on.
- The human behavior role in business triumph is going up, which means the need to predict its responsive behavior on the way to change. All these aspects are directly related to the cost issues, which step up the business activities.

Hugen et al. (2003) claimed that the upcoming day's simulation technology would get in touch with more and more applications. In the same context, Jain (1999) stated that simulation will become the way to do business in the future: he argued that making use of simulation modeling will extend from traditional applications in manufacturing and the logistics side to business processes and interactive simulation applications in training and sales. The following are some examples of applications and areas where simulation can be valuable:

1. Manufacturing: simulation can support successful manufacturing regarding product design, layouts, flow of materials, manufacturing processes and even the organization structure.
2. Conflict management: simulations enhance decision-making skills for these areas in supporting efforts for conflict evasion and conflict declaration (Oren, 2002).
3. Training: simulation can enhance an organization's efforts to train its staff or new employees about the significance and practice of cooperation or even use simulation as training system, making use of machine learning theories (Oren, 2002).
4. Judgment of manpower requirements.
5. Competitive market analysis.
6. Production planning and inventory control.
7. Corporate planning.
8. Man-machine interaction.

And other diverse applications and areas in which simulation can be used effectively.

SIMULATION ... SIMULATION

Up to now, simulation concept, the condition under which simulation is informed, and the relation between novel environment and simulation were established. The question arises: where is simulation in the information and knowledge world? When someone notifies you that the weather is cloudy then he may have knowledge different from that of you (see Figure 1).

Ali notifies Ahmad that the climate is cloudy; this means (knowledge) to some extent to Ahmad differs from that of Ali, where this meaning is associated to the necessities of each one, which may or may not be the alike. Figure 1 can be extended to the idea under consideration, that is, simulation. Imagine that the people in the above figure change to be an organization with knowledge resource, there will be area where the knowledge within its resource may mean many things according to each organization, these things result from the organization's diverse requirements, for instance, increasing market share as an information may mean making revenue and rising duty, the options depend on several factors: legal issues, competition status, and so on. In this and similar districts simulation will effectively enhance the decision–maker's efforts to seize

Figure 1. Knowledge conversion

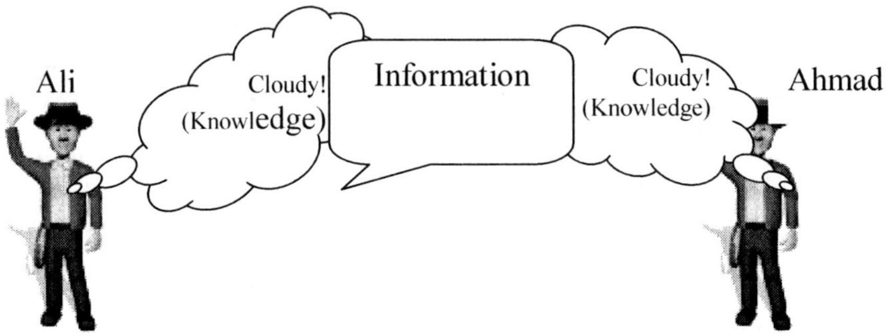

the proper decision. An important characteristic of simulation models is their ability to provide quantitative information, providing a foundation for assessment and comparisons of choice decision strategies to settle on whether that choice accomplishes the decision-maker's objectives or not. In the digital settings the business pressures are divided into three categories: market, societal, and technological, each one of these pressures calls for particular reaction types derived from certain requirements of the organization under consideration by making use of diverse responses (alternatives) simulating.

Business Process Simulation

Business logic is based on taking advantage or utilizing opportunity, nevertheless, it can be claimed that advantage or opportunity imply either cost or time in most cases of the business world. The organization may follow many tactics to achieve its objectives, for example, one organization may improve the way to reach its customers (demand pull/supply push), and another one may adjust its working processes, develop the working team or even take on new habits to everyday work. All the above tactics are related strongly to the inquiry mentioned earlier, to be precise, what if?

In the new economy, opportunity or advantage are robustly interrelated to the assets (information, knowledge) of organizations, so it can be argued that simulation aims to bring valuable information within the required time, which will lead at the end of the day to building many scenarios to support the decision-maker, who will agree on the appropriate alternative according to certain requirements. In the following section we will recognize the concept concerning business process simulation.

Business Process Elements

Tumay (1995) claimed that the four basic building blocks of a proper model are:

- Flow objects: it may be referred to as entities; these are objects that are processed by resources, for example, customer.
- Resources: these are agents that are used for accumulation value to flow objects; they are to be paid to activities, for example, service representatives.
- Activities: they are linked by routings to stand for the stream of objects through the simulation model, for example, batching.
- Routings: label the various types of associates between activities.

Model Performance Measures

Tumay (1996) suggested that the basic model performance measures are cycle time, entity count, resource utilization, and activity cost.

1. **Cycle time:** it is the entire time an entity uses during a process, this time incorporates: value added process time, waiting time, movement time, and so forth. One of the most precious outcomes of business process simulation is the automatic tracking and estimating of cycle time for each entity; furthermore, business process simulation tools present average and maximum values based on the total count of entities that pass through the process.
2. **Entity count**: it comprises the total number of entities that traverse a process or that are still being processes. This signifies that the total entities count is the sum of entities processed plus the entities that are in process. Business process simulation tools routinely track and evaluate entity counts for each type of entity in the model.
3. **Resource utilization**: throughout simulation resources change states from active to idle, from active to inverted. Resource utilization defines the percentage of time that a resource spends in each condition. The accessibility and transfer of resources shape the share of resources to activities in a model. So the resource uses results to provide helpful information in measuring and analyzing under-utilization or over-utilization of resources.
4. **Activity cost:** a resource is defined in a process model by the number of available units, handling overheads, system expenditure, and predetermined expenses. Activity cost is defined by the resources required to execute it, the time for the activity, and the entities that it processes. Activity cost calculations provide a sensible way for measuring and analyzing the cost of activities.

Simulation Life Cycle

Prior to discussing simulation life cycle, it should be concentrated on the idea that in simulation we are working with a model of the problem and this makes it possible to keep away from possible errors during implementation, such as discovering that the problem under consideration was not entirely covered. Since we simulate requirements that are changing repeatedly, simulation life cycle will be iterative in nature, and this nature entails assessment of exactness (i.e., validation, verification) after completing each phase of simulation study, which makes the reverse switch, is probable. Hlupic & Vreede (2005) suggested that the activities concerning business process simulation include the following steps:

a. Definition of modeling objectives,
b. Definition of model boundaries,
c. Data collection and analysis,
d. Development of business process simulation model,
e. Model testing,
f. Model experimentation,
g. Output analysis, and
h. Recommendations of business process change.

Definition of modeling objectives: any obstacle that binds the capability of making use of opportunity or taking advantage is a problem in the business world; once this problem is acknowledged it will be brought to the table to be solved. So the solution to this problem will be the vision of the upcoming model; for example, evaluating the consequence of entering WTO or evaluating the role of private sector may participate in developing economies. Subsequent to determining the modeling objectives, the question arises of how to achieve these objectives? The answer to this question will be shown through the following discussions.

Definition of model boundaries: within real

life there are a lot of problems where solution cost to these problems is high enough to convince the decision-maker to put down them as they are. So it is vital to verify the processes that can be considered before getting the point where we found that the problem wasn't well recognized.

Determining the processes that can be considered depend on the requirements, the objectives of modeling process, and their associations with the processes considered; it also it depends on the availability of the crucial resources: time, experts, or even the information itself.

Data collection and analysis: in the preceding step the availability of necessary resources was revealed. This border line is very important since we study a problem that will be modeled. So experts' ability to mine the information or even data from those experts, and time availability to obtain the associated data is very important factor in the series. There are numerous ways to gather the definite data required: interviews, direct observations, studying documents, and so forth. Following the required data collection, they should be analyzed by means of methodical approach to get to the goal of this step.

Development of business process simulation model: it relates to a simulation model enlargement using a simulation software package. Since simulation life cycle has an iterative nature, the software package should be prepared through an iterative and incremental process, and this entails adopting agile process models where the regularly changing requirements will be easily conducted for example: extreme programming, adaptive software development, starting with a simple model then, with the progress of ideas, this model will be extended and distinguished until an adequate model is obtained.

This is the case if the software is developed in-house, but if it is outsourced then the desirable characteristics are introduced through an RFP document.

Model testing: the point to be emphasized here is that testing must be conducted following each iteration throughout model growth; the purpose of this step is to handle any errors coming in or out of the model, studying the effect of these errors, and recording these errors to be under consideration in the scene. A series of different tests are conducted, each of which has explicit purpose although the final target is to verify that system elements have been properly incorporated and carry out allocated functions.

Model experimentation: formerly, model performance measures, model testing, were discussed; the next step will be for exercising the model by concerning the model performance measures through formal experimentation.

Experiments should be planned in such a way in an attempt to decrease arbitrary errors, and include a broad range of alternatives so that recommendations could be relevant for a variety of organizational units, the experiment should be as simple as possible, and a sound statistical analysis should be applied without making impractical assumptions related to the nature of business processes.

Output analysis: the tip to be stressed here is that, throughout several experiments conducted, major business interrelated key variables are estimated then the consequences explored. Subsequently, statistical tests can be used to verify whether there are noteworthy differences between key model output variables of various experiments.

Recommendations of business process change: simulation of business processes allow the simulation team to revise diverse possible scenarios, which will guide them to the most accurate scenario through which the organization can attain its objectives, followed by formulating the recommended scenario and fire it to the decision-maker who will revise the recommended scenarios resulting in adopting or rejecting the proposal following validating each choice. One of the regular scenarios resulting from simulation is the radical change in the course of actions of conducting certain process(s), that is, business process reengineering. In the following section we will give attention to the role of simulation in supporting BPR.

The Role of Simulation in Supporting BPR

In the previous sections, simulation perception was conversed taking into account the simulation life cycle. The question arises: what to simulate? Pressman (2005) indicated that within business processes people, equipments, material resources, and business procedures are pooled to generate a particular result. Levas (1995) claimed that the long-established sight of business process has been bringing down to a little degree; it is replaced by innovative pattern, where clients, dealer, the stream of work and the communication force supersede the organizational map. Earlier, it was stated that as complexity enhanced, simulation would be preferable; besides, the increase of risk entails that simulation tools be used. It is obligatory to recognize that human issues are fundamental in business cycles, so it is significant to study this factor's effects, trends, and skills. To emphasis that point, Levas (1995) stated: "We will need to move toward process representation and analysis that seeks to capture the unique skills and capabilities of each individual." So it is essential to realize the human capital, which plays a vital role in information and knowledge era. To illustrate the value of employees' role in business process reengineering scheme refer to Paper et al. (2003).

Bridgeland and Becker (1994) asserted that it is critical that a BPR modeling tool provides the way for capturing intellectual assets.

In the preceding sections it was stated that BPR is iterative process, so as long as we can minimize time required for iterations it will lead to successful BPR. Once information technology is involved within business process, the procedure's cycle time will be automatically minimized, but the problem arises where the time losses are related to human understanding, in which it will be a function of their willingness to utilize their skills to accelerate business process principally in new settings, where fluctuations are recurrent. In the following discussions, a variety of domains where simulation can play a vital role in supporting BPR will be considered, these domains include: business environment, business management, leadership, employee empowering, process improvement, ethical issues and stakeholders' management.

Business Environment Related Skills

Within the business environment there are numerous stress places, for example, if the vision of one element of the business cycle is not supported by the operational environment, sometimes even if the members of this environment are aware of the value of this vision, then stress will result. Here and in similar cases simulation as a prognostic tool can work effectively to minimize the probable risks. It must be illustrious that effective strategies can be constructed based on stresses thoughtfulness, which will assist in rising up these stresses that may appear in the upcoming days. Each category of these stresses may be faced with various optional strategies, for example, the way in which the operational environment members believe, act, or are energized, the organizational culture, sociability level, solidarity toward the targets—all of these issues must be well thought out to stimulate critical thinking within frail ends, manage probable reasons behind resistance, and hold the vision upon execution.

By applying simulation practices, the critical bounds, roles organizing, disseminating of responsibilities, and conflict management can be managed effectively. Still, it must be remembered that a dynamic business environment calls for dynamism of the stress places where frequent changes come to pass. Again simulation assists in minimizing the risks resulting from these frequent fluctuations.

Business Management Related Skills

Suppose that a corporation sells abroad a certain amount of its products globally to several markets, suddenly, a crisis take place with one or more of these markets, what is the solution? There are ROI losses; production size implies new storage facilities, which induce extra costs, and so forth. To be proactive, such economic uncertainties must be considered, all probable alternatives must be at the table, simulation seems to be useful tool to care for such economic uncertainties. In the new economy, international agreements are held—that is, WTO, which means new markets—at that moment, the problem is to determine the needs of such markets, and circumstances forced by these contracts. Simulation will support the efforts for balancing market needs, and the forecast of the possible revenues. A vital role of management is to create and facilitate the useful and possible change: as a preliminary stage, you as a manager must ask yourself:

1. Where are the changes required that lead to profitability?
2. What are the barriers that may face that change?

All of these questions represent the aspiration to induce change, and many alternatives are possible: from front line employees, middle management, or the client, the point is what will be the cost of each option? This may depends on the related issues of each option. Simulation is a technique that can be used to minimize the risk that may result from adopting one alternative over others. It is a vital point for management that all business procedures must be kept within the business cycle time line (task time), if any trouble appears, many solutions are available: cancel the unnecessary tasks, energize the weak points, dismissal of some employees, or even inserting new time management habits fitting the cases under consideration. Once these alternatives are on the table they must be simulated to adopt the appropriate one. Before starting any project the management gives enough time to select the working teams. Team's characteristics must concur with the organization vision to the gainful change.

In the new economy individualism disappears while team work character becomes stronger; the number of teams, individuals forming these teams and odd jobs are examples of what may be simulated to support a decision-maker, who will act together with a first round representation of what will occur later on.

Leadership Related Skills

Within the new economy, organizational culture plays a fundamental role in developing an organization's activities. Within operational environment present diverse workforce settings due to the diversity of their tacit assets and how these assets were fabricated, that is, the training through which they gain their assets, or the individual by whom their beliefs toward organizational culture were affected. Successful leadership enables the related leader to deal with diverse backgrounds and contrasting workforce age groups; for example, in an information era one comes across numerous types of workforces: some believe in experience character, others believes in building new techniques involving IT. Simulation is effective tool that supports efforts to identify the appropriate leadership for a certain type of workforce. Some managers are not aware of the hazard that may result when overlooking the fact that various workforce generations' beliefs ought to to be considered; this phenomenon is related directly to the loyalty level of the workforce to their organization. Practical experience indicates that the leader of any group will form a working model for this group, the members go behind his opinions, trends, and the ways he tracks to solve problems. The frequent fluctuations in the new economy's environment needs a further level of leadership dynamism, which necessitate a leader model of particular characteristics, these individualities must be verified depending on the outcomes of simulation study for performance measures before starting work; for example, a key success character is leadership hierarchy, that is where we will start to lead the team successfully? Frontline, managers, and so forth. Furthermore, one more important issue is to know how to lead, for example, in one case for successful leadership the working patterns must be revolutionized, another case requires taking into account the motivation factor. What's more, necessary communication skills for victorious and proper leadership must be confirmed. Bridgeland and Becker (1994) declared that communication skills encompass two purposes in the context of reengineering: to create an undeniable case for change and to generate a vision of what the company is to be. These skills lend a hand in periodic meetings with customers by serving the leader to bridge the gap between customer requirements and the organization products. So, effective leadership affects directly the revenue model of the organization. By simulating the surroundings within which the leader will work, the exceeding tips can be branded and the right personality can be picked. Simulation can effectively support an organization willing to study this type of skills.

Employees Empowering Level

According to Levas (1995) within the information era the worth of human being is not considered in unit\hours but in their involvement to upcoming victory. Bridgeland and Becker (1994) argued that the high crash speed of BPR schemes is due to inborn and ordinary variance of attention among workers and the organization as whole. The employee responsibility in potential success is linked strongly to the level this employee is motivated and recognized. In the preceding sections, workforce backgrounds and generations' character were discussed; this discussion leads to the thought that there are diverse groups of employees to be considered in the reengineering process. The needed efforts to systematize each class to change must be considered, as well, the communication skills to rejuvenate employees and communication skills for front line employees who deal directly with customers must be judged. Finally, each group of employees will require a certain type of management, which will forward the group efforts to profitable change. By simulating everyday jobs, roles, customer's culture, worker's qualifications and skills and then correlating them to the performance measures, then the required empowering level is identified and the incentives range are recognized.

Process Improvement

BPR is an approach that is generally used to drastically modify the process of coming with and creating novel and improved traditions to run a business (Levas, 1995). But the question that arises here is: What are the processes that will be modified? To answer this question various dimensions have to be taken into account, that is, organization vision and priorities, customer requirements and satisfaction, and so forth. Within the activities of business process progress, information resources and ways for information gathering must be identified. Considering "as is" a model is not enough for BPR use and it will go in front to risky "to-be" model (Levas, 1995). It is noted that customer requirements are ambiguous in most cases and they are changing repeatedly. Since simulation is a predictive tool, it can be used to minimize the risks that may result. To demonstrate the value of the simulation modeling efforts for the assessment of current performance levels and quantifying possible improvement, please refer to Hulpic and Vreede (2005).

Ethical Issues

Bhaskar (1994) asserted that employees have unstable level of influence and control, and use these personalities to carry or defend against the accomplishment of an economically wise reengineered process. For successful BPR it is essential to place the potential options of ethical matter sound effects at the table. As discussed earlier, dissimilar workforce age groups of employees, which have different settings and different viewpoints of how the business work runs, must be well thought-out. Ethical issues are not only distress employees, but also the client must be taken into account. The culture of the client, his/her consumerism, and his/her behaviors toward business products must be regarded. Simulating the interior and exterior settings will facilitate realizing the trends of individuals as well as organizations (competitors or friends) toward ethics. It appears that simulation can support efforts that are dedicated to revise ethical issues consequences on BPR.

Stakeholder's Management Skills

It was asserted earlier that the construction of a vision of what the company is to be is one of communication skills functions. Stakeholders are all the parties (individuals or groups) who deal with the change; these include the employee and managers (discussed early), clients, community, government, and so forth. In most cases stakeholders are concerned with what the company is to be. Unless you as manager can win over the stakeholders, especially effective ones, with the upcoming portrait of the organization you will lose their support. Each one of the stakeholders has a certain intuition regarding the organization vision and goals, this intuition relays robustly on their stakes of the change success. If the manager has the ability to recognize these visions he/she can prepare to the proper means to get their support. By determining the improvement level, procedures that need to be modified, performance measures, and the roles and responsibilities, one can readdress a certain group of stakeholder's influence to support the change not to resist it, and arrange to overcome this resistance if it take place. Simulation can support this manager in the effort to win in his/her battle. At the end of this section, it must be indicated that simulation supports diverse business process reengineering domains and facilitates:

- Minimizing risks.
- Desired change management.
- Expectation management.

Besides that, it is a tool that enables a decision-maker to model human responses either within the business cycle (employee) or those who have an effect on this cycle (external stakeholders). These entire capabilities enable a decision-maker to construct the right "to-be" model, which leads to effective execution of changes desired. The above discussions bring to light the role of simulation in supporting BPR, which is the most complex and painful period of transition to competitiveness.

In the following case study we will consider a comprehensive example for the role of simulation in business process reengineering.

CASE STUDY: TEAM-BASED HUMAN RESOURCE PLANNING MODEL

Cheng et al. (2005) proposed a team-based human resource planning model (THRP) with a center of attention on construction management process reengineering, where a team approach was applied in reorganizing the structure of a company to smooth the progress of newly designed process, and simulation was used to forecast labor power aptitude for the new organization after business process reengineering. The THRP method aims to determine the maximum loading of projects that can be held by the original labor power, in addition to identifying the range of labor power needed for the upcoming project loadings. The THRP method includes four phases, namely, process reengineering, data preparing, human resource allocation, and simulation. Using the THRP method, a company cannot only design a team-based organizational structure, but also assign human resources based on cross-functional processes. Furthermore, human resource utilizations before and after process reengineering can be assessed to evaluate the process reengineering practicability. Hence, optimal labor power can be assessed, and human resources allocated to fit the changing processes and situations of the growing business. Figure 2 shows THRP model.

To validate the soundness and feasibility of the THRP model Cheng et al. (2005) provided a case study. The THRP model was employed to assist "Company A" with reengineering of the construction planning process and evaluating the rationality of human resource use in the reengineered processes.

Process Reengineering Phase

Figure 3 shows the functional organization structure of "Company A." In the figure, the construction planning process was executed by the construction planning department. To execute different specific functional goals, the department was divided into three functional task groups. The planning process was enabled and split into (1) bidding/contracting, (2) estimation/budget and (3) purchasing sub-processes, which were carried out by the related task groups sequentially. However, due to the fact that task groups were accountable only for partial goals of the construction planning process, the three task groups hardly supported each other and some of them experienced overload leading to inefficient human resource deployment in functional organizations. Taking into account the ineffectiveness of previous construction planning, the manager had chosen the construction planning process to be reengineered.

Process Representation

The major rationale of processes representation is to develop a systematic definition of these processes. Two tasks have to be carried out:

Task 1. Activity Data Collection

To map a business process model from function-based to process-based organization, detailed information on the activities of functional departments is required. E-EPC diagram of the Architecture of Integrated Information System (ARIS) process modeling tool was used to outline both existing and the newly designed management processes of a construction company.

Task 2. Process Modeling

This is accomplished based on the collected data using a modeling tool, for example, the Architec-

Figure 2. The THRP model

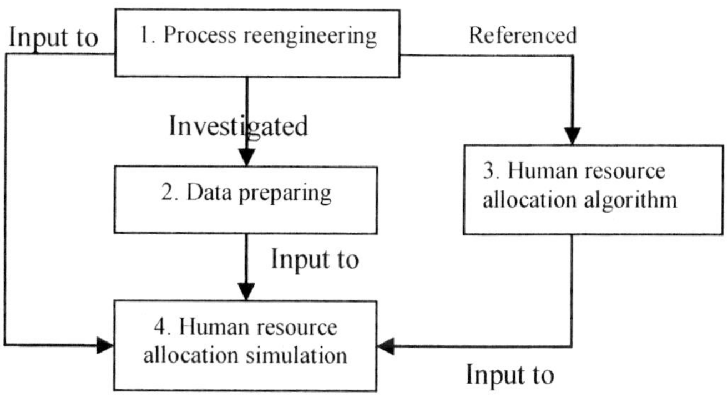

Figure 3. The organizational structure of Company "A" before BPR

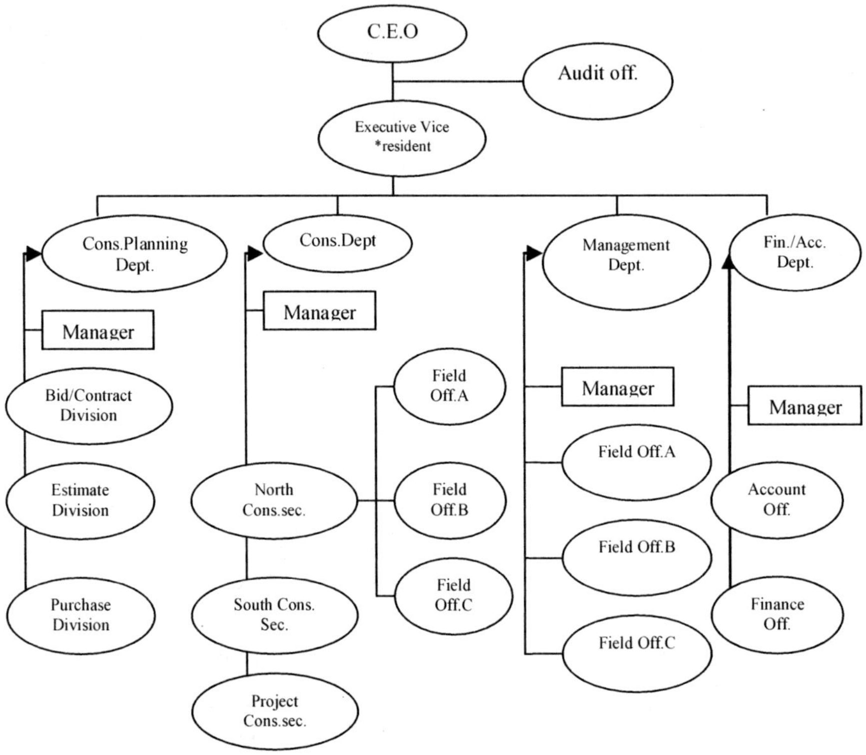

ture of Integrated Information System (ARIS) modeling tool.

Process Evaluation

The intention here is to analyze the rationality and effectiveness of process-based on the e-EPC process diagrams created in the process representation step. For example, hidden problems within the original bidding/contract processes were located as follows:

1. Only quantity surveys were implemented with computer-aided software while all other activities were completed manually; as a result, the activities efficiency and the labor power utilization were limited.
2. Job loading was not proportional to task divisions due to the magnitude of various construction projects. Actually, active assign of proper labor power actively to accurate groups in a functional organization structure is not easy.
3. No valid history reference data on material and labor was on hand to assist the estimator so that cost estimations are not up to snuff to correspond with current prices.
4. The time consumed by document circulation increased because all documents were required to be submitted to the managers.

Process Redesign

To fix the process defects, the process model was redesigned on process design principles and a new process model created. A cross-functional information system of cost estimation system was applied. Some activities could be integrated and executed by cost estimation system.

Team-Based Organization Creation

A team approach was applied to join multiple division functions into one unit which could facilitate functional interfaces and parallel process activities. Figure 4 shows the team-based organization structure of Company A corresponding to the new construction planning processes. The primary difference between the previous structure and the team-based structure is the appearance of the decision group on one hand and the two construction planning teams who are accountable for the entire construction planning process.

In the adjusted organization structure, the construction planning team is flexible in number depending on work loadings. As a reference for human resource allocation decision-making, an evaluation method with simulation tools was used to reveal the relation between work loading and the labor power of work teams so that the managers could assess the capability of labor power allocated in a team was used.

Preprocessed Data Phase

In the data preparation phase, the values of project parameters and process parameters were estimated according to the historical data of projects and activities of Company "A." Table 1 shows the project parameters of the Company "A."

Table 1. Project parameters of Company "A"

Project parameter	Function/Value
Start time of project	Uniform distribution
Success ratio of bidding	20%
Number of subcontracts	25
Required lab power	7 employees

The process parameters for both the original and the newly designed processes were estimated and then evaluated for labor power in activities, for probability distribution functions, and for durations with 95% confidence level.

Human Resource Simulation Phase

In this section, to validate the feasibility of the simulation system, the "construction planning process" of Company "A" was taken as an example. The current process model within the original organization structure was developed and simu-

Figure 4. The organizational structure of company "A" after BPR

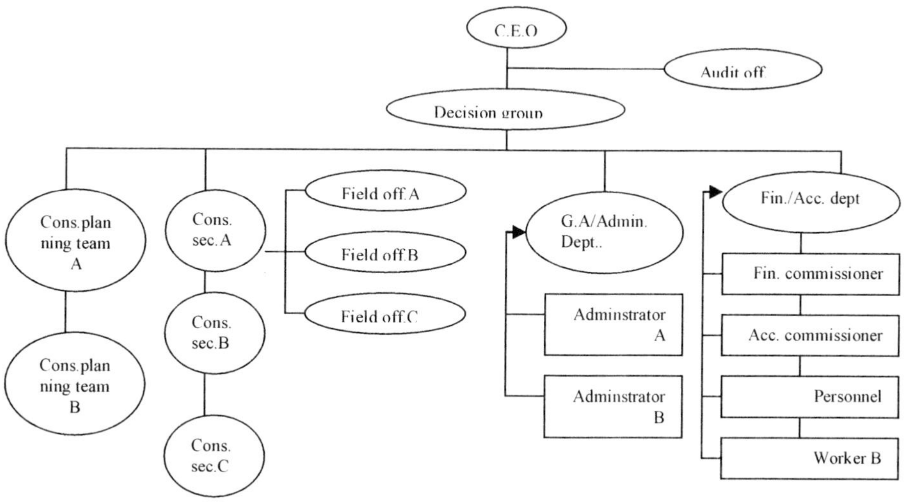

lated. Comparing the simulation results with the performance of the current process model, the simulation system was validated. The results of the model validation were very close to the real situations. For sixteen projects, the maximal project loading of seven workers was estimated by the simulation system with the test model. This result matched the real capability in the range of 15 to 18 projects estimated by the mangers of Company "A." Moreover, the average of idled labor power also was close to the real situation as evaluated by the managers with experience.

After the model test, the newly designed construction planning process was modeled in the eM-Plant system and evaluated with two situations: (1) the number of members of the construction planning team remained constant at seven, which was the total labor power of the construction planning department; (2) the project loading was taken as a function of the number of team members, and the combinations of labor power and project loading were estimated.

The main purpose of the first simulation is to estimate the potential project loading that current labor power can take. Therefore, the value of the current number of personnel available was set at seven workers. Moreover, each team consists of one senior engineer and at least one junior engineer, so there were eight possible labor power allocation alternatives for seven workers. Figure 5 shows the allocation alternatives and the amount of projects which were simulated.

As applying the forward scheduling method, the success ratio was always higher than 90% when the project loading was less than 25 projects. It decreased to 83% (less than the threshold of 90%) as the loading increased to 26 projects. Therefore, the maximum project loading for seven members was evaluated at 25 projects. Likewise, as the backward scheduling method was applied, the success ratio was always higher than 90% when the project loading was less 40 projects, but decreased to 80% as the loading increased to 41 projects. Therefore, the maximum project loading for seven members proved to be 40 projects when the backward scheduling method was applied.

Because forward scheduling deploys the maximum resource at the beginning of a project

Figure 5. The possible labor power deployment alternatives tree for C.P.T with NAP==7, NAP: number of personnel available, AOP: amount of projects

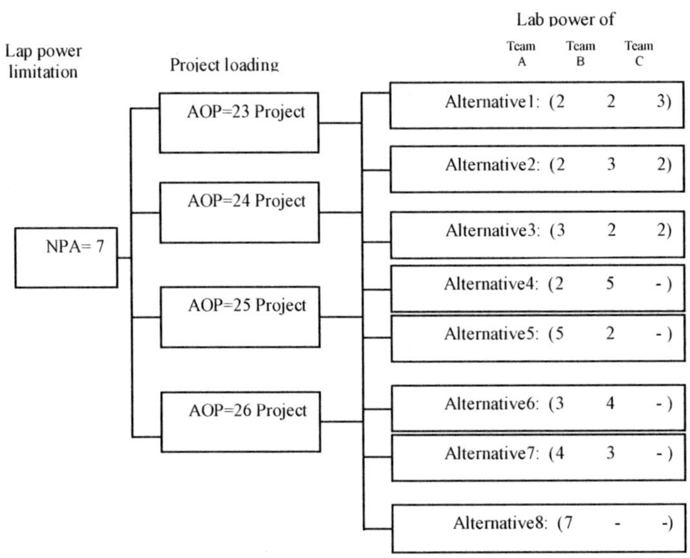

to accomplish the process as soon as possible, labor power capability might be limited by more resource conflicts than in the backward scheduling method. Therefore, it was guessed that optimum project loading falls between the two above referenced extreme cases. Based on this result, Company A's labor power margin was adapted to a minimum of 25 projects and a maximum of 40 projects.

In addition, the outputs of the simulation exhibit positive evidences of the advantages of process reengineering. That is, by comparing simulation results between the original process and the new, integrated construction planning process, we can see the labor power capability increasing from 16 projects to 40 projects, and idled labor power decreasing obviously due to the integration of functions.

For the second situation, this study extended the number of personnel available from 2 to 15 workers to realize the relation between labor power and project loading. In Figure 6, one NPA value corresponds to two project loadings; one is backward scheduling result and the other is forward scheduling result. As each NPA has been simulated, two curves could be finally sketched which present the relation of labor power and project loadings. Based on Figure 6, not only the capability range of specific labor power, but also the range of labor power requirement for specific project loading can be identified. Therefore, managers can estimate the efficiency of labor power or the amount of it needed based on the number of projects.

SUCCESSFUL SIMULATION

In the prior section the role of simulation in supporting BPR was discussed. Now, how to achieve successful simulation? According to Sadowski et al. (1999) successful simulation is one that brings functional information at the proper time to bear an evocative decision. Aguilar et al. (1999) acknowledged that the victory of a simulation project fundamentally depends on four factors: the process characteristics, the objectives of simulation, the quality of input data, and the

Figure 6. Simulated output curves of the new construction planning process

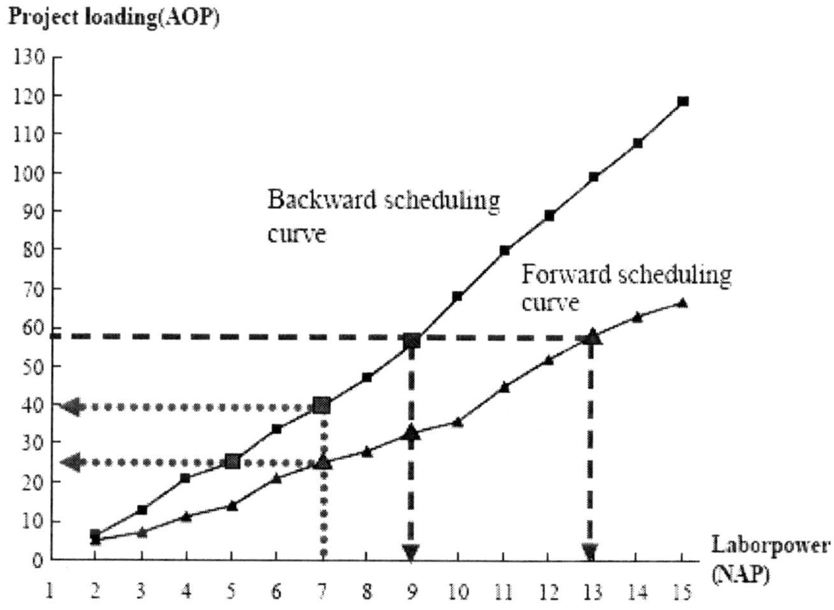

management of expectations. The key aspect of presenting the functional information is to look at it from the viewpoint of the audience for which it is intended.

- What they need to know
- Why they need to know
- Anticipate the questions they may ask
- Their view of the system
- Take time to introduce them to how you look at things and investigate how this varies from their point of view.

In the next discussion four aspects that affect the success of simulation will be underlined.

COMMUNICATION

Simulation models can be viewed as a problem recognition rather than a problem solving tool (Hlupic & Vreedi, 2005). In order to superiorly identify the problem it is essential to communicate the situation under consideration; if the situation communicated properly the problem to be solved will be recognized, defined and then appropriate formula for the problem will result. Through communication the relations between the situation problem and simulation intention will be defined leading to the implementation of the acceptable action. Robinson et al. (1998) claimed that the classic approach to signify human decision-making in a simulation model is to elicit the decision regulations from the decision-maker. This means that the communication channels with decision-makers are required to be sustained to identify the superlative match between different scenarios resulting from simulation, along with organization goals that will provide a solution approved by the decision-maker. Internal and external organizational environments have to be communicated; for example, employees, organizational chain of command, encouragement arrangement, market, customers, and competitors, are a number of issues have to to be regarded. Throughout communication the influence of diverse variables can be appraised, and the significance of each one can be labeled. One more party that must be communicated is the working team, that is, the team who is accountable for simulation process; this team must be supervised and led, as well as guided properly. Communication can be considered as the foundation from which either you tag along a mistaken path—meaning the risky one—resulting in organization failure or you tag on the precise path, which guides to success. The more properly and earlier that you handle the problem, the sooner that you can initiate your project (simulation). There are numerous ways to communicate with the above parties: interview is appropriate technique especially with top management, as well as observation of business process, besides several other techniques that can be used for this purpose. JAD sessions can be conducted to communicate all these parties, these meetings can be wise for eliciting requirements, brainstorming to analyze initiatives, collaboration and thorough analysis.

COMPLEXITY

In the former arguments it was acknowledged that simulation is chosen as complexity and risk of as-is as well as to-be models grows to be high. It is of the essence for simulation panel to go behind planned approach in their work, one key inspiration behind the use of such an approach is to administer the model complexity in order that the model can be effectively confirmed and certified (Balci, 1990). In the preceding aspect, that is, communication, the value of organization environments was discussed; within these settings we deal with employees, where each employee has personality venture, incentive style and grand (Bridgeland & Becker, 1994). What's more, by way of market instability with different input variables and the significance of each one to the business objectives and working business processes, simulation team selection plays a fundamental role. The bottleneck in the on-hand resources has to be considered; for example, time, people and tools. As this estimation encompass high accuracy, the decision-making value of business process simulation will be further be significant. Abstraction level is imperative for reducing complexity level in a simulation model, which then reduces essential time and resources dedicated to this effort. At the initial stages of simulation, it is noteworthy to gather as much information as possible: Benjamin et al. (1998) believed that it is crucial to start with low level of abstraction which imply huge amount of information. In addition, a system must be decomposed into subsystems to overcome its complexity, which means planning simulation project at proper level of details (divide and concur principle). Complexity reflection has to be linked to task worth analysis, that is to say, the tasks that represent keystones must be taken into account throughout the simulation work. On the other hand, the cost of each level of abstraction, that is, time, efforts, and resources analysis looked-for to accomplish the available and needed amount of information, in addition, the cost result from quality analysis must be thought about.

DYNAMISM

Hlupic & Vreedi (2005) emphasized that a simulation model can be easily customized to go behind modification besides utilizing it as a decision support tool for unbroken progress. The majority of these days' businesses are dynamic in nature and yet their objectives are habitually unpredictable due to the novel environment economy necessities. Significant assistance is the reality that experiments with business models can be reiterated, which facilitates the assessment of the sound effects of changes (Hlupic & Vreedi, 2005). In the framework of the above interpretation, it is essential to review the resulting model meticulously by the simulation team, focusing on the business aspirations that guide the simulation project. The effects of any adjustment call round the model have to be agreed upon between simulation team and business owner (or its agent); this will go ahead to enhanced communication and acquiring the necessary support of decision-maker. During the employment, new resources (time, personnel, etc.) may be required to keep on simulation project, in these cases action and reaction will not work, it is important to be proactive for these unexpected events. To overcome these and similar cases, it is necessary to have an expectations agenda and cost margin to go on with the project safely. Sadowski et al. (1999) argued that all the way throughout the project, suppleness is significant as circumstances come to pass, such as scope adjustment, difficulty with data gathering or professionals' accessibility. The simulation team has to look for innovative traditions to decipher evils.

SCOPE

As Sadowski et al. (1999) stated, "The most common types of misguided simulation studies are these where the scope is too ambitious or ill defined." In the two previous sections, task value analysis and cost analysis were pointed out as components of complexity factor examination, if the scope of simulation is amorphous everything appears to be significant according to the business under consideration. The scope stands for the boundaries of the work, Sadowski et al. (1999) asserted that the project originator must know what to wait for from simulation and the simulation team must know what is anticipated from them. So expectations management is one of the restrictions that affect simulation sensation. On the other hand, it is important that simulation concepts (for example, cycle time) have obvious denotation according to the related work. In the earlier discussions it was stated that successful simulation conveys precise information at the exact time to support an accurate decision; delivering information mostly depends on the individual, this information incorporates business rules and working processes, so the right individual is critical periphery in simulation project. One more boundary is the business objectives by which simulation work is bounded. Besides, business logic is a crucial character that is related to overall business settings that shape the margins of simulation plan. In order to obtain a proper scope a structured walkthrough must be accomplished principally with the dynamism attribute of new business environment.

CHALLENGES AND LIMITATIONS OF BUSINESS PROCESS SIMULATION

In the previous sections it was acknowledged that simulation is a predictive tool used to minimize the effects of probable risks. While simulation has numerous capabilities and characteristics that make it the best way to forecast the project future under certain circumstances, it has a lot of pitfalls:

1. Simulation is experience sensitive: the simulation consequences are strongly affected by the experience of simulation team, for example, studying diverse workforce generations necessitates adequate background in this field.
2. Simulation is the superlative option when the problem complexity is high: in straightforward cases decision-makers can use many other tools, for example, linear programming. If the problem complexity is not resolved accurately, the cost and efforts will not be easily justified when the stakeholders inquire about them.
3. Simulation is time sensitive: Hulpic & Vreede (2005) argued that as business surroundings and evils are turn out to be more complex, the time available to deliver solutions is more limited. Dynamic nature, new environment, and opportunities, become main concepts in business logic which is restricted in most cases by cost/benefit issues, so the rapid decisions necessitate that simulation timeline to be as minimum as possible.
4. Simulation is sensitive to "on-hand information:" unless the simulation team can effectively elicit the right information, the simulation consequences will be completely or at least partially distant from the acceptable solution, so it is necessary to engage the right people who have the right information; this obliges selecting the effective roles in the organization.
5. Simulation scope (as discussed in pervious section): this issue is in command of results by project limitations, business objectives, and so forth.

Hulpic & Vreede (2005) confirmed that the number of stakeholders, model building time and management awareness are the key challenges of simulation:

1. Number of stakeholders: the simulation team need to communicate properly and efficiently with all roles in the organization. They communicate to top management to understand the objectives of the business, with employees to recognize the proper methods to empower each one of them and to know how to plan the daily habits of each one of them; to revise staff age group styles diversity and even working processes must be communicated to study the running process stream. All of these roles are carried out by people, therefore those people have to be involved before the simulation life cycle starts, which means more time, efforts and costs.
2. Model building time: as discussed previously, the time is inadequate in the new

economy to think in all business situations. Unfortunately, simulation needs time, efforts, and human resources, and if simulation is not justified by the problem complexity along with its consequences it is favored to use a different tool.

3. Management awareness: management support is crucial in any activity success, in simulation case, it is necessary that management be aware of the advantages of simulation, the value of its outcomes, its responsibility in recognizing leadership skills, management skills, and so forth.

Besides these challenges, the culture is an additional challenge that must be concerned: at individual and national levels, this signifies the change acceptance level within the cognitive limit of the target society. Again, religion, habits, and traditions may make the predictive tool unable (even within a certain limit) to simulate the future. In order to overcome these challenges it is necessary to:

1. Select the appropriate simulation team.
2. Keep it simple: start with simple and known things on the road to further complex and unknown ones.
3. Divide and concur: exhaustive working may lead to disseminating simulation efforts; hence it is better to divide the work among simulation team.
4. To overcome time-consuming communication it is recommended to hold meetings for all the stakeholders within one session as possible; that is, JAD session.
5. It is recommended that agile methodologies are used to develop simulation software package, since agile approaches concern frequent changing, customer involvement, and so forth.
6. It is necessary to improve simulation team communication skills taking into account the cultural matters.

At the implementation level, the following are some issues that must be considered (Berio & Vernadat, 1999):

1. Provide a general model representation for the user (user interface).
2. Incremental modeling (concept of domains), because modeling is an iterative process.
3. Implementation of the view mechanism (for the management of, model complexity).
4. Distinction between material, information and control flows (for instance, using different graphical representations or notations).
5. Functional hierarchy for the decomposition of domain processes (top level), business process (intermediate level), and enterprise activities (lowest level).
6. Distributed simulation capabilities (to emulate concurrent processes and stand alone resource behaviors).

SUMMARY

The logic of the business world is to create an advantage and/or utilize an opportunity.

Customer, cost, and competition are the issue(s) that have an aptitude to drive any plausible business improvement. There are many approaches to change management; in the preceding discussion in this chapter the authors focused on total quality management (TQM), business process reengineering (BPR) and, knowledge management. Considering the rate of failure in reengineering projects was over 50%, one of the major tribulations that have a say to the breakdown of BPR projects is the need of tools for evaluating the sound effects of a considered solution before execution.

Complexity and risk are the main issues have to been emphasized when simulation activity is to be conducted. Flow objects, resources, activities, and routings are the basic building blocks of any proper model. Cycle time, entity count, resource utilization and activity cost were illustrated as the measures for any model performance. The chapter illustrated the model experimentation, output analysis, and recommendations of business process change as the major business process simulation steps. The number of stakeholders, model building time and management awareness were positioned as the key challenges of simulation. Throughout the preceding in this chapter the discussion on the effect of simulation on business environment related skills, business management related skills, leadership related skills, employees' empowerment level, process improvement, ethical issues, and stakeholders' management skills were discussed. Finally, for successful simulation communication, complexity, dynamism and scope must be considered and then simulation can be used in diverse applications and areas as outlined in this chapter.

REFERENCES

Ahadi, H.R. (2004). An examination of the role of organizational enablers in business process reengineering and the impact of information technology. *Information Resources Management Journal, 17*(4), 1-19.

Aguilar, M., Rautert, T.,& Pater, A.J.G. (1999). Business process simulation: Fundamental step supporting process centered management. In *Proceeding of the 31st Conference on Winter Simulation: Simulation - Bridge to the Future,* Phoenix, AZ, U.S. (pp. 1383-1392). New York: ACM Press.

Balci, O., (1990). Guidelines for successful simulation studies. In *Proceedings of the 22nd Conference on Winter Simulation,* New Orleans, LA, U.S. (pp. 25-32). Piscataway, NJ: IEEE Press.

Benjamin, P., Erraquntla, M., Delen, D., & Mayer, R., (1998). Simulation modeling at multiple levels of abstraction. In *Proceedings of the 30th Conference on Winter Simulation,* Washington, DC (pp. 391-398). Los Alamitos, CA: IEEE Computer Society Press.

Berio, G., &Vernadat, F.B. (1999). New developments in enterprise modeling using CIMOSA. *Computer In Industry, 40,* 99-114.

Bhaskar, R.,(1994). Analyzing and re-engineering business processes using simulation. In *Proceedings of the 26th Conference on Winter Simulation,* Orlando, FL, U.S. (pp. 1206-1213). San Diego, CA: Society for Computer Simulation International.

Bonser, C.F. (1992). Total quality education? *Public Administration Review, 52*(5), 504-512.

Bridgeland, D., & Becker, S. (1994) .Simulation satyagraha, a successful strategy for business process reengineering. In *Proceedings of the 26th Conference on Winter Simulation,* FL, U.S. (pp. 1214-1220). San Diego, CA: Society for Computer Simulation International.

Cheng, T.C.E. (1992). Computer simulation and its management applications. *Computer In Industry, 20,* 229-238.

Cheng, M., Tsai, M., & Xiao, Z. (2005). *Construction management process reengineering: Organizational human resource planning for multiple projects.* Article in press.

Davenport, T.H., & Short, J.E. (1990). The new industrial engineering: Information technology and business process redesign. *Sloan Management Review, 31*(4), 11-27.

Davenport, T.H. (1993). *Process innovation: Reengineering work through information technology.* Cambridge, MA: Harvard Business School Press.

Earl, M.J. (1994). The new and the old of business process redesign. *Journal of Strategic Information Systems, 3*(1), 5-22.

Ferrie, J. (1995). *Business processes – a natural approach.* ESRC Business Processes Resource Centre, University of Warwick. Retrieved from http:\\bprc.warwick.ac.uk\forum1.html

Garvin, D.A. (1991). How the Baldnge Award really works. *Harvard Business Review*, pp. 80-93.

Godfrey, A.B. (1993). Ten areas for future research in total quality management. *Quality Management Journal, 1*(1), 47-70.

Goll, E.O. (1992). Let's debunk the myths & misconceptions about reengineering. *APICS Magazine*, pp. 29-32.

Grant, R.M. (1996). Prospering in dynamically: Competitive environment: Organizational capability as knowledge integration. *Organization Science*, pp. 375-387.

Hammer, M. (1990). Reengineering work: Don't automate, obliterate. *Harvard Business Review, 68*(4), 104-112.

Hammer, M., & Champy, J. (1993). *Reengineering the corporation.* New York: Harper Collins Books.

Harrington, H.J. (1991). *Business process improvement.* New York: McGraw-Hill.

Hlupic, V., & Vreede, G. (2005). Business process modeling using discrete-event simulation: Current opportunities and future challenges. *International Journal of Simulation and Process Modeling, 1*(1/2), 72-81.

Hugan, J.C., Banks, J., Lendermann, P., Mclean, C., Page, E.H., Pegden, C.D., Ulgen,O., & Wilson, J.R. (2003). The future of simulation industry. In *Proceedings of the 35th Conference on Winter Simulation,* New Orleans, LA, U.S. (pp. 2033-2043).

Jain, S. (1999). Simulation in the next millennium. In *Proceeding of the 31st Conference on Winter Simulation: Simulation - Bridge to the Future,* Phoenix, AZ, U.S. (pp. 1478-1484). New York: ACM Press.

Juran, J.M. (1986). The quality trilogy. *Quality Process*, pp. 19-24.

Levas, A., Boyd, S., Jain, P., & Tulskie, W. (1995). Panel discussion on the role of modeling and simulation in business process reengineering. In *Proceedings of the 27th Conference on Winter Simulation,* Arlington, VA, U.S. (pp. 1341-1346). New York: ACM Press.

Liebowitz, J., & Beckman, T. (1998). *Knowledge organizations: What every manager should know.* Boca Raton, FL: CRC Press.

Liebowitz, J. (1999). *The knowledge management handbook.* Boca Raton, FL: CRC Press.

Liebowitz, J. (2000). *Building organizational intelligence: A knowledge management primer.* Boca Raton, FL: CRC Press.

Liebowitz, J. (2001). Knowledge management and its link to artificial intelligence. *Expert Systems with Applications, 20*,1-6.

Olian, J.D., & Rynes, S.L. (1991). Total quality work: Aligning organizational processes, performance measures, and stakeholders. *Human Resource Management, 30*(3), 303-333.

Omrani, D. (1992). Business process reengineering: A business revolution? *Management Services, 36*(10), 12-15.

Ören, T.I. (2002). Future of modeling and simulation: Some development areas. In *Proceedings of the 2002 Summer Computer Simulation Conference,* San Diego, CA, U.S.

Pall, G.A. (1987). *Quality press management.* Englewood Cliffs, NJ: Prentice-Hall.

Paper, D., Tingey, K.B., & Mok, W.(2003). *The relation between BPR and ERP Systems: A failed project.* Hershey, PA: Idea Group Publishing.

Pressman, R.S. (2005). *Software engineering: A practitioner's approach.* New York: McGraw Hill.

Robinson, S., Edwards, J.S., & Yonfa, W. (1998). An expert systems approach to simulating the human decision maker. In *Proceedings of the 30th Conference on Winter Simulation,* Washington, DC (pp. 1541-1546). Los Alamitos, CA: IEEE Computer Society Press.

Sadowski, D.A., & Grabau, M.R. (1999). Tips for successful practice simulation. In *Proceedings of the 31st Conference on Winter Simulation: Simulation – A Bridge to the Future (Vol. 1),* Phoenix, AZ ,U.S. (pp. 60-66). New York: ACM Press.

Saxena, K.B.C. (1996). Reengineering public administration in developing countries. *Long Range Planning, 29*(5), 703-711.

Sink, D.S. (1991). The role of measurement in achieving world class quality and productivity management. *Industrial Engineering, 70*, 23-28.

Swain, J.J. (1993). Flexible tools for modeling. *OR/MS Today*, 72-81.

Talwar, R. (1993). Business reengineering: A strategy-driven approach. *Long Range Planning, 26*(6), 22-40.

Turban, T., King, D., Lee, J.K., & Viehland, D. (2004). *Electronic commerce: A managerial perspective.* 3/E Prentice Hall.

Tumay, K. (1995). Business process simulation. In *Proceedings of the 27th Conference on Winter Simulation*, Arlington, VA, U.S. (pp. 55-60). New York: ACM Press.

Tumay, K. (1996). Business process simulation. In *Proceedings of the 28th Conference on Winter Simulation*, Coronado, CA, U.S. (pp. 93-99). New York: ACM Press.

This work was previously published in Simulation and Modeling: Current Technologies and Applications, edited by A. El Sheikh, A. Thyab Al Ajeeli, & E. Abu-Taieh, pp. 359-390, copyright 2008 by IGI Publishing, formerly known as Idea Group Publishing (an imprint of IGI Global).

Chapter IV
Environmental Drivers of E-Business Strategies Among SMEs

Alessandro Arbore
Bocconi University, Italy

Andrea Ordanini
Bocconi University, Italy

ABSTRACT

In front of traditional interpretations of the digital gap based on endogenous conditions of the firms, this chapter intends to emphasize the importance that some external pressures may have on the e-business strategy of small and medium enterprises (SMEs). The environmental factors analyzed here are market position, competitive intensity, and institutional pressures. SMEs have been grouped according to their level of e-business involvement, in relation to the number of e-business solutions adopted so far. Three layers are proposed: excluded, tentative, and integrated e-business SMEs. A multinomial logistic regression was used to predict these strategies. A general conclusion is that different models seem to explain exclusion and involvement. Specifically, two factors among those analyzed reveal to be more suitable in explaining e-business exclusion. They are the size of a SME and a lack of institutional pressures to adopt. On the other hand, e-business involvement seems to be primarily prompted by a selective competitive environment and not by imitative behaviors, as in the previous case.

INTRODUCTION

In this chapter, our general attention is on the adoption and diffusion of e-business solutions among small and medium enterprises (SMEs). More specifically, our interest is focused on some external factors that may affect this process, since we are persuaded that external forces are especially important within small organizations, while largely understated by the literature. We will try to analyze whether these factors do relate to the e-business involvement of an SME.

E-business is an umbrella term referring to a wide variety of Internet-based management solutions. The solutions considered here are: interactive Web sites, e-commerce platforms, e-procurement systems, customer relationship management systems, and telework.

BACKGROUND: SMES AND EXTERNAL FACTORS AFFECTING E-BUSINESS

Many researches explain the adoption of e-business solutions in terms of endogenous factors, that is variables which are internal to the organization. Among these factors, different typologies of variables are recursive: the level of financial resources able to affect any investment decision; the managerial culture, influencing the propensity to innovate; and the organizational readiness, which is relevant for the integration of new technologies (for a review, see Lee, Runge, & Baek, 2001). Conversely, the potential influence of exogenous pressures have been largely understated. Within this handbook, a review of internal factors is out of the scope of the current chapter. Instead, our goal is to deepen our understanding about the following environmental drivers: market position, competitive intensity, and institutional pressures.

When focusing on SMEs, environmental elements must be considered as especially important because of the high dependency of these organizations from the context: SMEs appear more sensible to external pressures, in terms of both competitive and social "rules of the game" (Fink, 1998). Therefore, important explanatory factors of adoption strategies shall be easily found by studying the environment where SMEs play, rather than focusing only on internal conditions. Above all, since e-business is basically considered an instrument to improve firm's competitiveness (Amit & Zott, 2000), we could expect that the competitive features of the arena where SMEs play require special attention.

Starting from the current literature, then, the environmental forces analyzed in this work are: (1) the level of perceived competition (Kuan & Chau, 2001; Riemschneider, Harrison, & Mykytn, 2003); (2) the pressure to be considered technology savvy (Iacovou, Benbasat, & Dexter, 1995; Zhu, Kremer, & Xu, 2003); and (3) the competitive position occupied in the marketplace (Daniel & Grimshaw, 2002; Lal, 1999).

Our chapter will briefly review the theoretical antecedents for each of these factors and then we will provide a set of hypotheses.

Competitive Intensity

According to the well known industrial organization framework (Andrews, 1971; Porter, 1985), it can be observed that an increasing competitive intensity worsens the balance between opportunities and threats, requiring firms to adopt more innovative strategies to survive and make profits.

Within this view, Gatignon and Robertson (1989) found that competitive pressure in the adopter industry has a positive impact on adoption of information and communication technologies. In the same way, Thong and Yap (1995) found that the CEO attitude towards new technologies adoption is positively correlated with the degree of competition faced in the market. Similarly, Premkumar and Roberts (1999) demonstrated that the degree of competitive rivalry in the adopter's industry affects the rate of adoption of digital technologies.

Also adopting the more recent resource-based approach (Barney, 1991; Peteraf, 1993), it could be observed that the strength of competition in the factor markets reduces the power of isolating mechanisms sustaining the competitive edge, thus requiring continuous innovation strategies. Within these contexts, innovations lead to resource substitution phenomenon, acting as basic conditions for rent seeking (Malerba & Orsenigo, 1997). Especially here, e-business solutions may contribute to the development of dynamic capabilities sustaining long-term competitive advantages (Teece, Pisano, & Shuen, 1997). This discussion leads to formulate our first hypothesis:

Hp1: The degree of perceived competition increases the intensity of e-business strategy among SMEs.

Institutional Pressures and Technology Legitimacy

According to the institutional theories, a firm's behavior has to be coherent with norms and social rules requested by their environment (Di Maggio & Powell, 1983; North, 1990).

Consistently, in order to gain access to specific resources, to collaborative networks, or to strategic alliances, a firm might be subject to legitimacy assessment by other social agents (competitors, partners, and other stakeholders). The requirements may be very selective especially for SMEs, since they are not usually perceived as legitimate players due to their lack of resources and capabilities (Grewal, Comer, & Metha, 2001).

Although for SMEs the last decision maker is generally the owner-manager, the pressure that she feels from other stakeholders (e.g., employees, customers, suppliers) remains an important determinant of technology adoption. Harrison, Mykytyn, and Riemenschneider (1997) found that similar unwritten norms, maintained by peers and society, strongly influence the intention to adopt information technologies in small businesses. Along the same line, Lee et al. (2001) posit that SMEs' managers hear about the relative advantages of digital technologies largely from the trade press, their friends, business competitors, and peer-social interactions.

This would create selective contexts, where it is important to be perceived as technology savvy and where e-business strategies may be driven, among the other things, by a relational need to be reputed as innovative and technology savvy. This leads to our second hypothesis:

Hp2: The need for a technology legitimacy increase the intensity of e-business adoption among SMEs.

Market Position

Given a certain level of competitive rivalry, a leading market position[1] may reveal better resources to exploit the potential of the new technologies. This, in turn, would be a further driver for e-business intensity. Moreover, early e-business adoption might be interpreted as a pre-emptive strategy of the leader. From this point of view, the leader would feel an external pressure to be the first mover, in order not to loose its supremacy.

From a theoretical point of view, there is a general consensus on the fact that the adoption of information technologies, by itself, has a marginal direct effect on firm performance, while significant impacts emerge only when such technologies are combined and integrated with other distinctive competencies (see, among the others, Clemons & Row, 1991; Mata, Fuerst, & Barney, 1995; Powell & Dent-Micallef, 1997).

A possible implication is that e-business solutions, like other ICTs, would have greater power in consolidating leading positions rather than reduce competitive gaps: the instrumental nature of technology makes e-business strategies viable only when there are some "business strategy" beyond them, thus suggesting that technology cannot fix a flaw process by itself, but it is able to improve, even significantly, an established process (Carr, 2001).

In other words, there is a "strategic necessity hypothesis" supporting the adoption of ICT technologies, and it is more likely that this necessity is present among firms with a solid market position (Clemons & Row, 1991).

Following these considerations, SMEs feeling in a leading market position would be more likely to adopt new technologies than "marginal" competitors, which would prefer to exploit existing knowledge and capabilities rather than exploring new possibilities (Leonard-Barton, 1992).

Hp3: Being in a leading market position increases the intensity of e-business among SMEs.

METHODOLOGY

Sampling and Collecting

The analysis is based on a survey of Italian SMEs. In this case, Italy can be considered as a meaningful field to investigate issues related to SMEs, given the high number of small organizations in most of the industries. A random stratified sample of 1,000 SMEs was selected, respecting the breakdown of SMEs among manufacturing and service industries, excluding firms with less than 50 employees, considered as very small, and with more than 500 employees, considered as large organizations. Data was collected through a questionnaire and firms were contacted by phone using the CATI technique during the period November/December, 2003.

A draft of the questionnaire was first tested on a random sample of 15 SMEs. The final version was modified accordingly. In order to reduce potential response bias, a unique key informant was chosen: the CEO was selected as the most appropriate respondent. In answering the entire questionnaire, 376 firms became the actual sample of this study.

Variables

The dependent variable of our model is the intensity of e-business adoption among SMEs. More precisely, we measure "e-business intensity" as a multinomial variable (EBUSINT) with three possible levels:

- 0, for SMEs which do not implement any kind of e-business strategy, and thus excluded from e-business trajectories (EXCLUDED)
- 1, for SMEs which tried to implement one e-business strategy among the following: interactive Web site, e-commerce, e-procurement, customer relationship management, and telework. This group of firms will be called TENTATIVE
- 2, for SMEs that integrated more than one e-business solutions in their processes, and for which e-business could be seen as a normal practice (INTEGRATED)

The intensity of competition perceived by a SME (variable "COMPETITION") has been measured through a five points likert-type scale (1= I completely disagree; 5 = I totally agree) for the following sentence: "In the market where we play, competition is extremely strong."

The intensity of technology legitimacy pressure perceived by a SME ("TECHLEGITIM") has been measured through a five point likert-type scale (1= I completely disagree; 5 = I totally agree) for the following sentence: "Given the market where we play, it is important for us to be considered as technology savvy."

The relative market position has been measured through a dummy variable ("LEADERSHIP"), as the answer to the following sentence: "Within your specific segment or niche, does your firm feel to be in a leading market position?" (1 = yes; 0 = no).

Since the range of firms' size in our sample is remarkable (from 50 to 250 employees), and since business size already proved to be a significant discriminator between IT adopters and non-adopters among SMEs (Fink, 1998), we controlled for size-effects (variable "SIZE"). To that end, we used the natural logarithm of the number of employees, considering that the probability to adopt an innovation increases with size, but at decreasing rates.

Last, we recognize that service sectors—for their intangible nature—may be more conducive of e-business strategy than manufacturing (Lucking-Reilly & Spulber, 2001). The dichotomous variable "SERVICE" (0 = manufacturing; 1 = service), then, is used to control for this industry specificity.

The Analytical Model

Multinomial logistic regression (MLR) is useful for situations in which you want to be able to classify subjects based on values of a set of predictor variables. This type of regression is similar to logistic regression, but it is more general because it can be applied when the dependent variable is not restricted to two categories.

Since we modeled our dependent variable as a multinomial variable with three levels (excluded, tentative, integrated), we applied the MLR procedure, which is essentially an extension of binary logistic regression to a polytomous multinomial (Agresti, 1999).

The method basically proceeds by comparing the effect of factors and covariates on the possibility of being in each of "*n-1*" categories (in our case, the "excluded" and the "integrated" categories) compared with the baseline category "*n*" (in our case, the "tentative" category).

This is conceptually equivalent to fitting "n-1" separate binary logistic models, comparing category 1 with category *n*, category 2 with *n*, and so on. Practically, the software usually estimates a simultaneous model which is more statistically sophisticated where, for each independent variable, we have "*n-1*" parameter estimates, each estimating the effect of a one-unit change in this variable on the log odds of being in category rather than in the baseline category (Long, 1997). In few terms, for each case, there will be n-1 predicted logits, one for each category relative to the reference or baseline category (Menard, 2002).

It could be noted that, when multiple classes of the dependent variable can be ranked, as for our case, ordinal logistic regression is sometimes preferred to multinomial logistic regression. Our choice to adopt MLR is due to the fact that our sample does not fully satisfy the test of parallel lines, which is mandatory to adopt the ordinary logistic regression (Menard). Moreover, MLR allows comparing the effects of independent variables (i.e., the drivers of e-business) across different categories of dependent variables, which is one important feature of our model. In any cases, when the ordered logit model is run adopting a logit as a link function, outcomes are largely similar to those obtainable through the multinomial logistic regression (Pampel, 2000).

FINDINGS

Table 1 shows the first outcome of the predictive model for the adoption of e-business solutions among SMEs. The reference category is "tentative," that is firms that adopted one, but only one, e-business solution.

The overall model fitting measures are all satisfactory.[2] We can focus, then, to parameter estimates and discuss our previous hypotheses. The findings are reported below:

1. The size of a SME appears to be a significant variable in explaining the leap from being "excluded" to become "tentative," but it does not appear as significant in explaining a further leap, the one from being "tentative" to become an "integrated" e-business firm. More precisely, a one unit increase in the natural logarithm of the number of employee of a SME (that is, an increase of about 170% in its size), reduces the odds ratio of being an "excluded" firm—instead of being at least a "tentative" one—by 34%.

2. The lack of competition would not prove to be a significant factor in explaining e-busi-

Table 1. Multinomial logistic regression: model fitting

Model Fitting Information

Model	-2 Log Likelihood	Chi-Square	df	Sig.
Intercept Only	762,955			
Final	717,061	45,895	10	0,000

Pseudo R-Square

Cox and Snell	0,115
Nagelkerke	**0,130**
McFadden	0,057

Likelihood Ratio Tests

Effect	-2 Log Likelihood of Reduced Model	Chi-Square	df	Sig.
Intercept	717,061	0,000	0	.
SIZE	723,692	6,631	2	**0,036**
TECHLEGITIM	725,818	8,758	2	**0,013**
COMPETITION	721,911	4,851	2	***0,088***
SERVICES	724,123	7,063	2	**0,029**
LEADERSHIP	730,237	13,176	2	**0,001**

The chi-square statistic is the difference in -2 log-likelihoods between the final model and a reduced model.
The reduced model is formed by omitting an effect from the final model.
The null hypothesis is that all parameters of that effect are 0.
This reduced model is equivalent to the final model because omitting the effect does not increase the degrees of freedom.

Classification

Observed	Predicted			
	EXCLUDED	TENTATIVE	INTEGRATED	Percent Correct
EXCLUDED	36	14	48	36,7%
TENTATIVE	17	26	71	22,8%
INTEGRATED	22	18	124	75,6%
Overall Percentage	19,9%	15,4%	64,6%	**49,5%**

*Table 2. Multinomial logistic regression: parameter estimates**

Parameter Estimates

		B	Std. Error	Wald	df	Sig.	Exp(B)	95% Confidence Lower Bound	95% Confidence Upper Bound
EXCLUDED	Intercept	2,947	1,012	8,476	1	0,004	.	.	.
	SIZE	-0,418	0,170	5,999	1	**0,014**	0,659	0,472	0,920
	TECHLEGITIM	-0,324	0,121	7,141	1	**0,008**	0,723	0,570	0,917
	COMPETITION	0,029	0,135	0,045	1	0,831	1,029	0,791	1,339
	SERVICES	-0,417	0,335	1,551	1	0,213	0,659	0,342	1,270
	LEADERSHIP	0,057	0,301	0,035	1	0,851	1,058	0,587	1,907
INTEGRATED	Intercept	-0,478	0,903	0,280	1	0,596	.	.	.
	SIZE	-0,093	0,143	0,423	1	0,515	0,911	0,689	1,205
	TECHLEGITIM	-0,043	0,112	0,146	1	0,702	0,958	0,770	1,193
	COMPETITION	0,250	0,125	3,983	1	**0,046**	1,284	1,004	1,642
	SERVICES	0,381	0,276	1,901	1	0,168	1,463	0,852	2,513
	LEADERSHIP	0,818	0,258	10,078	1	**0,002**	2,266	1,367	3,754

* *TENTATIVE is the reference category*

ness exclusion for a SME; on the contrary, the level of perceived competition appears significant in explaining the leap from "tentative" e-business to "integrated" e-business. This result would confirm our first hypothesis: the degree of perceived competition does affect the involvement in e-business strategies, even if it does not explain e-business exclusion *tout court*. More precisely, a one point increase in the five-point scale measuring the level of perceived competition increases the odds ratio of being an "integrated" e-business SME—instead of being just "tentative"—by 28.4%.

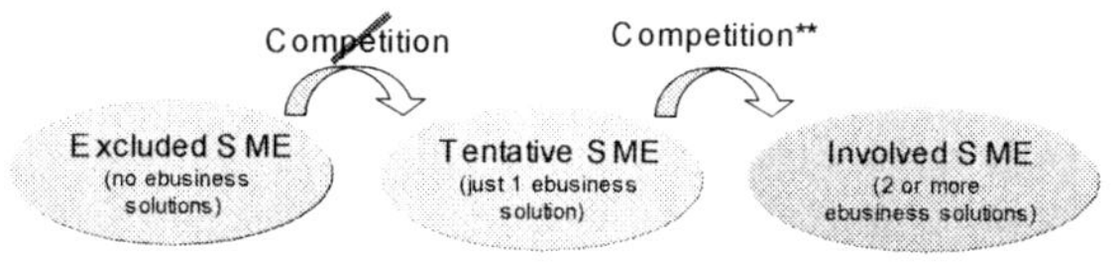

3. Low environmental pressures for being technology savvy prove to be a significant factor in explaining part of the e-business exclusion of a SME, but not a significant factor in explaining the leap from being "tentative" to become an "integrated" e-business firm. Accordingly, the second hypothesis would be confirmed by our evidence, but only in explaining e-business exclusion vs. adoption. This sample did not confirm any role of technology legitimacy requirements in explaining different level of e-business adoption. More precisely, a one point increase in the five-point scale measuring the intensity of this pressure reduces the odds ratio of being an "excluded" firm instead of being at least "tentative" by 27%.

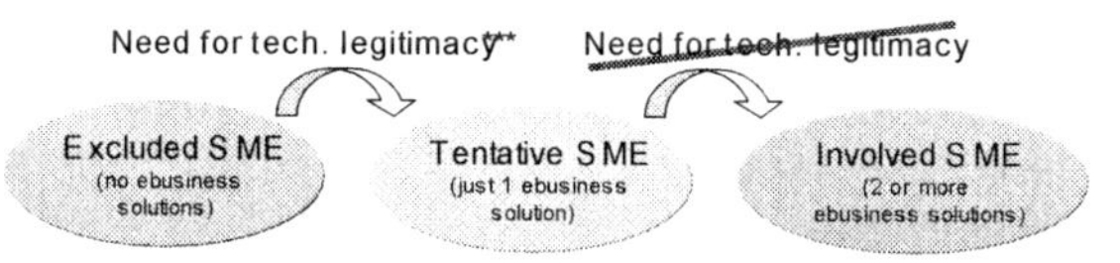

4. A (self-stated) leading market position is highly significant only in explaining the leap from being just "tentative" to be an "integrated" e-business firm: SMEs in a leading market position (or feeling so) more than double the odds ratio of being "involved" in e-business. In confirmation of our third hypothesis, then, it seems possible to conclude that a strong market position is positively related to higher levels of e-business involvement. More precisely, when an SME feels to be in a leading market position, the odds ratio of being an "integrated" e-business SME—instead of being just "tentative"—increases by 126.6%.

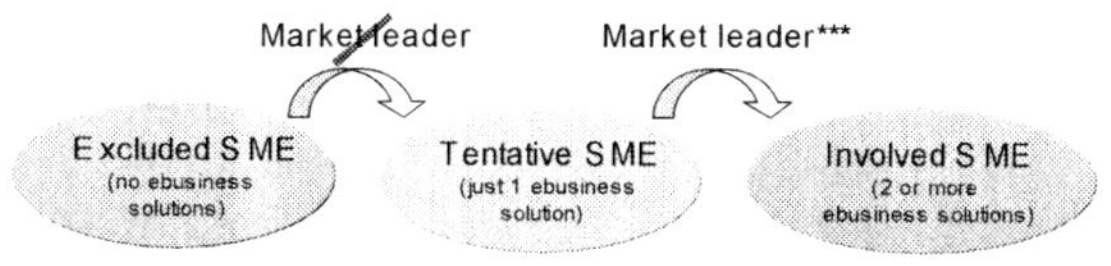

Finally, the role of the industry (namely, services vs. manufacturing) was controlled by the dichotomous variable "services." Even if the literature already proved the relevance of this factor, our sample produced a Wald statistics below the 10% level of significance for both the contrasts ("tentative" vs. "excluded" and "tentative" vs. "integrated"). Considering the two contrasts together, however, the χ^2 test on the difference between the full model deviance and the baseline model deviance shows an overall significance at the 5% level. The estimates indicate that belonging to a service sector, instead of a manufacturing one, would reduce the odds ratio of being "excluded" by 34%. Similarly, belonging to a service sector would increase the probability of being "integrated" (instead of just "tentative") by 46%.

IMPLICATIONS AND CONCLUSIONS

The very first conclusion that is possible to draw out is that different factors seem to explain the nonadoption of e-business solutions and different levels of e-business involvement. The analysis, in other words, confirms the opportunity to keep the two issues as separated: e-business exclusion and e-business involvement appear, at least partially, to be different phenomena that require different theoretical reasoning and modeling.

With specific regard to our study, two factors among those analyzed reveal to be more suitable in explaining e-business exclusion of some SMEs (but not to explain different levels of e-business adoption). They are the size of a SME and a lack of institutional pressures/inputs to adopt the innovations in point (see hypothesis two).

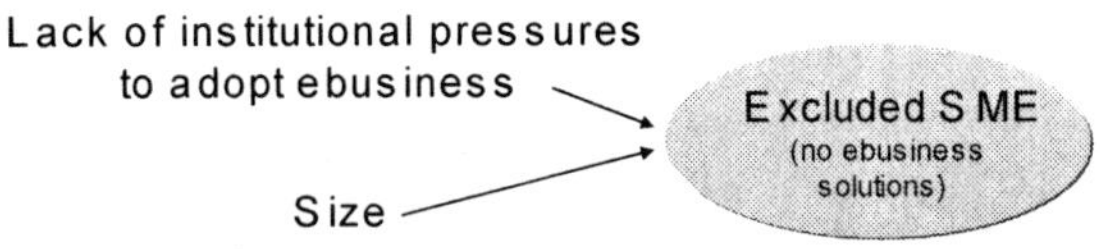

This means that:

1. When the adoption of e-business is just sporadic, almost casual (tentative, as said), this is generally because such an adoption roots mainly in imitating behaviors or external pressures, and less in the culture of innovation or in the search of competitive advantages.
2. It is also confirmed that the lack of adequate resources (tangibles and intangibles, as approximated by the variable size), may completely impair the adoption of any e-business solution, something well-known to the literature of innovations. SMEs in similar conditions need the special attention of e-business supporting policies, keeping in mind that pushing adoption, by itself, is not enough to let a firm enjoy the benefits of e-business.

The study, then, provides insights on e-business involvement, that is, on a further step to become firms developing more e-business integrated opportunities.

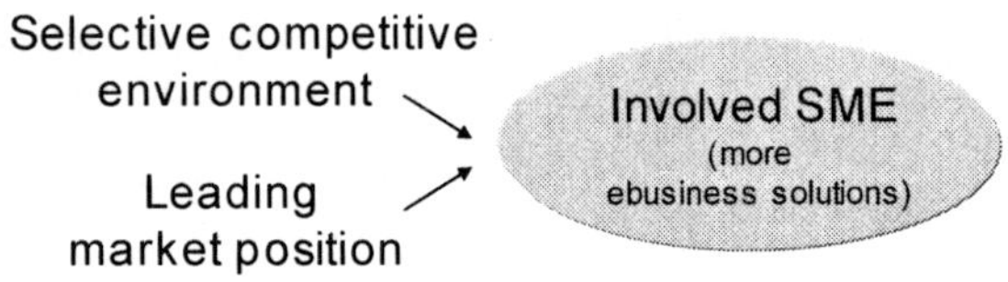

1. Interestingly, and significantly, this leap is prompted by a selective competitive environment, and not by imitative or induced behaviors, as for the previous, tentative step
2. An integrated e-business involvement, here, seems to be a requirement and an opportunity to remain competitive. Not by chance, in fact, these firms are the leading ones, feeling the necessity to stay on the edge.

Competition, then, would create the right conditions for driving the adoption of integrated e-business solutions among SMEs. Procompetitive policies, accordingly, would result in effective (and efficient) prodigitalization policies as well.

The results also lead to a related consideration: today, firms facing low levels of competition or low environmental pressures can still afford a low (or nought) e-business involvement and innovation. But how many arenas will have the fortune of maintaining a similar structure in the next future? The evidence tells us that these happy gardens are rarer and rarer, also because of technological changes. The management, here, should ask whether they are getting ready for the upcoming challenges or whether, instead, they are exposing their firms to some risky e-business run up.

Among the limitations of this study, it must be noted that a possible response bias exists. In fact, firms with a higher e-business involvement might be more inclined to answer the questionnaire. However, while this would bias the percentage of e-business adopters (statistical frequencies in Table 1), it should not bias the *relationships* that we discussed in this chapter.

Finally, as a suggestion for future research, the implications emerged in this study might be integrated by the analysis of further factors, both endogenous and exogenous, separately for e-business adoption and e-business involvement.

REFERENCES

Amit, R., & Zott, C. (2001). Value creation in e-business. *Strategic Management Journal, 22,* 493-520.

Andrews, K. (1971). *The concepts of corporate strategy.* Homewood, IL: Dow-Jones Irwin.

Barney, J. (1991). Firm resources and competitive advantage. *Journal of Management, 17*(1), 99-120.

Clemons, E., & Row, M. (1991). Sustaining IT advantage: The role of structural differences. *MIS Quarterly, 3,* 275-292.

Cohen, W.M., & Levin R.C. (1989). Empirical studies of innovation and market structure. In R. Schmalensee & R. Willig (Eds.), *Handbook of industrial organization* (pp. 1059-1107). Amsterdam: North Holland.

Daniel, E.M., & Grimshaw, D.J. (2002). An exploratory comparison of electronic commerce adoption in large and small enterprises. *Journal of Information Technology, 17,* 133-147.

Davidsson, P., Hunter, E., & Klofsten, M. (2006). Institutional forces – the invisible hand that shapes venture ideas. *International Small Business Journal, 24*(2), 115-131.

E-business-watch. (2003). *The 2nd European E-business Report.* European Commission.

Fink, D. (1998). Guidelines for the successful adoption of information technology in small and medium enterprises. *International Journal of Information Management, 18*(4), 243-253.

Gatignon, H., & Robertson, T.S. (1989). Technology diffusion: An empirical test of competitive effects. *Journal of Marketing, 53*(1), 35-49.

Grandon, E.E., & Pearson, J.M. (2004). Electronic commerce adoption: An empirical study of small and medium U.S. business. *Information & Management, 42,* 197-216.

Grewal, R., Comer, J.M., & Metha, R. (2001). An investigation into the antecedents of organizational participations in the business-to-business electronic markets. *Journal of Marketing, 65*(7), 17-33.

Harrison, D., Mykytyn, P.P., & Riemenschneider, C.K. (1997). Executive decisions about adoption of information technology in small businesses: Theory and empirical tests. *Information Systems Research, 8*(2), 171-195.

Iacovou, C.L., Benbasat, I., & Dexter, A.S. (1995). Electronic data interchange and small organizations: Adoption and impact of technology. *MIS Quarterly, 19*(4), 465-486.

Lal, K. (1999). Determinants of the adoption of information technology: A case study of electrical and electronic goods manufacturing firms in India. *Research Policy, 28,* 667-680.

Lee, J., Runge, J., & Baek, S. (2001). *Adoption of Internet technologies in small business.* In *Proceedings of Pacific Asia Conference on Information Systems (PACIS 2001),* Seoul, Korea.

Leonard-Barton, D. (1992). Core rigidities and core competencies. *Strategic Management Journal, 13,* 111-125.

Long, J.S. (1997). *Regression models for categorical and limited dependent variables.* Sage Publications.

Lucking-Reiley, D., & Spulber, D.F. (2001). Business to business electronic commerce. *Journal of Economic Perspectives, 15*(1), 55-68.

Malerba, F., & Orsenigo, L. (1997). Technological regimes and sectoral patterns of innovative actvities. *Industrial and Corporate Change, 6,* 83-117.

Mata, F.J., Fuerst, W.L., & Barney J.B. (1995). Information technology and sustained competitive advantage: A resource-based analysis. *MIS Quarterly, 19*(4), 487-505.

Menard, S. (2002). *Applied logistic regression analysis* (Rev. ed). Sage Series on Quantitative Applications in the Social Sciences. Newbury Park , CA: Sage.

North, D.C. (1990). *Institutions, institutional change and economic performance.* Cambridge, MA: Cambridge University Press.

Pampel, F.C. (2000). *Logistic regression. A primer.* Sage Series on Quantitative Applications in the Social Sciences, 132. Newbury Park, CA: Sage.

Peteraf, M.A. (1993). The cornerstones of competitive advantage: A resource-based view. *Strategic Management Journal, 14,* 179-192.

Pflughoeft, K.A., Ramamurthy, K., Soofi, E.S., Yasai-Ardekani, M., & Zahedi, F.M. (2003). Multiple conceptualizations of small business Web use and benefit. *Decision Sciences, 34*(3), 467-513.

Porter, M. (1980). *Competitive strategy.* New York: Free Press.

Powell, T.C., & Dent-Micallef, A. (1997). Information technology as competitive advantage: The role of human, business, and technology resources. *Strategic Management Journal, 18*(5), 375-405.

Premkumar, G., & Roberts, M. (1999). Adoption of new information technologies in rural small businesses. *Omega, International Journal of Management Science, 27,* 467-484.

Riemenschneider, C.K., Harrison, D.A., & Mykytn, Jr., P.P. (2003). Understanding IT adoption decisions in small business: Integrating current theories. *Information & Management, 40*(4), 269-285.

Teece, D.J., Pisano, G., & Shuen, A. (1997). Dynamic capabilities and strategic management. *Strategic Management Journal, 18*(7), 509-533.

Thong, Y., & Yap, C. (1995). CEO characteristics, organizational characteristics and information technology adoption in small businesses. *Omega, International Journal of Management Science, 23,* 429-442

Zhu K., Kremer, K., & Xu S. (2003). Electronic business adoption by European firms: A cross-country assessment of the facilitators and inhibitors. *European Journal of Information System, 12,* 251-268.

KEY TERMS

E-Business: An umbrella term referring to a wide variety of Internet-based management solutions, like a Web site, an e-commerce platform, or a customer relationship management system.

Web site: An organization's presence or an individual's presence on the World Wide Web. It is a structured collection of multimedia pages linked to each other and very often to pages on other Web sites (hyperlinks). A Web site is hosted on a server computer and, to qualify as a Web site, the server must be available on the Internet 24 hours a day.

E-Commerce: According to the American Marketing Association (AMA), an e-commerce strategy incorporates various elements of the marketing mix to drive users to a Web site for the purpose of purchasing a product or service.

E-Procurement: A structured information system adopted by some organizations for making business-to-business purchases over the Internet. Such a system can connect companies and their business processes directly with suppliers while managing all interactions between them. E-procurement is also referred to as *supplier exchange*.

Customer Relationship Management (CRM) System: a system combining database and computer technology with customer service to manage at best the relationships with clients. Automated CRM processes are often used to generate automatic personalized marketing actions based on the customer information stored in the system.

Telework: According to the European Commission, telework occurs when information and communications technologies (ICTs) are applied to enable work to be done at a distance from the place where the work results are needed or where the work would conventionally have been done.

Institutional Pressures: According to the Institutional Theory, institutions work as forces upon individuals and organizations by creating social pressures and restrictions, setting boundaries for what is accepted and what is not. Such an influence can be in the form of normative, coercive, and mimetic pressures (Davidsson, Hunter, & Klofsten, 2006). *Normative pressures* consist of social pressures on organizations and its members to conform to certain norms. *Coercive pressures* are often thought of as formal institutions of regulations or laws but can also be informal expectations on organizations (e.g., technical standards imposed by someone exerting power over another actor, as in a parent-subsidiary relationship). *Mimetic pressures* represent demands towards imitation of other organizations to cope with uncertainty.

ENDNOTES

1 A leading position for a SME, here, may also refer to a specific segment or niche of the market.

2 The likelihood ratio test on the entire model is highly significant: the independent variables, together, do have a significant effect on the e-business intensity among SME. With regard to the Nagelkerke pseudo R-square measure, it indicates a satisfactory level above the threshold value of 0.10. Also, the model is able to correctly classify 49.5% of the cases. This is an increase of 13.5% compared to its baseline: also in this case, a lift above 10% is largely considered as satisfactory.

This work was previously published in Handbook of Research on Global Diffusion of Broadband Data Transmission, edited by Y. Dwivedi, A. Papazafeiropoulou, & J. Choudrie, pp. 493-503, copyright 2008 by Information Science Reference, formerly known as Idea Group Reference (an imprint of IGI Global).

Section II
Development and Design Methodologies

Chapter V
Conflicts, Compromises, and Political Decisions:
Methodological Challenges of Enterprise-Wide E-Business Architecture Creation

Kari Smolander
Lappeenranta University of Technology, Finland

Matti Rossi
Helsinki School of Economics, Finland

ABSTRACT

This article describes the architecture development process in an international ICT company, which is building a comprehensive e-business system for its customers. The implementation includes the integration of data and legacy systems from independent business units and the construction of a uniform Web-based customer interface. We followed the early process of architecture analysis and definition over a year. The research focuses on the creation of e-business architecture and observes that instead of guided by a prescribed method, the architecture emerges through somewhat non-deliberate actions obliged by the situation and its constraints, conflicts, compromises, and political decisions. The interview-based qualitative data is analyzed using grounded theory and a coherent story explaining the situation and its forces is extracted. Conclusions are drawn from the observations and possibilities and weaknesses of the support that UML and RUP provide for the process are pointed out.

INTRODUCTION

Robust technical architecture is considered one of the key issues when building successful e-business systems. The design of technical architecture is usually seen as a set of trade-offs between available resources (such as available personnel and money) and operational requirements related to technical architecture, such as scalability, capacity, response times, security, and availability. The software architecture research provides design tools for technical architecture design, including, for instance, architecture description languages (Dashofy, Van der Hoek, & Taylor, 2005; Medvidovic & Taylor, 2000), common architectural patterns and styles (Monroe, Kompanek, Melton, & Garlan, 1997), architectural trade-off methods (Kazman, Klein, & Clements, 2000), architectural frameworks (Leist & Zellner, 2006), and technologies for e-business implementation (Bichler, Segev, & Zhao, 1998). In an ideal world, the work of an architect would be to find the explicit requirements for architecture, and select the best possible design tools and technologies to implement the architecture. Furthermore, the architecture development team would make rational trade-offs concerning the requirements, and produce the best realistic solution for the architecture with the selected design tools and implementation technologies.

However, the literature contains many examples of cases where technical rationality has not been sufficient for the success in IS projects (e.g. Sauer, Southon, & Dampney, 1997). Architecture researchers have found that the work of an architect and the usage of architecture are bound by more diverse organizational issues and limitations that the classical technical software architecture research ignores. These include for example the diverse role of an architect in an organization observed by Grinter (1999) and varying uses and meanings of architecture in practice (Smolander & Päivärinta, 2002a). The main message of these studies is that an architect has a social, and even political, role in an organization and that different stakeholders relate different meanings to architecture to fulfill their informational requirements in the development process. This phenomenon has remarkable similarities to information systems development in general. As pointed out by Klein & Hirscheim, the implicit assumption of rationality of the development processes hides the legitimating of the goals and differing political agendas of various stakeholders (Hirschheim & Klein, 1989).

To understand the issues involved in architecture development, we observed a project that was developing e-business architecture in an international ICT company. We interviewed various stakeholders to gain a deep insight into the process. The company already had several e-commerce systems in individual business units, but it needed a more uniform customer interface for its various systems. The e-business project included the integration of data and legacy systems from these units and the construction of a uniform Web-based customer interface hiding the differences of the business units. Our goal was to find ways for supporting architecture development by means of methods and description languages, such as UML. We were aware of efforts of supporting architecture design with UML (e.g., Conallen, 1999; Garlan & Kompanek, 2000; Hofmeister, Nord, & Soni, 1999b; Object Management Group, 1999, 2006), but these efforts were mostly targeted to technical software design and we did not know how well these would support a large socio-technical or organizational project, such as enterprise or e-business architecture development. Therefore we decided to observe a real world project and concentrate on the requirements that e-business architecture development in its complex organizational context state on description languages and development methods. Next, we decided to compare the observed requirements to the support that UML and RUP offer, because they, together, form the current methodological basis for many systems development organizations. UML is the de-facto standard language in software and systems development and RUP (Jacobson, Booch, & Rumbaugh, 1999) is a widely known process model that claims to improve development process maturity (Kuntzmann & Kruchten, 2003). We believed that this kind of knowledge would benefit both practitioners in process improvement and developers of UML extensions.

Another interest was to find out what factors influenced the creation of e-business architecture: was it designed purposefully by software architects through rational decisions and trade-offs, or did it emerge through somewhat non-deliberate actions obliged by the situation and its constraints, conflicts, compromises, and political decisions? This is a very important issue, as unlike software architecture, e-business architecture is very tightly coupled with the business models of the company and thus the architecture has a far more direct impact on business than for example low-level system architecture. Furthermore, if the business models are not supported by the e-business architecture, then the business strategy will not work (Ross, Weill, & Robertson, 2006).

We used open interviews of various actors in the projects to gather the necessary information about the project. We analyzed the qualitative data from the interviews using grounded theory (Glaser & Strauss, 1967) as the research method and concluded the analysis by categorizing the issues that had emerged using the taxonomy of Lyytinen (1987). Thus, we classified the issues as belonging into technical, language and organizational context. From this classification of issues, we extracted requirements for development methods when developing integrated e-business solutions and compared these requirements to the support that the combination of UML and RUP provides.

We observed that most of the problems encountered had very little to do with descriptions of the architecture per se. Rather what was problematic were the issues that architecture development exposed about the underlying organization. This is an important finding, as most of the research into architecture has been about effective description languages and design processes and there is a void of research about the organizational consequences of architecture development.

The article is organized as follows: we start by explaining in more detail what is meant by architecture in this article (section 2). In section 3, we describe the research process and method used. section 4 describes the situation the company is facing and the motives for the change and implementation of the e-business system. In section 5, we describe the situation and the context of the development project aiming at e-business implementation and the consequences of the situation for the progress of the development project. From the observed issues faced by the development project we draw conclusions and extract the requirements for development methods in e-business architecture development and compare the requirements to support that the combination of UML and RUP provides (section 6). We point out areas where current research is not supporting the needs of the practice of general and particularly e-business architecture development.

ARCHITECTURE IN SYSTEMS DEVELOPMENT

In this study, we describe a process where comprehensive e-business architecture is being created. In addition to e-commerce systems serving external customer transactions, e-business includes both the integration of and streamlining of internal information systems to serve the new digitally enabled business processes (Kalakota & Robinson, 2001) and the unified customer interface (Ross et al., 2006). For the sake of simplicity, we understand e-business here to cover both the transactions and processes within a firm and the integrated external e-commerce systems as in (Kalakota & Robinson, 2001). This enables us to interpret the process in the studied organization as the process of building an integrated e-business architecture. Ross et al. (2006) stress the architecture as the necessary foundation for execution of comprehensive, across the functions operating, e-business.

Conventionally, architecture is understood as a high-level logical abstraction of the system defining the main components of the system and their relationships. The term architecture is also used both in the context of an individual system and in the context of systems integration. The software architecture typically concentrates on the architecture of a single software system, whereas the terms information systems (IS) architecture and enterprise architecture (Kim & Everest, 1994; Ross et al., 2006; Sowa & Zachman, 1992) refer to the overall architecture of all information systems in an organization.

In practice, however, the borderline between a single system and a set of systems is difficult to determine. Practically no system today is isolated from other systems, and the relationship of a system to its environment may be architecturally more important than the inner structure of the system, especially when developing e-business systems. Usually, systems rely on a common technical infrastructure, (including networks, processing services, operation services, etc.) which is common for all the systems in an organization. Organizationally, architecture design is a co-operative effort involving many roles in the development environment. These roles include the role of an architect who is specifically associated with the task of architecture design. An architect needs contribution and commitment from many individuals, teams, and parts of organization to succeed in the effort (Grinter, 1999).

By architecture development, we mean a process where early design decisions are realized into an architecture defining that defines system's composition from various viewpoints. Architecture also contains the blueprints for system's implementation from conceptual and physical components. This process forms a set of documents which different stakeholders can use to relate their concerns to the issues made concrete by the architecture and discuss their needs in the terms defined by the common architecture. They can also make decisions concerning system development strategies and policies using architecture as a common reference. This conception sees architecture not only as a technical artifact but also as a boundary object (Star & Griesemer, 1989) having strong organizational connotations.

The conventional role of architecture is to serve as an enabler for further design and implementation (Hofmeister, Nord, & Soni, 1999a; Shaw & Garlan, 1996). Obviously, sound and well-designed technical architecture makes the detailed design and implementation of a system easier and less risky than it would be without such architecture. Architecture defines, for example, the modules or components which the system is composed of, and therefore it focuses and constrains the solution space of individual designers that develop individual components. This technical view of architecture has produced also studies related to UML. In the end of last decade, possibilities and weaknesses of UML as an architecture description language, and its complexity (Siau & Cao, 2001; Siau, Erickson, & Lee, 2005) were widely evaluated and enhancements were proposed (Conallen, 1999; D'Souza & Wills, 1998; Egyed & Medvidovic, 1999; Garlan & Kompanek, 2000; Hofmeister et al., 1999b; Medvidovic, Egyed, & Rosenblum, 1999; Rumpe, Schoenmakers, Radermacher, & Schürr, 1999). The recent developments in this area include the SysML extension of UML (Object Management Group, 2006). Different profiles and enhancements to UML have been proposed to tackle its limitations in electronic commerce (Dori, 2001).

RESEARCH PROCESS

The studied organization is a globally operating ICT company having thousands of employees worldwide. Its customers include both consumers and businesses for which the organization provides various products and services. Software is one of the key assets in the organization's service production and product development. Historically, the organization has had several independent business units targeted at diverging business sectors. In addition, the information management of the organization has been distributed to these business units and the functions of enterprise level information management have included mainly the provision of network infrastructure, enterprise level accounting, and basic office tools. Most of the information systems in use have been implemented and operated by the business units that have been quite independent in their decisions concerning strategies for information management. However, recent developments in markets and technology have led the organization to set its strategies to a more integrative direction. For this reason, the organization has set an objective to provide an integrated e-business solution to both its consumer and business customers. This will include both implementation of a uniform Web-based customer interface and sufficient integration between the distributed operative back-end information systems, such as customer management and billing systems.

The research process followed the grounded theory method (Glaser & Strauss, 1967), which is a research method developed originally for social sciences by Glaser and Strauss in the 1960s and later developed and re-interpreted by the original authors (e.g., Glaser, 1978; Strauss & Corbin, 1990) and others (e.g., Locke, 2001; Martin & Turner, 1986). Grounded theory promotes inductive theory creation from the data. The objective is not to validate or test theories but to create one. The analysis process of the grounded theory is explicitly defined and consists of several coding phases. The coding starts from *open coding* in which any incident, slice, or element of the data may be given a conceptual label for the identification of commonalities. These commonalities are called *categories* and they are described in terms of their properties (Fernández, Lehmann, & Underwood, 2002). The coding continues with *axial coding* (Strauss & Corbin, 1990) or theoretical coding (Glaser, 1978), where relationships between the categories are resolved. The coding ends at *selective coding* (Strauss & Corbin, 1990) where the resulting theory is "densified" (Glaser, 1978) or a core category selected (Strauss & Corbin, 1990) and theory about that is described. The data collection is based on the notion of *theoretical sampling*, which means adjusting the data collection process according to the requirements of the emerging theory. The sources of data may be adjusted during the process and the data collection can be stopped whenever a state of *theoretical saturation* is achieved, meaning a situation where no additional data would further develop the categories and their properties.

In the study, we interviewed 19 participants of the ongoing e-business system architecture design project during 2002, first in January and February and then later in November and December. The interviewees included six system architects, five enterprise system managers, three project managers, two software development managers, one project leader, one system analyst, and one marketing manager. Table 1 describes their relationship to the e-business development project. The interviews lasted from 45 to 120 minutes and they were completely transcribed as text.

The interview themes of this study were adjusted during the data collection to reflect better the developing theoretical understanding of the researchers and the specific knowledge of the interviewees. The emphasis of the interviews changed according to the interviewee and the special knowledge in his or her possession. Because the data collection proceeded partly in parallel with the analysis, the emerging theory also caused changes in the emphasis of the interview themes. In grounded theory this kind of adaptation is called *theoretical sensitivity*, and for theory-building research this is considered legitimate because "investigators are trying to understand each case individually and in as much depth as feasible" (Eisenhardt, 1989, p. 539). Eisenhardt calls the process where the emergence of a new line of thinking causes the altering of data collection *controlled opportunism* "in which researchers take advantage of the uniqueness of a specific case and the emergence of new themes to improve resultant theory" (Eisenhardt, 1989, p. 539).

Table 1. Interviewed persons and their roles

Role	Tasks	Interviews
System architect	Deals with technological solutions and architectural structures in the e-business development project	6
Enterprise system manager	Is responsible for a portfolio of systems and technologies that are used in a particular organization. Acts as a customer in the internal e-business development project or participates it as an expert.	5
Project manager	Manages resources and is responsible for the execution of a sub-project of the e-business development project	3
Software development manager	Is responsible for a permanent software development organization	2
Project leader	Manages the e-business development super-project and supervises its set of sub-projects.	1
System analyst	Participates the requirements gathering and analysis phases as an intermediate between customers and technical experts.	1
Marketing manager	Is responsible for the public image and services of the electronic channel. Requirements setter and a customer to the development project.	1

The analysis in this study started with the open coding phase. In the beginning, we did not have any explicit *a priori* constructs for the analysis. Our task was to search mentions from the interviews that could be interpreted as meaningful related to the research question, "What are the conditions and constraints for creating and designing architecture in a large information systems development project?" The identified mentions related to this question were categorized using the software tool ATLAS.ti. During the open coding phase, altogether 187 emergent categories were found, and the categories were assigned to emerging scheme of super categories or category families, including for instance changes, conflicts, consequences, experiences, problems, purposes, and solutions occurring during the e-business architecture design and implementation process.

The axial coding started in parallel with the open coding and causal relationships between categories were recorded with Atlas.ti's semantic network capability. Figure 1 shows an example of such a network diagram. In the figure, the boxes represent categories, the arrows between them interpreted causalities, and the lines associations between categories. The number of categories and the number of identified relationships between the categories added up to 187 categories and 200 relationships, which created a problem of how to report such a multitude of categories and relationships. The solution was sought through abstracting out those categories that were rarely occurring in the data and interpreted as not so relevant regarding the research question. In addition, more attention was paid to those categories that occurred frequently in the data.

Inductively, we produced an explaining story to the events and forces under which the e-business development project had to work. The organization is facing market changes and changing the organization according to the changing markets. The objectives for the e-business development emerge from these changes and because the change is continuous and it brings all the time new requirements for the e-business system, the objectives are quite fluctuating. In addition, the history and legacy structures of the organization cause conflicts and problems in the development when combined with the need for change. These fluctuating objectives and emerging conflicts and problems brought certain consequences to the e-business architecture development in the organization. The formation and description of this explaining story can be considered as selective coding (Strauss & Corbin, 1990) and its details

Figure 1. An example of a semantic network from axial coding

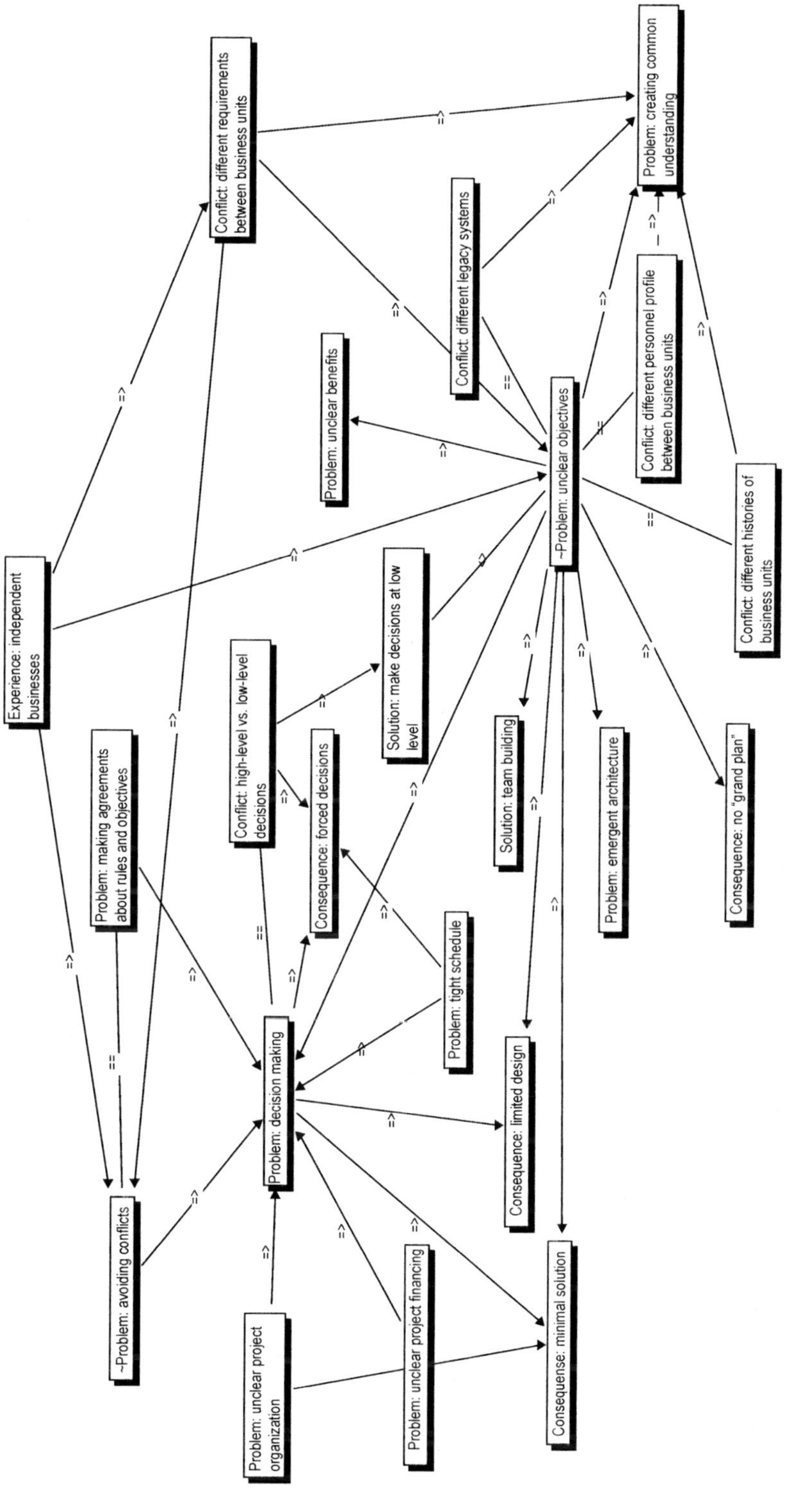

in the studied organization are explained in the next three sections.

The study has required extensive interpretation and exploration in the studied organization and therefore the main instruments of the research has been the researchers and their ability to interpret events and people's actions correctly. Robson (2002) lists three threats to validity in this kind of research, reactivity (the interference of the researcher's presence), researcher bias, and respondent bias, and strategies that reduce these threats. We have used these strategies in the following way:

- **Prolonged involvement:** Although this study lasted for one year, the research project altogether lasted for more than two years in the same organization and consisted of several phases and data collection rounds.
- **Triangulation:** The study has used data and observer triangulation as presented by Denzin (1978). To reduce the bias caused by researchers, we used *observer triangulation*, because the data collection was done by two researchers. The bias caused by data was minimized using *data triangulation*, where different sources of data were used. Interviews were the primary data collection method, but we also received many kinds of project and company documents and architecture descriptions.
- **Peer debriefing and support:** The research has included regular meetings and discussions with involved research participants from several research institutions. In addition, preliminary results of research phases have been presented and discussed in conferences and workshops (Smolander, 2003; Smolander, Hoikka, Isokallio et al., 2002; Smolander & Päivärinta, 2002a, 2002b; Smolander, Rossi, & Purao, 2002, 2005).
- **Member checking:** The interpretation of the data has been confirmed by presenting the results to company participants in the research project.
- **Audit trail:** All interviews have been recorded and transcribed. The notes and memos of the study have been preserved and data coding and analysis results are available through the analysis tool used, ATLAS.ti.

CHANGES AND THEIR EFFECTS IN THE DEVELOPMENT CONTEXT

Starting Point: Changing Markets, Changing Organization

During the time of the data collection, there was a considerable change going on in the ICT market and the organization under study had undergone a deep change. A few years ago, the strategies emphasized growth and utilization of the possibilities in the stock market. This enforced independent business units inside the organization since the growth was easier to handle through independency. Each of the business units built independent e-commerce solutions and customer extranets, which resulted to a fragmentary set of e-commerce solutions to customers with own Internet sites, sales and billing systems, and Web-based customer support.

When the beliefs in the possibilities of ICT sector's continuing growth diminished, the organization had to change its strategies from growth to profitability and from stock market to customer orientation. With independent business units, there was no authority in the organization, which would see a customer as a whole. Instead, each business unit kept track of the customers only in the context of its independent business. To produce a unified customer interface a profound change to the way of building information systems and an integrated e-business solution was needed. This change would also require changes in business practices and organization. The organization should operate in a more integrated fashion and the barriers between independent units should be lowered.

The organization began to see technical e-business architecture as an enabler of change. The IS organizations in independent business units were obliged to cooperate and enforce commitment to the integration of information systems. This also emphasized the role of central information management, which had been in a minor role this far. Now, its roles would include the enforcement of information systems integration and enabling the unification of the sales channels and customer management for the planned e-business solution. At this point, the organization decided to establish a working group of systems architects from various parts of the organization. In the following section, we shall describe the context and the forces under which this group of architects were developing and designing the unified e-business architecture.

Conflicts, Problems and Varying Purposes

The context for e-business architecture development included many issues, which the working group for technical architecture development had to face and be aware of. These included the market changes as described above, historical organizational inertia, fluctuating requirements and objectives, and conflicts and problems emerging from the market changes, inertia, and unclear objectives.

Historical Inertia

The organization's history with independent businesses and their diverging functions and objectives had both psychological and technical consequences causing slow progress and conflicts in the integrated e-business development. Each of the business units had legacy systems with incompatible information structures, technical architectures, and operating principles. It was not possible in practice to replace these systems with a uniform solution at once.

The historical inertia had effects also on the organization responsible for information management and information systems. Because of the independence, the organization had no clear central information management that could take responsibility of the e-business architecture development. Many of the conflicts and problems described later arose from this situation.

The Observed Objectives for the E-Business System

The fluctuating objectives, meanings, and requirements for the e-business architecture created another source of conflicts and problems. In a large organization with a high degree of independency, the conceptions among different business units and individuals about the purposes of an e-business solution vary considerably. Among the interviewees, we identified a large set of different purposes for the e-business system, which were then classified in five distinct classes:

- Creation of a unified electronic customer interface.
- Reduction of costs.
- Integration of information systems.
- Gaining business advantage.
- Implementing an organization change.

This list of observed purposes for the e-business system looks quite comprehensive and ambitious. Different interviewees emphasized the purposes differently and many saw that the only realistic objective was to implement a single sign-on procedure with a minimal level of customer information integration. The list anyhow shows the complicated and conflicting nature of objectives for the e-business system when it is developed for a large enterprise.

Emerging Conflicts and Problems

Changes in markets and organization, the history of the organization, and the complicated objectives for the e-business system put the architecture development group in a difficult situation. The group and its members were obliged to respond by some means and these responses shaped mitigated the role of deliberate design in the development process. In open coding, we identified in total 48 categories of conflicts and problems. This list was further combined to seven main categories, as follows:

- Varying requirements and unclear objectives
- Problems in the cooperation between technical and business people
- Conflict avoidance and problems in decision-making
- Problematic role of the central information management and its missing working practices
- Difficulties in creating common understanding about the architecture
- Difficulties in determining the level of integration
- Problems of implementing the integration

As described earlier, the purposes of the system were manifold and complicated and the requirements varied according to the business needs in the business units. The architects held this ambiguity of objectives and requirements as the biggest obstacle in the development. Those in the managerial level recognized the problem as well, but explained it as unavoidable in the situation and expected that the first prototypes of the system will bring more clarity to the objectives. This resembles the chicken-egg problem: architects must know well the objectives to design the architecture, but the objectives are further clarified only after the first version of the architecture is built.

There were several mentions about the problems in the cooperation between technical and business people. Architects expected the business managers to explicate clear requirements and objectives for the system and its architecture. However, they considered the task impossible, because they thought that the business managers do not possess enough understanding about the possibilities of current technology. They felt that this leads to unrealistic objectives, which were manifested especially when considering the possibilities of legacy systems integration: people with business background had far more optimistic views than architects.

Conflict avoidance and problems in decision-making slowed the progress. Again, because of the history of independency, a central authority that could take care of the architectural decisions for the integrated e-business solution was missing. Because nobody took a full responsibility of the situation, this led to avoidance of conflicts and enforced the tendency towards compromises. A frequently occurring phrase among the architects included the term "lowest common denominator," which was usually noting to the compromised solution with a single sign-on procedure and a minimal level of customer information integration.

The role of the central information management was unclear and it was lacking the routine of large development efforts. The independency of businesses and the minor role of central information management had implications on the working practices. The architectural and development practices of the business units contained considerable differences implying that also common working practices needed to be established for the development process of the e-business system.

Even the understanding of the designed architecture and related technical solutions were difficult to communicate across the organization. Since the business units have had their own histories and produced their own legacy systems and information architectures, the interpretations on the situation and objectives diverged. This, combined with changing organization, unclear objectives, and missing common working practices, created difficulties in understanding and transferring architectural knowledge between the participants from different business units.

It was also difficult to determine the level of integration between the systems. The ownership of the information becomes an issue even in the most modest single sign-on e-business solution serving the whole organization. The question becomes, "who owns the customer information?" and relates to determining the integration level to the currently independent back-end legacy systems. The more ambitious integration, the more out-of-control the customer information (and possibly other information too) shifts from the business units.

In addition to determining the integration level, the actual implementation of integration proved to be problematic. Since the diverging legacy systems could not be replaced, they all had to be interfaced. Of the seven conflicts and problems occurring when creating e-business architecture, only the problem of implementing the integration was mainly a technical problem. The others were more related to the change in organization and practices that happen when developing an e-business system in a large organization with independent businesses. In the following, we shall look closer on what consequences these conflicts and problems cause for the architecture design and development process.

CONSEQUENCES: LIMITED DESIGNS AND MINIMAL SOLUTIONS

In the beginning of the project a unified architecture was seen as a panacea for solving the problems of systems integration, streamlining the organization and unifying the customer interface. However, during the project it became clear that the aforementioned conflicts and problems would have some unfavorable consequences. While it was of paramount importance for the company to be able to streamline its systems and develop a more coherent architecture enabling the creation of an e-business system, the realities of legacy systems and the organization led to situation where it was best to seek satisfying, even minimal, solutions instead of optimal ones.

In the early phases of the project architecture was seen as general blueprints or roadmaps, largely drawn from scratch. Soon, however, the technical experts realized that evolutionary prototyping was the only possibility for progress in the architecture development. Because the schedule was tight, the objectives and requirements unclear and changing, and because the business units were rather independent, it was hard to achieve common understanding and commitment. With prototyping, it would be possible to clarify objectives and commit stakeholders by showing them visible results and benefits. This could be seen as "extreme" architecture design (Merisalo-Rantanen, Tuunanen, & Rossi, 2005). This could however lead to new problems. The technically oriented architects were specially worried that, combined with the quarter-based reporting system in the organization, evolutionary prototyping can easily produce quick-and-dirty and ad hoc solutions. We could classify the interviewees to those with positive attitudes towards prototyping and to those with negative or doubtful attitudes. In general, the project management believed positively that "somehow" the prototypes would transform to the final e-business solution, whereas technical architects presented more doubts and wanted to have explicit requirements and objective statements before committing to certain architectural solutions.

Prototyping and minimal solutions formed a vicious circle that made the development of robust and clear architectures nearly impossible by severely limiting the options available for the architecture developers. Existing legacy systems, the evolutionary approach, varying requirements, unclear objectives, difficulties in creating common understanding, and problems in decision making created a complex situation where textbook methods, description languages, and rational architecture design, as it is conceived in the literature, had no possibilities for immediate success. The degrees of freedom of design became limited. The system and its architecture could not be designed rationally as a whole, but rather one needed to accept the conditions and limitations caused by the factors above and to keep the day to day operations running while the new systems are continuously created through evolution.

The situation had also organizational consequences. We found clear hints of low-level networking and formation of shadow organizations as the result of unclear project organization and problems of decision-making and objective setting. As the organization and responsibilities change, new and perhaps inexperienced persons come into crucial official positions related to the e-business development. At the same time, the experienced architects and other key persons continued to stay in contact with each other. This unofficial shadow organization balanced the mismatch in skills and experience that might otherwise seriously impede the development.

The final consequence from all the above is, that in fact the e-business architecture becomes emergent: it is created gradually through compromises, constraints, and conflicts (c.f., Ciborra, 2000; Hanseth, Monteiro, & Hatling, 1996). The exact objectives and responsibilities will be resolved as the architecture emerges through evolutionary prototyping. Compared to the conventional view on software architecture design (Hofmeister et al., 1999a), most of the claimed benefits of rigorous architecture development seem to be lost. There is no "grand plan" since the work is proceeding in a day-to-day basis and the well defined responses and interfaces between systems do not necessarily emerge in a rationally planned way, but rather most duplicate functions are kept and there is agreement only on a few items that become the "architecture."

DERIVED REQUIREMENTS FOR E-BUSINESS SYSTEMS DEVELOPMENT METHODOLOGY

From the previous observations and explanations, we can derive a set of requirements that an e-business systems development methodology should meet. The grounded theory process resulted in an explanation model (Figure 2), from which a set of methodological requirements can be extracted. Changing markets and organization, historical inertia, and unclear objectives for the development produced a complex combination of conflicts and problems that brought various difficult consequences to the e-business development process. We analyzed the complex socio-technical situation

Figure 2. Deriving the methodology requirements

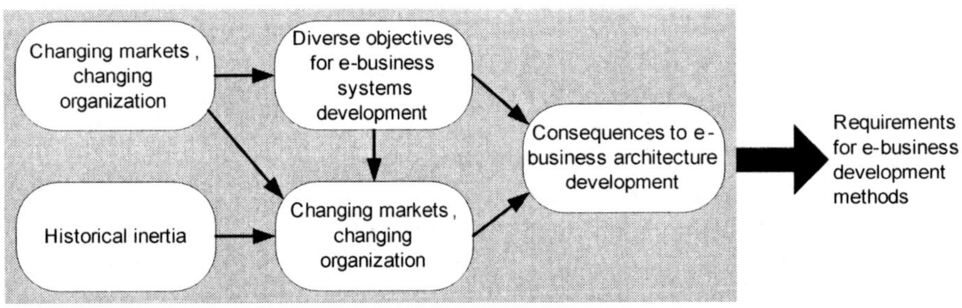

and its consequences and reasoned the set of most pertinent methodological requirements. This was done by identifying and coding the methodological requirements in the interview transcripts and further combining them in 13 requirements as described below.

According to Lyytinen et al. a design methodology should conform to a set of key requirements (Lyytinen, Smolander, & Tahvanainen, 1989). It must embed several conceptual structures and description languages, and support several levels of abstraction at which the development process takes place. It should also cover the whole spectrum of activities in information systems development (ISD), include a prescribed model of activities to be carried out during the development process, include a model of the organizational form of the development (a set of human roles), and try to reuse existing descriptions and implementations. Tools for drawing, manipulating, and managing the descriptions should also support the methodology, in a balanced manner.

We can further elaborate this conception of ISD methodology by distinguishing between three separate contexts in ISD, namely the technical, language, and organization contexts (Lyytinen, 1987). The technical context is concerned with the technical components of the system (like hardware and software), language context forms the environment for linguistic communication, and the organization context provides the environment for systematic human interactions, including decision-making and operative control. An ISD methodology includes assumptions, models, languages, and tools related to these three contexts. In the following, we shall extract from the case the general requirements for e-business development methodology and classify them according to these contexts. The objective of this classification is to illustrate the nature and requirements of e-business architecture development in large organizations with several business areas and to highlight the areas with a weak methodical support.

Lyytinen commented already in 1987 that most development methodologies have too limited scope and they tend to concentrate on technological issues late in the development lifecycle (Lyytinen, 1987). This limited scope omits most of the institutional and governance issues which seemed to be central for most stakeholders according to this study on architectural practice. One could argue that the organizational context is particularly relevant for e-business area, as most proponents of e-business emphasize the changes it brings about to work processes and organizations (Kalakota & Robinson, 2001).

The research into e-business architecture development is in a relatively immature stage. Previous literature has largely assumed that it solves technical issues for known problems (Taylor, McWilliam, Forsyth, & Wade, 2002). However, from the previous passages it has become obvious that methods for forming the problem statement and reaching a mutual agreement on what the architecture is in the end of the day are crucial. In this section, we take this as a starting point and observe the issues that rose in the described case starting from the inner, technical context and ending to the general organizational issues. This corresponds to Lyytinen's idea that the contexts are hierarchically ordered, because languages are presented by material carriers of technology context and language is needed for organized social action (Lyytinen, 1987). We identify e-architecture approaches in these areas and show how they propose solutions to the issues raised in our study.

In the following, we shall present the methodological requirements for each context. We also refer to the rows in Table 1 with the notation R1-R13.

Requirements from the Technology Context

Observed Requirements

The technical requirements of e-business development methods do not differ much from those of methods for traditional transaction-based information systems. E-business system development includes methodical requirements concerning e.g. distribution, error recovery, and networking, but those requirements can be met without a special "e-business support." A standard way to describe such technical solutions is of course required /R1/.

Integrated e-business architecture necessitates the integration of information systems in the organization and the rationalization of technology and development processes. Existing legacy systems will be integrated to the e-business functionality. This requires the selection of an integrative technology and the construction of development processes supporting the implementation of the integration. Because the integration is the basis and characteristic to e-business development, the development methodology should have specialized and usable techniques for describing information systems integration /R2/.

The key issue in the development of e-business systems is the keeping of the day-to-day operations running and at the same time implementing the integration between existing legacy systems and the new e-business functionality. This means that the nature of development is in many cases more analogous to a maintenance project than to a green-field development project. Current systems development methodologies and models of thought are mostly aimed at designing new systems instead of changing existing ones. This problem has been recognized before the advent of e-business, but it becomes more critical in the e-business development. From this we can derive a requirement that the development methodology for e-business systems should support evolutionary approaches to architectures and systems /R3/.

Existing Solutions

Most research on e-business systems development in general, and e-business architecture in particular, concentrates on this view. Much of the support that UML and RUP or their derivatives provide seems to concentrate on this area. Component aware methodologies, such as the Catalysis extension to UML, seem suitable for e-business. In addition, there are UML 2.0 extensions, such as SysML (Object Management Group, 2006), that provide better support for technical architecture design. Bischler and Segev (Bichler et al., 1998) investigate the possibilities of component oriented approach for e-business. They take a technical viewpoint, and provide a useful listing of enabling technologies for e-business. An applicable standard in this area is the SysML extension to UML (Object Management Group, 2006). A work by Rossi & Schwabe (Rossi & Schwabe, 2000) uses patterns and frameworks as building blocks for e-business systems. This kind of approach could be particularly useful for a relatively well-specified domain, such as trade processes, which are assumed to be generic in nature. Baskerville & Pries-Heje see a relatively fixed architecture as a common ground, on top of which e-business systems can be built (Baskerville & Pries-Heje, 2001).

As mentioned earlier, in the e-business domain there are several layers of components available. The InterNCA architecture in (Lyytinen, Rose, & Welke, 1998) describes some of these and outlines needs for new breed of development methodologies, which would take into the account the particular problems of e-business systems development. Greunz & Stanoevska-Slabeva present an extension of UML, which can be used to realize systems on top of "media platform" architecture (Greunz & Stanoevska-Slabeva, 2002).

Requirements from the Language Context

The language context provides a means and an environment for linguistic communication which encompasses the use, nature, content, context and form of signs (Lyytinen, 1987). The methodology requirements coming from the language context deal with the ability of stakeholders to communicate successfully during the e-business architecture development process.

Observed Requirements

The chicken-egg problem between objectives and architecture becomes problematic in e-business development. To design a robust technical architecture, one must have clear objectives, and to select realistic objectives, one must understand the possibilities of the technical architecture. To overcome this problem, it is necessary to have a close cooperation between technical architects and those responsible of the business. This, however, induces a language problem. These groups often do not have a common language. To overcome the language problem, we need architecture description languages that business managers understand /R4/ and business descriptions that are explicit enough for technical people /R5/.

The problems of objectives and integration culminate on architecture design because the designs and prototypes related to technical architecture become the first concrete artifacts in the development showing implications of decisions to businesses and to the information management. Before architecture design, the plans and designs have been on the "PowerPoint presentation" level, showing ambiguous and general roadmaps and noble objectives. The more concrete the architecture becomes, the more various stakeholders become aware of the consequences, conflicts, and problems they will be facing. This leads to two distinct requirements for the development methodology: the methodology should take the development to a very concrete level (both politically and technically) very soon after the project initiation /R6/ and the architecture designs and descriptions (and their implications) should be approachable and intelligible by the various stakeholders participating the process /R7/.

Existing Solutions

As a description language, UML and its extensions offer a fairly strong support for engineering in the language context. Yet, there are very few articles describing these issues of having a common language in e-business area, but one could expect that methodologies used in other domains for participative processes and joint application development could be applied here (August, 1991). In this context, architecture serves as a language between the participants in the development process, enabling communication and making the consequences of the implementation concrete to the participants. Using architecture as an enabler of communication between a diverse set of participants (including various levels of management and technical experts) requires informal and expressive approaches, which are practically non-existent in the field of software architecture research. This kind of conception of "architecture as language" can be associated with approaches that include rich and informal description techniques, like "rich pictures" in (Wood-Harper, 1985), the wall-charting technique (Saaren-Seppälä, 1988), and genre-based approaches (Päivärinta, Halttunen, & Tyrväinen, 2001).

Requirements from the Organization Context

Observed Requirements

These problems formed the largest bulk in our study. They included issues such as organizational inertia as well as environmental limitations, characteristics of a given business environment, codes of conduct in business, and regulatory and societal factors. These factors form together the 'ballpark' for an organization to act in relationship with its providers and customers.

The first organizational requirement comes from the overall conclusion of the case. The transition from heterogeneous e-commerce to integrated e-business is not only technically challenging. It is more a profound change to the organization. In fact, the primary challenge is in the change of the organization, not in the implementation of the technology. Therefore, e-business systems development methodology should support also the description of organizational change /R8/.

In this change of organization and implementation of technology, the role of central information management or some kind of central authority in the organization is crucial. The central authority should take care of the multitude of conflicts occurring when aiming at integration and coordinate the creation of objectives for the system. An e-business development methodology should enable the creation of a common vision /R9/, which can then be enforced by the central authority.

Evolution with modest but growing objectives may be the only way to develop integrated e-business systems. To foster commitment, some immediate benefits should be shown with the prototypes for each stakeholder. However, at the same time, the path to robust architecture should also be secured and enough time and resources must be given to technical architects. This very difficult and complex trade-off must be made in every e-business project /R10/.

The implementation of e-business integration deals not only with technical issues but also with difficult political ones. An organization shifting to integrated e-business must resolve issues concerning the internal ownership of information related for instance to customers, sales, contracts, and products. The ownership and responsibilities related to information must be decided and described during the development process. The development methodology should include descriptions for organizational responsibilities and ownership of information /R11/.

Identifying and agreeing about objectives became the most difficult problem in this case. Thus, to become valuable in practice, e-business development methodology should support not only the formation and recording of objectives but also measuring of success related to objectives /R12/.

The requirements directed to an e-business development organization are quite conflicting. On the other hand, the development requires a strong authority that can control the process through conflicts, and on the other hand, the formation of unofficial and shadow organization (peer-level networking) should be fostered to allow creative solutions and frictionless cooperation between businesses /R13/. This requirement is, however, not a new one when developing organizations.

Existing Solutions

From a more managerial and decision oriented view one could look at business- and strategy development methods, which aim at creation of a common understanding and vision of business strategy. This view sees building of architecture as a common vision building effort rather than a system building effort. It could also be argued that e-business architecture building is quite similar to organizational change processes, especially the introduction of enterprise wide information systems, such as ERP. Koontz has argued for this by presenting e-business architecture development model, which is very generic (Koontz, 2000).

Organizational issues are largely neglected by the traditional systems development methodologies, but form important context and frame for the implementation of the e-business systems and architectures. The work on organizational change and observation of the power-play could be fruitful if applied to early stages of architecture development. However, they do merely observe the issues than provide solutions. Checkland's SSM methodology is one of the few general-purpose methodologies that identifies and models the "essence" of the organizational idea of the system and then proceeds to actual development of the system (Checkland & Scholes, 1990). It is clear from the observations in this case study that the explicit identification and framing of the problem to be solved, and then resolving the actual goals of the architecture forms the basis for architecture development.

Most studies thus far seem to assume that the development of e-architecture and infrastructure can be guided by the deliberate actions and decisions of management. However, as can be seen here the technological changes often evolve from designers' and users' experience with such technologies and are often unpredictable (Ciborra, 2000).The problem of loosing the original target while developing partial solutions and prototypes (e.g., see R10) could be helped by explicitly recognizing emergent and opportunistic possibilities created on the process.

Summary of Issues

The list above shows that most solutions and research this far, has concentrated on the technical level. Unfortunately, most of the problems seem to be non-technical in nature, they are rather more of the linguistic or organizational. E-business cuts across functional borders in organization and is built on a complex infrastructure of ERP and legacy systems and it shares many of the challenges and opportunities of these organizational technologies.

Table 2 summarizes these derived requirements for e-business development methodology. The requirements and their rationale are described in the text above. The 'Type' column places the requirement to the appropriate context or contexts (T: technology, L: language, O: organizational). The last column in the table ("Support in RUP employing UML") analyzes how unified modeling language (Object Management Group, 2005) and the Unified Process (Rational Software Corporation, 2001) support the e-business specific characteristics of the development process. This is important, because UML and RUP together form the current methodological basis for many software organizations. The column shows that the support is generally poor. The e-business specific requirements are not met by UML and RUP —only the standard technical issues are well covered. This conclusion calls for method development supporting better these e-business specific requirements.

In the technical context we noted that e-business development would benefit from method enhancements in IS integration and evolutionary development. However, the language and especially the organization context appeared to have more importance in the development. In the language context, there was an urgent need for more understandable and concrete architecture descriptions that could be used among many groups involved in the process, including technical and non-technical people. The organization context appeared as the most important target for research and practical methodical improvements. In that context, we could identify a multitude of issues requiring improvements, including better understanding and usable methods for the design and implementation of organization change, organizational vision, organizational ownership of information, and organizational responsibilities.

Figure 3 shows concisely our findings. When creating e-business or enterprise architecture, the major problems to be solved are organizational. This does not align with the support that UML and RUP provides, because they mostly concentrate on solving the problems in the language and technical contexts. It is the task of future research to provide improvements to this, but, as can be seen from Table 2, it might need quite radical extensions or changes to UML and RUP to be able to support effectively the formation of e-business architecture.

Figure 3. Support and requirements

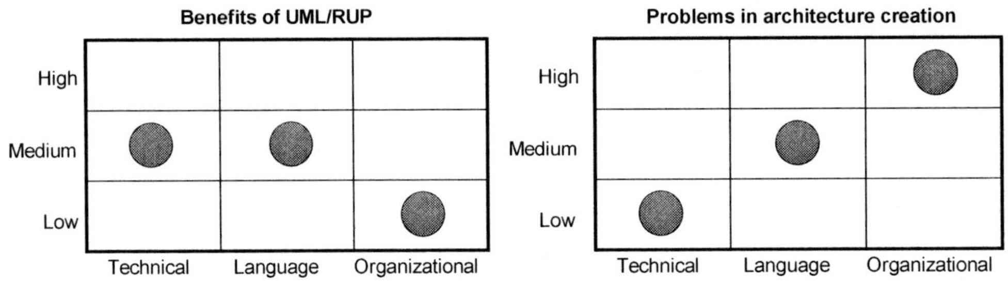

Table 2. Summary of the requirements for e-business development methodology

	Requirement	Type	Rationale	Support in RUP employing UML
R1	Technical issues (like distribution, error recovery, and networking) must be described in a standard way.	**T**	These issues will occur as in all modern systems development	Good; this is what UML and RUP are for
R2	Specialized techniques for describing the information systems integration	**T**	IS integration is characteristic to e-business development	Poor; no specialized technique for the description of integration in standard UML. Some UML 2.0 extensions are however available.
R3	The development methodology should support evolutionary approaches to architectures and systems.	**L/T**	The change and maintenance of existing systems forms a major part of the e-business systems development	Moderate; UML and RUP are mainly targeted at the development of new systems
R4	Architectural description languages that business managers understand	**L**	To enable realistic objective selection, business managers must have some understanding on architecture	Poor; the descriptions necessitate too much technical skills and knowledge
R5	Business descriptions that are explicit enough for technical people	**L**	To understand the objectives, technical people must have understanding on business	Moderate; no description techniques showing overall aggregate view
R6	The methodology should take the development to a very concrete level (both politically and technically) soon after the project initiation	**T/L/O**	The more architecture becomes concrete, the more stakeholders become aware of the consequences, conflicts, and problems	Good (technically), none (politically)
R7	The architecture designs and descriptions (and their implications) should be approachable and intelligible by the various stakeholders participating the process	**L/O**	To enable wide understanding to the consequences of architectural selections (cf. R4).	Moderate; no relevant description technique besides Use Case diagrams
R8	Support for the description of organizational change	**O**	e-business involves deep changes to organization	Poor; some thoughts of "organization engineering" in RUP's Business Architecture
R9	Support for the description of a common vision	**O**	Resolve conflicts, build objectives	Poor; no common language for all stakeholders
R10	Both prototyping and careful architecture design needed	**T**	Gain commitment and resolve objectives through prototyping, aim at robust architecture	Moderate; iterative basis in RUP, but its implementation is difficult in practice
R11	Methodology should contain descriptions for organizational responsibilities and ownership of information	**L/O**	The ownership of information becomes an issue when aiming at e-business integration	Poor; only general thoughts

Table 2. Summary of the requirements for e-business development methodology

	Requirement	Type	Rationale	Support in RUP employing UML
R12	e-business development methodology should support the formation and recording of objectives and measuring of success related to objectives	L/O	Identifying and agreeing about objectives is one of the most difficult issues in e-business development	Poor; the objectives are mostly supposed to be given to the development project
R13	The development process should support organizationally both effective control structures and flexibility	O	Strong authority is needed to handle the conflicts and unofficial structures for creative solutions	Poor; development organization "design" in a general level

CONCLUSION

We have described a process where a large ICT company is building architecture for a comprehensive e-business system. From the case, we extracted 13 requirements for methodology supporting integrated e-business systems development and classified the requirements to technology, language, and organization contexts. We also compared the requirements to the support that UML and RUP offers and concluded that the e-business specific requirements are not met in UML and RUP. Successful e-business development requires alternative approaches that support better organization change, communication between stakeholders, systems integration, objective formation, and evolutionary development.

In our study, architecture manifested itself as a catalyst that makes business and organizational conflicts and problems concrete. When making decisions about architecture, the systems architects had to take into account the organizational situation in the company. At the same time the architecture starts shaping and changing the organization, thus forming a double mangle (e.g., Jones, 1998). The architects also realized that technical rationality is not enough for success in this kind of a situation. To succeed in e-business architecture development, one has to be aware of the political and organizational forces that are driving the development and its objectives. E-business architecture development can therefore be characterized as a process of seeking boundaries, finding sufficient consensus, and identifying commonalities across organizational borders. Most previous literature on architectural methods has neglected this and sought to develop description languages for describing the actual architectures for systems with clear problem statements, whereas we claim that it would be more important to seek tools that aid in building common understanding about the system and its architecture and tools for processing the emerging conflicts. Thus, we maintain that the field of architecture for e-business would benefit from tools that help to identify and process the emerging conflicts than tools that aid in developing a technically "perfect" and optimized solution. These tools could be used in early phases of development to augment UML and RUP based tools. Examples of such tools are group support systems and different participation facilitation systems. Thus we do not call for replacing UML, but rather adding tools that can be used to communicate with nontechnical people about the architecture.

ACKNOWLEDGMENTS

We would like to thank the anonymous reviewers of this paper for their valuable instructions and especially the reviewer that gave us the simple idea of Figure 3.

REFERENCES

August, J. H. (1991). *Joint application design: The group session approach to system design*. Englewood Cliffs, NJ: Yourdon Press.

Baskerville, R., & Pries-Heje, J. (2001, July 27-29). *Racing the e-bomb: How the internet is redefining information systems development methodology*. Proceedings of the IFIP TC8/WG8.2 Working Conference on Realigning Research and Practice in Information Systems Development: The Social and Organizational Perspectice (pp. 49-68). Boise, Idaho.

Bichler, M., Segev, A., & Zhao, J. L. (1998). Component-based e-commerce: Assesment of current practices and future directions. *SIGMOD Record, 27*(4), 7-14.

Checkland, P. B., & Scholes, J. (1990). *Soft system methodology in action*. Chichester: John Wiley and Sons.

Ciborra, C. (2000). Drifting: From control to drift. In K. Braa, C. Sorensen & B. Dahlbom (Eds.), *Planet internet*. Lund: Studentlitteratur.

Conallen, J. (1999). Modeling web application architectures with UML. *Communications of the ACM, 42*(10), 63-70.

D'Souza, D. F., & Wills, A. C. (1998). *Objects, components, and frameworks with UML: The catalysis approach*: Addison-Wesley.

Dashofy, E. M., Van der Hoek, A., & Taylor, R. N. (2005). A comprehensive approach for the development of modular software architecture description languages. *ACM Transactions on Software Engineering and Methodology, 14*(2), 199-245.

Denzin, N. K. (1978). *The research act: A theoretical introduction to sociological methods*: McGraw-Hill.

Dori, D. (2001). Object-process methodology applied to modeling credit card transactions. *Journal of Database Management, 12*(1), 4.

Egyed, A., & Medvidovic, N. (1999, Oct). *Extending Architectural Representation in UML with View Integration*. Proceedings of the 2nd International Conference on the Unified Modelling Language (UML), (pp. 2-16). Fort Collins, CO.

Eisenhardt, K. M. (1989). Building theories from case study research. *Academy of Management Review, 14*(4), 532-550.

Fernández, W. D., Lehmann, H., & Underwood, A. (2002, June 6-8). *Rigour and relevance in studies of IS innovation: A grounded theory methodology approach*. Proceedings of the European Conference on Information Systems (ECIS) 2002, (pp. 110-119).Gdansk, Poland.

Garlan, D., & Kompanek, A. J. (2000). *Reconciling the needs of architectural description with object-modeling notations*. Proceedings of the Third International Conference on the Unified Modeling Language - UML 2000, (pp. 498-512). York, UK.

Glaser, B. (1978). *Theoretical sensitivity: Advances in the methodology of grounded theory*. Mill Valley: Sociology Press.

Glaser, B., & Strauss, A. L. (1967). *The discovery of grounded theory: Strategies for qualitative research*. Chigago: Aldine.

Greunz, M., & Stanoevska-Slabeva, K. (2002). *Modeling business media platforms*. 35th Annual Hawaii International Conference on System Sciences, Maui, HI.

Grinter, R. E. (1999). Systems architecture: Product designing and social engineering. *ACM SIGSOFT Software Engineering Notes, 24*(2), 11-18.

Hanseth, O., Monteiro, E., & Hatling, M. (1996). Developing information infrastructure: The tension between standardization and flexibility. *Science, Technology & Human Values, 21*(4), 407-426.

Hirschheim, R., & Klein, H. K. (1989). Four paradigms of information systems development. *Communications of the ACM, 32*(10), 1199-1216.

Hofmeister, C., Nord, R., & Soni, D. (1999a). *Applied software architecture*. Reading, MA: Addison-Wesley.

Hofmeister, C., Nord, R., & Soni, D. (1999b). *Describing software architecture with UML*. Proceedings of the First Working IFIP Conference on Software Architecture (WICSA1), (pp. 145-160). San Antonio, TX.

Jacobson, I., Booch, G., & Rumbaugh, J. (1999). *The unified software development process*. New York: Addison-Wesley.

Jones, M. (1998). *Information Systems and the Double Mangle: Steering a Course Between the Scylla of Embedded Structure and the Charybdis of Strong Symmetry*. IFIP WG8.2/8.6 Joint Working Conference, Helsinki, Finland.

Kalakota, R., & Robinson, M. (2001). *e-Business 2.0: Roadmap for Success*: Addison-Wesley.

Kazman, R., Klein, M., & Clements, P. (2000). *ATAM: Method for Architecture Evaluation* (Technical report No. CMU/SEI-2000-TR-004): Software Engineering Institute.

Kim, Y.-G., & Everest, G. C. (1994). Building an IS architecture: Collective wisdom from the field. *Information & Management, 26*(1), 1-11.

Koontz, C. (2000). Develop a solid e-commerce architecture. *e-Business Advisor*(January).

Kuntzmann, A., & Kruchten, P. (2003). The rational unified process—an enabler for higher process maturity. Retrieved April 19, 2007 from http://www-128.ibm.com/developerworks/rational/library/content/03July/0000/0579/Rational_CMM_WhitePaper.pdf.

Leist, S., & Zellner, G. (2006, April 23-27). *Evaluation of current architecture frameworks*. SAC'06, (pp. 1546-1553). Dijon, France.

Locke, K. (2001). *Grounded theory in management research*: SAGE Publications.

Lyytinen, K. (1987). A taxonomic perspective of information dystems fevelopment: Theoretical constructs and recommendations. In R. J. Boland, Jr. & R. A. Hirschheim (Eds.), *Critical issues in information systems research* (pp. 3-41): John Wiley & Sons.

Lyytinen, K., Rose, G., & Welke, R. (1998). The brave new world of development in the internetwork computing architecture (InterNCA): Or how distributed computing platforms will change systems development. *Information Systems Journal, 8*(3), 241-253.

Lyytinen, K., Smolander, K., & Tahvanainen, V.-P. (1989). *Modelling CASE environments in systems development*. Proceedings of CASE'89 the First Nordic Conference on Advanced Systems Engineering, Stockholm.

Martin, P. Y., & Turner, B. A. (1986). Grounded theory and organizational research. *The Journal of Applied Behavioral Science, 22*(2), 141-157.

Medvidovic, N., Egyed, A., & Rosenblum, D. S. (1999). *Round-trip software engineering using UML: From architecture to design and back*. Proceedings of the 2nd Workshop on Object-Oriented Reengineering (WOOR), Toulouse, France, Sept. 1999, 1-8.

Medvidovic, N., & Taylor, R. N. (2000). A classification and comparison framework for software architecture description languages. *IEEE Transactions on Software Engineering, 26*(1), 70-93.

Merisalo-Rantanen, H., Tuunanen, T., & Rossi, M. (2005). Is extreme programming just old wine in new bottles: A comparison of two cases. *Journal of Database Management, 16*(4), 41.

Monroe, R. T., Kompanek, A., Melton, R., & Garlan, D. (1997). Architectural styles, design patterns, and objects. *IEEE Software, 14*(1), 43-52.

Object Management Group. (1999). *UML Profile for Enterprise Distributed Object Computing: Request for Proposals (ad/99-03-10)*: OMG.

Object Management Group. (2005). *Unified modeling language: Superstructure version 2.0* (No. formal/05-07-04).

Object Management Group. (2006). *OMG SysML Specification (ptc/06-05-04).*

Päivärinta, T., Halttunen, V., & Tyrväinen, P. (2001). A genre-based method for information system planning. In M. Rossi & K. Siau (Eds.), *Information modeling in the new millennium* (pp. 70-93). Hershey, PA: Idea Group.

Rational Software Corporation. (2001). Rational Unified Process [Online documentation, Version 2001A.04.00].

Robson, C. (2002). *Real world research, (2nd ed.).* Blackwell Publishing.

Ross, J. W., Weill, P., & Robertson, D. C. (2006). *Enterprise architecture as strategy: Creating a foundation for business execution*: Harvard Business School Press.

Rossi, G., & Schwabe, D. (2000). Object-oriented web applications modeling. In M. Rossi & K. Siau (Eds.), *Information modelling in the next millennium.* Hershey: IDEA Group Publishing.

Rumpe, B., Schoenmakers, M., Radermacher, A., & Schürr, A. (1999). *UML + ROOM as a Standard ADL.* Fifth IEEE International Conference on Engineering of Complex Computer Systems, (pp. 43-53).

Saaren-Seppälä, K. (1988). *Wall chart technique: The use of wall charts for effective planning.* Helsinki: Kari Saaren-Seppälä Ky.

Sauer, C., Southon, G., & Dampney, C. N. G. (1997). *Fit, failure, and the house of horrors: Toward a configurational theory of IS project failure.* Proceedings of the eighteenth international conference on Information systems, (pp. 349-366). Atlanta, Georgia.

Shaw, M., & Garlan, D. (1996). *Software architecture: Perspectives on an emerging discipline*: Prentice Hall.

Siau, K. & Cao, Q. (2001). Unified modeling language (UML) — a complexity analysis. *Journal of Database Management, 12*(1), 26-34.

Siau, K., Erickson, J., & Lee, L. Y. (2005). Theoretical vs. practical complexity: The case of UML. *Journal of Database Management, 16*(3), 40-57.

Smolander, K. (2003, January 6-9,). *The birth of an e-business system architecture: Conflicts, compromises, and gaps in methods.* Hawaii International Conference on System Sciences (HICSS'36), Hilton Waikoloa Village, Big Island, Hawaii.

Smolander, K., Hoikka, K., Isokallio, J., Kataikko, M., & Mäkelä, T. (2002, April, 8-11). *What is included in software architecture? A case study in three software organizations.* Proceedings of 9th annual IEEE International Conference and Workshop on the Engineering of Computer-Based Systems (pp. 131-138). (ECBS) 2002, Lund, Sweden.

Smolander, K., & Päivärinta, T. (2002a, May 27 - 31). *Describing and communicating software architecture in practice: Observations on stakeholders and rationale.* Proceedings of CAiSE'02 - The Fourteenth International Conference on Advanced Information Systems Engineering, (pp. 117-133).Toronto, Canada.

Smolander, K., & Päivärinta, T. (2002b, Aug 25-30). *Practical rationale for describing software architecture: Beyond programming-in-the-large.*

Software Architecture: System Design, Development and Maintenance - IFIP 17th World Computer Congress - TC2 Stream / 3rd Working IEEE/IFIP Conference on Software Architecture (WICSA3), (pp. 113-126). Montréal, Québec, Canada.

Smolander, K., Rossi, M., & Purao, S. (2002, December 18). *Software architecture: Metaphors across contexts.* AIS Theory Development Workshop, Barcelona.

Smolander, K., Rossi, M., & Purao, S. (2005, May 26-28). *Going beyond the blueprint: Unraveling the complex reality of software architectures.* 13th European Conference on Information Systems: Information Systems in a Rapidly Changing Economy, Regensburg, Germany.

Sowa, J. F., & Zachman, J. A. (1992). Extending and formalizing the framework for information systems architecture. *IBM Systems Journal, 31*(3), 590-616.

Star, S. L., & Griesemer, J. R. (1989). Institutional cology, "translations" and boundary objects: Amateurs and professionals in berkeley's museum of vertebrate zoology, 1907-39. *Social Studies of Science, 19*, 387-420.

Strauss, A. L., & Corbin, J. (1990). *Basics of qualitative research: Grounded theory procedures and applications.* Newbury Park, CA: Sage Publications.

Taylor, M. J., McWilliam, J., Forsyth, H., & Wade, S. (2002). Methodologies and website development: A survey of practice. *Information and Software Technology, 44*(6), 381-391.

Wood-Harper, T. (1985). Research methods in information systems: Using action research. In E. Mumford, R. A. Hirschheim, G. Fitzgerald & T. Wood-Harper (Eds.), *Research methods in information systems.* New York: North-Holland Publishers.

This work was previously published in Journal of Database Management, Vol. 19, Issue 1, edited by K. Siau, pp. 19-40, copyright 2008 by IGI Publishing, formerly known as Idea Group Publishing (an imprint of IGI Global).

Chapter VI
Nazar Foods Company: Business Process Redesign Under Supply Chain Management Context

Vichuda Nui Polatoglu
Anadolu University, Turkey

EXECUTIVE SUMMARY

Nazar Group of Companies has been a leading producer and distributor of cookies, crackers, cakes, chocolate, and other products in Turkey for more than 40 years. This case is about the group's management roles in transforming the companies into a more consumer-focused orientation using supply chain management philosophy as a strategic framework. Descriptions of supporting business systems were summarized along with the challenges and problems facing managers in effective utilization of these systems in practice.

ORGANIZATIONAL BACKGROUND

Nazar Cookies Company (NCC) was founded in 1961 by an entrepreneur who had seen a business opportunity in providing new cookie varieties for Turkish consumers. Having graduated from a European university with a management degree, he was expected to manage the family business of flour milling. After a short stay in his father's business, however, he decided to go on his own way with a clear vision of bringing new tastes to Turkish consumers at the highest possible quality. He also decided to establish his company in his hometown, which is a strategically located central Anatolian city that already had considerable industrial activity.

After a year of intensive work both in product and process development, NCC could begin production in 1962 with a capacity of three tons per day of a few varieties of products that already existed in the market. Since NCC was essentially a production-focused company, and since there had not been any other marketing companies to work with, the products were sold in bulk (4-5 kg boxes) to individual merchants at the factory door, who would then distribute them to retail shops in their own territories.

During the first few years, workers, foremen, engineers, and the owner were all working together very closely and with high motivation toward getting a share in the market, which was dominated by three major players, all of which were located in Istanbul, the heart of trade in Turkey. In addition to his quick learning ability, the owner/president was very successful in transferring a few critical people from competitors and bringing know-how through his European friends and their networks.

The company established the first semi-automatic production line in Turkey in 1967. NCC grew rapidly by the addition of new production lines and new brands. In 1971, NCC became a family-owned company under the trade name of Nazar Food Company (NFC). In 1975, together with its major competitor today, NFC successfully employed the packaging machines, which were able to produce individually wrapped portions in its process lines. This led these two companies to differentiate their products and earn strong consumer acceptance in the marketplace. Also, in the same year, management decided to lease a computer from IBM to handle personnel files and payroll, which marked itself in history as the first private organization using a computer in Turkey. In 1979, a machinery company (Nazar Machinery Company) was established in the city industrial zone to produce special bakery machines both for Nazar companies and others. Also, during that time, the accounting activities were fully computerized.

As NFC was about to become the market leader in 1980 with sales reaching 39,400 tons, the country experienced its strongest social unrest, which created unfortunate problems with worker unions. The operations had suffered for almost a year, during which the two companies faced grave financial problems. In 1981, the president decided to establish a new production company (Bonjuu Food Company) in the industrial zone and a new marketing company (Nazar Marketing Company) in the city, both with the minor partnership of a big industrial conglomerate.

Until 1990, the Nazar Group of Companies experienced stagnation. Computerization reached operational levels in each company. The marketing company organized wholesalers across the country and executed its sales operations through them. There were about 50 large wholesalers who sold Nazar products to more than 2,000 smaller local wholesalers, who also could procure directly from NFC. The transportation between the factories and wholesalers was outsourced.

In 1993, the president decided to establish a new and modern production facility for NFC in the industrial zone and to transfer the production in the old factory entirely to the new one in time. This new plant started production in 1995 with one highly automated production line. In 1997, the marketing company was moved to Istanbul, and the sales operations were reorganized under a new distribution system where individual and exclusive distributors were hired as business partners. Most of the old wholesalers became exclusive distributors of Nazar brand products.

Between 1990 and 2000, the business grew on the average of 5% every year, reaching about 74,000 tons annually (see Exhibit 1 in the Appendix). Until that time, export business had been given little attention. In 2000, however, the export directorship was formed within the marketing company, and exclusive distributorships were initiated in about 40 countries. In 2001, a new approach to production planning was implemented, which transformed then predominantly production-focused system into a sales-driven system.

The Nazar group management decided to enter into the chocolate business, and a new chocolate factory was built in 2003 in the industrial zone under NFC. By the end of that year, the marketing company sold about 111,000 tons of about 80 different Nazar brands, including cookies, crackers, digestives, light products, baby biscuits, specialties, cakes, pies, wafers, and breakfast cereals, out of which 21,000 tons were exports. The revenue exceeded $250 million US, while the group had almost no debt (see Exhibit 1). Nazar brand became one of the top five brands recognized in Turkey.

According to Nielsen data, between 2000 and 2003, the Turkish packaged bakery products market was stagnant. Since per capita consumption of packaged bakery products is about 3.8 kg in Turkey, which is well below developed countries (e.g., 7.2 kg in Germany, 11.4 kg in England, 14.2 kg in Holland), the reason for market stagnation was explained by the economic crisis that the country had been going through in recent years that adversely affected disposable incomes of the people (Euromonitor, 2003). Therefore, as economy improved in Turkey, the market was expected to grow considerably. This expectation had been luring most of the multinational companies and local industrial conglomerates to move into FMCG market through acquisitions, joint ventures, or direct investments.

In this market, from 2000 to 2003, Nazar's share rose from 29% to 33% (see Exhibit 1), while its major competitor's share declined from 59% to 50%. The rest of the market was filled by almost 50 small, mostly local producers, the largest of which had 5% share. The duopolistic market structure created by Nazar and its major competitor had been a big entry barrier for the newcomers. Both had established very strong brands and distribution patterns during the past 40 years. While Nazar's major competitor had been successfully moving into different food categories, from beverages to cooking oil, during the past few years, Nazar had chosen to remain focused at its core business until recently when it had moved into the chocolate business.

Nazar production companies currently operate under ISO 9002 quality standard leading towards TQM. This is in compliance with the group's objective of producing and selling the best quality products at affordable prices to Turkish consumers. In the late 1990s, NFC had turned down a joint venture deal with a giant multinational food corporation, closing the opportunity for higher competition in this market.

Among the distribution channels, the chain stores sales in Turkey had been rising from 19% in 2000 to about 40% in 2003, still far below developed countries, while the individual grocery stores' share dropped to 52% from 71% in terms of Nielsen's Retailer Measurement Index. The rest of the channel comprises confectionary stores, kiosks, gas stations, and so forth remain about the same. Nazar's distribution pattern altered similarly in that the share of national chain stores rose up to about 15% in 2003 in volume.

Nazar Marketing Company (NMKC) is the only customer of the two production companies and functions as a service (transportation, sales, marketing, etc.) provider for them. By design, these four companies cannot function independently in that together they form a big supply chain that is administered by the Group Management Team (see Exhibit 2 for the list of group managers.) Some of the members of this team have been elected for the Management Council, which the president established in 1999 (see the list of council members in Exhibit 3.) The council sets strategic directions and gives organizational and financial decisions regarding the group of companies.

All of the Group Management Team members are placed under the payroll of NFC. Also, NFC holds the industrial property rights of Nazar branded products. On the other hand, each company has a general manager who is responsible for its board, which is comprised of family members, professionals, and a few external consultants (see top levels of the organizational charts of NMKC and NFC in Exhibit 4.) Vice President of Procurement oversees the Procurement Director who manages a group of officers responsible for executing the MRP system through which the material requirements of the production companies are satisfied collectively. They communicate with the Supply Chain Group Manager and the factories' planning managers.

Vice President of Planning and IT oversees the Supply Chain Group Manager, the Information Systems Group Manager, and a number of technical analysts, and administers the Production Inventory Management System (PIMS), which is the key interface between sales and production functions. The Supply Chain Group Manager communicates with the procurement officers, Sales Forecast Manager, and country managers in the NMKC and planning managers in the production companies. The Information Systems Group Manager administers central data processing, the help desk for the Nazar intranet, and computer program development projects. The Vice President is also responsible for corporate governance and strategic planning, for which he or she establishes and coaches project groups to satisfy certain organizational needs.

The Technical Coordinator oversees the Quality Assurance Group Manager and a number of technical analysts and administers the use of technology and feasibility of investments in the production companies. The manager also coordinates group resources for process design, facility layout, Total Productive Maintenance projects, and quality assurance activities.

The NMKC has Marketing, Sales, Exports, and Planning directorships located at the head office in Istanbul, who report to the General Manager. NMKC has eight regional sales offices, each with sizable warehouses geographically dispersed across Turkey. Each office has a regional manager directly reporting to the Sales Director. There are about 150 distributors who execute exclusive sales routes. These distributors are individual merchants who serve about 180,000 sales points, including small kiosks, confectioneries, gas stations, groceries, and local chain stores. Each distributor is served by a Distribution Manager, who reports to the Regional Manager, who looks after daily local business affairs in addition to administration of financial and operational obligations of the distributors towards NMKC. Distributors own their service trucks, which are driven by their sales representatives who are trained and equipped according to the standards established by the Sales Director. Each sales representative carries a hand-held terminal through which they view the individual account of a sales point, issue an invoice, take backorders, or view promotion programs. The Sales Director designs and administers incentive packages for distributors, which include various operational and financial targets. If a distributor meets these criteria, he or she earns additional sales premiums.

The Marketing Director oversees a number of brand managers who are assigned to certain product groups. Brand managers administer standing of brands in the market, monitor competitors' activities, design promotion programs, develop brand advertisements, conduct consumer surveys, and contribute new product development projects. In addition, there is a Sales Forecast Manager under the Marketing Director who operates the Demand Forecasting and Production Order System (DFPOS) in collaboration with the Supply Chain Group Manager.

The Export Director and a number of country managers operate the Export Order Management System (EOMS) in collaboration with the Supply Chain Group Manager. The Planning Director of NMKC administers improvement projects as a project leader, which involves cost cutting, technology implementation, TQM, and other organizational issues. The Director also manages a local IT group, which acts as a help desk for the Distributor Management Information System (DMIS).

The General Managers in two production companies oversee Production, Technical, Planning, Quality Assurance, Finance, and Personnel Managers. The production companies are organized along the production processes, where each process has an owner who reports directly to all of the managers. Planning Managers operate PIMS in collaboration with the Supply Chain Group Manager.

SETTING THE STAGE

Prior to 1990, computer utilization had been limited to data processing for payroll and accounting purposes, which was administered under the Finance Coordinator. This involved a backroom operation lacking a clear vision or strategy. In 1990, Deniz Batu was hired as the Vice President responsible for planning and IT. His main task was to identify critical business processes and to develop IT applications to enhance and, if necessary, to redesign them according to a priority given for him at that time. Batu's concerns were on redesigning business processes using an IT-enabled approach to organizational change (Al-Mashare & Zairi, 2000; Davenport & Short, 1990; Davenport & Stoddard, 1994; Grover et al., 1993).

Until 1990, there had been an officer working under the General Manager of NFC who would communicate with NMKC through telephone, receive sales information, negotiate with them, and establish a production scheduling program for the following month. The manager would take into account capacity limitations, material, and workforce requirements based on some scheduling patterns coming from personal experience. Batu thought that this approach had been successful in the past when the system was compact enough, but then it eventually became too ad hoc and myopic, which did not allow structural business growth. He envisioned a new approach.

Batu decided to start from the business transactions of the wholesalers; that is, he formed a project group that developed an IS for order processing, credit status reporting, and payment collection. Shortly after the implementation of this system, the project group developed an additional IS module, which included warehouse inventory management and shipment operations.

Having collected sizable data through the use of this IS platform, Batu decided in 1992 to develop a performance measurement system that summarized financial and operational data as graphs and tables in order to support business decision making as well as to measure the performance of the marketing and production companies. This approach, however, changed the atmosphere of the group management meetings adversely, because until then the decision makers were used to relying on their instincts and limited information. The production people were more reluctant to accept the measurement results, while marketing people were disturbed mostly by someone else watching their operations.

One of the positive outcomes of the performance measurement system, however, was that the group management realized that the overall profitability of the group had been affected adversely by demand fluctuations. Thus, a lesser degree of demand variation would lead to less shortages, lower inventories, and higher capacity utilization. The group management started to search for remedies.

The friction between Batu and the rest of the group, however, did not stop him from proceeding. As a next step forward, he initiated another project group to work on sales forecasting. This group developed an IS module that generated monthly sales forecasts for each SKU based on the past 36 months' sales data. Users would input pricing and promotion information and choose among alternative analytical and subjective forecasting tools. As a result, the program would output forecast intervals (minimum and maximum values) for the following three months. Unfortunately, even though the users in NMKC liked the idea of forecasting, they were not willing to adapt for change. Thus, the use of this system failed in the implementation stage.

Batu's next target was to improve the procurement operation performance, measured as production loss due to material shortages. To this end, he decided to develop an MRP system for the Procurement Director and his team. He formed a project group that included production people and procurement officers. This group developed an MRP platform, which was essentially a decision support system to optimize total cost of procurement while improving the relationship between production planning and material availability. The system has been upgraded several times since its launch in 1995.

In about 1994, based on performance measurement results, the group management started to exercise the idea of implementing an exclusive distributorship instead of working with wholesalers. Even though the operational cost of a distributor system would be higher, it was believed that, among other benefits, this system would yield more accurate sales forecasts, which, in turn, would improve the overall performance of the Nazar group.

In 1996, the group management made its decision in favor of distributorship. Thus, Batu decided to develop an operation management system that would replace the existing system for the management of wholesalers. To this end, the Distributor Management Information System (DIMS) was developed and implemented in 1997. DMIS included order processing, inventory and account management, and promotion and pricing modules, which were presented as a decision support platform for the distributors. On the other end, the financial and operational performance of each distributor was monitored daily, since the system was synchronized by dial-up connections every night.

Together with DMIS, a newer version of the sales forecasting IS, called Demand Forecasting and Production Order System (DFPOS) was also launched. Being a monthly-operated, three-month planning horizon system, DFPOS was designed to administer production orders for Nazar production companies based on sales forecasts. In the first phase of the run, each Distribution Manager (64 individuals at that time) entered their subjective views as a function of 10 critical factors, including competitors' activities, new product launches, and distributors' stocks for each SKU. This information then was provided for each Regional Manager as a regional sum, and their acceptance or revision was asked.

Following this stage, the regional forecasts were integrated together with the analytical forecasts obtained by running three forecasting methods using the past 36 months' sales data, corrected for seasonality, price, promotion, and advertisement effects. The resulting forecast intervals for each SKU were passed into the second phase of DFPOS run, where the weekly production orders for the next 12 weeks were obtained. In this process, annual budget figures and market research parameters also were taken into account.

Implementation of DMIS continued smoothly, since there was an urgent need for such an operating system to run the new distributor system. DFPOS was launched in 1997; however, it could not be implemented successfully, because between 1997 and 1998, the top management of NMKC had been almost completely renewed, and there were more urgent organizational problems to deal with.

Between 1997 and 1999, Nazar Group's operations grew considerably, which required more synergy between the production and marketing companies. However, it seemed to Batu that the production companies were making their production plans on their own, while NMKC was trying to respond to market dynamics in the short term. As a result, the group management meetings were dominated by inconclusive discussions between the marketing and production people.

In the Management Council, Batu argued that the group management team had not been able to manage the Nazar supply chain efficiently. Thus, the subsystems developed that far had to be integrated further in order to establish more group synergy. Batu commented:

From my side, supply chain management concept is a management model which extensively utilizes the systematic approach to run the business. ... Our efforts/practices could not be seen as the picture of a developed supply chain and its administration, but only a part of it. These efforts only show our consciousness on the way to have a supply chain management system and its practice. The transition is still going on. (See Chandra and Kumar, 2000; Ho, et al., 2002; Kopczak and Johnson, 2003; Larson and Halldorsson, 2002; Mentzet et al., 2001; for reviews of supply chain management).

After long discussions, the Management Council accepted Batu's proposal and, in addition, decided to move the group management from production-focused (push-type) orientation to a more customer–focused (pull-type) one.

In 1999, the General Manager of NFC and the Technical Coordinator left the group, which was the initial sign of change. Batu had to revise his implementation strategy; thus, he had to determine where to start the integration project and how to proceed. In 2000, a new Technical Coordinator was hired as a council member, who also had background in supply chain management. He became Batu's major partner in system design.

CASE DESCRIPTION

In mid 2000, Batu decided to start the integration project right at the interface between Production and Sales, where the majority of management problems originated. He formed a steering committee, which assigned certain projects to cross-functional project groups. The steering committee reported to the Management Council. The objective of the initiative was to develop and implement an IS, called Production-Inventory Management System (PIMS), which would integrate sales forecasts coming from NMKC and production planning, while optimizing the overall operational efficiency of the Nazar supply chain.

Prior to the PIMS project, Batu pointed out that production companies were undertaking pseudo-production planning activities without an obligation to meet production orders taken from DFPOS. Although a production order for each product was given each month, orders were rarely met. For this reason, production cost control in that kind of environment had been very difficult. Finch and Luebbe (1995) state that planning for operations is essential because operation function controls a large percentage of a firm's resources, including inventories, capacities, and workforce.

Basic supply chain components of Nazar Group are shown in Exhibit 5, where the system boundaries of PIMS and its relational diagram also are indicated. Having looked at this picture, Batu realized that in the first stage of the project, conceptualization of PIMS had to be agreed upon collectively. To this end, many project meetings were organized where production, marketing, and procurement people were presented with a number of alternative approaches to system design. After many discussions, a list of protocols was established between marketing and production, and another one between production and procurement functions under which the selected system (shown in Exhibit 6) was defined.

The protocols were designed to underline the responsibilities of both parties and to resolve or avoid conflicts. For instance, under the protocol between marketing and production, the planning period was established as 12 weeks rolling horizon and the time step was taken as one week. Therefore, NMKC had to enter the sales forecasts for 12 weeks for each SKU. That is, every week, sales forecasts for the following 11 weeks could be revised, and the 12th week had to be entered for the first time. Sales forecasts, however, only could be revised under certain revision limits that were previously agreed upon. The correlation between weekly sales forecasts (revised) and actual shipments was a part of performance measurement for NMKC. On the other hand, the production company was responsible for the realization of production orders and preparation of stocks, including safety stocks, for shipment in the beginning of the assigned week. The correlation between production orders and actual production was a part of the performance measure of the production company.

Under the protocol between production and procurement, the production company was responsible for validating daily raw material usage, while it was procurement's responsibility to update supplier information, net cost of procurement, batch sizes, and so forth. Also, it was the procurement department's responsibility and its performance measure to provide the correct materials at the required time. To this end, the materials were divided into two groups; namely, major and minor materials, where the major materials were the ones with high usage, short shelf-life, or short leadtimes (less than two days), and minor materials were the ones with low usage or long leadtimes. It was agreed under the protocol that the procurement department would have to provide minor materials needed at the beginning of the week and provide major materials not longer than two days before their use. The timing of usage of the materials was given by the Production Planning Program (PPP) output (see Exhibit 7).

Having established the systems concept, Batu decided to move forward to the next stage, where a number of project groups would examine the MRP, production, production planning, human resources, and warehousing functions in order to identify their weaknesses under the new system requirements. After several upgrading studies, these functions were improved, especially, in terms of IT and decision-making abilities. User terminals were transformed into Web-based, and the underlying database operations were streamlined to achieve a higher speed of data exchange. Also, the connections to remote locations, especially within factory floors or warehouses, were improved.

In the mean time, a group of analysts started the development of PPP with an objective of generating a 12-week production plan that utilized production means and sources in the most economical way. To this end, PPP was designed as a hierarchical optimization model (Schneeweiss, 1999), as shown in Exhibit 7. At the Master Production Schedule (MPS) level, the optimal weekly production plan for the 12-week planning horizon was determined. This plan optimized the use of production line capacities in order to fulfill the sales forecasts and safety stock requirements so that shortages and inventory carrying costs were minimized. MPS was modeled as a periodic review, partial backlogging, and capacitated production-inventory model (Hax & Candea, 1984).

The output of MPS (weekly production quantities) was entered into the Scheduling Model. This model used a heuristic solution procedure to obtain the detailed production schedules for 63 shifts (three weeks) that minimized the completion times and setup losses. The output of the Scheduling Model was entered into the Assignment Model, which determined the optimal workforce assignments for the 63 shifts given by the Scheduling Model so that the use of workforce skills was maximized. Under this hierarchical structure, an iterative method was used so that the lower-level optimization programs checked feasibility of the higher-level program solutions. If the feasibility test did not pass, then the higher-level program searched for the next solution. The iterations ended when a feasible and satisfactory solution was obtained.

The MPS model, developed for one of NFC's plants where 120 SKUs were produced in 12 production lines, was structured as a Mixed Integer Programming (MIP) model with about 10,000 constraints and 5,000 decision variables. The Scheduling and Assignment models also were designed as MIP models with 52,000 constraints and 41,000 decision variables, and with 4,500,000 constraints and 5,350,000 variables, respectively. The optimization models were developed using GAMS modeling tool. The iterative hierarchical solution procedure was developed in-house using a C++ code, which called in Cplex solver for MIP. The entire system is located in a server with 2 GB RAM and 2.4 GHz Pentium IV microprocessor. It took 90 minutes for the program to obtain a satisfactory solution.

One of the critical success factors of the project was the effective use of IT so that the resulting system would allow fast and accurate decision making and be open for future system extensions. This required a careful database management on the mainframe, because there were many distributed network users from different disciplines, and their interactions involved data entry, report/graph viewing, and local decision making.

In the next phase of system integration, Batu decided to launch user training programs. MRP users were trained for the use of materials management according to new rules. Human resource departments at the production companies were trained for updating operator skill levels, developing operator training programs, and getting performance measurement information. Also, the production planning people at the production companies were trained for updating product and process parameters, setup times, operator skill definitions, and so forth.

In the last quarter of 2001, Batu decided to launch the PIMS system starting at one of NFC's production plants. There were minor IT- or IS-related problems, which were solved immediately. However, there was major resistance from both production and marketing users, but not from the procurement people. In fact, in the beginning of 2001, a new general manager was hired for NFC and appointed to the Management Council as well, who was hesitant to show leadership for implementation, since most of the major decisions were made before him.

The production people also were arguing strongly about the success of the new production paradigm (customer-focused, planned production), and they were defending the performance of the old paradigm (production-focused, myopic production planning), where they enjoyed full control of production resources. For instance, they claimed that the finished goods inventories were higher compared to one year before. However, after a short analysis, it was shown that the difference originated partly from the safety stocks, which did not exist before, and the rest of the stocks on weighted average were moving at a rate faster than before. Batu thought that the production people were used to giving short-term tactical decisions, which mostly optimized local factors, and they were not willing to see easily that PIMS was concerned about group-wide optimization that involved longer-term strategic decisions; for this reason, the model outputs seemed flawed to most users.

Marketing people also were resisting change. The sales forecasts coming through DFPOS were still short-sighted. They were complaining about PIMS not being able to adapt to changes in the market quick enough, which, they argued, had been leading the company to a high loss of sales.

Amidst all these low user adoptions, the system was operating technically quite smoothly. Batu was able to reply to almost all of the complaints with performance measures. These complaints continued until mid-2002, when Batu decided to move ahead and promote his project leader as Supply Chain Group Manager, thereby collecting most planning decisions under one manager. From that point on, PIMS was administered by this group manager, who was knowledgeable about the entire system.

In 2002, the sales grew 12%, and the market share rose 2%, while the Management Council decided to remain neutral about PIMS. In 2003, Batu decided to include the other NFC plant and Bonjuu Foods under PIMS. The implementation took about nine months with almost no implementation problems on the production side. DMIS also was upgraded from a dial-up connection to a Web-based application in 2003, adding features to streamline the process and adding value for the distributors. Since the distributors are Nazar's customers in its supply chain, this application is hoped to form a basis for more collaboration. (See Fawcett and Magnan, 2002, for a study of supply chain integration practice; and Lancioni, et al., 2003, for Internet application trends in SCM.)

CURRENT CHALLENGES/ PROBLEMS FACING THE ORGANIZATION

By the end of 2003, all existing production lines were administered under PIMS except for those in the new chocolate plant, which would be joined later. It seemed to Batu that a procurement and production mechanism was built, which operated at a reasonable efficiency; however, the sales forecast errors were still too high to get the most out of this system. The marketing people were still operating the system with shortsighted forecasts, which led to imposing too many forecast changes and thus, higher stock levels than expected. In return, this often caused wrong management concerns about the effectiveness of PIMS. It seemed to Batu that adapting marketing people to change would take longer than expected, and he had to initiate another process to motivate them.

Batu also believed that the group management organization was not adequate anymore for the current size of the overall supply-chain operations. Under the current group management structure, the cross-functional decisions were not made as fast nor as effectively as they should have been. As a result, the implementation of PIMS was affected adversely by the lack of a collaborative group management platform. In fact, all collaborative group operations, such as product development, were affected adversely by the current management structure. Thus, the problem would have to be solved through a holistic strategic management approach.

On the other hand, users were complaining about the long response time of the system, as they were trying to test the performance of several implementation scenarios. Batu believed that there were still a number of improvements to be realized about the optimization algorithms within the PIMS and MRP systems in order to speed up the overall solution time. The current runtime of about 90 minutes seemed to be a practical limit to undertake what-if type manual decision interventions regarding the use of production resources, such as overtime or hiring/firing decisions.

In addition, there had been a strong demand from users in that they needed more variations about the output report formats. Batu considered these continuous improvement projects as a step toward higher user adoption, where he placed utmost emphasis.

NOTE

Dedicated to the memory of Mustafa Ozturk.

REFERENCES

Al-Mashari, M., & Zairi, M. (2000). Revisiting BPR: A holistic review of practice and development. *Business Process Management Journal, 6*(1), 10-31.

Chandra, C., & Kumar, S. (2000). Supply chain management in theory and practice: A passing fad or a fundamental change? *Industrial Management & Data Systems, 100*(3), 100-113.

Davenport, T., & Short, J. (1990). The new industrial engineering: Information technology and business process redesign. *MIT Sloan Management Review, 31*(4), 11-27.

Davenport, T., & Stoddard, D. (1994). Reengineering: Business change of mythic proportions? *MIS Quarterly, 18*(2), 121-127.

Fawcett, S. E., & Magnan, G. M. (2002). The rhetoric and reality of supply chain integration. *International Journal of Physical Distribution & Logistics Management, 32*(5), 339-361.

Finch, B. J., & Luebbe, R. L. (1995). *Operations management: Competing in a changing environment.* Dryden Press.

Grover, V., Teng, J., & Fiedler, K. (1993). Information technology enabled business process redesign: An integrated planning framework. *Omega: The International Journal of Management Science, 21*(4), 433-447.

Hax, A. C., & Candea D. (1984). *Production and Inventory Management*. Englewood Cliffs, NJ: Prentice-Hall.

Ho, C. K., Au, K. F., & Newton, E. (2002). Empirical research on supply chain management: A critical review and recommendations. *International Journal of Production Research, 40*(17), 4415-4430.

Kopczak, L. R., & Johnson, M. E. (2003, Spring). The supply-chain management effect. *MIT Sloan Management Review*, 27-34.

Lancioni, R. A., Smith, M. F., & Schau, H. J. (2003). Strategic Internet application trends in supply chain management. *Industrial Marketing Management, 32*, 211-217.

Larson, P. D., & Halldorsson, A. (2002). What is SCM? And, where is it? *Journal of Supply Chain Management, 38*(4), 36-44.

Mentzer, J. T., et al., (2001). Defining supply chain management. *Journal of Business Logistics, 22*(2), 1-21.

Schneeweiss, C. (1999). *Hierarchies in distributed decision making*. Springer Verlag.

APPENDIX

Exhibit 1. Financial data: Nazar Group of Companies

Year	2003	2002	2001	2000	1999
Total Sales (tons)	111,214	101,887	90,817	74,462	62,816
Total Revenue (million USD)	260	175	145	153	126
Export (% of Total Revenue)	13.6	9.83	13.8	6.7	0.4
Market Share (%)*	33	32	30	29	30

**Nielsen Data.*

Exhibit 2. List of Group Management Team Members, all placed under the payroll of NFC

- President (family member)
- Vice President of Procurement, (family member)
- Vice President of Planning and IT
- R&D Coordinator (family member)
- Technical Coordinator
- Finance Coordinator
- Human Resource Coordinator
- Group Auditor

Exhibit 3. List of Management Council Members

- President (family member)
- Vice President of Procurement, (family member)
- Vice President of Planning and IT
- R&D Coordinator (family member)
- Technical Coordinator
- General Manager of Nazar Marketing Company
- General Manager of Nazar Foods Company
- External Consultant for Finance
- External Consultant for Public Relations
- Two Family Members

Exhibit 4. Top Level Organization Charts of Nazar Foods and Nazar Marketing Companies

Nazar Foods Company Board
- General Manager
  - Production Manager
  - Production Planning Manager
  - Technical Manager
  - Quality Assurance Manager
  - Finance Manager
  - Personnel Manager
  - Plant Manager (Rusk Factory)
  - Plant Manager (Chocolate Factory)

Nazar Marketing Company Board
- General Manager
  - Marketing Director
    - Sales Forecast Manager
  - Sales Director
    - 8 Regional Managers
    - Chain Stores Manager
    - Transportation Manager
  - Export Director
    - Country Managers
  - Planning Director
  - Finance Manager

Exhibit 5. IS components under Nazar group supply chain

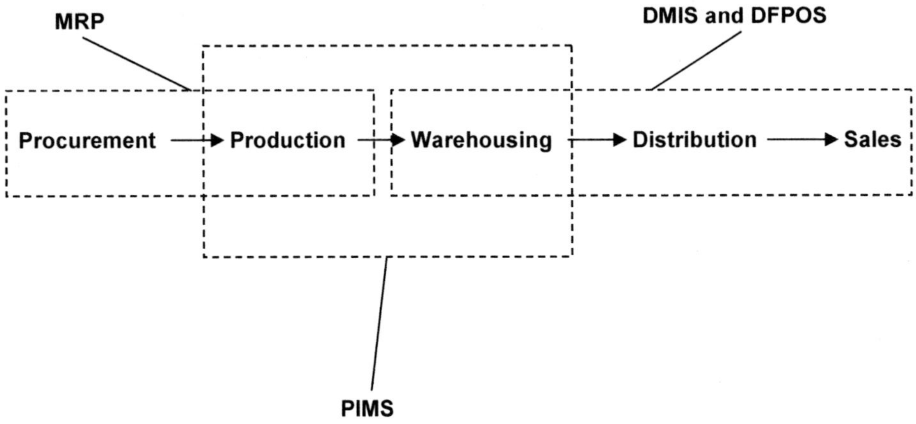

Exhibit 6. Conceptual overview of production-inventory management system (PIMS)

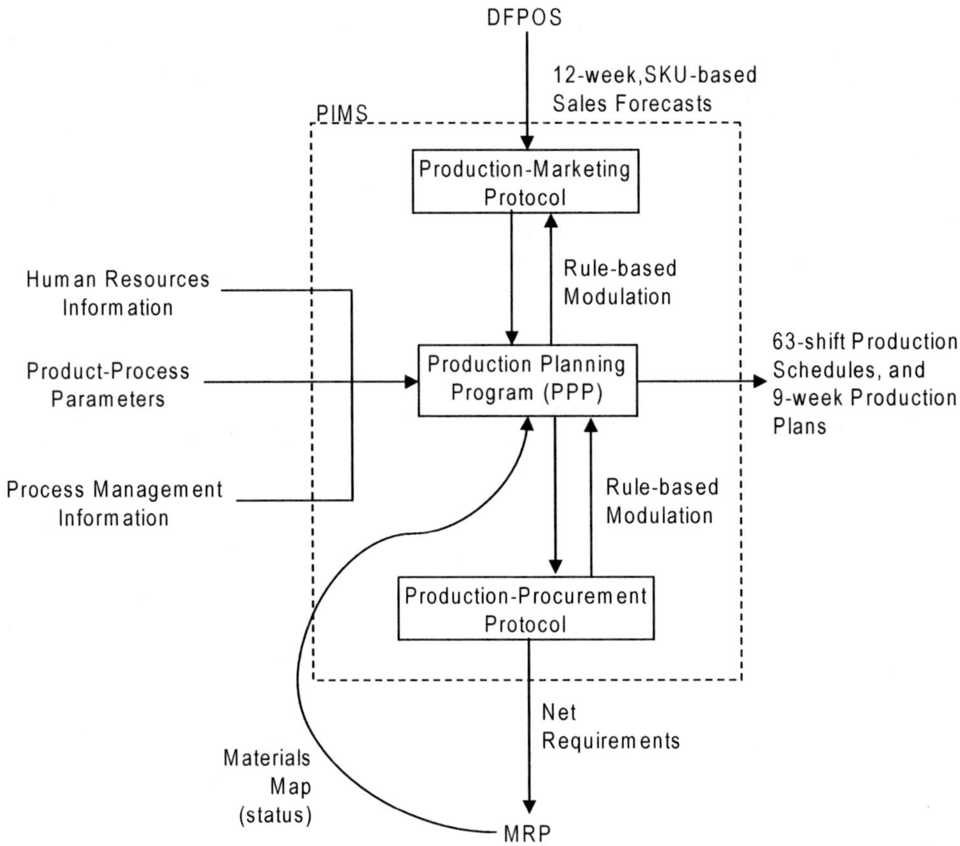

Exhibit 7. Production planning program (PPP) system design

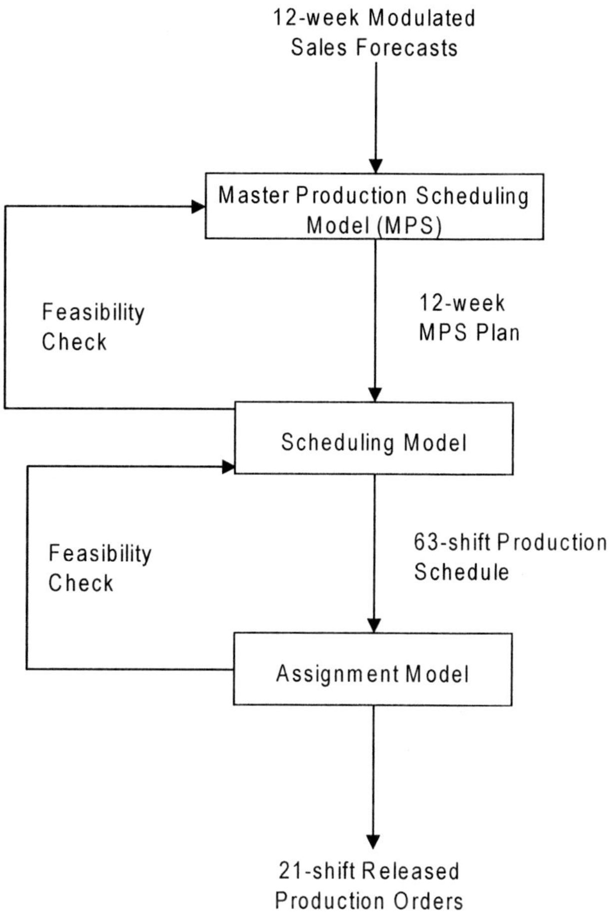

This work was previously published in Journal of Cases on Information Technology, Vol. 8, Issue 1, edited by M. Khosrow-Pour, pp. 49-62, copyright 2006 by IGI Publishing, formerly known as Idea Group Publishing (an imprint of IGI Global).

Chapter VII
BROOD:
Business Rules-driven Object Oriented Design

Pericles Loucopoulos
Loughborough University, UK

Wan M.N. Wan Kadir
Universiti Teknologi Malaysia, Malaysia

ABSTRACT

A critical success factor for information systems is their ability to evolve as their environment changes. There is compelling evidence that the management of change in business policy can have a profound effect on an information system's ability to evolve effectively and efficiently. For this to be successful, there is a need to represent business rules from the early requirements stage, expressed in user-understandable terms, to downstream system design components and maintain these throughout the lifecycle of the system. Any user-oriented changes could then be traced and if necessary propagated from requirements to design specifications and evaluated by both end-users and developers about their impact on the system. The BROOD approach, discussed in this article, aims to provide seamless traceability between requirements and system designs through the modelling of business rules and the successive transformations, using UML as the modelling framework.

INTRODUCTION

The ubiquitous nature of information systems and the increasing dependency of organizations, government and society on such systems highlight the importance of ensuring robustness in their operation. At the same time rapid changes in the environment of information systems places an increasing emphasis on the ability of these systems to evolve according to emerging requirements. A large proportion of a total systems' lifecycle cost is devoted to introducing new requirements, and removing or changing existing system functionality (Grubb & Takang, 2003). Software evolution therefore is considered as a key challenge in the development and maintenance of information systems (Erlikh, 2000).

In recent years there has been an increasing interest of the IS community in business rules, which has resulted in dedicated rule-centric modeling frameworks and methodologies (Ross & Lam, 1999; Zaniolo et al., 1997), international initiatives for the investigation of business rules' role in the context of knowledge management (Hay & Healy, 1997), conferences, workshops and tutorials (Mens, Wuyts, Bontridder, & Grijseels, 1998), and rule-centric rule management tools and application development support environments (e.g., Blaze Advisor Builder, BRS RuleTrack, Business Rule Studio, Haley Technologies, ILOG Rules, Platinum Aion, Usoft Developer and Visual Rule Studio). Whilst these efforts make significant contributions in their own right, a key challenge remains unanswered namely the *linking of business rules specifications to software designs*.

The aim of the BROOD (business rules-driven object oriented design) approach is to address the issue of software evolution from both *requirements* and *design* perspectives. This confluence should provide a seamless and traceable facility that arguably should bring about a more effective way of dealing with software evolution, by aligning changes of the information system to changes in its environment. BROOD adopts as its methodological paradigm that of object orientation with UML as its underlying graphical language. It augments UML by explicitly considering business rules as an integral part of an object-oriented development effort. To this end BROOD aims:

i. To explicitly model business rules in a manner understandable to end-user stakeholders.
ii. To map these to formal descriptions amenable to automation and analysis.
iii. To provide guidelines on the deployment of business rules in the development process.
iv. To provide guidelines on the evolution of requirements and related design specifications.

The article is organized as follows. Section 2 discusses the background to business rules modeling. Section 3 introduces the motivation for BROOD. Section 4 introduces the BROOD metamodel as the foundation for modeling business rules. Section 5 discusses the manner in which business rules are linked to design components via the concept of 'rule phrase.' The BROOD process is detailed in section 6. The BROOD approach is supported by an automated tool and this is briefly discussed in Section 7. The article concludes with an overview of BROOD, observations on its use on a large application and comparisons with traditional approaches.

The language details for business rules definition are given in appendix A. The BROOD approach is demonstrated through an industrial application which is described in appendix B. This application had originally been developed using a traditional approach. Therefore, it proved useful not only as a means of providing a practical grounding on BROOD but also on comparing and contrasting the use of BROOD with a traditional development effort.

BUSINESS RULES MODELLING

The motivation of BROOD is to provide a development environment whereby the business analysis and system design domains are supported by business rules modeling with the specific aim to facilitating more effective software evolution.

The term "business rule" has been used by different authors in different ways. For example, in (Rosca, Greenspan, Feblowitz, & Wild, 1997), business rules are:

statements of goals, policies, or constraints on an enterprise's way of doing business.

In (Herbst, 1996a), they are defined as:

statements about how the business is done, i.e.

about guidelines and restrictions with respect to states and processes in an organization.

Krammer considers them as "programmatic implementations of the policies and practices of a business organization" (Krammer, 1997) whilst Halle states that:

depending on whom you ask, business rules may encompass some or all relationship verbs, mathematical calculations, inference rules, step-by-step instructions, database constraints, business goals and policies, and business definitions. (Halle, 1994).

In general, business rules in the information systems field may be viewed in terms of two perspectives: (a) business rules as applied to conceptual modeling and (b) business rules as applied to evolvable software systems development.

Business Rules in Conceptual Modeling

1. Business rules as part of requirements gathering and systems analysis have not been ignored by structured analysis, information engineering or object-oriented analysis approaches (Moriarty, 1993) which, to varying degrees, subsume or represent business rules as part of notation schemes used to specify application requirements (Gottesdiener, 1997) Ross (1997) comments that traditional IS methodologies have addressed rules poorly, and only relatively late in the system development lifecycle. (Hay & Healy, 1997) mention that rules dealing with information structure may be represented by any of several flavors of entity—relationship or object class diagrams, and responses to events may be shown via essential data flow diagrams (McMenamin & Palmer, 1984) or as entity life history diagrams (Robinson & Berrisford, 1994).

From a conceptual perspective there are approaches that consider business rules as an integral part of the modeling and analysis of systems' requirements. An early effort in this direction was the *RUBRIC* project (Loucopoulos & Layzell, 1986; van Assche, Layzell, Loucopoulos, & Speltinex, 1988) parts of which were integrated into the information engineering (Martin, 1989) method.

In *BROCOM* (Herbst, 1996b, 1997), the rule language is a type of structured English, and therefore it is highly expressive. Moreover, rules are organized according to a rich meta-model, and can be retrieved based on a number of different criteria. As far as methodological guidance is concerned, Herbst proposes the development of various models which are helpful during the analysis phase, but the process of creating and using them is not clearly defined. The transition from analysis to design and implementation has not been addressed by this approach.

The *DSS* approach (Rosca, Greenspan, & Wild, 2002; Rosca et al., 1995) focuses on the analysis phase of IS development by supporting the rationale behind the establishment of rules. DSS adopts the ECA (event-condition-action) paradigm for structuring rule expressions and also links these expressions to the entities of an underlying enterprise model. The absence of a formal rule language confines the use of DSS on modeling tasks.

The Business Rules Group (*BRG*), formerly known as the GUIDE Business Rule Project (Hay & Healy, 1997), investigated an appropriate formalization for the analysis and expression of business rules (Hay & Healy, 2000). This approach identifies terms and facts in natural language rule statements, and consequently, it offers a high level of expressiveness. The meta-model it provides for describing the relations between these terms and facts is very detailed. Therefore, rule models are (a) highly manageable and (b) formal and fully consistent with the information models of a specific organization.

The *IDEA* method (Zaniolo et al., 1997) focuses on the maintenance of formality and consistency with underlying business models. The method offers guidance for every activity being involved in the development of a rule-centric information system. The IDEA method is directed towards the use of specific active and deductive databases, and of the corresponding rule languages. As a result of this, (a) IDEA rules are rather difficult to be expressed or even understood by business people; and (b) the choice of technologies to be employed for the development of an information system is rather limited.

The *BRS* approach (Ross, 1997) is formal, in accordance with the underlying data models of an organization, offers sufficient methodological guidance, and allows management of rule expressions based on a very detailed meta-model. It is also one of the few methods that adopts a graphical notation for expressing rules. Regarding the development process, BRS introduces a business rule methodology called BRS Proteus™ methodology that defines a number of steps for both business and system modeling (Ross, & Lam, 2003). BRS also provides the BRS RuleTrack™, an automated tool for recording and organizing business rules.

The object constraint language (*OCL*) of UML (Eriksson & Penker, 2000) is tightly bound with the widely accepted UML but lacks methodological guidance for the collection of rules. Rule structures are implied by the allocation of rules to classes, attributes, associations and operations.

Table 1. Comparative evaluation of business rule in conceptual modeling

Criteria \ BR Approach	BRG	BROCOM	BRS
Concepts			
Business Rule Definition	IS	IS	Business
Business Rule Taxonomy			
- Structural Rules	High (10)	Low (0)	Medium (1)
- Behavioural Rules	Medium (8)	High (>30)	Medium (8)
- Derivation	Medium (2)	Low (0)	Medium (2)
Bus. Rule Management Elements	Medium (5)	Medium (9)	High (>30)
Modelling Language			
Understandability	Medium	Medium	High
Expressiveness (business rules)	Medium	High	High
Unambiguity	Medium	High	Medium
Formality	Medium	Medium	High
Evolvability	Medium	Medium	High
Process			
Lifecycle coverage	A	A	A + D
Process description	N/A	High	High
Coherence	N/A	High	High
Support for evolution	No	Yes	Yes
Pragmatics			
Communicability	Medium	High	High
Usability	Medium	High	High
Resources availability	Low	Medium	High
Openness	High	Medium	High

Lifecycle coverage: A-Analysis, D-Design, I-Implementation, M-Maintenance

A comparative evaluation of the treatment of business rules for conceptual modeling by three widely used approaches is shown in Table 1.

Business Rules in Evolvable Software Evolution

The majority of approaches in this category aim to improve the understanding and evolution of a software system by logically and physically separating business rule components from other software components.

The adaptive object model (*AOM*), which is also known as the dynamic object model (Riehle, Tilman, & Johnson, 2000), is *"a system that represents classes, attributes, and relationships as metadata"* (Yoder, Balaguer, & Johnson, 2001). Unlike traditional object-oriented design, AOM is based on objects rather than classes. It provides descriptions (metadata) of objects that exist in the system. In other words, AOM provides a meta-architecture that allows users to manipulate the concrete architectural components of the model such as business objects and business rules. These components are stored as an object model in a database instead of in code. The code is only used to interpret the stored objects. Thus, a user only needs to change the metadata instead of changing the code to reflect domain changes.

The *coordination contract* method aims to separate coordination from computation aspects (or core components) of a software system (Andrade, Fiadeiro, Gouveia, & Koutsoukos, 2002). It is motivated by the fact that there should be two different kinds of entities in a rapidly changing business environment—core business entities which are relatively stable and volatile business products which keep changing for the business to remain competitive (Andrade & Fiadeiro, 2000). Volatile business products are implemented as contracts. A contract aims to externalize the interactions between objects (core entities) by explicitly define them in the conceptual model. It extends the concept of association class by adding a coordination role similar to other components in architecture-based software evolution such as architectural connectors (Oreizy, Medvidovic, & Taylor, 1998), glue (Schneider, 1999), actor (Astley & Agha, 1998) or change absorbers (Evans & Dickman, 1999).

Business Rule Beans (*BRBeans*), formerly known as accessible business rules (Rouvellou, Degenaro, Rasmus et al., 1999; Rouvellou, Degenaro, Rasmus et al., 2000), is a framework that provides guidelines and infrastructures for the externalization of business rules in a distributed business application (IBM, 2003). Business rules are externally developed, implemented and managed to minimize the impact of their changes on other components such as core business, application, and user interface objects. They are implemented as server objects, which are fired by embedded trigger points in application objects. A rule management facility is provided to help users to understand the existing rules and to locate the rules when changes are required. BRBeans is implemented as a part of WebSphere Application Server by IBM *"to support business applications that externalize their business rules"* (Kovari, Diaz, Fernandes et al., 2003).

A comparative evaluation of the treatment of business rules evolvable software systems development by the three approaches is shown in Table 2.

MOTIVATION FOR THE BROOD APPROACH

According to Lehman's laws (Lehman & Belady, 1985), a software system that is used in a real-world environment inevitably must change or become progressively less useful in that environment. Lehman's laws also state that the software structure tends to become more complex due to the implemented changes and its size must continue to grow to accommodate new user requirements. Therefore, there is a need to introduce a method

Table 2. Comparative evaluation of business rules in evolvable software systems

Criteria \ BR Approach	Adaptive Object Model (AOM)	Coordination Contract	Business Rule Beans (BRBeans)
Concepts			
Business Rule Definition	Implicit	Implicit	Explicit
Business Rule Taxonomy	primitive, composite, workflow	ECA	derivation, constraint, invariant, script, classifier
Business Rule Management Elements	Nil	Nil	Yes
Modelling Language			
Understandability	High	Medium	Medium
Expressiveness (business rules)	Low	Medium	Medium
Formality	Low	High	Medium
Evolvability	High	High	High
Process			
Lifecycle coverage	(Evolutionary)	D + I + T + M	A + D + I + T + M
Process description	Low	Medium	High
Coherence	Medium	Medium	Medium
Support for evolution	Low	Medium	High
Pragmatics			
Communicability	High	Medium	Medium
Usability	Low	Medium	Medium
Resources availability	Medium	Medium	High
Openness	Medium	Medium	Low

that facilitates the management of the increasingly complex and larger size software system due to its evolution.

The position put forward in this article is that developers need to identify the sources of changes for software evolution in the system's environment and that some of the most volatile of these components tend to be business rules. In section 0 many contemporary approaches were reviewed all of which aim to externalize business rules from software components.

At the conceptual modeling level, there are approaches that separate syntax and semantics for modeling business rules. This effort localizes the changes to business rule components, and also increases the understanding and maintainability of business rules specification. This category of approaches provides a great deal of help in dealing with the concepts related to business rules, but they provide relatively little description on the design and implementation aspect of business rules.

At the implementation level, approaches create separate software components that implement business rules. As a result, the business rule changes will only localize to such components, and reduce the impact of changes to the overall software structure. This group of approaches provides very good facilities for developing evolvable software components but is less helpful in representing business rules at the conceptual business level.

The BROOD approach addresses both business modeling and the linking of business model components to software architecture components. By focusing on the conceptual level, BROOD attempts to externalizing changes from software components. This user-oriented view enhances understandability and maintainability since it encourages the direct involvement of business stakeholders in the maintenance of their business rules.

By introducing a linking component between the conceptual model of business rules and software design, BROOD attempts to increase business rule traceability. Traceability is highly desirable since one can keep 'forward' and 'backward' tracks of changes between business and software.

BROOD considers both *product* and *process* perspectives of the development and evolution of a software system. The *product* is defined using the BROOD metamodel, which specifies the structure for business rule specification, software design, and their linking elements. The *process* refers to a set of systematic and well-defined steps that should be followed during software development and evolution. The BROOD process emphasizes several important activities in a software lifecycle that contribute to a more resilient software system.

THE BROOD METAMODEL

The initial concept of the metamodel was introduced in (Wan Kadir & Loucopoulos, 2003; Wan Kadir & Loucopoulos, 2004). The metamodel is complemented by a language definition based on the context-free grammar EBNF, which is included in appendix A. The language definition defines the allowable sentence patterns for business rule statements and describes the linking elements between business rules and the related software design elements.

At the outset, three main desirable characteristics were set for developing an appropriate business rule metamodel, which would be consistent with the aims of BROOD:

- It should have an exhaustive and mutually exclusive typology to capture different types of business rules.
- It should have the structured forms of expressions for linking the business rules to software design.
- It should include rule management elements to improve business rule traceability in a business domain.

These three characteristics form the basis for the development of the business rule metamodel, which is shown in Figure 1. This figure shows the business rules metamodel together with parts of the UML metamodel that deal with static (classes) and dynamic (actions and events) aspects. The key requirement of BROOD for tracing changes from business to software through the use of business rules is achieved by integrating these three metamodels.

Business Rules Typology

The metamodel classifies business rules into three main types, which are constraint, action assertion, and derivation.

Constraints

Constraint rules specify the static characteristics of business entities, their attributes, and their relationships. They can be further divided into attribute and relationship constraints. The former specifies the uniqueness, optionality (null), and value check of an entity attribute. The latter asserts the relationship types as well as the cardinality and roles of each entity participating in a particular relationship.

Figure 1. The BROOD business rule metamodel

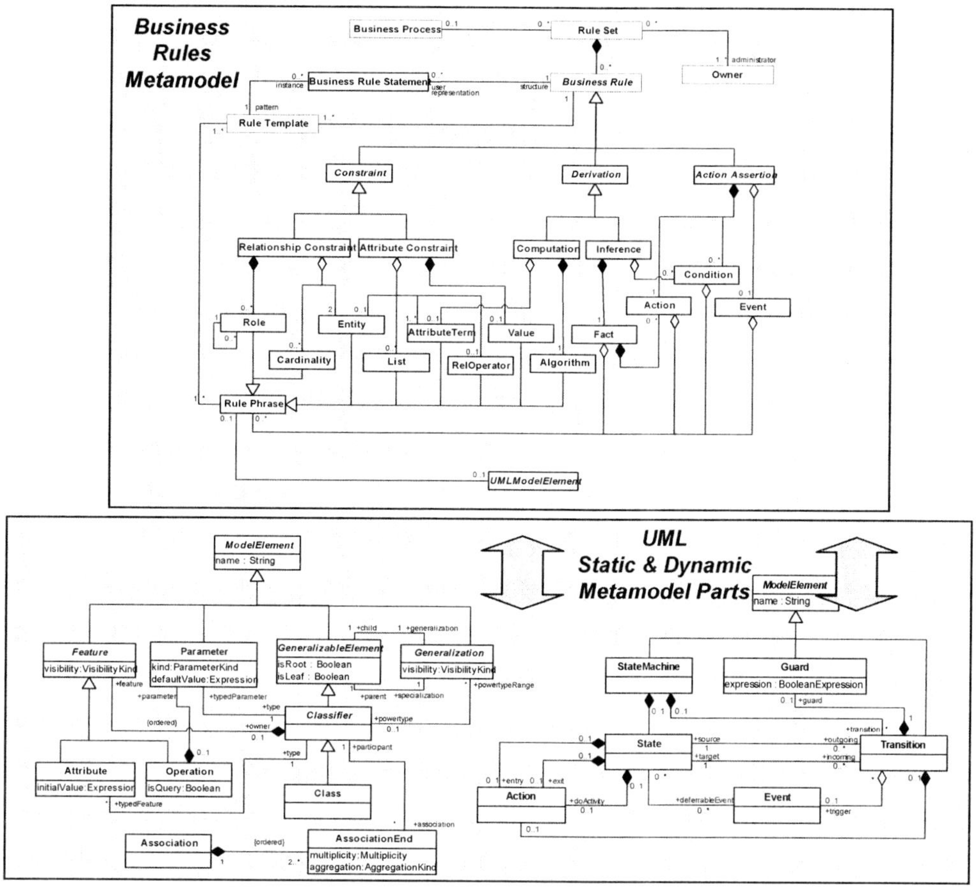

Examples of attribute constraints from the MediNet application expressed according to the BROOD syntax (see `attribute constraint` definition in appendix A) are the following:

Patient must have a unique patient registration number.
Patient may have a passport number.
Bill must have a unique bill number.
The amount of Bill must be less than the maximum bill amount set by the paymaster.
An employee level of a Panel Patient must be in {employer, executive, production operator}.

Examples of relationship constraints for MediNET (see `relationship constraint` definition in appendix A) are:

Clinic item is a/an item type of bill item.
Bill must have zero or more bill item.
HCP Service Invoice is a/an Invoice.

Actions

Action assertion concerns a behavioral aspect of the business. Action assertion specifies the *action* that should be activated on the occurrence of a certain *event* and possibly on the satisfaction of certain *conditions*. An event can be either a simple or a complex event where the latter is constructed by one or more simple events using the logical connectives AND/OR. A condition may be a simple or complex condition. A simple condition is a Boolean expression which compares a value of an entity attribute with any literal value or the value of another entity attribute using a relational operator. It can also be an inspection of the existence of a value of an entity attribute in a list of values.

An action is performed by a system in response to the occurrence of an event and the satisfaction of the relevant condition. The execution of action may change the state of the system. An action may be a simple action or a sequence of simple actions. Simple actions can be further categorized into three different types, trigger actions, object manipulation actions, and user actions. Trigger action invokes an operation, a process, a procedure, or another rule under certain circumstances. Object manipulation action sets the value of the attribute or create/delete an instance of an entity. User action is a manual task that is done by system users. During implementation, user action is often implemented as a message displayed to the user.

Examples of action assertion for MediNET (see `action assertion` definition in appendix A) are:

When new invoice created then calculate invoice end date.
When patient consultation completed then removed the patient from consultation queue and create bill for the patient.
When invoice entry updated if stock of drug smaller than re-order threshold then reorder the drug.

Derivation

A derivation rule derives a new fact based on existing facts. It can be of one of two types, *computation*, which uses a mathematical calculation or algorithm to derive a new arithmetic value, or *inference*, which uses logical deduction or induction to derive a new fact. Typically, an inference rule may be used to represent permission such as user policy for data security. An example of a computation derivation rule such as "The amount HCP MediNET usage invoice is computed as the amount of transaction fees, which are calculated as the transaction fee multiply by the total number of transactions, plus the monthly fee" would be expressed as:

let a = transaction_fee;
let b = number_of_treated_patient;
transaction_fees = a * b;
invoice_amount = transaction_fees + monthly_fee;

Examples of inference rules are given below:

If the paymaster's last quarter transaction is more than RM12,000.00 and the paymaster has no past due invoices then the paymaster is a preferred customer.
If the user type is equal to HR Officer and the user company is equal to patient paymaster then the user may view the patient's medical certificate.

The Rule Template

Rule templates are the formal sentence patterns by which business rules can be expressed. They are provided as a guideline to capture and specify business rules as well as a way to structure the business rule statements. Each rule template consists of one or more well-defined rule phrases, which are discussed in section 0.

By using the available templates, an inexperienced user may easily produce a consistent business rule statement. Rule templates help users to avoid tedious and repeated editing when creating many similar rules; and ensure uniformity by restricting the type of rules that can be written by business users. The use of templates also allows the precise linking of business rules to software design elements. The templates can be directly derived from the rules definition in Appendix A. Business rules templates are shown in Table 3.

Table 3. Business rule templates

Types	Templates
Attribute Constraint	<entity> must have | may have [a unique] <attributeTerm>. <attributeTerm1> must be | may be <relationalOperator> <value> | <attributeTerm2>. <attributeTerm> must be in <list>.
Relationship Constraint	[<cardinality>] <entity1> is a/an <role> of [<cardinality>]<entity2>. [<cardinality>] <entity1> is associated with [<cardinality>]<entity2>. <entity1> must have | may have [<cardinality>] <entity2>. <entity1> is a/an <entity2>.
Action Assertion	When <event> [if <condition>] then <action>. *The templates of <event> :* <attributeTerm> is updated <entity> is deleted | is created <operation>|<rule> is triggered the current date/time is <dateTime> <number> <timeUnit> time interval from <dateTime> is reached <number> <timeUnit> after <dateTime> <userEvent> *The templates of <condition> :* <attributeTerm1> <relationalOperator> <value | attributeTerm2> <attributeTerm> [not] in <list> *The templates of <action> :* trigger <process> | <operation> | <rule> set <attributeTerm> to <value> create | delete <entity> <userAction>
Computation	<attributeTerm> is computed as <algorithm>
Derivation	if <condition> then <fact>. *The templates of <fact> :* <entity> | <attributeTerm> is [not] a <value> <entity> may [not] <action>

The Rule Management Elements

Management elements are also included in the BROOD metamodel for facilitating the organization and management of business rules. These elements include the *rule set*, *business process*, and *owner*.

Rule set is used to group business rules into a set of closely interrelated rules. Each business rule model must have a single rule set, which is considered as the root rule set. This rule set must have at least one rule statement or another rule set.

One of the popular ways to identify a rule set is through its related business process. For example, the rules 'The bill amount is calculated as the sum of amounts of all bill items' and 'If a patient is a panel patient and his paymaster pays the bill in full, the balance is set to 0 and the bill status is set to paid' can be grouped in a rule set which is related to 'bill preparation' process. By properly organizing rules, the complexity of managing a large set of rules can be reduced.

Each business rule model must have an owner. An owner may also be defined for a rule set. The owner of a parent rule set is assumed to be the owner of its child rule set if the child does not define its owner. It is important to define the owner information in a business rule model to determine the access rights and responsibility to a business rules repository, especially for software systems with multiple user groups that possess different business rules. An owner may be an organizational unit, an individual user, a user group or role that is responsible for the management of the respective business rules. During business rule implementation, each rule set, business process, and owner is given a unique identifier.

THE RULE PHRASE

A rule phrase in BROOD links a user-oriented business rule definition to a software design component. There are alternative ways in which this may be achieved. For example, using a rule object or rule engine, or making use of OCL. The use of rule object or rule engine increases the semantic distance between analysis and design and imposes implementation considerations. The use of constraints expressed using OCL may provide a link between business rule specifications and software design but OCL is still hard to understand by business users although OMG claims that no mathematical background is required in using OCL.

Rule phrases are considered as the building blocks for rule statements. They can be maintained independently during implementation, in other words, they are not deleted when a business rule is deleted. However, the modification and deleting of a rule phrase is not recommended since a careful effort is needed in reviewing its aggregated business rules. In addition to playing a role as the building blocks for business rule statements, rule phrases are also important in linking business rules to software design elements.

The mappings between rule phrase types and UML model elements are summarized in Table 4. Most of the rule phrases are directly linked to class diagram model elements. Entity and attribute term are directly connected to the respective class and attribute in the class diagram. Cardinality and role are correspondingly linked to multiplicity and role of an association end of a relationship. Algorithm is linked to operation specification.

Rule phrases for event, condition, and action, which are the building blocks for action assertion rules, are naturally linked to statechart diagram. Event, condition, and action are respectively linked to event, guard, and action of a state transition in a statechart diagram. Consequently, event and action may be linked to a class operation, and guard may be linked to an operation specification,

Table 4. Association between rule phrases and design elements

Rule Phrase Type	Software Design Elements
Entity	Class
Attribute Term	Attribute
Operation Term	Operation
Attribute Constraints	Attribute.isUnique, Attribute.notNull
Cardinality	AssociationEnd.multiplicity
Role	AssociationEnd.role
Event	Transition.event → Class.operation
Condition	Transition.guard, Operation.specification
Action	Transition.action → Class.operation
Algorithm	Operation.specification
Value	- (literal value), Operation.
List	- (enumeration), Operation
Relational Operator	- (enumeration)

in a class diagram. List and relational operator contain enumerated values whilst value contains a literal value. However, value and list can be linked to an operation that return a single and multiple values respectively.

THE BROOD PROCESS

The BROOD process is described using the process model based on the syntax and semantics of the OMG software process engineering metamodel (SPEM). SPEM was developed by the Object Management Group to provide a metamodel and notations for specifying software processes and their components (OMG, 2002). SPEM extends the unified modeling language (UML) (OMG, 2001) metamodel with process specific stereotypes. A part of SPEM that shows most of the important components of a process structure is shown in Figure 2.

In SPEM, a *work product* is an artifact produced, consumed, or modified by a process. It may be a piece of information, a document, model, or source code. It is either used as an input by workers to perform an activity, or a result or an output of such activities. A work product is called a deliverable if it is needed to be formally delivered by a process. The examples of work products in BROOD are class diagram, statechart diagram, and business rule specification. Each work product is associated with a process role that is formally responsible for its production.

A *process role* defines the responsibilities of an individual, or a group of individuals working together as a team. Each process role performs or assists with specific activities.

The core activities of the BROOD process are situated in the analysis, design, and evolution phases. Analysis phase produces analysis model that contains two main work products: the initial business rule specification and preliminary software design models. Both work products are refined and linked during the design phase to produce a more traceable and consequently evolvable software system. The flow of activities in each BROOD phase is shown in Figure 3.

The Analysis Phase

As shown in Figure 4, the analysis phase starts with an architectural analysis activity that considers the work products from requirements phase such as use-case model, business model, initial architecture descriptions, and supplementary requirements. A software architect performs architectural analysis by identifying the analysis packages based on the functional requirements

Figure 2. An excerpt from OMG software process engineering metamodel (OMG, 2002)

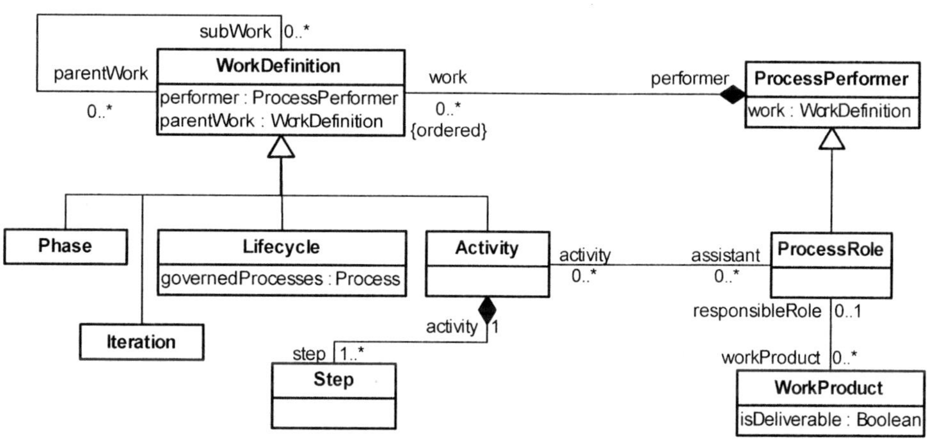

Figure 3. The flow of activities in the BROOD process

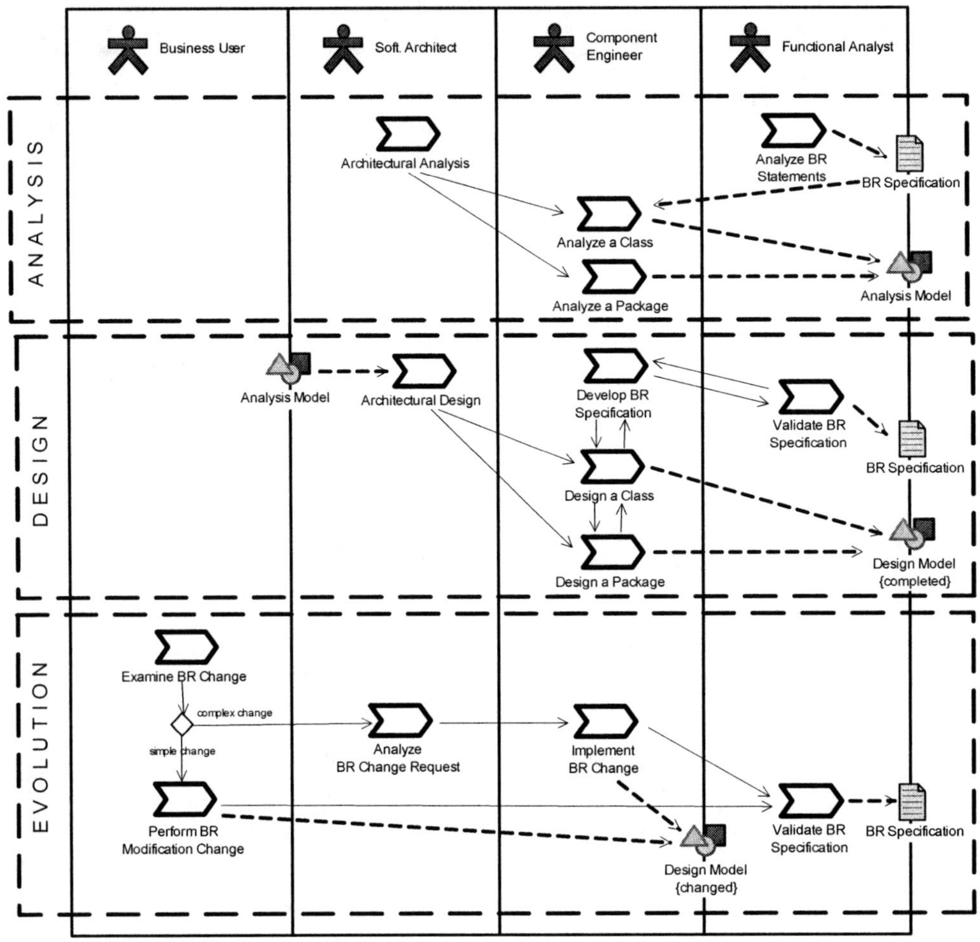

Figure 4. Packages for the MediNet application

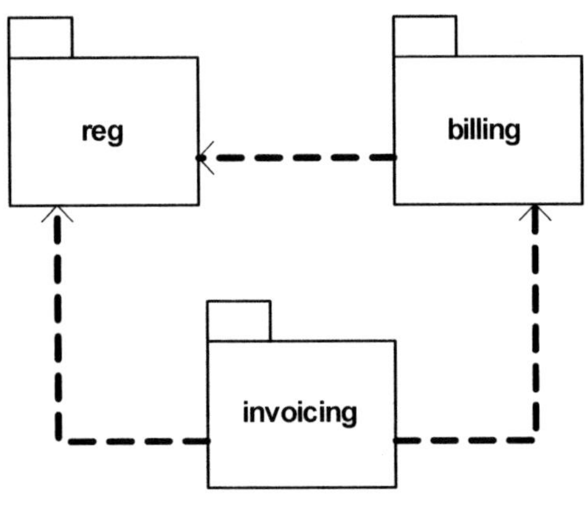

and knowledge of the application domain. Each package realizes a set of closely related use cases and business processes to minimize the coupling between packages, which in turn localizes business changes. This activity identifies analysis classes and outlines their name, responsibilities, attributes, and relationships. In order to extract more information about the behavior of the classes, collaboration or interaction diagrams can be developed based on the process flows (scenario) in the use case models. The main work products produced by this activity are analysis class diagrams and packages in their outline version.

Considering the MediNet application, architectural analysis resulted in three packages *business processes* i.e. *registration*, *billing*, and *invoicing*. The registration package groups all classes related to patient registration such as Patient, Paymaster, HCProvider, Clinic, User, and RegLocation. Billing package contains classes related to billing and drugs inventory such as Bill, BillPayment, Bill _ Item, TransType, TransItem, and ExpenseItem. Invoicing package includes classes related to invoicing and invoice payment for example Invoice, InvoiceItem, Payment, and PaymentAllocation.

The outline of analysis class diagrams and packages are further refined by class analysis and package analysis activities, respectively. A component engineer identifies more detailed information about responsibilities and attributes of each class. Different types of relationships between classes such as association, aggregation, and inheritance are also identified. The possible states and their transitions can be identified to understand the behavior of objects from certain classes. These steps are repeated until a complete analysis class diagram, statechart diagram and package are achieved.

The activity of business rule modeling considers the informal statements captured during initial requirements and identifies the types for each business rule statement based on the BROOD typology. Business rule statements are transformed into more structured business rule specifications according to the templates' definition.

Table 5 shows a set of structured rules for the MediNet application. This template provides the means of managing rules as they get discovered and analyzed and acts as a 'repository' of rules for their entire lifecycle.

Table 5. Business rule statements for the MediNET application

Business Process	Business Rule Example	Rule Type
Registration	A patient must have a unique registration number.	Att. Constraint
	A patient may have more than one paymaster.	Rel. Constraint
	If a patient has an outstanding balance, then the patient should be banned from consultation registration	Action Assertion
	When consultation registration is successfully completed, then put the patient into the consultation queue.	Action Assertion
	If a patient's condition is critical then the patient is an emergency patient.	Inference
Billing	The amount of a panel patient's bill must not exceed the maximum bill amount set by the paymaster.	Att. Constraint
	Each bill item is associated with an item from the clinic transaction items	Rel. Constraint
	When consultation is completed then create bill.	Action Assertion
	If the bill is a panel patient's bill then create panel transaction item.	Action Assertion
	The amount of a bill is computed as the sum of all amounts of bill items.	Computation
	The amount of bill item is computed as the unit amount multiply by the quantity.	Computation
	A bill can be modified only if the user role is Chief Clinic Assistant.	Inference
Invoicing	One invoice must have zero or more payments.	Rel. Constraint
	When a payment is not received within 30 days from the invoice date, then the first reminder will be sent.	Action Assertion
	The amount of HCP MediNET usage invoice is computed as the sum of monthly subscription fee plus transaction fees.	Computation
	A paymaster (panel company) is under probation if the paymaster has an invoice with category 1 past due and the current balance is more than RM 5,000.00.	Inference

The Design Phase

The design phase involves the identification of application-specific and application-general subsystems. The application-specific subsystems are related to packages that group a set of closely related services in an application domain. The application-general subsystems are related to implementation technology decisions such as the introduction of user interface and database connectivity layers. The MediNet subsystems definition is shown in Figure 5.

The class design activity elaborates further the static and dynamic information of classes that were defined during the analysis phase. Additional information on the operations, attributes, and relationships can be added to each class. The specification of operations and attributes is made using the syntax of the chosen programming language. If necessary, the methods that specify the algorithm for the implementation of operations are specified.

The class design activity for the MediNet application resulted in detailed specification of for the three packages of registration, billing and invoicing. The class association diagram of Figure 6 shows the class details for invoicing. In order to reduce diagrammatic complexity all parameters and return values are hidden in the class operations.

The calculation of invoice amount is different for different types of invoice. The amount for healthcare service invoice is calculated as the total of its item amounts after applying additional computation rules such as bill limit, invoice limit and discount. MediNET uses the open item invoicing method that allows an invoice issuer to track each unpaid invoice as an individual item for aging purposes. Panel patient bills are considered as the items for HCP MediNET usage and HCP service usage invoices. For HCP MediNET usage invoice, the number of bills issued by a particular HCP is counted as the number of transactions, which is later used in the invoice amount calculation.

Figure 5. Software architecture for the MediNet application

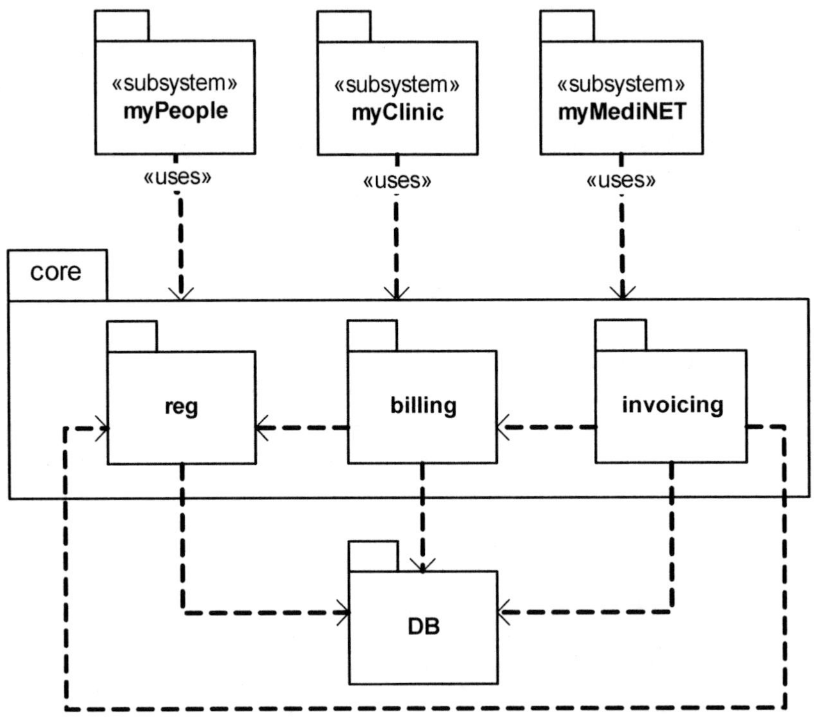

Figure 6. Class association diagram for invoicing for the MediNet application

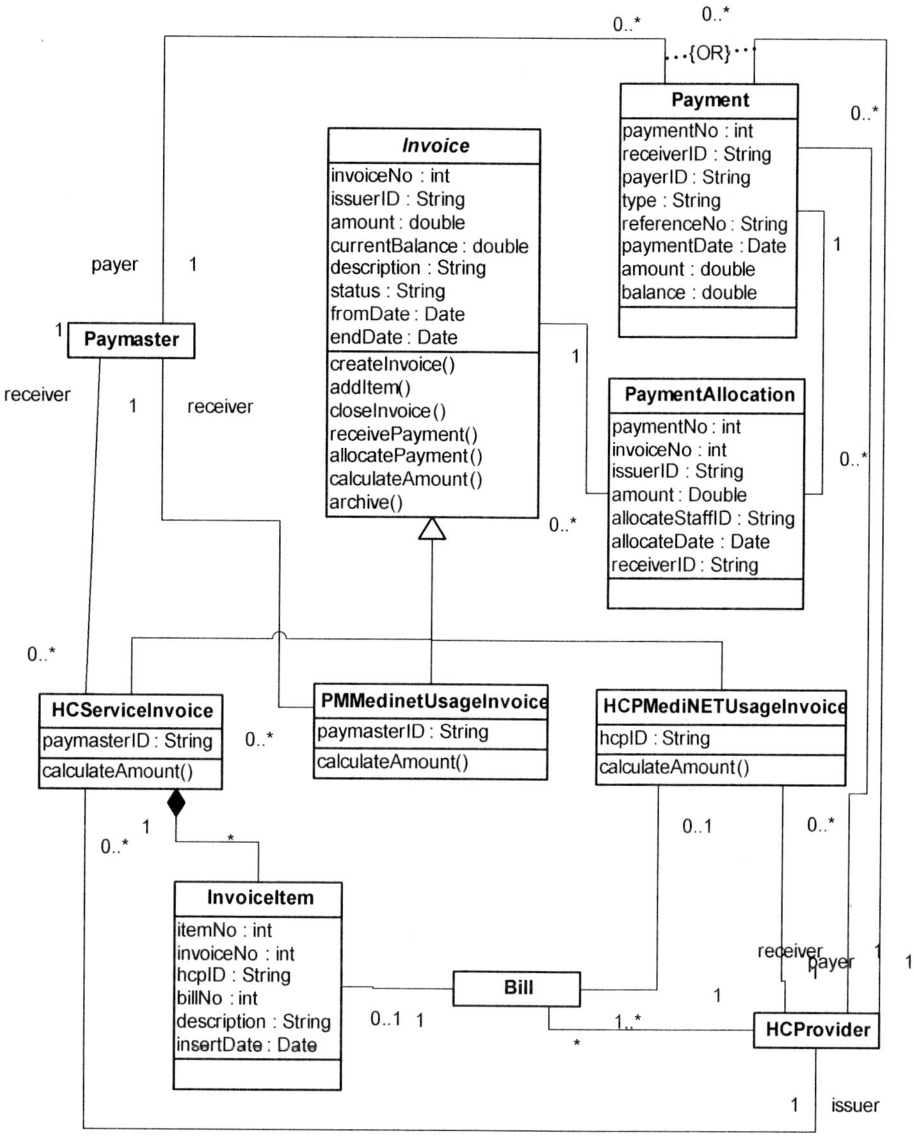

In terms of payment, MediNET allows balance forward invoicing method in addition to open item method.

Within the design process classes are further elaborated in terms of the events and conditions that trigger their transition from one state to another. These are shown as statechart diagrams. For example, a statechart diagram for the `HCServiceInvoice` object is shown in Figure 7.

Within the BROOD design phase, rule phrase specifications are developed. Each rule phrase definition is stored in the repository called rule phrase entries. The possible values for rule phrase may be a set of enumerated values or the values of the linked software design element. A component engineer may define certain attributes for each business rule specification such as rule priority, owner, and business process. Each business rule

Figure 7. The STD `HCServiceInvoice` *object for the MediNet application*

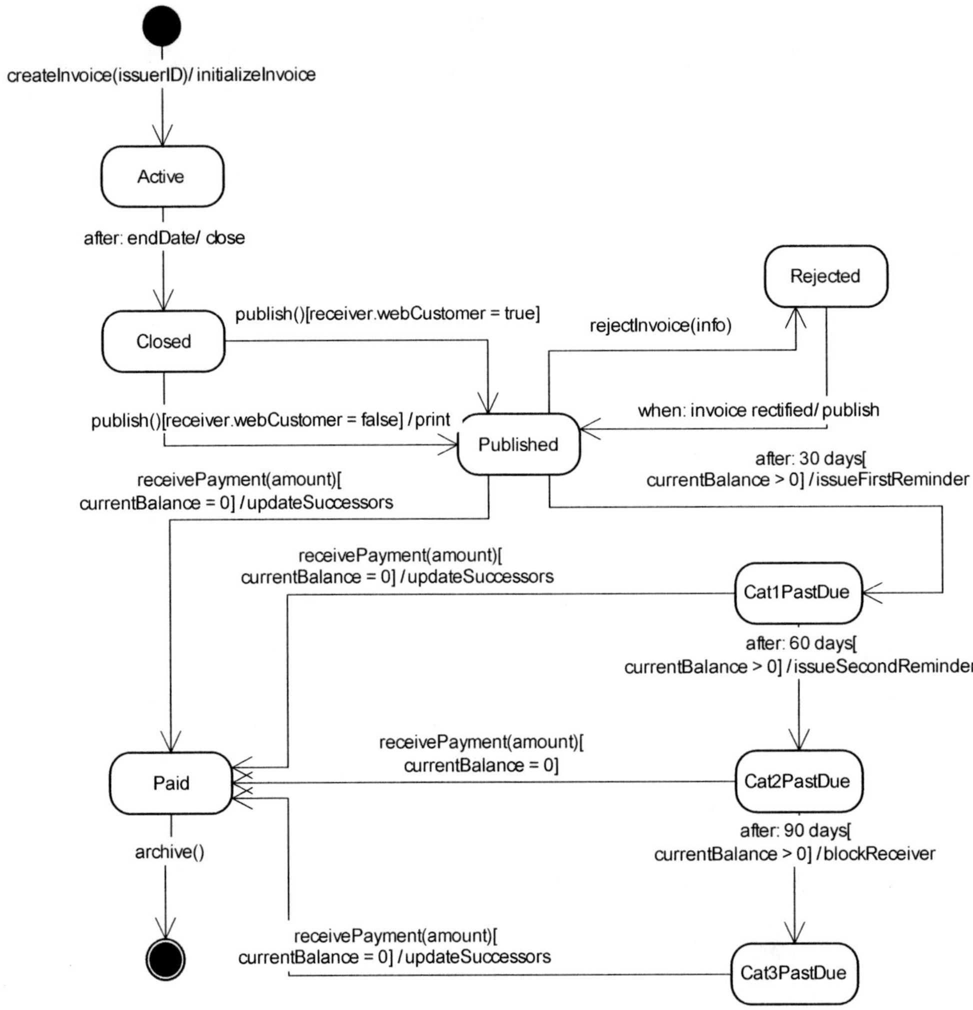

statement can also be arranged in an appropriate rule set to assist the future management of the business rules.

For the MediNet application, the rules shown in Table 5 are specified according to rule phrases syntax as shown in Table 6.

The first rule in Table 6 shows the rule phrase derived from the attribute constraint rule, informally defined in the analysis phase as "A patient must have a unique registration number." The rule phrases '`a patient`' and '`registration number`' are respectively linked to `Patient` class and `patRegNo` attribute. The keywords '`must have`' and '`a unique`' are not statically linked to any design element. Instead, they are used to dynamically toggle the optionality and uniqueness values of `patRegNo` attribute during the creation or modification of the business rule statement. In other words, they are used to enable the automated change propagation to software design.

The second rule in Table 6 shows a relationship constraint., The rule phrases '`clinic item`' and '`bill item`' are respectively linked to `TransItem` class and `Bill _ Item` class. The rule phrases '`one and only one`' and '`clinic item`' play a similar role to keywords as in the attribute constraint rule, that is their purpose is to

Table 6. Rule phrases and linked software design elements for the MediNet application

B Rule Category	Business Rule Phrases	Software Design Elements
Attribute Constraint	<entity> = 'a patient'	Patient (class)
	'must have'	- (patRegNo.optionality)
	'a unique'	- (patRegNo.uniqueness)
	<attributeTerm> = 'registration number'	Patient.patRegNo (attribute)
Relationship Constraint	<cardinality> = 'one and only one'	- (AssociationEnd.multiplicity)
	<entity> = 'transaction item'	TransItem (class)
	<role> = 'item type'	- (AssociationEnd.name)
	<entity> = 'bill item'	Bill_Item (class)
Action Assertion	<event> = '30 day after the creation date of the invoice'	- (Trans1.event.spec)
	<condition> = 'current balance of the invoice is greater than 0'	- (Trans1.guard.body)
	<action> = 'trigger issue the first reminder'	- (Trans1.action.initialiseInvoice().spec)
Computation	<attributeTerm> = 'the amount of HCP MediNET Usage invoice'	HCPMediNETUsageInvoice.amount
	<algorithm> = 'the sum of monthly subscription fee plus transaction fee'	HCPMediNETUsageInvoice. calculateA-mount().specification
Inference	<attributeTerm> = 'a paymaster status'	Paymaster.status
	<value> = 'under probation'	- (literal value)
	<condition> = 'the paymaster has an invoice with category 1 past due' AND 'the current balance is greater than RM 5,000.00'	Paymaster.getStatus().specification

propagate business changes to design elements. The former specifies the multiplicity of an association end whilst the latter specifies the role of an association end.

In the *action assertion* rule "When a payment is not received within 30 days from the invoice date, then the first reminder will be sent," the rule phrases that represent the event, condition, and action are not directly linked to any design element but they are respectively used to generate the specifications of the transition's event, guard, and action in the HCP service usage invoice STD. Since event, condition, and action rule phrases are themselves composed by other rule phrases, they may be indirectly linked to the related design components via these rule phrases.

The *computation* and *inference* rules are linked to the operation specification —the computation rule is linked to the specification of `calculateAmount()` operation in `HCPMediNETUsageInvoice` class and the inference rule is linked to `getStatus()` operation from `Paymaster` class. During the development of an inference rule, a new operation is often needed to be added in its associated class to perform the derivation and return the inferred value.

The Evolution Phase

In general, business rule changes may be classified into simple and complex changes. A simple change is concerned with the modification, addition, or deletion of business rules that do not need to introduce new rule phrases or design elements. A complex change involves the addition or deletion of rule phrases or design elements.

Ordinarily, *simple business rules changes* could be performed by business users. The examples of five change scenarios that require simple business changes in MediNET system are shown in Table 7.

Table 7. Simple change scenarios for the MediNet application

Change Scenarios	Changed Business Rules
1. HCP allows patients to make 'more than one payment for their bills' instead of the previously set 'single payment for each bill'.	One patient bill is associated with zero or more payments.
2. HCP makes small changes on the conditions to issue the reminder and block paymaster.	WHEN *15 days* from the invoice date IF a payment is not received THEN issue the first reminder. WHEN *30 days* from the invoice date IF the payment is not received THEN issue the second reminder. WHEN *45 days* from the invoice date IF the payment is not received THEN block the paymaster.
3. The MediNET supplier offers a more attractive usage charge to HCPs. They are charged based on the number of treated patients regardless the number of patient visits.	The amount of HCP usage invoice IS CALCULATED AS if (opt new package) then the transaction fee multiply by the number of registered patients, else, the transaction fee multiply by the number of treated patients, plus the monthly fee.
4. HCP introduces 5% discount to its internet customer.	If the paymaster is an internet customer, then give 5% discount to their invoices.
5. The HCP decides that each expense item must belong to one of the pre-defined types.	Zero or more expense item is associated with one and only one transaction item.

The implementation of a *complex* business rule change requires more effort than that of simple change. It involves the introduction of new rule phrases or design elements, which is needed to be performed by an individual with the knowledge of software design. In addition to technical skills, it often requires creative skills in making a design decision. Three examples of complex rules changes are shown in Table 8.

The first scenario initiates the modification of two existing business rule statements, the calculation of bill and the calculation of invoice amount. These business rule changes consequently lead to a minor change in software design, that is the introduction of `hasMaxBill` attribute in the `Paymaster` class.

In the second scenario, the paymaster decided to introduce different healthcare benefit coverage to different levels of their payees. For example, executive staff is entitled to any medical treatment and medical procedures whilst production staff is only paid for outpatient treatments. It is obvious that simply implementing this new requirement into the existing `Paymaster` or `PanelPatient` class may increase the complexity of these classes. Therefore, additional classes that are responsible to manage the healthcare benefit coverage are required to be added to the existing software design. The possible candidates for these classes include `BenefitCoverage`, `SelectedClinic`, `MedicalProcedure`, and `Entitlement`.

The third scenario requires the intervention of a software developer. This scenario requires a number of new inference rules to be added to define a loyal, potential, and good paying customer. In addition to these business rules, an action assertion rule that initializes the value of the invoice discount during invoice creation should also be added. The introduction of the new inference rules consequently requires `isLoyal()`, `isPotential()`, and `isGoodPaying()` operations to be added to the `Paymaster` class. Similarly, the newly introduced action assertion rule requires component engineers to modify the action component of the

Table 8. Complex change scenarios for the MediNet application

Change Scenarios	Changed Business Rules

1. HCP introduces new package for paymaster. In this package, the paymaster may limit the maximum amount of each patient bill to RM 20.00, and the excessive cost is absorbed by HCP. However, the paymaster must pay a monthly fee of RM5.00 for each patient.	The amount of a bill is computed as
	let amount = the sum of all amounts of bill items
	if (patient is a panel patient) AND (paymaster has maximum bill amount) AND (amount > RM 20.00)
	amount = 20
	The amount of HCP service invoice is computed as
	let amount = the total of the invoice items
	if (paymaster has maximum bill amount)
	amount = amount + 5 * the number of paymaster's patients

2. Paymaster wishes to provide different healthcare benefit coverage for different groups of its payees.	If (the patient is a panel patient) AND (the patient is an executive staff) then the patient is entitled to any type of treatments and medical procedures. If (the patient is a panel patient) AND (the patient is a production staff) then the patient is entitled for an outpatient treatment.

3. HCP would like to introduce a 5% discount on the invoices to preferred paymasters as a way to express gratitude to the loyal, potential, and good paying paymasters.	If (a paymaster has been a paymaster panel for more than 5 years) then (the customer is a 'loyal' customer).
	If (a paymaster has an average of at least RM24000.00 for the invoices over the last five years) then (the paymaster is considered as a 'potential' customer).
	If (a paymaster never has a past due invoice for the last two years) then (the paymaster is considered as a good paying paymaster).
	When (the invoice in created) if (the paymaster is a loyal, potential and good paying customer) then (set the discount of the invoice to 5%)

transition from the initial state to '`Active`' state in the STD for `HCServiceInvoice` object.

THE BROOD SUPPORT TOOL

The BROOD process introduces several additional activities to the traditional object-oriented software design process. These additional activities include the documentation of business rules and their linking to software design components. To assist a developer with these BROOD-specific activities, a tool has been developed that supports the activities of business rule specification and management, software design editing, and business rule change propagation.

The BROOD tool was developed on top of the generic modeling environment (GME) (Ledeczi et al., 2001; VU, 2003), which is a configurable modeling environment.

The metamodel and templates, which are discussed in section 0, were used to implement the BROOD tool environment.

GME was used to visually edit the software design models, business rule specification, and rule phrase entries. Three main modules (known as interpreters in GME) were developed to simplify the rule phrase management, business rule composition, and business rule modification. These modules also perform the *automated propagation* of business rule changes to the respective software design elements, since a manual undertaking of such propagation would be impractical for most applications.

The BROOD tool has been designed to be used by both software developers and business users. A user-friendly interface is provided to ease the management and traceability of business rules by non-IT users. An overview of the BROOD support tool is shown in Figure 8.

The metamodel, the graphical model editor, the rule phrase management, the business rules composition and the business rules modification functions are part of the core component and user application layer in the BROOD tool architecture.

Figure 8. Overview of the BROOD tool

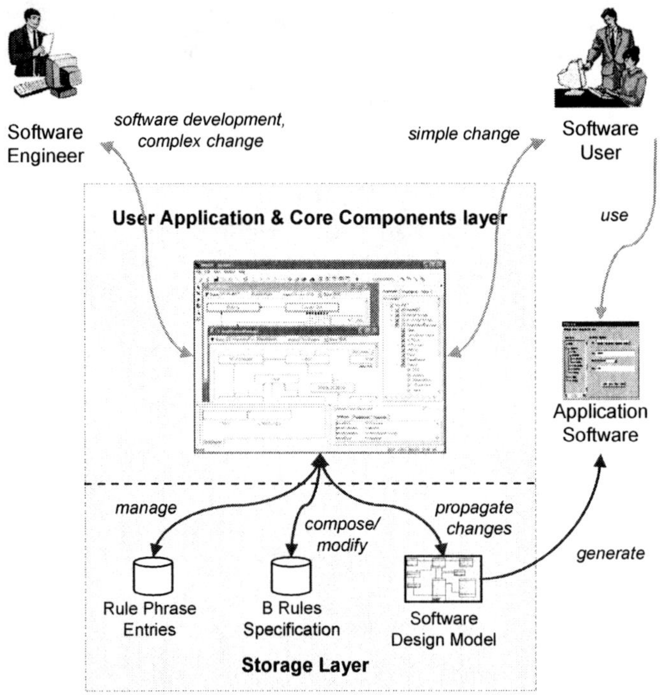

The rule phrase entries, business rule specification, and software design models are stored in the storage layer.

The BROOD tool maintains the consistencies between business rule and the linked software design each time a business rule is created or modified. It provides full automated support in performing simple changes and partial support for complex changes since these require creative skills of software engineers in making a design decision.

There are four main types of model that can be managed using the BROOD tool: rule phrase entries, business rule, class diagram, and statechart diagram. Users may select the type of model to be created from a set of choices. An example of the BROOD model editor is shown in Figure 9. The model editor provides a convenient way to create a model and also to connect it or parts of it to other models.

While graphical model editing is convenient for visual models such as those of class and statechart diagrams, it is less helpful for business rules specification.

The graphical model editor can be used for some simple business rules definition such as cardinality, relational operator, list, and optionality but for more complex rules the BROOD tool offers a dedicated rule editor, the add business rule (ABR) module. This module performs two main tasks: business rule composition and software design updating. In business rule composition mode, rule phrases are used to construct a business rule statement. In software design updating mode the module updates the software design model that corresponds to the composed rule.

The BROOD tool also helps with the implementation of business rule changes. The modify business rule (MBR) module was developed to assist tool users in performing this task, an example of which is shown in Figure 9.

A full description of the tool is beyond the scope of this article. It should be stressed however, that the tool plays an important part in the

Figure 9. Example of the BROOD model editor

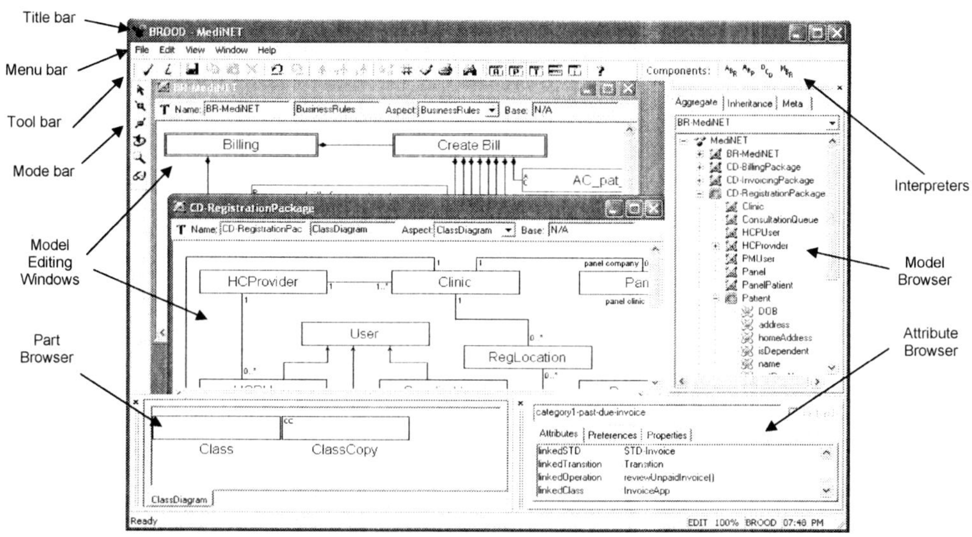

effective application of the BROOD approach by simplifying a sometimes tedious, error-prone, and time-consuming task of linking and propagating business rule changes to software design components.

DISCUSSION

The main aim of BROOD has been to facilitate the process of software evolution through: (a) externalization of business rules and their explicit modeling and (b) the linking of each modeled business rule with a corresponding software component. This approach provides full traceability between end-user concepts and software designs. By combining BROOD to design traceability in source code (Alves-Foss, Conte de Leon, & Oman, 2002), it is possible to achieve effective traceability in a software system.

The BROOD metamodel offers a complete foundation and infrastructure for the development of a software system that is resilient to business rule changes.

With regard to business rule typology, BROOD introduces three main business rule types: constraints, action assertion, and derivations. These types are further divided into an adequate number of sub-types and templates. In contrast to BRG, BROCOM, and BRS approaches, BROOD attempts to remove the redundancy by reducing the unnecessary business rule types. At the same time, it improves the incompleteness of business rule types in AOM, coordination contract, and BRBeans approaches. In terms of business rule management elements, BROOD provides the concept of *ruleset* to organize the groups and hierarchy of the closely related business rules.

In terms of its modeling language, BROOD offers a high level of expressiveness. The keywords in the language definition and a sufficient number of sentence templates should provide adequate representation constructs. In general, achieving total expressiveness of the modeling language business rules is relatively hard to achieve due to the large number of ways of expressing business rules in a natural language. The usability of BROOD in this context will be proved in due course once the approach has been applied on different domains and applications. BROOD was found to have a high level of un-ambiguity by the introduction of the appropriate typology and templates. BROOD provides a mutually exclusive set of business rule types and removes the superfluous templates in order to avoid conflict and redundancy in representing the meaning of business rules.

In practical terms, BROOD can be applied using the UML-based SPEM metamodel, which provides a set of concepts and notations to describe various software process components such as lifecycle phases, activities, process roles, and work products. The use of business rule templates and UML improves the usability of the BROOD approach. The templates allow users to create a business rule statement by simply composing the existing rule phrases whilst UML provides abstractions for users to naturally design a software system. Moreover, the detailed process description is provided to guide users especially in performing complex tasks such linking business rules to software design and handling different types of changes.

The utility of BROOD was demonstrated in this paper through the use of the MediNet industrial application. This application had originally been developed using a standard object-oriented approach. It was therefore possible (and indeed desirable) to use the case study not only as a way of demonstrating BROOD but also for comparing and contrasting BROOD to a traditional development approach.

By considering UML for software design, BROOD maintains the well-known object-oriented design quality attributes such as modularity, high cohesion, low coupling, efficiency, and portability. BROOD however provides additional quality attributes such as *requirements traceability*, *software evolvability*, and *approach usability*.

The traditional approach deployed for MediNet did not provide explicit traceability of business policy defined during the requirements specification phase. Instead, it provides a so-called 'seamless transition' from the use case models that document the user requirements to the analysis and design models. This resulted in business rules being embedded in both requirements specification and software design models. In contrast, with BROOD there was a natural transformation of the MediNET requirements into the structured business rules specification and in turn this specification was directly related to software design components.

Concerning software evolution, the implementation of changes using the traditional approach required the use of expertise with specific knowledge of the MediNET software design. Since software engineers do not normally initiate business changes, they had to repeat all phases in MediNET development lifecycle especially requirements and analysis phases. Locating the related software design components was hard since there was no explicit link between the MediNET design models and its user requirements.

In relation to approach usability, the traditional approach was easier to apply during development since it did not have to deal with additional steps that were added to explicitly specify, document, and link business rules specification to software design. These steps were found to increase the complexity and duration of software development process. However, the availability of the business rule typology and templates, which provide the guidelines for the analysis of business rule statements and the identification of rule phrases, were found useful in minimizing these problems. The business rule templates have improved the MediNET system understandability and increased the involvement of business users in the MediNET development. During evolution, BROOD was found easier to be used than the traditional approach. Using BROOD, business users could perform the simple business rule changes as demonstrated in the MediNET application. Rapid change implementation is important especially in business critical applications with intolerable downtime. The detailed process description facilitated the implementation of complex changes in MediNET.

In summary, BROOD contributes to three critical areas namely business rules specification, object-oriented design, and software evolution process. The proposed business rule specification extends the state-of-the-art approaches to business rule representation by reducing redundancy and avoiding conflict among business rule types in its typology. The structures of rule templates have been defined so as to make them suitable for linking to software designs in support of future software evolution. A specification is aligned to changing user requirements via the linking of business rules to software designs through a detailed transformation of business rule into the specification of related software design components. Thus, the externalization of frequently changing aspects of a system into detailed business rules and the maintenance of associations between these and corresponding software components should provide a strong framework for effective software evolution.

ACKNOWLEDGMENT

The authors would like to thank the human resource department of Universiti Teknologi Malaysia (UTM) for partially sponsoring this research, and Penawar Medical Group, Malaysia for the permission to use its MediNET healthcare information system requirements specification as the case study. The authors wish to also express their gratitude to the three anonymous reviewers and to the editor of the special issue, Professor Dinesh Batra, whose insightful and detailed comments have contributed to the production of a much improved version of this article.

REFERENCES

Alves-Foss, J., Conte de Leon, D., & Oman, P. (2002). *Experiments in the use of xml to enhance traceability between object-oriented design specifications and source code.* Paper presented at the 35th Annual Hawaii International Conference on System Sciences.

Andrade, L., & Fiadeiro, J. (2000, October 15-19). *Evolution by contract.* Paper presented at the ACM Conference on Object-Oriented Programming, Systems, Languages, and Applications 2000, Workshop on Best-practice in Business Rules Design and Implementation, Minneapolis, Minnesota USA.

Andrade, L., Fiadeiro, J., Gouveia, J., & Koutsoukos, G. (2002). Separating computation, coordination and configuration. *Journal of Software Maintenance and Evolution: Research and Practice, 14*(5), 353-359.

Astley, M., & Agha, G. A. (1998, 20-21 April). *Modular construction and composition of distributed software architectures.* Paper presented at the Int. Symposium on Software Engineering, for Parallel and Distributed Systems, Kyoto, Japan.

Eriksson, H.-E., & Penker, M. (2000). *Business modelling with uml*: OMG Group, Wiley Computer Publishing, John Wiley & Sons, Inc.

Erlikh, L. (2000). Leveraging legacy system dollars for e-business. *IEEE IT Professional, 2*(3), 17 - 23.

Evans, H., & Dickman, P. (1999, October). *Zones, contracts and absorbing change: An approach to software evolution.* Paper presented at the Conference on Object-Oriented Programming, Systems, Languages and Applications (OOPSLA '99), Denver, Colorado, USA.

Gottesdiener, E. (1997). Business rules show power, promise. *Application Development Trends, 4*(3, March 1997).

Grubb, P., & Takang, A. A. (2003). *Software maintenance: Concepts and practice*. Singapore: World Scientific Publishing.

Halle, B. V. (1994). Back to business rule basics. *Database Programming and Design*(October 1994), 15-18.

Hay, D., & Healy, K. A. (1997). *Business rules: What are they really?* GUIDE (The IBM User Group). Retrieved from http://www.BusinessRules-Group.org/):.

Hay, D., & Healy, K. A. (2000). *Defining business rules ~ what are they really?* (No. Rev 1.3): the Business Rules Group.

Herbst, H. (1996a). *Business rule oriented conceptual modelling*. Verlag: Physica .

Herbst, H. (1996b). Business rules in system analysis: A meta-model and repository system. *Information Systems, 21*(2), 147-166.

Herbst, H. (1997). *Business rule-oriented conceptual modeling*. Germany: Physica-Verlag.

IBM (Cartographer). (2003). *Ibm websphere application server enterprise*

Kovari, P., Diaz, D. C., Fernandes, F. C. H., Hassan, D., Kawamura, K., Leigh, D., et al. (2003). *Websphere application server enterprise v5 and programming model extensions: Websphere handbook series* (First Edition ed.): International Business Machines Corporation.

Krammer, M. I. (1997). Business rules: Automating business policies and practicies. *Distributed Computing Monitor*(May 1997).

Ledeczi, A., Maroti, M., Bakay, A., Karsai, G., Garrett, J., Thomason, C., et al. (2001, 17 May). *The generic modeling environment.* Paper presented at the Workshop on Intelligent Signal Processing, Budapest, Hungary.

Lehman, M. M., & Belady, L. A. (1985). *Program evolution: Processes of software change*. London: Academic Press, Inc.

Loucopoulos, P., & Layzell, P. J. (1986, 1987). *Rubric: A rule based approach for the development of information systems.* Paper presented at the 1st European workshop on fault diagnosis, reliability and related knowledge based approaches, Rhodes.

Martin, J. (1989). *Information engineering*: Prentice-Hall.

McMenamin, S. M., & Palmer, J. F. (1984). *Essential systems analysis.* Englewood Cliffs, NJ: Yourdon Press.

Mens, K., Wuyts, R., Bontridder, D., & Grijseels, A. (1998). *Tools and environments for business rules.* Paper presented at the ECOOP'98, Brussels, Belgium.

Moriaty, T. (1993). The next paradigm. *Database Programming and Design.*

OMG (Cartographer). (2001). *Omg unified modeling language specification*

OMG (Cartographer). (2002). *Software process engineering metamodel specification*

Oreizy, P., Medvidovic, N., & Taylor, R. N. (1998, April 19-25). *Architecture-based runtime software evolution.* Paper presented at the International Conference on Software Engineering 1998 (ICSE'98), Kyoto, Japan.

Riehle, D., Tilman, M., & Johnson, R. (2000). *Dynamic object model* (No. WUCS-00-29): Dept. of Computer Science, Washington University.

Robinson, K., & Berrisford, G. (1994). *Object-oriented ssadm.* Englewood Cliffs, NJ: Prentice Hall.

Rosca, D., Greenspan, S., Feblowitz, M., & Wild, C. (1997, January 1997). *A decision support methodology in support of the business rules lifecycle.* Paper presented at the International Symposium on Requirements Engineering (ISRE'97), Annapolis, MD.

Rosca, D., Greenspan, S., & Wild, C. (2002). Enterprise modeling and decision-support for automating the business rules lifecycle. *Automated Software Engineering, 9*(4), 361 - 404.

Rosca, D., Greenspan, S., Wild, C., Reubenstein, H., Maly, K., & Feblowitz, M. (1995, November 1995). *Application of a decision support mechanism to the business rules lifecycle.* Paper presented at the 10th Knowledge-Based Software Engineering Conference (KBSE95), Boston, MA.

Ross, R. G. (1997). *The business rule book: Classifying, defining and modelling rules*: Data Base Newsletter.

Ross, R. G., & Lam, G. S. W. (1999). *Ruletrack: The brs meta-model for rule management*: Business Rule Solutions, Inc.

Ross, R. G., & Lam, G. S. W. (2003). *The brs proteus(tm) methodology* (Fourth ed.): Business Rule Solutions.

Rouvellou, I., Degenaro, I., Rasmus, K., Ehnebuske, D., & McKee, B. (1999, November 1-5). *Externalizing business rules from enterprise applications: An experience report.* Paper presented at the Conference on Object-Oriented Programming, Systems, Languages, and Applications, Denver, Colorado.

Rouvellou, I., Degenaro, L., Rasmus, K., Ehnebuske, D., & McKee, B. (2000, June). *Extending business objects with business rules.* Paper presented at the 33rd International Conference on Technology of Object-Oriented Languages and Systems (TOOLS Europe 2000), Mont Saint-Michel/ St-Malo, France.

Schneider, J. (1999). *Components, scripts, and glue : A conceptual framework for software composition.* Bern:University of Bern.

van Assche, F., Layzell, P. J., Loucopoulos, P., & Speltinex, G. (1988). *Rubric: A rule-based representation of information system constructs.* Paper presented at the ESPRIT Conference, Brussels, Belgium.

VU (Cartographer). (2003). *Gme 3 user's manual*

Wan Kadir, W. M. N., & Loucopoulos, P. (2003, 23-26 June). *Relating evolving business rules to software design.* Paper presented at the International Conference on Software Engineering Research and Practice (SERP), Las Vegas, Nevada, USA.

Wan Kadir, W. M. N., & Loucopoulos, P. (2004). Relating evolving business rules to software design. *Journal of Systems Architecture, 50*(7), 367-382.

Yoder, J. W., Balaguer, F., & Johnson, R. (2001, October 14-18). *Adaptive object models for implementing business rules.* Paper presented at the Third Workshop on Best-Practices for Business Rules Design and Implementation, Conference on Object-Oriented Programming, Systems, Languages, and Applications (OOPSLA 2001), Tampa Bay, Florida, USA.

Zaniolo, C., Ceri, S., Faloutsos, C., Snodgrass, R., Subrahmanian, V. S., & Zicari, R. (1997). *Advanced database systems*: Morgan Kaufmann.

APPENDIX A. SPECIFICATION OF BROOD

Part I: The BROOD Metamodel

Business Rule Organisation and Typology

business_rule_model = rule_set, owner;

rule_set = (rule_set | rule_statement), {rule_set | rule_statement}, [owner], [business_process];

business_rule = (constraint | action_assertion | derivation), name, [is_mandatory], [priority], [is_propagatable];

Contraint

constraint = att_constraint | rel_constraint;

Attribute Constraint

att_constraint = entity, ('must have' | 'may have'), ['a unique'], att_term
| att_term, ('must be' | 'may be'), relational_op, (value | att_term)
| att_term, 'must be in', list;

att_term = attribute, 'of', entity;

Relationship Constraint

rel_constraint = ([cardinality], entity, 'is a/an', role, 'of', [cardinality], entity
| [cardinality], entity, 'is associated with', [cardinality], entity
| entity, ('must have' | 'may have'), [cardinality], entity
| entity, 'is a/an' entity),
{Association};

Action Assertion

action_assertion = 'WHEN', event, ['IF', condition], 'THEN', action, {StatechartDiagram, Transition};

Event

event = simple_event | complex_event;

simple_event = (change_event | time_event | user_event), {Class, Operation};

change_event = att_term ('is updated' |) |
entity ('is deleted' | 'is created')
(operation | business_rule), 'is triggered';

time_event = date_time |
n, time_unit, 'time interval from', date_time , 'is reached' |
number, time_unit, 'after', date_time;

user_event = string;

complex_event = simple_event, {('Or' | 'And'), simple_event {('Or' | 'And'), simple_event}

Condition

condition = simple_condition | complex_condition;

simple_condition = ['Not'], attribute_term, relational_op, (value | attribute_term) | attribute_term, ('in' | 'not in'), list;

complex_condition = simple_condition, ('Or' | 'And'), simple_condition, {('Or' | 'And'), simple_condition};

Action

action= simple_action | action_sequence;

simple_action = trigger_action | object_ manipulation_action | user_action,

{Class, Operation};
trigger_action = 'trigger', (process | operation | business_rule);
object_manipulation_action = 'set', att_term, 'to', value |
('create' | 'delete'), object;
action_sequence = simple_action, {simple_action};

Derivation

derivation = computation | inference;
Computation
computation = attribute_term, 'is computed as', algorithm, {Class, Operation};
algorithm = string;
(* i.e. any specification language for specifying the algorithm e.g., OCL, pseudo-code, etc. *)
Inference
inference = 'If', condition, 'then', fact;
fact = (attribute_term | entity), relational_op, ['a'], value) |
entity, ('may' | 'may not'), action, {Class, Operation};

Rule Phrases / Linking Elements / Low-Level Definitions
(* Some low level non-terminal symbol such as <real>, <integer> and <string> are not defined. **** *)
entity = phrase, Class;
attribute = phrase, Class, Attribute;
operation = phrase, {Class, Operation};
cardinality = phrase, maxCard, minCard;
eventPhrase = phrase, event, {Class, Operation};
actionPhrase = phrase, action, {Class, Operation};
role = string;
list = string,{string};
phrase = string;
value = string | integer | real | date | time;
number = real | integer;
time_unit = 'second' | 'minute' | 'hour' | 'day' | 'month' | 'year';
relational_op = 'equal' | 'not equal' | 'less than' | 'less than or equal' | 'greater than' | 'greater than or equal';
name = string;
priority = 'high' | 'medium' | 'low';
is_mandatory = boolean;
is_propagatable = boolean;
boolean = 'true' or 'false';

Part II: The BROOD Process

The following specification is based on OMG Software Process Engineering Metamodel.

Process: **Business Rule-based Object-Oriented Design (BROOD)**

Phase: **Analysis**

Activity: **Analyze Business Rule Statements**
ProcessRole: **Functional Analyst**
ActivityParameters {kind: input}
WorkProduct: **Use-Case Model** {state: **revised**}
WorkProduct: **Business Rule Statements** {state: **revised**}
ActivityParameters {kind: output}
WorkProduct: **Business Rule Specification** {state: **initial draft**}
Steps
Step: **Identify business rule type**
Step: **Rewrite business rules according to sentence templates**
Step: **Resolve rule conflicts and redundancy**

Activity: **Architectural Analysis**
ProcessRole: **Software Architect**
ActivityParameters {kind: input}
WorkProduct: **Use-Case Model** {state: **revised**}
WorkProduct: **Business Model** {state: **completed**}
WorkProduct: **Architecture Description** {state: **initial draft**}
WorkProduct: **Supplementary Requirements** {state: **revised**}
ActivityParameters {kind: output}
WorkProduct: **Analysis Class Diagram** {state: **outline**}
WorkProduct: **Analysis Package** {state: **outline**}
WorkProduct: **Architecture Description** {state: **revised draft**}
Steps
Step: **Identify analysis packages**
Step: **Identify analysis classes**
Step: **Describe analysis object interactions**

Activity: **Analyze a Class**
ProcessRole: **Component Engineer**
ActivityParameters {kind: input}
WorkProduct: **Analysis Class Diagram** {state: **outlined**}
ActivityParameters {kind: output}
WorkProduct: **Analysis Class Diagram** {state: **completed**}
Steps
Step: **Identify class responsibilities**
Step: **Identify class attributes**
Step: **Identify class relationships**

Activity: **Analyze a Package**
ProcessRole: **Component Engineer**
ActivityParameters {kind: input}
WorkProduct: **Analysis Package** {state: **outlined**}
WorkProduct: **Architecture Description** {state: **revised draft**}

ActivityParameters {kind: output}
WorkProduct: **Analysis Package** {state: **completed**}
Steps
Step: **Analyze the cohesiveness of each package**
Step: **Analyze the dependencies between packages**
Phase: **Design**
Activity: **Architectural Design**
ProcessRole: **Software Architect**
ActivityParameters {kind: input}
WorkProduct: **Use-Case Model** {state: **revised**}
WorkProduct: **Analysis Model** {state: **completed**}
WorkProduct: **Architecture Description** {state: **revised draft**}
WorkProduct: **Supplementary Requirements** {state: **revised**}
ActivityParameters {kind: output}
WorkProduct: **Design Class Diagram** {state: **outline**}
WorkProduct: **Design Package** {state: **outline**}
WorkProduct: **Architecture Description** {state: **revised**}
Steps
Step: **Identify subsystems and their interfaces**
Step: **Identify architectural significant classes**
Step: **Identify generic design mechanisms**

Activity: **Design a Class**
ProcessRole: **Component Engineer**
ActivityParameters {kind: input}
WorkProduct: **Design Class Diagram** {state: **outlined**}
ActivityParameters {kind: output}
WorkProduct: **Design Class Diagram** {state: **completed**}
WorkProduct: **Design Statechart Diagram** {state: **completed**}
Steps
Step: **Identify operations**
Step: **Identify attributes**
Step: **Identify relationships**
Step: **Describe method**
Step: **Describe state**
Step: **Link Statechart diagram element to class diagram**

Activity: **Design a Sub-System**
ProcessRole: **Component Engineer**
ActivityParameters {kind: input}
WorkProduct: **Sub-System** {state: **outlined**}
WorkProduct: **Architecture Description** {state: **revised**}
ActivityParameters {kind: output}
WorkProduct: **Sub-System** {state: **completed**}

Steps

Step: **Design sub-system dependencies**

Step: **Design sub-system interfaces**

Activity: **Develop Business Rule Specifications**

ProcessRole: **Component Engineer**

ActivityParameters {kind: input}

WorkProduct: **Business Rule Specifications** {state: **initial draft**}

ActivityParameters {kind: output}

WorkProduct: **Business Rule Specifications** {state: **revised draft**}

Steps

Step: **Define rule phrases**

Step: **Link rule phrase to design elements**

Step: **Form structured rule statements**

Step: **Populate rule attributes**

Step: **Organize rule set**

Activity: **Validate Business Rule Specifications**

ProcessRole: **Functional Analyst / Business User**

ActivityParameters {kind: input}

WorkProduct: **Business Rule Specifications** {state: **revised draft**}

ActivityParameters {kind: output}

WorkProduct: **Business Rule Specifications** {state: **completed**}

Steps

Step: **Ensure correctness of business rule specifications**

Step: **Ensure understandability of business rule specifications**

Phase: **Evolution**

Activity: **Examine Business Rule Change Request**

ProcessRole: **Business User / Functional Analyst**

ActivityParameters {kind: input}

WorkProduct: **Business Rule Change Request** {state: **initial**}

WorkProduct: **Business Rule Specifications** {state: **completed}**

ActivityParameters {kind: output}

WorkProduct: **Business Rule Change Request** {state: **revised**}

Steps

Step: **Determine the type of business rule change**

Step: **Revise business rule change request (for complex change)**

Activity: **Perform Business Rule Modification Change**

ProcessRole: **Business User / Functional Analyst**

ActivityParameters {kind: input}

WorkProduct: **Design Model** {state: **completed}**

ActivityParameters {kind: output}

WorkProduct: **Design Model** {state: **changed}**
Steps
Step: **Locate the relevant business rule specification**
Step: **Perform change on business rule specification**
Step: **Propagate change to software design**

Activity: **Analyze Business Rule Change Request**
ProcessRole: **Software Architect**
ActivityParameters {kind: input}
WorkProduct: **Business Rule Change Request** {state: **revised**}
WorkProduct: **Design Model** {state: **completed}**
ActivityParameters {kind: output}
WorkProduct: **Business Rule Change Plan** {}
Steps
Step: **Identify the effect of changes**
Step: **Produce the detailed change plan**

Activity: **Implement Business Rule Change**
ProcessRole: **Component Engineer**
ActivityParameters {kind: input}
WorkProduct: **Business Rule Change Plan** {}
ActivityParameters {kind: output}
WorkProduct: **Design Model** {state: **changed**}
Steps
Step: **Review the change plan**
Step: **Perform the changes**

APPENDIX B. THE MEDINET APPLICATION

MediNET is a suite of internet applications that addresses the administrative and back-end processing requirements of the healthcare business community. It acts as a secondary layer to the existing administrative and information systems. MediNET allows various components of the healthcare industry to exchange business data instantaneously and automate their routine administrative tasks. Therefore, facilitated businesses are able to reduce their administrative burdens, become more efficient and make better informed business decisions. In contrast to the traditional applications, MediNET does not require its users to maintain separately installed software. It allows its users to leverage the power of technology without having to bear massive development, acquisition, infrastructure or maintenance costs.

MediNET users only need to pay as and when they use the application. In general, MediNET users can be divided into three categories: paymasters, healthcare providers (HCPs), and supplier. Paymasters are those who pay for medical or healthcare services, for examples employers, insurers and managed care organizations. They use MediNET to maintain the basic parts of the patient records such as performing their payee registration and defining the healthcare benefit coverage of their payees. HCPs are the professionals who dispense medical treatment, for examples general practitioners (GPs), hospitals and dentists. HCPs use MediNET to manage patient records, patient billing and paymaster invoicing.

The current implementation of MediNET is only limited to employers as the paymasters and GPs as the HCPs. The supplier is the company who owns, provides and maintains the MediNET application. It rents MediNET to HCPs and paymasters as and when the applications are needed and charges them based on the number of performed transactions.

MediNET was chosen as a case study due to the various frequently changing business rules introduced by its different users. For example, HCPs provide different packages to the paymasters that constrain the way they perform the patient billing and paymasters invoicing. Paymasters may also want to introduce different healthcare benefit coverage to different staff levels that control the eligibility of the staff's treatments. The business rules related to the packages and benefit coverage are frequently changed by the HCPs and paymasters. Other common changes to business rules include the introduction of invoice discounts, the rule to block non-paying paymasters, and the conditions to issue reminder for past due invoices. These frequent changes indicate the need for an approach to simplify the implementation of changes in MediNET software system.

This work was previously published in Journal of Database Management, Vol. 19, Issue 1, edited by K. Siau, pp. 41-73, copyright 2008 by IGI Publishing, formerly known as Idea Group Publishing (an imprint of IGI Global).

Chapter VIII
Best Practice in Company Standardization

Henk J. de Vries
Erasmus University, Rotterdam, The Netherlands

Florens J.C. Slob
Van Gansewinkel Zuid-Holland, Vlaardingen, The Netherlands

ABSTRACT

This article describes a best practice model for standardization within companies, based on a process approach to the development of company standards. Per process, a best practice is developed based on an investigation within six multinational companies and a review of literature, if any. The findings are benchmarked against experiences in three comparable fields: IT management, quality management, and knowledge management. Though the number of company standards exceeds by far the number of external standards, they have been neglected in standardization research. The authors hope that standards practitioners will benefit from their study and that it will stimulate researchers to pay more attention to this topic.

INTRODUCTION

By the end of 2003, the People's Republic of China had 20,226 national standards (including adopted international standards), more than 32,000 professional standards, more than 11,000 local standards, and more than 860,000 company standards (When, 2004). Most other countries do not have a central registration of company standards, but it can also be expected in other parts of the world, the number of company standards outweighs to a large extent the number of other standards. This huge difference is not reflected in the amount of attention to company standards in scientific literature. Main exceptions are some German books in the series DIN Normungskunde (Adolphi, 1997; Hesser & Inklaar, 1997; Schacht, 1991; Susanto, 1988). Professional publications on company standardization include AFNOR (1967), Bouma and Winter (1982), British Standards Society (1995), Nakamura (1993), Ollner (1974), Simons and de Vries (2002), Toth (1990), Verity Consulting (1995), Wenström, Ollner, and Wenström (2000), and Winter (1990). Publications on IT standardization that touch the topic of company standardization include Cargill (1997) and Rada and Craparo (2001). In this article, we will contribute to a better understanding of company standardization by investigating how company standards are developed in company practice and in developing a best practice for this.

A company standard is the result of the standardization by a company or other organization for its own needs (Düsterbeck et al., 1995). Company standardization includes developing standards for use within the company and developing standards to be used in the company's relations with its direct business partners (de Vries, 1999). Developing does not mean that each company standard has to be designed from scratch. A company standard may have the form of the following (de Vries, 1999):

- A reference to one or more external standards officially adopted by the company
- A company modification of an external standard
- A subset of an external standard (i.e., a description of the company's choice of competing possibilities offered in an external standard, or a subset of the topics covered in the external standard)
- A standard reproduced from (parts of) other external documents (i.e., suppliers' documents)
- A self-written standard

Companies may prefer external standards from IEEE, for example, but these do not meet all their needs, and therefore, they complement these with all forms of company standards just mentioned. In most companies, the number of company standards exceeds the number of external standards.

This research project stems from a wish of five big Dutch companies to try to improve their own company standardization performance by learning from each other. At a later stage, a sixth one joined the group. The research project aimed at developing a best practice for company standardization. This best practice should be established by comparing the standardization activities of the six companies and, subsequently, by choosing the best way to perform them.

RESEARCH DESIGN

In order to be able to compare the companies, a common model was needed. The model should describe the processes needed for developing and implementing a company standard. For determining *best*, the expected contribution of standards to business results was chosen as a starting point. For *best practice* of a process, its expected suitability for contributing to a successful company standard was the criterion. In order to assess this, findings in company practice were completed by insights from (standardization) literature, as far as relevant. Although the majority of standards are company standards, scientific standardization literature pays little attention to them.

Steps to Company Standardization Success

As we want to determine best practice, we need to define success; when is it possible to say that company standardization has been successful? Because there is not much literature about the subject of (company) standardization, we had to look mainly at the practical situation within the six companies. The definition of success resulted from the interviews carried out within the companies and from discussions with people who work with or who are professionally engaged with standardization. These findings were completed with insights from literature.

In line with ISO 9001 (ISO, 2000b), we can define success as user satisfaction. We will use the term *direct user* for people that read the standard. Other users use products, services, systems, and so forth, in which the standard has been implemented. Because of the diversity of standards and user categories, it is difficult to measure this satisfaction and, subsequently, to relate it to best practices in the way of preparing the standards. The success of company standardization results from the processes that constitute it (see Figure 1). Therefore, we relate success to these processes. We can distinguish three steps.

Figure 1. Company standardization model

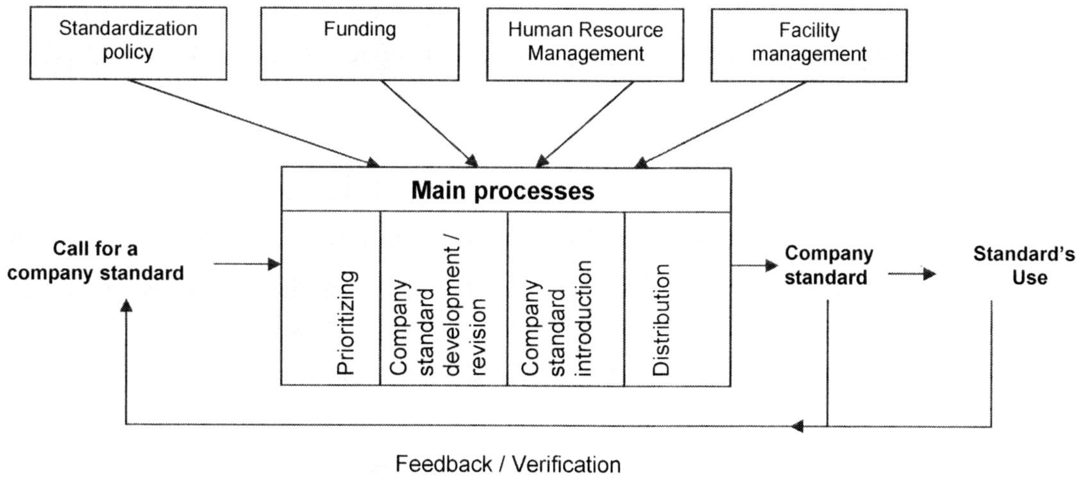

Step 1: The Standard Should Be There.

The demand for a (company) standard starts either within the organization or arises from external obligations (e.g., legislation). Then, this demand should be assessed, and it should be decided whether or not to develop the standard. Such a decision should be based on standardization policy, and the possible development of the proposed standard should be balanced against other requests for standards development: prioritizing.

The development of the standards is the next process, which consists of the composition of a draft version of the standard and commentary rounds, the writing of the final version of the standard, and the approval of this standard. The output is an approved company standard (or normative document). To develop the standard, there is a need of competent personnel (Human Resource Management); the standard has to be paid for (funding process); and IT tools should be in place to support standards development (facility management).

Step 2: The Standard Is Known and Available.

When a standard has been developed (and accorded for), the next step toward success is the standards becoming available to the intended users and they are aware of its existence. This is a second prerequisite for success.

During this introduction process, the potential direct users should become informed about the standard's existence and its potential fitness for use (Juran, 1988). The benefits of the standard and the reasons for certain choices in the standard can be explained. The more and better the standard is known, the higher the chance they will actually use it and do so in the way intended by the standard's developers. In our model, the output of a process forms the input of the following process. However, practice can be less rigid. For instance, it can be important to start with the introduction (promotion) of the standard already during its development. Also, after the introduction period, the promotion of the standard can continue.

For the standard's availability to the direct users (physically), a distribution process should be in place. This process should ensure that the standards reach the direct user in a fast and easy way. This can be done, for instance, by subscription, ordering on demand, or publishing on demand using an intranet. An extra success factor is that the direct user always works with the right version of the standard. After a period of time, the standard may be revised, so the distribution process has to be defined in such a way so as to make sure that the right version of the standard always is being used.

Step 3: The Standard Is Used.

Company standardization only can be a success when the standard is used in practice (in the right way). A standard that is of a high quality but is not used in practice has no value; there has to be a market for the standard. So, the potential direct users must be willing to use the standard and be capable of understanding and using it. We even can define the success one step further when we look at our standardization definition. The product of the company standardization—the company standard—has to solve the matching problem. The standard has to be the answer to the demand out of the organization, which was the starting point of the process.

Evaluation of the standard's use may form the basis for withdrawing, maintaining, or changing the standard. The developed standard should be an answer to the question for which it was produced: Are the (potential) users of the standard satisfied? Therefore, user feedback to those who have decided to make the standard as well as to the people who have developed it is essential. The picture shows one feedback loop, but this is a simplification; more might be drawn because the (quality) management of each process needs a form of feedback, as in the Deming circle—plan, do, check, act. A process approach that uses feedback and aims at enhancing customer satisfaction by meeting needs is characteristic of the ISO 9000:2000 quality management approach (ISO, 2000a, 2000b).

Measuring Company Standardization Success

In the research project, it appeared to be difficult to measure the success, mainly because of difficulty in measuring the real usage of a standard and its impact on business performance. Therefore, we have chosen an indirect way to assess best practice, taking the example of Chiesa et al. (1996), who have developed a technical innovation audit. They divide the innovation process into subprocesses (main processes and facilitating processes), and for every subprocess, they define characteristics that are associated with success or failure of the subprocess and the overall innovation process. All these characteristics are put in a statement on a scorecard. The answer on the statement can be put in a scale (e.g., from 1-5, from not applicable at all to completely applicable). Innovation and company standardization have a lot in common. Innovation is concerned with the development of a new product or process, or the improvement of an existing product or process. The innovation process can only be really successful when there is a market for this product or process. In company standardization, a standard is developed or revised. This also can only be called a success when there is a market for the standard. As the success of the company standardization process depends on the use of the standards, we have tried to find factors that positively influence the use of the standards. The factors can be related to the elements of our model. By defining these factors, the companies can be compared to each other. The companies can be scored per factor with a score on a pre-defined scale. This appeared to be an applicable method for the best practice study.

The scorecard method is also very useful to compare the different practices and to develop a best practice. For every process of the model in Figure 1, we, therefore, have developed scorecards with propositions that define a (supposed) best-practice situation—best in the sense of the expected contribution of the process to the overall success of company standardization. The statements have been developed on the basis of discussions with specialists from both the practical area (the users and developers of company standards) and the professional area (university staff and experts from the national standards body). Company standardization literature has played a minor role, as, in general, it does not provide in-depth best-practice data. Each proposition could be answered on a scale from 1 (not applicable at all) to 5 (completely applicable). The score of 5 is considered to be best practice.

For every company, the scorecards were filled in both by the companies and the researchers (objective party). The scores have been put together with the scores of the other companies, and a mean-score has been determined. These figures have been presented in tables, the most interesting ones also in graphs. This has been done per process. For every process, the order of companies was different so the companies could not recognize which score belonged to which company. By comparing their own scores with the best practice and with the other companies, it was possible for the cooperating parties to distinguish gaps between their practice and best practice, think about reasons for this, and decide on focus and improvement points for their future policies on company standardization.

Moreover, besides an overall research-report for all companies, a small report per company was made with a description of their actual company standardization and the focus points for them to work toward best practice. This has been supported by a presentation within the company for a group of people involved in the different processes of standardization. In this session, there was also the possibility to discuss the best-practice situation in relation to the possibilities of the company. Of course, best practice can have a different follow-up in each company. Besides the report, these individual sessions were seen as a helpful method to analyze the status of the current situation on company standardization and to identify focus points for its future optimization. In this discussion, the presented model for company standardization appeared to be very helpful in order to make the discussion more clear and structured.

To elucidate the scorecards method, we will give an example—a graph of three different criteria out of the scorecard for the company standard development process.

These propositions describe the importance of involving the (potential) users of a standard in the development process. This is to make sure that the standard is user-friendly, that it can be used in practice (and not only in a theoretical situation), and that it really helps the user. In addition, the standard must be a solution for the initial demand out of the organization.

The scores of the six companies on these three propositions are visualized in a graph (Figure 2). The picture shows seven pairs of bars. The first six represent the scores of the six companies, the seventh the mean scores on these criteria. Now the companies can compare their scores with those of the other companies, the mean scores, and the best practices. When most of the companies score low at a certain proposition, it is a point of attention for the companies on which they can do better, or it might be a weak point in the best practice.

Table 1. Score card method example—three criteria for the company standard development process

Nr.	Description	Score
1.	The party that demands for a new or revised company standard is involved in the development process of the standard.	
2.	During the development process of the standard the potential users of the standard are involved.	
3.	It is possible for contractors or suppliers to give input for a company standard.	

Figure 2. Scorecard graph example—Three criteria for the company standard development process

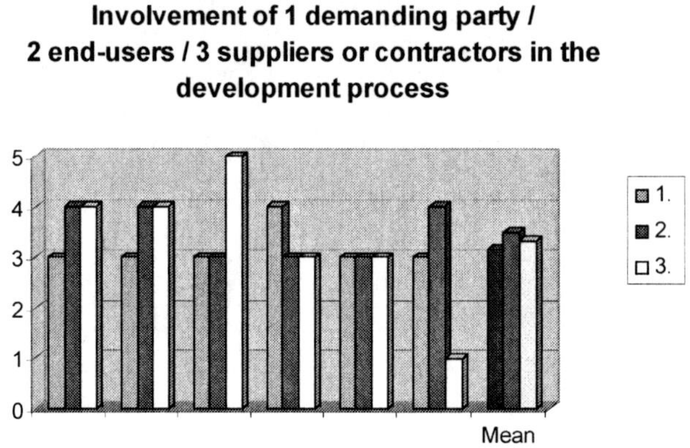

BEST-PRACTICE EXAMPLES

The result of the research study is a best practice model. The best practice can be divided in best practices for each process. Every company has its own specific needs, culture, and ways of doing things. So, the best practices have to be adapted to the specific situation of a company, and, therefore, a company best practice can differ from company to company. The model presented here was deducted partly from literature, but the bigger part was based on real practices.

Steering Group

Standardization work always can be postponed for a day; direct productive labor always comes first. But postponing may lead to doing nothing at all. Without a clear standardization policy and an organization structure to fulfill this policy, standardization is not effective. Having a company standardization steering group is an important part of best practice. A few of the investigated companies have such a group. The steering group develops the policy, and the board of directors approves this policy. The steering group consists preferably of (technical) managers from the several departments or business units. The standardization activities have to be linked to the interests of these business units/departments. The line management has to commit itself to the year's plan drawn up by the steering group.

The standardization department acts as the steering group's secretary and brings in standardization skills. The standardization department coordinates and supports the standardization activities; the business unit managers can be addressed for providing their technical experts (with their skills). The standardization policy has to be a deduction of the general company policy. To support this, a steering group membership of a general (technical) director can be very helpful.

Adolphi (1997) is the main scientific study on the organization of company standardization. Neither he nor other scientific literature mentions the idea of a steering group. Some professional studies do (De Gelder, 1989; Simons & de Vries, 2002). The British Standards Society (1995) mentions a standards committee but does not talk about a real steering responsibility. ANSI's best practice research (Verity Consulting, 1995) apparently did not find steering groups in the multinational companies they investigated.

Adolphi (1997) pays a lot of attention to the role of a central standardization department. Other sources do this as well, whereas the British Standards Society (1995) only mentions a standards specialist, whereas in an earlier edition of this publication (British Standards Institution, 1970), they mentioned a standards department.

Indeed, it can be observed that the number of companies that operate a special (staff) department on standards has diminished, despite all its advantages. This is reflected in the diminishing number of members of national standards users' organizations in most countries. Companies that have maintained a standardization department have reduced their size. Philips, for instance, has a Corporate Standardization Department consisting of about 20 employees, whereas 20 years ago, the department employed 150 people. However, big and medium-sized companies will need one or more full-time or part-time standards specialists somewhere in the organization.

User Participation

Crucial in the development of standards is the way the actual users of the standards participate in this process. The investigated companies recognize the importance of user participation but often still give it too little attention. From both literature (particularly, Nakamura [1993]) and practice, it is known that involving the users in the (company) standards development process has a positive influence on their actual usage. User involvement makes standards more acceptable and applicable, and for this reason, acceptance rate increases. Because in practice it is impossible to involve all users, a group of representatives is the best option. So, not only one specialist develops the standard, but an entire committee does. After completing a draft version of the standard, other users and specialists can be involved through commentary rounds.

Of course, the amount of user involvement and the advantages related to that should be balanced with the cost—time is money. Diverging user opinions may hinder standards development, but it is better to discover these and reach consensus (including the option to stop further development) than to develop standards that the intended users do not want.

During the research, not only the six companies were visited but also several contractors and suppliers. These external parties were obliged to use the (technical) company standards, although sometimes they had a better alternative. This cannot be called best practice. Increasingly, engineering is outplaced. We concluded that involving the user is important, and therefore, external parties also should be involved in developing certain company standards. Best practice, in this case, balances the advantages and disadvantages of the company and its suppliers.

Automatic Usage of Standards

A direct user reads the paper or electronic version of the standard. It is not self-evident that the user then really will understand and use it properly. Sometimes, the standard's contents can be built into, for instance, software, drawings, specifications, machine settings, forms, or gauges. In this way, the standard is used automatically. The only literature in which we found something about automatic standards was Dutch professional standards literature (Bouma & Winter, 1982; Simons & de Vries, 2002).

SCORECARD EXAMPLE

We now will discuss one of the scorecards in more detail; particularly, the scorecard policy making—strategic level. Policy making was the only process that has been divided in three parts; namely, strategic, tactical, and operational levels. Because best practice includes management support for company standardization, we have chosen this one. After discussing the strategic level, we add some remarks on the tactical and operational levels.

Policy Making—Strategic Level

To make company standardization work, there has to be a (organizational) framework and a policy within which the standardization activities are executed. There has to be enough engagement to the policy by the people that have to carry out the standardization activities and their management (and the higher levels of management). In our best practice, top management is represented in company standardization or at least supports it. The most effective way to make this work is by means of a steering group in which the standardization department, (technical) managers from business units, and a member of a top-level management (e.g., technical director) are represented.

Figure 3 presents a possible organizational structure. For making a good standard, the technical expertise of one or more technical experts (who, in general, work within the business units) should be combined with the standardization expertise of a standards engineer (who may work within a standardization department). A networking structure, in one way or another, is expected to be the best way to do this.

All the companies have filled in the score presented in Table 2, and the score has been discussed. In the following section, we will present a few of the graphs that can be constructed out of the answers of the six companies.

Table 2. Scorecard for the policy making process at the strategic level

Scorecard Policy Making – Strategic level		
Nr.	**Description**	**Score**
1.	There is a clear strategic policy on company standardization.	
2.	At the corporate level a clear framework has been for operating company standardization.	
3.	At the corporate level tasks, competencies and responsibilities for company standardization have been defined.	
4.	Standardization expertise has sufficient influence on the company's strategic policy.	
5.	At the corporate level, management is aware of the importance and benefits of having (company) standards and standardization.	
6.	The maintenance of the existing system of company standards is a part of the strategic policy on company standardization.	
7.	The business units have sufficient influence on the strategic policy on company standardization (to make sure that their needs in this area are met).	
8.	The business units commit to the strategic policy on company standardization.	
9.	The strategic policy on company standardization is derived from the general strategic policy of the company (it supports the general policy and it does not conflict with it).	
10.	In this strategic policy on company standardization the goals are clearly defined.	
11.	The management is willing to steer company standardization at a high (top) level in the organization in order to minimize the danger of sub-optimization.	
12.	The management is aware that by using (company) standards company-wide the company can achieve cost-benefits for the purchasing of materials.	
13.	The management is aware that by using (company) standards company-wide the company can reduce cost of engineering and maintenance.	
14.	The management is aware that (company) standards use is needed to assure a specified quality-level of the company.	
15.	The management recognizes company standardization as an essential activity and steers this activity at a corporate level.	
16.	Corporate management has authorized the strategic level company standardization.	
17.	The strategic policy on company standardization has enough status and is being pursued by the total company.	

Figure 3. Possible organizational structure for company standardization

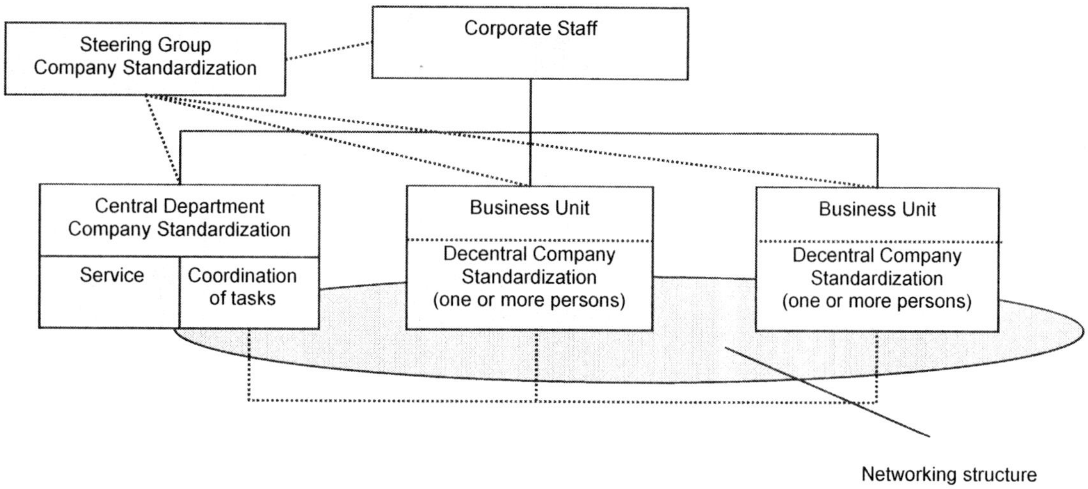

Statement 17: The strategic policy on company standardization has enough status and is being pursued by the total company.

Statement 17 is one of the statements in which there is a variation between the scores of the different companies. These are the more interesting statements. It can mean three things: either this part of the best practice does not fit within the culture of this company; this is not best practice; or it is a focus point for the company to improve its process. These statements have been the focus points in the discussions with the companies. All companies saw Statement 17 as best practice and, therefore, as an important focus point when they scored low.

It is important that company standardization has enough status in order to make sure that standards are being developed and used. It helps a lot when company standardization is supported at a corporate level within the organization, because frequently, the company focus is on short-term moneymaking. The graph in Figure 4 shows that most companies do not score high on this statement. To give company standardization enough status, it is helpful when, at a corporate level in the organization, the importance of standardization and the benefits that it can bring are recognized and formalized. Subsequently, when this policy is communicated in the right way, it is more likely that company standardization becomes a success.

Companies that scored low on the status also scored low in the participation of the business units in the definition of a strategic policy on company standardization (see Figure 5). Although recognition of the importance of standardization at a high level within the organization is an essential factor, this is not enough. In order to make it work also on the other levels, these levels must be involved in the formulation of the strategic policy. In practice, the importance of this fact was recognized, but not many of the companies did, in fact, involve the BUs in strategic policy development.

Now we will address in short the tactical and operational level in policy making. The best-practice statements related to these levels can be found in Appendix 1.

Policy Making: Tactical Level

Additionally, on this level, the participation of the business units is important for the overall

Figure 4. Scorecard graph example—Status of company standardization policy

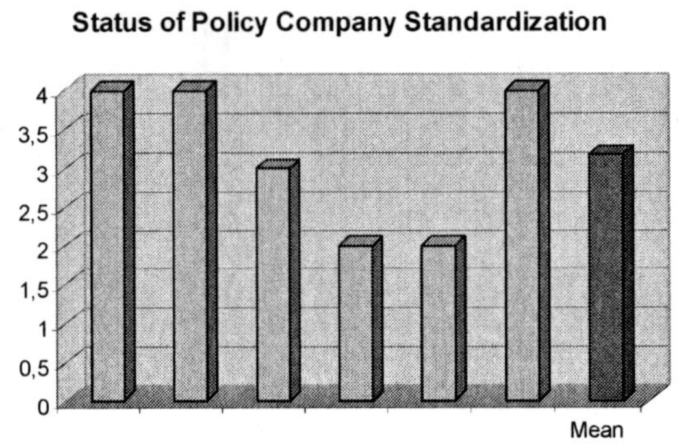

Figure 5. Scorecard graph example—The influence of business units on the strategic policy concerning company standardization

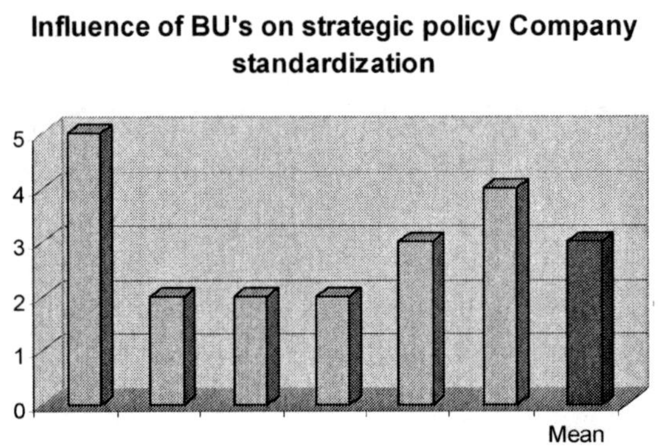

commitment toward (company) standardization. In a situation where a staff function (as a company standardization department often is) has to work in a demand-driven market situation, it is important to know what that market wants. The market concerns the demand for standards within the company. Therefore, that market, the (potential) users of the standards, should be given a possibility to speak. They should be involved in the prioritizing process, including setting criteria for prioritizing and the recognition of certain areas of attention (see Figure 6).

Policy Making: Operational Level

At the operational level, there is an important point of interest. A lot of the input for standards comes from technical experts. In general, they work within a BU, so there is no hierarchical relationship between the standardization department management and these experts. Standardization is only one of their activities. These technical experts have to report to their line management in their BU. Often, these BU managers do not consider standardization a top priority. Their lack of support is related to the fact that, for the most part, they are not involved in the corporate policy-making process on standardization. This makes it very difficult for the standardization department to really manage company standardization. The way to solve this is by involving BU management in corporate standardization management.

Figure 6. Scorecard graph example—The influence of business units on criteria for the prioritizing process

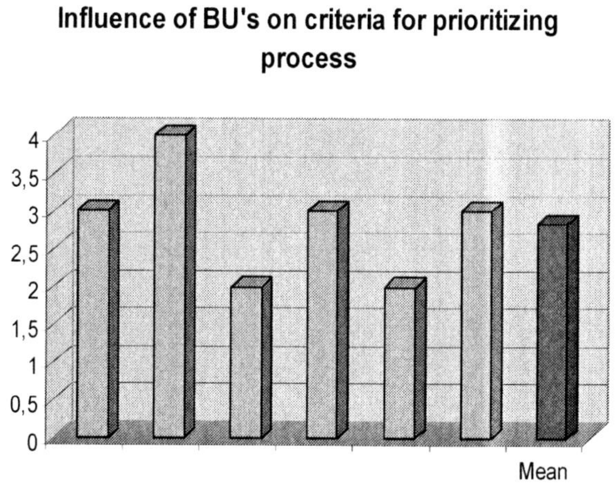

ANALYSIS

Our best practice in company standardization may be benchmarked with best practices in comparable fields, especially with quality management, IT management, and knowledge management.

IT Management Benchmark

Developing and implementing a standard may be compared with developing and implementing an IT system. Kocks (1997) analyzes the rather common failure of project management in automation projects and discusses two approaches used for such projects: the *waterfall approach* and the *evolutionary approach.*

In the waterfall approach, product specifications form the basis for the design of the project. The final product as well as some in-between milestones are defined. However, experiences in EDP auditing show that often the predefined specs are not met. The main reasons for this are the following:

- A lack of knowledge in extracting user needs from the clients.
- A lack of knowledge in deriving a process design from the prespecified product.
- Problems linking people to the process (even with a perfect process design, if people do not do what they are expected to do, the project will fail).

The evolutionary approach reflects the other side of the spectrum of possible approaches. In this approach, the project team starts without knowing the final result. Hope for a positive result is based mainly on trust in the personal skills of the people who carry out the project. Project planning is vague, and the budget cannot be estimated easily. The characteristics of a successful evolutionary approach are flexibility, smooth communication, fast decision making, and professional people.

Company standardization naturally resembles the waterfall approach. It may share drawbacks that are inherent to this approach, such as problems in specifying the standard needed, difficulties in designing the process to arrive at that standard, and difficulties in handling unforeseen human behavior. In best practice, these drawbacks are tackled as follows:

- During the prioritizing process, the company's standardization department makes a proposal for the project, including planning and budget, in cooperation with (representatives of) the intended participants. This resembles the functional specification of an automation system and the plan for making it, though in a limited sense.
- Best practice for the standard developing process includes measures to assure arrival at a product that meets user needs. Milestones are draft standards that already have the form of the final standard. The process usually has a standard design; it is not adapted to the specific requirements of the standard. The only specific thing concerns the selection of the people; representatives of all interested parties join.
- The third drawback is intrinsic to making use of codesigning customers (de Vries, 1999) but can be restricted by having a skilled standardization department. During the whole process, intended users are involved.

All three reasons for failure of the waterfall approach apply to company standardization, but the best practice includes measures to avoid this, mainly in the form of user involvement.

Standardization practice has at least some characteristics of the evolutionary approach. During the process, unexpected circumstances have to be attended to so that the final result, if any, does not always meet the criteria set at the outset. However, experience shows that unstructured standards development leads to low priority of company standardization. Company standards themselves provide structure, and the process of developing them should not contradict this. However, problems related to the waterfall approach can be solved partly by learning from the evolutionary approach that the project manager (i.e., the standards officer) should manage flexibility, informal communication, and informal pre-decision making.

Luitjens (1997) mentions five key success factors for complex governmental automation projects:

1. **A Pronounced Assignment.** Without a clear assignment, projects fail. This is reflected in the best practice for the prioritizing process.
2. **Financing Schedule from the Outset.** From the very beginning, a clear financing schedule for the whole project should be established and agreed upon. This includes giving an estimate of the costs and a list of parties that have expressed their willingness to pay. Salami tactics mostly fail. Prioritizing and funding best practice provide solutions for this.
3. **Understanding Complexity.** Complexity consists of product complexity, the technical complexity of the system that has to be built, and process complexity, which includes the different stakeholders with diverging interests and mutual relations and financial possibilities. Not all individual standards are complex, but the whole collection of interrelated standards is. Best practice separates process design and product (standard) design and provides solutions for stakeholder involvement and resource management.
4. **Creating a Basis for the Project.** The different actors should support the project. To attain this, it is important to make explicit the arguments for them to start and maintain their participation. Joint conceptualization appears to be a prerequisite for this—the more people are involved in finding solutions and balancing alternatives, the more they will be willing to support the final choice. The policy, prioritizing and standards development processes, and user involvement in all processes provide a sound basis for the project.

5. **Personal Skills.** Some people manage, whereas others in comparable circumstances fail. Common sense and a sense of humor appear to be prerequisites. This is the only missing element in the company standardization best practice model.

Quality Management Benchmark

Company standardization and quality management can be compared at two levels. First, quality management includes developing, maintaining, and improving a quality management system. This may be compared with developing, maintaining, and improving a standards collection. More than that, such a collection may form part of a quality management system. Secondly, quality management includes the development of procedures and instructions, which can be regarded as company standards. Therefore, quality management theory can form a benchmark for company standardization at both levels.

At the first level, quality management literature pays a lot of attention to quality as a line function vs. quality as the activity of a separate department or quality manager. Dale and Oakland (1991) and many others emphasize that quality should be managed in the line functions. However, "there is a role for a quality management representative, at board or senior management level, but this is concerned with facilitation, support, planning, promotion and co-ordination. Quality planning, review, and re-planning are the foundations of quality improvement. Without this basis the development of product and service designs, specifications, operational specifications and instructions, quality manuals, reviews and evaluation procedures will be poorly structured and badly focused" (Dale & Oakland, 1991, p. 228). Therefore, in order to arrive at quality management for the line, they advise a form of central support. The same can be seen in the best practice model: line management establishes policy (policy process) and sets priorities (prioritizing process), and users are involved in all other processes, which are supported by a standardization department or standards officer. Dale and Oakland (1991) stress the importance of user involvement. The quality circles they advise can be compared with working groups that develop a standard.

At the second level, developing procedures and instructions, our own experience demonstrates the comparability of both. We developed a book and a course on developing procedures for an ISO 9000-based quality management system based on our experience in company standardization (de Vries, 2002). Feedback from dozens of people who have read the book or joined the course confirms that this approach is fruitful for developing procedures. Conversely, the book was used for developing the company standardization best practice.

Knowledge Management Benchmark

Company standardization can be regarded as a form of knowledge management, where tacit knowledge is transformed into explicit knowledge. Slob (1999) has compared the conclusions of the best-practice study (real practice) with literature on knowledge management (the English-language sources were Brown [1991], Essers and Schreinemakers [1996], Kriwet [1997], Nonaka [1991, 1994], Nonaka and Takcuchi [1995], Polanyi [1966], Schreinemakers [1996], and Thayer [1968]) and concludes that knowledge management literature does not add real new insight to the best practice founded during the practical research. This underpins that it is really a best practice.

Company standardization can be seen as a way to manage technical knowledge. Figure 7 shows the way company standardization often is organized in organizations. The technical specialist(s) together with the standardization department are responsible for the realization of the standard. Knowledge is recorded (in the standard) and transferred to the other workers/users. Knowledge management literature (Verkasalo,

Figure 7. Model for company standardization (the old way)

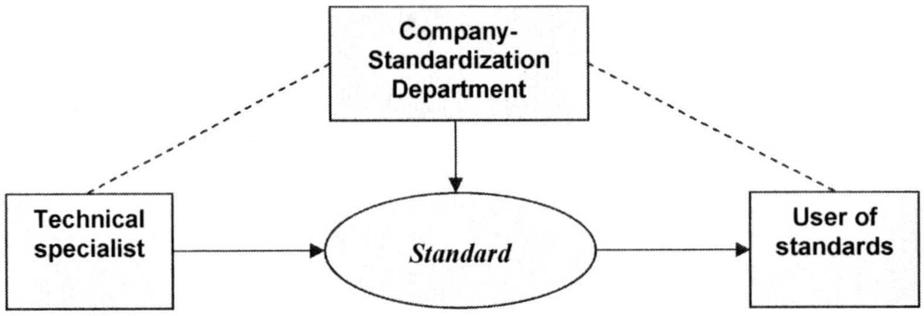

1998) distinguishes between the knowledge domain of the providers of the knowledge (in our case, the technical specialists) and the receivers of the recorded knowledge (in our case, the workers/direct users of standards). Both have their own knowledge domain. This has to be an important consideration when the knowledge is recorded.

Slob (1999) focuses mainly on standard development. It appears to be successful when the (technical) knowledge that is captured in standards is available for the direct users *and* the standards are actually used within the company. To achieve this, the standard should be user-friendly. To arrive at this situation, the actual user should play an important role in the standard development process. In practice, this is done too little. Arguments for user involvement can be found in several sources of literature, such as Nakamura (1993), Adolphi (1997), Brown and Duguid (1991), Gouldner (1954), De Gelder (1989), and Winter (1990). These findings in the area of standardization are supported by experiences and literature in knowledge management (Nonaka, 1991, 1994).

This leads to a slightly different model for company standardization (see Figure 8). In this model, the practical knowledge and experience of the user is connected with the technical knowledge of the specialist and with the standardization knowledge of the company standardization department. By involving the user in the development of standards, experience and practical knowledge flow into the standards. Even more important is that their knowledge about using standards can help to make the standards user-friendlier. A user-friendly standard influences the actual using of the standard positively.

Slob (1999) concludes the following:

- Company standardization is a way to manage technical (company) knowledge.
- Standardization is a structured way to transfer tacit into explicit knowledge.

Figure 8. Model for company standardization (best practice way)

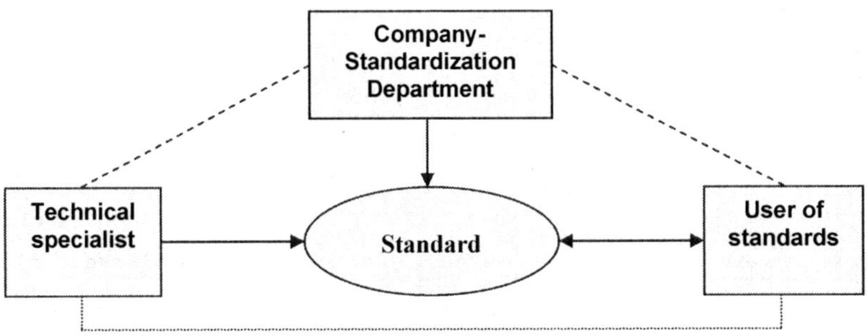

- When tacit knowledge is made explicit, it should be considered by whom this codified knowledge will be used in the future.
- It also should be considered that there can be an important difference in the knowledge domain of the specialist(s) or writer(s) of the standard and the intended direct users of that standard.
- These users of the standards, therefore, should be drawn into their development.

The presented new model for company standardization (Figure 8) compromises these conclusions.

CONCLUSION

In this article we have developed a process-based model for company standardization and a best practice for the processes that constitute company standardization. Best practice has been developed by examining practices in six big companies in the Netherlands and by using insights from standardization literature. The latter appeared to be incomplete, especially where academic literature was concerned.

The main benchmark for *best* in best practice is the success of the company standard. A company standard is successful when it is used and appears to solve the problem for which it was developed. Success results from a combination of successful performance of the company standardization processes that can be distinguished and that are shown in the company standardization model. Therefore, for each of these processes, several good practice indicators have been developed. The starting point for this was the way the six companies carry out their activities. The best practice of these was assessed by professionals as well as the research team. Where possible, standardization literature was used as an additional benchmark, but in several cases, this was not possible simply because literature on company standardization appeared not to address the topics concerned. Afterwards, the best-practice findings were confirmed by comparing them with insights from literature in the areas of IT management, quality management, and knowledge management.

Findings have been presented in the form of scorecards. Using these scorecards, the individual companies could benchmark themselves against the others, the mean score, and the best practice. The six companies differ in scores. No one is overall the best or the worst. Each one has good as well as bad performances in different areas.

The participating companies and other companies that develop many company standards can use the results to improve the performance of their company standardization processes and, in this way, improve the effectiveness and efficiency of their company standardization activities.

DISCUSSION

The research project did not concern IT standards but rather engineering standards used by multinational chemical and petrochemical companies. The following remarks can be made concerning the applicability of the results for other companies and for the typical domain of IT standards.

- The investigated companies use the standards mainly for the quality and safety of their installations, for the compatibility of parts thereof, and for avoiding an unnecessary variety of these parts. This can be compared with IT standards used by big companies, though in that case, there is more emphasis on compatibility (e.g., companies may face the problem of which external IT standards to choose for their systems or which options within or versions of these standards). So, the function of IT standards is, to a large extent, identical to the one of engineering standards in process industries, although the research, in fact, does not concern the standards contents but the process of developing them. In any case, it may be expected that results equally apply to IT standards.

- An exception to this conclusion may concern the best way of organizing standardization. In many cases, companies will have a central IT department. This department, instead of a central standardization department, might support the standardization activities. In this case, the advantage of having specialist knowledge of IT should be balanced against the possible disadvantages of having less standardization expertise and of additional coordination to manage interrelations between IT and non-IT standards.
- In most branches of business, standards related to the products or services are the most important ones. In the case of IT companies, these are product- or service-related IT standards. The main purpose of such standards is to support the market success of the products or services. Compared to our study, the role and benefits of such standards differ, but the way they are prepared may be identical. Therefore, there is no reason why company standardization and the best practices for it are fundamentally different. However, the participants will differ as standardization in such companies will be more directly linked with product or service development and marketing. This may result in a different organizational setting and governance structure for company standardization (Adolphi, 1997).
- The advantages of some of the company standards increase with growth in company size. For instance, quantity rebates related to preference ranges of software packages are more feasible in big companies. Small companies will not always have the possibilities to have a standardization department, a steering group, an intranet, and so forth. Small enterprises need less formalization, so their need for standards is less. But they will need standards, and the processes described apply to them, as well. Best practice for them may be expected to be more low-profile.
- Another difference may concern intellectual property rights (IPRs). IPRs hardly apply to engineering standards but may be important for product standards. Therefore, in IT standardization, it may be an additional best practice to have standardization and IPR closely related (Clarke, 2004).
- Possibly, some of the best practices are typically Dutch, and in other cultures, other practices would be better. Some differences between Dow Chemical (with a culture that mixes American and Dutch influences) and the other companies suggest this. For reasons of confidentiality, we cannot mention examples. In general, corporate culture of all such multinational companies is becoming increasingly international.

These issues are possible topics for future research. Other future research items may include the following:

- Practice as well as best practice of IT (company) standardization within companies that produce IT products or services and within (big) organizations that use IT systems to support their functioning.
- The relation between best practice and cost reduction, taking into account the cost of (human and other) resource allocations, transaction costs (for standards development and implementation), and total cost of ownership (of the IT systems).
- Balancing between developing a company standard or using an external standard.
- Possibilities for modification of the practice model for use by standards-developing organizations. In the available best practice study on national standardization organizations (Bonner & Potter, 2000), such a model is missing.

- Role of company standards in case of outsourcing of activities (this applies to process industries that outsource engineering or maintenance of plants as well as to companies that outsource IT system development, support, or maintenance).
- Completion of the comparisons with IT management, quality management, and knowledge management in the form of a more thorough review of the literature.
- Comparison of user involvement in company standardization with user involvement in formal standardization and consortia.
- (Best practice) field research in other branches of industry; for instance, mechanical engineering or service industries.

REFERENCES

Adolphi, H. (1997). *Strategische Konzepte zur Organisation der Betrieblichen Standardisierung.* Berlin: Beuth Verlag.

AFNOR. (1967). *La normalisation dans l'entreprise.* Paris: Association Française de Normalisation.

Bloemen, F. E. M., Van den Molegraaf, J. C. M., & Van Mal, H. H. (1992). Normalisatie Vermindert Levensduuruitgaven van Chemische Installaties Aanzienlijk. *B&Id, 4*(8), 17-20.

Bonner, P., & Potter, D. (2000). *Achieving best practices in national standardisation—A benchmarking study of the national standardisation systems of Finland, Sweden, Denmark and Italy.* Helsinki, Finland: Ministry of Trade Industry.

Bouma, J. J., & Winter, W. (1982). *Standardization fundamentals.* Delft: Nederlands Normalisatie-instituut.

British Standards Institution. (1970). *The operations of a company standards department.* London: British Standards Institution.

British Standards Society. (1995). *Standards and quality management—An integrated approach.* London: BSI.

Brown, J., &. Duguid, P. (1991). Organizational learning communities of practice: Toward a unified view of working, learning and innovation. *Organization Science, 2*(1), 40-57.

Cargill, C. (1997). *Open systems standardization—A business approach.* Upper Saddle River, NJ: Prentice Hall.

Chiesa, V., et al. (1996). Development of a technical innovation audit. *Journal of Production Innovation Management, 13*, 105-136.

Clarke, M. (2004). *Standards and intellectual property rights: A practical guide for innovative business.* London: NSSF.

Dale, B., & Oakland, J. (1991). *Quality improvements through standards.* Leckhampton, Cheltenham, UK: Stanley Thornes.

De Gelder, A. (1989). *Opstellen van normen.* Delft: Nederlands Normalisatie-Instituut.

de Vries, H.J. (1999). *Standardization: A business approach to the role of national standardization organisations.* Boston: Kluwer Academic Publishers.

de Vries, H.J. (2002). *Procedures voor ISO 9000:2000.* Delft, The Netherlands: NEN.

Düsterbeck, B., Hesser, W., Inklaar, A., & Vischer, J. (1995). Company standardization. In W. Hesser, & A. Inklaar (Eds.), *An introduction to standards and standardization* (pp. 99-138). Berlin: Beuth Verlag.

Essers, J., & Schreinemakers, J. (1996). The conceptions of knowledge and information in knowledge management. *Proceedings of the Fourth International ISMICK-Symposium*, Würzburg, Germany.

Gouldner, A. W. (1954). *Patterns of industrial bureaucracy.* New York: The Free Press.

Hesser, W., & Inklaar, A. (Eds.). (1997). *An introduction to standards and standardization.* Berlin: Beuth Verlag.

ISO. (2000a). *Quality management systems—Fundamentals and vocabulary.* Geneva: International Organization for Standardization.

ISO. (2000b). *Quality management systems—Requirements.* Geneva: International Organization for Standardization.

Juran, J. M. (1988). *Juran on planning for quality.* London: The Free Press.

Kocks, C. (1997). Het échec van projectmanagement in de systeemontwikkeling. *Informatie, 39*(4), 6-11.

Kraaijeveld, P. (2002). *Governance in the Dutch banking industry—A longitudinal study of standard setting in retail payments.* Rotterdam: Rotterdam School of Management/Faculteit Bedrijfskunde.

Kriwet, C. (1997). *Inter- and intraorganizational knowledgetransfer* [doctoral thesis]. Bamberg: Difo Druck: Universität St-Gallen.

Luitjens, S. (1997). Interorganisatorische informatiseringsprojecten bij de overheid. *Informatie, 39*(4), 18-22.

Nakamura, S. (1993). *The new standardization—Keystone of continuous improvement in manufacturing.* Portland, OR: Productivity Press.

Nonaka, I. (1991). The knowledge creating company. *Harvard Business Review, 6*, 96-104.

Nonaka, I. (1994). A dynamic theory of organizational knowledge creation. *Organization Science, 5*(1), 14-37.

Nonaka, I., & Takeuch, H. (1995). *The knowledge creating company.* New York: Oxford University Press.

Ollner, J. (1974). *The company and standardization* (2nd edition). Stockholm: Swedish Standards Institution.

Oly, M. P., & Slob, F. J. C. (1999). *Benchmarking Bedrijfsnormalisatie—Een Best Practice Voor de Procesindustrie.* Rotterdam: Erasmus Universiteit Rotterdam.

Polanyi, M. (1966). *The tacit dimension.* Gloucester: Peter Smith.

Rada, R., & Craparo, J. S. (2001). Standardizing management of software engineering projects. *Knowledge Technology and Policy, 14*(2), 67-77.

Schacht, M. (1991). *Methodische Neugestaltung von Normen als Grundlage für Eine Integration in Den Rechnerunterstützten Konstruktionsprozeß.* Berlin: Beuth Verlag GmbH.

Schreinemakers, J. F. (Ed.). (1996). Knowledge management—Organization competence and methodology. *Proceedings of the Fourth International ISMICK Symposium*, Würzburg, Germany.

Simons, C.A.J., & de Vries, H.J. (2002). *Standaard of maatwerk—Bedrijfskeuzes tussen uniformiteit en verscheidenheid.* Schoonhoven, The Netherlands: Academic Service.

Slob, F. J. C. (1999). *Bedrijfs-normalisatie—De Schakel Tussen Tacit en Explicit Knowledge.* Rotterdam: Erasmus Universiteit Rotterdam.

Susanto, A. (1988). *Methodik zur Entwicklung von Normen.* Berlin: Beuth Verlag GmbH.

Thayer, L. (1968). *Communication and communication systems.* Homewood, IL: Richard D. Irwin.

Toth, R.B. (Ed.). (1990). *Standards management—A handbook for profits.* New York: American National Standards Institute.

Verity Consulting. (1995). *Strategic standardization—Lessons from the world's foremost companies*. New York: ANSI.

Verkasalo, M., & Lappalainen, P. M. (1998). A method of measuring the efficiency of the knowledge utilization process. *IEEE Transactions on Engineering Management, 45*(4), 414-423.

Wen, Z. (2004). Reform and change—An introduction to China standardization. *Proceedings of the 11th International Conference of Standards Users*, Amsterdam.

Wenström, H., Ollner, J., & Wenström, J. (2000). *Focus on industry standards—An integrated approach*. Stockholm: SIS Förlag.

Winter, W. (1990). *Bedrijfsnormalisatie*. Delft: Nederlands Normalisatie-Instituut.

ENDNOTE

* The author would like to thank Michiel Oly and Florens Slob who did the field work. Special thanks to Florens for acting as a sparring partner during the development of this chapter.

APPENDIX

Standardization policy: Strategic level
See the main text.

Standardization policy: Tactical level

- (Line) managers of experts involved in company standardization are involved in setting the company standardization policy.
- People responsible for setting company standardization policy at the tactical level have enough knowledge to be able to do so.
- The Company Standardization Department (CSD) is involved in establishing (separate scores):
    - the way of funding company standardization activities;
    - the status of company standards (voluntary or compulsory);
    - priority areas (for instance, 'engineering standards' or 'standards to assure and improve environmental performance');
    - criteria for prioritizing.
    - Business units (BUs) are involved in establishing (separate scores):
    - the way of funding company standardization activities;
    - the status of company standards (voluntary or compulsory);
    - priority areas (for instance, 'engineering standards' or 'standards to assure and improve environmental performance');
    - criteria for prioritizing.
    - There is a clear company standardization policy deployment to all people concerned.
    - CSD informs all people concerned on company standardization issues.

Standardization policy: Operational level

- CSD co-ordinates the operational standardization activities and monitors progress.
- Progress of activities is evaluated on a regular basis.
- CSD reports delays, line management decides on corrective and actions, if any.
- People involved in standardization are encouraged to propose suggestions for improvement of standardization policy.
- Standardization policy at the operational level is evaluated on a regular basis.

Prioritising process

- Each employee is authorized to submit proposal for developing, changing or withdrawing company standards.
- (Final) users are encouraged to submit (change) proposals.
- CSD co-ordinates gathering proposals.
- Company standardization expertise is used in prioritizing.
- Criteria for prioritizing are in line with general company policy.
- Criteria for prioritizing are evaluated on fitness for use on a regular basis.
- Optimal overall company results prevail over BU benefits (no sub-optimalization).
- Once priorities have been set, CSD makes a proposal for planning and budget in co-operation with (representatives of) the intended participants.

- Planning and budget are realistic and performable.
- CSD informs the interested parties on the annual planning and makes it available to them.
- CSD monitors whether set priorities are being realized.
- In the case of an absence of agreed-upon expert-involvement in developing a company standard, CSD is responsible to ask the heads of these experts to charge them to pick up their duties.

Company standard development process

- Those who have asked for standards become involved in their development.
- Intended standards users become involved in their development.
- Supplier and/or contractors can provide input in the company standard development process.
- Standards writers communicate with stakeholders during the development process.
- Each company standard is assessed on its expected fitness to contribute to business results.
- The company has a meta-standard that provides criteria for its company standards.
- This meta-standard is known by all involved in company standards development and they apply it.
- On a regular basis, the requirements in this meta-standard are assessed on topicality and fitness for use.
- Company management has authorized this meta-standard.
- The company standard is not just based on the personal opinion of one expert but it is broadly based.
- Participants in standard development consider their task as important and urgent.
- The status of writing standards equals the status of carrying out projects.
- There are enough competent employees for writing new standards and maintaining the quality and consistency of the existing standards collection.
- A 'why-document' is attached to each company standard. It provides the underpinning of the most important choices/decisions that have been made during standards development.
- A draft of each new company standard is sent out for comments to a relevant group of people within the company.
- There is a procedure for processing comments.
- Everybody is allowed to comment on draft standards.
- CSD co-ordinates comments processing.
- Comments, if any, are sent to the development team. They decide on adoption or rejection.
- In the case of rejection they give the reasons why.
- CSD checks the standard against the requirements in the meta-standard.
- Company management authorizes the standard.
- IT tools are used in developing and writing the standard.

Company standards introduction process

- CSD is the central help-desk for questions concerning company standardization.
- CSD is able to answer questions concerning company standards or to refer to experts who can answer these questions.
- CSD announces new, modified and withdrawn standards, when necessary via BU officers responsible for standardization or via certain (other) users within the organization.
- CSD is able to communicate with the rest of the organization about new, modified and withdrawn standards.
- There is a procedure for how to announce company standards.
- CSD is able to tailor information to the needs of specific user groups.
- CSD monitors user satisfaction concerning the provision of standards-related information.

- Each BU has appointed one or more officers responsible for the diffusion of standards-related information.
- CSD uses IT tools for standards introduction.
- The information concerning changes in the standards collection includes reasons for the (new / modified) standard and for major choices within the standard, and expected advantages. In the case of withdrawal, the reasons for this are mentioned.

Distribution process

- CSD makes standards available.
- Company standards can be obtained on request or by subscription to the whole collection or to a part of it.
- CSD can advise on searching and ordering standards.
- CSD operates a database with bibliographical data on all company standards.
- Out-dated versions of existing standards and withdrawn standards remain available for consultation.
- CSD operates a system that shows who has which standard, including the version of this standard.
- In the case of a new version all users of the replaced version get the announcement.
- Users can get standards in a form (electronic and/or paper) and format that suits them.
- The version of a standard is clear to the users.
- CSD publishes company standards in electronic format and makes them available in a virtual way.
- Virtual company standards are, as far as the text is concerned, available in text mode (not in pixel mode only), which enables text search on headwords.
- On a regular basis, CSD monitors the effectiveness and topicality of its subscription system. Subscriptions include department name and name of the employee concerned.

Facility management

- CSD monitors the market for IT tools that may support its processes.
- CSD has a budget for investments in facilities.
- IT facilities to support company standardization should fit with IT used elsewhere within the organization.
- IT facilities to support company standardization should fit with IT used by the national standards body for producing, making available, distributing, and searching its standards.
- The company operates an intranet and uses it for standards-related information.
- Within the company e-mail can be used for communication about company standards.

Funding

- Funding for the maintenance of the system of company standards is assured.
- Funding for company standards that are essential for the company is assured.
- Fixed costs for CSD are charged on the company as a whole.
- Corporate management decides on the way these fixed costs are charged on the BUs.
- Variable costs for company standardization are paid by those that have caused these costs (the part of the company for which the standard has been developed).

This work was previously published in International Journal of IT Standards and Standardization Research, Vol. 4, Issue 1, edited by K. Jacobs, pp. 62-85, copyright 2006 by IGI Publishing, formerly known as Idea Group Publishing (an imprint of IGI Global).

Section III
Tools and Technologies

Chapter IX
Best Practice in Leveraging E-Business Technologies to Achieve Business Agility

Ehap H. Sabri
University of Texas at Dallas, USA

ABSTRACT

This chapter explains the best practice in implementing e-business Technologies to achieve business cost reduction and business agility. Many companies started to realize that gaining competitive advantage is no longer feasible by only managing their own organizations; it also requires getting involved in the management of all upstream supply organizations as well as the downstream network. E-business technologies present huge opportunities that are already being tapped by several companies and supply chains. Although the benefits of implementing e-business technologies are clear, enterprises struggle in integrating e-business technologies into supply-chain operations. The author illustrates the strategic and operational impact of e-business technologies on supply chains and explains the performance benefits and challenges firms should expect in implementing these technologies. Also, the author provides the best-practice framework in leveraging e-business applications to support process improvements in order to eliminate non-value-added activities and provide real-time visibility and velocity for the supply chain. Finally, this chapter presents the future trends of using e-business in transformation programs.

INTRODUCTION

Executives realized that producing high-quality products is not enough in today's competitive environment; the new challenge is to get products to customers when and where they need them, exactly the way they want them, with a competitive price and in a cost-effective manner. Many factors are making this challenge more complicated; globalization, increased complexity of supply chains (SCs) with outsourcing and the move to mass customization and build-to-order (BTO) environments, the need for a shorter time to market to gain competitive advantage, and the shift from vertical to horizontal supply chains make an efficient integration with suppliers and customers more critical.

E-business technologies address the above challenges by enabling enterprises to collaborate with their internal and external suppliers and customers, providing visibility, automating the paper-driven business processes, and interconnecting inventory, logistics, and planning systems.

The way to survive the competition in today's business world is to stay ahead of competitors. Leveraging e-business technologies effectively is key to staying competitive and achieving business agility. Although the benefits of implementing e-business technologies are clear, enterprises struggle with integrating e-business technologies into supply-chain operations. Decision makers find themselves asking the most fundamental questions. How can we do it? What is the best practice? Does it apply to us? Does technology add value? If so, what is the best way to quantify it and then maximize it? Since many have failed in achieving value, how can we make sure that we will not be one of them and will be able to minimize the risk? What does senior management need to do to support transformation initiatives? This chapter gives powerful tools for answering these questions.

This chapter addresses the strategic and operational impact of e-business technologies on supply chains and explains the performance benefits and challenges firms should expect in implementing e-business technologies. Also, it provides the best-practice framework in leveraging e-business technologies to support process improvements in order to achieve cost reduction and velocity for the supply chain. This framework includes a practical and effective return-on-investment (ROI) model to calculate the benefits of e-business transformation programs.

The objectives of this chapter can be summarized as follows.

- Provide a good understanding of the challenges in today's business environment
- Identify the impact of e-business technologies on enterprise processes
- Highlight the benefits of implementing e-business technologies
- Provide guidelines and a framework for implementing e-business technologies successfully

The concepts in this chapter are presented in an easy-to-understand manner that is intended for any reader interested in learning about e-business technologies. Because e-business can be leveraged by several functions within the organization, this chapter has been written for the wide audience that is interested in learning how to leverage e-business techniques in improving processes and slashing waste. This chapter provides strategies for senior managers to use in planning for transformation programs, and also provides middle mangers with tools to effectively manage and implement the best practice. Graduate students can use this chapter to gain an excellent understanding of how e-business technologies work, and then use this knowledge to either extend the research in this field or implement the concepts learned from this chapter in the industry.

BACKGROUND

Valencia and Sabri (2005) stated that the widespread use of the Internet has turned the eyes of many companies to the numerous solutions that the Internet provides. E-business technologies have helped many companies in improving their overall processes and performances.

On the other hand, Handfield and Nichols (2002) mentioned that integrated supply-chain management (SCM) is now recognized as a strategy to achieve competitive advantage. When pressed to identify how to achieve this strategy, however, the path forward for executives is not clear. Numerous solution providers offer the "silver bullets" to supply-chain integration, yet the results are never guaranteed." Devaraj and Kohli (2002) mentioned that executives are concerned that even when there is promise of a payoff, the assumptions may change and payoffs may never be realized.

Rigby, Reichheld, and Schefter (2002) mentioned that, in a survey conducted by a CRM (customer-relationship management) forum, when asked what went wrong with their CRM projects, 4% of the managers cited software problems, 1% said they received bad advice, but 87% pinned the failure of their CRM projects on the lack of adequate change management.

Any transformation program should encompass three specific phases: initial enablement, followed by implementation, and finally ongoing support and maintenance. An effective transformation plan must support these three phases and address all the challenges around selecting the right strategy, change management, and software provider; maintaining upper management buy-in; managing by metrics; and rolling out a maintenance strategy.

Valencia and Sabri (2005) mentioned the several guidelines that are important to consider when e-business technologies are implemented. These guidelines can be grouped as follows.

- **Initial enablement:**
  - Synchronize e-business objectives with corporate initiatives
  - Use e-business as a driver for significant process improvement
  - Identify operational and financial benefit metrics
  - Clearly identify the process and the scope of the transformation program
  - Obtain consensus from all process stakeholders
- **Implementation:**
  - Simplify processes by eliminating non-value-added activities
  - Deploy in small phases with compelling ROI
  - Consider proactive enforcement of to-be processes in the solution
  - Enable exception-based problem resolution
- **Ongoing support and maintenance:**
  - Define the ongoing process for capturing, monitoring, and analyzing metrics data

E-Business Definition

E-business can be defined as the use of the Internet to facilitate business-to-business (B2B) or business-to-consumer (B2C) transactions and includes all operations before and after the sale. E-business can also be defined as the adoption of the Internet to enable real-time supply-chain collaboration and integration of the planning and execution of the front-end and back-end processes and systems. E-business has already impacted the industry significantly by providing important benefits like cost reduction, visibility improvement, lower inventory, streamlined processes, better response time, faster time to market, better asset utilization, higher shareholder value, fulfillment lead-time reduction, flexibility improvement, revenue increases by penetrating new markets, improvement in customer satisfaction, and better standards of living.

E-business, or the Internet computing model, has emerged as perhaps the most compelling enabler for supply-chain integration. Because it is open, standard based, and virtually ubiquitous, businesses can use the Internet to gain global visibility across their extended network of trading partners and respond quickly to changing business conditions such as customer demand and resource variability.

The Internet is considered to be the enabler for e-business technologies, while e-business is the enabler for supply-chain collaboration and integration. E-business technologies can support different environments: business to employee (B2E), B2C, and B2B. The B2E environment links the ERP (enterprise resource planning), SCM, warehousing, shipping, and human-resources systems together into a Web-based system. B2E focuses on the internal transactions of a company and affects the internal supply-chain process. The B2C environment allows customers to place, track, and change orders online, and allows sellers to gather information about the consumer in real time. B2C is sometimes referred to in the literature as e-commerce. Other literature differentiates between the direct business customer and the end customer (consumer). The B2B environment links B2E and B2C to the systems of the suppliers and affects the external supply-chain processes. The best practice is to have all of the three environments (B2E, B2B, and B2C) under one portal for seamless information transfer between them.

E-business technologies can also be divided into two types: (a) process-focused technologies like online auctions and (b) infrastructure-focused technologies like Web services (XML [extensible markup language], SOAP [simple object access protocol], UDDI [universal description, discovery, and integration], and WSDL [Web service description language]), the wireless application protocol (WAP), the global positioning system (GPS), bar coding, and radio-frequency identification (RFID) to transmit the data into computer applications. Web services are built on platform-independent standards that enable e-business applications to share information over the Internet between internal and external systems.

XML provides the best way for companies to pass data and coordinate services over the Internet. In essence, XML is a file format that allows users to include definitions of terms and processing rules within the same file (Harmon, 2003). SOAP and UDDI are additional software protocols, where SOAP is a protocol that enables one computer to locate and send an XML file to another computer, and UDDI is a protocol that allows one company to query another company's computers to determine how certain kinds of data are formatted. WSDL is the language in which the UDDI protocol is implemented.

There are still issues to be resolved, and many groups are working on middleware and security standards to make XML more flexible and secure (Harmon).

TODAY'S BUSINESS CHALLENGES

Executives face many challenges today in every aspect of their operations and enterprise integration. The following are considered to be the top 10 challenges.

- The need to be customer oriented and at the same time manage cost more efficiently
- Information delay, which is considered to be a typical concern. Since the processes are the ones that realize the information flow between partners, enterprises need to redesign their business processes to address this challenge.
- Globalization, which intensifies the competition and makes competitive advantage crucial
- The increased complexity of supply chains and the growing need for a tighter control of over it. The supply chain can be defined as a network of facilities (manufacturing plants, assembly plants, distribution centers, warehouses, etc.) that performs the function of the transformation of raw materials into intermediate products and then finished products, and finally the distribution of these products to customers. The increased complexity may result from the involvement of one company in multiple supply chains, the growing complexity of products, the growing complexity of managing information flows, and the increasing trends of third-party logistics and subassembly (contract) manufacturers.

- Long and unpredictable product life cycles. It is important to shorten the product-introduction cycle and be faster to react to the market needs to gain competitive advantage.
- The shift from vertical integration to horizontal supply chains, which calls for more efficient collaboration with suppliers and customers. The new trend is for companies to buy out competitors in the same business or merge with them (consolidation) instead of buying their suppliers (i.e., to expand vertically instead of horizontally); this requires the synchronized addressing of collaboration, planning, and procurement issues.
- Outsourcing and having suppliers across the world. Companies nowadays outsource assembly work, information-systems management, call centers, service-parts repair and management, and product engineering to contractors. The bigger challenge is to decide what to outsource, and how to make sure that customer satisfaction, delivery service, or quality are not impacted.
- Expensive cost structure, especially when companies are facing intensified competition. Related to this is the increase in shipping costs due to outsourcing.
- The disruption to the supply chain from demand and supply mainly caused by the supply-chain dynamics.
- Supporting the redesigned processes with leading-edge technology that is easy to integrate, cheap to maintain, fast to achieve results, and low in risk

In order to address the previous challenges in today's environment, companies should look for certain key enablers to implement in their operations. These key enablers can be grouped as follows.

1. **Cross-organizational collaboration:** This can reduce lead time, improve efficiency, reduce quality risk, and streamline processes.
2. **Flexibility:** Flexibility should be built into product designs and manufacturing processes to become more customer oriented and mitigate the challenge of supply and demand fluctuations by providing the ability to change plans quickly. Flexibility is measured based on the ability to shift production load (flexible capacity), change production volumes and product mix, and modify products to meet new market needs. It is important to mention that cost-reduction initiatives usually inversely impact flexibility.
3. **Visibility:** Real-time visibility reduces the uncertainty and nervousness in the supply chain, reduces safety stock (i.e., reduces cost), and increases customer satisfaction (i.e., increases revenue) by presenting the real picture and providing the ability to solve potential problems ahead of time. It will also reduce the impact of disruption to the supply chain caused by demand and supply.
4. **Process innovation:** This enabler addresses the following types of questions. How can companies reengineer their processes to increase speed when introducing new products? What supply-chain-process improvements and tools should companies invest in to gain competitive advantage? How can companies restructure their supply chains to reduce cost and increase profitability across their total global network? How can companies reduce their supplier base?
5. **Risk management:** This enabler addresses the new risks related to product quality and service delivery that arise from outsourcing, locating supply-chain activities across the world, and the acceleration of new product introductions. It also addresses the security concerns after September 11, 2001.

6. **Technology:** Technology should be adopted to enable and support the new or modified processes, and reduce the supply-chain complexity.

E-business is the major driver to implement the first, third, and last enablers, while best practice is the major driver for the rest of the enablers. These two drivers (e-business and best practice) will be discussed later in this chapter. The following section will provide the benefits of implementing the best practice, which is enabled by the right e-business technology.

THE IMPACT OF E-BUSINESS TECHNOLOGIES ON SCM, CRM, & SRM SUPERPROCESSES

The e-business technologies available through the Internet, combined with ongoing advances in advanced planning and scheduling (APS) software development, have given SCM an enormous boost and helped in maximizing business agility. APS is a constraint-based planning logic that emerged in the early 1990s, and it is considered to be the major breakthrough after MRP (material resource planning) logic. SCM is defined as the process of optimizing the flow of goods, services, and information along the supply chain from supplier to customer. It is also the process to strategize, plan, and execute business processes across facilities and business units. It focuses on the internal supply chain, which is under the direct control of the enterprise.

Information at all points along the supply chain is captured and well presented by e-business technologies (in a B2E environment), enabling better decision making in SCM businesses processes, especially regarding maintaining appropriate inventory levels and the efficient movement of products to the next production or distribution process, and supporting sales and operations planning (S&OP). E-business has replaced excess inventory with accurate, inexpensive, and real-time information. Also, real-time information about the supply and the ability to collaborate with customers on the forecast have helped producers to balance and match supply with demand. All the above have enabled many companies to transform their supply operations from build to stock (BTS) and mass production to BTO and mass customization. Anderson (2003) defined build to order as the on-demand production of standard products, while mass customization is the on-demand production of tailored products.

Supplier-relationship management (SRM) is the process of supporting supplier partnerships in the supply chain, and coordinating processes across product development, sourcing, purchasing, and supply coordination within a company and across companies. CRM is the process of covering all customer needs throughout the phases of customer interaction. CRM is also defined as the process of allocating organizational resources to activities that have the greatest return on profitable customer relationships. Since the best practice of SRM and CRM are built around supply-chain integration, e-business is considered as the enabler for these superprocesses. The B2B environment is typically leveraged for SRM, while the B2C environment is typically leveraged for CRM.

Organizations utilize e-business solutions (a solution is a combination of best-practice processes and enabled technology) in the SRM area to eliminate paperwork, streamline shipment and payments, reduce the cycle time of finding and acquiring suppliers, easily monitor contract terms, leverage spend consolidation by supplier and part rationalization, increase supplier awareness during the design and production phases, and automate the procurement process.

On the other hand, organizations utilize e-business solutions in the CRM area to automate order receiving; to capture, analyze, and leverage customer information; and to reduce order-to-delivery cycle time and expediting costs.

We will drill down in the next section to detail

the SCM, SRM, and CRM business processes and highlight the impact e-business has on them. We will mention the related pain points and show the potential benefits of addressing them using e-business technologies in addition to several success stories in this area.

SRM, SCM, AND CRM business processes; Pain Points; benefits of adopting e-business technology; and success stories

Each superprocess (like SCM, SRM, and CRM) consists of several business processes. Each key business process is defined (see Table 2), and typical challenges in the current practice (as-is process) are highlighted. The chapter shows how e-business technology and its different application levels can address these challenges, and finally typical benefits resulting from adopting e-business technology are mentioned.

Key Business Processes

Table 1 shows the key business processes in each superprocess of SCM, SRM, and CRM. Although the name and scope of these processes may vary across different industries, this table and the following process definitions give companies a good idea on how to map their business to this table and understand the impact of e-business on their own processes. The criteria used to link certain business processes to the appropriate superprocess are the following.

- If a business process has a direct relationship with suppliers based on the best practice, it would belong to the SRM superprocess.
- If a business process has a direct relationship with customers based on the best practice, it would belong to the CRM superprocess.
- If a business process has a direct relationship with neither suppliers nor customers, and it helps in balancing supply and demand, it would belong to the SCM superprocess.
- If a business process is in the gray area where it spans across two superprocesses, its own subprocesses should be evaluated, and the business process will be linked to the corresponding superprocess to which the majority of the subprocesses belong to.

In the second dimension of Table 1, the criteria that have been used to decide the level a certain business process belongs to are as follows.

- If a business process is used mainly to generate strategies to run the business, it would belong to the strategic level.
- If a business process is used mainly to generate a plan to operationalize the strategies, it would belong to the tactical level.
- If a business process is used mainly to execute the plans to realize the strategies, it would belong to the operational and execution level.

Table 1. Business-process distribution

		Superprocess		
Level		SRM	SCM	CRM
	Strategic	Strategic Sourcing	Supply-Chain Design	Marketing Management
	Tactical	Product Design	Sales & Operations Planning	Selling Management
	Operational	Procurement	Order Fulfillment	Customer-Service Management

The strategic level is considered to be the long-term process, the tactical level is the midterm process, and the operational level is the short-term process, which includes execution (for simplicity). Going up the levels from the operational to the tactical to the strategic, the percentage of cost savings goes up and the impact of decisions on the success of the organization is higher.

Strategic Sourcing

Strategic sourcing is defined as the process of identifying the best sourcing strategy to reduce cost and raw-material supply risk, and to achieve a long-term relationship with suppliers. One of the major challenges (pain points) in this process is the inability to identify and manage the total supplier spend and demand because of complex, disconnected purchasing systems. Another disconnection is between the engineering and purchasing systems, which causes the lack of visibility to the design engineers of the approved vender list (AVL). Another related challenge is the inability to consider supplier performance during sourcing decisions by design engineers or purchasing analysts.

Product Design

Product design is the process of collaboration among companies, partners, and suppliers to share product design, schedules, and constraints to arrive at a single bill of material for a finished product effectively. It is a critical process due to its ability to facilitate bringing innovative and profitable products to the market quickly, and to ensure product quality. The product design consists of three phases: concept, development, and pilot. It also includes product-engineering changes (product revisions) as a subprocess. These changes can be due to component-cost change, product improvements, process change, quality corrective actions, material shortages, or product obsolescence. Product revisions involve design engineers, procurement, suppliers, manufacturing and process engineers, contract manufacturers, and service support. Product design is tightly integrated with PDM (product-definition management), which is the database for all designed parts.

Product design has several challenges like intensified competition, which increases the need to introduce new products to the market more quickly; complex products, which make optimizing the design more challenging; frequent design changes, which increase prototype-part cost due to the late involvement of suppliers in the design phase; and the inability to identify the right products to launch or fund, the right suppliers to collaborate with during the design, and the right standard items to reuse. Also, subcontracting and outsourcing extends the need for real-time collaboration with partners and suppliers.

Procurement

Procurement is the process of executing the selected sourcing strategies by performing a request for quote, reverse-auction, bid-analysis, and contract-processing work flows to select the source of supply, and then managing all daily activities of procurement with the selected suppliers. It is also the process of managing two-way real-time communications with suppliers regarding the part or raw-material supply to achieve and execute a synchronized procurement plan.

There are three key pain points for this process. First is the lack of intelligent visibility and consistent supplier performance throughout the life cycle of the purchase order. This results from the inability to conduct reliable bid analysis considering different criteria in addition to the price, the lack of early problem detection for the inbound material and mismatch-resolution framework, a costly and difficult-to-maintain EDI (electronic data interchange) because different versions of the software may result in transmission errors, and the inability to capture supplier performance data.

The second key pain point is the many non-value-added and time-consuming (paper-based) activities in this process, like manual RFQ and contracting processes, the checking of shipment status, and paper invoices. The high cost of both expedition and mismatch resolution between the receipt and the invoice is the third key pain point.

Supply-Chain Design

SC design is a long-term planning process to optimize the supply-chain network or configuration and material flow. The primary objective of this process is to determine the most cost-effective SC configuration, which includes facilities; supplies; customers; products; and methods of controlling inventory, purchasing, and distribution on one hand; and the flow of goods throughout the SC on the other hand. Sabri and Beamon (2000) mentioned that strategic supply-chain design concerns are the location of facilities (plants and distribution centers), the allocation of capacity and technology requirements to facilities, the assignment of products to facilities, and the distribution of products between facilities and to customer regions.

The major pain points or challenges of this process are the inability of the inflexible supply-chain configuration to react efficiently to the variability in demand and supply, or to the introduction of new products into the market. The shift from mass production to customized products forces companies to rethink about their physical SC configurations, and nonrepeatable and manual processes.

Sales and Operations Planning

The APICS (American Production and Inventory Control Society) dictionary defines sales and operations planning as "a process that provides Management the ability to strategically direct its businesses to achieve competitive advantage on a continuous basis by integrating customer-focused marketing plans for new and existing products with the management of the supply chain." The main objective of this process is to balance demand and supply, which is not an easy exercise due to the dynamic nature and continuous fluctuation of demand and supply. Historically, supply and demand balancing has been done reactively by sales, marketing, and operations teams allocating constrained products to customer orders, expediting product shipments, or reconfiguring products to create the required models. This business process consists of several subprocesses like demand forecasting, inventory planning, master planning, and revenue planning.

Some of the major pain points of this process are the inability to generate a unified demand plan and to reach consensus across multiple departments, demand and supply volatility, the lack of historical data related to supply and transportation lead-time variability, and the lack of visibility downstream and upstream the supply chain after unexpected events happen.

Order Fulfillment

Order fulfillment is a process of providing accurate, optimal, and reliable delivery dates for sales orders by matching supply (on-hand, in-transit, or planned inventory) with demand while respecting delivery transportation constraints and sales channels or distribution centers' allocations. It is the process of promising what the company can deliver, and delivering on every promise. It is tightly integrated with the selling-management process under CRM.

The major pain points for order fulfillment are the inability to provide visibility across the supply chain to ensure on-time delivery to the customer, and the inability to provide flexibility in meeting customer's expectations. The Internet market forces companies to deal with small shipment sizes more frequently, and changes the destination of deliveries to residential areas.

Marketing Management

Marketing management is the process of creating effective marketing programs to increase revenue, and to increase demand for the products in profitable market segments. It is also the process of generating new customers in a profit-effective manner and providing the best mix of products and services. The marketing process is an input to the demand forecasting subprocess to communicate the projected demand upstream for planning and forecasting purposes. The traditional marketing process is company centric, where phone or face-to-face meetings are the primary marketing media.

In the past, manufacturing controlled the market by determining the price, quality, specifications, and delivery parameters of their products. Company-centric organizations were organized as isolated departments, each dedicated to specific fulfillment functions along the supply chain (Curran & Ladd, 2000).

The other main pain points for this process are the inability to identify appropriate market segments for incentives and promotions, the inability to create effective marketing programs to achieve revenue and profitability objectives while considering supply-chain constraints, and lost revenue due to ineffective new-product launches.

Selling Management

It is the process of helping and guiding the customer to decide on what to buy, and providing accurate and reliable information on the price, delivery, and configuration options. Selling management is the trigger point for sales order processing, which is a subprocess under order fulfillment.

The main pain points in the current practice are the inability to match offerings to customer needs profitably through intelligent pricing, the configuration and availability checking, and the inability to provide the sales agents with guided selling, pricing, and order-promising information to ensure accurate order generation and provide the best product-service bundle to the customer.

Sabri (2005) summarized the challenges that the retail industry faces in the area of selling management.

1. Managing the complicated pricing process
2. Managing the growing product catalog with the challenge of limited space
3. The need for speed in the complex supply network of short-life products
4. Managing promotions and discounts effectively, and the need for markdown optimization
5. Managing product assortments, phasing out products, and seasonality

Customer-Service Management

Customer-service management usually starts through the signing up of a service agreement with the customer, which includes several contract items like discounts on replacement parts, guaranteed response time, technicians' hourly rates, and support time (Curran & Keller, 2000). This process consists of service planning and scheduling, service contract management, service order processing, replacement-part delivery, damaged-part recycling or returns, call centers, and billing. The call center or help desk is the traditional channel for receiving the service order notification, which represents a request for a customer-service activity that can be used to plan specific tasks related to the usage of spare parts and resources, allocate resources to the service task, monitor the performance of the conducted service tasks, and settle service costs.

Some of the CSM-process pain points are the complexity of today's products, which makes managing this process more difficult; customer dissatisfaction due to service-part shortage; inaccurate forecasting for service parts that are considered of high-dollar value, and slow-moving items; and the fact that customer service is becoming a competitive advantage due to the intensified competition and the need to compensate for revenue losses in a flat economy.

E-Business Application Levels and Benefits

Application Levels of E-Business

Before discussing how e-business can address the aforementioned pain points and provide benefits, let us first discuss the different application levels of e-business technology as shown in Figure 1.

There are four application levels of e-business as shown in Figure 1. The higher one goes in the pyramid, the more impact these levels have on the success of the organization and business agility. It is important to mention that achieving the higher levels depends on mastering the lower levels. In Level 1 (the base of the pyramid), information is extracted from data. Then, knowledge is extracted from information in Level 2, and wisdom is obtained in Level 3; this enables companies to accelerate to Level 4.

Level 1: SC Visibility

SC visibility refers to sharing data across different participants of the supply chain, and presenting the needed information extracted from data to all participants, depending on their roles, online and on a real-time basis. Some examples of data include forecast data, inventory pictures, capacity plans, promotion plans, shipment schedules, and production schedules. SC visibility addresses the challenge of supply and demand uncertainty by providing visibility to supply events like supplier shortages, and demand events like changes to customer orders. SC visibility provides several benefits like forward (proactive) visibility, early problem detection, and increased productivity and efficiency.

E-business software providers like i2 Technologies support several important capabilities for this level, like a centralized view into critical supply-chain information, and multiple modes of notification (e-mail, e-mail digests, pagers, or cell phones).

Savi Technologies is an example of a company that makes use of RFID technologies to track individual products, containers, and transportation vehicles as they move through the supply chain.

Figure 1. Application levels of e-business

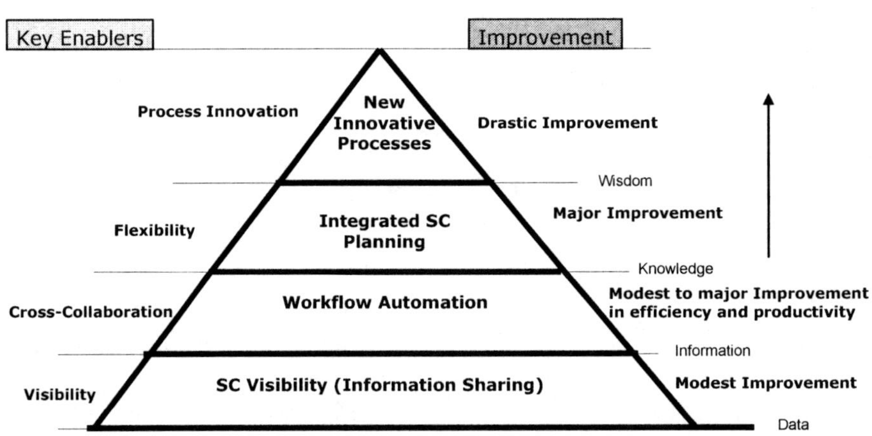

The information is put on the Internet so that real-time visibility of movements can be obtained (Lee & Whang, 2001).

Another example for providing visibility to in-transit products and for improving the order-fulfillment process is of a contract trucking company that uses a two-way mobile satellite-communication and position-reporting system to monitor the location of its trucks in order to improve performance under just-in-time programs (Ballou, 2004).

Level 2: Work-Flow Automation

Work-flow automation refers to the automation and streamlining of activities between supply-chain participants. For example, the request for a quote (a subprocess of procurement) and the related activities between buyers and suppliers can be automated and tightly coupled to increase productivity and reduce cycle time. Another example is the automation of the request for information (a subprocess of product design) between engineers in the buying organization and suppliers; here, productivity and quicker-time-to-market gains are achieved. In Level 2, shared information (from Level 1) is taken one step further by collaborating on it or resolving mismatch problems (exceptions). In this level, exceptions are prioritized so that the most important supply-chain disruptions are dealt with in the quickest and most optimal manner; this provides the SC partners the ability to respond to problems in real time to minimize the impact of disruptions on the supply chain, which means cost-effective, speedy, reliable, and almost-error-free SC activities.

The automation of critical (core competency) business processes should be done after improving the as-is process by eliminating nonvalue activities, simplifying and streamlining processes, and removing barriers (disconnects) between processes or functions. This means the automation should be done for the redesigned modified to-be process, and the software needs to be customized to follow and support the process to maintain the competitive advantage. On the other hand, automating noncore competency processes can be done by either using out-of-the-box work flows provided by software companies by which such processes are changed accordingly (no value in tailoring the software to fit the process), or by outsourcing the management of these processes to a third party.

A good example of work-flow automation is the application of electronic exchange portals in the area of procurement, such as Covisint for the automobile industry, e2open for the electronics industry, and Transora for the grocery industry.

Level 3: Integrated SC Planning

The integrated-SC-planning level allows companies to respond quickly and effectively to unplanned supply and demand events that may disrupt information and material flow in the supply chain as one unit. It allows a company to plan based on real-time execution data, and execute based on an up-to-date plan. Integrated SC planning provides a process-centric view coordinating different business subprocesses like product introduction, forecasting, replenishment, manufacturing, fulfillment, and procurement with suppliers and customers, while enabling event management. For example, it supports event-triggered planning and replanning. This level blends information gathered from users using collaboration in Level 2 and multiple transactions and planning systems to allow the exchange of knowledge by the SC partners and create synchronized plans and one global view of the supply chain.

Each supply-chain member (buyer, supplier, carrier, third-party logistics, contract manufacturer, etc.) often operates independently and only responds to immediate requirements. If the Internet is integrated with the SC planning process, SC members can share needed information on a real-time basis, and react quickly and efficiently to changes in demand, material shortages, transportation delays, and supplier inability to replenish. One example is the collaborative planning, forecasting, and replenishment (CPFR) initiative.

McDonald's Japan is a good example of the successful use of CPFR. McDonald's Japan established a process around the Internet whereby stores, marketing, distribution centers, and suppliers would communicate and collaborate via the company's Web site to agree on order sizes and supply-replenishment delivery schedules (Ballou, 2004).

TaylorMade (a large golf supplier) leveraged integrated SC planning to improve the order-fulfillment process. TaylorMade adopted Provia Software as the warehouse-management system and integrated it smoothly with i2's planning and fulfillment systems to prioritize orders based on service level, order volume, promised delivery date, and transport mode (Bowman, 2002).

Level 4: New Innovative Processes

Once companies master e-business application levels, they start to think of adopting new strategies and models for conducting business, seeking not only incremental improvements, but drastic ones. They might seek to reengineer (redesign) their processes to leverage the most out of e-business technologies. Sometimes, companies start to define new processes, seeking new business opportunities or trying to penetrate new markets and customer segments that were neither apparent nor possible prior to the e-business. Companies seek the new-generation business models to achieve competitive advantage and significant benefits. One example is what Dell Computer did when it adopted the build-to-order strategy and provided flexible configuration capability for customers online. The following are examples that show the range of possibilities for companies that pioneered in these areas.

Example 1: Mass Customization

The Internet and e-business technologies facilitate mass customization and allow customers to configure specific order options tailored to their preferences.

Mass customization is the centerpiece of a strategy that woke the big golf supplier TaylorMade and propelled it ahead of the competition in terms of agility and innovation. Today, TaylorMade can customize virtually any aspect of a club. The results to date are impressive (Bowman, 2002).

Example 2: Public Marketplaces

The Internet and e-business technologies helped many companies do business online using a secured specialized Web site. One example is World Chemical Exchange, providing a global market for chemical and plastic manufacturers and buyers. More than 2,500 members can now conduct around-the-clock trading of chemicals and plastics of all types (Lee & Whang, 2001).

Example 3: Supply-Chain Redesign

A good example is what many remote discount computer-hardware and -supply houses did to compete with local retail stores. Many of them used the Internet technologies as a strategy to compress the order cycle time and improve the order-fulfillment process: A customer enters the order through the company's Web site, the inventory and payment are checked, and the order is filled from the warehouse and shipped using UPS, FedEx, or other carriers directly to the end customer.

Example 4: Value-Added Replenishment Programs

Companies as part of lean initiatives are trying to focus on value-added activities to cut waste in the supply chain and reduce overhead cost. Therefore, manufacturers are moving away from making products to stock and sell them later. They are moving away from procuring based only on forecast. Vendor-managed inventory (VMI) is a replenishment program that helps companies achieve their objectives. VMI delays the ownership of goods until the last possible moment and delegates managing the stock to the supplier.

Western Publishing is using a VMI program in its Golden Book lines. It develops a relationship with its retailers in which these retailers give Western point-of-sale data. Ownership of the inventory shifts to the retailer once the product is shipped (Ballou, 2004).

Kanban replenishment is another program in which replenishing parts is based on part consumption. It avoids the inaccuracy in forecasting and eliminates the need for inventory.

Example 5: Online Retailing

Amazon.com understood e-business technologies very well. It has based its business model around it. Amazon.com depends on its efficient supply chain to satisfy customer needs worldwide. It mastered the selling-management process by improving the Web shopping experience through providing quick and reliable promises, and suggesting product bundles, among many other features. This makes Amazon.com one of the biggest and early adopters of e-business technologies.

Benefits of Adopting E-Business Application Levels

Tables 2, 3, and 4 illustrate how the four application levels of e-business can address the challenges of SCM, SRM, and CRM business processes that were mentioned in the beginning of this section. These tables also show the potential benefits of adopting e-business strategies.

Tables 2, 3, and 4 show the operational and financial benefits of adopting e-business application levels. The operational benefits can be grouped under inventory reductions, cycle-time reductions, productivity increase, supplier performance improvement, and customer-service-level increase. The financial benefits are driven from the operational benefits and can be grouped as follows.

- Cost reduction due to cost savings. The tight integration of supply-chain processes reduces the cost and time needed to exchange transactions and allows efficient procurement, which helps the purchasing staff to focus more on strategic activities like building supplier relationships than managing day-to-day transactions.
- Revenue growth and profit increase due to increased customer satisfaction by delivering on every promise and responding quickly to customer needs, and the ability to penetrate new markets.
- Better asset utilization by replacing inventory with real-time visibility
- Higher shareholder value due to growing profit.

The next section will provide the needed guidelines to implement e-business technologies successfully. Finally, a case study will be presented.

A FRAMEWORK FOR SUCCESSFUL IMPLEMENTATION OF E-BUSINESS TECHNOLOGIES

Many companies are struggling with implementing e-business technologies and achieving the promised value or ROI. In addition, companies are looking for guidelines and strategies for ongoing operational management and support after the go-live, which includes rolling more customers,

Table 2. The impact of e-business application levels on SRM processes

	SRM Business Processes			
E-Business Application Levels	**Strategic Sourcing**	**Product Design**	**Procurement**	**Benefits**
SC Visibility	Sharing AVL with design and procurement departments	Real-time visibility on engineering change requests (ECRs)	Sharing supplier and shipment information, real-time exception visibility, audit-trail notification, alerts, and tracking	• Reducing part-inventory obsoleteness • Improving inventory turns • Reducing safety stock • Reducing expedition cost
Work-Flow Automation	A single user interface for design, sourcing, and procurement with flexible and configurable work flows	Shared design workbench	Automated procurement subprocesses, bid analysis, and resolution work flow	• Reducing design rework • Reducing process cycle time • Improving productivity
Integrated SC Planning	Consolidation of enterprise spend/demand across separate systems	Tightly integrated to PDM and AVL	Synchronized replenishment, supporting different replenishment types, and matching execution documents like purchase orders, ASN, and invoices	• Increasing reuse of existing parts in the design • Improving on-time delivery
New Innovative Processes	Analyzing supplier and SC performance (slice and dice by site, commodity, time, supplier, and KPI)	Design collaboration	Auctions, marketplace exchanges	• Reducing development cost • Improving time to market • Reducing part/raw-material cost • Improving quality

Table 3. The impact of e-business application levels on SCM processes

	SCM Business Processes			
E-Business Application Levels	**Supply-Chain Design**	**Sales and Operations Planning**	**Order Fulfillment**	**Benefits**
SC Visibility	Providing an aggregated view on the SC performance and strategic information	Real-time visibility to unexpected events in the SC and audit-trail data	Real-time SC visibility for the order-delivery life cycle including contract manufacturers, distribution centers, and logistic providers	• Reducing uncertainty and safety stock • Early issue detection
Work-Flow Automation	Consistent process with friendly user interface	Unified demand plan across different departments	Exception work-flow resolution for demand changes and fulfillment delays	• Increasing efficiency • Fast response
Integrated SC Planning	Integration with strategic sourcing to reduce supplier base	Synchronized marketing, sales, production, and procurement plans	CPFR	• Speed • Accuracy
New Innovative Processes	SC redesign	Mass customization	Build to order	• Flexibility • Penetrating new markets • Customer satisfaction

Table 4. The impact of e-business application levels on CRM processes

E-Business Application Levels	Marketing Management	Selling Management	Customer-Service Management	Benefits
SC Visibility (Information Sharing)	Capturing feedback from the customers, providing a mix of products and service offerings customized to customer needs	Providing up-sell and cross-sell product recommendations and product bundles, flexible pricing models for markdown and rebates	Providing service order status and highlighting exceptions	• Publicizing product information • Increasing customer satisfaction • Reduce Inv.
Work-Flow Automation	Capturing log records for every visit of a user in the Web servers' log file, including pages visited, duration of the visit, and whether there was a purchase, demand collaboration with customers	Product configuration, quotation processing	Service order logging, billing of services	• Better prediction of customer demand • Improving response time • Improving productivity
Integrated SC Planning	Considering the supply-chain constraints while executing the marketing campaigns, providing customer profiling and segmentation	Supporting different channels for order capturing (Web based, call center, EDI, phone, e-mail, or personnel meeting)	Warranty check, service order processing, integrating the call center	• Increasing revenues and profit • Creating new market/distribution channels • Accurate promising date
New Innovative Processes	Real-time profiling that tracks the user click stream, allows the analysis of customer behavior, and makes instantaneous adjustments to the site's promotional offers and Web pages	Online flexible configuration and real-time promise date	Dealing with products and services as one package during selling	• Long-term relationship and trust with the customer • Gaining competitive advantage

suppliers, and new business units when implementing e-business solutions to improve SRM, SCM, and CRM superprocesses.

According to a survey of 451 senior executives, one in every five users reported that their CRM initiatives not only had failed to deliver profitable growth, but also had damaged long-standing customer relationships (Rigby et al., 2002).

Currently, there is uncertainty and doubt among organizations regarding the new Internet technologies, and although the appeal for best practice and the benefits of implementing e-business technologies are clear, enterprises struggle in integrating them into supply-chain operations because they are encountered by many challenges like the inability to master change management, the need for new skills to support processes that span across suppliers and partners, the need for e-business strategy and continuous upper management support, the lack of comprehensive metrics and continuous monitoring, and the inability to select the right software-providing partner.

Figure 2 is proposed to address these challenges and provide best-practice guidelines to implement e-business program transformation successfully.

E-Business Strategy and Goals

A clear strategy is the first step for a successful transformation. Executives need to understand the big picture, the interactions between all the processes, and the e-business applications to help them in creating an e-business strategy.

Benchmarking

Benchmarking is the process of comparing and evaluating a firm or a supply chain against others in the industry to help in identifying the gaps and areas of improvement. Benchmarking is used to validate the potential benefit and gain in performance measures from implementing e-business applications.

Process Analysis

The purpose of process analysis (also called design and requirements) is to use modeling (process mapping) methods to analyze "as-is" business processes, capture the existing challenges and pain points in the current process and the supply chain, design and validate the to-be process improvements against best-practice benchmarks, determine the extent of process and technology changes possible in the currently existing systems, and identify the additional software (application) capabilities that are required to support the to-be process that cannot be supported by the existing systems. This requirements list will be the base for selecting the new software.

Select the Right E-Business Software

As a best practice, organizations need to identify the best-of-breed solution that is most suitable for the required functionality for their business, taking into consideration software-technology maturity and sustainability. Supporting leading industry standards for e-business technology like Java, XML, Linux, and Web services is crucial during the selection process.

Cost and Benefit Analysis

Cost and benefit analysis is the process that determines the potential benefits from implementing the combination of the best-practice process

Figure 2. Framework for implementing e-business transformation programs

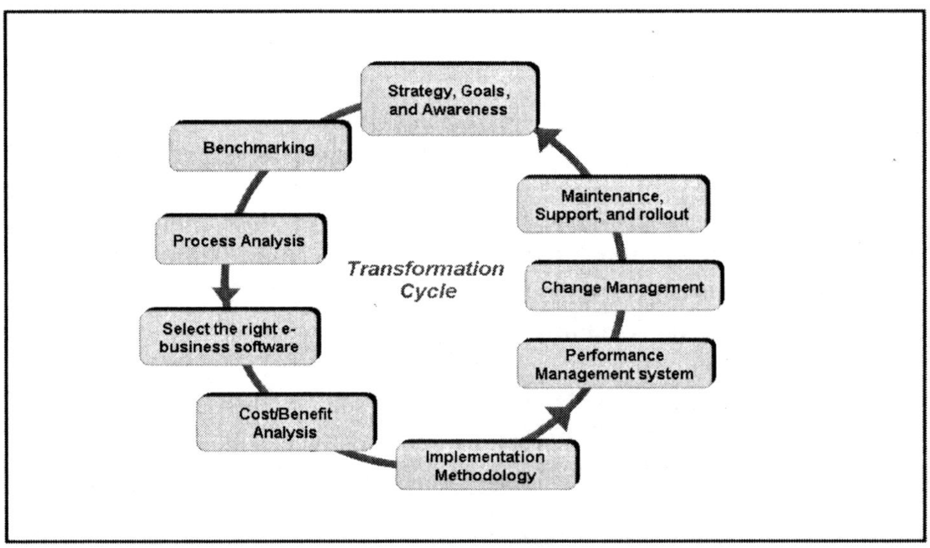

and the new application or software. It addresses questions like the following. What is the potential value of increasing the loyalty of our customers when new marketing-management software is implemented? What is the cost of implementing the new solution?

Adopt a Value-Driven Implementation Methodology

Adopting a value-driven approach to conduct the e-business transformation programs like Six Sigma is very critical. An effective transformation program typically takes 2 to 5 years, with several intermediate checkpoints (go-lives) to achieve the value needed to pay for the rest of the program.

Performance-Management System

A performance-management system consists of two phases. The first phase is to establish a consistent metrics-tracking and -publishing process, and this phase should finish before the implementation of the transformation program. The second phase is to continue measuring the benefits and ROI, which should start during and after the implementation.

Since the performance-management system depends mainly on monitoring the metrics (KPIs), it is critical to spend enough time on defining these metrics. The performance-management system should manage and coordinate the development of these metrics. Melnyk, Stewart, and Swink (2004) mentioned that metrics provide the following three basic functions.

- **Control:** Metrics enable managers to evaluate and control the performance of the resources.
- **Communication:** Metrics communicate performance to internal and external stakeholders.
- **Improvement:** Metrics identify gaps (between actual performance and expectation) that ideally point the way for intervention and improvement.

Sabri and Rehman (2004) provided guidelines for identifying and maintaining metrics based on best practice, recommended to capture all operational metrics because improvement in one area could be at the expense of another, and suggested to summarize benefits in six key areas: revenue increase, cost reduction, process lead-time reduction, asset reduction, customer benefits, and supplier benefits.

Change Management

Effective change management for e-business transformation programs should consider gaining and keeping executive sponsorship. Without executives' buy-in and support, a transformation program would be much closer to failure than success. It should also involve all SC partners in developing the new to-be process, and should establish a benefit-sharing and incentives mechanism.

Maintenance, Support, and Rollout

Although companies acknowledge the importance of ongoing operational management and support, few of them think ahead of time and allocate the right resources for it. Once the e-business application links are in place, companies find themselves with an urgent need to manage the ongoing maintenance and rollout. Ongoing monitoring and maintenance are necessary to ensure 100% uptime and compliance. The lack of a defined and clear plan for maintenance and rollout might impact the whole transformation program negatively. The ongoing maintenance and rollout process should include adding new SC organizations and removing existing ones as necessary. It includes training programs and process compliance by monitoring related metrics. It also includes the identification and description of all user groups, and the process of adding new users, making changes to user authorization levels, maintaining profiles, and deleting users. Finally, contingency plans should be reviewed periodically to make sure its readiness. Contingency plans represent predefined courses of actions to be followed in case of the occurrence of a drastic event like when the sources for inbound information go down.

Case Study

This case study is based on an article published in October 2004 by Reuben Slone in *Harvard Business Review* (HBR), which is about the supply-chain turnaround by Whirlpool in the last 4 years. Whirlpool makes a diverse line of products like washers, dryers, refrigerators, dishwashers, and ovens, with manufacturing facilities in 13 countries. This case study is a real-life example of a company that adopted many of the best-practice guidelines of implementing e-business applications that were highlighted previously in this section.

Strategy

Whirlpool needed a strategy that not only addresses the current needs, but also anticipates the challenges of the future. Whirlpool wanted a strategy that can optimize supply-chain performance at minimum cost, and include new e-business technology, processes, roles, and talents to achieve competitive advantage. Its strategy was to focus on customer requirements first and proceed backward. Therefore, Whirlpool and Sears as a customer studied consumers' desires with regard to appliance delivery. They found that consumers are asking for accurate promises as a first requirement: "Give a date, hit a date."

Benchmarking and Process Analysis

Whirlpool benchmarked its competitors and obtained cross-industry information and competitive intelligence from AMR, Gartner, and Forrester Research. Then it mapped out what is considered best-practice performance along 27 different SC-capability dimensions. This exercise helped identify areas of improvement.

Cost and Benefit Analysis

The program transformation team had to build a compelling business case to get the buy-in from upper management. They had to justify their program wholly on expense reductions and working capital improvements.

Effective Transformation Plans

Effective transformation plans include a value-driven implementation methodology (Six Sigma), performance-management system, change management, and rollout plans.

Whirlpool started with improving the S&OP process. Its current process was inadequate with Excel spreadsheet feeds. Now, Whirlpool is able to generate synchronized long and short plans that consider marketing, sales, finance, and manufacturing constraints or requirements. Then, it launched a CPFR pilot to share forecasts using a Web-based application and to collaborate on the exceptions, which enabled it to cut forecast accuracy error in half within 30 days of launch. In January 2002, Whirlpool implemented a suite of software products from i2 to reduce inventories while sustaining high service level. By May 2002, a blind Internet survey showed Whirlpool to be "most improved," "easiest to do business with," and "most progressive" in the eyes of their trade partners.

It segmented its products and followed a different strategy for each product group. For high-volume SKU like dishwashers, refrigerators, and washing machines, it used the build-to-stock replenishment technique with its customers. For smallest volume SKUs, they followed the pull replenishment technique with the more flexible build-to-order process. The inventory savings on the small-volume SKUs can balance out the costs of stocking up on the high-volume SKUs. Whirlpool also started to move away from having one service level across all products, recognizing that some products are more important or more profitable than others and should have higher service levels.

Recently, there has been a focus on system-to-system transactions, in which the Whirlpool system talks directly to a customer's system for purposes of transmitting purchase orders, exchanging sales data, and submitting invoices and payments. At the same time, customers can check availability and place orders via the Internet. Whirlpool is also looking to implement an event-management capability that provides a notification whenever an action in the process has taken place.

A couple things were absolutely critical to keep the transformation program schedule on track: a highly disciplined transformation program office and an effective management system. The key was to think big but focus relentlessly on near-term deadlines. Whirlpool organized the change effort into 30-day chunks, with three new capabilities or business releases rolling out monthly, some on the supply side and some on the demand side. The main job of the program transformation office, which adopted Six Sigma methodology, was to ensure the completion of projects on time, on budget, and on benefit.

The transformation program office contracted Michigan State University and the American Production and Inventory Control Society to develop a competency model that can outline the skills and roles required in a top-tier organization. Whirlpool also expanded the compensation system to allow employees to be rewarded for increasing their expertise even if they are not being promoted into supervisory roles. It also put a huge emphasis on developing employees' management skills and used a model developed by Project Management Institute (PMI) as a standard for evaluating and enhancing the organization's project-management capabilities. Finally, it assembled a supply-chain advisory board to provide guidance and assess the transformation program results and direction.

To summarize, Whirlpool followed the best practice in leveraging e-business technologies, and in return, it has much to show for its transformation efforts. Today, its product-availability service level is more than 95%. The inventory of finished goods has dropped from 32.8 to 26 days. In one year, it lowered its working capital by almost $100 million and supply-chain costs by $20 million with an ROI equal to 2.

CONCLUSION

E-business technologies present huge opportunities that are already being tapped by many companies and supply chains. Leveraging e-business technologies effectively is key to gaining competitive advantage, streamlining processes, slashing waste, and eventually achieving business agility, which is significantly needed in the new age of globalization and intensive competition.

More companies will start to realize that gaining competitive advantage is no longer feasible only by managing their own organizations. They need to get involved in the management of all upstream organizations that are responsible for the supply, as well as the downstream network that is responsible for delivery and the after-sales market. The challenge for companies for the rest of this decade is synchronization across supply-chain processes, from product design and procurement to marketing and customer-service management, in order to be more responsive to customer needs. The new trend of mergers and acquisitions will continue to rise, and big companies that are buying out smaller ones will grow even bigger in the complexity of their supply chains. This will increase the need for e-business technologies to streamline the process of collaboration between the different entities.

Therefore, in the next few years, we will see the explosion of e-business-applications use as companies utilize e-business to redefine supply-chain processes that span across suppliers and customers, which will result in a significant improvement in efficiency and will help companies achieve competitive advantage. Companies that do not come on board will realize that they are losing ground and customers soon.

The widespread use of e-business will lead to new options for improving business-to-business and business-to-consumer collaborations like multitier collaborations and root-cause analysis for exceptions in the supply-chain performance. In addition, it will open new ways of integration between supply-chain partners like system-to-system integration using Web services (e.g., integrating one firm's inventory-control system and another's logistics-scheduling environment), the use of wireless devices, and the tight integration of the Web site with the back-end systems of supply-chain partners. Eventually, e-business technologies will replace electronic data interchange, the benefits of which never materialized for midsized companies because of its high cost.

We also expect SMEs (small and medium-sized enterprises) to realize the importance of e-business and to follow one of the following arrangements in adopting e-business technologies depending on the business requirements and cost factors.

- **Microsoft arrangement:** Easy to implement due to wide familiarity with the product and its selling process through partners, cheap license, cheap maintenance, and tight integration with other Microsoft products like Excel
- **Public Web-enabled arrangement:** Prebuilt solution by a Web-enabled applications provider at a fixed monthly cost, no need for software to be present on the company's internal network, no maintenance fees, and lower risk due to almost zero-down investment

Intelligent performance-management systems that can capture negative performance trends and select the correct resolutions are expected to come into widespread use in the next few years.

To summarize, we will witness, for the rest of this decade, what is called a tightly integrated environment in which supply-chain interactions involve tightly integrated databases and applications; processes are significantly redesigned and streamlined to eliminate redundancies and nonvalue activities.

REFERENCES

Anderson, D. M. (2003). *Build-to-order & mass customization.* Cambria, CA: CIM Press.

Ballou, R. H. (2004). *Business logistics/supply chain management* (5th ed.). Upper Saddle River, NJ: Prentice Hall.

Bowman, R. J. (2002). TaylorMade drives supply-chain efficiency with 24 hour club. *SupplyChainBrain.com.* Retrieved December 10, 2004, from *http://www.supplychainbrain.com/archives/10.02.TaylorMade.htm?adcode=5*

Curran, T. A., & Ladd, A. (2000). *SAP R3 business blueprint: Understanding enterprise supply chain management* (2nd ed.). Upper Saddle River, NJ: Prentice Hall.

Devaraj, S., & Kohli, R. (2002). *The IT payoff: Measuring the business value of information technology investment.* Upper Saddle River, NJ: Prentice Hall.

Handfield, R. B., & Nichols, E. R. (2002). *Supply chain redesign: Transforming supply chains into integrated value systems.* Upper Saddle River, NJ: Prentice Hall.

Harmon, P. (2003). *Business process chain: A*

manager's guide to improving, redesigning, and automating processes. San Francisco: Morgan Kaufmann Publishers.

Lee, H., & Whang, S. (2001). E-business and supply chain integration. *Stanford Global Supply Chain Management Forum*, 1-20.

Melnyk, S. A., Stewart, D. M., & Swink, M. (2004). Metrics and performance measurement in operations management: Dealing with the metrics maze. *Journal of Operations Management, 22*, 209-217.

Rigby, D., Reichheld, F., & Schefter, P. (2002). Avoid the four perils of CRM. *Harvard Business Review*, 1-9.

Sabri, E. (2005). *Value chain management to achieve competitive advantage in retail industry.* Paper presented at the Middle East Retail Conference, United Arab Emirates.

Sabri, E., & Beamon, B. (2000). A multi-objective approach to simultaneous strategic and operational planning in supply chain design. *OMEGA: The International Journal of Management Science, 28*(5), 581-598.

Sabri, E., & Rehman, A. (2004). *ROI model for procurement order management process.* Paper presented at the Lean Management Solutions Conference, Los Angeles.

Slone, R. E. (2004). Leading supply chain turnaround. *Harvard Business Review*, 1-9.

Valencia, J. S., & Sabri, E. H. (2005). *E-business technologies impact on supply chain.* Paper presented at the 16th Annual Conference of POMS, Chicago.

This work was previously published in Enterprise Service Computing: From Concept to Deployment, edited by R. Qiu, pp. 356-287, copyright 2007 by IGI Publishing, formerly known as Idea Group Publishing (an imprint of IGI Global).

Chapter X
Building Dynamic Business Process in P2P Semantic Web

Timon C. Du
The Chinese University of Hong Kong, Hong Kong, China

Eldon Y. Li
National Chengchi University, Taiwan & California Polytechnic State University, USA

ABSTRACT

Business process management systems such as the workflow management system and the enterprise application integration system manage process flow on a minute-by-minute basis in various application domains. In the conventional approach, the business process must be predefined before it is implemented. However, involving business users in the early stage of the design phase is neither efficient nor realistic in the dynamic business world. This study proposes a framework to implement a dynamic business process in the P2P Semantic Web, which provides the flexibility to dynamically alter business process and to take semantic data into consideration. The system is demonstrated by a case of a manufacturer that is processing an order.

INTRODUCTION

In the past decade, the Internet technology boom has encouraged the development and sharing among people, organizations, and enterprises of vast ranges of information. However, most of that information is written in hypertext markup language (HTML), which mainly follows a predefined format to express the content, where well-formatted information is normally written for human comprehension rather than machine automation. This means that when the information volume grows, the time to locate and digest the information increases even more rapidly. In this way, users need to make a tremendous effort to locate information that fits their needs. There are many possible solutions to resolve the information overloaded problem, such as paying money to the search engine to improve visibility, which is called "paid placement" or "paid inclusion." Sophisticated solutions such as allowing users to write a query paragraph rather than simply inputting keywords are also possible. In the years to come, we will see many more innovative solutions to the problem.

The Web has also evolved to become a service-providing medium. Web services use software applications to provide interoperability, whereby they discover, describe, and access other services from the Internet, Intranets, and Extranets. This leads to the adoption of XML (extensible markup language) technology in which information is shared in text format. Note that XML provides independence of applications and data, which allows data to be shared among applications. However, the problem lies in determining what kinds of information can be shared and how it can be shared. As the Web is no longer a media for human-to-human communication because the information available is overwhelming, there is a need to seek help from machines in organizing and locating specific information. The evolution will take place in two dimensions: from syntactic to semantic and from static to dynamic. This will move the Web toward being a Semantic Web and Web service, and then advance the Web service into an intelligent Web service and the Semantic Web into Semantic Web services.

The Semantic Web structures Web content into semantic data for both humans and machines. The semantic data are the information and the meaning of the information. These are presented as structured collections of information and sets of rules. Although both the knowledge representation and rules have been studied for years in the area of artificial intelligence, the traditional approaches have rigid structures to ensure that new knowledge can be inferred from existing data and rules. In contrast, the decentralized nature of the Semantic Web allows individual Web sites to represent knowledge in their own ways. This provides an opportunity for Web sites to grow independently and diversely.

This study will use the properties provided in the Semantic Web to build dynamic business processes, where "a business process is a collection of related structure activities that produce a specific outcome for a particular customer" (http://en.wikipedia.org). The process can be defined by attributes such as name, description, date, version, component, operation, and so forth. It is worth noting here the difference between workflow and business process. A workflow is a complex business process that normally involves many *tasks*; it is static and has to be well defined before applying. This also means that the *roles* assigned to specific tasks are predefined even though the *users* that are assigned to roles can be dynamically identified. A workflow can be activated many times, and each implementation is called a *case*, which has a unique identity and a limited lifetime. In this case, the business process is a concept mingling the workflow and the case because it indicates which task must be carried out for a specific customer. As workflow schemas are static and predefined, they are difficult to adopt in the rapidly changing environment, particularly for collaboration among partners (Zeng et al., 2003). Moreover, problems of consistency after changing the workflow, resource optimization in the dynamic environment, the reuse of workflow, the workflow engine that is used to manage the changing workflow, and the flexibility to adapt workflow to new environments are all our concerns (Cichocki & Rusinkiewicz, 2004).

In this study, the business process is developed in the peer to peer (P2P) architecture of the Semantic Web. The P2P architecture is used as a communication platform in which each party (node) has a similar role and a similar ability to handle business processes with other parties directly or through a community service (http://searchnetworking. techtarget.com). Moreover, each node is built with Semantic Web technology that allows the semantics of Web content to be included in the handling of business processes. The advantages of this approach are: (1) Web sites that participate in the business process are dynamically selected (for example, the selection of suppliers); (2) information and support for implemented tasks are dynamically collected (for example, order processing); (3) the implementation of business processes can be automated (such as in outsourcing); and (4) the business process can be dynamically modified (such as in business process collaboration). Figure 1 exhibits an example of how a business process is dynamically modified. The remaining sections are organized as follows: A brief introduction to the links between business and the Semantic Web, an illustration of the architecture, a demonstration, and discussion.

Business Process and Semantic Web

A business process defines the activities, including input, output, and method, that are necessary to complete a specific assignment. A business process is created to deal with a specific *case* in

Figure 1. An example of dynamically modifying a business process

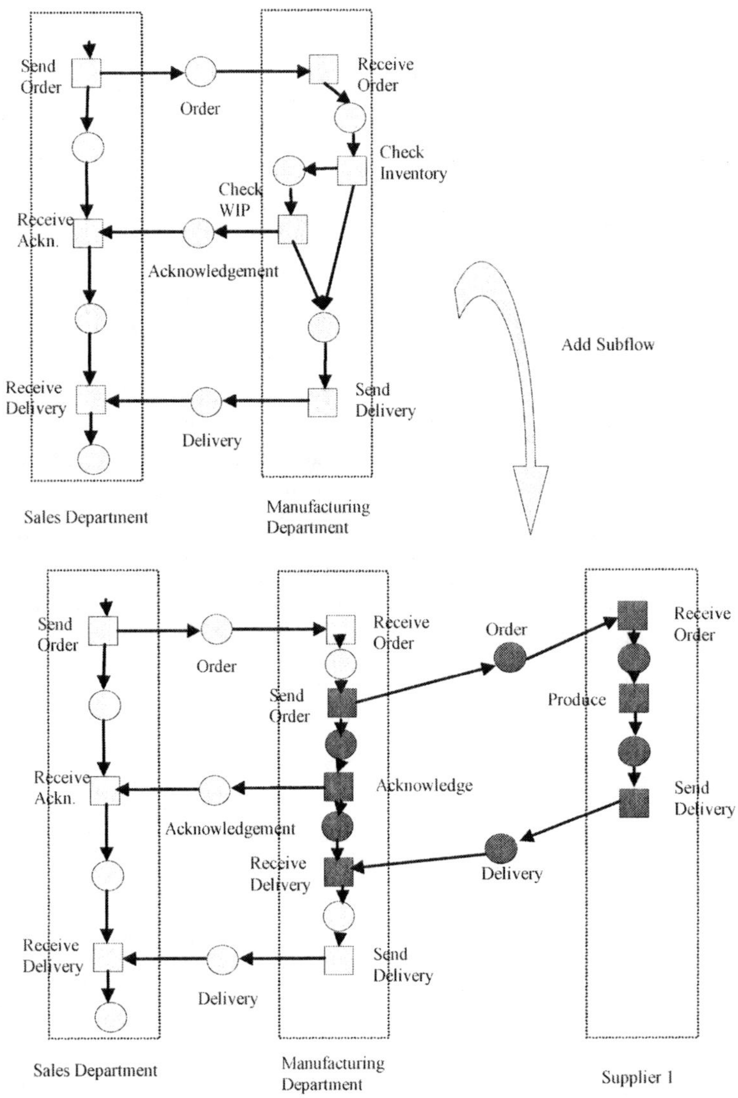

an organization, such as applying for a mortgage, placing orders or proceeding with engineering tests. The structure of a business process can be very complex. It can be composed of many subprocesses (also called processes), such as a workflow. The work in a business process can be identified as a *task*, which represents the indivisible unit of work. The task is carried out by a *process*. When the processes are carried out in a business process they follow a specific sequence that determines which task needs to be performed next. A case should be completed within a certain time limit and should exit the system when the work is completed. This also means that attributes are needed to describe the state and content of the process.

There are four different types of sequences in a complex business process: *sequential*, *parallel*, *selective*, and *iterative* routings. Sequential routing confines one task to be executed before another task, whereas parallel routing allows two tasks to be performed without feedback from each other. Selective routing provides a choice between or among tasks, and iteration allows the same task to be performed more than once.

During implementation, the process must be enacted to perform a task. Tasks are assigned to designated *roles* following principles such as the separation of duties, least privilege assignment and data abstraction (Sandhu, Coyne, Feinstein, & Youman, 1996). These principles ensure the successful implementation of the business process. For example, the separation of duties assigns two sensitive tasks to two exclusive roles so that conspired perpetration can be avoided. This principle is easily adopted within an organization (by using an Intranet) and can be accepted in supply chain collaboration (by using an extranet), but it is difficult to use on the Internet, in which the new assignments can go to any participant. In a client-server type of community, the duty to maintain the principle is normally assigned to a community server, which becomes a bottleneck because it needs to trace every business process. This study uses P2P architecture to develop the business process. As stated earlier, P2P architecture offers the advantage of sharing workloads (King, Ng, & Sia, 2004). Hence, the duty to maintain the principle should fall on any node in the community that uses the business process. Similarly, the least privilege policy, also called the "need to know" policy (Castano, Fugini, Martella, & Samarati, 1995), provides only minimum information for completing the task. Information sharing between nodes is also based on this principle, whereby only the minimum information is carried via agents that roam between nodes. However, as information is limited, when one node receives separate information from two sources that belong to the same business process that information cannot be composed back to the original message, which means that sensitive data can be leaked.

A business process management system manages the process flow on a minute to minute basis in various application domains such as office automation, finance, healthcare, telecommunication, manufacturing and production (Bertino, Jajodia, & Smarati, 1999). As has been discussed, in conventional business process systems, such as the workflow management system (WFMS), the process is static and predefined. However, it is unrealistic to apply a static and predefined process in a dynamic business world. Much research has tried to resolve dynamic business process problems. Examples of these problems include (1) evolving the process when the system parameters, the relationships among parameters, or communication among different partners in the supply chain changes (Rouibah & Caskey, 2003); (2) differentiating a shared public workflow from a private workflow to alleviate the effect of a change in a public workflow on a private domain (van der Aalst, 2003); (3) using different agents to manage the variation of workflows, in which the interagent workflow concerns control flow, data flow, and material flow between agents, and the intra-agent workflow provides flexibility in performing the activities on the work-list (Zhuge, 2003); (4)

applying knowledge-based techniques to make workflow systems more adaptive and to provide more flexible process management (Chung et al., 2003); and (5) not forming the business process until runtime to tolerate the dynamics (Zeng et al., 2003; Su, Meng, Krithivasan, Degwekar, & Helal, 2003)

The_Semantic Web brings structure to the meaningful content of Web pages, whereby software agents roam from one page to another to carry out sophisticated tasks for users (Berners-Lee, Hendler, & Lassila, 2001) . The implementation of the Semantic Web should be decentralized, with structured information and tasks carried out by the software agents, and with sets of inference rules helping the software agents to retrieve information. Most current studies on the Semantic Web focus mainly on the services carried out by software agents, such as ontology design, the visual environment for browsing, RDF (resource description framework) model and syntax specification, and Web services with ontologies, as opposed to individual servers (http://www.w3.org/). Less attention has been paid to the coordinated efforts of the servers to form a group ideology.

A Semantic Web is similar to a deductive database and a knowledge-based system, where new knowledge is deduced by applying rules to existing facts (Du, 2002). The differences between these systems are that the knowledge-based system does not use secondary storage to house data as do deductive databases and the Semantic Web, and both the knowledge-based system and deductive database apply rigid structures to the knowledge representation and deduction rules to ensure that new knowledge can be obtained from inference. In contrast, the Semantic Web allows Web sites to represent the knowledge and the relationships of the knowledge in their own ways. The information on Web sites can then be shared for use in different domains. For example, a query can be interpreted by the semantics interpreter through the query statement in such a way that the query results are more relevant (Jain, Aparicio, & Singh, 1999; Karvounarakis et al., 2003).

In the Semantic Web, the software agent is used to roam from page to page to carry out tasks that are assigned by users. However, it can do more than being a messenger because a mobile agent is an autonomous object that is created for dynamic and distributed applications that execute designated tasks. Referring to Wooldridge (Wooldridge & Jennings, 1995), agents can be identified as either *strong* or *weak*. Strong agents are capable of mentalist notions, rationality, veracity, adaptability, and learning. These capabilities come mainly from the technology of artificial intelligence. Weak agents, in contrast, can complete tasks autonomously, interact with external objects, and are reactive or proactive toward environmental change based on a pre-planned scheme. Software agents have been implemented in many distributed environments to share system loading and increase flexibility. Several applications have been successfully developed using mobile agents: for example, the supply chain SMART project (http://smart.npo.org), the virtual enterprise (Jain et al., 1999), information retrieval (Cabri, Leonardi, & Zambonelli, 2000), the Internet-based auction house (Sandholm & Huai, 2000), secured transactions (Castano et al., 1995), and distributed network management (Du, Li, & Chang, 2003). Some studies have further integrated mobile agents with CORBA, such as MESIS resource management (Bellavista, Corradi, & Stefanelli, 2000) and broadband intelligent networks (Chatzipapadopoulos, Perdikeas, & Venieris, 2000). In general, the software agent system can be applied to the areas of electronic commerce, personal assistance, secure brokering, distributed information retrieval, telecommunication network services, workflow applications and groupware, monitoring and notification, information dissemination, and parallel processing (Lange & Oshima, 1998).

The Architecture of Semantic Business Process

To implement a P2P framework, a node must first download a P2P networking program, such as IBM's advanced peer-to-peer networking (APPN), and a semantic business process program, such as semantics flow builder (SFB) and mobile agents. The SFB supports four functions—implementation manager, process planner, resource manager, and process monitor—and three mobile agents—a configure agent, a runtime agent, and a supervise agent—as shown in Figure 2. The three agents and four SFB functions interact as shown in Table 1.

SFB Functions

Four SFB functions are responsible for different duties. The *Process Planner* is used to design business processes and assign the processes to roles (Web sites). The Planner sends the configure agent to search for another network member that can implement the next task through community directory services (similar to UDDI). Once the agent finds another qualified network member, it

Figure 2. The architecture of the semantics business process

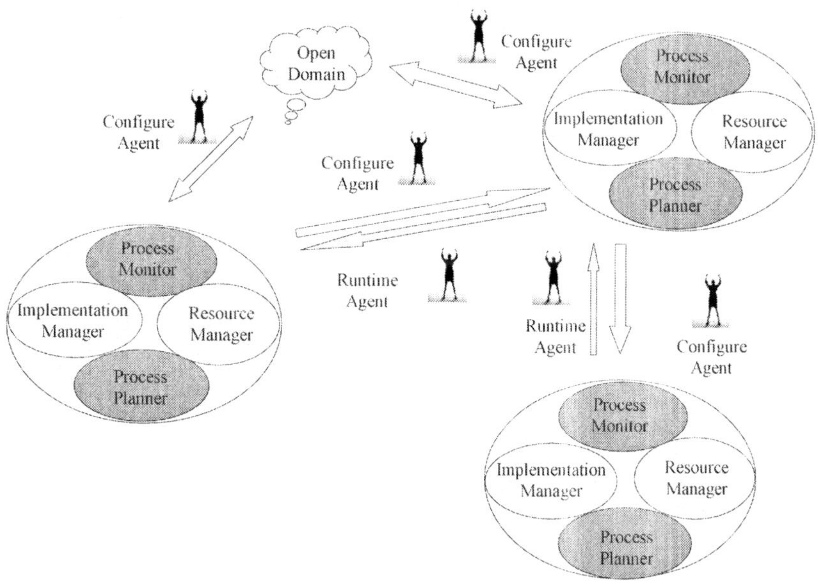

Table 1. The correlation of builder functions and mobile agents

	Process Planner	Resource Manager	Process Monitor	Implementation Manager
Configure Agent	✓	✓		✓
Runtime Agent	✓			✓
Supervise Agent			✓	

connects to that member and then carries the job assignment to the Web site (on a need-to-know basis). If none of members (Web sites) qualifies, then the Planner aborts the process. If more than one candidate Web site is found, then the configure agent activates the Resource Manager to determine which web site should be chosen (the separation of duty is sustained at this moment).

When a new task arrives at the next member, the Process Planner of the new Web site activates a runtime agent, which is dispatched to collect data, report to the initiated Web site whenever needed, and execute the task and work locally with the Implementation Manager (which will be explained later). When the task is completed, the member either returns the work to the initiated web site or searches for a new member to continue the work, depending on the business process. In the latter case, a new configure agent is sent to the community directory service to search for another member that can be the candidate for the next task. This procedure repeats until it reaches to the end of the process blueprint designed by the initiated Web site. Meanwhile, a member may need to interact with previous members or the initiated Web site if it needs more information to execute its work. When a Web site encounters the completion of the process, it should report to the web site that activated it (stacking).

It should be noted that this design allows a member to dynamically modify the business process according to local needs. This is based on the understanding that the local member should have a better knowledge of how to implement a particular task than any other member. However, when authority is given to a Web site, the business process can grow unpredictably. Therefore, it is the duty of the local Process Planner to check the soundness if the Web site extends the business process (this will be discussed later.) Fortunately, based on the hierarchical conceptualization of workflow theory, a complex workflow can be divided into many sub-flows, and if the sub-flows are sound the parent flow is also sound (Aslst & Hee, 2002). Formally, business processes are modified as: Business process *BP(W, T, F)* where W is the finite set of Web sites, w; T is a finite set of tasks, t, ($W \cap T = \varnothing$); and $F \subseteq (W \times T) \cup (T \times W)$ is a set of flow relations.

If *inf(M)* is a strictly increasing function of the distance between current belief τ' and original belief τ; *inf(M)*=$|\tau' - \tau| = \sum_{i=1}^{m} (\tau_i - \tau'_i)^2$ is the change of belief due to semantic information; and $t_1 \notin t$ where t_1 is the new task to implement τ'

then BP ⊂ BP' where F' ⊆ (W' × T') È (T' × W') and w ⊆ w'
dispatch Configure Agent
activate Resource Manager
call Reachability Graph checking
endif

The *Resource Manager* is responsible for assigning activities to resources. This manager should interact with the Implementation Manager to execute the task and the Process Monitor to ensure that constraints are upheld. Moreover, the Resource Manager has guidelines (such as separation of duty) to determine the allocation of sources when more than one Web site is found. This is where the Semantic Web can play a significant role. In general, the guidelines can be as simple as providing rules of thumb, such as the cheaper the better or the faster the better, or more advanced rules, such as providing resource clustering, preconditioning, exclusion, or case attributes. The selection should refer to the semantic data. Note that the semantics refers to the meanings and the logic of the requisition. It is important for the Resource Manager to make the right selection based on sufficient information.

The *Process Monitor* oversees the activities of the business process and uses the Supervise Agent to communicate with participating members. The main duties include alerting the Web site if the task is delayed and aborting the process if no member can be assigned to the next task.

The duty of the *Implementation Manager* is relatively straightforward: it completes the task assignment. The task can be executed immediately, at a preset time, or after a series of events. When the assignment is completed, the Implementation Manager informs the Process Planner to dispatch a Configure Agent to locate Web site for the next task assignment. However, the Implementation Manager notices the encountered circumstance and needs to consider more factors: in other words, if the information *inf(M)* is a strictly increasing function of the distance between current belief τ' and original belief τ, then the Implementation Manager activates the Process Manager again, and the business process can be modified accordingly.

Mobile Agent Function

Mobile agents travel around Web sites as messengers or information locators. In the design, a *Configure Agent* locates a candidate Web site for the next process and providing instructions to the new selected member. That is, the Configure Agent takes the blueprint of a business process, the participant list, the data for implementing the task, and the duty and instructions of task assignment to the next Web site. When it arrives at a new Web site, the local Implementation Manager is enacted immediately, at a preset time or when certain events occur.

The second agent is a *Runtime Agent*, which is responsible for supporting the execution of a business process. It is the duty of the Runtime Agent to obtain augmented information to support the execution of the Implementation Manager. In a P2P Semantic Business Process, every participating member relies on the monitoring function.

As the participating members are dynamically selected and the process flow is modifiable, a *Supervise Agent* is used to monitor the activities of the members based on the most current status reported to and stored in the Process Monitor of the initiated Web site. That is, the Supervise Agent is sent by the initiated Web site to the member Web sites periodically (predefined by timers) or actively (triggered by events) to ensure that the business process operates smoothly.

The Advantages of a Semantic Business Process

The semantic business process takes advantage of the Semantic Web to implement business processes. The first advantage of this approach is a flexible data structure. The conventional Web page presents content and links to a database when a large volume of information is associated with it. As the databases are all using the relational data model, the data structure is rigid and it is difficult to provide personalized service. However, this is not the case in Semantic Web, where data is stored in the format of XML/RDF and is suitable for dynamic environments.

The second advantage is that the Semantic Web can act as a medium to support decision-making rather than simply to provide information, as does the conventional HTML Web page. This is because the content that is embedded in the RDF provides additional information in its tag that can be directly employed in user applications.

The third advantage is that the conventional Web allows users to specify keywords for searching relevant content. However, in the Semantic Web, the system knows more about both information providers and requesters, and then matches the information that is most useful for the requesters. For example, when a user searches for "industrial engineering" on the Web, university departments such as "system engineering" may not appear in the results, even though the courses offered are actually close to what the user is looking for. In the Semantic Web, the search can be further conducted against the course descriptions and program tags, and "system engineering" results can also be included.

IMPLEMENTATION AND DEMONSTRATION

This section demonstrates how the business process can be built and expanded in the Semantics Web. The example shown in Figure 3 represents a PC manufacturer receiving orders from buyers. The manufacturer first checks its inventory for finished products, work in process, and the capacity of its own factories. If it cannot fill the orders from its own capacity, then the manufacture outsources all or a part of them to collaborative partners. Depending on the semantic data, such as quality and collaboration history, the system recommends different supplier lists to the manufacturer.

Web Ontology and Semantics

The ontology defines the meaning and the relationship of a particular subject area. To implement the Semantic Web, the ontology of the subject area must be predefined.

The resource description framework (RDF) can be used to represent machine-processable information in the World Wide Web using a triple format: subject, predicate, and object (http://www.w3.org/TR/2004/REC-rdf-concepts-20040210/). RDF uses XML to allow users to define their own document formats to represent statements.

In this demonstration, RDF mainly defines database content that stores information about products, suppliers and the community. The content in these files can be embedded into Web pages to create "semantic" Web files. Here, we separate the content into four RDF files for demonstration. All the RDF files have been validated by the W3C RDF validation service at http://www.w3.org/RDF/Validator/. The structure graph of the major data fraction representation is shown in Figure 4.

Figure 3. An illustration of the order fulfillment of one manufacturer

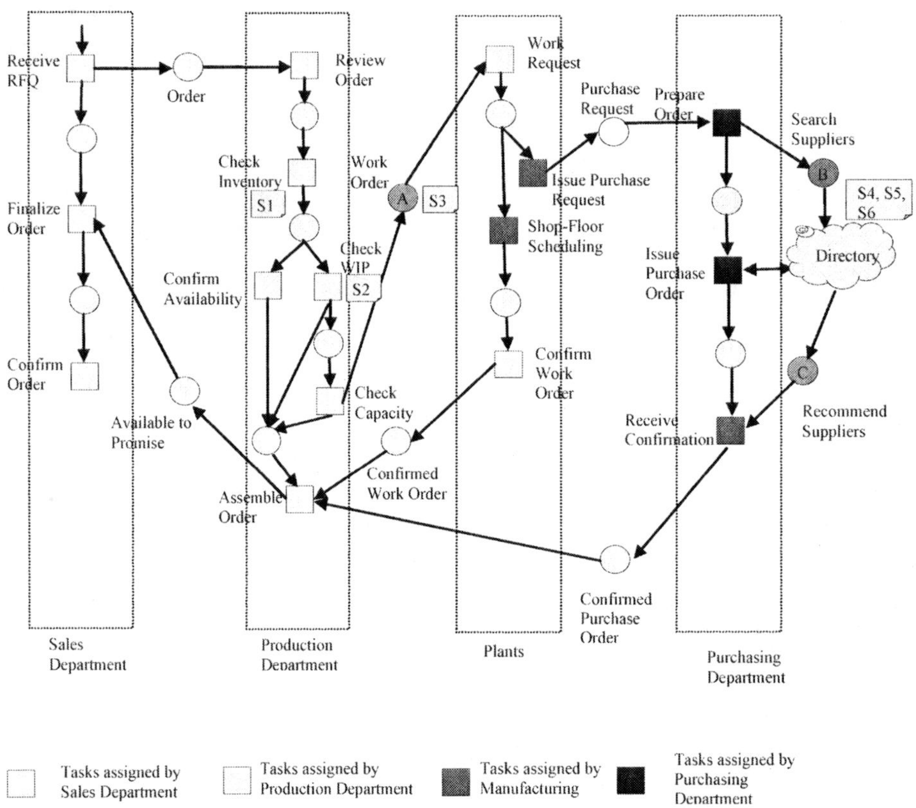

Figure 4. Graphical presentation of four RDF files.

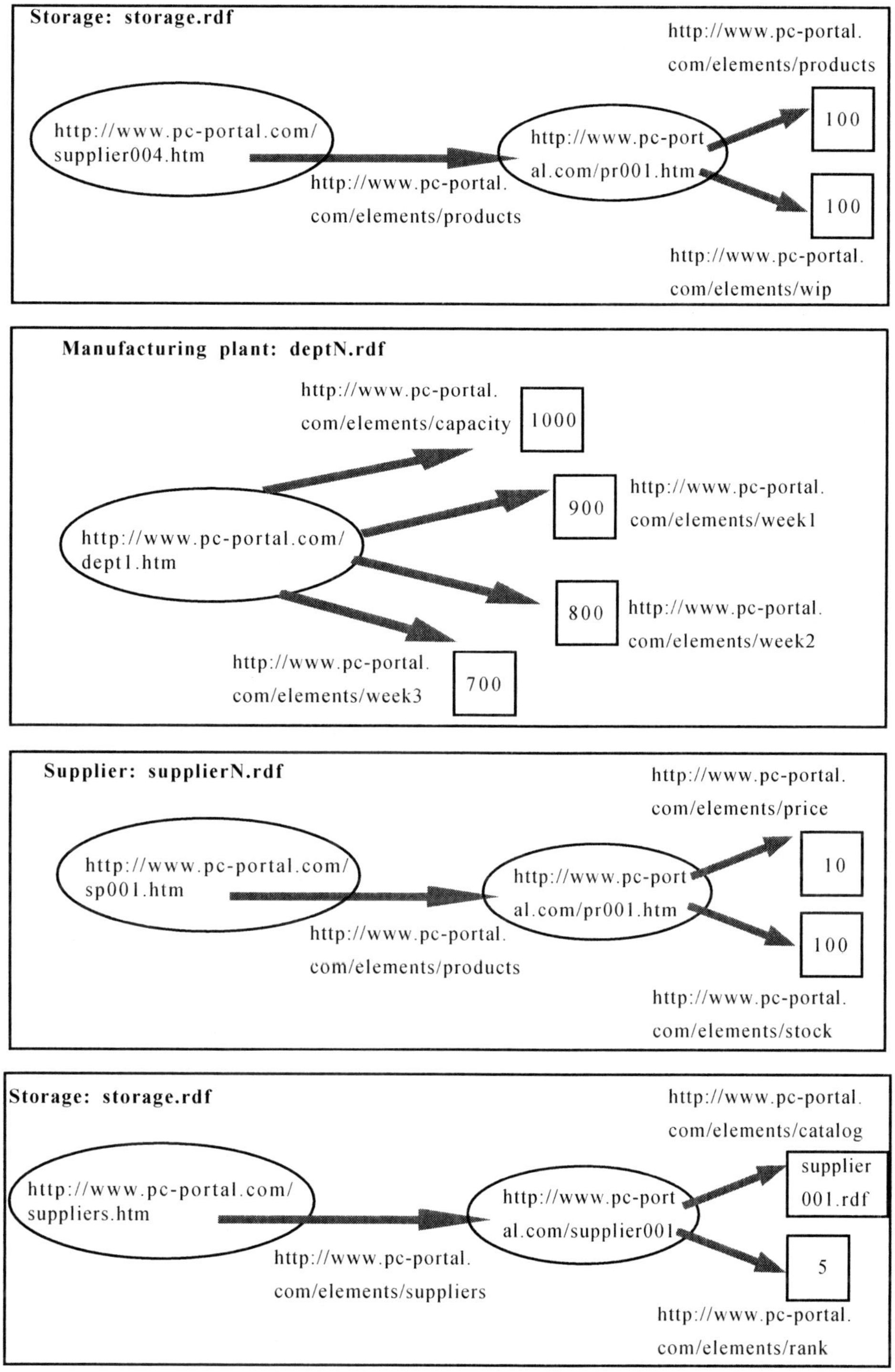

1. Storage.rdf stores data about the finished products and work-in-process products that are either current inventory items or available-to-promise items.
2. DeptN.rdf stores data about manufacturing departments and production capacities in recent weeks.
3. SupplierN.rdf stores data about collaborative partners, such as locations, prices, specifications, and stocks of different products.
4. Resource-manager.rdf acts as a coordinator to determine the selection of collaborative partners. The file also contains information that is related to the collaboration history and ratings of the suppliers.

System Development

This system was developed with the following tools: (1) Macromedia Dreamweaver MX for building common HTML files and dynamic JavaServer Pages (JSP) Web pages; (2) Jbuilder X for building Java files and classes (JSDK 1.4.3 included); (3) Jena 2.1 for building Semantic Web applications, including creating, modifying and querying RDF files, and providing a programmatic environment for RDF, RDFS, and OWL, including a rule-based inference engine; (4) RDQL for querying RDF content; and (5) Tomcat 5.1 for building JSP files to execute on a server.

Four classes with many methods have been built, and the use case is shown in Figures 5 and 6.

1. *Class Storage* is designed to store Information about the product inventory. Two methods are used:
   - getStock(String product): to get the number of finished goods of the specified product in stock; and
   - getWip(String product): to get the number of works in process in stock of the specified product.
2. *Class Department* is designed to store information about manufacturing plants. Two methods are used:
   - getCapacity(String week): to get the capacity of the specified week; and

Figure 5. Graphical ontology of the order placing process.

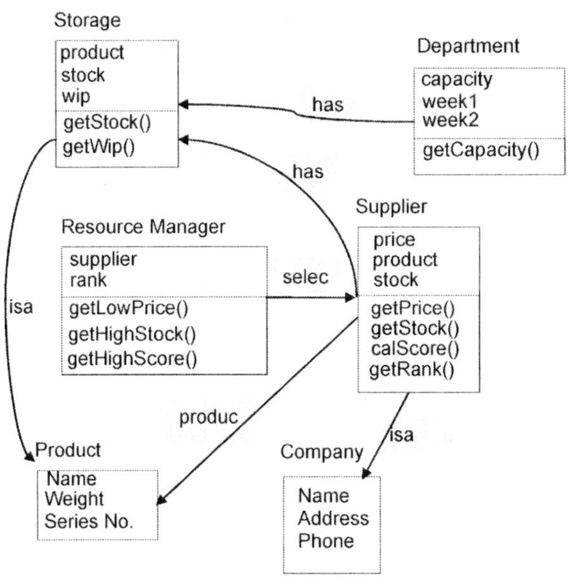

Figure 6. A graphical use case presentation

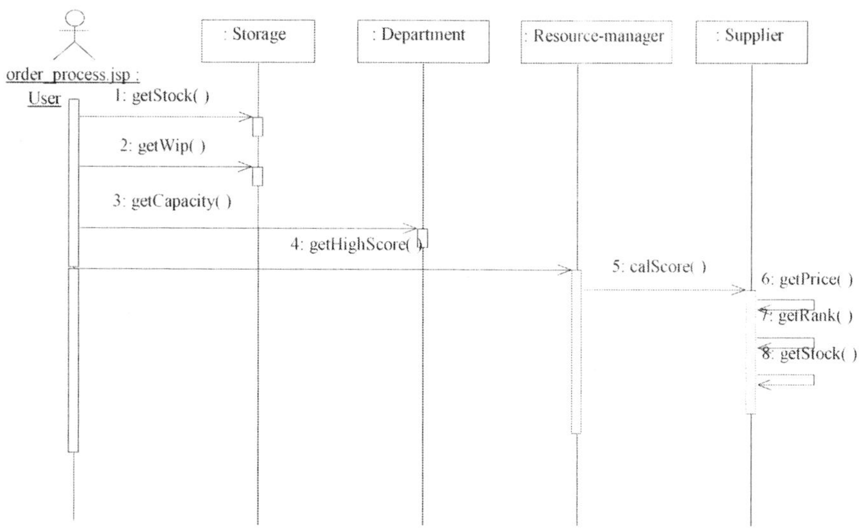

- getCapacity(int n): to get the total capacity of n weeks from now.

3. *Class Resource Manager* is designed to store Information about the collaborative partners. One method is used:
    - getHighScore(String product): to find the supplier with the highest score under the current conditions.
4. *Class Supplier* is designed to store information about selected suppliers. Four methods are used:
    - getPrice(String product): to get the price offered by the supplier of the specified product;
    - getStock(String product): to get the stock of the specified product that the supplier owns;
    - getRank(): to get the ranking of the supplier, which is stored on the community page (and thus suppliers are not allowed to modify their own scores); and
    - calScore(String product): to calculate the score for suppliers under different conditions.

Illustration

This section uses the example in Figure 3 for illustration. The scenario is that a manufacturer checks the inventory and work-in-process products to ascertain whether the available-to-promise amount is sufficient when a new order is placed. The manufacturer has three plants, each has a different capacity and inventory. If the internal capacity cannot satisfy the order, the purchasing department of the company will outsource a part or all of the order to collaborative partners. Assuming that the current inventory of available-to-promise finished product is 100 and of work-in-process product is 100, then the manufacturing lead time is one week. In Figure 3, node A represents the Implementation Manager of the manufacturer, node B represents the Resource Manager of the manufacturer, and node C represents the Implementation Manager of suppliers.

Scenario 1: *The order amount is 50 and the delivery date is two weeks from now. After receiving an order, the company first checks whether or not the inventory of finished goods in stock is sufficient. If the finished goods in stock are enough to cover the* *order, then it will be confirmed. In this scenario, the finished product is sufficient to promise the order, and the order is thus confirmed.*

Scenario 2: *The order amount is 150 and the delivery date is two weeks from now. As the finished product is insufficient, the system will check the work-in-process product. In this scenario, adding the amount of the finished product and work-in-process product is sufficient to promise the order. The order is confirmed.*

Scenario 3: *The order amount is 900 and the delivery date is two weeks from now. As the available-to-promise amount is not enough, the system will check whether the 3 production plants (plants 1-3) are able to produce the outstanding amount within the required delivery time. If they can, then jobs will be assigned to the plants according to their remaining capacities in the required time. That is, the order will first go to the plant with the largest remaining capacity. For example, as shown in Table 2, in the two week period, plant 1 can produce 300, plant 2 can produce 300, and plant 3 can produce 500. As the capacity is sufficient to meet the order, the order is confirmed. The shortage of this order is 700 (order—inventory—work in process), and the order will be spilt into 500 units for plant 3 and 200 units for plant 1.*

Scenario 4: *The order amount is 1400 and the delivery date is two weeks from now. The demand is larger than the remaining capacities and the inventory of the three plants, so the purchasing department searches for suppliers to outsource the order. The system sends Configure Agents to the community directory to find a list of suppliers that have sufficient stock to cover the outstanding amount (order amount—finished goods—work in process—maximum amount that the departments can produce). As more than one supplier can supply the products, the system will recommend a list of best matching suppliers based on the "semantic" information written in RDF/XML files. For example, there are many factors, such as price, reputation, collaborative history, and current stock, to consider when choosing a supplier. After determining the supplier, the Process Planner of the purchasing department will alter the current business process to include other business processes, such as quality control and delivery service, from the supplier. Again, it is the duty of the purchasing department to check the soundness of the business process. The order is then confirmed.*

Table 3 shows the data that is used in this demonstration. When more than one supplier is qualified, it is the task of Resource Manager to prioritize the suppliers. The algorithm is as follows: if the outstanding amount is less than 10% of the total order, then price will be considered as the most critical factor and given a weight of 50%, with stock given a weight of 30% and reputation given a weight of 20% for selecting the supplier. If the outstanding amount is more than 10% but

Table 2. The capacity and work-in-process of three plants

Plant	Capacity	Week 1	Week 2	Week 3	Week 4	Week 5
1	1000	900	800	700	500	600
2	800	600	700	600	500	400
3	800	500	600	600	400	500

Table 3. The price, stock, and reputation of three suppliers

Supplier		Price	Stock	Reputation
1	Product001	10	100	5
	Product002	20	150	
1	Product001	15	200	4
	Product002	25	200	
3	Product001	20	150	4
	Product002	20	200	

less than 20% of the total order, then stock is considered to be the most critical factor (50%), followed by price (30%) and reputation (20%). If the outstanding amount is more than 20% of the total order, then reputation becomes the most critical factor (50%), followed by stock (30%) and price (20%). The rational is that when the outsource amount is very large, the manufacturer pays special attention to elements of reputation such as technology level, quality, and experience. The calculation is conducted by assuming that three suppliers all meet the requirements.

The price, stock and reputation of the three suppliers are represented as p1, p2, and p3, s1, s2, and s3, and g1, g2, and g3. The higher score is given to the higher preference, such as low price, high stock, and good reputation. The total score is then multiplied by the weights. In this scenario, as the 1300 units can be produced by the three plants in two weeks, 100 units will be outsourced. Therefore, price is considered to be the most critical factor as the outstanding amount is 7% of the total order. The system thus places supplier 001 at the top of the recommendation list. However, the list is only given to the Resource Manager of the manufacturer as a reference. The Resource Manager should refer to other criteria such as the collaboration history of the suppliers.

Scenario 5: *The order amount is 1500 and the delivery date is two weeks from now. As the outsourced amount is 200 units (13% of the total order), current stock is considered to be the most critical factor. The system thus recommends supplier 002 first.*

Scenario 6: *The order amount is 1700 and the delivery date is two weeks from now. As the outsourced amount is 400 units (23% of the total order), reputation is considered to be the most critical factor. The system thus recommends supplier 001 first.*

CONCLUSIONS AND FUTURE STUDY

This study has argued that current business process systems, such as the workflow management system, need to define the whole process before implementing it. This, however, is not suitable for the dynamic business world because collaboration is dynamic. This study has presented a system that uses the Semantic Web to build dynamic business processes. The system is built on top of a P2P architecture that allows each Web site (member) to operate independently and collaboratively through the community directory. In this design, each member has the functions of Process Planner, Resource Manager, Process Monitor, and Implementation Manager. Three mobile agents are used for the communication: a Configure Agent, a Runtime Agent, and a Supervise Agent. The system is illustrated with the case of the order handling process of a manufacturer. The illustration demonstrates that the business process can be extended when necessary, and that the operation of the business processes can take semantics data, defined in RDF and XML, into consideration.

This study does not consider areas of security such as access control. Future studies could address the issues of sharing information when the business process is extended indefinitely. Moreover, the directory service is relatively simple in this study. A related future study on Web service could be used to improve this issue. Another plausible issue is how to select suppliers when thousands of Web sites are qualified or when business processes are interrelated.

REFERENCES

Aslst, W., & Hee, K. (2002). *Workflow management: Models, methods systems.* Cambridge, MA: MIT Press.

Bellavista, P., Corradi, A., & Stefanelli, C. (2000). An integrated management environment for network resources and services. *IEEE Journal on Selected Areas in Communications, 18*(5), 676-685.

Berners-Lee, T., Hendler, J., & Lassila, O. (May, 2001). The semantic web. *Scientific American, 284*(5), 34-44.

Bertino, E., Jajodia, S., & Smarati, P. (1999). A flexible authorization mechanism for relational data management systems. *ACM Transactions on Information Systems, 17*(2), 101-140.

Cabri, G., Leonardi, L., & Zambonelli, F. (2000, February). Mobile-agent coordination models for internet applications. *IEEE Computer, 33*(2), 82-89.

Castano, S., Fugini, M., Martella, G., & Samarati, P. (1995). *Database security.* Harlow, UK, UK: Addison-Wesley and ACM Press.

Chatzipapadopoulos, F., Perdikeas, M., & Venieris, L. (2000, June). Mobile agent and CORBA technologies in the broadband intelligent network. *IEEE Communication Magazine, 38*(6), 116-124.

Chung, P. W. H., Cheung, L., Stader, J., Jarvis, P., Moore, J., & Macintosh, A. (2003, April). Knowledge-based process management-an approach to handling adaptive workflow. *Knowledge-Based Systems, 16*(3), 149-160.

Cichocki, A., & Rusinkiewicz, M. (2004). Providing transactional properties for migrating workflows. *Mobile Networks and Applications, 9*, 473-480.

Du, T. (2002, June). Techniques and applications of emerging database system architectures. In C. T. Leondes (Ed.), *Database and Data Communication Network Systems.* Burlington, MA: Academic Press.

Du, T., Li, E., & Chang, A.-P. (2003, July). Mobile agents in distributed network management. *Communications of ACM, 46*(7), 127-32.

Jain, A., Aparicio, M., & Singh, M. (March 1999). Agents for process coherence in virtual enterprises, *Communications of the ACM, 42*(3) 62-69.

King, I., Ng, C. H., & Sia, K. C. (2004, July). Distributed content-based visual information retrieval system on peer-to-peer networks, *ACM Transactions on Information Systems* 22, no. 3, 477-501.

Karvounarakis, G., Magganaraki, A., Alexaki, S., Christophides, V., Plexousakis, D., Scholl, M., & Tolle, K. (2003, August). Querying the semantic web with RQL. *Computer Networks* 5, *42*(5), 617-640.

Lange, D., & Oshima, M. (1998). *Programming and deploying java mobile agents with aglets.* Reading, MA: Addison-Wesley.

Rouibah, K., & Caskey, K. (2003, September). A workflow system for the management of inter—company collaborative engineering processes. *Journal of Engineering Design, 14*(3), 273-293.

Sandholm, T., & Huai, Q. (2000, March/April). Nomad: Mobile agent system for an Internet-based auction house. *IEEE Internet Computing, 4*(2), 80-86.

Sandhu, R. S., Coyne, E. J., Feinstein, H. L., & Youman, C. E. (1996, February). Role-based access control models. *IEEE Computer*, 38-47.

Su, S. Y. W., Meng, J., Krithivasan, R., Degwekar, S., & Helal, S. (2003, January). Dynamic inter-enterprise workflow management in a constraint-based e-service infrastructure, *Electronic Commerce Research, 3*(1-2) 9-24.

van der Aalst, W. M. P. (2003, October). Inheritance of interorganizational workflows: How to agree to disagree without losing control. *Information Technology and Management, 4*(4), 345-389.

Wooldridge, M. J., & Jennings, N. R. (1995, February). Agent theories, architectures and languages: A survey. *Lecture Notes in Computer Science,* 890, 1-39.

Zeng, L., Benatallah, B., Lei, H., Ngu, A., Flaxer, D., & Chang, H. (2003, June). Flexible composition of enterprise web services. *Electronic Markets, 13*(2), 141-152.

Zhuge, H. (2003, May). Workflow- and agent-based cognitive flow management for distributed team cooperation. *Information and Management, 40*(5), 419-429.

This work was previously published in Advances in Electronic Business, Volume 2, edited by E. Li, and T. Du, pp. 180-198, copyright 2007 by Information Science Publishing (an imprint of IGI Global).

Chapter XI
Patterns for Designing Agent-Based E-Business Systems

Michael Weiss
Carleton University, Canada

ABSTRACT

Agents are rapidly emerging as a new paradigm for developing software applications. They are being used in an increasing variety of applications, ranging from relatively small systems such as assistants to large, open, mission-critical systems like electronic marketplaces. One of the most promising areas of applications for agent technology is e-business. In this chapter, we describe a group of architectural patterns for agent-based e-business systems. These patterns relate to front-end e-business activities that involve interaction with the user, and delegation of user tasks to agents. Patterns capture well-proven, common solutions, and guide developers through the process of designing systems. This chapter should be of interest to designers of e-business systems using agent technology. The description of the patterns is followed by the case study of an online auction system to which the patterns have been applied.

INTRODUCTION

Agents are rapidly emerging as a new paradigm for developing software applications. They are being used in an increasing variety of applications, ranging from relatively small systems such as assistants to large, open, mission-critical systems like electronic marketplaces. One of the most promising areas of applications for agent technology is e-business (Papazoglou, 2001). In this chapter, we describe a group of architectural patterns for agent-based e-business systems. These patterns relate to front-end e-business activities that involve interaction with the user, and delegation of user tasks to agents.

The chapter is structured as follows. First, we provide a background on patterns and their application to the design of agent systems. Then, we discuss the forces or design constraints that need to be considered during the design of agents for e-business systems. This is followed by a description of the agent patterns for e-business. A number of examples illustrate the application of these patterns. Finally, we discuss current trends and opportunities for future research and offer concluding remarks.

BACKGROUND

Patterns are reusable solutions to recurring design problems and provide a vocabulary for communicating these solutions to others. The documentation of a pattern goes beyond documenting a problem and its solution. It also describes the forces or design constraints that give rise to the proposed solution (Alexander, 1979). These are the undocumented and generally misunderstood features of a design. Forces can be thought of as pushing or pulling the problem towards different solutions. A good pattern balances these forces. A set of patterns, where one pattern leads to other patterns that refine or are used by it, is known as a pattern language. A pattern language can be likened to a process: it guides designers who wants to use those patterns through their application in an organic manner. As each pattern of the pattern language is applied, some of the forces affecting the design will be resolved, while new unresolved forces will arise as a consequence. The process of using a pattern language in a design is complete when all forces have been resolved.

There is by now a growing literature on using patterns to capture common design practices for agent systems. Aridor and Lange (1998) describe domain-independent patterns for the design of mobile agent systems. They classify mobile agent patterns into traveling, task, and interaction patterns. Kendall, Murali Krishna, Pathak, et al. (1998) use patterns to capture common building blocks for the architecture of agents. They integrate these patterns into the layered agent pattern, which serves as a starting point for a pattern language for agent systems based on the strong notion of agency. Schelfthout, Coninx, et al. (2002), on the other hand, document agent implementation patterns suitable for developing weak agents.

Deugo, Weiss, and Kendall (2001) identify a set of patterns for agent coordination, which are, again, domain-independent. They classify agent patterns into architectural, communication, traveling, and coordination patterns. They also describe an initial set of global forces that push and pull solutions for coordination. Kolp, Giorgini, and Mylopoulos (2001) document domain-independent organizational styles for multi-agent systems using the Tropos methodology. Weiss (2004) motivates the use of agents through a set of patterns that document the forces involved in agent-based design and key agent concepts.

On the other hand, Kendall (1999) reports on work on a domain-specific pattern catalog developed at BT Exact. Several of these patterns are documented using role models in a description of the ZEUS agent building kit (Collis & Ndumu, 1999). Shu and Norrie (1999) and the author in a precursor to this chapter have also documented domain-specific patterns, respectively, for agent-based manufacturing and electronic commerce. However, unlike most other authors, they present the patterns in the form of a pattern language. This means that the relationships between the patterns are made explicit in such a way that they guide a developer through the process of designing a system.

Lind (2002) and Mouratidis, Weiss, and Giorgini (2006) suggest that we can benefit from integrating patterns with a development process, while Tahara, Oshuga, and Hiniden (1999) and Weiss (2003) propose pattern-driven development processes. Lind (2002) suggests a view-based categorization scheme for patterns based on the MASSIVE methodology. Mouratidis et al. (2006) document a pattern language for secure agent systems that uses the modeling concepts of the Tropos methodology. Tahara et al. (1999) propose a development method based on agent patterns and distinguish between macro and micro architecture patterns. Weiss (2003) documents a process for mining and applying agent patterns.

FORCES

The design of agent-based systems in the e-business domain is driven by a number *forces*, including autonomy, the need to interact, information overload, multiple interface, ensuring quality, adaptability, privacy concerns, search costs, and the need to track identity. Not all of these forces can be equally satisfied by a given design, and trade-offs need to be made. The patterns described in this chapter help with making informed trade-offs.

AUTONOMY

The currently dominant metaphor for interacting with computers is direct manipulation. Direct manipulation requires the user to initiate all tasks explicitly and to monitor all events. For example, a user searches the Web for an auction that offers the desired item for sale, and subsequently monitors the state of the auction. The obvious drawback of this approach is that most of the time the user is occupied in tasks that are peripheral to the primary objectives. The user's ability to find the best deal available at any of the many online auctions in operation is also greatly limited.

Agents can be used to implement a complementary interaction style, in which users *delegate* some of their tasks to software agents which then perform them autonomously on their behalf. This indirect manipulation style engages the user in a cooperative process in which human and software agents both initiate communication, monitor events, and perform tasks. Autonomy is the capability of an agent to follow its goals without interactions or commands from the user or another agent. An autonomous agent does not require the user's approval at every step of executing its task, but is able to act on its own.

With agents performing autononmous actions, users are now facing issues of trust and control over their agents. The issue of *trust* is that by engaging an agent to perform tasks (such as selecting a seller), the user must be able to trust the agent to do so in an informed and unbiased manner. The agent should not, for example, have entered contracts with sellers to favor them in return for a cut on their proceeds to the developer of the agent or the server that hosts and executes the agent. The user would also like to specify the *degree of autonomy* of the agent. For example, the user may not want to delegate decisions to the agent that have legal or financial consequences, although a buyer agent is capable of not only finding the cheapest seller, but also placing a purchase order.

NEED TO INTERACT

Agents typically only have *a partial representation* of their environment, and are thus *limited* in their ability—in terms of their expertise, access to resources, location, and so forth—to interact with it. Thus, they rely on other agents to achieve goals that are outside their scope or reach. They also need to coordinate their activities with those of other agents to ensure that their goals can be met, avoiding interference with one another. The behavior of an individual agent is thus often not comprehensible outside its social structure—its relationships with other agents. For example, the behavior of a buyer agent in an auction cannot be fully explained outside the context of the auction itself, and of the conventions that govern it (for example, in which order—ascending or descending—bids must be made, and how many rounds of bidding there are in the auction).

An important issue in designing systems of interacting agents is dealing with *openness*. The Internet and e-business applications over the Internet are both examples of open systems. Open systems pose unique challenges in that their components are not known in advance; they can change unexpectedly, and they are composed of heterogeneous agents implemented by different developers at different times with different tools and methodologies. Similarly, as we do not control all the agents, one can also not assume that the agents are cooperative. Some agents may be benevolent and agree on some protocol of interaction, but others will be *self-interested* and follow their own best interests. For example, in an electronic marketplace, buyer and seller agents are pursuing their own best interests (making profit) and need to be constrained by conventions.

INFORMATION OVERLOAD

People and organizations wish to find relevant information and offerings to make good deals and generate profit. However, the large set of sellers, in conjunction with the *multiple interfaces* they use, makes it difficult for a human to overview the market. One solution has been to provide *portals* or common entry points to the Web. These portals periodically collect information from a multitude of information sources and condense them to a format that users find easier to process, typically taking the form of a hierarchical index. One disadvantage of this solution is that the categories of the index will be the same for every user. Individual preferences are not taken into account when compiling the information, and niche interests may not be represented at all.

MULTIPLE INTERFACES

One of the difficulties in finding information (e.g., when comparing the offerings of different sellers) is the large number of different interfaces used to present the information. Not only are store fronts organized differently, sellers do not follow the same conventions when describing their products and terms of sale. For instance, some sellers include the shipping costs in the posted price; others will advertise one price, but add a handling charge to each order. A solution is to agree on *common vocabularies*, but these must also be widely adopted. With the introduction of the extensible markup language (XML) for associating metacontent with data and current developments in the Semantic Web such as ontology representation languages (OWL), this is slowly becoming a reality. For example, a price in a catalog can be marked up with its currency whether it already includes the shipping cost. However, the difficulty with any standard format is that it takes a considerable amount of time to find agreement among the interested parties. One also needs to allay the fear of sellers in losing business to competitors once their product information becomes easily accessible.

ENSURING QUALITY

Shopping online lacks the immediate mechanisms for establishing trustworthiness. How can you trust a seller, with whom you have had no previous encounter, whether the order you placed will be fulfilled satisfactorily? For example, any seller in an online auction could claim that the item offered for sale is in superior condition, when the buyer cannot physically verify that claim. One solution is to solicit *feedback* about the performance of a seller (respectively, buyer) from buyers (respectively, sellers) after order fulfillment. For example, the online auction site eBay keeps records of how a seller was rated by other buyers. Potential new buyers will take the ratings from previous buyers into account before considering buying from a seller. However, eBay's solution falls short in two ways. Old low ratings are not discarded or discounted when more recent ratings are higher. Also, if a seller gets a low overall rating, it is easy for the seller to assume a new identity and start afresh with a new rating. A mechanism for ensuring quality must avoid this, as discussed in the context of reputation system design by Zacharia, Moukas, and Maes (1999).

ADAPTABILITY

Users differ in their status, level of expertise, needs, and preferences. The issue of adaptability is that of tailoring information to the features of the user, for example, by selecting the products most suitable for the user from a catalog, or adapting the presentation style during the interaction with the user. Any approach to tailoring information involves creating and maintaining a user model. When creating a user model, two cases need to be distinguished (Ardissono, Barbero, et al., 1999): for first time visitors, no information about them is available, and the user characteristics must be recognized during the interaction; on subsequent visits, a detailed user model about a visitor is already available and can be used to tailor the information.

Several design considerations for user modeling are detailed in Ardissono et al. (1999). Users need to register permanently with the system to have their data stored; otherwise user models will only be maintained during a single interaction. In the context of online shopping, a system must also deal with direct and indirect users. A customer of a Web store may browse for products for himself, as well as for other people (indirect users), who have different needs and preferences. Finally, the user model must be able to reflect changes in interest over time. One approach to collecting user information is to ask the user to provide the information explicitly, for example, by filling out a form. This allows one to create a profile of the user that is potentially very accurate, and to provide personalized service to the user from the beginning. However, there are at least two problems with this solution. First, by requiring the user to provide this information upfront; the threshold for the user to do so is very high. Only very advanced users will want to tune their own profiles. Second, when the user's interests change, this will not be reflected in the profile, unless the user keeps updating her profile. Again, in practice, users do not update their profiles after installation.

PRIVACY CONCERNS

Personalization requires the collection and release of personal information to the agent providing the personalized service. One way of personalizing interactions between buyers and sellers is for the seller to collect information about a buyer from the buyer's behavior (e.g., their clickstream). The buyer may not be aware of the information collected, nor does she always have control over what information is gathered about her. Although effective from the seller's perspective, this is not a desirable situation from the perspective of the buyer. Users are typically not willing to allow just anyone to examine their preferences and usage patterns, in particular without their knowledge or consent. They want to remain in control, and decide on an interaction-by-interaction basis which information is conveyed to the seller. A solution that addresses the force of privacy concerns must put the user in charge of which information is collected and who it is made available to. An additional complexity results from the desire of some buyers to remain anonymous. If a buyer remains anonymous, a seller cannot provide personalized service. Thus, generally, users are willing to share personal information with sellers, if the expected gains outweigh the possible threats for their privacy.

SEARCH COSTS

It can be expensive for buyers and sellers to find each other. In a static marketplace, each buyer can store a contact list of sellers for each product, and then quickly locate an appropriate seller when a particular product is needed. However, an electronic marketplace is dynamic. Buyers and sellers can join and leave the marketplace, and change their requirements and offerings qualitatively and quantitatively at any point in time. It, therefore, becomes impossible for a market participant to maintain an up-do-date list of contacts. Another problem is that of restricting the buyer's options. If each buyer maintains its own list of contacts, they run the risk of not being aware of better deals available elsewhere. One possible solution to these problems is to use a mediator which can match potential trading partners in the market. With the introduction of mediators, buyers and sellers no longer maintain their own lists of contacts, or need to contact a large number of alternative trading partners to find the optimal one. One trade-off of this solution is, however, that individual preferences or history of interaction with a particular trading partner cannot be accounted for by a mediator. Thus, it is reasonable to maintain individual lists of trading partners that one has dealt with in the past, keeping track of the quality provided and using this personalized ranking of partners to filter the list of contacts provided by a mediator.

IDENTITY

For various reasons, buyers and sellers need to be represented by unique identities. The most important reasons are authentication, nonrepudiation, and tracking. One way of assigning a unique identity to trading partners is to use one of the many unique labels which are readily available on the Internet, for example, an e-mail address, or a Yahoo! account name. A problem with this approach is that it is also very easy to obtain a new identity, thus making authentication, nonrepudiation, or tracking schemes that rely on such identities impractical. Similarly, a user could obtain multiple identities and pretend to represent multiple different parties, where instead there is only one. A solution that remedies this situation must make it advantageous for individuals to keep their identities over those users who change them often (Zacharia et al., 1999).

PATTERNS

The patterns we identified and their relationships are shown in Figure 1. The arrows indicate refinement links between the patterns. Each arrow in the diagram points in the direction from a "larger" pattern to a "smaller" pattern. The starting point for the language is the AGENT SOCIETY pattern, which motivates the use of agents for building the application. At the next level of refinement, the diagram leads the designer to consider the patterns agent as DELEGATE, AGENT AS MEDIATOR, AND COMMON VOCABULARY.[1]

agent as delegate and the patterns it links to deal with the design of agents that act on behalf of a single user. The agent as mediator pattern guides the designer through the design of agents that facilitate between a group of agents and their users. COMMON VOCABULARY provides guidelines for defining exchange formats between agents. The rest of Figure 1 shows refinements of the AGENT AS DELEGATE pattern. For example, the USER AGENT pattern prescribes to use a single locus of interaction with the user and represent the concurrent transactions a user participates in as buyer and seller agents. User interaction also includes profiling the user (USER PROFILING) and subscribing to information (e.g., the status of an auction) relevant to the user (NOTIFICATION).

In the following, each pattern is represented by its context, the problem it addresses, a discussion of the forces, its solution, and a resulting context. The context is represented by the dependencies between the patterns. The problem is a succinct statement on what problem the pattern addresses. The solution takes the form of a role diagram. These roles will be filled by agents. For example, consider the USER AGENT pattern. It is applied after AGENT AS DELEGATE, and, in turn, refined by USER PROFILING and NOTIFICATION. The it addresses the problem of how users instruct agents to act on their behalf (as buyers and sellers) and how they keep in control over what the agent does (e.g., does it have authority to complete a trade?). The role

Figure 1. Patterns for e-business agents and their dependencies (arrows indicate dependencies and dashed lines patterns that are not described here)

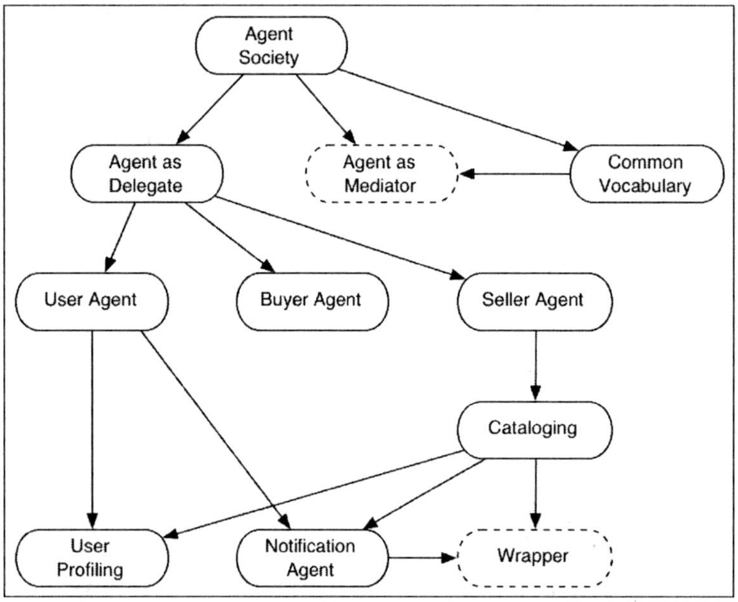

diagram for the USER AGENT pattern is shown in Figure 2. Role diagrams and their semantics are discussed further in AGENT SOCIETY. The resulting context points to related patterns in this pattern language.

AGENT SOCIETY

Context

Your application domain satisfies at least one of the following criteria: your domain data, control, knowledge, or resources are decentralized; your application can be naturally thought of as a system of autonomous cooperating entities, or you have legacy components that must be made to interoperate with new applications.

Figure 2. Role diagram for the USER AGENT pattern

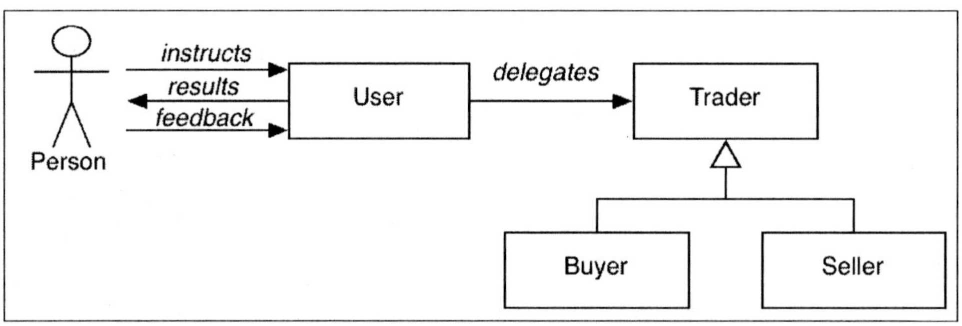

Problem

How do you model systems of autonomous co-operating entities in software?

Forces

- Autonomy
- Need to interact

Solution

Model your application as a society of agents. Agents are autonomous computational entities (autonomy), which interact with their environment (reactivity) and other agents (social ability) in order to achieve their own goals (proactiveness). Often, agents will be able to adapt to their environment and have some degree of intelligence, although these are not considered mandatory characteristics. These computational entities act on behalf of users or groups of users (Maes, 1994). Thus, agents can be classified as *delegates*, representing a single user and acting on his behalf, or *mediators* or *intermediaries* acting on behalf of a group of users, facilitating between them.

It is important to point out that objects cannot achieve these goals directly. A differentiating characteristic between agents and objects is their *autonomy*. Autonomy is here used in an extended sense. It not only comprises the notion that agents operate in their own thread of control, but also implies that agents are long-lived (they execute unattended for long periods), take initiative (they do not simply act in response to their environment), react to stimuli from the environment as guided by their goals (the *receiving* agent decides whether and how to respond to a stimulus), and interact with other agents to leverage their abilities in support of their own as well as collective goals. *Active objects*, on the other hand, are autonomous only in the first of these senses.

A society of agents can be viewed from two dual perspectives: either a society of agents emerges as a result of the interaction of agents, or the society imposes constraints and policies on its component agents. Both perspectives, which we can refer to as micro and macro view of the society, respectively, mutually reinforce each other, as shown in Figure 3. For example, emergent behaviors such as specialization of agents leads to the notion of roles that agents play, which

Figure 3. Micro-macro view of an agent society

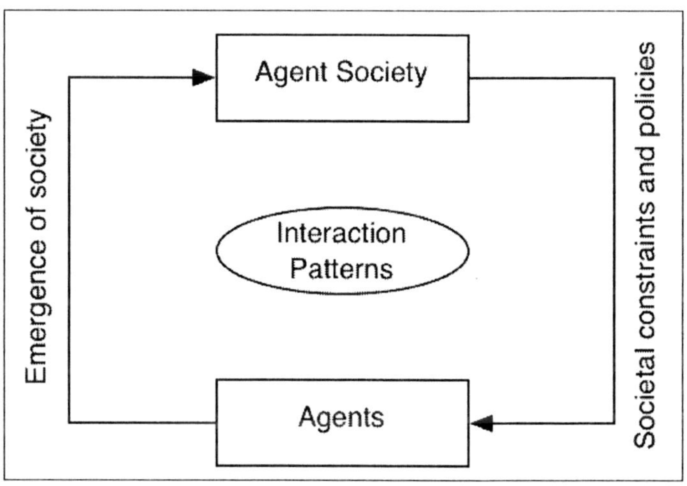

allow us to codify expectations about an agent. Roles, in turn, impose restrictions on the possible behaviors of agents (Ferber, 1999).

This suggests two approaches to systematically designing agent societies. In the first approach, we identify top-level goals for the system and decompose them recursively, until we can assign them to individual agents. In the second approach, we construct an agent society incrementally from a catalog of interaction patterns (Kendall et al., 1999). These interaction patterns are described in terms of roles that agents can play and their interactions and may also specify any societal constraints or policies that need to be satisfied. Roles are *abstract* loci of control (Ferber, 1999; Kendall, 1999; Riehle & Gross, 1998). Protocols (or patterns of interaction) describe the way the roles interact. Policies define constraints imposed by the society on these roles (Weiss, Gray, & Diaz, 1997; Zambonelli, Jennings, et al., 2001). As an example of a policy, consider an agent-mediated auction, which specifies conventions specific to its auction type (for example, regarding the order of bids; ascending in an English auction, descending in a Dutch auction) that participating agents must comply with in order for the auction to function correctly.

Many types of applications, including electronic commerce systems, can be modeled using User, Task, Service, and Resource roles, and their subtypes. Figure 4 depicts these roles and their subtypes used in this chapter in a role diagram, using the notation introduced in Kendall (1999). *Role diagrams* are more abstract than class diagrams. Each role in the diagram defines a position and a set of responsibilities. A role has collaborators—other roles that it interacts with. Arrows between roles indicate dynamic interactions between roles; their direction represents the direction in which messages are sent. The triangle indicates a subtyping relationship between roles; subtypes inherit the responsibilities of their parent roles and add responsibilities of their own (e.g., Buyer from Trader).

The User role encapsulates the behavior of managing a user's task agents, providing a presentation interface to the user and collecting profile information about the user, among other responsibilities. A Task role represents users in a specific task, typically a long-lived, rather than one-shot transaction. In this context, we only consider Trader agents, which can either represent the user as a Buyer or Seller. The common functionality of both roles (for example,

Figure 4. Top-level roles and their subtypes in this pattern language

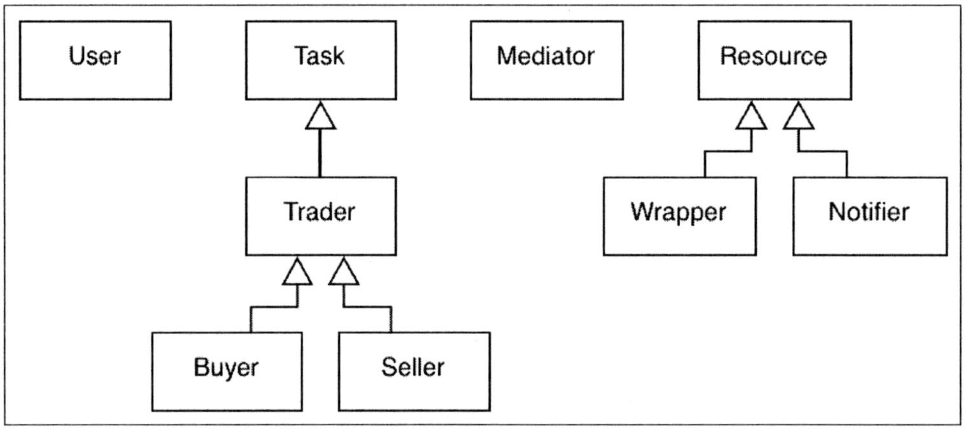

they represent the negotiation strategies of their users) is represented in the trader role. Another example of a Task role would be a search role that encapsulates the behavior of making queries to the Web on the user's behalf and filtering the results. One could also model transactions as a separate Transaction role as proposed by Ulmer (2004), representing the transactions a Task agent engages in.

A Mediator role typically provides a service to a group of users. It mediates the interaction between two or more agents through this service. One example is a directory agent that provides a reference to an agent given its name (white pages agent), or references to agents that can provide a certain product or service (yellow pages agent). More advanced services facilitate more complex interactions between agents, for example, enforcing an auction protocol. For example, see the recommender agents described in Weiss (2004) or the direction and auction agents in Fonseca, Griss, and Letsinger (2001).

The Resource role abstracts information sources. These can be legacy data sources wrapped by "glue" code that converts generic requests from other agents to the API of the data source. These can be agents that process more complex queries by first breaking them down into subqueries and then collating the results. Resource agents are a form of Indirection Layer (Avgeriou & Zdun, 2005). Notifier agents also belong in this category; they can be instructed to generate an alert when a certain condition in a data source is being met. For example, the Amazon Deliver's agent sends e-mails to users, when a book meeting user-specified criteria (such as author) is added to a catalog.

Resulting Context

For members of an agent society to understand each other, they need to agree on common exchange formats, as described in COMMON VOCABULARY. For agents that act on behalf of a single user, which is what e-business front-end system are concerned with, consult AGENT AS DELEGATE. For agents that facilitate between a group of users and their agents, refer to AGENT AS MEDIATOR described in more detail in Weiss (2004).

AGENT AS DELEGATE

Context

You are designing your system as a society of autonomous agents (AGENT SOCIETY) and want to delegate a user's time-consuming, peripheral tasks to software assistants.

Problem

How do you instruct assistants? How much discretion should you give to assistants? How do you manage the assistants that perform tasks on your behalf?

Forces

- Information overload
- Search costs

Solution

Use agents to act *on behalf* of the user. They are the system's interface to the user and manage task-specific agents such as buyer or seller agents on the user's behalf. User agents can also learn about the needs of the user by building a user profile from a history of interactions. This user profile allows sellers to customize their offerings to specific user tastes, while the user agents control what part of a profile sellers can access.

The structure of this pattern is shown in Figure 5. This role diagram shows the roles agents need to fill in the pattern. Note that we introduced the role of a Trader agent, as discussed in AGENT SOCIETY, which contains the beliefs and behavior common to both Buyer and Seller agents. For

Figure 5. Role diagram for AGENT AS DELEGATE

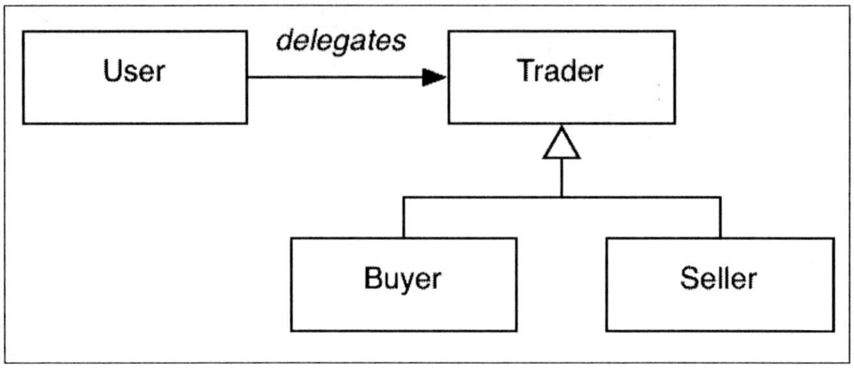

example, both Buyer and Seller agents have a belief for the desired price and make offers and counter-offers to other agents.

Resulting Context

For the interaction with the user to gather their requirements and feedback on the quality of the service received by a seller and for managing Task agents, consult USER AGENT. Also consult USER AGENT for measures to control access to user profiles. For the design of Trader agents, see BUYER AGENT and SELLER AGENT.

COMMON VOCABULARY

Context

When agents in an AGENT SOCIETY interact, they need to agree on common exchange formats. One scenario is that you are using agents to represent customers and sellers in individual transactions—BUYER AGENT and SELLER AGENT. Buyer and seller agents need to understand each other in order to exchange messages with one other. Another scenario is that you need to derive a user profile from user interactions—USER PROFILING—and you require your information sources such as product catalogs to be well structured.

Problem

How do you enable agents (for example, buyer and seller agents) to interact? How can you make it easier for a comparison-shopping agent to extract data from a catalog?

Forces

- Multiple interfaces

Solution

In the example, for buyer and seller agents to understand each other, they need to agree on a common message format that is grounded in a common ontology. The ontology defines product-related concepts that each party must use during interaction, their attributes, and valid value ranges. On receiving a message, the seller agent translates the request to a seller-specific format and fetches the contents of the product database.

It is generally impractical to define a general-purpose ontology for agent interaction. These are unlikely to include the intricacies of all possible domains. Instead, the common ontology will be application-specific. Given such a shared ontology, the communicating agents need to map their internal representations to the shared ontology. Much progress has been made on XML-based ontologies for electronic commerce, for example, xCBL, cXML, and RosettaNet, in recent years. Given that buyer and seller agents adopt one of these standards as their internal representation of domain concepts, the problem remains of building inter-ontology translators. One pragmatic approach to ontology mapping using XSLT (XML stylesheet language transformation) is described in Carlson (2001). However, refer to the references in the Resulting Context for more complex mappings.

The structure of this pattern is shown in Figure 6. This figure was adapted from Collis and Lee (1999).

Resulting Context

This pattern does not itself lead to other patterns in this pattern language. But patterns for ontologies have been documented elsewhere (Aranguren, 2005; Reich, 2000). A current overview on techniques for ontology mapping, which could be mined for further ontology mapping patterns, can be found in Staab and Stuckenschmidt (2006).

USER AGENT

Context

You are delegating tasks to an agent—AGENT AS DELEGATE—which autonomously performs the task on behalf of the user. Now you want to create a locus of control through which the users can interact with the agents created on their behalf.

Problem

How do you manage the user's profile and control access to it and the various (concurrent) transactions in which the user participates?

Forces

- Privacy concerns
- Ensuring quality

Solution

User agents form the *interface* between the user and the system receive the user's queries and feedback, and present information *tailored* to users. A user agent delegates the user's queries or orders (offers to buy/sell an item) to a trader agent and manages the various buyer and seller agents on behalf of its user. The user agent manages the user's profile and controls who can access it. The Open Profiling Standard (W3C, 1997) was an early example of employing user agents in this way. In this proposal, profile information for different sellers was stored in a personal profile repository. Sections of the profile could be restricted to a subset of the sellers. In thc SOaP system (Voss & Kreifelts, 1997), user agents track all task agents for tasks in which a user is engaged.

Figure 6. Role diagram for COMMON VOCABULARY

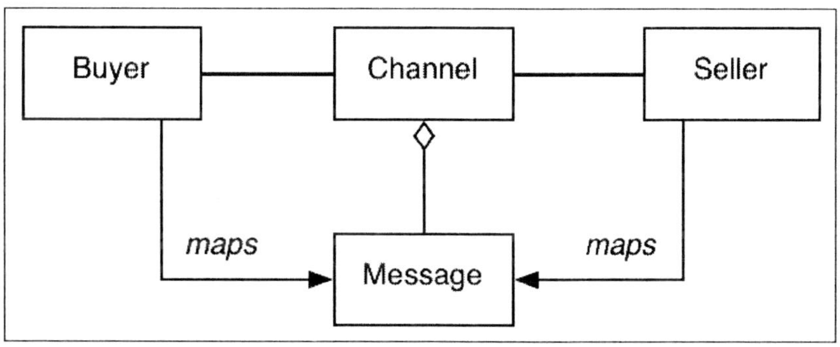

The structure of this pattern is shown in Figure 7.

Resulting Context

A user can subscribe to the progress of a query or an order by instructing a NOTIFICATION AGENT to monitor its status. For more on modeling the user that requires explicit user input is kept at a minimum; consult USER PROFILING.

BUYER AGENT

Context

You are delegating tasks to an agent—AGENT AS DELEGATE—and provide a locus of control where users can interact with their agents—USER AGENT. You need an agent to represent a user as a customer in a transaction with sellers in an electronic marketplace.

Problem

How do you communicate your goals and buying strategy?

Forces

- Autonomy

Solution

A buyer agent can *tailor* the selection and presentation of products to the needs of its user. It *locates* seller agents that offer the requested product or service and negotiates with them about price and other terms of sale (e.g., shipping). Kasbah and Tete-a-Tete (Guttman & Maes, 1999) are systems that use this approach. In these systems, each buyer agent is given such information as the desired price, the maximum price to pay, and the time by which a purchase needs to be completed. In Tete-a-Tete, the agents are negotiating about other criteria than just price such as shipping terms or extended warranties. The virtual marketplace architecture in Greengrass, Sud, and Moore (1999) uses mobile buyer agents to represent the user in a particular transaction. A further consideration is whether a buyer agent needs final approval to complete a transaction.

The buyer role is defined as a subrole of the trader role in Figure 7 above.

Resulting Context

For buyer and seller agents to understand each other, they need to agree on a COMMON VOCABULARY for exchanging messages during the negotiation. Buyer and seller agents find each other through AGENTS AS MEDIATORS (Weiss, 2004). In Greengrass et al. (1999) and Fonseca et al. (2001), a directory facilitator plays the role of a mediator.

Figure 7. Role diagram for USER AGENT

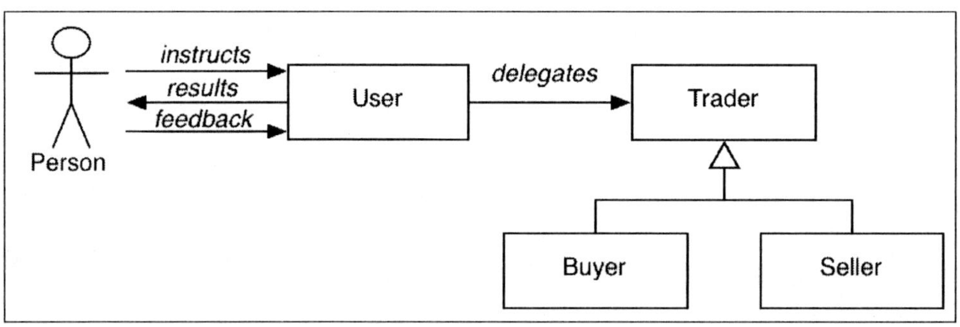

SELLER AGENT

Context

You are delegating tasks to an agent—AGENT AS DELEGATE—and provide a locus of control where users can interact with their agents—USER AGENT. You now need an agent to represent a seller in a transaction with customers in an electronic marketplace.

Problem

How do you communicate your selling strategy to an agent?

Forces

- Autonomy

Solution

A seller agent *offers* products and services to buyer agents (directly or through a market). It answers queries for information about its owner's products or services, responds to RFPs, and enters into negotiation with buyer agents. A seller agent encapsulates its *execution state* and the seller's selling *strategy* (e.g., a function for setting bids). In Kasbah (Guttman & Maes, 1999) seller agents periodically send offers to buyer agents, each time adjusting their offers according to a concession strategy. In the virtual marketplace by Greengrass et al. (1999) stationary seller agents negotiate with mobile buyer agents. In the mobile shopper scenario in Fonseca et al. (2001), seller agents bid in competition with one another to satisfy a buyer agent's call for proposal.

The seller role is defined as a subrole of the trader role in Figure 7.

Resulting Context

For buyer and seller agents to understand each other, they need to agree on a common exchange format, as described in a COMMON VOCABULARY. Buyer and seller agents find each other through AGENTS AS MEDIATORS (Weiss, 2004). If you wish to make different offers to different buyers, creating a custom catalog for each buyer by tailoring the contents of a generic catalog to the buyer's profile, consult CATALOGING.

USER PROFILING

Context

You provide a locus of control—USER AGENT—where users can interact with their agents. You receive instructions and feedback from the user. You want to derive a profile that describes the user from these interactions. Once you have deduced a user profile, you can provide it to sellers who want to personalize the customer's experience, for example, by creating a custom catalog based on the user's preferences and buying pattern.

Problem

How can you capture the users' profiles without requiring too much explicit input? This can become involved, if you want to track users' profiles as their interest changes.

Forces

- Adaptability

Solution

During the interaction with a user, the system builds a user profile by static user modeling, classifying the user into predefined user classes (stereotypes), or dynamic user modeling (monitoring user activity and changing the profile dynamically). For example, in Ardissono et al. (1999), user profiles contain a collection of interests in addition to generic information about the user. Interests contain descriptions of the topics the user is interested in. Interests may also contain weights (e.g., fuzzy logic quantifiers) that define the degree of interest the user has in a topic. The agent may also tailor its interaction style, providing more or less detail depending on the user's receptivity.

It is desirable to limit the amount of explicit input required from the user, for example, in the form of rules. Although manual setting of the user profile results in a very precise profile, this is difficult to perform correctly except for an advanced user (Brenner et al., 1998). On the other hand, it is advantageous to know as much as possible about the user to start with in order to keep the learning phase short. The user agent can request the user to provide demographic information such as sex, age, and profession, which allow us to group the user into a class. The interests of the user are then initialized to those typical for this class of users.

From the point of view of limiting user input, initializing the user profile by observing the user's behavior over time is most desirable (Brenner, Zarnekow, & Wittig, 1998). The user's personal preferences can then be deduced using cluster analysis. This has the added advantage that it is easy to adapt the user profile to changes in their interests. Once the user profiles have been initialized, the user agent can update the profile by soliciting feedback on query results from the user, or to rate a seller on her quality of service after the order has been fulfilled. A typical example for learning a user profile from user feedback is the Letizia user agent (Lieberman, 1998). The Sporas system for reputation management (Zacharia et al., 1999) ranks sellers on their past performance as assessed by user feedback.

In Figure 7, the arrow labeled "feedback" indicates how the user agent receives feedback from the user after evaluating the quality of the result returned.

Resulting Context

To construct complex user profiles (e.g., based on user navigation patterns), the information sources such as product catalogs must be well structured—COMMON VOCABULARY—and comparable on the basis of their content. If the items in an information source cannot be compared in terms of attributes, collaborative filtering can still help you create useful simpler user profiles—RECOMMENDER (Weiss, 2004).

CATALOGING

Context

You are deriving a user profile from user interactions—USER PROFILING. You are using an agent to represent a seller in a transaction in a marketplace—SELLER AGENT. You wish to tailor the contents of your catalog to individual buyers based on their user profiles.

Problem

How do you customize a catalog?

Forces

- Information overload
- Multiple interfaces

Solution

A product extractor dynamically creates a customized view on the catalog. It selects the products that best match the customer's preferences by comparing the product features with those contained in the profile. A user profile contains predictive information about the user's preferences toward product features as defined by the product categories. The view may also be customized regarding generic traits of the user (e.g., his level of expertise, job, or age).

Tailoring the product catalog to the user resolves the force of information overload. A large electronics parts catalog, for example, may contain 50,000 parts, of which only a small subset are relevant to the needs of an individual customer. By extracting a customized view of the catalog we show only those parts matching features specified in the user profile. An example of using this pattern is the personalized Web store architecture presented in Ardissono et al. (1999).

Existing product catalogs can be integrated with the agent-based subsystem through catalog agents. Each catalog agent is a WRAPPER (Weiss, 2004) that "agentifies" an existing catalog, converting a catalog-specific schema to a common schema used by the product extractor. In addition to filtering the contents of the catalog against the buyer's profile, discounts can also be offered to individual customers to entice existing customers to remain loyal to the business, as well as to attract new customers.

The structure of the pattern is shown in Figure 8.

Resulting Context

To control what information is disclosed to the seller, the user profile should be maintained by the user agent, and supplied to the seller agent on request. For addressing privacy concerns when accessing user profiles, consult USER AGENT. For a discussion on obtaining the user profiles for tailoring the content of a generic catalog to a buyer's profile, consult USER PROFILING. Consult NOTIFICATION AGENT, if you want to notify the customer about changes to the catalog (e.g., the addition of a new widget that matches the user's profile). Each catalog agent is a wrapper, that agentifies an existing catalog, converting a catalog-specific schema to a common schema—WRAPPER (Weiss, 2004).

NOTIFICATION AGENT

Context

You provide a locus of control—USER AGENT—where users can interact with their agents, and

Figure 8. Role diagram for CATALOGING

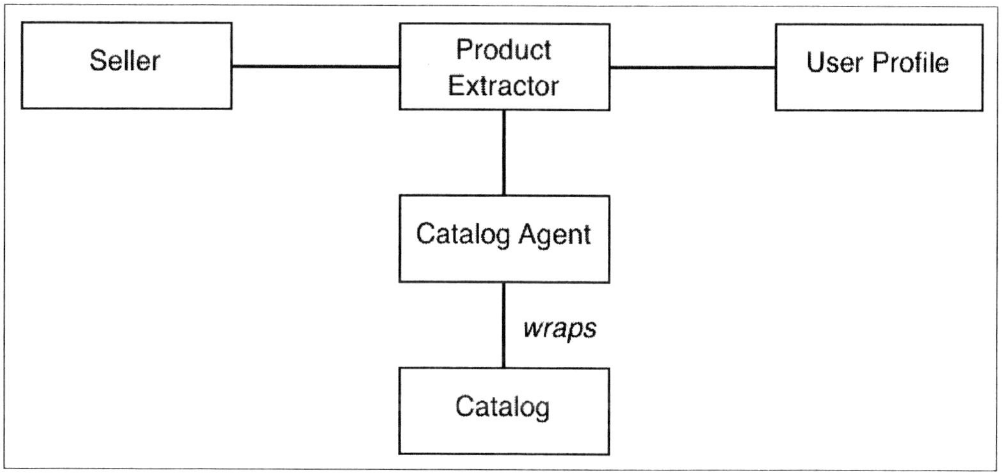

want to subscribe to the progress of a transaction. You want to notify the customer about changes to the catalog—CATALOGING. In both cases, you need to monitor a data source (e.g., a product catalog) for changes or the progress of a transaction.

Problem

How to keep users informed about changes of interest to them.

Forces

- Information overload

Solution

The solution involves a notification agent that resides close to the information source. It monitors the information source for changes of interest by registering with the information source or by continuously polling it. Notification agents can be considered a special type of mobile agent that only move to a single remote location. A notification agent is created with a condition, typically comprising an event (such as the posting of a product for sale) and a boolean expression on the event data (such as the name of a product). Whenever it detects an event of the specified type at the remote location, it evaluates this condition. If the condition is satisfied, the agent notifies the user agent.

The benefits of using this pattern are similar to those of sending a mobile agent to another host and letting it interact remotely. It reduces the number of messages between the user agent and the information source. The example of a meta-auction engine such as AuctionWatcher (2002) makes this clear: it creates an agent that monitors the progress of an auction on the user's behalf and notifies the user about events of relevance, for example, when the user has been outbid and when the user should increase her maximum bid. Without a meta-auction engine, the user agent would have to poll the state of the auction periodically.

The structure of this pattern is shown in Figure 9.

Resulting Context

You want to use the same notification agent with multiple sellers. Therefore, you decide to employ WRAPPER (Weiss, 2004) agents that translate from the format of seller-specific information sources to that understood by the notification agent.

Examples

The following examples illustrate some uses of the patterns described in this chapter. The first example, an online auction, demonstrates how agents can be used in the negotiation phase (Guttman & Maes, 1999) of an e-business transaction, in which buyers and sellers negotiate the terms

Figure 9. Role diagram for NOTIFICATION AGENT

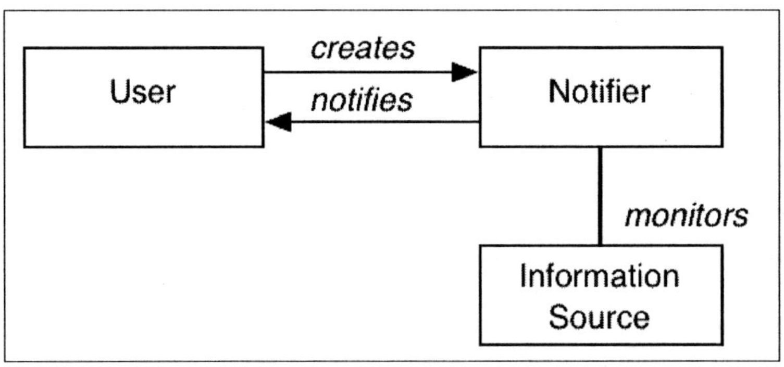

of a transaction (such as price and warranty). The second and third examples show agents in operation during the information phase (Guttman & Maes, 1999), in which buyers navigate product catalogs and use mediators to locate sellers that offer a certain product or establish their actual needs.

Online Auction

In this example, in an online auction, users post items for sale, while other users place bids on those items. A user may be represented—AGENT AS DELEGATE—by multiple BUYER and SELLER AGENTS in concurrent transactions. These agents are all managed by a USER AGENT that provides a single interface to the user. In our example, the user Bob is represented in the auction by a seller agent, while the users Alice and Mary act as buyers via their buyer agents, as shown in Figure 10. The auction mechanism is implemented by a mediator agent—AGENT AS MEDIATOR. This agent provides a MEETING PLACE (Deugo et al., 2001) for buyers and sellers. It maintains a catalog of items for sale and a list of auctions with administrative information for each one (highest bid, reserve price, and remaining duration of the auction). The mediator receives requests from sellers to create an auction, bids from buyers, and, if the type of auction allows it (e.g., in an English auction), informs each buyer agent about a new bid, as well as the outcome.

Buyer agents implement the bidding strategies of their users (characterized by parameters such as starting price, maximum price, and rate of increase). They also inform them about important events regarding the current auction (e.g., if they are winning or losing the auction). While buyer agents only notify a user about the current auction, notifier agents—NOTIFICATION AGENT—can be used to monitor other auctions on a user's behalf. The user creates a notifier agent by initializing it with a specification of the product or service she is looking for. On receiving a NOTIFICATION about an auction, a user can decide to create a new buyer agent to join it.

Locating Sellers by Product or Service

This example switches the positions of buyer and seller agents in the online auction example. Bob wants to buy a certain product or service and, via his USER AGENT, creates a BUYER AGENT and initializes it with a specification of the product or service. This buyer agent queries a MEDIATOR AGENT—in this case, a search agent or a directory agent—for the locations of sellers for the product or service in question. At this architectural level, we could use static or mobile agents to represent

Figure 10. Collaboration diagram for the agent-based online auction example

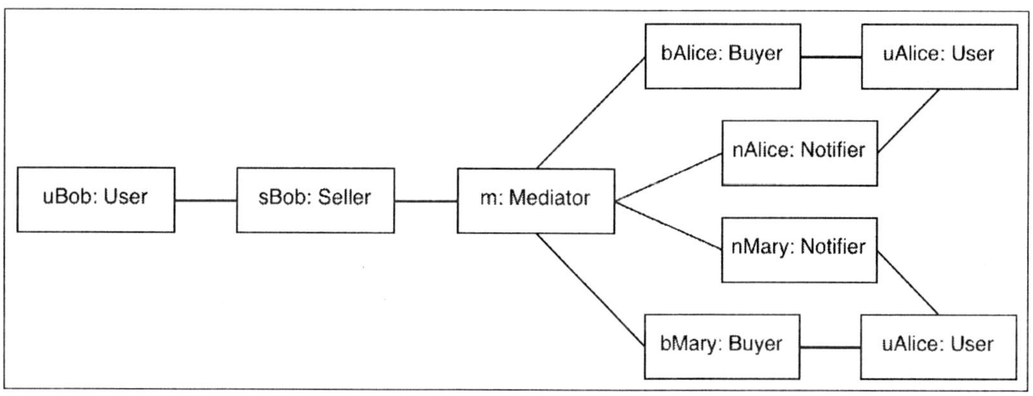

buyer agents. Greengrass et al. (1999) describe a mobile agent scenario in which a buyer agent moves to the known site of a directory agent, queries this directory agent, and obtains an itinerary of the locations of SELLER AGENTS to visit. Fonseca et al. (2001) document a mobile shopping system, where an agent representing a shopper in a mall contacts a directory facilitator agent on entry to the mall, and obtains directions to stores which carry products of interest to the user, provides those directions to the user, and allows him to check the prices of other stores. For further details on this case study, and an illustration of how the patterns can be used as part of a pattern-driven design process, see Weiss (2003).

Customizing Navigation

Another example is using agents to assist users in navigating through an (online) product catalog. From a front-end perspective, a USER AGENT can be used to collect profile information about a user and control how this information is made available to seller agents. The profile information for different sellers is stored in a personal profile repository in the user agent—USER PROFILING. Sections of the profile can be restricted to a subset of the sellers only. Using the profile information, the seller agent can classify the user into predefined stereotypes and thus infer a profile of product preferences—USER PROFILING. With these preferences, a product extractor agent—CATALOGING—can tailor the contents of the product catalog, such as in the personalized Web store in Ardissono et al. (1999). In addition to filtering the catalog contents against the buyer's profile, the product extractor can propose discounts to retain existing or attract new customers.

Although we have focused on using user profiles in the front-end, this is not to say that they cannot equally be used in the back-end. However, the basic trade-off in this case is that users will have less control over profiles collected and stored by sellers. Customers may decide to do business with sellers who do not collect profiles in this way, or make the process of collecting profiles transparent and the profiles themselves accessible.

CONCLUSION

In this chapter, we described a group of architectural patterns for designing agent-based e-business systems and gives several examples illustrating their use. These patterns relate to front-end e-business activities that involve interaction with the user and delegation of tasks from users to agents. Future work will describe patterns for back-end e-business activities that do not involve direct interaction with the user, but rather depict mechanisms for mediating between agents representing users. These patterns will expand on the description of mediator agents in this chapter. Together, these patterns are just the beginnings of a pattern language for agent-based e-business system design, based on our current understanding of the technology. As the use of agent technology in e-business matures, this language will evolve as well. It is our hope that the proposed set of patterns and the pattern format may provide a starting point for future effort in this direction.

FUTURE RESEARCH DIRECTIONS

To date, only a subset of the patterns of agent-based e-business systems have been documented. This provides many opportunities for future research. These opportunities can be grouped into two areas. On one hand, a better understanding of using agent patterns as part of a pattern-driven design process (Weiss, 2003) is required; we need to be able to reason about design trade-offs between patterns; see Mussbacher, Amyot, and Weiss (2007) for a typical approach and survey of related efforts, and capture pattern knowledge in pattern repositories (Knublauch & Rose, 2002) that can be consulted by developers to address specific design problems during the development of an agent-based system. Finally, we want to generate code for specific agent frameworks from those patterns.

On the other hand, many more agent patterns in the e-business domain remain to be mined and documented. Areas of particular interest are patterns where agents are used as mediators, ranging from directory agents to sophisticated broker and market maker agents (Deugo et al., 2001), and patterns for agents that provide mobile, context-aware services. One example of current research in this area is a set of auction patterns documented by Jureta, Faulkner, and Kolp (2005). However, this would also include patterns for search, reputation management, and integration. A taxonomy of e-business agents, which could provide a suitable starting point for a systematic mining effort is given in Papazoglou (2001).

Conceptual frameworks for these activities are also required. Weiss (2003) proposes a pattern-driven design framework for harvesting recurring design solutions and documenting them as patterns, and guiding the designer through the selection of patterns appropriate to their specific design context. The approach suggests a five step process, the first three related to mining patterns: identify the forces in a domain, document the roles of pattern participants, and document patterns and their dependencies. The last two apply to patterns: identify the overall design goals and select patterns.

Finally, we need to document patterns for nonfunctional design issues such as deployment, scalability, and security of agent-based e-business systems, and we must gain a better understanding of how to integrate such patterns with the current agent development processes. Some progress along these lines has been made in the area of agent security patterns. A good starting point is Mouratidis et al. (2006).

ACKNOWLEDGMENT

An earlier version of this chapter was accepted for PLoP 2001 (Weiss, 2001). Thanks go to my shepherd Dirk Riehle for his valuable comments. The material in this chapter has benefited from feedback in several tutorials and classes held since on this material and was expanded to reflect the recent progress in the area of agent patterns.

REFERENCES

Alexander, C. (1979). *The timeless way of building*. Oxford University Press.

Aranguren, M. (2005). *Ontology design patterns for the formalisation of biological ontologies.* Master's Thesis, Manchester University.

Ardissono, L., Barbero, C., et al. (1999). An agent architecture for personalized Web stores. In *Proceedings of the Conference on Autonomous Agents* (pp. 182-189). ACM.

Aridor, Y., & Lange, D. (1998). Agent design patterns: Elements of agent application design. In *Proceedings of the Conference on Autonomous Agents* (pp. 108-115). ACM.

AuctionWatcher (2002). Retrieved August 14, 2007, from http://www.auctionswatch.info

Avgeriou, P., & Zdun, U. (2005). Architectural patterns revisited: A pattern language. In *Proceedings of the European Conference on Pattern Languages of Programs.*

Brenner, W., Zarnekow, R., & Wittig, H. (1998). *Intelligent software agents: Foundations and applications.* Springer.

Carlson, D. (2001). *Modeling XML applications with UML: Practical e-business applications.* Addison-Wesley.

Collis, J., & Lee, L. (1999). Building electronic marketplaces with the ZEUS agent tool-kit. *Lecture Notes in Artificial Intelligence, 1571,* 1-24.

Deugo, D., Weiss, M., & Kendall, E. (2001). Reusable patterns for agent coordination. In A. Omicini et al. (Eds.), *Coordination of Internet Agents* (pp. 347-368). Springer.

Ferber, J. (1999). *Multi-agent systems: An introduction to distributed srtificial intelligence* (pp. 13-16). Addison-Wesley.

Fonseca, S., Griss, M., & Letsinger, R. (2001). *An agent-mediated e-commerce environment for the mobile shopper* (HP Labs Tech. Rep. No. HPL-2001-157).

Greengrass, E., Sud, J., & Moore, D. (1999, June). Agents in the virtual marketplace: Component dtrategies. In *Proceedings of SIGS* (pp. 42-52).

Griss, M. (1999). *My agent will call your agent ... but will it respond?* (HP Labs Tech. Rep. No. HPL-1999-159).

Guttman, R., & Maes, P. (1999). Agent-mediated integrative negotiation for retail electronic commerce. *Lecture Notes in Artificial Intelligence, 1571,* 70-90.

Jureta, I., Faulkner, S., & Kolp, M. (2005). Best practices agent patterns for on-line auctions. In *Proceedings of the International Conference on Enterprise Information Systems* (pp. 814-822).

Kendall, E. (1999). Role models: Patterns of agent system analysis and design. In *Proceedings of the Agent Systems and Applications/Mobile Agents.* ACM.

Kendall, E., Murali Krishna, P., Pathak, C., et al (1998). Patterns of intelligent and mobile agents. In *Proceedings of the Conference on Autonomous Agents.* ACM.

Kolp, M., Giorgini, P., & Mylopoulos, J. (2001). A goal-based organizational perspective on multi-agent architectures. In *Proceedings of the Workshop on Agent Theories, Architectures, and Languages* (LNCS 2333, pp. 128-140). Springer.

Lieberman, H. (1998). *Integrating user interface agents with conventional applications.* Paper presented at the Conference on Intelligent User Interfaces. ACM.

Lind, J. (2002). Patterns in agent-oriented software engineering. In *Proceedings of the Workshop on Agent-Oriented Software Engineering* (LNCS 2585, pp. 45-58). Springer.

Maes, P. (1994, July). Agents that reduce work and information overload. *Communications of the ACM,* pp. 31-41.

Mouratidis, H., Weiss, M., & Giorgini, P. (2006). Modelling secure systems using an agent-oriented approach and security patterns. *International Journal on Software Engineering and Knowledge Engineering, 16*(3), 471-498.

Mussbacher, G., Amyot, D., & Weiss, M. (2007). Formalizing patterns with the user requirements notation. In T. Taibi (Ed.), *Design Pattern Formalization Techniques.* Hershey, PA: IGI Global.

Noriega, P., & Sierra, C. (1999). Agent-mediated electronic commerce. *Lecture Notes in Artificial Intelligence, 1571.* Springer.

Papazoglou, M. (2001, April). Agent-oriented technology in support of e-business. *Communications of the ACM,* pp. 71-77.

Reich, J. (2000). *Ontological design patterns: Modelling the metadata of molecular biological ontologies, information and knowledge.* Paper presented at the Conference on Database and Expert System Applications.

Riehle, D., & Gross, T. (1998). Role model based framework design and integration. In *Proceedings of the Conference on Object-Oriented Programs, Systems, Languages, and Applications* (pp. 117-133). ACM.

Schelfthout, K., Coninx, T., et al (2002). *Agent implementation patterns.* Paper presented at the OOPSLA Workshop on Agent-Oriented Methodologies.

Shu, S., & Norrie, D. (1999). *Patterns for adaptive multi-agent systems in intelligent manufacturing.* Paper presented at the International Workshop on Intelligent Manufacturing Systems.

Staab, S., & Stuckenschmidt, H. (Eds.). (2006). *Semantic Web and peer-to-peer.* Springer.

Steinmetz, E., Collins, J., Jamieson, S., et al. (1999). Bid evaluation and selection in the MAGNET automated contracting system. *Lecture Notes in Artificial Intelligence, 1571*, 105-125.

Tahara, Y., Oshuga, A., & Hiniden, S. (1999). *Agent system development method based on agent patterns.* Paper presented at the International Conference on Software Engineering. ACM.

Ulmer, D. (2004). *Architectural solutions to agent-enabling e-commerce portals with pull/push abilities.* Unpublished doctoral thesis, Pace University.

Voss, A., & Kreifelts, T. (1997). *SOaP: Social agents providing people with useful information.* Paper presented at the Conference on Supporting Groupwork. ACM.

W3C. (1997). *Open profiling standard* (version 1.0, note 1997/6).

Weiss, M. (2001). *Patterns for e-commerce agent architectures: Agents as delegates.* Paper presented at the Conference on Pattern Languages of Programs.

Weiss, M. (2003). Pattern-driven design of agent systems: Approach and case study. In *Proceedings of the Conference on Advanced Information System Engineering* (pp. 711-723). Springer.

Weiss, M. (2004). A pattern language for motivating the use of agents. In *Agent-Oriented Information Systems: Revised Selected Papers* (LNAI 3030, pp. 142-157). Springer

Weiss, M., Gray, T., & Diaz, A. (1997). Experiences with a service environment for distributed multimedia applications. feature interactions in telecommunications and distributed systems, IOS, 242-253.

Wooldridge, M., & Jennings, N. (1995). Intelligent agents: Theory and practice. *The Knowledge Engineering Review, 10*(2), 115-152.

Zacharia, G., Moukas, A., & Maes, P. (1999). *Collaborative reputation mechanisms in electronic marketplaces.* Paper presented at the Hawaii International Conference On System Science. IEEE.

Zambonelli, F., Jennings, N., et al. (2001). Agent-oriented software engineering for Internet applications. In A. Omicini, et al. (Eds.), *Coordination of Internet Agents* (pp. 326-346). Springer.

ADDITIONAL READING

Deugo, D., Kendall, E., & Weiss, M. (1999). Agent pPatterns. Tutorial at the *International Symposium on Agent Systems and Applications/Mobile Agents.* Retrieved August 15, 2007, from http://www.scs.carleton.ca/~deugo/Patterns/Agent/Presentations/AgentPatterns

Jureta, I., Faulkner, S., & Kolp, M. (2005). Best practices agent patterns for on-line auctions. *International Conference on Enterprise Information Systems* (pp. 814-822).

Knublauch, H., & Rose, T. (2002). Tool-supported process analysis and design for the development of multiagent systems. *Workshop on Agent-Oriented Software Engineering* (LNCS 2585, pp. 186-197). Springer.

Mussbacher, G., Amyot, D., & Weiss, M. (2007). Formalizing patterns with the user requirements notation. In T. Taibi (Ed.), *Design Pattern Formalization Techniques*. Hershey, PA: IGI Global.

ENDNOTE

[1] It is customary to indicate references to patterns through a SMALL CAPS font.

This work was previously published in Agent Systems in Electronic Business, edited by E. Y. Li, S. T. Yuan, pp. 1-24, copyright 2008 by Information Science Reference, formerly known as Idea Group Reference (an imprint of IGI Global).

Chapter XII
Performance Evaluation of Consumer Decision Support Systems

Jiyong Zhang
Ecole Polytechnique Fédérale de Lausanne (EPFL), Switzerland

Pearl Pu
Ecole Polytechnique Fédérale de Lausanne (EPFL), Switzerland

ABSTRACT

Consumer decision support systems (CDSSs) help online users make purchasing decisions in e-commerce Web sites. To more effectively compare the usefulness of the various functionalities and interface features of such systems, we have developed a simulation environment for decision tasks of any scale and structure. Furthermore, we have identified three criteria in an evaluation framework for assessing the quality of such CDSSs: users' cognitive effort, preference expression effort, and decision accuracy. A set of experiments carried out in such simulation environments showed that most CDSSs employed in current e-commerce Web sites are suboptimal. On the other hand, a hybrid decision strategy based on four existing ones was found to be more effective. The interface improvements based on the new strategy correspond to some of the advanced tools already developed in the research field. This result is therefore consistent with our earlier work on evaluating CDSSs with real users. That is, some advanced tools do produce more accurate decisions while requiring a comparable amount of user effort. However, the simulation environment will enable us to efficiently compare more advanced tools among themselves, and indicate further opportunities for functionality and interface improvements.

INTRODUCTION

With the rising prosperity of the World Wide Web (WWW), consumers are dealing with an increasingly large amount of product and service information that is far beyond any individual's cognitive effort to process. In early e-commerce practice, online intermediaries were created. With the help of these virtual storefronts, users were able to find product information on a single Web site that gathers product information from thousands of merchants and service suppliers. Examples include shopping.yahoo.com, froogle.com, shopping. com, cars.com, pricegrabber.com, and so forth. However, due to the increasing popularity of electronic commerce, the amount of online retailers proliferated. As a result, there are now easily millions (or 16-20 categories) of brand-name products available on a single online intermediary Web site. Finding something is once again difficult, even with the help of various commercially available search tools.[1] Recently, much attention in e-commerce research has focused on designing and developing more advanced search and product recommender tools (Burke, Hammond, & Young, 1997; Pu & Faltings, 2000; Reilly, McCarthy, McGinty, & Smyth, 2004; Shearin & Lieberman, 2001; Shimazu, 2001; Stolze, 1999). However, they have been not employed in large scales in practicing e-commerce Web sites. Pu and Kumar (2004) gave some reasons as to why this is the case and when such advanced tools are expected to be adopted. This work was based on empirical studies of how users interact with product search tools, providing a good direction as to how to establish the true benefits of these advanced tools. However, insights gained from this work are limited. This is mainly due to the lack of a *large* amount of *real* users for the needed user studies and the high cost of user studies, even if real users were found. Each of the experiments reported in Pu and Kumar (2004) and Pu and Chen (2005) took more than 3 months of work, including the design and preparation of the study, the pilot study, and the empirical study itself. After the work was finished, it remains unclear whether a small amount of users recruited in an academic institution can forecast the behavior of the actual user population, which is highly diverse and complex.

Our main objective in this research is to use a simulation environment to evaluate various search tools in terms of interaction behaviors: what users' effort would be to use these tools and what kind of benefits they are likely to receive from these tools. We base our work on some earlier work (Payne, Bettman, & Johnson, 1993) in terms of the design of the simulation environment. However, we have added important elements to adapt such environments to online e-commerce and consumer decision support scenarios. With this simulation environment, we hope to more accurately forecast the acceptance of research tools in the real world, and curtail the evaluation of each tool's performance from months of user study to hours of simulation and a week of fine tuning the simulation results against a small but diverse amount of real users. This should allow us to evaluate more tools and, more importantly, discover design opportunities of new tools.

Our initial work of measuring the performance of various decision support strategies in e-commerce environments was reported in a conference paper (Zhang & Pu, 2005). The current article is an extended version of the conference paper. Besides adding significantly more details on the work already reported, there are a number of important and new contributions:

- In the conference paper, we only reported the performance evaluation results of various decision strategies such as the lexicographical (LEX) strategy, the elimination-by-aspects (EBA) strategy, and so forth; in this paper, we consider the evaluation of a consumer decision support system as an integral unit compromising decision strategies, user interfaces, and the underlying product catalog;
- In the extended effort-accuracy framework described in the conference paper, we only used a classical definition of decision accuracy; here we propose two new definitions of decision accuracy that correspond more

precisely with a user's choice behavior in e-commerce situations rather than the classical choice problem in decision literature;
- Based on the new definitions, we were able to draw more conclusions from the simulation results: not only can we establish that hybrid decision approaches can reduce user's effort while achieving a high level of decision accuracy, but we can also see some opportunities for improving consumer decision support systems by designing better interfaces and decision approaches, courtesy of the simulation environment.

This paper is organized as follows: the second section reviews some related research work; the third section defines the consumer decision support system (CDSS) and clarifies its relationship with our earlier published concepts on multi-attribute decision problem (MADP) and various decision strategies; the fourth section describes in detail the simulation environment for the performance evaluation of CDSSs; the fifth section describes the extended effort-accuracy framework consisting of three performance criteria: cognitive effort, elicitation effort, and decision accuracy; the sixth section reports the performance evaluation of various CDSSs with respect to a set of simulated MADPs and user preferences; the seventh section discusses the main research results obtained, followed by the conclusion section.

RELATED WORK

In traditional environments where no computer aid is involved, behavioral decision theory provides adequate knowledge describing people's choice behavior, and presents typical approaches of solving decision problems. For example, Payne et al. (1993) established a well-known effort-accuracy framework that described how people adapted their decision strategies by trading off accuracy and cognitive effort to the demands of the tasks they faced. The simulation experiments carried out in that work were able to give a good analysis of various decision strategies that people employ, and the decision accuracy they would expect to get in return.

In the online electronic environment where the support of computer systems is pervasive, we are interested in analyzing users' choice behaviors when tools are integrated into their information processing environments. That is, we are interested in analyzing when given a computer tool with its system logic, how much effort a user has to expend and how much decision accuracy he or she is to obtain from that tool. On one hand, though the decision maker's cognitive effort is still required, it can be significantly decreased by having computer programs carry out most of the calculation work automatically; on the other hand, the decision makers must expend some effort to explicitly state their preferences to the computer according to the requirements of the underlying decision support approach employed in that system. We would like to call this extra user effort (in addition to the cognitive effort) preference elicitation effort. We believe that elicitation effort plays an important role in the new effort-accuracy model of users' behavior in online choice environments.

Many other researchers have carried out simulation experiments in evaluating the performance of their systems or approaches. Payne et al. (1993) introduced a simulation experiment to measure the performance of various decision strategies in off-line situations. Recently, Boutilier (Boutilier, Patrascu, Poupart, & Schuurmans, 2005) carried out their experiments by simulating a number of randomly generated synthetic problems, as well as user responses to evaluate the performance of various query strategies for eliciting bounds of the parameters of utility functions. In Reilly et al. (2005), various users' queries were generated artificially from a set of off-line data to analyze the recommendation performance of the incremental critiquing approach. These related works generally suggest that simulating the interaction between users and the system is a promising methodology for performance evaluation. In our work, we go further in this direction and propose the general simulation environment that can be adopted to evaluate the performance of various CDSSs systematically within the extended effort-accuracy framework. To the best of our knowledge, our simulation work is the first attempt in systematically evaluating the performance of various CDSSs with simulation methodology.

CONSUMER DECISION SUPPORT SYSTEM

In a scenario of buying a product (such as a digital camera), the objective of consumers is to choose the product that most closely satisfies their needs and preferences (decision result), and furthermore, they are not likely to regret the products that they have bought (how accurate their decision is). They usually face a large amount of product alternatives (or options) and need a decision support system in order to process the entire product catalog without having to examine all items exhaustively. Therefore, a consumer decision support system consists of three components: (1) the product catalog that is accessible to consumers via an interface; (2) the underlying decision support approach that helps a consumer to choose and determine the product most satisfying his or her preferences; (3) the user interface with which a consumer interacts in order to state his or her preferences. We will now introduce these three components respectively.

The product catalog or more precisely an electronic product catalog (EPC) (Palmer, 1997; Torrens, 2002) provides a list of products, each one represented by a number of attributes. The process of determining the most preferred product from the EPC can be formally described as solving a multi-attribute decision problem[2] $\Psi = \langle \mathbf{X}, \mathbf{D}, \mathbf{O}, \mathbf{P} \rangle$, where $\mathbf{x}=\{x_1, ..., x_n\}$ is a finite set of attributes the product catalog has, $\mathbf{D}=D_1 \times ... \times D_n$ indicates the space of all possible products in the catalog (each $D_i (1 \leq i \leq n)$ is a set of possible domain values for attribute X_i), $\mathbf{O}=\{O_1,...,O_m\}$ is a finite set of available products (also called alternatives or outcomes) that the EPC offers, and $\mathbf{P}=\{P_1,...,P_t\}$ denotes a set of preferences that the decision maker may have. Each preference P_i may be identified in any form as required by the decision methods. The solution of a MADP is an alternative O most satisfying the decision maker's preferences.

In traditional decision making environments, consumers usually adopt various decision strategies such as EBA or LEX to obtain decision results (Payne et al., 1993). In a computer assisted scenario, the distribution of work is quite different. It is the CDSS that will perform these decision strategies to help the consumer to make decisions. The consumer is only required to input his or her preferences as required by the specific decision strategy; and then the solution can be chosen for the consumer automatically. When a decision strategy is adopted in the consumer decision support system, we also say it is a decision support approach for that system. In this paper, we focus on the following decision strategies and study the performance of CDSSs based on these decision strategies.

1. The weighted additive (WADD) strategy. It is a normative approach based on multi-attribute utility theory (MAUT) (Keeney & Raiffa, 1993). In our simulation experiment, we use it as the baseline strategy.
2. Some basic heuristic strategies. They are the equal weight (EQW) strategy, the elimination-by-aspects strategy, the majority-of-confirming dimensions (MCD) strategy, the satisficing (SAT) strategy, the lexicographic (LEX) strategy and the frequency of good and bad features (FRQ) strategy. Their detailed definitions can be found in Payne et al. (1993) and Zhang and Pu (2005).
3. Hybrid decision strategies. Besides the basic

heuristic strategies, people may also use a combination of several of them to make a decision to try to get a more precise decision result. These kinds of strategies are called hybrid decision strategies. As a concrete example of hybrid decision strategies, The C4 strategy (Zhang & Pu, 2005), which is a combination of four basic heuristic strategies: EBA, MCD, LEX, and FRQ, is also studied in this paper.

In a CDSS, the user-interface component is used to obtain the consumers' preferences. However, such preferences are largely determined by the underlying decision support approach that has been adopted in the system. For example, the popular ranked list interface is in fact an interface implementing the lexicographical strategy. Also, if we adopt the weight additive strategy in a consumer decision support system, the user interface will be designed in the manner of asking the user to input corresponding weight and middle values for each attribute. In our current work, we assume the existence of a very simple user interface. Thus, we regard the underlying decision support approach as the main factor of the consumer decision support system.

SIMULATION ENVIRONMENT FOR PERFORMANCE EVALUATION

Our simulation environment is concerned with the evaluation of how users interact with consumer decision support systems (CDSSs), how decision results are produced, and the quality of these decision results.

The consumer first interacts with the system by inputting his or her preferences through the user interface. With the help of decision support, the system generates a set of recommendations to the consumer. This interactive process can be executed multiple times until the consumer is satisfied with the recommended results (i.e., a product to purchase) or gives up due to loosing patience.

As shown in Figure 1, for a given CDSS, we evaluate its performance in a simulated environment by the following procedure: (1) we generate a set of MADPs using Monte Carlo method to simulate the presence of an electronic catalog up to any scale and structure characteristics; (2) we generate a set of consumer preferences also with the Monte Carlo method, taking into account user diversity and scale; (3) we carry out the simulation of the underlying decision ap-

Figure 1. An architecture of the simulation environment for performance evaluation of a given consumer decision support system

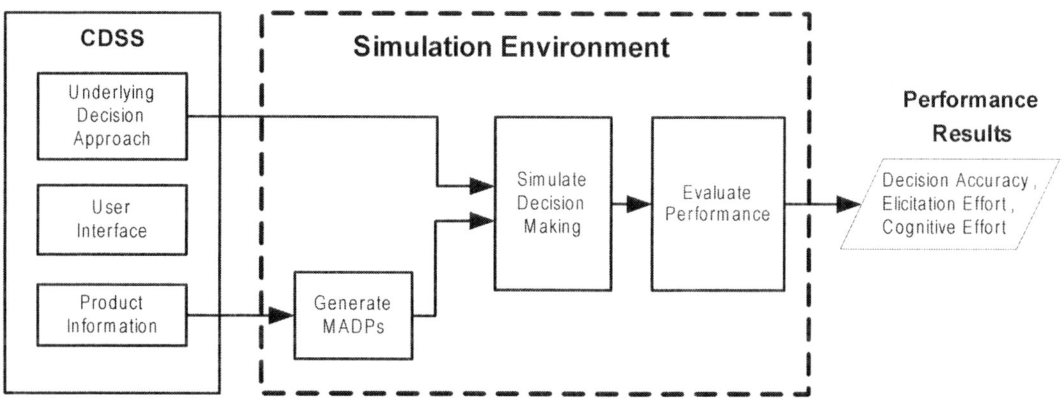

proach of the CDSS to solve these MADPs; (4) we obtain associated decision results for the given CDSS (which product has been chosen given the consumer's preferences); and finally, (5) we evaluate the performance of these decision results in terms of cognitive effort, preference elicitation effort, and decision accuracy under the extended accuracy-effort framework (detailed discussion of this framework in the next section).

The simulation environment can be used in many ways to provide different performance measures of a given CDSS. For instance, if both the detail product information of CDSS and the consumer's preferences are unknown, we can simulate both the alternatives and the consumer's preferences, and the simulation results would be the performance of the CDSS independently of users and the set of alternatives; if the detail product information of the CDSS is provided, we then only need to simulate the consumer's preferences, and the alternatives of the MADPs can be copied from the CDSS instead of being randomly generated. The simulation results would be the performance of the CDSS under the specified product set.

As a concrete example to demonstrate the usage of such a simulation environment, we will show a procedure in evaluating the performance of various CDSSs in terms of the scale of the MADPs, which is determined by two factors: the number of attributes n and the number of alternatives m. Since we are trying to study the performance of different CDSSs (currently built on heuristic decision strategies) in different scales of MADPs, we assume that users and alternatives are both unknown and they are simulated to give results independently of the user and the system. More specifically, we classify the decision problems into 20 categories according to the scales of n (the number of attributes) and m (the number of alternatives): n has five values (5, 10, 15, 20, and 25), and m has four (10, 100, 1,000, and 10,000). To make the performance evaluation result more accurate, each time we randomly generate 500 different MADPs in the same scale and use their average performance as the final result. The detail simulation result will be reported in the experimental result section.

THE EXTENDED EFFORT-ACCURACY FRAMEWORK

The performance of the system can be evaluated by various criteria such as the degree of a user's satisfaction with the recommended item, the amount of time a user spends to reach a decision, and the decision errors that the consumer may have committed. Without real users' participation, the satisfaction of a consumer with a CDSS is hard to measure. However, the other two criteria can be measured.

The amount of time a user spends to reach a decision is equivalent to the amount of time he or she uses to express preferences and process the list of recommended items in order to reach a decision. The classical effort-accuracy framework mainly investigated the relationship of decision accuracy and cognitive effort of processing information by different decision strategies in the off-line situation. In the online decision support situation, however, the effort of eliciting preferences must be considered as well.

Furthermore, most products carry a fair amount of financial and emotional risks. Thus, the accuracy of users' choices is extremely important. That is, there is a posterior process where users evaluate the search tools in terms of whether the products they have found via the search tool are really what they want and whether they had enough decision support. This is what we mean by decision accuracy.

We therefore propose an extended effort-accuracy framework by explicitly measuring three factors of a given consumer decision support system: cognitive effort, elicitation effort, and decision accuracy. In the remainder of this section, we first recall the measurement of cognitive effort in the classical framework, we give various definitions of accuracy, and then we detail the method of measuring elicitation effort. Finally, the cognitive and elicitation effort of these decision strategies are analyzed in section 5.4, in an online situation.

Measuring Cognitive Effort

Based upon the work of Newell and Simon (1972), a decision approach can be seen as a sequence of elementary information processes (EIPs), such as reading the values of two alternatives on an attribute, comparing them, and so forth. Assuming that each EIP takes equal cognitive effort,[3] the decision maker's cognitive effort is then measured in terms of the total number of EIPs. Conformed with the classical framework, a set of EIPs for the decision strategies is defined as (1) READ: read an alternative's value on an attribute into short-term memory (STM), (2) COMPARE: compare two alternatives on an attribute, (3) ADD: add the values of two attributes in STM, (4) DIFFERENCE: calculate the size of the difference of two alternatives for an attribute, (5) PRODUCT: weight one value by another, (6) ELIMINATE: eliminate an alternative from consideration, (7) MOVE: move to next element of the external environment, and (8) CHOOSE: choose the preferred alternative and end the process.

Measuring Decision Accuracy

Accuracy and effort form an important performance measure for the evaluation of consumer decision support systems. On one hand, consumers expect to get highly accurate decisions. On the other hand, they may not be inclined (or able) to expend a high level of cognitive and elicitation effort to reach a decision. Three important factors influence the decision accuracy of a consumer decision support systems: the underlying decision approach used; the number of interactions required from the end user (if a longer interaction is required, a user may give up before he finds the best option); the number of options displayed to the end user in each interaction cycle (a single item is likely to miss the target choice compared to a list of items; however, a longer list of items requires more cognitive effort to process information). In our current framework, we investigate the combined result of these three factors (i.e., decision approach as well interface design components) of a given consumer decision support system.

In the following sections, we start with classical definitions of decision accuracy, analyze their features and describe their weaknesses for the online environments, and then we propose two definitions, which we have developed, that are likely to be more adequate for measuring decision accuracy in e-commerce environments. To eliminate the effect of a specific set of alternatives on the decision accuracy results, in the following definitions we assume that there is a set of *N* different MADPs to be solved by a given consumer decision support system that implements a particular decision strategy *S*. The accuracy will be measured in average among all those MADPs.

Accuracy Measured by Selection of Nondominated Alternatives

This definition comes from Grether and Wilde (1983). After adapting it to decision making with the help of a computer system, this definition says that a solution given by CDSS is correct if and only if it is non-dominated by other alternatives. So the decision accuracy can be measured by the numbers of solutions which are *Pareto optimal* (i.e., not dominated by other alternatives, see also Viappiani, Faltings, Schickel-Zuber, & Pu, 2005). We use O^i_S to represent the optimal solution given by the CDSS with strategy S when solving $MADP_i (1 \leq i \leq N)$. The accuracy of selection of nondominated alternatives $Acc_{NDA}(S)$ is defined as the following:

$$Acc_{NDA}(S) = \frac{N - \sum_{i=1}^{N} \text{Dominated}(O_S^i)}{N}, (1)$$

where

$$\text{Dominated}(O_S^i) = \begin{cases} 1 & \text{if } O_S^i \text{ is dominated in } MADP_i \ (1 \le i \le N) \\ 0 & else \end{cases}$$

According to this definition, it is easy to see that a system employing the WADD strategy has 100% accuracy because all the solutions given by WADD are *Pareto optimal*. Also, this definition of accuracy measurement is effective only when the system contains some dominated alternatives, otherwise the accuracy of the system is always 100%.

This definition of accuracy can distinguish the errors caused by choosing dominated alternatives of the decision problems. However, measuring decision accuracy using this method is limited in e-commerce environments. In an efficient market, it is unlikely that the consumer products or business deals are dominated or dominating. That is, it is unlikely an apartment would be both spacious and less expensive compared to other available ones. We believe that although this definition is useful, it is not helpful to distinguish various CDSSs in terms of how good they are for supporting users to select the best choice (not just the nondominated ones).

Accuracy Measured by Utility Values

This definition of measuring accuracy was used in the classical effort-accuracy framework (Payne et al., 1993). Since no risk or uncertainty is involved in the MADPs, the expected value of an alternative is equivalent to the utility value of each alternative. The utility value of each alternative is assumed to be in the weight additive form. Formally, this accuracy definition can be represented as:

$$Acc_{UV}(S) = \frac{\sum_{i=1}^{N} \frac{V(O_S^i)}{V(O_{WADD}^i)}}{N}, \quad (2)$$

where $V(O^i_S)$ is the value function given by the WADD strategy in $MADP_i$. In this definition, a system employing the WADD strategy is also 100% accurate because it always gives out the solution with the maximal utility value.

One advantage of this measure of accuracy is that it can indicate not only that an error has occurred, but also the severity of the error of the decision making. For instance, a system achieving 90% accuracy indicates that an average consumer is expected to choose an item that is 10% less valuable from the best-possible option. While this definition is useful for choosing a set of courses to take for achieving a particular career objective, it is not most suitable in e-commerce environments. Imagine that someone has chosen and purchased a digital camera. Two months later, she discovers that the camera that her colleague has bought was really the one she wanted. She did not see the desired camera, not because the online store did not have it, but because it was difficult to find and compare items on the particular e-commerce Web site. Even though the camera that she bought satisfied some of her needs, she is still likely to feel a great sense of regret, if not outright disappointment. Her likelihood of returning to that Web site is in question. Given that bad choices can cause great emotional burdens (Luce, Payne, & Bettman, 1999), we have developed the following definition of decision accuracy.

Accuracy Measured by Selection of Target Choice

In our earlier work (Pu & Chen, 2005), we defined decision accuracy as measured by the percentage of users who have chosen the right option using a particular decision support system. We call that option the target choice. In empirical studies with real users, we first asked users to choose a product with the consumer decision support system, and then we revealed the entire database to them in order to determine the target choice. If the product recommended by the consumer decision support system was consistent with the target choice, we said that the user had made an accurate decision.

In simulation environment, we take the WADD strategy as the baseline. That is, we assume the solution given by WADD is the user's final most-preferred choice. For another given strategy *S*, if the solution O^i_S is the same as the one determined by WADD, then we count it as one *hit* (this definition is called the *hit ratio*). The accuracy is measured statistically by the ratio of hit numbers to the total number of decision problems:

$$Acc_{HR}(S) = \frac{\sum_{i=1}^{N} Hit(O^i_S)}{N}, \quad (3)$$

where

$$Hit(O^i_S) = \begin{cases} 1 & \text{if } O^i_S = O^i_{WADD} \text{ in } MADP_i \\ 0 & \text{else} \end{cases}$$

This measure of decision accuracy is ideally consistent with the consumers' attitude towards the decision results. However, by this definition, it is assumed that the consumer decision support system only recommends one product to the consumer each time. In reality, the system may show a list of possible products to the consumer, and the order of the product list is also important to the consumer: the products displayed at the top of the list are more likely to be selected by the consumer. Therefore, we have developed the following definition to take into account that a list of products is displayed, rather than a single product.

Accuracy Measured by Selection of Target Choice Among K-best Items

Here we propose measuring the accuracy of the system according to the ranking orders of the K-best products it displays. This is an extension of the previous definition of accuracy. For a given $MADP_i$, instead of using strategy *S* to choose a single optimal solution, we can use it to generate a list of solutions with ranking order $L^i_S = \{O^i_{S,1}, O^i_{S,2}, \ldots, O^i_{S,K}\}$, where $O^i_{S,1}$ is the most-preferred solution according to the strategy S, and $O^i_{S,2}$ is the second-preferred solution, and so on. The first *K-best* solutions consist of the solution list. If the user's final choice (which is assumed to be given by the WADD strategy O^i_{WADD}) is in the list, we assign a *rank value* to the list according to the position of O^i_{WADD} in the list. Formally, we define this accuracy of choosing K-best items as:

$$Acc_{HR\_in\_Kbest}(S) = \frac{\sum_{i=1}^{N} RankValue(L^i_S)}{N}, \quad (4)$$

where

$$RankValue(L^i_S) = \begin{cases} 1 - \frac{k-1}{K} & \text{if } O^i_{S,k} = O^i_{WADD} \text{ in } MADP_i \quad (1 \le k \le K, 1 \le n \le N) \\ 0 & else \end{cases}$$

According to this definition, the WADD strategy still achieves 100% accuracy and is used as the baseline. A special case of this accuracy definition is that when *K=1*, it degenerates to the previous definition of *hit ratio*. In the simulation experimental results that we will show shortly, we have set *K* to 5.

In practice, it is required to eliminate the effect of random decision, and we expect that the strategy of *random choice* (selecting an alternative randomly from the alternative set, denoted as *RAND* strategy) could only produce *zero* accuracy. By doing so, we define the *relative accuracy* of the consumer decision support system with strategy *S* according to different definitions as:

$$RA_Z(S) = \frac{Acc_Z(S) - Acc_Z(RAND)}{1 - Acc_Z(RAND)}, \quad (5)$$

where

Z= NDA, UV, HR, or HR_in_Kbest.

For example, $RA_{HR}(LEX)$ denotes the relative accuracy of the *LEX* strategy under the accuracy measure definitions of *hit ratio*.

From the previous definitions, we can see that each definition represents one aspect of the accuracy of the decision strategies. We think that the definitions of *hit ratio* and *K-best items* are more suitable to measure the accuracy of various consumer decision support systems, particularly in e-commerce environments. In the sixth section, we will study the performance of various decision strategies with these accuracy measurement definitions.

Measuring Elicitation Effort

In computer-aided decision environments, a considerable amount of decision effort goes into preference elicitation since people need to "tell" their preferences explicitly to the computer system. So far, no formal method has been given to measure the preference elicitation effort. An elicitation process can be decomposed into a series of basic interactions between the user and the computer, such as selecting an option from a list, filling in a blank, answering a question, and so forth. We call these basic interaction actions elementary elicitation processes (EEPs). In our analysis, we define the set of EEPs as follows: (1) SELECT: select an item from a menu or a dropdown list, (2) FILLIN: fill in a value to an edit box, (3) ANSWER: answer a basic question, (4) CLICK: click a button to execute an action.[4]

It is obvious that different EEPs require different elicitation effort (for instance, the EEP of one CLICK would be much easier than an EEP of FILLIN a weight value for a given attribute). For the sake of simplification, we currently assume that each EEP requires an equal amount of effort from the user. Therefore, given a specific decision approach, elicitation effort is measured by the total amount of EEPs it may require.

This elicitation effort is a new factor for the online environment. The main difference between cognitive effort and elicitation effort lies in the fact that cognitive effort is a description of the mental activities in processing information, while the elicitation effort is about the interaction effort between the decision maker and the computer system through predesigned user interfaces. Even though the decision makers already have clear preferences in their mind, they must still state their preferences in a way that the computer can "understand." With the help of computer systems, the decision maker is able to reduce the cognitive effort by compensating with a certain degree of elicitation effort.

Let us consider a simple decision problem with three attributes and four alternatives. When computer support is not provided, the cognitive effort of solving this problem by the WADD strategy will be 24 READS, 8 ADDS, 12 PRODUCTS, 3 COMPARES, and 1 CHOOSE. The total number of EIPs is therefore 48.[5]

However, with the aid of a computer system, the decision maker could get the same result by spending two units of elicitation effort (FILLIN the weight value of first two attributes) and one unit of cognitive effort (CHOOSE the final result).

Analysis of Cognitive and Elicitation Effort

With the support of computer systems, the cognitive effort for WADD, as well as the basic heuristic strategies, is quite low. The decision maker inputs his or her preferences, and the decision support system executes that strategy and shows the proposed product. Then the decision maker chooses this product and the decision process is ended. Thus, the cognitive effort is equal to one EIP: CHOOSE the final alternative and exit the process. For the *C4* strategy, the cognitive effort of solving an MADP with *n* attributes and *m* alternatives is equal to that of solving a problem with *n* attributes and *4* alternatives in the traditional situation, the cognitive effort of which has been studied in (Payne et al., 1993).

According to their definitions, various decision strategies require that preferences with different parameters be elicited. For example, in the WADD strategy, the component value function and the weight for each attribute must be obtained, while for the EBA strategy, the importance order and cutoff value for each attribute are required. The required parameters for each strategy are shown in Table 1.

For each parameter in the aforementioned strategies, a certain amount of elicitation effort is required. This elicitation effort may vary with different implementations of the user interface. For example, to elicit the weight value of an attribute, the user can just FILLIN the value to an edit box, or the user can ANSWER several questions to approximate the weight value. In our analysis and the following simulation experiments, we follow the *at least* rule: the elicitation effort is determined by the least number of EEP(s). In the above example, the elicitation effort for obtaining a weight value is measured as 1 EEP.

SIMULATION RESULTS

In this section, we report our experimental results of the performance of various consumer decision support systems under the simulation environment that was introduced earlier. To simplify the experiments, we only evaluate those CDSSs built on the decision strategies listed in Table 1. Without loss of generality, we will also use the term *decision strategy* to represent the CDSS built on that decision strategy.

Table 1. Elicitation effort analysis of decision strategies

Strategy	**Parameters required to be elicited**
WADD	Weights, component value functions
EQW	Component value functions
EBA	Importance order, cutoff values
MCD	None
SAT	Cutoff values
LEX	Importance order
FRQ	Cutoff values for good and bad features
C4	Cutoff values, importance order

For each CDSS, we first simulate a large variety of MADPs, and then run the corresponding decision strategy on the computer to generate the decision results. Then the elicitation effort and decision accuracy are calculated according to the extended effort-accuracy framework. For each MADP, its domain values for a given attribute are determined randomly: the lower bound of each attribute is set to 0, and the upper bound is determined randomly from the range of 2 to 100. Formally speaking, for each attribute X_i, we define $D_i = [0,z_i]$ where $z_i \in [2,100]$.

As shown in Table 1, each decision strategy (except MCD) requires the elicitation of some specific parameters such as attribute weights or cutoff values to represent the user's preferences. To simulate the component value functions required by the WADD strategy, we assume that the component value function for each attribute is approximated by three midvalue points, which are randomly generated.[6] Thus, each component value function requires three units of EEPs. Other required parameters, such as the weight and cutoff value (each requires one unit of EEP) for each attribute are also simulated by the random generation process. The order of importance is determined by the weight order of the attributes for consistency.

In our simulation experiments, the WADD strategy is appointed as the baseline strategy, and the relative accuracy of a strategy is calculated according to equation (5). The elicitation effort is measured in terms of the total number of EEPs required by the specific strategy, and the cognitive effort is measured by the required units of EIPs. Since the relationship between accuracy and cognitive effort has already been studied and analyzed by Payne et al. (1993), in this section, we only focus on the performance of each strategy in terms of decision accuracy and elicitation effort.

Figure 2 shows the changes in *relative accuracy* with four different accuracy measure definitions for the listed decision strategies as *the number of attributes* increases in the case that each MADP has 1,000 alternatives. In all cases, the WADD is the baseline strategy; thus it achieves 100% accuracy. When measured by the selection of nondominated alternatives (RA_{NDA}), the relative accuracy of each heuristic strategy increases as the number of alternatives increases. This is mainly because the alternatives are more likely to be *Pareto optimal* when more attributes are involved. Furthermore, the RA_{NDA} of all strategies could achieve 100% accuracy when the attributes number is 20 or 25. This shows that the RA_{NDA} is not able to distinguish the decision errors occurred with the heuristic strategies in the simulated environment. When the accuracy is measured under the definitions of RA_{UV}, RA_{HR} and $RA_{HR\_in\_Kbest}$, the EQW strategy achieves the highest accuracy besides the baseline WADD strategy, and the SAT strategy has the lowest relative accuracy. The four basic heuristic strategies EBA, MCD, LEX, and FRQ are in the middle-level range. The LEX strategy, which has

Figure 2. The relative accuracy of various decision strategies when solving MADPs with different number of attributes, where m*(number of alternatives)* = 1,000

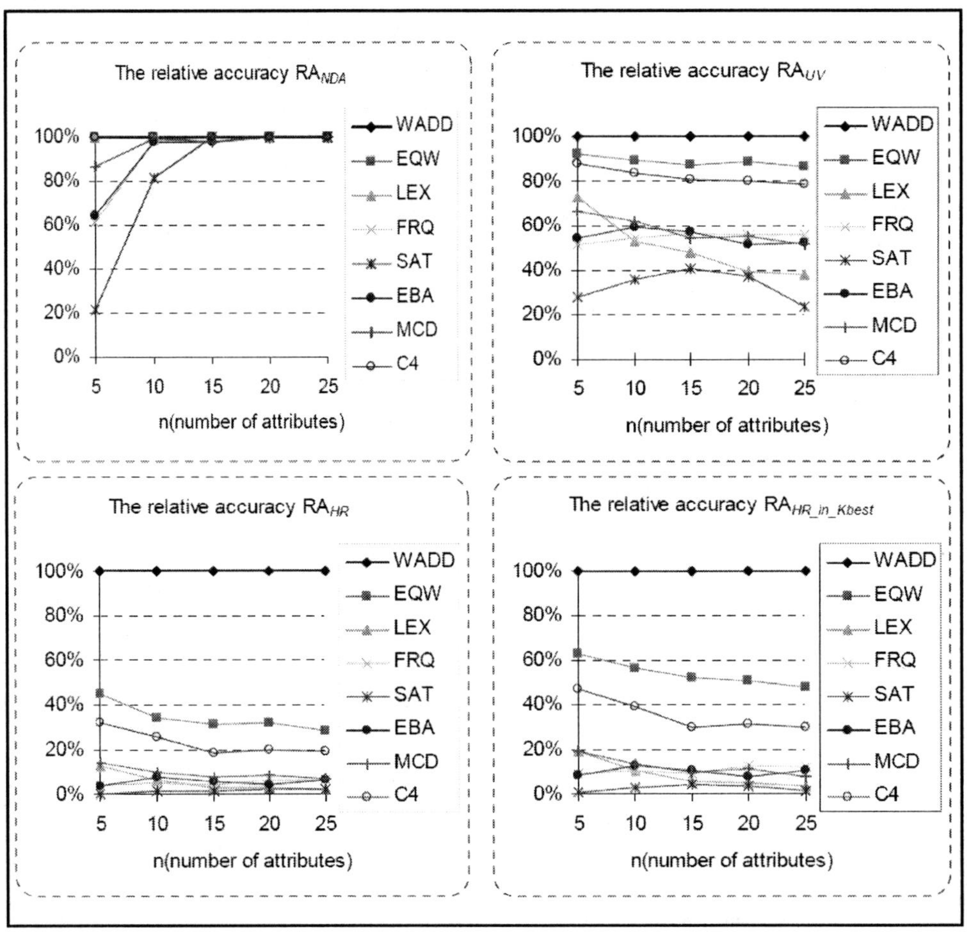

been widely adopted in many consumer decision support systems, is the least accurate strategy among the EBA, FRQ, and MCD strategies when there are over 10 attributes. When the accuracy is measured by RA_{UV}, the EQW strategy could gain over 90% relative accuracy, while it could only achieve less than 50% relative accuracy when measured by RA_{HR}. This comparison generally suggests that most of the decision results given by EQW strategy may be very close to a user's target choice (which is determined by the WADD strategy), but are not identical. Also, in all cases, the accuracy measured by $RA_{HR\ in\ Kbest}$ (where *K=5* in the experiment) is always higher than that measured by RA_{HR} (which is a special case of $RA_{HR\ in\ Kbest}$ when *K=1*). This shows that under this definition, the possibility of containing the final target choice in a K-item list is higher when K is larger. Of particular interest is that the proposed *C4* strategy, which is a combination of the four basic strategies, could achieve a much higher accuracy than any of them alone. For instance, when there are 10 attributes and 1,000 alternatives in the MADPs, the relative accuracy of *C4* strategy could exceed the average accuracy of the four basic strategies by over 27% when the definition of $RA_{HR\ in\ Kbest}$ is adopted.

Figure 3. The relative accuracy of various decision strategies when solving MADPs with a different number of alternatives, where n*(number of attributes)* = 10

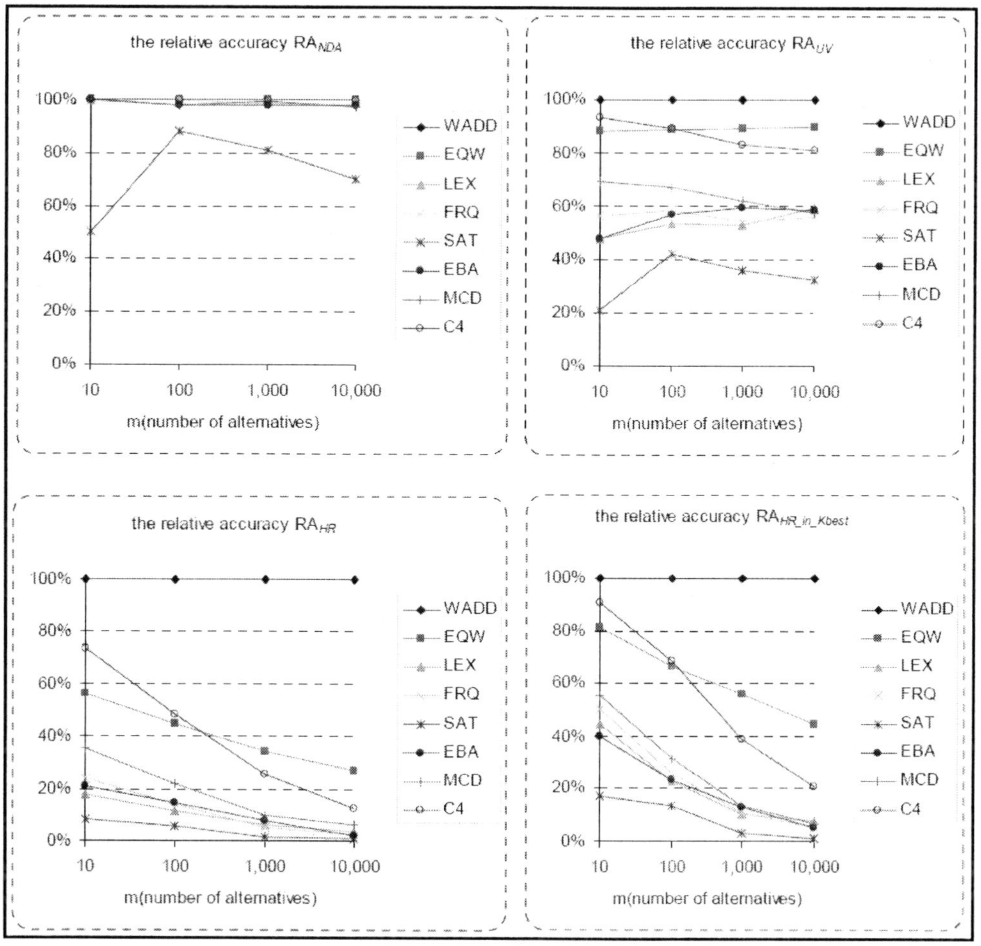

Figure 3 shows the relationship between *relative accuracy* and *the number of alternatives* (or the number of available products in a catalog) for the listed decision strategies. When the accuracy is measured by the selection of nondominated alternatives (RA_{NDA}), all strategies except SAT could gain nearly 100% of relative accuracy without a significant difference. This generally shows that the RA_{NDA} is not a good definition of accuracy measurement in the simulated environment. When the accuracy is measured by the utility values (RA_{UV}), the accuracy of the heuristic strategies remains stable as the number of alternatives increases. With the definitions of *hit ratio* (RA_{HR}) and *hit ratio in K-best items* ($RA_{HR\_in\_Kbest}$), however, the heuristic strategies strongly descend into a lower range of accuracies as the size of a catalog increases. This corresponds to the fact that consumers have increasing difficulties finding the best product as the number of alternatives in the catalog increases. The *C4* strategy, though its accuracy decreases when the number of alternatives increases, could still maintain a considerably higher relative accuracy than that of the EBA, MCD, LEX, and FRQ strategies when using the accuracy definition of RA_{HR} and $RA_{HR\_in\_Kbest}$.

The effect of the number of attributes on elicitation effort for each strategy is shown in Figure 4. As we can see, the elicitation effort of the heuristic strategies increases much slower than that of the WADD strategy as the number of attributes increases. For instance, when the number of attributes is *20*, the elicitation effort of the FRQ strategy is only about *25%* of that of WADD strategy. The FRQ and SAT strategies require the same level of elicitation effort, since both of them require the decision maker to input a cutoff value for each attribute. Except the MCD strategy, which requires no elicitation effort in the simulation environment, the LEX strategy is the one that requires the least elicitation effort in all cases among the listed strategies. The combined C4 strategy, which could share preferences among its four underlying basic strategies, requires only a slightly higher elicitation effort than the EBA strategy.

Figure 5 shows the relationship between *elicitation effort* and *the number of alternatives* for each strategy. As the number of alternatives increases exponentially, the level of elicitation effort for WADD, EQW, MCD, SAT, and FRQ strategies remains unchanged. This shows that the

Figure 4. The elicitation effort of various decision strategies when solving MADPs with a different number of attributes, where m*(number of alternatives)* = 1,000

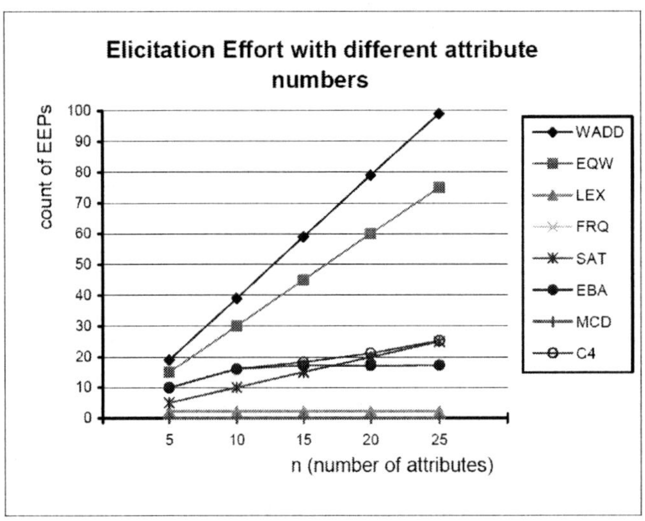

Figure 5. The elicitation effort of various decision strategies when solving MADPs with a different number of alternatives, where n*(number of attributes)* = 10

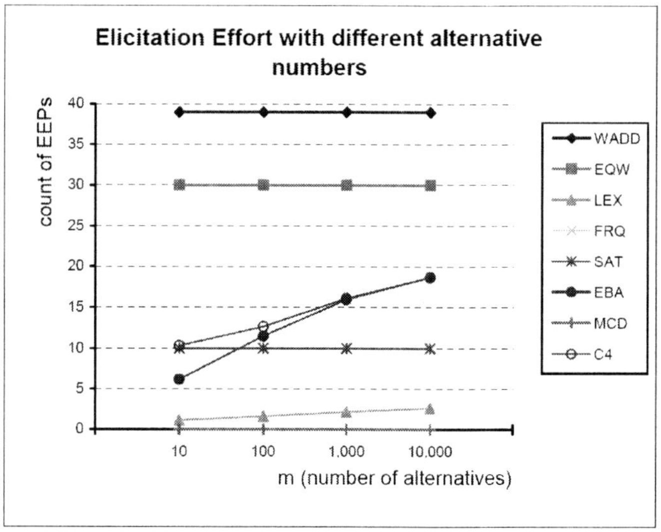

elicitation effort of these strategies is unrelated to the number of alternatives that a decision problem may have. For the LEX, EBA, and *C4* strategies, the elicitation effort increases slowly as the number of alternatives increases. As a whole, Figure 5 shows that the elicitation effort of the studied decision strategies is quite robust to the number of alternatives that a decision problem has.

A combined study from Figure 2 to Figure 5 can lead to some interesting conclusions. For each category of MADPs, some decision strategies, such as WADD and EQW, could gain relatively high-decision accuracy with proportionally high-elicitation effort. Other decision strategies, especially *C4*, MCD, EBA, FRQ, and LEX, could achieve a reasonable level of accuracy with much lower elicitation effort compared to the baseline WADD strategy. Figure 6 illustrates the relationship between elicitation effort and $RA_{HR\ in\ Kbest}$ for various strategies when solving different scales of decision problems. For the MADPs with 5 attributes and 100 alternatives, the MCD strategy could achieve around *35%* relative accuracy without any elicitation effort. The *C4* strategy, in particular, could achieve over *70%* relative accuracy while only requiring about 45% elicitation effort compared to the WADD strategy.

For all the decision strategies we have studied here, we say that a decision strategy *S* is *dominated* if and only if there is another strategy *S'* that has higher relative accuracy and lower cognitive and elicitation effort than *S* in the decision problem. Figure 6 shows that when the MADPs have 10 attributes and 1,000 alternatives, the WADD, EQW, *C4*, and MCD are nondominated approaches. However, for a smaller scale of MADPs (5 attributes and 100 alternatives), only the WADD, *C4,* and MCD strategies have the possibility of being the optimal strategy. This figure also shows that if the user's goal is to make decisions as accurately as possible, WADD is the best strategy among the listed strategies; while if the decision maker's goal is to have reasonable accuracy with a certain elicitation effort, then the *C4* strategy may be the best option.

Figure 6. Elicitation effort/relative accuracy trade-offs of various decision strategies

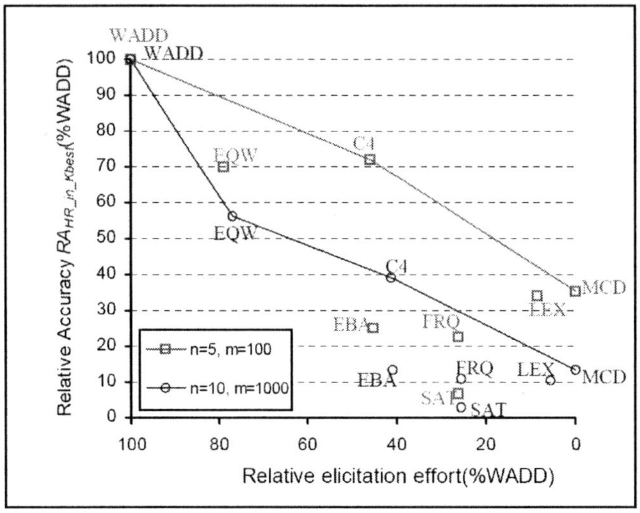

DISCUSSION

The simulation results suggest that the tradeoff between decision accuracy and elicitation effort is the most important design consideration for inventing high-performance CDSSs. That is, while advanced tools are desirable, we must not ignore the effort that users are required to make when stating their preferences.

To show how this framework can provide insights to improve user interfaces for the existing CDSSs, we have demonstrated the evaluation of the simplest decision strategies: WADD, EQW, LEX, EBA, FRQ, MCD, and SAT (Payne et al., 1993). The performance of these strategies was measured quantitatively in the proposed simulation environment within the extended effort-accuracy framework. Since the underlying decision strategy determines how a user interacts with a CDSS system (preference elicitation and result processing), the performance data allowed us to discover better decision strategies and eliminate suboptimal ones. In this sense, our work provides a new design method for developing user interfaces for consumer decision support systems.

For example, LEX is the underlying decision strategy used in the ranked list interface that many e-commerce Web sites employ (Pu & Kumar, 2004). However, our simulation results show that LEX produces relatively low-decision accuracy, especially as products become more complex. On the other hand, a hybrid decision strategy, *C4*, based on any combinations of LEX, EBA, MCD, and FRQ was found to be more effective. Combining LEX and EBA together, for example, we can derive an interface that looks like SmartClient. EBA (elimination by aspect) corresponds to eliciting constraints from users, and this feature was implemented as a constraint problem-solving engine in SmartClient (Torrens, Faltings, & Pu, 2002). After users have eliminated the product space by preference constraints, they can use the LEX strategy (ranked list) to further examine the remaining items. Even though this hybrid strategy does not include any interface features to perform trade-off navigation, the simulation results are still consistent with our earlier empirical work on evaluating CDSSs with real users (Pu & Chen, 2005; Pu & Kumar, 2004). That is, advanced tools such as SmartClient can achieve a higher accuracy while requiring users to expend slightly extra cognitive and elicitation effort than the basic strategies it contains.

The strongest implication of the simulation results is that we will be able to efficiently evaluate more-advanced tools and compare them in terms of effort and accuracy. Our plan for the future therefore includes evaluating SmartClient (Pu & Faltings, 2000) and its trade-off feature, FindMe (Burke et al., 1997), Dynamic Critiquing (Reilly et al., 2004), and Scoring Trees (Stolze, 2000), and comparing their strengths and weaknesses. We will also perform more simulations using different scales of *K* with the accuracy definition of $RA_{HR\_in\_Kbest}$. Because *K* is the size of the result set displayed in each user interaction cycle, we hope to gain more understanding on the display strategy used for CDSSs.

Finally, we do emphasize that the simulation results need to be interpreted with some caution. First of all, the elicitation effort is measured by approximation. As mentioned earlier, we assumed that each EEP requires an equal amount of effort from the users. Currently, it is unknown whether this approximation would affect the simulation results largely. In addition, when measuring the decision accuracy, the WADD strategy is chosen as the baseline, assuming that it contains no error. However, this is not the case in reality. Moreover, as the MADPs in the simulation experiments are generated randomly, there is a potential gap between the simulated MADPs and the product catalog in real applications. We are currently addressing these limitations, and fine-tune some of the assumptions with real user behaviors.

CONCLUSION

The acceptance of an e-commerce site by consumers strongly depends on the quality of the tools it provides to help consumers reach a decision that makes them confident enough to purchase. Evaluation of these consumer decision support tools on real users has made it difficult to compare their characteristics in a controlled environment, thus slowing down the optimization process of the interface design of such tools. In this paper, we described a simulation environment to evaluate the performance of CDSSs more efficiently. In this environment, we can simulate the underlying decision support approach of the system based on the consumers' preferences and the product catalog information that the system may have. The decision results can then be evaluated quantitatively in terms of decision accuracy, elicitation effort, and cognitive effort described by the extended effort-accuracy framework. More importantly, we were able to discover new decision strategies that led to interface improvements of existing CDSSs. Even though this is the first step, we hope to be able to evaluate and design new user interfaces for high performance CDSSs, and forecast users' acceptance of a new interface based on benefits such as effort and accuracy.

ACKNOWLEDGMENTS

Funding for this research was provided by the Swiss National Science Foundation under grant 200020-103490.

REFERENCES

Boutilier, C., Patrascu, R., Poupart, P., & Schuurmans, D. (2005). Regret-based utility elicitation in constraint-based decision problems. In *Proceedings of the International Joint Conferences on Artificial Intelligence (IJCAI'05)*, Edinburgh, Scotland, UK (pp. 929–934).

Burke, R. D., Hammond, K. J., & Young, B. C. (1997). The FindMe approach to assisted browsing. *IEEE Expert, 12*(4), 32–40.

Grether, D. M., & Wilde, L. L. (1983). Consumer choice and information: New experimental evidence. *Information Economics and Policy, 1*, 115-144.

Keeney, R. L., & Raiffa, H. (1993). *Decisions with multiple objectives: Preferences and value tradeoffs*. Cambridge, UK: Cambridge University Press.

Luce, M. F., Payne, J. W., & Bettman, J. R. (1999). Emotional trade-off difficulty and choice. *Journal of Marketing Research, 36*(2), 143–159.

Newell, A., & Simon, H. A. (1972). *Human problem solving*. Englewood Cliffs, NJ: Prentice-Hall.

Palmer, J. W. (1997). Retailing on the WWW: The use of electronic product catalogs. *International Journal of Electronic Markets, 7*(3), 6–9.

Payne, J. W., Bettman, J. R., & Johnson, E. J. (1993). *The adaptive decision maker*. Cambridge, UK: Cambridge University Press.

Pu, P., & Chen, L. (2005). Integrating tradeoff support in product search tools for e-commerce sits. In *Proceedings of the ACM Conference on Electronic Commerce (EC'05)*, Vancouver, Canada (pp. 269–278).

Pu, P., & Faltings, B. (2000). Enriching buyers' experiences: The SmartClient approach. In *Proceedings of the SIGCHI Conference on Human Factors in Computing Systems*, The Hague, The Netherlands (pp. 289–296).

Pu, P., & Kumar, P. (2004). Evaluating example-based search tools. In *Proceedings of the ACM Conference on Electronic Commerce (EC'04)*, New York (pp. 208–217).

Reilly, J., McCarthy, K., McGinty, L., & Smyth, B. (2004). Dynamic critiquing. In *Proceedings of the 7th European Conference in Case-Based Reasoning (ECCBR 2004)*, Madrid, Spain (pp. 763–777).

Reilly, J., McCarthy, K., McGinty, L., & Smyth, B. (2005). Incremental critiquing. *Knowledge Based Systems, 18*(2-3), 143–151.

Shearin, S., & Lieberman, H. (2001). Intelligent profiling by example. In *Proceedings of the International Conferences on Intelligent User Interfaces (IUI'01)*, Santa Fe, New Mexico (pp. 145–151).

Shimazu, H. (2001). Expertclerk: Navigating shoppers buying process with the combination of asking and proposing. In *Proceedings of the 17th International Joint Conference on Artificial Intelligence (IJCAI'01)*, Seattle, Washington (pp. 1443–1448).

Stolze, M. (1999). Comparative study of analytical product selection support mechanisms. In *Proceedings of INTERACT 99*, Edinburgh, UK (pp. 45–53).

Stolze, M. (2000). Soft navigation in electronic product catalogs. *International Journal on Digital Libraries, 3*(1), 60–66.

Torrens, M. (2002). *Scalable intelligent electronic catalogs*. Doctoral dissertation no. 2690, Swiss Federal Institute of Technology (EPFL), Lausanne, Switzerland.

Torrens, M., Faltings, B., & Pu, P. (2002). Smart clients: Constraint satisfaction as a paradigm for scaleable intelligent information systems. *CONSTRAINTS: An International Journal, 7*(1), 49–69.

Viappiani, P., Faltings, B., Schickel-Zuber, V., & Pu, P. (2005). Stimulating preference expression using suggestions. In *Workshop Notes of the IJCAI-05 Multidisciplinary Workshop on Advances in Preference Handling*, Edinburgh, UK (pp. 186–191).

Zhang, J., & Pu, P. (2005). Effort and accuracy analysis of choice strategies for electronic product catalogs. In *Proceedings of the 20th ACM Symposium on Applied Computing (SAC-2005)*, Santa Fe, New Mexico (pp. 808–814).

ENDNOTES

1. Search tools and consumer decision support systems are two terms used interchangeably throughout this article although the latter is considered to be more advanced in terms of its implementation and interface features.
2. It is also known as multicriteria decision making (MCDM) problem (Keeney & Raiffa, 1993). Our definition emphasizes on the term *attribute*, which is an objective aspect of products, not related to the decision maker's preferences.
3. Though this assumption is obviously imprecise, more studies by assigning different weighting of effort for the various EIPs show that the key relationships between the decision strategy and the decision environments were largely unchanged. See page 137 of Payne et al. (1993).
4. We assume that the actions are in their basic forms only. For example, the FILLIN operation is not allowed to elicit more than one value or even an expression. Otherwise a usability issue will arise.
5. The detail analysis is given at pages 80–81 of Payne et al. (1993). This example assumes the values of all attributes are numeric and consistent with the decision maker's preferences.
6. The procedure of assessing component value functions with midvalue points is introduced in page 120 of Keeney and Raiffa (1993).

This work was previously published in International Journal of E-Business Research, Vol. 2, Issue 3, edited by I. Lee, pp. 28-45,

Chapter XIII
E-Business Technologies in E-Market Literature

Nikos Manouselis
Agricultural University of Athens, Greece

ABSTRACT

E-business processes are implemented through existing, as well as novel technologies. This book chapter focuses on the field of electronic markets (e-markets), and studies the technologies and solutions that are applied and proposed in this field. In particular, the chapter reviews e-market literature in order to identify which are the technological trends that have appeared in the e-markets field during the last decade. A conceptual model that allows for the classification of e-market research literature according to a number of technical topics is first introduced. Then, e-market literature is reviewed, and the technologies that seem to be attracting more research attention are identified. Representative contributions are discussed, and directions for future research are indicated. The overall aim of this chapter is to provide a blueprint of the literature related to e-business technologies for e-markets.

INTRODUCTION

According to the 2005 report of the United Nations Conference on Trade and Development (UNCTAD, 2005), e-commerce continues to grow in all sectors. In the United States (the largest e-commerce market), e-commerce is still most prominent in manufacturing and wholesale trade, but on the other hand, growth rates are highest in retail trade (B2C) and services. In the United States, the largest global e-commerce market, e-commerce sales have continuously grown during the last years. With a growth rate (24.7%) significantly higher than for total retail trade (4.3%), the share of e-commerce in total retail trade is also growing. The latest available figures indicate that its share has more than doubled (UNCTAD, 2005). Eurostat data (http://epp.eurostat.cec.eu.int/) show that for the European Union (EU), e-commerce sales over the Internet increased from 0.9% in 2002 to 2.2% in 2004. Compilations by the OECD suggest that online sales represent a small but growing share of total sales in most EU member countries, and that there is solid growth in B2C e-commerce (OECD, 2004).

As a result, numerous electronic markets (e-markets) are continuously being deployed. For instance, the European Observatory of e-Markets eMarketServices (http://www.emarketservices.com) has listed, until January 2006, about 905 e-markets from various business sectors. E-markets aim to facilitate information exchange and support activities related to business process management and transactions. They are characterized by a frictionless and very low-cost flow of information between buyers and sellers. Moreover, they allow sellers to reach a wider consumer base, and buyers to have access to a large number of sellers. E-markets are therefore expected to create economic value for buyers, sellers, market intermediaries, and for society as a whole (Bakos, 1998; Grieger, 2003).

In e-markets, proposed technologies and solutions vary from simple online catalogues that provide more information about products to interested customers, to sophisticated collaborative project management and supply-chain-management environments (Dai & Kauffman, 2002b). They address various technical topics, such as architectures, interoperability, services, protocols, data management, and networking. Nevertheless, there has not been, so far, a comprehensive overview of the technologies proposed, the dimensions addressed, or the solutions tested. This chapter aims to cover this aspect by providing a blueprint of research literature and e-business technologies for e-markets.

An attempt to review and classify published research in this field can be an interesting and useful contribution to e-business researchers, managers, and practitioners/implementers. It can answer questions such as the following: which technical topics attract more attention in the field of e-markets? What are the proposed technologies and solutions? What are possible future directions of their development? Within this context, the aim of this chapter is to provide an overview of recent technological contributions in the field of e-markets. More specifically, it reports results from a study of e-market research that has been published during the past decade in scientific journals. The results provide interesting insight about the technologies for e-business processes in e-market environments, and outline implications for practice and research.

The chapter is structured as follows. The "Background" section provides some background on e-markets, as well as an overview of relevant studies. "Methodology" presents the methodology followed in order to identify and classify e-market literature around technical topics. "Results" presents and discusses the results of the classification and reviews representative contributions. Finally, "Conclusion" provides the conclusions of this study and outlines some implications for related research.

BACKGROUND

E-Markets

In the influential paper of Malone, Yates, and Benjamin (1987), e-markets have been defined according to the traditional market paradigm: structures that coordinate the flow of materials or services, through supply and demand forces, as well as through external transactions between different individuals and firms. Market forces determine the design, price, quantity, and target delivery schedule for a given product, which will serve as input into another process. The buyer of the good or service compares its many possible sources, and makes a choice based on the best combination of these attributes. Another prevailing definition, which has a more technological focus, was given by Bakos (1991): an electronic marketplace (or electronic market system) is an interorganizational information system that allows the participating buyers and sellers to exchange information about prices and product offerings. As Bakos (1991) notes, this definition of e-markets has a narrower, system-oriented focus in comparison to the more general definition of Malone et al. (1987), which refers to an e-market as a governance mechanism. As Internet became more and more widespread, providing a cheap and easy way for market participants to communicate and exchange information, the term "e-markets" tended to concern the systems described by Bakos (1991). Thus, nowadays, an e-market can be considered as an information system that intends to provide market participants with online services that will facilitate information exchange between them, with the purpose of facilitating their business transactions.

Thus, e-markets can support one or more phases of a transaction process, starting from information finding and ending with after-sales service support (Strader & Shaw, 1997). Different types of e-markets have been identified in the literature. First of all, depending on the nature of transactions they support, e-markets can be classified according to the combination of parties they involve. Therefore, most of the existing e-markets can be classified as business-to-consumer (B2C), business-to-business (B2B), and consumer-to-consumer (C2C) ones. Other, less popular, types also exist, such as government-to-consumer (G2C) and government-to-business (G2B) e-markets (Turban,, King, Lee, & Viehland., 2004).

Depending on their target audience, e-markets can be distinguished as buyer-oriented, seller-oriented, or neutral (Grieger, 2003). Buyer-oriented e-markets mainly aggregate buyers, allowing them to also aggregate their expenditure, reduce administration costs, increase visibility, and facilitate global sourcing. Seller-oriented e-markets concentrate on bringing multiple sellers together into a central catalogue and product information repository, in order to allow them to achieve higher visibility and conduct trade with as many buyers as possible. Moreover, e-markets can be either characterized as vertical or horizontal (Grieger, 2003). Horizontal e-markets cover the needs of a wider audience, offering a broad range of products or services that are related with this audience. On the other hand, vertical e-markets offer a class of products or services that aim to one or more particular industry sectors (Wellman, 2004). E-markets can also be distinguished as open/public and closed/private ones (Grieger, 2003; Wellman, 2004). Stanoevska-Slabeva (1999) identifies, as single or homogeneous e-markets, those that are developed by a single enterprise in order to support online distribution of the enterprises' products. Similarly, multiple or heterogeneous e-markets are those where multiple enterprises participate. Other classifications have also been introduced in the literature. Grieger (2003) presents some of them: e-markets with fixed vs. variable pricing mechanisms; e-markets that support information exchange, negotiation, or settlement of after-sales respectively; e-markets that use an aggregation vs. a matching market mechanism; e-markets that support different business objectives (manufacturing vs. operating inputs, and spot vs. systematic sourcing).

Literature Reviews and Case Study Surveys

One of the first papers reviewing the e-market field has been the one from Bakos (1991). It performed a strategic analysis of e-markets based on economic models of search, and reviewed some characteristic applications that adopted principles from traditional markets theory, and implemented them in an electronic way. This analysis particularly focused on the services that its selected case studies offered, but did not provide much information about the technologies used in each case. In two other studies, Strader and Shaw (1997, 1999) analyzed the impact of e-markets from a transaction cost perspective, and referred to a number of e-market examples. A particular technology-related topic that they identified is the use of widely accepted standards for the description of products and services in an electronic format, so that interoperability between different electronic markets can be accomplished. In a similar manner, an overview of the e-markets' area was presented by Segev, Gebauer, and Faerber (1999). In this study, five representative examples of Internet-based e-markets were reviewed, and common elements and features were outlined. They discussed different policies for admitting new participants, various revenue models, quality of the product catalog, as well as services to support a transaction process. Again, the back-office technologies for these features are not discussed. In the study of Timmers (1998), a review of e-market business models was provided. The author described characteristic business models and referred to representative e-market examples implementing them, without analyzing the supporting technologies.

The paper of Smith, Bailey, and Brynjolfsson (1999) has been, to our knowledge, the first important overview and assessment of the area of online markets. It mainly addressed ways to measure efficiency in online markets, focused on potential sources of price dispersion, and introduced important developments to watch in e-markets. In this review, technology-related topics were not addressed. A very comprehensive literature review in the area of e-markets is the one of Grieger (2003) that focused on the supply chain dimension of e-markets. In this study, the author examined several e-markets, and classified them according to several dimensions. Technical dimensions were not used for this classification. Furthermore, Anandalingam, Day, and Raghavan (2005) presented an introductory survey of essential literature on e-markets. Although several mechanisms and settings have been reviewed, the authors' focus seemed to be more on auctions. Therefore, aspects such as mechanisms to facilitate multi-item auctions or the winner determination auction have been described. Finally, technical topics that concern e-markets have been partially covered in the context of the larger e-commerce literature review from Kauffman and Walden (2001). This study analyzed e-commerce literature on several levels, including a technology one. It addressed several technical topics, such as agent technologies, network infrastructures, and structural standards.

There are also publications that focus on specific segments or industries of e-markets. The study by Kollmann (2000) has focused specifically on the sector of German-language online markets for used cars. It provided a business-oriented evaluation tool for e-markets in the form of a competition analysis matrix, which did not include any technological characteristics. Rosson and Davis (2004) focus on Canadian e-markets, presenting a survey of 13 existing case studies. They discuss characteristics such as the e-market scope (vertical vs. horizontal) and type (sell-side, buy-side, etc.), but do not examine the technologies supporting the covered e-markets. In Dai and Kauffman (2002b), an analytic framework is used to study and classify business-to-business (B2B) e-markets. In their study, B2B e-markets are also analyzed from a technological perspective, according to the type of e-market functions their services support. Moreover, the role of some B2B e-markets as technology adapters is described, offering some insight to the technologies they offer to e-market participants that allow integration of e-commerce systems, provision of technological standards, and implementation of outsourced services. Holzmueller and Schluechter (2002) also focus on B2B marketplaces, for the country of Germany. They examine the future of German B2B e-markets using a Delphi survey from e-market experts, and they identify how these experts weight the importance of various services that a B2B e-market may offer (e.g., e-mail, EDI, online communication, search possibilities, etc.). In the study of Lenz, Zimmermann, and Heitmann (2002), a survey of 248 European B2B e-markets is carried out. They also examine various e-market services, classifying them into wider categories (such as collaboration services, financial services, shopbots, negotiation, etc.), and examining their current status of development in the European e-markets.

In general, previous studies either focus on the analysis of the literature, or provide a survey of e-market case studies. Only one study (Holzmueller & Schluechter, 2002) was based on the opinion of e-market experts. This difference in employed methods has been also reflected in their results: the studies focusing more on proposed technologies for e-markets have been the ones based on surveys of existing case studies. On the contrary, e-market literature reviews generally adopted an economic or business perspective, neglecting the technology aspects. To our knowledge, there has not been, so far, an overview of e-market literature from the perspective of technology. In our opinion this is an important shortcoming, since new and innovative technologies are usually first proposed and tested in relevant research studies. Therefore, academic literature can be a valuable source for identifying which technologies are proposed, which dimensions have been addressed, or which solutions have been tested in e-markets. We therefore decided to examine e-market literature of the last decade, in order to identify the most important technological trends in the field of e-markets.

METHODOLOGY

In order to classify e-market research papers that deal with technical topics, we reviewed relevant classification frameworks. First of all, we reviewed e-commerce research classifications such as the ones of Kauffman and Walden (2001), Urbaczewski, Jessup, and Wheeler (2002), Ngai and Wat (2002), and Turban et al. (2004). We also considered the Information Systems research classifications of Liang and Chen (2003) and Orlikowski and Iacono (2001). Finally, we examined the reference framework that has been engaged by the e-Commerce Working Group of the European Standardization Committee CEN/ISSS to analyze and categorize e-commerce models and architectures (CEN, 2001).

It has been concluded that the framework proposed by Urbaczewski et al. (2002) covers the generic e-market topics with the organizational, economic, technical, and other topic areas. In this light, these topic areas are used to specify our framework. The topics of each area have been appropriately elaborated to cover the characteristics and particularities of the e-market research field. This process led to the development of an overall classification framework for e-market research, which is presented in Figure 1 and described in detail elsewhere (Manouselis, 2005). The focus of this chapter is on technical dimensions, therefore only the topics relevant with technical research have been selected from the framework. These technical topics have been identified in related classification frameworks, and were appropriately refined after the e-market literature review. Table 1 further describes the topics in the technical research area.

The proposed framework is used for classifying the papers of an e-market literature review. The review is based on a study of publications in scientific journals with a long tradition, as well as journals specifically focusing on e-commerce that have appeared during the late 1990s. It has been carried out by examining 18 journals that were considered as well-accepted publication outlets for e-commerce research. Year 1995 was chosen as a starting date for our review, since our study revealed that e-market papers started appearing systematically in these journals from that year and forth.

The examined journals' contents have been thoroughly reviewed in order to locate papers relevant to e-markets. More specifically, the papers that were initially identified, included in their title, abstract, keywords or full text one or more related keywords such as electronic or online "markets," "marketplaces," "auctions,"

Figure 1. A classification framework for e-market research

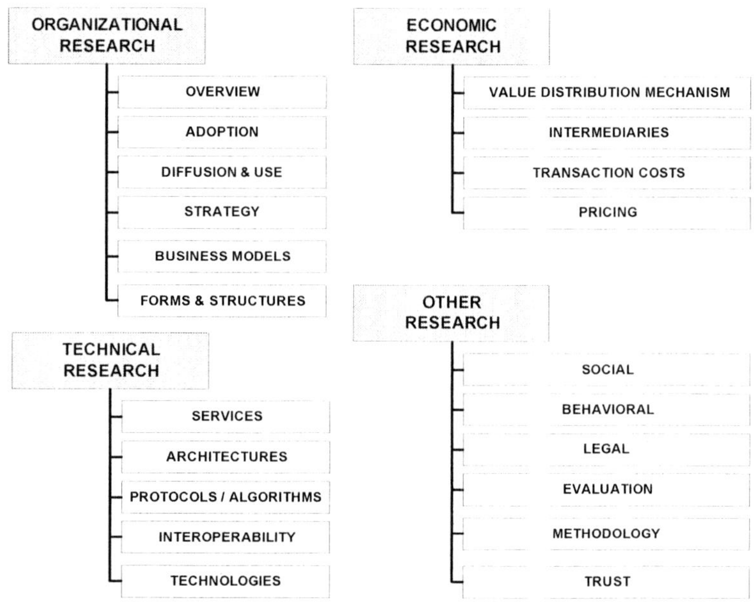

Table 1. Technical research topics

Technical Research	
Architecture	Papers dealing with architectures for e-markets, including modeling e-markets as well as designing/developing infrastructures for e-markets.
Interoperability	Papers that specifically address the interoperability issues of e-markets. Business process modeling (using a common language such as ebXML, 2005) or interoperable product catalogs are issues classified in this category.
Services	Papers that specifically focus on services that e-markets offer.
Protocols / Algorithms	Papers presenting different protocols and algorithms implementing e-market mechanisms, such as value distribution ones.
Technologies	Papers discussing proposed technologies for e-markets, such as the use of Web services or XML, with data management models and techniques used specifically in e-market implementation, and with the network-level implementation of e-markets.

"exchanges," "negotiations," "trading," "shop," "mall," and so forth. More than 400 papers have been initially collected in this way. We briefly examined each one of these papers in order to filter out those that were not directly relevant to the field of e-markets, or were considered too generic for the scope of our study. Finally, 248 papers were identified as appropriate.

Figure 2 illustrates the journals covered in this study, ranked according to the number of identified e-market papers. The journal with the highest number of e-market papers is the *Electronic Markets* journal (50 papers). This was expected, since this journal focuses particularly on e-market topics. Second is *Decision Support Systems*, which has published 35 e-market related papers so far (including papers "In Press"). Other journals with a high number of e-market papers are *International Journal of Electronic Commerce* (27 papers), *Communications of the ACM* (22 papers), and *Electronic Commerce Research & Applications* (20 papers). Since several of the

Figure 2. Distribution of identified e-market papers per examined journal

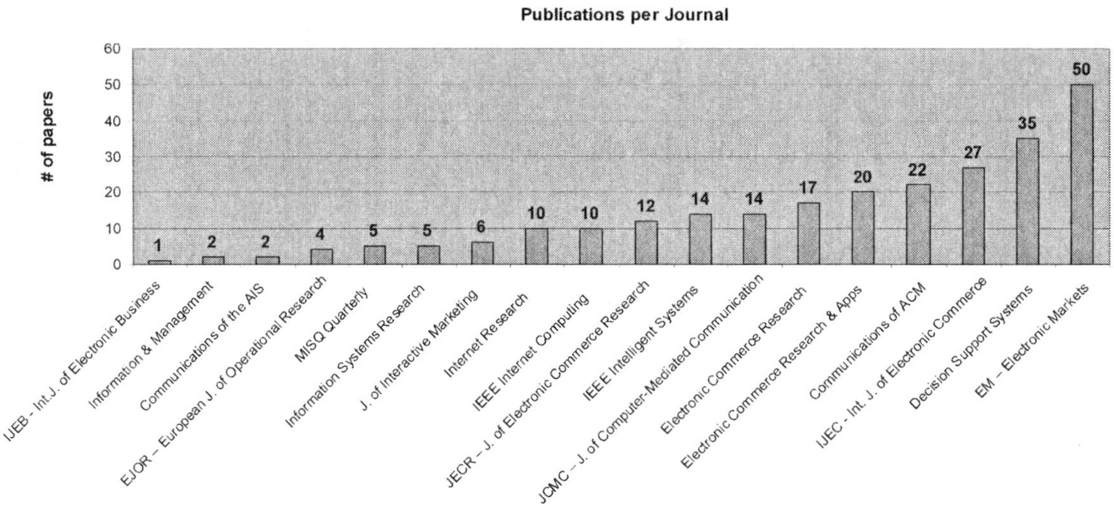

specialized e-commerce journals have launched their operation after the Dot.com explosion of 1999, newer journals (such as *Electronic Commerce Research & Applications*) might not have the opportunity to publish, so far, as many e-market papers as more traditional journals (such as *Decision Support Systems*). We further investigated this point by calculating the rate of e-market papers each journal has published per examined year. Figure 3 presents the ranking of journals according to this annual e-market publication rate. Again, *Electronic Markets* seems to be the journal publishing the highest number of e-market papers (about 8 papers per year). We note, though, that two relatively new e-commerce journals follow: these are *Electronic Commerce Research & Applications* (about 7 papers per year) and *Electronic Commerce Research* (about 4 papers per year). Traditional journals also publish e-market research regularly. For instance, *Decision Support Systems* and *International Journal of Electronic Commerce* publish about 3 e-market papers per year.

It has to be noted that the coverage of our review had some limitations. In most cases, we collected all e-market papers that were published in the examined journals from 1995 to 2005. In two particular cases though, *Electronic Markets* and *Information Systems Research*, the review started from later years (1999 and 2002, respectively) since we did not have full access to the older contents of the journals. In addition, there are some high quality journals (such as *Journal of Organizational Computing and Electronic Commerce* and *Harvard Business Review*) that we did not include in this review. The main reason is that at the time of this study, we did not have access to the journals' full contents. Therefore, we could not exhaustively search all issues for published e-market papers. Additionally, focusing on journals that published primarily e-commerce research, we did not extend our review to other publications that may have included some papers about e-markets (such as economic journals). Nevertheless, we consider the list of journals covered rather extensive: it includes 10 out of the 15 most appropriate journals for e-commerce research, and 8 out of the 10 journals for e-commerce research with highest quality, according to the rankings provided by Bharati and Tarasewich (2002). Although this review was not exhaustive, it serves as a comprehensive base for an understanding of e-market research.

Figure 3. Estimated annual rate of e-market papers per examined journal

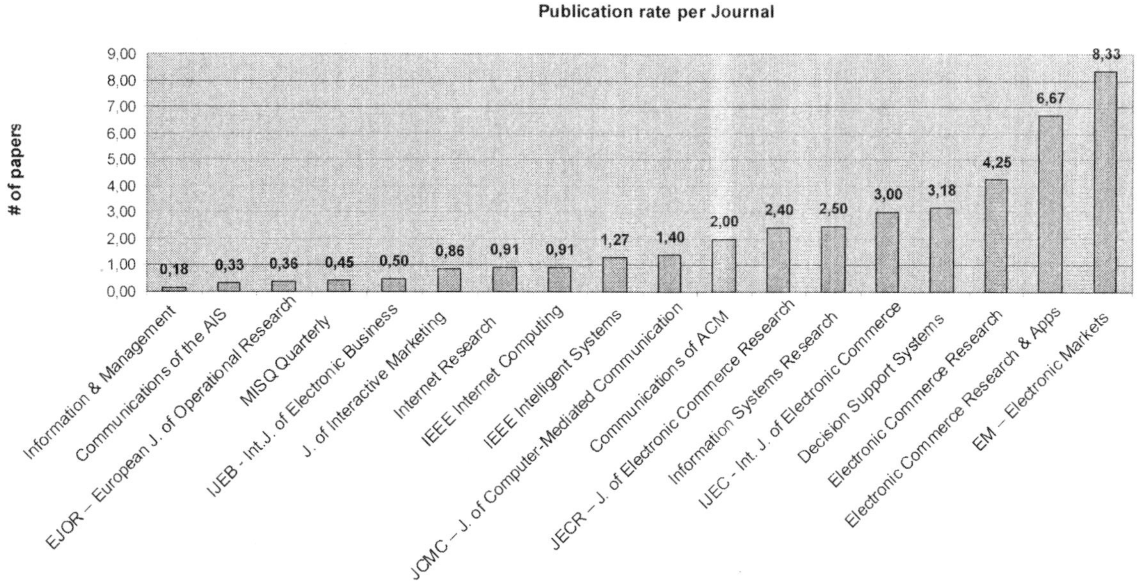

RESULTS

Initially, we classified all 248 e-market papers in the four general topic areas that are described in Figure 1. The result of this initial classification is presented in Figure 4. This figure indicates that the highest percentage of examined publications belongs to the Economic and the Technical areas (35% and 30% of the total respectively). Organizational Research also attracts important research interest, since 21% of the published papers cover this area. Finally, about 14% of e-market papers cover Other Research topics. In this chapter, we focus on the 28% of e-market papers (that is, 118 papers) that mainly focus on technical topics.

Figure 5 presents the distribution of these 118 papers according to the topics in the Technical topic area. It is interesting to note that Architectures (with 39% of total Technical Research papers) and Protocols/Algorithms (with 32.2%) monopolize this e-market research area. Topics such as Interoperability (which is identified as a key issue from e-commerce experts, as discovered by Dai & Kauffman, 2002a) and Technologies

Figure 4. Distribution of e-market papers per topic area

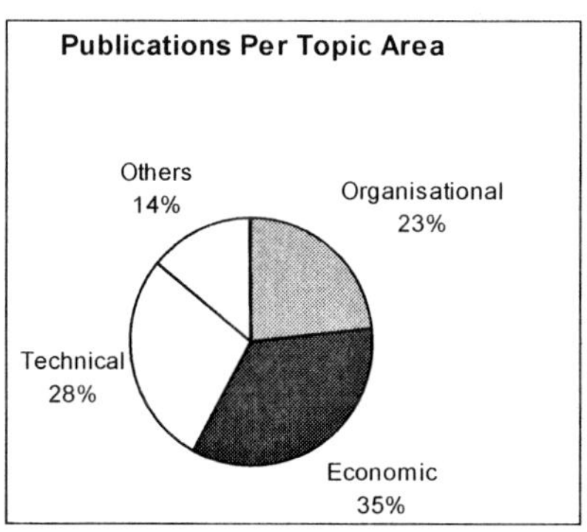

Figure 5. Distribution of publications per category of the technical area

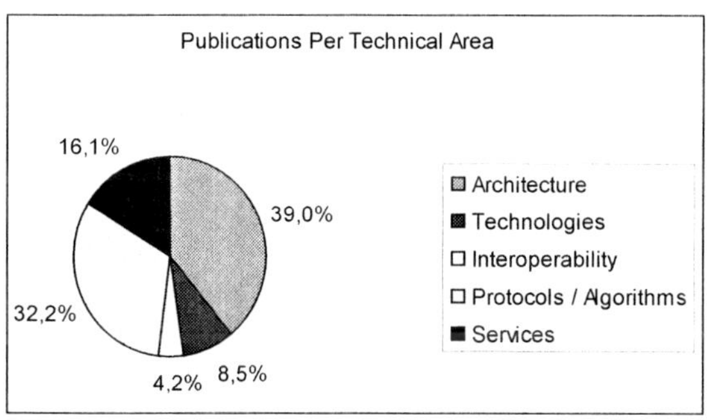

Figure 6. Publications related to the technical area, per journal

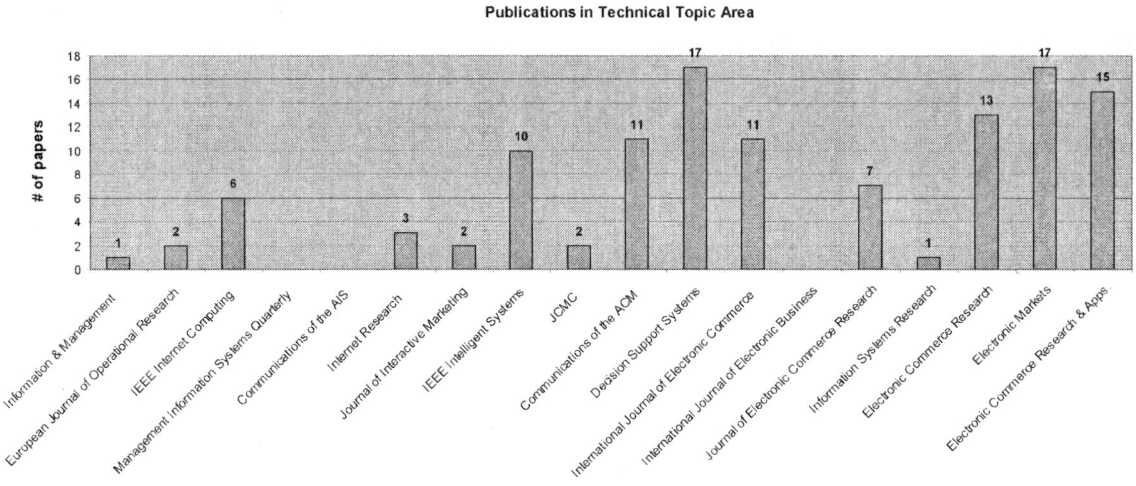

have been slightly covered. Nevertheless, this can be due to the fact that such papers are published in journals other than the ones examined, as well as the fact that low-level technical solutions are usually covering all e-commerce fields and not e-markets in particular. Finally, e-market Services seem to be attracting an important degree of attention: about 16.1% of Technical Research papers are about Services.

Figure 6 presents the classification of papers covering technical topics per journal examined. The majority of the papers in *Decision Support Systems* (20 out of the 35 e-market papers that are published in this journal), *Electronic Markets* (20 out of the 50 papers), *Electronic Commerce Research & Applications* (16 out of the 20 papers), and *International Journal of Electronic Commerce* (15 out of the 27 papers), are around technical topics. In the following paragraphs, we review the open issues around each technical topic, as well as the representative publications.

Architecture

The technical topic of *architecture* refers to approaches for modeling and developing of e-market architectures. In particular, it concerns the design and development of e-market models, such as conceptual models and frameworks for e-markets, models for negotiation mechanisms in e-markets, as well as metamodels for the analysis or classification of e-market components. Additionally, it concerns the design, specification, and implementation of e-market infrastructures, such as the design of e-market applications, e-market simulators, and e-market tools (matching mechanisms, product catalogs, recommendation services, etc.). These major issues are presented in Table 2. The most important contributions and representative references are also reported.

There are several studies in the e-market literature reporting contributions in the areas presented. First of all, there are contributions presenting conceptual models or frameworks that represent e-market architectural elements. Such is the work of Wang (1997), Kain et al. (1999), Brandtweiner and Scharl (1999), Baghdadi (2004), Wicke (1999), Gomber and Maurer (2004), and Blecker et al. (2004). Models or frameworks for particular types of markets also exist, such as the ones proposed for secure e-markets from Roehm and Pernul (2000), Mandry et al. (2001), and Jaiswal et al. (2004). Apart from viewing e-market architectures in total, such contributions can also focus on architectures of e-market modules. For example, negotiation mechanism architectures

Table 2. Issues, contributions, and representative references in the topic of architecture

Issues	Contributions	Representative References
Models	E-market conceptual models and frameworks	Baghdadi, 2004; Blecker, Abdelkafi, Kreutler, & Kaluza., 2004; Brandtweiner & Scharl, 1999; Gomber & Maurer, 2004; Jaiswal, Kim, & Gini., 2004; Kain, Aparicio, & Singh, 1999; Mandry, Pernul, & Roehm, 2001; Roehm & Pernul, 2000; Wang, 1997; Wicke, 1999
	Designing e-market models	Fontoura, Ionescu, & Minsky, 2005; Geyer, Kuhn, & Schmid, 1997; Hamalainen, Whinston, & Vishik, 1996; Mullen & Breese, 2000
	E-market negotiation mechanisms models	Chiu, Cheung, Hung, Chiu, & Chung, in press; Srivastava & Mohapatra, 2003
	E-market metamodels	Bhargarva, Krishnon, & Mueller, 1997; Lindemann & Schmid, 1999
Infrastructure	Infrastructure design of e-market applications	Collins, Ketter, & Gini, 2002; Fan, Stallaert, & Whinston, 1999; Gates & Nissen, 2001; Harrison & Andrusiewicz, 2004; Jannsen & Sol, 2000; Kaihara, 2003; Karacapilidis & Moraitis, 2000; Karacapilidis & Moraitis, 2001; Liu, Wang, & Teng, 2000; Maamar, Dorion, & Daible, 2001; Teich, Wallenius, Wallenius, & Zaitsev, 1999b; Wang, Tan, & Ren, 2004
	Simulators of e-markets	DiMicco, Maes, & Greenwald, 2003; Kearns & Ortiz, 2003; Praca, Ramos, Vale, & Cordeiro, 2003; Zimmerman, Thomas, Gan, & Murillo-Sanchez, 1999
	Infrastructure for automated matching mechanisms in e-markets	Chkaiban & Sonderby, 2000; Dumas, Benatallah, Russel, & Spork, 2004; Ha & Park, 2001; Lin & Chang, 2001
	Infrastructure for virtual field experiments	Kim, Barua, & Whinston, 2002
	Infrastructure for mediating product catalogs	Lincke & Schmid, 1998
	Auction decision support system infrastructure	Gregg & Walczak, in press
	Infrastructure for mobile e-market services	Kwon, in press
	Infrastructure for supply chain e-markets	Gerber & Klusch, 2002; Gerber, Russ, & Klusch, 2003
	E-market recommendation service infrastructure	Ha, 2002

can be found modeled in a conceptual way (Chiu et al., in press; Srivastava & Mohapatra, 2003). Other contributions include papers regarding the design of e-market architectures (Fontoura et al., 2005; Geyer et al., 1997; Hamalainen et al., 1996; Mullen & Breese, 2000). An important strand of related work concerns proposed metamodels for describing, analysing, and/or specifying e-markets. Characteristic examples are the papers of Bhargarva et al. (Bhargava, Krishnan, & Mueller,1997) and Lindemann and Schmid (1999).

Another dimension of the e-market architectures area concerns contributions about architectures that are implemented through proposed infrastructures. The most common case is papers presenting the architecture of implemented e-markets (Collins et al., 2002; Fan et al., 1999; Gates & Nissen, 2001; Harrison & Andrusiewicz, 2004; Jannsen & Sol, 2000; Kaihara, 2003; Karacapilidis & Moraitis, 2000; Karacapilidis & Moraitis, 2001; Liu et al., 2000; Maamar et al., 2001; Teich et al., 1999b; Wang et al., 2004). Other infrastructure implementations are also presented, including automated matching mechanisms (Chkaiban & Sonderby, 2000; Dumas et al., 2004; Ha & Park, 2001; Lin & Chang, 2001) as well as other special types of e-market infrastructures. Examples include:

- The e-market infrastructure for virtual field experiments of Kim et al. (2002)
- The infrastructure for mediating e-market catalogs of Lincke and Schmid (1998)
- The infrastructure of an auction decision support system presented by Gregg and Walczak (in press)
- The infrastructure for an e-market with mobile services described by Kwon (in press)
- The infrastructure for supply chain management e-markets that Gerber and Klusch (2002) and Gerber et al. (2003) implemented for trading timber
- The infrastructure for e-market recommendation services that Ha (2002) describes

A class of such contributions with particular interest are e-market simulators. These are infrastructures that allow for simulating e-market participants behaviours in different application domains, such as electric power markets (Praca et al., 2003; Zimmerman et al., 1999), financial markets (Kearns & Ortiz, 2003), and simulators for studying dynamic pricing strategies in markets (DiMicco et al., 2003).

From the review of these contributions, it can be concluded that research in the topic area of e-market architectures has particularly focused on ways of modelling and metamodelling e-markets, as well as in studying the development of various infrastructures related to e-market services. Modelling e-markets can greatly facilitate their analysis and implementation; therefore, additional focus should be given on the use of software-related tools, such as the Unified Modelling Language (UML), and their combination with widely accepted software development approaches, such as the rational unified process (RUP), in order to provide e-market developers with formal tools for the specification of e-market architecture, that can be reused in more than one implementation. In addition, metamodelling of e-markets can help in the identification of their most important components and characteristics, contributing, for instance, to their development and description as independent components or services; for example, according to the emerging paradigm of Web services (Beneventano, Guerra, Magnani, & Vincini, 2004). Another dimension is the use of the e-market metamodels in order to facilitate the users' access to e-markets; for example, by developing Internet-based directories or online recommendation services for e-markets (Manouselis & Costopoulou, 2005a; Manouselis & Costopoulou, 2005b).

INTEROPERABILITY

Interoperability refers to the ability of different systems to interoperate, that is, to cooperate and exchange information in preagreed, well-defined formats. In e-market literature, interoperability concerns various issues, such as the exchange of business documents in a format that different systems may understand, the description of products in electronic catalogs in an interoperable manner, the use of appropriate technical markup languages such as XML, and the definition of appropriate semantics, as well as the exchange of interoperable messages between systems. These topics, the most important contributions, and representative references are presented in Table 3.

There are a few studies in the e-market literature concerning interoperability issues in e-markets. Such papers cover issues such as interoperable business document exchange (Glushko et al., 1999), e-catalog and product description/classification interoperability (Baron et al., 2000; Beneventano et al., 2004; Fensel et al., 2001), XML language use and semantics (Smith & Poulter, 1999), and communication/messages semantic interoperability (Vaishnavi & Kuechler, 2003).

Interoperability is an issue of extreme importance in e-business, and extended work is carried out in standardization bodies and specification groups, such as the European Committee for Standardization CEN (CEN, 2001). More work

Table 3. Issues, contributions, and representative references in the topic of interoperability

Issues	Contributions	Representative References
Interoperability	Interoperable business document exchange	Glushko, Tenenbaum, & Meltzer., 1999
	E-catalog and product description/ classification interoperability	Baron, Shaw, & Bailey, 2000; Beneventano et al., 2004; Fensel, Ding, Omelayenko, Schulten, Botquin, Brown, & Flett, 2001
	XML language use and semantics	Smith & Poulter, 1999
	Communication/messages semantic interoperability	Vaishnavi & Kuechler, 2003

is required in the field of e-markets, in order to facilitate the reusability of e-business information from different systems, as well as the communication among different systems and technologies. The range of topics includes electronic data interchange (e.g., the Open-EDI reference model ISO/IEC 14662), classification of products (e.g., the UN/CEFACT UNSPSC product and services classification, http://www.unspsc.org/), multilingual electronic catalogues (e.g., BMEcat, http://www.bmecat.org/), e-invoicing (e.g., CEN/ISSS, 2003a), and description of core business processes and messages (e.g., ebXML bpPROC, 2001).

TECHNOLOGIES

This topic refers to particularly applied technologies, as well as issues relevant to networking and data management in e-markets. It concerns the study of technologies such as agent technologies, particular implementations of e-markets, human computer interaction (HCI) issues in e-markets, and networking issues. These issues, the most important contributions, and representative references are presented in Table 4.

There are several studies in the e-market literature reporting contributions in these areas. First of all, there are contributions presenting the application of technologies related with agents in e-markets. Such contributions include reviews of agent technologies in e-markets (Gregg & Walczak, 2003; Maes, 1999; Maes, Guttman, & Moukas, 1999) and studies of e-markets that are enabled from using agent technologies (Crowston & MacInnes, 2001). Other contributions deal with details of implementing particular technical solutions, such as the specifications of the eCo initiative for business documents exchange (Glushko et al., 1999) and the HealthTex extranet implementation (Angeles, 2001). Moreover, there are contributions dealing with interactivity tech-

Table 4. Issues, contributions, and representative references in the topic of technologies

Issues	Contributions	Representative References
Agent technologies	Agent technologies in e-markets	Gregg & Walczak, 2003; Maes, 1999; Maes et al., 1999
	E-markets enabling agent-oriented queries	Crowston & MacInnes, 2001
Technical implementations	eCo initiative for business documents exchange	Glushko et al., 1999
	Extranet implementation	Angeles, 2001
Interactivity (HCI) technologies	Virtual world environments	Shen et al., 2002
	Multimedia cues use	Vishwanath, 2004
Technical requirements	B2B e-markets	Feldman, 2000
Networking	Network congestion pricing	Henderson et al., 2001

nologies in e-markets, such as the development of virtual world environments (Shen, Radakrishnan, & Georganas, 2002) and the use of multimedia cues (Vishwanath, 2004). Some contributions also refer to technical requirements for e-markets, such as Feldman (2000) does for the particular case of B2B e-markets. Finally, a small number of papers concerns networking technologies issues, since such aspects of e-markets are usually covered by specialized publications and do not appear in e-market research. The only indicative example we identified deals with networking congestion and pricing schemes (Henderson, Crowcroft, & Bhatti, 2001).

The small number of purely technical contributions in the e-market area is explained if we consider that these topics are e-commerce wide and not e-market specific, and that the coverage of this review has not included many technical journals. On the other hand, in our opinion, further work is definitely required on technical topics such as the use of Web services for the implementation of e-market services, as well as the exploration of HCI issues concerning e-market environments.

PROTOCOLS/ALGORITHMS

This technical topic refers to the design and development of e-market mechanisms and services, implementing various e-market protocols or algorithms. It concerns issues such as the design and development of pricing algorithms, trading algorithms, as well as buyers' decision support algorithms. The issues currently covered in e-market literature are presented in Table 5. The most important contributions and representative references are also reported.

There are several studies in the e-market literature reporting contributions in this area. First of all, there are some contributions that discuss pricing algorithms. These include the works of Zacharia, Evgeniou, Moukas, Boufounos, and Maes (2001) and Deck and Wilson (2002). Moreover, there are some contributions that present algorithms that aim to support the purchase decision process, such as algorithms for auction support systems (Bapna, Goes, & Gupta, 2003; Teich, Wallenius, Wallenius, & Zaitsev, 2001) and algorithms that support recommendation services (Linden, Smith, & York, 2003; Tewari, Youll, & Maes, 2002).

Table 5. Issues, contributions, and representative references in the topic of protocols/algorithms

Issues	Contributions	Representative References
Pricing algorithms	Pricing algorithm analysis	Deck & Wilson, 2002; Zacharia et al., 2001
Trading algorithms	Review of trading algorithms	Sandholm, 2000a; Sandholm, 2000b; Stroebel, 2000; Teich et al., 1999a; Teich et al., 2004
	Modelling trading algorithms	Dumas et al., 2002; Stroebel, 2001
	Designing automatically trading algorithms	Cliff, 2003
	Agent-automated trading algorithms	Collins et al., 2001; Deveaux et al., 2001; Dumas et al., 2005; Goldman & Kraus, 2004; Greenwald & Stone, 2001; Ito et al., 2002; Kitts & LeBlanc, 2004; Ono et al., 2003; Padovan et al., 2002; Sandholm, 1999; Teuteberg, 2003; Vulkan & Preist, 2003; Wellman et al., 2003a; Wellman et al., 2003b; Wellman et al., 2001; Wurman et al., 1998; Yuan & Lin, 2004
	Examination of nonautomated trading algorithms	Bichler & Kalagnanam, in press; Burmester et al., 2004; Deck & Wilson, 2002; Di Noia et al., 2003; Gerber et al., 2004; Kalagnanam et al., 2001; Seifert et al., 2004; Tallroth, 2004
Decision support algorithms	Auction decision support	Bapna et al., 2003; Teich et al., 2001
	Recommendation	Linden et al., 2003; Tewari et al., 2002

Nevertheless, most contributions fall into the category of trading algorithms. There exist papers that review families of trading algorithms (Sandholm, 2000a; Sandholm, 2000b; Stroebel, 2000; Teich, Wallenius, & Wallenius, 1999a; Teich, Wallenius, Wallenius, & Koppius, 2004), papers that propose methodologies to model algorithms and protocols (Dumas, Governatori, Ter Hofstede, & Oaks, 2002; Stroebel, 2001), as well as novel contributions proposing automatic design of trading algorithms (Cliff, 2003). Most contributions, though, present agent-automated algorithms, including Wellman, Cheng, Reeves, and Lochner (2003a); Wellman, Greenwald, Stone, and Wurman (2003b); Wellman, Wurman, O'Malley, Bangera, Lin, Reeves, and Walsh (2001); Greenwald and Stone (2001); Wurman, Walsh, and Wellman (1998); Sandholm (1999); Ito Hattori, and Shintani (2002); Ono, Nishiyama, and Horiuchi (2003); Yuan and Lin (2004); Deveaux, Paraschiv, and Latourrette (2001); Dumas, Aldred, Governatori, and Ter Hofstede (2005); Goldman and Kraus (2004); Kitts and LeBlanc (2004); Teuteberg (2003); Collins, Bilot, Gini, and Mobasher (2001); Padovan, Sackmann, Eymann, and Pippow (2002); and Vulkan and Preist (2003). Finally, many papers examine algorithms for nonautomated trading environments, although they sometimes engage an automated trading simulation to study these algorithms. Such papers include algorithms on optimal allocation (Seifert et al., 2004), multiattribute auctions (Bichler & Kalagnanam, in press), low price matching (Deck & Wilson, 2002), clearing continuous double auctions (Kalagnanam, Davenport, & Lee, 2001), uncoercible bidding games (Burmester, Magkos, & Chrissikopoulos, 2004), multiquote double auctions (Tallroth, 2004), as well as algorithms for matching buyers and sellers (Di Noia, Di Sciascio, Donini, & Mongiello, 2003; GerberTeich, Wallenius, & Wallenius, 2004).

Extensive work has been carried out in the topic area of algorithms and protocols, and most topics are covered to a satisfactory extent. In addition, this is an area of e-market technologies that has very strong roots in theoretical contributions in the field of e-markets (e.g., game theory and consumer behaviour analysis).

SERVICES

This topic concerns types and categories of services that e-markets offer to their users. These concern descriptions of typical e-market services, analyses of various case studies, as well as studies of the evolution of e-market services in the course of time or for particular business sectors. The major issues currently covered by e-market papers, most important contributions, and representative references are presented in Table 6.

There are several studies in the e-market literature reporting contributions in these areas. First of all, there are contributions that review and classify typical e-market services. These include examination of services in specific e-market business models (Timmers, 1998), e-market services classified by actor role (O'Daniel, 2001), by interaction degree required (Akkermans, 2001), by the type of the e-market (Raisinghani & Hanebeck, 2002) and by the e-market channels engaged (Simons, Steinfield, & Bouwman, 2002).

Moreover, there are contributions presenting specific case studies of services provided by e-markets. Such case studies include mass customization services (Warkentin et al., 2000), product representation services (Koppius et al., 2004), pre- and postpurchase services (Cao & Gruca, 2004), agent-based services (Liang & Huang, 2000; Moukas et al., 2000; Silverman et al., 2001). Other studies concern the services of particular case studies of e-markets, such as real-estate e-market services (Crowston & Wigand, 1999), financial e-market services (Gallaugher & Melville, 2004; Minakakis & Rao, 1999), and software e-market services (Elfatatry & Layzell, 2004).

Table 6. Issues, contributions, and representative references in the topic of services

Issues	Contributions	Representative References
Typical e-market services	Per business model	Timmers, 1998
	Per actor role	O'Daniel, 2001
	Per e-market type	Raisinghani & Hanebeck, 2002; Wang & Archer, 2004
	Per interaction degree	Akkermans, 2001
	Per market channels	Simons et al., 2002
Case study analysis	Mass customization	Warkentin, Bapna, & Sugumaran, 2000
	Product representation	Koppius, van Heck, & Wolters, 2004
	Pre- and postpurchase services	Cao & Gruca, 2004
	Agent-based services	Liang & Huang, 2000; Moukas, Zacharia, Guttman, & Maes, 2000; Silverman, Bachann, & Al-Akharas, 2001
	Real-estate e-markets	Crowston & Wigand, 1999
	Financial services e-markets	Gallaugher & Melville, 2004; Minakakis & Rao, 1999
	Software services e-markets	Elfatatry & Layzell, 2004
Status & evolution of e-market services	Analysis of B2B market services	Raisinghani & Hanebeck, 2002
	Participants expectations about B2B market services	Holzmueller & Schluechter, 2002
	Operators perspective on B2B market services	Holzmueller & Schluechter, 2002; Lenz et al., 2002; Wang & Archer, 2004
	Trust services use	Palmer, Bailey, & Faraj, 2000

Finally, there are contributions examining the current status and the future evolution of e-market services. Such contributions include the analysis of services that are offered by B2B e-markets (Raisinghani & Hanebeck, 2002), e-market participants' expectations about B2B market services (Holzmueller & Schluechter, 2002), e-market operators perspective on B2B market services (Holzmueller & Schluechter, 2002; Lenz et al., 2002; Wang & Archer, 2004), as well as the use of trust-related services in e-markets (Palmer et al., 2000).

The topic area of e-market services is expected to constantly grow, as new services for supporting the phases of a transaction process are introduced. In addition, apart from their apparent consumer orientation, e-markets are also considered as powerful business tools that can facilitate the proper operation of the whole supply chain (Grieger, 2003). Dai and Kauffman (2002b) have provided a very enlightening framework of services that B2B e-markets may offer, which includes (among others) workflow management, collaborative project management, supply chain management, system integration, and compliance with standards.

CONCLUSION

This chapter aimed to provide an overview of recent technological developments and trends in the field of e-markets. More specifically, it reported results from a review of e-market papers that have been published during the past decade in scientific journals, and that particularly focused on topics related to the application of e-business technologies in e-markets. The review covered 18 journals that publish e-commerce research, and selected the 118 (out of the overall sample of 248) papers that cover some technical topic. Using a classification framework for e-market research, five technical topic areas have been identified: e-market architectures, interoperability, services, protocols/algorithms, and technologies. The most important issues in each topic area have been discussed, and representative contributions have been reviewed. The results of this review provided interesting insight about the current status, as well as the future perspectives, of e-business technologies in e-market research.

In particular, it has been identified that the topic areas attracting more attention in e-market research have been architectures and protocols/algorithms. On the other hand, there seems to be a shortage of research related to more low-level technical topics, such as the ones covered by the technologies and interoperability areas. Our study revealed several directions where future research could be focused. First of all, particular importance should be given to the exploration of models, techniques, and languages for the description of e-market components in terms of Web services (Beneventano et al., 2004), as well as business processes and documents (eBXML, 2005). For this purpose, additional research is required towards the implementation of interoperability specifications and standards. This may, in turn, facilitate the automated business information exchange between e-market systems, and the integration of already existing information in different e-market systems (a topic termed as the *reusability* of business information). A future perspective that attracts more and more attention is the cooperation of e-markets in networks called e-market "federations" (Stanoevska-Slabeva, 1999). Furthermore, international standardization bodies (CEN/ISSS, 2003b) focus on the development of open source solutions for enterprise uses, particularly in the case of small and medium enterprises (SMEs). Another open issue is the further exploration of decision support algorithms, models and systems for e-market buyers and sellers (Manouselis & Costopoulou, 2005b). Finally, the application of novel technologies will allow the deployment of a new generation of e-market services. Examples include the exploration of ambient or virtual e-market environments that will intelligently help the users carry out their transactions (Shen et al., 2002), as well as mobile devices that will allow for on-site customer service (Vrechopoulos, O'Keefe, Doukidis, & Siomkos, 2004) integrated with shopping, working, or living environments of the users.

The analysis presented in this chapter took place in the context of a wider e-market literature review that covered all e-market research topic areas. In this chapter, we particularly focused on the 118 e-market papers of our sample that covered technical topics. There may be some additional papers, outside the coverage of our review that may be addressing e-market technical issues. Therefore, the list of reviewed contributions should be not considered exhaustive. On the contrary, the primary concern of the chapter has been to identify the main contributions related to technical topics, and to serve as an initial road-map to relevant research. This chapter engages a systematic way for classifying and examining e-market literature; therefore, it could be possibly used as a case study for studying any other topic area of Figure 1. As a matter of fact, we aim to perform such focused studies for the rest of the topic areas in the future. In addition, future work will include covering publications from other important sources, such as key conferences and the "grey" literature of the e-business area, in order to give a more complete picture of technologies and solutions for e-business process management in e-markets.

REFERENCES

Akkermans, H. (2001). Intelligent e-business: From technology to value. *IEEE Intelligent Systems, Special Issue on Intelligent E-Business, 16*(4), 8-10.

Anandalingam, G., Day, R. W., & Raghavan, S. (2005). The landscape of electronic market design. *Management Science, 51*(3), 316-327.

Angeles, R. (2001). Creating a digital marketspace presence: Lessons in extranet implementation. *Internet Research: Electronic Networking Applications and Policy, 11*(2), 167-184.

Baghdadi, Y. (2004). ABBA: An architecture for deploying business-to-business electronic commerce applications. *Electronic Commerce Research & Applications, 3*, 190-212.

Bakos, Y. (1991). A strategic analysis of electronic marketplaces. *Management Information Systems Quarterly, 15*(3), 295-310.

Bakos, Y. (1998). The emerging role of electronic marketplaces on the Internet. *Communications of the ACM, 41*(8), 35-42.

Bapna, R., Goes, P., & Gupta A. (2003). Replicating online yankee auctions to analyze auctioneers' and bidders' strategies. *Information Systems Research, 14*(3), 244-268.

Baron, J. P., Shaw, M. J., & Bailey, A. D.Jr. (2000). Web-based e-catalog systems in B2B procurement. *Communications of the ACM, 43*(5), 93-100.

Beneventano, D., Guerra, F., Magnani, S., & Vincini, M. (2004). A Web service based framework for the semantic mapping amongst product classification schemas. *Journal of Electronic Commerce Research, 5*(2), 114-127.

Bharati, P., & Tarasewich, P. (2002). Global perceptions of journals publishing e-commerce research. *Communications of the ACM, 45*(5), 21-26.

Bhargava, H. K., Krishnan, R., & Mueller, R. (1997). Decision support on demand: Emerging electronic markets for decision technologies. *Decision Support Systems, 19*, 193-214.

Bichler, M., & Kalagnaman, J. (in press) Configurable offers and winner determination in multi-attribute auction. *European Journal of Operational Research.*

Blecker, T., Abdelkafi, N., Kreutler, G., & Kaluza, B. (2004). Auction-based variety formation and stering for mass customization. *Electronic Markets, Special Issue on Innovative Auction Markets, 14*(3), 232-242.

Brandtweiner, R., & Scharl, A. (1999). An institutional approach to modeling the structure and functionality of brokered electronic markets. *International Journal of Electronic Commerce, 3*(3), 71-88.

Burmester, M., Magkos, E., & Chrissikopoulos, V. (2004). Uncoercible e-bidding games. *Electronic Commerce Research, 4*, 113-125.

Cao, Y., & Gruca, T. S. (2004). The influence of pre- and post-purchase service on prices in the online book market. *Journal of Interactive Marketing, 18*(4), 51-62.

CEN. (2001). *Summaries of some frameworks, architectures and models for electronic commerce*, CWA 14228:2001E, European Committee for Standardization.

CEN/ISSS. (2003a). *Report and recommendations of CEN/ISSS e-invoicing focus group on standards and developments on electronic invoicing relating to VAT directive*. 2001/115/EC, European Committee for Standardization CEN/ISSS.

CEN/ISSS. (2003b). *CEN/ISSS roadmap for addressing key eBusiness standards issues 2003-2005*. eBusiness Standards Focus Group, European Committee for Standardization CEN/ISSS.

Chiu, D. K. W., Cheung, S. C., Hung, P. C. K., Chiu, S. Y. Y., & Chung, A. K. K. (in press) Developing e-negotiation support with a meta-modeling approach in a Web services environment. *Decision Support Systems.*

Chkaiban, G., & Sonderby, M. (2000). AATP: Auction agent transfer protocol. *Electronic Markets, 10*(2), 94-101.

Cliff, D. (2003). Explorations in evolutionary design of online auction market mechanisms. *Electronic Commerce Research & Applications, 2*, 162-175.

Collins, J., Bilot, C., Gini, M., & Mobasher, B. (2001). Decision processes in agent-based automated contracting. *IEEE Internet Computing*, 61-72.

Collins, J., Ketter, W., & Gini, M. (2002). Multi-agent negotiation testbed for contracting tasks with temporal and precedence constraints. *International Journal of Electronic Commerce, 7*(1), 35-57.

Crowston, K., & MacInnes, I. (2001). The effects of market-enabling Internet agents on competition and prices. *Journal of Electronic Commerce Research, 2*(1), 1-22.

Crowston, K., & Wigand, R. T. (1999). Real-estate war in cyberspace: An emerging electronic market?. *Electronic Markets, 9*(1/2), 37-44.

Dai, Q., & Kauffman, R. J. (2002a). B2B e-commerce revisited: Leading perspectives on the key issues and research directions. *Electronic Markets, 12*(2), 67-83.

Dai, Q., & Kauffman, R. J. (2002b). Business models for Internet-based B2B electronic markets. *International Journal of Electronic Commerce, 6*(4), 41-72.

Deck, C. A., & Wilson, B. J. (2002). The effectiveness of low price matching in mitigating the competitive pressure of low friction electronic markets. *Electronic Commerce Research, 2*, 385-398.

Deveaux, L., Paraschiv, C., & Latourrette, M. (2001). Bargaining on an Internet agent-based market: Behavioral vs. optimizing agents. *Electronic Commerce Research, 1*, 371-401.

Di Noia, T., Di Sciascio, E., Donini, F. M., & Mongiello, M. (2004). A system for principled matchmaking in an electronic marketplace. *International Journal of Electronic Commerce, 8*(4), 9-38.

DiMicco, J. M., Maes, P., & Greenwald, A. (2003). Learning curve: A simulation-based approach to dynamic pricing. *Electronic Commerce Research, 3*, 245-276.

Dumas, M., Aldred, L., Governatori, G., & Ter Hofstede, A. H. M. (2005). Probabilistic automated bidding in multiple auctions. *Electronic Commerce Research, 5*, 25-49.

Dumas, M., Benatallah, B., Russel, N., & Spork M. (2004). A configurable matchmaking framework for electronic marketplaces. *Electronic Commerce Research & Applications, 3*, 95-106.

Dumas, M., Governatori, G., Ter Hofstede, A. H. M., & Oaks, P. (2002). A formal approach to negotiating agents development. *Electronic Commerce Research & Applications, 1*, 193-207.

ebXML (Electronic Business using eXtensible Markup Language). (2005). Retrieved January 29, 2006, from http://www.ebxml.org/

ebXML bpPROC. (2001). *Catalog of common business processes v1.0*. ebXML Business Process Team, UN/CEFACT and OASIS.

Elfatatry, A., & Layzell, P. (2004). Negotiating in service-oriented environments. *Communications of the ACM, 47*(8), 103-108.

Fan, M., Stallaert, J., & Whinston, A. B. (1999). The design and development of a financial cybermarket with a Bundline Trading Mechanism. *International Journal of Electronic Commerce, 4*(1), 5-22.

Feldman, S. (2000). Electronic marketplaces. *IEEE Internet Computing, 4*(4), 93-95.

Fensel, D., Ding, Y., Omelayenko, B., Schulten, E., Botquin, G., Brown, M., & Flett, A. (2001,

July/August). Product data integration in B2B e-commerce. *IEEE Intelligent Systems*, 54-59.

Fontoura, M., Ionescu, M., & Minsky, N. (2005). Decentralized peer-to-peer auctions. *Electronic Commerce Research*, *5*, 7-24.

Gallaugher, J. M., & Wang, Y.-M. (1999). Network externalities and the provision of composite IT goods supporting the e-commerce infrastructure. *Electronic Markets*, *9*(1/2), 14-19.

Gates, W. R., & Nissen, M. E. (2001). Designing agent-based electronic employment markets. *Electronic Commerce Research*, *1*, 239-263.

Gerber, A., & Klusch, M. (2002, January/February). Agent-based integrated services for timber production and sales. *IEEE Intelligent Systems*, 33-39.

Gerber, A., Russ, C., & Klusch, M. (2003). Supply web co-ordination by an agent-based trading network with integrated logistics services. *Electronic Commerce Research & Applications*, *2*, 133-146.

Gerber, C., Teich, J., Wallenius, H., & Wallenius, J. (2004). A simulation and test of OptiMark's electronic matching lorithm and its simple variations for institutional block trading. *Decision Support Systems*, *36*, 235-245.

Geyer, G., Kuhn, C., & Schmid, B. (1997). Designing a market for quantitative knowledge. *International Journal of Electronic Commerce*, *1*(4), 89-108.

Glushko, R. J., Tenenbaum, J. M., & Meltzer, B. (1999). An XML framework for agent-based e-commerce. *Communications of the ACM*, *42*(3), 106-114.

Goldman, C. V., & Kraus, S. (2004). The value of temptation. (2004). *Electronic Commerce Research*, *4*, 415-454.

Gomber, P., & Maurer, K.-O. (2004). Xetra bEST - Intregration of market access intermediaries' requirements into market design. *Electronic Markets, Special Issue on Innovative Auction Markets*, *14*(3), 214-222.

Greenwald, A., & Stone, P. (2001). Autonomous bidding agents in the trading agent competition. *IEEE Internet Computing*, *5*(2), 52-60.

Gregg, D. G., & Walczak, S. (in press). Auction advisor: An agent-based online-auction decision support system. *Decision Support Systems*.

Gregg, D. G., & Walczak, S. (2003). E-commerce auction agents and online-auction dynamics. *Electronic Markets*, *13*(3), 242-250.

Grieger, M. (2003). Electronic marketplaces: A literature review and a call for supply chain management research. *European Journal of Operational Research*, *144*, 280-294.

Ha, S. H. (2002, November/December). Helping online customers decide through Web personalization. *IEEE Intelligent Systems*, 34-43.

Ha, S. H., & Park, S. C. (2001, July/August). Matching buyers and suppliers: An intelligent dynamic exchange model. *IEEE Intelligent Systems*, 28-40.

Hamalainen, M., Whinston, A. B., & Vishik, S. (1996). Electronic markets for learning: Education brokerage on the Internet. *Communications of the ACM*, *39*(6), 51-58.

Harrison, J. V., & Andrusiewicz, A. (2004). A virtual marketplace for advertising narrowcast over digital signage networks. *Electronic Commerce Research & Applications*, *3*, 163-175.

Henderson, T., Crowcroft, J., & Bhatti, S. (2001, September-October). Congestion pricing: Paying your way in communication networks. *IEEE Internet Computing*, 85-89.

Holzmueller, H. H., & Schluechter, J. (2002). Delphi study about the future of B2B marketplaces in Germany. *Electronic Commerce Research & Applications*, *1*, 2-19.

ISO/IEC 14662. (2004). *Information technology—open-EDI reference model.* ISO/IEC JTC 1. Retrieved January 29, 2006, from http://www.disa.org/international/is14662.pdf

Ito, T., Hattori, H., & Shintani, T. (2002). A cooperative exchanging mechanism among seller agents for group-based sales. *Electronic Commerce Research & Applications, 1*, 138-149.

Jaiswal, A., Kim, Y., & Gini, M. (2004). Design and implementation of a secure multi-agent marketplace. *Electronic Commerce Research & Applications, 3*, 355-368.

Janssen, M., & Sol, H. G. (2000). Evaluating the role of intermediaries in the electronic value chain. *Internet Research: Electronic Networking Applications and Policy, 10*(5), 406-417.

Kaihara, T. (2003). A study on virtual market model for e-marketplace server. *Electronic Commerce Research & Applications, 2*, 278-285.

Kain, A. K., Aparicio, M., & Singh, M. P. (1999). Agents for process coherence in virtual enterprises. *Communications of the ACM, 42*(3), 62-69.

Kalagnanam, J. R., Davenport, A. J., & Lee, H. S. (2001). Computational aspects of clearing continuous call double auctions with assignment constraints and indivisible demand. *Electronic Commerce Research, 1*, 221-238.

Karacapilidis, N., & Moraitis, P. (2000). Intelligent agents as artificial employees in an electronic market. *Journal of Electronic Commerce Research, 1*(4), 133-142.

Karacapilidis, N., & Moraitis, P. (2001). Building an agent-mediated electronic commerce system with decision analysis features. *Decision Support Systems, 32*, 53-69.

Kauffman, R. J., & Walden, E. A. (2001). Economics and electronic commerce: Survey and directions for research. *International Journal of Electronic Commerce, 5*(4), 5-116.

Kearns, M., & Ortiz, L. (2003). The Penn-Lehman automated trading project. *IEEE Intelligent Systems, Special Issue on Agents and Markets, 18*(6), 22-31.

Kim, B., Barua, A., & Whinston, A.B. (2002). Virtual field experiments for a digital economy: A new research methodology for exploring an information economy. *Decision Support Systems, 32*, 215-231.

Kitts, B., & LeBlanc, B. (2004). Optimal bidding on keyword auctions. *Electronic Markets, Special Issue on Innovative Auction Markets, 14*(3), 186-201.

Kollman, T. (2000). Competitive strategies for electronic marketplaces: A study of German-language trading sites for used cars on the WWW. *Electronic Markets, 10*(2), 102-109.

Koppius, O. R., van Heck, E., & Wolters, M. J. J. (2004). The importance of product representation online: Empirical results and implications for electronic markets. *Decision Support Systems, 38*, 161-169.

Kwon, O. (in press). Multi-agent system approach to context-aware coordinated web services under general market mechanism. *Decision Support Systems.*

Lenz, M., Zimmermann, H.-D., & Heitmann, M. (2002). Strategic partnerships and competitiveness of business-to-business e-marketplaces: Preliminary evidence from Europe. *Electronic Markets, 12*(2), 100-111.

Liang, T. P., & Chen, D.-N. (2003). Evolution of information systems research. In *Proceedings of the Pacific Asian Conference on Information Systems*, Adelaide, Australia (pp. 834-842). Atlanta, GA: Association for Information Systems.

Liang, T.-P., & Huang, J.-S. (2000). A framework for applying intelligent agents to support electronic trading. *Decision Support Systems, 28*, 305-317.

Lin, F.-R., & Chang, K.-Y. (2001, July/August). A multiagent framework for automated online bargaining. *IEEE Intelligent Systems*, 41-47.

Lincke, D.-M., & Schmid, B. (1998). Mediating electronic product catalogs. *Communications of the ACM, 41*(7), 86-88.

Lindemann, M. A., & Schmid, B. F. (1999). Framework for specifying, building, and operating electronic markets. *International Journal of Electronic Commerce*, *3*(2), 7-21.

Linden, G., Smith, B., & York, J. (2003, January-February). Amazon.com recommendations: Item-to-item collaborative filtering. *IEEE Internet Computing*, 76-80.

Liu, H., Wang, S., & Teng, F. (2000). Real-time multi-auctions and the agent support. *Journal of Electronic Commerce Research*, *1*(4), 143-151.

Maamar, Z., Dorion, E., & Daigle, C. (2001). Toward virtual marketplaces for e-commerce support. *Communications of the ACM, 44*(12), 35-38.

Maes, P (1999). Smart commerce: The future of intelligent agents in cyberspace (keynote speech at Direct Marketing Association Conference, 1998). *Journal of Interactive Marketing, 13*(3), 66-76.

Maes, P., Guttman, R. H., & Moukas, A. G. (1999). Agents that buy and sell. *Communications of the ACM, 42*(3), 81-91.

Malone, T. W., Yates, J., & Benjamin, R. I. (1987). Electronic markets and electronic hierarchies. *Communications of the ACM, 30*(6), 484-497.

Mandry, T., Pernul, G., & Roehm, A. W. (2001). Mobile agents in electronic markets: Opportunities, risks, agent protection. *International Journal of Electronic Commerce*, *5*(2), 47-60.

Manouselis, N. (2005). *Electronic markets: Literature review, classification, and identification of open issues* (Tech. Rep.). Athens, Greece: Agricultural University of Athens, Informatics Laboratory. Retrieved January 29, 2006, from http://e-services.aua.gr

Manouselis, N., & Costopoulou, C. (2005b). Designing an Internet-based directory service for e-markets. *Information Services & Use*, *25*(2), 95-107.

Manouselis, N., & Costopoulou, C. (2005a). Towards a metadata model for e-markets. In *Proceedings of the 12th Research Symposium on Emerging Electronic Markets (RSEEM 2005)* (pp. 169-184). Amsterdam, Netherlands: Vrije University.

Minakakis, L., & Rao, B. (1999). Competing in online markets: Financial services as a case in point. *Electronic Markets*, *9*(4), 263-268.

Moukas, A., Zacharia, G., Guttman, R., & Maes, P. (2000). Agent-mediated electronic commerce: An MIT Media Laboratory perspective. *International Journal of Electronic Commerce*, *4*(3), 5-22.

Mullen, T., & Breese, J. (2000). Experiments in designing computational economies for mobile users. *Decision Support Systems*, *28*, 21-34.

Ngai, E. W. T., & Wat, F. K. T. (2002). A literature review and classification of electronic commerce research. *Information and Management*, *39*, 415-429.

O'Daniel, T. (2001). A value-added model for e-commerce. *Electronic Markets*, *11*(1), 37-43.

OECD. (2004). *Information technology outlook.*

Ono, C., Nishiyama, S., & Horiuchi, H. (2003). Reducing complexity in winner determination for combinatorial ascending auctions. *Electronic Commerce Research & Applications*, *2*, 176-186.

Orlikowski, W. J., & Iacono, S. (2001). Research commentary: Desperately seeking the IT in IT research—a call to theorizing the IT artifact. *Information Systems Research*, *12*(2), 121-134.

Padovan, B., Sackmann, S., Eymann, T., & Pippow, I. (2002). Prototype for an agent-based secure electronic marketplace including reputation-tracking mechanisms. *International Journal of Electronic Commerce, 6*(4), 93-113.

Palmer, J. W., Bailey, J. P., & Faraj, S. (2000). The role of intermediaries in the development of trust on the WWW: The use and prominence of trusted third parties and privacy statements. *Journal of Computer-Mediated Communication, 5*(3).

Praca, I., Ramos, C., Vale, Z., & Cordeiro, M. (2003). MASCEM: A multiagent system that simulates competitive electricity markets. *IEEE Intelligent Systems, Special Issue on Agents and Markets, 18*(6), 54-60.

Raisinghani, M. S., & Hanebeck, H.-C. L. (2002). Rethinking B2B e-marketplaces and mobile commerce: From information to execution. *Journal of Electronic Commerce Research, 3*(2), 86-97.

Roehm, A. W., & Pernul, G. (2000). COPS: A model and infrastructure for secure and fair electronic markets. *Decision Support Systems, 29*, 343-355.

Rosson, P., & Davis, C. (2004). Electronic marketplaces and innovation: The Canadian experience. *International Journal of Information Technology and Management, 3*(1), 41-58.

Sandholm, T. (1999). Automated negotiation. *Communications of the ACM, 42*(3), 84-85.

Sandholm, T. (2000a). Approaches to winner determination in combinatorial auctions. *Decision Support Systems, 28*, 165-176.

Sandholm, T. (2000b). Issues in computational Vickrey auctions. *International Journal of Electronic Commerce, 4*(3), 107-129.

Segev, A., Gebauer, J., & Faerber, F. (1999). Internet-based electronic markets. *Electronic Markets, 9*(3), 138-146.

Seifert, R. W., Thonemann, U. W., & Hausman, W. H. (2004). Optimal procurement strategies for online spot markets. *European Journal of Operational Research, 152*, 781-799.

Shen, X., Radakrishnan, T., & Georganas, N. D. (2002). vCOM: Electronic commerce in a collaborative virtual world. *Electronic Commerce Research & Applications, 1*, 281-300.

Silverman, B. G., Bachann, M., & Al-Akharas, K. (2001, July/August). Do what I mean: Online shopping with a natural language search agent. *IEEE Intelligent Systems*, 48-53.

Simons, L. P. A., Steinfield, C., & Bouwman, H. (2002). Strategic positioning of the Web in a multichannel market approach. *Internet Research: Electronic Networking Applications and Policy, 12*(4), 339-347.

Smith, H., & Poulter, K. (1999). Share the ontology in XML-based trading architectures. *Communications of the ACM, 42*(3), 110-111.

Smith, M. D., Bailey, J., & Brynjolfsson, E. (1999). Understanding digital markets: Review and assessment. In Brynjolfsson E. & Kahin B. (Eds.), *Understanding the digital economy.* Cambridge, MA: MIT Press.

Srivastava, V., & Mohapatra, P. K. J. (2003). PLAMUN: A platform for multi-user negotiation. *Electronic Commerce Research & Applications, 2*, 339-349.

Stanoevska-Slabeva, K. (1999). The concept of federated electronic markets. In *Proceedings of the 2nd Workshop on Advanced Issues of E-Commerce and Web-Based Information Systems (WECWIS 1999)* (pp. 164-167). Santa Clara: IEEE Computer Society Press.

Strader, T. J., & Shaw, M. J. (1997). Characteristics of electronic markets. *Decision Support Systems, 21*, 185-198.

Strader, T. J., & Shaw, M. J. (1999). Consumer cost differences for traditional and Internet markets. *Internet Research: Electronic Networking Applications and Policy, 9*(2), 89-492.

Stroebel, M. (2001). Design of roles and protocols for electronic negotiations. *Electronic Commerce Research, 1*, 335-353.

Stroebel, M. (2000). On auctions as the negotiation paradigm of rlectronic markets. *Electronic Markets, 10*(1), 39-44.

Tallroth, E. (2004). Continuous trading in thin private value markets: The multiple-quote double auction. *Electronic Markets, Special Issue on Innovative Auction Markets, 14*(3), 223-231.

Teich, J., Wallenius, H., & Wallenius, J. (1999a). Multiple-issue auction and market algorithms for the world wide web. *Decision Support Systems, 26*, 49-66.

Teich, J., Wallenius, H., Wallenius, J., & Koppius, O. R. (2004). Emerging multiple issue e-auctions. *European Journal of Operational Research, 159*, 1-16.

Teich, J., Wallenius, H., Wallenius, J., & Zaitsev, A. (1999b). A multiple unit auction algorithm: Some theory and a Web implementation. *Electronic Markets, 9*(3), 199-205.

Teich, J. E., Wallenius, H., Wallenius, J., & Zaitsev, A. (2001). Designing electronic auctions: An Internet-based hybrid procedure combining aspects of negotiations and auctions. *Electronic Commerce Research, 1*, 301-314.

Teuteberg, F. (2003). Experimental evaluation of a model for multilateral negotiation with fuzzy preferences on an agent-based marketplace. *Electronic Markets, 13*(1), 21-32.

Tewari, G., Youll, J., & Maes, P. (2002). Personalized location-based brokering using an agent-based intermediary architecture. *Decision Support Systems, 34*, 127-137.

Timmers, P. (1998). Business models for electronic markets. *Electronic Markets, 8*(2), 3-8.

Turban, E., King, D., Lee, J., & Viehland, D. (2004). *Electronic commerce: A managerial perspective 2004*. Upper Saddle River NJ: Prentice Hall.

UNCTAD. (2005). *Information economy report 2005* (UNCTAD/SDTE/ECB/2005/1). Geneva: United Nations Conference on Trade and Development.

Urbaczewski, A., Jessup, L. M., & Wheeler, B. (2002). Electronic commerce research: A taxonomy and a synthesis. *Journal of Organisational Computing and Electronic Commerce, 12*(4), 263-305.

Vaishnavi, V. K., & Kuechler, W. L. (2003). An approach to reducing e-commerce coordination costs in evolving markets using a semantic routing protocol. *Journal of Electronic Commerce Research, 4*(3), 113-127.

Vishwanath, A. (2004). An empirical investigation into the use of heuristics and information cues by bidders in online auctions. *Electronic Markets, Special Issue on Innovative Auction Markets, 14*(3), 178-185.

Vrechopoulos, A. P., O'Keefe, R. M., Doukidis, G. I., & Siomkos, G. J. (2004). Virtual store layout: An experimental comparison in the context of grocery retail. *Journal of Retailing, 80*(1), 13-22.

Vulkan, N., & Preist, C. (2003). Automated trading in agent-based markets for communication bandwidth. *International Journal of Electronic Commerce, 7*(4), 119-150.

Wang, H. (1997). A conceptual model for virtual markets. *Information and Management, 32*, 147-161.

Wang, S., & Archer, N. (2004). Strategic choice of electronic marketplace functionalities: A buyer-supplier relationship perspective. *Journal of Computer-Mediated Communication, 10*(1). Retrieved December 6, 2006 from http://jcmc.indiana.edu/vol10/issue1/

Wang, Y., Tan, K.-L., & Ren, J. (2004). PumaMart: A parallel and autonomous agents based internet marketplace. *Electronic Commerce Research & Applications, 3*, 294-310.

Warkentin, M., Bapna, R., & Sugumaran, V. (2000). The role of mass customization in enhancing supply chain relationships in B2C e-commerce markets. *Journal of Electronic Commerce Research, 1*(2), 45-52.

Wellman, M. P. (2004). Online marketplaces. In M. P.Singh (Ed.), *Practical handbook of Internet computing.* Boca Raton FL: CRC Press LLC.

Wellman, M. P., Cheng, S.-F., Reeves, D. M., & Lochner, K. M. (2003a). Trading agents competing: Performance, progress, and market effectiveness. *IEEE Intelligent Systems, Special Issue on Agents and Markets, 18*(6), 48-53.

Wellman, M. P., Greenwald, A., Stone, P., & Wurman, P. R. (2003b). The 2001 trading agent competition. *Electronic Markets, 13*(1), 4-12.

Wellman, M. P., Wurman, P. R., O'Malley, K., Bangera, R., Lin, S., Reeves, D., & Walsh, W. E. (2001, March-April). Designing the market game for a trading agent competition. *IEEE Internet Computing*, 43-51.

Wicke, G. A. (1999). Electronic markets - A key to mobility. *Electronic Markets, Special Issue on Electronic Commerce and Logistics, 9*(3), 162-168.

Wurman, P. R., Walsh, W. E., & Wellman, M. P. (1998). Flexible double auctions for electronic commerce: Theory and implementation. *Decision Support Systems, 24*, 17-27.

Yuan, S.-T., & Lin, Y.-H. (2004). Credit based group negotiation for aggregate sell/buy in e-markets. *Electronic Commerce Research & Applications, 3*, 74-94.

Zacharia, G., Evgeniou, T., Moukas, A., Boufounos, P., & Maes, P. (2001). Economics of dynamic pricing in a reputation brokered agent mediated marketplace. *Electronic Commerce Research, 1*, 85-100.

Zimmerman, R. D., Thomas, R. J., Gan, D., & Murillo-Sanchez, C. (1999). A web-based platform for experimental investigation of electric power auctions. *Decision Support Systems, 24*, 193-205.

This work was previously published in E-Business Process Management: Technologies and Solutions, edited by J. Sounderpandan & T. Sinha, pp. 68-95, copyright 2007 by IGI Publishing, formerly known as Idea Group Publishing (an imprint of IGI Global).

Section IV
Utilization and Application

Chapter XIV
Process-Oriented Assessment of Web Services

Jan-Hendrik Sewing
Siemens Management Consulting, Germany

Michael Rosemann
Queensland University of Technology, Australia

Marlon Dumas
Queensland University of Technology, Australia

ABSTRACT

Though Web services offer unique opportunities for the design of new business processes, the assessment of the potential impact of Web services is often reduced to technical aspects. This paper proposes a four-phase methodology which facilitates the evaluation of the potential use of Web services in e-business systems both from a technical and from a strategic viewpoint. It is based on business process models, which are used to frame the adoption of Web services and to assess their impact on existing business processes. The application of this methodology is described using a procurement scenario.

INTRODUCTION

Web services (WS) is an emerging set of technologies that aims at facilitating the flexible and standardised implementation of interoperable software systems. Considerably hyped in recent years, Web services are expected to ease many current IT problems, such as the large-scale integration of heterogeneous software applications or the cost-effective establishment of E-business interactions. From a more technical viewpoint, investment in Web services is seen as a prerequisite to adopt a service-oriented architecture.

Although the intensity of development efforts and standardisation activities is very high, systematic assessment approaches of the actual impact of Web services on existing IT infrastructures are still rare. Thus, many organisations are still struggling to assess the real impact of Web services and the accompanying opportunities and threats. Without appropriate business alignment, however, Web services might be perceived as a technical solution without a clear value proposition, in the sense that its potential benefits might not justify associated software reengineering efforts. This constitutes a potential risk factor in light of current IT spending practice and could eventually hamper a wide adoption.

Addressing the alignment of Web services to business priorities is therefore a critical step towards the success of this emerging technology: it will determine whether Web services can fit into (and more importantly improve) existing business practices and thus increase the competitiveness of the organisations that adopt them.

Business process modelling encapsulates all forms of graphically visualising business processes and related elements such as data, resources, and so on for a wide variety of possible purposes including among others process documentation, process improvement, compliance, software implementation, or quality certification (Becker, Rosemann, & Von Uthmann, 2000; Curtis, Keller, & Over, 1992). It is an established approach for analysing and improving existing business processes. Business process models, extended with relevant information, have the potential to serve as a decision support instrument for assessing the potential of Web services. They are able to show the process context and ways of how Web services can enable business process innovation.

This paper proposes a methodology for identifying and assessing opportunities for introducing Web services into organisations by means of business process modelling. After briefly outlining and justifying the research approach, a framework is presented for selecting the most appropriate processes for incorporating Web services. Following this, information domains and types are identified that need to be contained in a business process model to support systematic Web services assessments and to facilitate Web services deployment. This information is then mapped into a specific representation in the context of the ARIS Toolset (Scheer, 1998a), a widely used solution for business process modelling. This mapping as well as the conceptual possibilities of the methodology are then illustrated through an example from the area of e-procurement. Finally, conclusions and directions for future work are outlined.

RESEARCH APPROACH

The proposed assessment methodology is grounded in related literature and complemented by focus group discussions with early and prospective Web services adopters. The purpose of the focus groups was to explore the current practice of Web service implementations, and industry's perception and approaches on how to address the challenge of business alignment. Specifically, two focus groups were organised: one for discussing the uptake and adoption of Web services technologies and a second one for discussing the use of business process models for assessing Web services adoption opportunities.

The participants of the focus groups were selected on the basis of their experience with Web services or their affiliation to organisations that were considering the deployment of Web services. The choice of participants was also guided by the objective of covering different organisations and industry sectors, and striking a balance between participants with a technical and a management background. Overall, the focus groups included 15 participants from eight organisations and covering four different groups (IT users, vendors, consulting firms, and research).

The reason for choosing focus groups as the empirical basis for this study lies in their effectiveness for gathering the general opinion of a target audience by providing an environment that allows probing for clarification and justification of opinion (Morgan, 1988; Saulnier, 2000). Focus groups are especially suitable for generating hypotheses when little is known in a specific research area (New Mexico State University–College of Agriculture and Home Economics, 1999). Sofaer, Kreling, Kenney, Swift, and Dewart (2001) suggest that if the previous work in a field is limited (which is the case here) then the research needs to be, at least initially, exploratory in approach (Sofaer et al., 2001).

WEB SERVICES ASSESSMENT METHODOLOGY

Two main assessment scenarios can be differentiated: (1) an organisation has a specific need and wants to evaluate the applicability of Web services within a selected business process, or (2) an organisation wishes to identify those business processes, which would benefit most from the deployment of Web services. In both cases it is assumed that the organisation has conducted business process modelling and business process redesign activities beforehand, in order to start from an informed perspective.

Decision Methodology: Overview

In the following, a general decision methodology for the introduction of Web services is proposed for scenario (2). It is shown what information would be required at which phase and to what extended business process models can be utilised.

The methodology is intended to serve as a guideline for systematically assessing the potential of business processes regarding the deployment of Web services and selecting the most appropriate processes and Web services. It helps answer "outside-in" questions (Bibby & Brea, 2003), such as "to what business processes could Web services be best applied?" and "what economic impact could that have?"

The methodology consists of a framework that follows a top-down structure with four decision phases. It includes several checklists to make it a practical instrument. A process Web services potential, that is, the technical and economic feasibility and suitability of Web services integration within a selected business process is the main outcome of this methodology. The assessment is based on a scoring model, in which criteria and their weighting can be adapted and modified, making the tool highly flexible.

The assumed starting input are business process models, which could be the result of a comprehensive process modelling or business process improvement project. In the *first phase*, this existing set of business processes is evaluated against a shortlist of criteria, which allows to immediately disqualify some business processes for the deployment of Web services. These criteria could be that the processes are definitely unable to be Web services enabled or are already working very well so that running the risks associated with the change process would be unreasonable.

Within the *second* phase, the remaining subset of processes is evaluated regarding its "Web service—process suitability". Processes can be classified into four categories based on organisation-independent characteristics, that is, (a) strong Web service suitability, (b) Web service "learning chance", (c) future Web service potential, and (d) limited Web service applicability.

The processes which fall into the categories (a), (b), and (c) are subject to further investigation within a *third* phase. Here, organisation-dependent criteria come into play, further reducing the set of potentially suitable business processes. This includes among others an assessment of the strategic importance of Web services for the organisation.

During the *fourth* and final phase, the organisation finally prioritises the remaining potential Web services projects, largely based on methods and measures known from conventional evaluation of alternative IT investments such as Return on Investment and Net Present Value (Remenyi, Money, Sherwood-Smith, & Irani 2000).

The following sections describe the different phases and the required input in more detail.

First Phase: Process Rejection Based on Disqualifying Criteria

At this phase business processes that match at least one of a list of the disqualifying criteria are rejected. These organisation-independent criteria should be easy to assess without requiring a detailed investigation of the process models. Care must be taken to ensure that the criteria are chosen in such a way that they do not reject potential processes over-hastily. On the other hand they should be selective enough to reject as many unsuitable processes as possible and reduce the effort of detailed evaluations in the following phase. Thus, there is a trade-off between the amount of accidental disqualification of business processes and the workload at the following decision point.

Given that Web services are driven towards automated program-to-program interactions, and given the cost of reengineering existing processes and software to introduce Web services, a conservative set of criteria could be:

- The process involves only physical performance that cannot be digitised;
- Human intelligence or sophisticated interpretation is required; and
- Isolated process which is working well, stable, efficient, and cannot be leveraged (i.e., does not represent "hidden value").

Second Phase: Assessing General Web Services Suitability

At this phase the remaining subset of business processes from the first phase is evaluated using a "Web Service—Process Suitability" scoring table. The criteria are still independent from the specifics of an individual organisation. The goal of the scoring table is to assess the suitability of the business process for the application of Web services based on two dimensions.

- The first dimension measures whether the *business* needs match with potential business drivers for Web services.
- The second dimension evaluates whether the *technical* requirements could currently be met by available Web services technology.

Each dimension is represented by a number of criteria which can be weighted and contain weighted sub-criteria. For both dimensions possible criteria are summarised in Table 1. The criteria and framework are based on criteria proposed by (Burdett, 2003; Hagel III & Brown, 2002; Hagel III, Brown, & Layton-Rodin, 2002; Linthicum, 2002; Patricia Seybold Group, 2002; Robins, Sleeper, & McTiernan, 2003; The Stencil Group, 2002; Wilkov, 2002; Wright, 2002), and findings from our two focus groups.

Scores are then calculated independently for both dimensions. Every criterion which has been answered with a "yes" gets a score of one, every "no" results in a score of zero. The scores are then weighted and added as shown in Table 2. It is not in the scope of this work to determine how the scores should or could be derived, but we can note that traditional multi-criteria decision-making methodologies (Keeney & Raiffa, 1992) could be employed for this purpose.

The resulting score for each dimension of the business process under evaluation can then be visualised as a dot in a two dimensional matrix which represents its potential for Web services deployment. A possible matrix is given in Figure 1.

Table 1. Process evaluation for Web services

Second Phase: Qualifying Analysis Criteria	
Business Need	**Business Process Characteristics**
Reduction of asset investment:	Unique expensive resources are currently used to support the process and could be replaced
Reuse and easier maintenance:	Redundant functionality in several application systems exists and shall be reduced/existing functionality shall be leveraged
Support for heterogeneous endpoints:	Business process requires support for multiple, heterogeneous interfaces
Automation of manual interventions and intensive data entry (human intervention for exceptions only):	Multiple manual, error-prone interventions dealing with digitized data are currently required for the business process
Automation of transaction chains:	Multi-step process, involving different business parties, shall be automated
Introduction of Self-service mechanism (enabling direct access to core system rather than cached or replicated data):	A batch process shall be replaced by a self-service, real-time mechanism
Higher transparency/visibility:	Frequent access to dynamically produced data has to be supported
Ad-hoc business:	Ad-hoc business with previously unknown parties shall be supported
Higher flexibility and business agility, dynamic process support:	"On demand" reconfiguration of business process required
Low impact of failure:	Financial risk of system failure is low for the business process
Technical Need	**Business Process Characteristic**
Processing speed:	No extremely short responses are required
Processing time guarantees:	No precisely predictable response time is required
Distribution of transaction volume:	Low transaction burst probability
Response to failure:	No failure compensation, roll-back, "state capture" are required
Security Requirements:	No non-repudiation, "chains of trust" and tamper-proofness are required
Semantic heterogeneity:	Shared meaning can be defined
Process repetition:	High repetition frequency
Process stability:	Process and involved application systems are likely to change over time
Transaction mode:	Real-time mode is required
Support for heterogeneity:	Multiple, diverse hardware and software systems are involved
Implementation effort:	Significant custom development would be required for conventional approach

Table 2. Simple scoring table for each of the two dimensions

Characteristic	[No = 0, Yes = 1]	Weight; Σ(rows) = 1 (each ranging [0..1])	Score per Characteristic
xyz	{0;1}	[0..1]	= ({0;1} x [Weight])
…	…	…	…
		Σ(rows) = 1	Σ(rows)

Figure 1. Web services suitability matrix

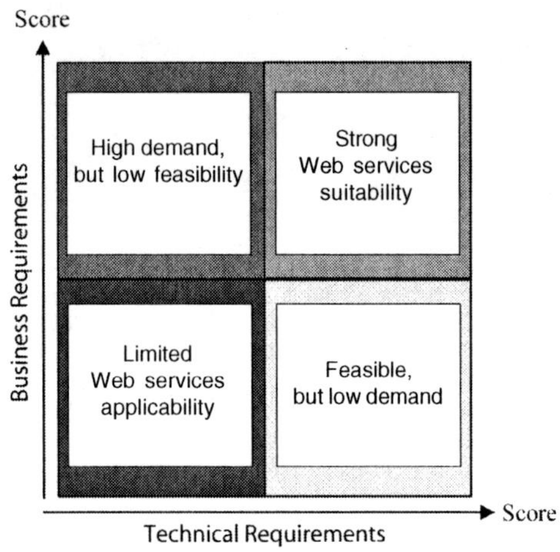

Third Phase: Organisational Characteristics

The third phase evaluated the general process suitability for Web services. After this phase, at least the processes marked with "limited applicability" can be eliminated. The following evaluation is not based on general process characteristics anymore but on *organisational-dependent* criteria. Here, it has to be established whether the qualified processes from Phase 2 are suitable for Web services with regard to the specific characteristics of the organisation.

For example, in spite of high costs and risks, an organisation could decide to experiment with a "future Web service" application, and so on. Potential questions leading to assessment criteria were identified with the help of the focus group sessions:

- Who are the involved business partners for the business process under consideration? What is the level of trust and the level of knowledge about their internal processes and systems? Do the partners already use standardised data formats or are they in the process of adopting Web services?
- Would the required technical resources be available?

Table 3. Organisational assessment criteria

Organisational Assessment Criteria	
Internal Factors	
Funding & Backing:	Business units specify and fund most major IT projects
Role of IT for organisation:	Use of IT is a competitive advantage
Role of innovation for organisation:	Innovation is a competitive advantage, organisation is risk taking
Current application architectures:	IT maintenance and integration costs are high
Importance of optimisation:	Increasing productivity is a strategic need
Current IT resources:	Current development & deployment platforms support Service-Oriented Architectures
Current available IT skills:	Adequately skilled personnel is available
External Factors	
Industry characteristics regarding specified data formats:	Industry uses standardised data formats (esp. XML)
Industry characteristics regarding data regulations:	Use or sharing of data is regulated by law
Industry e-commerce capabilities:	Industry has experience using B2Bi
Support from current IT vendors:	IT vendors have strategic support for Web services
Current business partners IT capabilities:	Partners have heterogeneous B2B capabilities
Market structure:	Oligopoly, more than one dominating player are present
Current business relationship characteristics:	Several trust-based relationship with deep mutual understanding of internal structures exist

Figure 2. Matrix for WS strategic importance with respect to organisational criteria

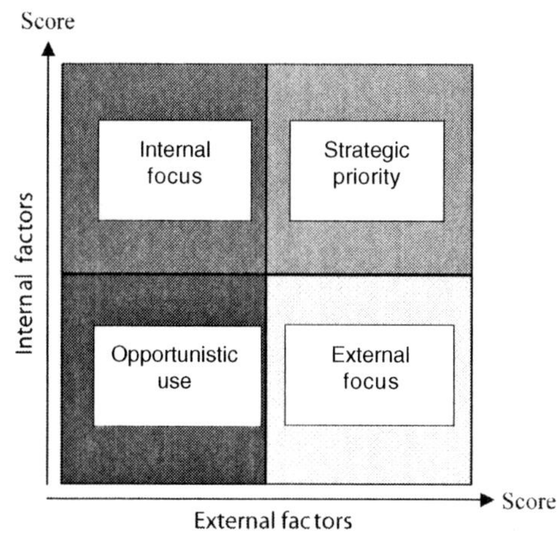

- Would the required skill set be available?
- Are there example implementation and/or best practice available?
- What are potential risks? Consider risk affinity.

Some of these questions relate to internal organisational factors while others deal with external market characteristics. Clearly, the organisational assessment of Web services should consider criteria along both of these categories. The set of criteria presented in Table 3 derive from the previous questions as well as relevant literature (Chen, 2003; Christiansen, 2002; The Stencil Group, 2002).

Scores can then be calculated and combined in the same way as for the process analysis in phase 2. The resulting degree of current importance of Web services for an organisation could be again visualised as a dot in a two-dimensional matrix similar to the process evaluation phase. This is shown in Figure 2 and Table 4.

Fourth Phase: Assigning Web Services Implementation Priority

The remaining business processes that were generally suitable regarding their process characteristics (second phase) and met the organisations' specific situation (third phase) are prioritised in a last step. The goal here is to define what processes should be Web service-supported first. This can be determined by considering organisation-dependent factors. A list of proposed factors is presented in Table 5. Different weights could be assigned to the factors depending on the importance the

Table 4. Explanation of the cells in the matrix of Figure 2

Field in Matrix	Description	Likely Approach	Potential Risks
NE = Strategic priority	Web services should represent a significant element of the overall IT strategy. Strategic business processes will be affected. All major IT efforts should be considered in the context of fulfilling the SOA vision.	Going for vision of service-oriented enterprise	Over architecting
NW = Internal focus	The organisation is positioned to make use of Web services. However, many of the partners and customers may not be. Therefore it makes most sense to look at how Web services-based integration can optimise internal processes and help better utilise existing assets.	Focusing on fixing while ensuring performing applications	Ignoring interesting market opportunities
SE = External focus	Web services represent an important way to connect to customers and business partners because of market dynamics. Web services-based offerings could represent a potential competitive advantage for first movers.	Using innovation for competitive advantage	Opening holes regarding security and scalability
SW = Opportunistic use	Web services may be an appropriate solution for specific projects. However, they do not represent a critical element of the overall IT strategy. Nevertheless, developers should be encouraged to experiment with the Web Service standards and related software tools.	Small steps for incremental benefits	Missing the strategic vision

Table 5. Priority criteria

4th phase: Priority criteria
Choose main "pain areas" where business partner or customers would like to be able to do things they cannot do at the moment
Consider importance of involved business partner/customer for organisation.
Choose projects where a new business need has to be satisfied and aggregated applications from remote systems can be leveraged.
Choose projects for identified stable (proven) core business functionalities. However, the pilot area should not endanger established, mission-critical processes.
Choose highly repeatable scenarios.
Evaluate project's feasibility.
Analyse of value proposition with (risk-adapted) return on investment analysis, economic value added (EVA) etc. for Compare estimated costs.
• Compare estimated project duration.
• Compare potential benefits.
• Compare potential risks.
Financial decision for evaluating investment alternatives, likely to be based on strategic cost management methods like total cost of ownership.

organisation attaches to them. The set of criteria is based on Christiansen (2002), Estrem (in press), Hammer and Champy (1993), Hagel and Brown (2002), Patricia Seybold Group (2002), Samtani and Sadhwani (2002), and the focus groups.

Based on these outlined logical steps an organisation should be able to systematically integrate Web service technology as a facilitator of its business processes. The questions proposed for an assessment and their sequence guarantee that the

Figure 3. Identifying and evaluating Web service opportunities

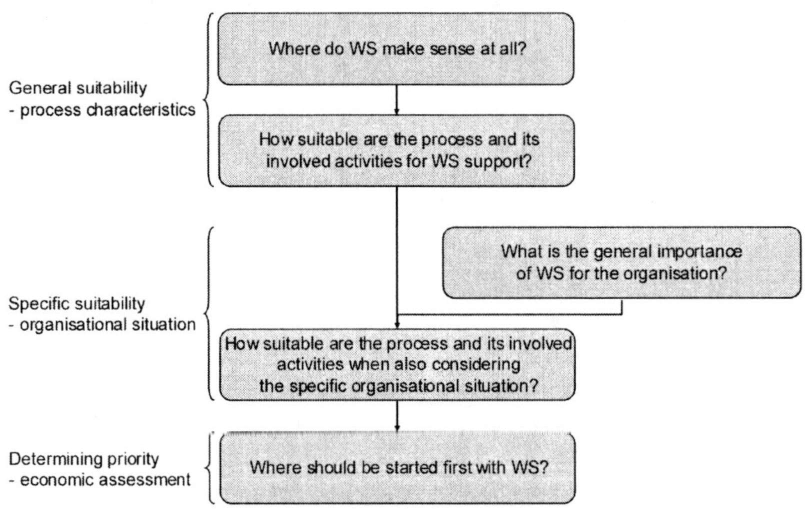

most suitable and feasible activities and business processes for Web services support are identified. The framework can moreover be tailored to the individual characteristics of an organisation, as the criteria and their weighting are adaptable. Figure 3 summarises the outlined phases.

SUPPORT THROUGH BUSINESS PROCESS MODELLING

Required Information for the Assessment of Web Service Potential

Business process modelling can support the decision making process described earlier in all phases. Apart from presenting an overview of an organisation's processes, assigned actors and resources and their interrelationships, which is of great value in order to gain a fundamental understanding of how the enterprise works (e.g., compare with Schmelzer & Bloomberg, 2002), a wide spectrum of information can be captured in the process model and help answer the questions noted previously. A list of identified critical information for the evaluation of Web services and their deployment is presented in Table 6 and Table 7. This list was developed based on the information which has been identified as important for the different evaluation phases as well as with the help of additional literature (e.g., ebXML Business Process Team, 2002; Papazoglou, 2003). Furthermore, a classification into separate domains has been carried out.

Required Information for Web Services Deployment

Apart from supporting the *identification and evaluation* of opportunities for Web services integration to improve business processes, business process models are also a valuable tool for facilitating Web services deployment. Business process models could capture (a) patterns, (b) Web services taxonomies, and (c) Web services semantics.

Patterns may be identified in Web services practices and added as additional, classifying information to a model. Once patterns are identified and captured they provide opportunities for simplifying structures and processes. Besides, these identified patterns promote the re-use of knowledge and functionality which reduces the development effort. Encouraging and reinforcing consistency and standardisation (e.g., compare with Glushko & McGrath, 2002) this can also lead to reduced maintenance. IBM, for example, offers a set of e-Business patterns to facilitate the process of developing Web-based applications. As a general rule, they expect that the emerging Web services affect the implementation of all their presented patterns, that is, business, integration, and application patterns, whenever there is a boundary between businesses, applications, or logical components of a solution across which information must be exchanged (Adams, Gisolfi, Snell, & Varadan, 2002).

Because Web services are presumed to be re-used, a prerequisite for efficient service development is also the creation of a comprehensive reusability strategy. One of the bases for this strategy should be a taxonomy of services (Scholler, 2003). *Web service taxonomies* help categorise Web services, for example, based on their role or function they provide within an overall enterprise. Scholler (2003), for instance, proposes a 2x2 matrix taxonomy consisting of the dimensions provider scope (e.g., the provider may be a particular organisational unit, and its associated applications or the provider may also be enterprise wide in scope) and consumer scope (e.g., consumers may be local to a particular organisation, or the consumers may be global and outside the boundaries of the enterprise). These dimensions result in at least four classes of services with accompanying different strategies

Table 6. Information for Web service evaluation: Processes and transactions characteristics

Related Phase	Information Domain and Type	Detailed Description
	Process characteristics	
2	**Process stability**	Adaptability requirements (process' ability/likelihood to change)
2	**Process repetition frequency**	Frequency process is carried out with
2, 4	**Process's level of mission-criticality**	Degree to which the organisation relies on the process under consideration
2, 4	**Process's estimated monetary value if quantifiable**	Quantification of the value of the business process if possible
	Transactions characteristics	
2	**Business transaction type** E.g. Request/confirm, Request/ response, Notification, Distribution	Transaction type information supports an estimation of the degree of complexity of a potential service
2	**Composition requirements**	Required interrelations with other services, supports an estimation of the degree of complexity of a potential service
2	**Transaction mode** Synchronous, asynchronous or "as-agreed-by-parties"	"As-agreed-by-parties" indicates that the flow of control would be specified in trading partner agreements
2	**Message delivery requirements**	
	Reliable messaging	Delivery of message until acknowledged
	Message sequencing	Sequencing requirements
	Two Phase Commit	"All or nothing" synchronisation
	Message expiry	Definition of validity of involved message
2	**Processing speed requirements**	Time constraints that have to be met
2	**Processing speed guarantees**	Accepted level of speed/time deviation
2	**Throughput requirements**	Rate (and peak rate) at which potential service is required to be able to process requests
2	**Scalability requirements**	Based on estimation of service's future use
2	**Security requirements**	
	Authentication	Identification and validation of message sender
	Authorization	Assignment of rights to message sender
	Confidentiality	Transport security/encryption requirements
	Data integrity	To ensure that data has not been altered between communication entities
	Non-repudiation	To ensure that transaction route is traceable and no aspect of the transaction can be denied
2	**Failure response requirements**	Compensation requirements for sub-transactions, roll-back, sub-transactions might also produce valuable results that should not be completely lost in case of failure (state capture)

Table 7. Information for Web service evaluation: Systems, data and partners characteristics

Related Phase	Information Domain and Type	Detailed Description
	Involved systems' characteristics	
1, 2	Description of modules and functionality	Description of functionality to track redundancies, encourage re-use etc.
2	**Capacity utilisation level**	Description of system's current degree of utilisation and relationships to processes
2	**Costs (initial & maintenance)**	Description of current costs for, supporting potential reduction of asset investments etc.
2	**Existing interfaces**	Description of interfaces to asses degree of required support for heterogeneity
2	**Used communication protocols**	Description of communication protocols
2	**Systems ability to change**	System's adaptability support and requirements
	Involved data's characteristics	
3	**Data format & standards compliance**	Description of data structure
2	**Dynamics, frequency of change**	Description of current level of dynamics of involved data
2	**Importance of timeliness**	Requirements for timeliness of involved data
2	**Required level of data security**	Description of required degree of end-to-end security for data
	Involved business partners' characteristics	
2, 3	**Total number of involved parties**	Higher number usually means higher complexity that has to be supported
4	**Assumed frequency of cooperation**	Information could be used for assigning priority to potential supporting IT project
4	**Importance of business partner to organisation**	Information could be used for assigning priority to potential supporting IT project
3	**Autonomy, degree of individuality**	Partner's IT compliance to existing "global" standards and agreements
3	**Existing level of business trust**	A high level of business trust is especially considered to be important for near-term external Web Service projects
3	**Existing process insight, manageability, shared meaning**	External visibility, understanding, and manageability of partners' applications
3	**Existing technological base**	Description of partners' current IT systems
3	**Existing IT skill base**	Description of partners' current IT skills

that should be followed (Scholler, 2003). Other examples for possible Web services taxonomies include the business purposes that trigger Web services implementations. Web services taxonomy information could be attached to the Web services implementations that are captured in business process models.

Apart from capturing patterns and Web service taxonomies, *Web service semantics* (i.e., service capabilities, additional functional and non-functional properties) can also be recorded in business process models to facilitate Web services deployment. Documentation of Web services capabilities and additional functional properties will support the re-use of services and facilitate communication with internal and external parties involved in the Web services implementations. Furthermore, capturing non-functional service properties will be necessary for Web services (provider) evaluation.

Table 8 lists information that is important for Web services deployment and can be captured in a business process model. The information domains and types presented are based on ebXML Business Process Team (2002), National Health Supply Chain Taskforce Interoperability Working Group (2002), and Scholler (2003).

Table 8. Identified critical information for Web service deployment

Information Domain and Type	Detailed Description
Business purpose for web service	
Capturing the business purpose of Web services implementations provides a basis for identifying knowledge and know-how for future implementation projects.	
Interaction pattern	
Web services transactions could potentially also automate more complex interaction patterns to great advantage in the future. Capturing the interaction patterns supported by existing Web services implementations would offer the chance to identify reusable knowledge if the same interaction pattern was to be supported in a new project.	
Simple Transaction (1:1)	Any Web services where the objective is for the provider to execute an operation on behalf of the consumer. (E.g. order taking, billing, buying, reporting, finding, reserving)
Agent (1:1:n)	A Web services that acts as an agent providing intelligence in the selection of other services. (E.g. search engine, travel agent that maintains up-to-date arrangements, automatic trading agent)
Dealer/Intermediary (n:1:n)	A third party that locates, aggregates, potentially inserts value-adding services
Auction (1:n)	An auction service allows an individual or enterprise to offer various forms of auction service on a private or public basis. (E.g. personal auction service, bid processes)
Virtual hub (n:n)	Core business services are exposed and executed directly by other parties in a collaborative process. (E.g. supply chain process)
Relationship type	
Buyer to major supplier, Buyer to small supplier, Buyer/supplier via e-Marketplace, Buyer/supplier via a third party ("exchange hub"), Ad-hoc, previously unknown	Identified patterns would encourage re-use of functionalities, thus facilitate deployment etc.
Service semantics	
Service ontology & capabilities	Description of what the service is about and how it can be discovered (e.g. synonyms for name etc.)
Functional service properties e.g. identification, location, etc.	Potentially supporting re-use of services and communication with business partners
Non-functional service properties e.g. availability, costs, ownership, quality, etc.	Potentially supporting provider evaluation etc.

INTEGRATION IN ARIS AND EXAMPLE

This section discusses how the proposed methodology for Web services assessment and deployment can be supported by a mainstream business process modelling solution, namely ARIS. The implementation of the methodology is then illustrated through an e-procurement scenario.

Introduction to ARIS

ARIS is a mature business modelling tool, which is regularly ranked in market studies as the most advanced solution for process modelling and analysis. Its sophisticated capabilities and its wide distribution is practice motivated us to select ARIS for the purpose of this research. ARIS (Architecture of Integrated Information Systems) is a process-oriented business process documentation, analysis, and improvement framework (supported by a toolset) that attempts to span the gap between business theory and information/communication technology (Scheer, 1998a). In ARIS, business processes are represented in diagrammatic form as chains of events and functions (EPCs). Apart from processes, ARIS can be used to model systems, resources, data, software, information flow, organisation, knowledge, skills, business objectives, risks, and costs (Davis, 2001). The result is a highly intricate model which is divided into views in order to reduce its complexity. With such division, the contents of the individual views can be described by special methods. The description may either be performed from a purely functional point of view, or the applications may be considered from the point of view of the data. A third perspective is the organisational one, where organisational units and responsibilities are presented. In order to maintain the relational structure between functions, data, and organisation, the control view shows, for instance, what data is processed by which functions (Scheer, Abolhassan, Jost, & Kirchmer, 2002, p.17). A fifth view, the output view, represents resulting products and services. Output is the result of processes and describing output is seen as one of the key processes in describing business processes (Scheer, 1998b, p.93).

The ARIS Toolset supports a range of modelling techniques. Several model types were evaluated regarding their suitability for supporting the integration of the identified critical information for Web service assessment and deployment. Among them are the extended Event-Driven Process chain (eEPC), Column eEPC, Process Chain Diagram (PCD), and the recently introduced E-Business Scenario Diagram. In our example, the latter was used for the top-level modelling. The extended event-driven process chain is the chosen model type for modelling greater levels of detail. Both techniques, e-business scenario diagram and the event-driven process chain, are also used within the enterprise System SAP. Thus, we believe that our examples can easily be understood by the wide community involved in SAP-related modelling activities.

ARIS Model Types Employed

EPCs are activity-oriented diagrams which are depicted in the process view. The structure of an EPC is that of a directed graph with active nodes ("functions") and passive nodes ("events"). A process is described via an EPC as a chain of business functions, where each function describes an activity and is preceded by and succeeded by events. The latter represent the prior and subsequent situation regarding the function (Soderstrom, 2002). In ARIS, events are graphically represented by a hexagon shape; functions are displayed as soft rectangles. In addition to that, rule operators, represented by circles, illustrate AND, OR, and XOR decisions and are used to model the internal structure of a process (e.g., branching, re-branching, parallel sub-processes, etc.). Dotted arrows connect the elements depicting the control flow.

eEPCs are event-driven process chains which are "extended" by the inclusion of elements that are specified in greater detail in other views. That way eEPCs can represent how the available resources implement a process and how the process interacts with its environment. Based on such a model the following types of questions could be answered: (a) who does it? (organisational unit); (b) what do they do? (function, information carrier); (c) how do they do it? (knowledge, application system); (d) why do they do it? (objective); and (e) when do they do it? (event) (Davis, 2001, pp. 162-163).

Table 9 shows common object types that were also used for the implementation of the exemplary business process model presented later. Their description has been adapted from the ARIS Methods Manual (IDS Scheer AG, 2002).

To facilitate the modelling of e-business processes, the ARIS framework incorporates a dedicated type of diagram, namely "e-business scenario diagram". Using this type of diagram it is possible to view a value-added chain holistically, that is, from the end customer through all the companies involved in the process. By adopting the column representation style, the e-business scenario diagram provides an abstraction of the interfaces between different process partners.

Table 9. Common objects within the ARIS Toolset

Symbol	Object Type Name	Description
	Event	Events trigger functions and are the results of functions.
	Function	A function is a technical task or activity performed on an object.
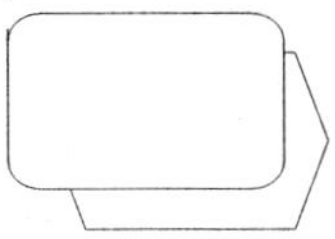	Process Interface	A process interface indicates from which process the related event has been created, or which process the event triggers.
	Rules X-OR AND OR	The rules describe how the events and functions are related. The X-OR means that one and only one input/output is possible, the AND that all the inputs or outputs must be true, and the OR when any combination may be possible.
Resource objects		
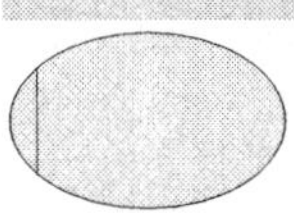	Organisational Unit Type	An organisational unit type represents a typification of individual organisational units, i.e. performers of the tasks required to attain the business objectives.
	Information Carrier	An information carrier is a means to store information.
	Cluster	A cluster represents the logical view on a collection of entity types and relationship types of a data model.
	Application System Type	The Application System Type is representative of a related group of IT systems.
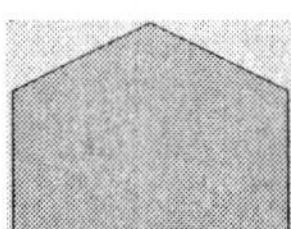	Objective	An objective is the definition of future company goals
	Knowledge Category	A knowledge category is used to classify knowledge by topic

Apart from involved business participants that are placed in the "header row" and the central elements, business processes, different information carrier objects (e.g., Internet) are also available to present the underlying media by which business documents are passed across boundaries (Davis, 2001, p. 345). Business component objects, which represent the application system type used in normal eEPCs, can also be included. Furthermore, security protocol objects can be attached to the business documents to specify security requirements. As with eEPCs, the organisational, data and systems description can be specified in greater detail within additional assignable models. The symbols (representing different objects) offered by the E-business Scenario Diagram type are shown in Figure 4.

Description of Relevant Modelling Constructs in ARIS

The following sections present the modelling constructs and techniques that could be used—in addition to the standard elements "function", "state", "operator", and "connection"—to capture the information relevant to Web services assessment and deployment (hereafter referred to as "Web service modelling") in an ARIS business process model.

Hierarchical Decomposition

It is a natural design technique to start by creating a high-level concept and then to drill down into successive levels of detail (Davis, 2001, p. 242). Process decomposition is achieved by assigning hierarchies of eEPCs to functions (Davis, 2001, p. 243). Apart from that, most model assignments in ARIS are made to models that provide additional details about the particular object. The most relevant for this work are presented in Table 10.

Figure 4. Modelling symbols for e-business scenario diagrams

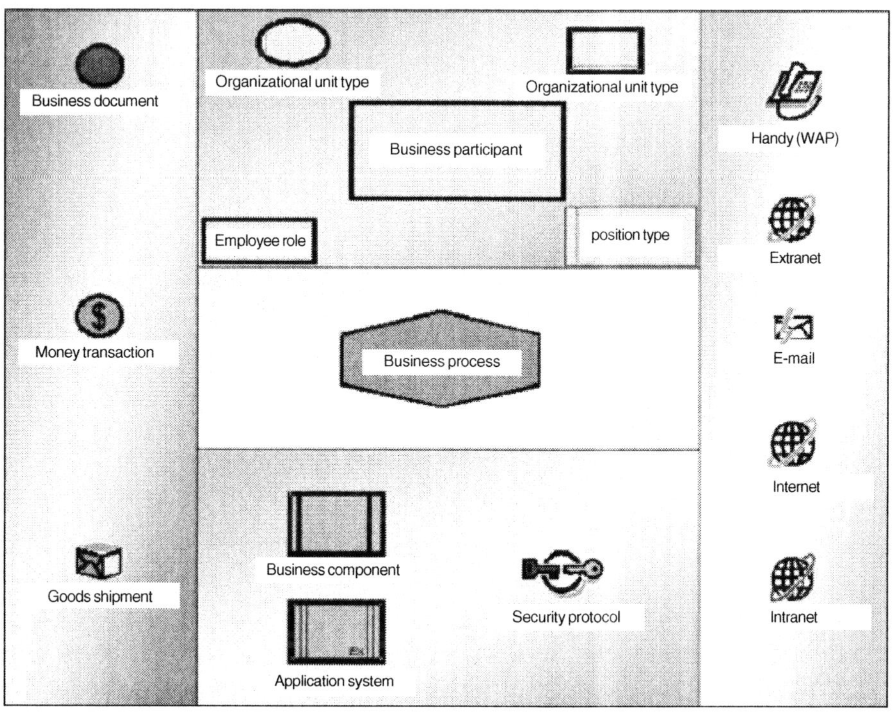

Table 10. Hierarchical models in ARIS that can be assigned to objects, adapted from (Davis, 2001)

Object	Assigned Model	Hierarchical Representation
Function	eEPC	Decomposition of the Function into a more detailed sub process
Application System Type	Application System Type Diagram	Decomposition of the systems into sub-systems, modules and IT functions
Organisational Unit Type	Organisation Chart	Description of the organisational set-up of the involved businesses
Information Carrier	None	However, the Technical Terms Model or the eERM Model can be assigned to show structure of carried data
Cluster	eERM Model	Formal description of the data structure
Technical Term	Technical Terms Model	Decomposition of the Technical Term into its information structure
Knowledge Category	Knowledge Structure Diagram	Description of the structure of business knowledge
Business Objective	Objective Diagram	Composition / decomposition of the business objectives and description of related critical factors

Attributes

Attributes are populated with values either through the process of drawing the models or by inserting them manually. Apart from storing modelling related information that is necessary for the administration of the databases, models and its objects, additional information about the real world items that the model represents can be added. Special attributes further allow for linking business documents and Web sites or other applications to objects, models, and databases. Thus, although ARIS' attributes are not intended for storing vast amounts of detailed information about the items themselves, a business process model can act as a central repository (Davis, 2001, pp. 25, 97). For convenience, the attributes can also be displayed directly on the model graphic (Davis, 2001, p. 91).

Organisational Objects

Organisational objects represent information on business participants that are involved in the process tasks. Many practitioners model every organisational object, be it a single person, department or a whole organisation, as an organisational unit object which is feasible and keeps the models simple (Davis, 2001, pp. 145, 147). However, a hierarchical approach is more appropriate if complex projects shall be modelled and shared to ensure a common, standard-based approach. Therefore, the detailed relationships between organisational objects can be modelled within the organisational chart model. In both model types, eEPCs and e-business scenario diagram, it is possible to assign organisational chart models to organisational objects (Davis, 2001, p. 145).

Application System Objects

Application system objects represent the IT assets in ARIS that are used to support the business. Many objects exist to define detailed hierarchies of systems, sub systems, software modules, and even specific IT functions. Although in practice only the application system type element is used within the majority of eEPCs, an application system's internal relationships can be displayed in the assignable application system model type (Davis, 2001, p. 148).

If processes are entirely carried out by application systems the corresponding function symbol can be replaced by a designated object called system function (Davis, 2001, p. 150).

Data Objects

Involved data in IT systems and communication can be modelled formally, that is, using recognised modelling standards such as ER-diagrams, or less formally using "business language". Whereas the technical term object is used for modelling data informally from a business perspective, the cluster, entity type and attribute objects represent formal data modelling in ARIS (Davis, 2001, 150). Their internal relationship can be shown via the eERM model type. The technical terms model can be used to model how technical terms map to clusters, entities and attributes of the formal data model (Davis, 2001, p. 151).

Information Carrier Objects

Information carriers can be thought of defining how the data is stored and delivered or "carried" to and from the functions (Davis, 2001, p. 155). Symbols are available for EDI, intranet, Internet, e-mail, fax, and so on. Explicit relationships between the involved data and its carrier can also be modelled (resulting in so called "secondary relationships)" (Davis, 2001, p. 157). However this relationship cannot be modelled (visually) in the e-business scenario diagram type.

Objective Objects

A hierarchy of business objectives and related critical success factors can be modelled within the objectives diagram model. The specific objectives could then be added to an eEPC and assigned on a Function/EPC level to show which process steps support their realisation (Davis, 2001, p. 161).

Knowledge Objects

Knowledge is considered everything that is known to be of relevance to a process (Davis, 2001, p. 158). In process modelling one would not want to try to model all of the knowledge related to the process but only where it was key to a process step (Davis, 2001, p. 158). The ARIS object chosen for knowledge here is the knowledge category object. For more detailed levels, e.g. to represent the structure of knowledge or interrelationships, specific designated model types exist as with the other resources as well. The knowledge structure diagrams are useful models for representing and structuring aspects of business knowledge, thus also facilitating communication and re-use of the latter. For Web services modelling they can be redefined in order to depict available case studies, benefits realised through Web services application, and so on.

Matching Web Service Information with ARIS Constructs

In the following, it is outlined how necessary information supporting Web services evaluation and deployment could be captured as elements of a collaborative business process model created with the ARIS Toolset. Here, a matching between the identified critical information supporting Web services assessment and deployment (Table 6, Table 7, and Table 8) on the one hand and the outlined appropriate ARIS constructs for representation in a collaborative business process model on the other hand is performed. The outcome is shown in Table 11, Table 12, and Table 13.

E-Procurement Scenario

Figure 5 depicts the high-level business processes of the e-procurement scenario modelled with the ARIS Toolset. These processes are presented in an e-business scenario diagram. The header row contains the involved business parties; the following row holds the related business processes and resources. This model is of the "swim lane" type. The column presentation therefore visualises the interface between the two business partners. Electronic communication takes place in form of business document exchanges. Most of the busi-

Table 11. Capturing WS-relevant process and transaction characteristics in process models

Phase	Information domain and type	How to capture in a process model?
	Process characteristics	
2	**Process stability**	To be specified on Function/EPC level as discrete attribute (predefined list)
2	Process repetition frequency	To be specified on Event level as attribute
2, 4	**Process' level of mission-criticality**	To be specified on Function/EPC level as discrete attribute (predefined list) or through colour coding (i.e. representing value of attribute by displaying corresponding Function objects in different, designated colours)
2, 4	**Process's estimated monetary value if quantifiable**	To be possibly specified on Function/EPC level as attribute or through colour coding
	Involved electronic transaction characteristics	
2	**Business transaction type**	Information implicitly available through process structure
2	**Composition requirements**	Relationships of constituting parts of transaction are implicitly available through process structure
2	**Transaction mode**	To be modelled as a discrete attribute (predefined list)
2	**Message delivery requirements**	Information may be attached as to Information Carrier or Function
2	**Failure response requirements**	Information may be attached to Information Carrier or Function
2	**Required processing speed**	To be specified on functional level as attribute
2	**Processing speed guarantees**	To be specified on functional level as attribute
2	**Throughput requirements**	To be specified on functional level as attribute
2	**Scalability requirements**	To be specified on functional level as attribute
2	**Security requirements**	Can be modelled in E-Business Scenario Diagram as designated symbol with own attributes. However, no mapping of the symbol to other diagrams (e.g. eEPCs) is possible. Could alternatively be modelled as attributes of other practical object that was assignable to information carriers or as direct attributes of Information carrier or Function.

ness processes carry an "assignment" symbol in their bottom right corner which depicts the fact that an associated eEPC is available that further details the business process. The user can quickly browse through the models with the help of these visual links. The modelling symbols have been introduced in Figure 4.

The scenario starts with the product catalogue provision by the seller. The catalogue can be provided as a Web services which would be a service to the buyer. An advantage would be the support for heterogeneous systems, that is, the catalogue Web services could be integrated on a Web site, as a small desktop application at the buyer's site, and so on. Upon identification of a specific product need, a purchase requisition is triggered on the buyer's side, who assigns a source of supply which may lead to an update of contract information. Thereafter a purchase order (PO) is created and the material planning system is updated. Upon reception of the purchase order the seller validates it and creates a sales order (SO). A PO acknowledgment (PO Ack) is sent to the buyer who changes the status of the purchase order. The seller provides the required goods and sends an advanced shipping notification (ASN) to the buyer which leads to another update of the PO at the buyer's side. Finally the goods are shipped and an invoice is created and transmitted to the buyer. Although no examples could be found, the invoicing process might prove suitable for Web services integration. The buyer confirms the reception of the goods, updates his material planning, and verifies the invoice upon arrival. A payment notification is sent to the seller when the invoice has been verified. In addition, message

Table 12. Capturing WS-relevant system, data and partners characteristics in process models

	Information domain and type	How to capture in a process model?
	Involved systems' characteristics	
1, 2	**Description of internal structure and functionality**	To be described as attribute of Application System Type Module or IT Function
2	**Capacity utilisation level**	To be specified as attribute of Application System or Module
2	**Costs (initial & maintenance)**	Same as above
2	**Existing interfaces**	Supported input and output formats to be specified as Data objects and/or as attributes of Application System
2	**Used communication protocols**	Depicted through information carrier
2	**Systems ability/likelihood to change**	To be specified as discrete attribute (predefined list) of Application System or Module
	Involved data's characteristics	
3	**Data format, standards compliance**	To be described as attribute of Cluster object and specified in eERM model if complex
2	**Dynamics, frequency of change**	To be specified as attribute of Cluster object
2	**Importance of timeliness**	To be specified as discrete attribute (predefined list) of Cluster object
2	**Required level of data security**	To be described as attribute of Cluster object
	Involved business partners' characteristics	
2, 3	**Total number of involved parties**	Derived from relationships with Organisational Units
4	**Frequency of cooperation**	Discrete attribute (predefined list) of Organisational Unit
4	**Importance of business partner**	As above
3	**Autonomy, degree of individuality**	As above
3	**Existing level of business trust**	As above
3	Existing process insight and manageability, shared meaning	As above (possibly multiple attributes)
3.	**Existing technological base**	Implicitly contained in model through Application Systems if process & resource insight is granted
3.	**Existing IT skill base**	Same as **Frequency of cooperation**
	Types of characteristics of the involved business parties could also be modelled as redefined Knowledge Category objects and be assigned to the organisational objects representing the business participants via the Knowledge Map model type.	
	Examples, first implementations and maturity, risks, and pitfalls	
3, 4	Can be referenced as attribute on Function/EPC level. Colour coding could be used to assign the implementation's level of maturity on the Function/EPC level (designated colours for discrete levels of maturity). Could alternatively be modelled as redefined Knowledge Category objects that could be assigned on Function/EPC level and colour coded according to the maturity. The advantage of using Knowledge Category objects is that they could carry further details (e.g. experienced issues, benefits) in assigned Knowledge Structure Diagrams.	

Table 13. Capturing information for Web service deployment in a business process model

Information domain and type - Web Service deployment -	How to capture in a process model?
Business purpose for Web Service	
Business drivers could be captured in several plausible ways, as: a) a discrete attribute (predefined list + free text if value not yet in list) on Function/EPC level. b) redefined specific Knowledge Category objects. The advantage would be that these objects could then be directly assigned to Functions as well as be included in Knowledge Structure diagrams detailing known Web Service implementations. Objective objects can only be assigned to Functions. c) a discrete attribute (predefined list + free text if value not yet in list) of the Knowledge Category objects which refer to first implementations and are assigned to Functions. d) Objective objects in a hierarchical Objective Diagram + assigned on Function/EPC level after first Web services projects.	
Interaction patterns	
Interaction type classifications could be captured in several plausible ways, as: a) a discrete attribute (predefined list + free text if value not yet in list) on Function/EPC level. b) redefined specific Knowledge Category objects (that could be part of a Knowledge Structure Diagram attached to a Knowledge Category object for first implementations) c) Comments, after first own or reported projects. d) a discrete attribute (predefined list + free text if value not yet in list) of the Knowledge Category objects which refer to first implementations and are assigned to Functions. This is recommended, because it constitutes a simple, discrete type of information.	
Relationship type	
See **Interaction patterns** above	
Service semantics	
Functional service properties	To be described on Function/EPC level as attributes or as attributes of the Knowledge Category objects representing Web services examples
Non-functional service properties	To be described on Function/EPC level as attributes or as attributes of the Knowledge Category objects representing Web services examples
Service ontology & capabilities	To be described on Function/EPC level as attributes or as attributes of the Knowledge Category objects representing Web services examples
Misc.	
Information can be included that is critical or has proven to be important in the past	To be captured in model as attributes, Comments or Knowledge Objects

exchange is required for PO amendment, status querying, and further notifications. Existing Web services solutions are attached to the model in the form of comments. Comments are also attached to processes where Web services applications should be clearly considered, for example, automation of (parts of) contracts, support for the invoice process, and purchase order changes.

Figure 6 depicts the process "Create ASN" in greater detail. The representation chosen is an eEPC model. The column type gives a corresponding "swim lane" view on the involved business parties. In ARIS the model shows up after a double click on the assignment symbol of the "Create ASN" process in the e-business diagram. The model shows the required activities and resulting states to carry out the business process. It also includes involved application systems, data and information carriers and their interrelationships. Applications systems and data can be further detailed in related diagrams such as the eEPC in Figure 6. The activities (function objects) supported through Web services carry a Knowledge object that represents the corresponding type of Web services example, differentiated according to their maturity, that is, research prototype, vendor proposal, success

Figure 5. High-level processes for e-procurement in e-business diagram

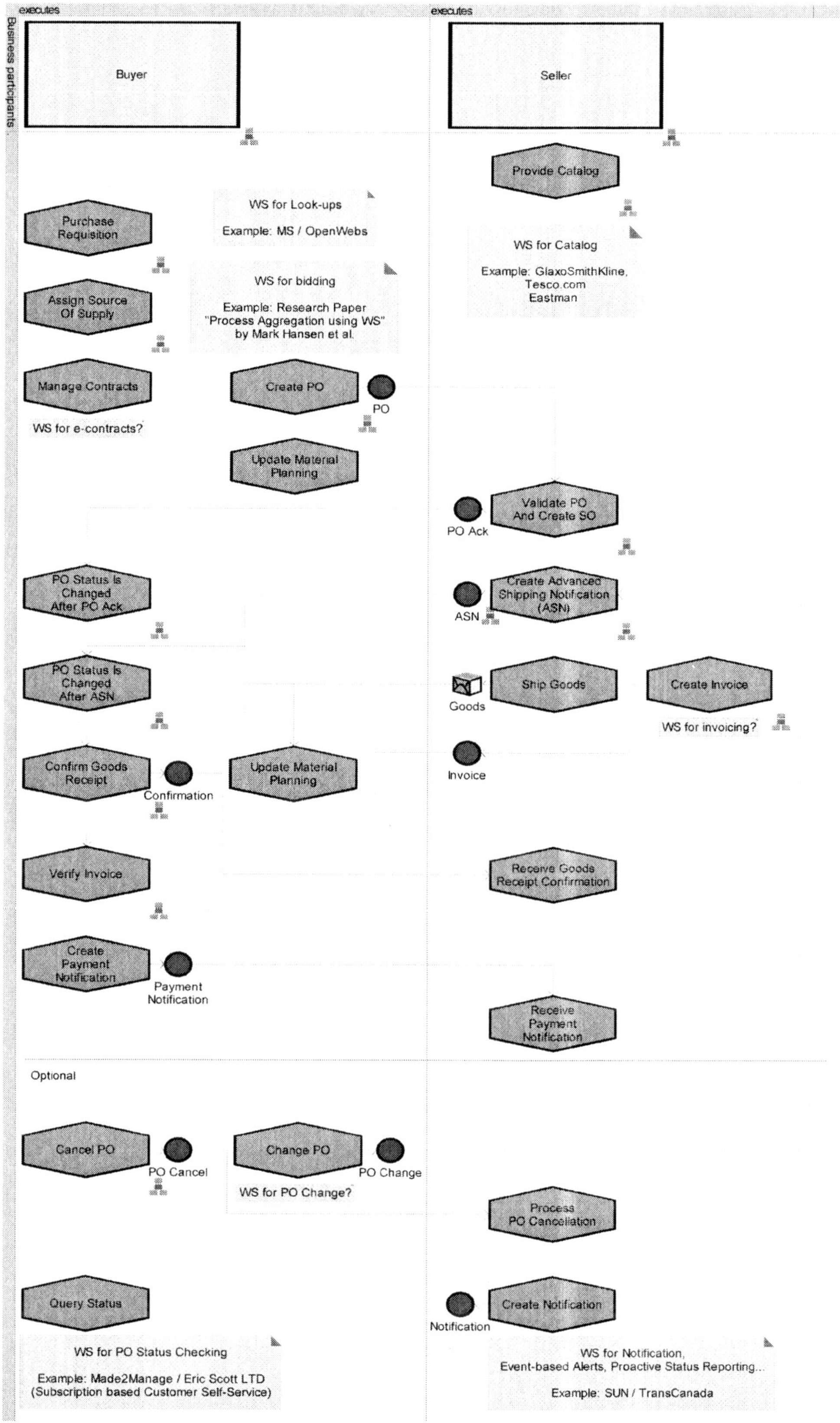

Figure 6. Seller's process "Create ASN" in greater detail via an eEPC

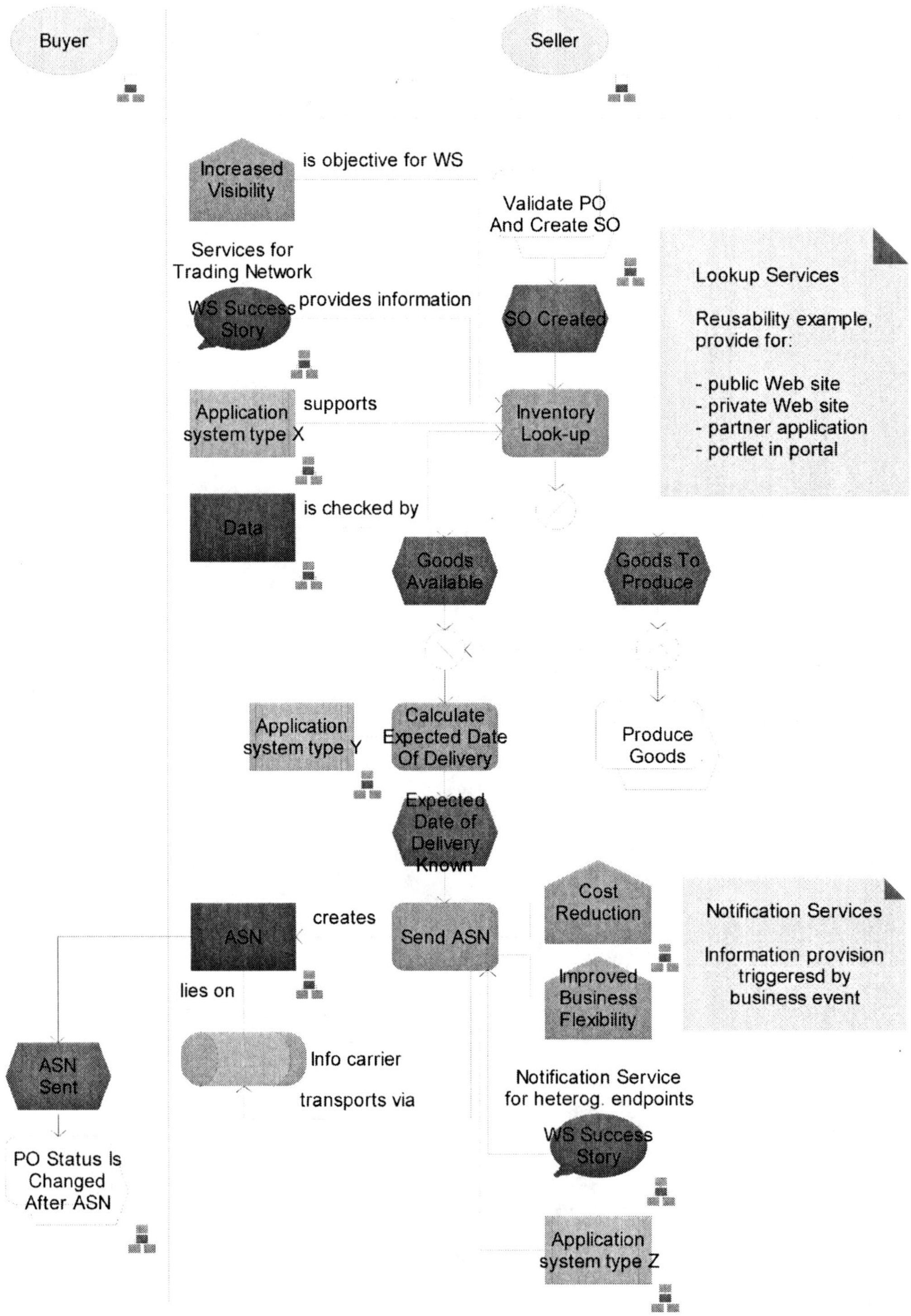

story. The different degree of maturity is depicted through colour coding of the knowledge objects (i.e., predefined colours for low maturity, moderate maturity, high maturity: red (darker shade), yellow (lighter shade), and green (medium shade). The Web services examples can be detailed in knowledge structure diagrams, which can include information about benefits, issues and hyperlinks to relevant documents.

CONCLUSION

This paper addressed one of the currently perceived issues surrounding Web services, namely the lack of a sound methodology to demonstrate the actual business impact of Web services adoption in specific settings. The main contributions are: (a) a process-oriented framework for systematic assessment of Web service adoption opportunities including checklists and scoring tables; (b) a structured set of identified critical information for Web services evaluation and deployment through business process models; and (c) a mapping of this information types into ARIS constructs, thus enabling the representation of this information in a business process model.

The study has drawn on an extensive review of the literature as well as reported case studies and best practices. From these resources, a list of assessment criteria for potential application areas of Web services could be derived. These criteria were then tested through an e-procurement scenario and refined through feedback obtained from focus groups.

Further research leading to the refinement, extension, and testing of the proposed assessment methodology is needed. In particular, the methodology could be extended by depicting trade-offs between benefits and risks of Web services deployment. Also, additional requirements for the methodology should be identified through further case studies, and the implementation of the proposed methodology in other tools than ARIS should be considered. Finally, it would be highly desirable to test the proposed methodology with potential users in order to identify and understand the risks and pitfalls of its application.

Another relevant direction for future work is the exploration of requirements that collaborative e-business interactions impose on business process modelling and Web services as well as their implications. Issues that still need to be addressed and overcome include dealing with business trust, semantic heterogeneity and exceptions, all of which were identified as crucial during the focus groups.

ACKNOWLEDGMENTS

The authors are grateful to the participants of the focus groups who remain anonymous due to a confidentiality agreement. The work of the third author has been partly funded by a Queensland Government "Smart State Fellowship" co-sponsored by SAP Research.

REFERENCES

Adams, H., Gisolfi, D., Snell, J., & Varadan, R. (2002). *Best practices for Web services: Back to the basics, Part 2*. IBM Developer Works.

Becker, J., Rosemann, M. & Von Uthmann, C. (2000). Guidelines of business process modeling. In W. van der Aalst, J. Sedel, & A. Oberweis (Eds.), *Business process management: Models techniques and empirical studies* (pp. 30-49). Berlin: Springer-Verlag.

Bibby, A. & Brea, C. (2003). Business process reengineering through Web services: A user-experience perspective. *Web Services Journal, 2*(9), 39-42.

Bielski, L. (2003). Web services goes live: One deployment at a time. *ABA Banking Journal, 95*(7), 49-58.

Burdett, D. (2003). *The business Web services scorecard: Using Web services for business—The present and the future*. Commerce One Operations Inc.

Chen, M. (2003). Factors affecting the adoption and diffusion of XML and Web services standards for E-business systems. *International Journal of Human-Computer Studies, 58*(3), 259.

Christiansen, S. (2002, December 8-13). *The business case for XML Web services*. Paper presented at the XML Conference 2002, Baltimore, MD.

Curtis, B., Keller, M. I., & Over, J. (1992). Process modeling. *Communications of ACM, 35*(9).

Davis, R. (2001). *Business process modelling with ARIS: A practical guide*. London: Springer.

ebXML Business Process Team. (2002). *Business process and business document modeling worksheets and guidelines*. Retrieved June 1, 2003, from http://www.collaborativedomain.com/standards/documents/bpWS-1.05-2%20DRAFT%20(May%2016).doc

Estrem, W. A. (in press). An evaluation framework for deploying Web Services in the next generation manufacturing enterprise. *Robotics and Computer-Integrated Manufacturing* (Corrected Proof).

Glushko, R. J. & McGrath, T. (2002). Document engineering for e-business. *Proceedings of the 2002 ACM Symposium on Document Engineering* (pp. 42-48). ACM Press.

Hagel, J., III & Brown, J. S. (2002). *Orchestrating business processes—Harnessing the value of Web services technology*. Retrieved June 1, 2003, from http://www.johnhagel.com/paper_orchestratingwebservices.pdf

Hagel, J., III, Brown, J. S., & Layton-Rodin, D. (2002). *The secret to creating value from Web services today: Start simply*. Retrieved June 1, 2003, from http://www.johnhagel. com/paper_startsimply.pdf

Hammer, M. & Champy, J. (1993). *Reengineering the corporation. A manifesto for reengineering*. New York: Harper Business.

IBM. (2003). *IBM patterns for e-business*. Retrieved September 1, 2003, from http://www-106.ibm.com/developerworks/patterns/

IDS Scheer (2002). *ARIS Methods (for Version 6)*. Technical manual, IDS Scheer, Sarbrucken, Germany.

Jost, W. & Wagner, K. (2002). The ARIS Toolset. In A. W. Scheer, F. Abolhassan, W. Jost, & M. Kirchmer (Eds.), *Business process excellence: ARIS in practice* (pp. 16-31). Berlin Heidelberg New York: Springer.

Keeney, R. & Raiffa, H. (1993). *Decisions with multiple objectives: Preferences and value tradeoffs*. Cambridge University Press.

Linthicum, D. S. (2002). *An application integration value-add? expoQ's David Linthicum on Web services in EAI*. Retrieved August 18, 2003, from http://searchwebservices.techtarget.com/originalContent/0,289142,sid26_gci 788646,00.html

Morgan, D. L. (1988). *Focus groups as qualitative research* (Vol. 16). Newbury Park, California: SAGE Publications.

National Health Supply Chain Taskforce Interoperability Working Group. (2002). *Electronically connecting trading partners: A proposed interoperability standard*. National Health Supply Chain Taskforce Interoperability Working Group.

New Mexico State University - College of Agriculture and Home Economics. (1999). *1999-2003 evaluation handbook*. Retrieved June 1, 2003, from http://www.cahe.nmsu.edu/grants/evaluation/eval_section2.html#focus

Papazoglou, M. (2003). Web services and business transactions. *World Wide Web Journal, 6*(1), 49-91.

Patricia Seybold Group. (2002). *An executive's guide to Web services*. Patricia Seybold Group.

Remenyi, D., Money, A., Sherwood-Smith, M., & Irani, Z. (2000). *Effective measurement and management of IT costs and benefits* (2nd ed.). Butterworth-Heinemann.

Robins, B., Sleeper, B., & McTiernan, C. (2003). *Web services rules: Real-world lessons from early adopters*. The Stencil Group.

Samtani, G. & Sadhwani, D. (2002). ROI and Web services. In *Web service business strategies and architectures*. New York: Expert Press.

Saulnier, C. F. (2000). Groups as data collection method and data analysis technique: Multiple perspectives on urban social work education. *Small Group Research, 31*(5), 607-627.

Scheer, A. W. (1998a). *ARIS - Business process frameworks*. Berlin: Springer.

Scheer, A. W. (1998b). *ARIS - Business process modelling*. Berlin: Springer.

Scheer, A. W., Abolhassan, F., Jost, W., & Kirchmer, M. (2002). *Business process excellence: ARIS in practice*. Heidelberg: Springer.

Schmelzer, R. & Bloomberg, J. (2002, June 18). *Want to service-enable your enterprise? Model first!* Retrieved June 1, 2003, from http://searchwebservices.techtarget.com/tip/1,289483,sid26_gci833705,00.html

Scholler, D. (2003, April 7). *Web services architecture: Part 1—Service development excellence*. Retrieved June 1, 2003, from http://www.ge-bac.com/article.php?story= 20030407225246949

Singh, M. P. & Huhns, M. N. (2005). *Service-oriented computing: Semantics, processes, agents*. John Wiley & Sons.

Soderstrom, E., Andersson, B., Johannesson, P., Perjons, E., & Wangler, B. (2002). Towards a framework for comparing process modeling languages. In A. Banks, Pidduck et al. (Eds.), *Proceedings of CAiSE 2002* (pp. 600-611). Heidelberg: Springer.

Sofaer, S., Kreling, B., Kenney, E., Swift, E. K., & Dewart, T. (2001). Family members and friends who help beneficiaries make health decisions. *Health Care Financing Review; Washington, 23*(1), 16.

The Stencil Group. (2002). *The laws of evolution: A pragmatic analysis of the emerging Web services market*. The Stencil Group.

Wilkov, R. (2002). *How to get real value from Web services... today*. Retrieved June 1, 2003, from http://www.ebizq.net/topics/dev_tools/features/1567.html

Wright, D. (2002). *Beyond the hype: How to make Web services work for your organization, Part 2—How to begin to use Web services in your business*. Retrieved June 1, 2003, from http://www.lightshipinc.com/lightship/download/download.aspx? Title=BeyondHypePart2

This work was previously published in International Journal of E-Business Research, Vol. 2, Issue 1, edited by I. Lee, pp. 19-44, copyright 2006 by IGI Publishing, formerly known as Idea Group Publishing (an imprint of IGI Global).

Chapter XV
Application of Web Services in the Context of E-Procurement: An SME Foci

Stanley Oliver
University of Bolton, UK

Kiran Maringanti
University of Bolton, UK

ABSTRACT

This chapter highlights the importance of e-procurement and the barriers affecting its widespread adoption in the context of small and medium enterprises. The chapter takes a technical perspective and critically analyzes the importance of information systems in the procurement domain and the integration challenges faced by SMEs in today's digitally networked economy. Next, the role of XML-based Web services in solving the integration challenges faced by SMEs is discussed. Subsequently, a procurement transformation framework enabled by Web services which provides a clear methodology of the way in which information systems should be introduced in the procurement domain is discussed. The chapter concludes by a discussion of the measures that must be undertaken by various stakeholders like the government and universities in increasing the awareness levels of SMEs to the latest e-business mechanisms.

INTRODUCTION

Micro, small and medium-sized enterprises (SMEs) play a central role in the world economy. They are a major source of entrepreneurial skills, innovation, and employment. There are an estimated 75 million SMEs worldwide, which represent about 99 percent of all companies (IBM, 1998). Zheng, Caldwell, Harland, Powell, Woerndl, and Xu (2004) find that the "Internet presents many opportunities for SMEs to harness the benefits of Information and Communications Technologies (ICT)" (p. 27-39). E-procurement, which is the utilization of the Internet in enabling and streamlining the entire procurement cycle, has been identified as a very important area of concentration for SMEs (ABI, 2003; OGC, 2005). "Electronic procurement specifically and eCommerce generally will knit supplier and buyer business processes together to deliver seamless transactions" (Cavinato & Kauffman, 2000). Large enterprises have already invested huge amounts of resources in e-procurement and are reaping the benefits of it. E-procurement is being championed by larger enterprises, mainly to save transaction costs and reduce prices. But potentially they also offer opportunities for SMEs to find new business partners and to benefit from closer integration into the value chains of large companies (ABI, 2003).

It is pertinent to study the impact of e-procurement on SMEs owing to many factors:

1. Many large organizations' supplier base consists of small and medium enterprises (SMEs), and without the full participation of these SMEs, the initiatives of large corporations will not be successful.
2. The application of emerging information technologies (IT) has often proven to be a complex job for SMEs.
3. SMEs are often at a disadvantage in terms of finance, technology, human resource development, and networking (UN-ECE, 1997); in the case of information technologies, the task seems even more daunting, owing to the highly complex evolving process and also the challenge in successfully deciphering a business case for the justification of its investment.

In this chapter, we will look at the evolution of procurement and look at the importance of e-procurement for SMEs. We will also look at the barriers to the widespread adoption of e-procurement and how the deployment of Web services will help overcome those barriers.

BACKGROUND

This section offers primary insight into procurement, e-procurement, inter-organizational information systems, and supply chain management. We believe these areas are closely knitted and usually overlapping.

Procurement

Every business, irrespective of its size and sector, are involved in some form of buying and selling. Procurement is an unavoidable and important business function. A typical firm spends at least half of its revenues on external purchases of goods and services (Markham, Morales, & Slaight, 2000). Procurement is defined by Gebauer, Beam, and Segev (1998) as "including all activities involved in obtaining, transporting and moving material towards the production process." Though procurement has long been overlooked as a backwater, repetitive function, nevertheless it is indispensable, it forms the bedrock of the company, and it is a core business function. A study made by AT Kearney on European and North American manufacturers found that in 1985, 30% of the total manufacturing cost stemmed from purchased material and services. In 1995, the figure rose to 55%, and for 2005, it was estimated to rise to 85%, which makes procurement a very important function (Knusden, 2003). Since the procurement process is located at the beginning of the value chain, any ripples created here will be echoed right across the supply chain. But traditional procurement processes are muddled with inefficiencies, and leave scope for non-compliance with existing procurement policies.

Procurement, purchasing, and supply management are simply different terms used in the literature to describe the same activity. But we prefer the usage of the term "procurement." Knusden (2003) justifies the usage of the term "procurement" by asserting that "it neither rules of the operational nor the strategic aspect of acquiring external resources." Procurement is the name given to a very broad purchasing function which includes basic steps like making a requisition for goods, to much more complex aspects like sourcing and logistics. Thus, the scope of procurement is very wide, making it a very important component of supply chain management. Typically, a company's procurement function is subdivided into strategic and operational processes, since activities and priorities in these two areas are entirely different (Kaufmann, 1999; Lamming, 1995), as depicted in Figure 1.

However, traditionally procurement was often neglected as a back room function. A glance at the organization chart of many organizations reveals that purchasing departments are located in many areas of the organization. Separate purchasing departments for manufacturing and sales made it difficult to have a centralized purchasing policy. Heywood, Barton, and Heywood (2002, p. 8) note that "traditional buyers have long argued that their work does not lend itself to automation because much of the information that appears on a purchase order or contract is unstructured text, and most purchasing systems find this difficult to accommodate. A blank purchase order with terms and conditions written in the very small lettering on the back is the way they like to work. Because there was never a big push from the buyers to automate, traditional purchasing departments were usually left to their own devices and persisted with manual paper systems that satisfied only the needs of the buyers."

This is one of the reasons why procurement functions were never automated, as insufficient emphasis was placed on this important corporate function. Neef (2001) notes "traditionally, the external resources that were acquired by the company have been broken down into two major categories, that is, Direct and Indirect goods."

1. **Direct goods:** Typically, direct goods are 80% by value and 20% by volume of many organizations expenditure on procurement. Direct goods include goods which are used in the production of core products and services of the company. Direct goods are central to the running of the business, and are very crucial because any disruption in this area of purchasing can cause havoc and ultimately challenge the survival of the company. Procurement strategies for direct goods assume the highest significance for any company and have to be planned with utmost care. They improve the efficiency of the company, which in turn will help it in gaining competitive advantage in the market.
2. **Indirect goods:** Typically, indirect goods are 20% by value and 80% by volume. Indirect goods can be classified as goods which aid in the running of the business. Indirect goods are classified again as below.
   - **Maintenance, retail, and operation (MRO):** MRO goods are very crucial to the business as these include obtaining parts for the various machinery

Figure 1. Procurement classification model (Source: Authors)

Procurement	
Strategic	**Transactional**
Sourcing • Define suppliers • Prequalify suppliers • Establish contracts • Manage supplier relationships	*Purchasing* • Recognize need • Generate order • Receive materials • Settle invoice

and other high-end instruments which perform the actual production.

- **Office supplies:** Office supplies include all other expenditure which is helpful in performing routine jobs. These include stationery, lighting, and so forth. These are not mission-critical goods and can be bought at any period with off-contract suppliers as they can be substituted easily.

Complexity is an inherent attribute of procurement. Companies have always been trying to simplify this extremely crucial aspect of their business, in extracting optimal quality and accurate transactions at a lowest possible cost. For example, Figure 2 demonstrates the routine tasks involved on the operational side of a traditional procurement life cycle. As garnered, the process was very labor-intensive, which was a source of inefficiency in most organizations. The solution to cut down drastically on the inefficiency was through the introduction of information systems. Thus, the concept of inter-organizational information systems (IOIS) came to the fore.

Inter-Organizational Information System (IOIS)

Generally, the need for sharing procurement-related information is found to be on a higher scale between participant organizations. The emergence of IOIS attempted to solve that problem. An IOIS is defined as a computer and communication infrastructure, crossing company boundaries and enabling information sharing (Cash & Konsynski, 1985). IOIS facilitate technology-based cooperation across organizations (Bakos, 1991). Basically, IOIS enables two companies to exchange business-related documents in some pre-agreed proprietary format. As processes evolved, we saw the rise of electronic data interchange (EDI), a variant of IOIS during the period of the 1980s.

Figure 2. Traditional procurement process (Source: Heywood et al., 2002)

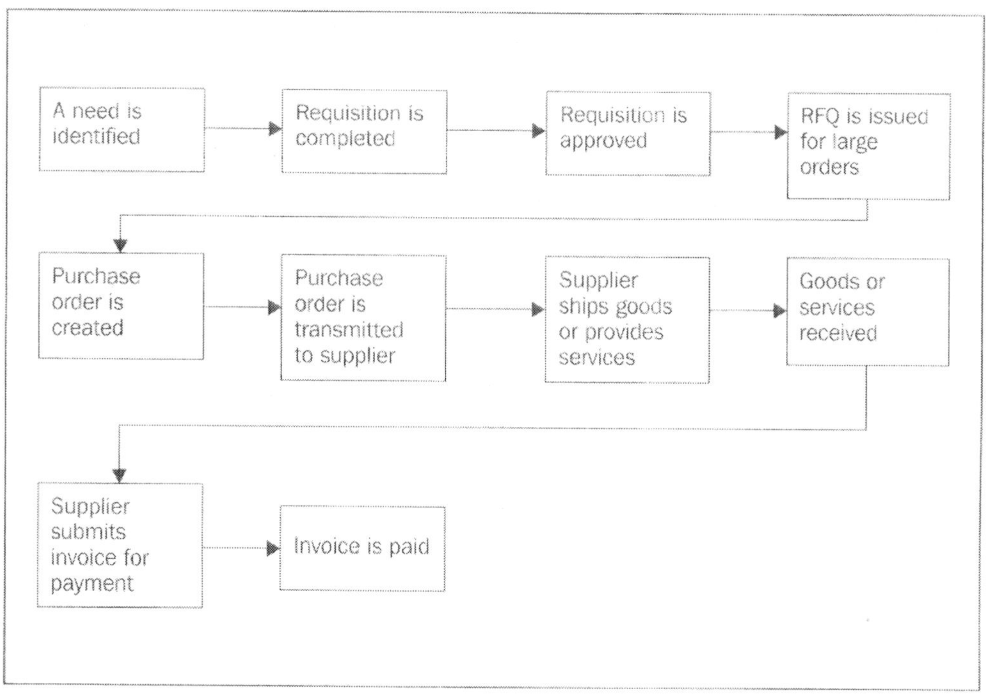

Electronic Data Interchange (EDI)

Electronic Data Interchange has been around for a long time and has been widely used for the exchange of business documents by large firms. EDI is often confined to data exchange using EDI VAN (value added network) or EDI standard protocols such as UN/EDIFACT (United Nations/EDI for Administration, Commerce and Transport) and ANSI (American National Standards Institute) ASC (Accredited Standards Committee) x12 (Shimada, 2004). Many large firms have been applying technology to the purchasing process for several decades through electronic data interchange (EDI). It was still expensive to implement, often running into millions of dollars (Presutti, 2002). However, the high costs associated with EDI can be afforded only by the large companies (Khazanchi, 1999). Competing standards, high-entry barriers and lack of suitability for real-time transactions meant that EDI was not an option for SMEs. But with the anvil of e-business, the concept of doing business electronically with a multitude of partners has become affordable for even the SME community.

E-Business

Human race has been involved in buying and selling of products and services to each other for as long as recorded history. McMillan (2002) notes that the "trading of goods and services for other goods or for money is central to the concept of human socialization." While the basic philosophy has remained the same, means of achieving the ends have changed profoundly. The success of the PC-based model of computing, coupled with the emergence of the World Wide Web, has opened up new and exciting opportunities for businesses. The Internet in general, and in particular, e-business has changed the centuries-old practices/methods dramatically at an unprecedented pace. Businesses all over the globe wanted to gain the benefits offered by this new channel of communication. While the most visible manifestation of the Internet has been in the emergence of electronic commerce as a new retail channel, it is likely that the Internet will have a profound impact on business-to-business interaction, especially in the area of supply chain integration.

The consumer-centric business-to-commerce (B2C) model dominated the embryonic stages of the Internet. But it will be their B2B successors who will leverage the full potential of this new-found electronic economy. Gartner Group, an IT research firm, predicted that the worldwide B2B market would be $ 7.2 trillion by 2003. True to predictions, B2B/e-business is already the fastest growth area in the superheated new Internet economy and carries potential almost beyond measure. In the field of e-business, e-procurement is regarded as having far greater potential for cost savings and business improvements than online retailing or enterprise resource planning systems (Aberdeen, 2000; Neef, 2001). Many studies have clearly indicated that the biggest savings from e-business initiatives will occur in the area of e-procurement (Knusden, 2003).

Supply Chain Management (SCM)

Supply chain management can be described as the chain linking each element of the manufacturing and supply process from raw materials to the end user, encompassing several organizational boundaries (New & Payne, 1995; Scott & Westbrook, 1991). Increasingly, organizations are looking to squeeze costs out of the supply chain to gain competitive advantage over other firms. Christopher (1998) also notes that the goal of supply chain management is to link the marketplace, the distribution network, the manufacturing process, and the procurement activity in such a way that customers are serviced at higher levels but at lower total cost. Seventy percent of a firm's sales revenues are, on average, spent on supply chain-related activities from material purchases to the distribution and service of finished products to the final customer (Presutti, 2002). Supply chain management has thus evolved into a very important area of study for many researchers and companies attributable to the symbiotic relationship between supply chain and organizational performance. Supply chain management is seen as paramount to delivering high customer satisfaction with reduced lead times and costs (Bhattacharya, Coleman, & Brace, 1996).

The emergence of e-business has provided a fresh impetus for re-invigorating the supply chain. Today, there is an increased use of geographically-dispersed suppliers by firms to retain their competitive advantages. This act requires a high degree of orchestration between the geographically-dispersed partners. The role played by information technology in synchronizing these partners is profound. Cagliano, Caniato, and Spina (2003) note that "e-business is particularly important for the supply chain literature as a consequence of the increasing need to integrate activities and information flows and to optimize the processes not only at the single company level, but also at the level of inter-company processes." Chen and Meixell (2003) point towards the symbiotic relationship between supply chain management and information technology. Due to the dynamic nature of supply chain management, new breed information technologies can offer significant contributions in optimizing supply chains for better performance. This makes SCM more responsive to the dynamics of the marketplace. E-procurement is a subset of supply chain management.

E-PROCUREMENT AND SMES

E-procurement is a collective term for a range of e-business software solutions which utilize the latest information and communication technologies (especially the Internet), that can be employed to automate the internal and external processes associated with strategic sourcing and purchasing, which includes catalogue search, item requisition request, approval, purchase order, delivery, receiving, payment, identification of sourcing opportunities, supplier evaluation, negotiation, and contract. Examples of the e-business software solutions include e-procurement software, business-to-business (B2B) auctions, B2B market exchanges, purchasing consortia, e-tendering, e-auctions, e-marketplaces, and e-sourcing.

The e-business software solutions that aid the procurement process automation utilize the latest information and communication technologies, such as electronic data interchange, Internet, e-mail, software and hardware, but excludes other means of communication such as telephone, fax, and so forth. E-procurement technologies fundamentally aim to hammer out inefficiencies associated with manual-based procurement systems.

From the above discussion, we can deduce that e-procurement is mainly the effective utilization of the modern Internet standards for streamlining the entire corporate procurement activities. The emergence of e-procurement, which leverages the potential of the Internet to improve the procurement process, has gathered considerable interest amongst academia and business practitioners.

Benefits of E-Procurement to SMEs

We spoke about how e-procurement can help organizations in improving over traditional procurement processes. Especially for an SME, if they adopt electronic procurement, a small percentage of savings in procurement expenses can help them reduce operation costs and improve the profit margin considerably, as procurement is an expensive business activity. This improves their competitiveness as well, which would ultimately benefit the economy (Chan & Lee, 2003).

This section lists the benefits of e-procurement which are exclusive to SMEs, as highlighted by many authors (ABI, 2003; NEPP, 2004; Office of Government Commerce, 2002):

- Competition with any other supplier, regardless of their size; any supplier with access to the Internet is now on a par with even the largest suppliers
- Being strategically valuable, as it helps them to win other business elsewhere
- Receiving payment more quickly as there is less of a paper chase at the buyer end
- Business does not need to be limited to one geographical area
- Removal of some of the process costs associated with supplying to government
- Efficiency (doing things better through pure cost reduction in current procurement and selling business processes)
- Effectiveness (doing better things, through supply chain integration driving costs out of the supply chain, and strategic sourcing to establish new competitive supply sources)
- Evolution (doing things differently promoted through transparency and intelligence)
- B2B re-engineering (promoting business intelligence and transparency in the customer and supply chain partners and encouraging innovation through collaboration)

But on a precautionary note, it must be understood that e-procurement does not replace procurement. E-procurement is only a strategic tool that enhances the entire procurement operation. The aim that an e-procurement system attempts to achieve could be divided into two categories, that is, internal and external, as depicted in Figure 3.

The functionality that is set forth to be achieved on the internal side of e-procurement could be achieved through either:

- An ERP system
- Specialized e-procurement software

The functionality that is set forth to be achieved on the external side of e-procurement could be achieved through:

- B2B marketplaces
- E-auctions
- e-tendering

There is no particular variant of e-procurement that will dominate the entire industry. Different models are suitable for different industries, and the kind of solution to be embraced is also dictated by the size of the company. Davila, Gupta, and Palmer (2003) note that "e-procurement software and B2B auctions are better suited to the needs of large corporations, while market exchanges and purchasing consortia better serve the needs of smaller companies and non-profits." Thus, electronic marketplaces have been identified as the preferred way for SMEs to conduct electronic procurement.

New, Meakin, and Southworth (2002) note that "one of the most misleading aspects of much

Figure 3. Essentials of a good e-procurement system

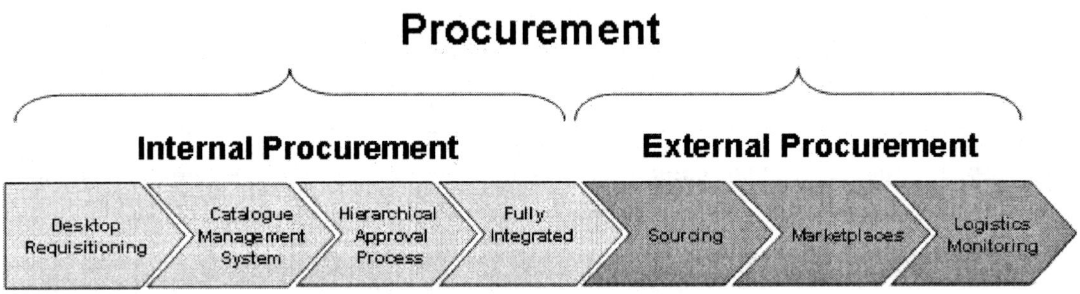

that has been written about the Internet and its effects on organizations is the lumping together of different types of organizations operating in different types of markets. Firms differ in many significant ways." Echoing the above thoughts, firms, especially SMEs, vary significantly in their procurement patterns, and it is often difficult to prescribe a particular model for a group of firms. Instead, SMEs have to mix and match solutions that best serve their purpose from the wide gamut of e-procurement solutions available.

B2B Marketplaces

B2B marketplaces are the umbrella term which embraces all variants of external e-procurement models. There are many names by which B2B marketplaces are addressed. In this chapter, they would be addressed as B2B marketplaces as they focus on business-to-business transactions and engage in product, service, or information exchange between buyers and sellers. "The existence of Marketplaces in human society has a long history from before the agora of Ancient Greece to the online trading places of the 21st century" (Stockdale & Standing, 2004). The concept of an Electronic Marketplace dates back to the mid-1940s, when the first documented EM system, known as Selevision, was used to remote-market Florida citrus (Henderson, 1984).

B2B marketplaces basically provide the infrastructure for the transfer of information, service, or product between the concerned partners. The ability of the marketplaces to interoperate extends the idea of liquidity and network effect by joining more buyers with more suppliers, but does not sacrifice the ability of each marketplace to be highly specific to the supply-chain node or target buyer group it serves. B2B marketplaces have emerged as the best mechanism to unlock that value, which aligns buyers and sellers in product or industry-focused Internet marketplaces for the exchange of goods and services (Aberdeen Group, 2001).

Schmid (1993) and Bakos (1991) consider B2B marketplaces as manifestations of the neo-classical market ideal, reducing transaction costs to a negligible minimum. Malone, Yates, and Benjamin (1987) conclude that markets are the preferred coordination mechanism for products with low asset specificity and low product description complexity. B2B marketplaces offer compelling features like price discovery, aggregation of buyers and sellers, automation of processes, and expanding markets to buyers and sellers (Bakos, 1998; Kaplan & Sawhney, 2000). However, there have been various viewpoints on the positioning of B2B marketplaces:

- Is a B2B/e-marketplace an inter-organizational information system? (Bakos, 1991)
- Is a B2B/e-marketplace an e-procurement solution? (Segev & Gebauer, 1999)
- Is a B2B/e-marketplace a medium? (Schmid & Lindemann, 1998)
- Is a B2B/e-marketplace a meeting point? (Kaplan & Sawhney, 2000)
- Is a B2B/e-marketplace an intermediary? (Dai & Kauffman, 2000)
- Is a B2B/e-marketplace just a listing? (Bradley & Peters, 1997)

We consider that B2B marketplaces fall under the ambit of e-procurement, which is consistent with Segev and Gebauer (1999) who note that "compared to many other electronic procurement solutions, electronic marketplaces represent a relatively neutral position between buyer and seller, providing services to both sides of a transaction. An electronic marketplace represents a virtual place where buyers and sellers meet to exchange goods and services."

The electronic markets hypothesis (EMH) by Malone, Yates, and Benjamin (1987) predicted that electronic marketplaces will be the favored mechanisms for coordinating material and information flows among organizations in the presence of electronic communication technologies. True to their hypothesis, the rise of the B2B marketplaces has been stupendous. Technically, e-marketplaces are more strategic by enabling firms to interact with other firms in a market setting than electronic data interchange (EDI) systems in a relational setting (Grewal, Comer, & Mehta, 2001).

B2B Marketplaces Classification

Generally, B2B marketplaces can be classified into public, private, and industrial/consortia marketplace.

- **Public marketplace***:* A public marketplace could also be termed as a third-party or a neutral marketplace. They provide content, value-added services, and transaction capabilities.
- **Private marketplace:** Private marketplaces are exclusively the networks built by large enterprises to deal with their group of suppliers. In these kinds of marketplaces, the establisher of the network provides the infrastructure, and thus it is tightly integrated with the enterprises and its suppliers. Typical examples of such kind of marketplaces are Click2Procure (Siemens), Wal-Mart, and UPS.
- **Industrial or consortia marketplace:** Industrial marketplaces are generally established by a group of large enterprises to leverage their buying power. In these kinds of environments, the marketplaces are integrated with the establishing enterprises. Examples of such marketplaces are Covisint, E2Open, and so forth.

Barriers to Electronic Procurement for SMEs

Numerous studies highlight the fact that the adoption of e-business among SMEs is not in tune with the expectations, and the reasons cited are numerous. Many studies have been conducted to investigate the inhibitors to the adoption of e-business among SMEs. MacGregor and Vrazalic (2005) summarize the inhibitors to the adoption of e-business among SMEs.

A study conducted by Davila et al., (2003) has pointed out that user's of e-procurement technologies report that they can acquire goods over the Internet from only 15% of the supply base. A majority of suppliers in the supply base are SMEs because of their common role as suppliers for dominating manufacturers (Hauser, 2000).

This indicates that the uptake of e-procurement is low among small and medium enterprises. However, the barriers related to the adoption of e-procurement among SMEs and the solutions to overcome those barriers is an under-researched area, and there exists very little rigorous academic

Figure 4. B2B marketplaces classification

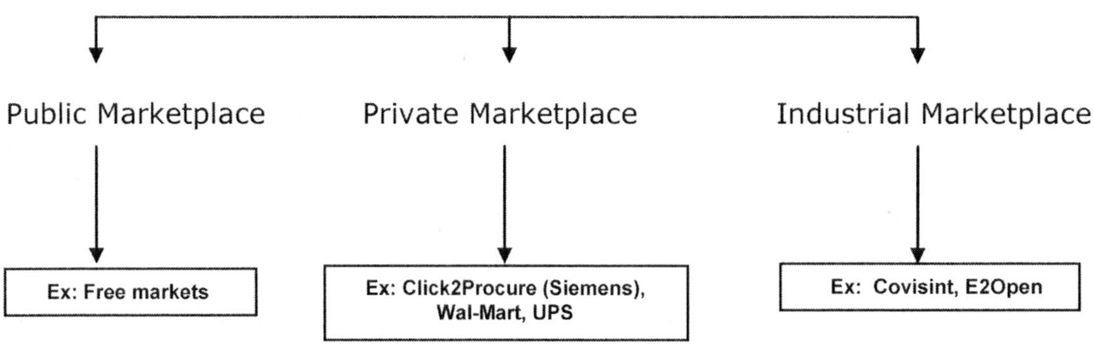

Table 1. Summary of the inhibitors to e-business adoption amongst SMEs (Source: MacGregor & Vrazalic, 2005)

Barriers to E-Commerce Adoption	Related Literature
High cost of e-commerce implementation; Internet technologies are too expensive to implement	Iacovou et al. (1995), Quayle (2002), Purao and Campbell (1998), Lawrence (1997), Riquelme (2002), and Van Akkeren and Cavaye (1999)
E-commerce is too complex to implement	Quayle (2002)
Small businesses require short-term ROI and e-commerce is a long-term investment	Lawrence (1997) and McGowan and Madey (1998)
Organisational resistance to change because of the fear of new technology amongst employees	Lawrence (1997) and Van Akkeren and Cavaye (1999)
Preference for and satisfaction with traditional manual methods, such as phone, fax, and face to face	Lawrence (1997), Venkatesan and Fink (2002), and Poon and Swatman (1999)
Lack of technical skills and IT knowledge amongst employees; lack of computer literate/specialised staff	Quayle (2002), Lawrence (1997), Riquelme (2002), Van Akkeren and Cavaye (1999), Iacovou (1995), and Chau and Turner (2001)
Lack of time to implement e-commerce	Walczuch et al. (2000), Lawrence (1997), and Van Akkeren and Cavaye (1999)
E-commerce is not deemed to be suited to the way the organisation does business, or the way our clients do business	Hadjimonolis (1999) and Iacovou et al. (1995)
E-commerce is not deemed to be suited to the products/services offered by the small business	Walczuch et al. (2000), Kendall and Kendall (2001), and Hadjimonolis (1999)
E-commerce is perceived as a technology lacking direction	Lawrence (1997)
Lack of awareness about business advantages/opportunities that e-commerce can provide	Iacovou et al. (1995) and Quayle (2002)
Lack of available information about e-commerce	Lawrence (1997)
Concern about security of e-commerce	Quayle (2002), Purao and Campbell (1998), Riquelme (2002), Van Akkeren and Cavaye (1999), Poon and Swatman (1999), and Hadjimonolis (1999)
Lack of critical mass among customers, suppliers and business partners to implement e-commerce	Hadjimonolis (1999)
Heavy reliance on external consultants (who are often considered by small businesses to be inadequate) to provide necessary expertise	Lawrence (1997), Van Akkeren and Cavaye (1999), and Chau and Turner (2001)
Lack of e-commerce standards	Tuunainen (1998)

and empirical research in these areas. Since there is a wealth of information available on the barriers to the adoption of e-procurement among large corporations, a summary of the barriers is presented in Table 2. These barriers were summarized by Hawking and Stein (2004) from their study of 38 major Australian firms' e-procurement adoption.

Hawking and Stein (2004) note that "the main barriers to the uptake of e-procurement are infrastructure, technology, and integration-based. This seems to indicate that the complex technological issues—both within and between organisations in the procurement process—are crucial."

A study was commissioned by IMPAQ (which specializes in developing e-procurement technologies to enable SMEs to trade with blue-chip customers) on top FTSE 350 companies to identify the extent to which e-procurement is enabling blue-chip buying organizations to enhance trading with SME suppliers. The study signifies that "61% of the blue-chip buyers felt the need to promote the adoption of e-procurement among SMEs." Corporate buyers perceive that the lack of understanding of e-procurement and the cost of the technology are the main barriers to adoption by SMEs (IMPAQ, 2004).

Table 2. Summary of e-procurement barriers among large organizations (Source: Hawking & Stein, 2004)

E-Procurement Barriers
Inadequate Technical Infrastructure
Lack of Skilled Personnel
Inadequate Technological Infrastructure of Business Partners
Lack of Integration with Business Partners
Implementation Costs
Company Culture
Inadequate Tech Infrastructure of Partners
Regulatory and Legal Controls
Security
Cooperation of Business Partners
Inadequate E-Procurement Solutions
Upper Management Support

Bennett, Managing Director of IMPAQ (2004), notes that "whilst Britain's largest companies are seeing tangible benefits from e-procurement, many are not recognizing the technology's full potential due to the overriding issue of getting buy in from the SME supplier community."

Another study conducted on the adoption of e-procurement by SMEs in Canada concludes that e-procurement in Canadian SMEs has a slow acceptance rate compared to other Internet-based solutions. Multiple factors such as lack of management support, high cost, and uncertainty about benefits of e-procurement were the major barriers cited by the respondents and, surprisingly, information and data security were not considered a significant barrier (Cuthbert, Hamzic, & Archer, 2003). This study was conducted between June and July, 2003. A total of 53 companies responded to the questionnaire in a survey distributed primarily by email.

A recently-released benchmarking survey report on SME e-procurement adoption in the Northwest of England notes that "the rate of adoption of e-procurement by SMEs in the Northwest of England is extremely low. Multiple factors such as technical integration problems and lack of top management support were cited as barriers to the adoption of e-Procurement" (Bigonline.org, 2005). This benchmarking survey was conducted on 50 manufacturing SMEs in the Northwest of England. The methodology employed was mixed methods, which involves the sequential usage of quantitative and qualitative methodologies. For the first phase of the study, a quantitative survey was conducted on 50 SMEs to understand the adoption trend of e-procurement among them. Poon and Swatman (1998) have indicated that "the survey provides the broad and unbiased overview and generic understanding of key issues related to small-business Internet use in a non-anecdotal manner. For the second phase of study, five SMEs were selected from the respondent SMEs, and case studies were conducted on them. The multiple case-study research then served as a flexible and adaptive means to pursue the investigation of these issues in an in-depth manner." Gallivan (1997) indicates that in studying the impact of new technologies on organizations such as e-commerce, the use of mixed method studies provides opportunities to gather mixed-level data, which can be useful in linking the individual to the organizational level of analysis.

CASE STUDY

This section presents two case studies of SMEs, highlighting the challenges to their adoption of e-procurement.

Case Study 1

Company A are designers, builders, and installers of high-quality windows, doors, and conservatories for over 25 years. It employs modern manufacturing methods which incorporate the use of computer-aided design and manufacture, which ensures the production of precision window frames. Currently, the company has an annual turnover of £3.5 million and employs 50 people.

Profile of Company A

Number of employees:	50
Industry sector:	Manufacturer
Turnover:	£ 3.5 million
Number of computers:	5
Position:	IT Manager/Buyer

Company A uses basic Microsoft Word and Excel for record-keeping and communication, and a bespoke program for designing windows. At present, the organization conducts most of the procurement-related tasks manually. There is a facility in the bespoke program for stock-keeping, stock control, and purchasing which are not used currently. The organization issues 200-300 purchase orders per month, and currently there are five buyers involved in the procurement process. The organization sends purchase orders via fax, as only one PC has Internet access. No procurement-related information goes directly into their financial system (Sage Line 50). There is no integration between the systems of the organization to enable a better coordinated flow of procurement-related information. The company is planning to implement a network server in the future, which will facilitate other PCs in the manufacturing side with Internet access to place purchase orders electronically via e-mail or suppliers Web-based ordering systems.

Issues Affecting Adoption of E-Procurement

The purchasing and IT manager of Company A notes that the main reasons for the lack of implementation of e-procurement are:

- **Lack of knowledge and awareness about the benefits offered by e-procurement:** He notes that:

  unless I understand what's involved, how it works you are in a disadvantage position. (Anon, A., personal communication, June 2005)

- **Lack of top management support and the willing to do is missing:** On the issue of non-implementation of the modules in the Be-spoke package, he notes:

  I have been pushing to take that module option but from the M.D's view it is an expense which he will manage without. But from my point of view it is money well spent, because basically as a business I process windows and when orders go out automatically reallocate stock and re-order as and when required, which to me is excellent but he won't go that route yet. (Anon, A., personal communication, June 2005)

Case Study 2

Company B provides anechoic and screened room solutions for all EMC and RF Protection environments. It also manufactures cabinets for the telecommunications industry and various other subcontractor works. Their two main clients are British Telecom and Marconi Systems, for which Company B makes cabinets and private telephone exchanges. This case company also makes cabinets for a high speed ADSL Internet service provider. The company employs 55 and has an annual turnover of £4 million.

Profile of Company B

Number of employees:	55
Industry sector:	Engineering
Turnover:	£ 4 million
Number of computers:	> 20
Average IT spending:	£ 5,000 – £ 15,000
Position:	IT/Production Engineer/Buyer

Current Status of the Organization

With an annual procurement expenditure of around £2 million and issued purchase orders nearing 200 per month, procurement occupies a pivotal role in this company. At present, the organization has an in-house developed internal procurement system. Currently, the stock levels are driven straight out of the database. The company runs SAGE Line 100 software which generates the requirements and, depending on how the supplier wants to receive the orders, they are sent out via fax, e-mail, or post. Currently, the organization has a supply base of around 900 suppliers who cover a multiplicity of products and services. These suppliers cover most of the procurement needs of the organization. The company realizes that it is a burden to maintain such a vast array of suppliers and has started a disembarkation program. The supply base has been trimmed down to around 600. IT manager, Mr. X, justifies having such a vast supply base and notes that "since our procurement is so diverse, it is warranted that we have such a range of suppliers." The company's supply base consists of a diverse mix starting with a micro-company in Aston to a large global distributor like TDK.

Issues Affecting Adoption of E-Procurement

This diversity causes the potential problem of having to deal with different suppliers in different ways. A micro-SME would not be able to receive orders electronically, while a medium to large company might possess the capability to trade electronically. The IT manager feels that currently smaller suppliers are not yet ready to deal with them electronically and that integration of systems with heterogeneous suppliers is still a pain point.

He further adds that:

Technically it is a big challenge for the other parties to implement or consume information in real-time. For me, a proper e-procurement system would be for us feeding data direct from our database to supplier's database, so that is real time. Basically at the moment it is halfway there. We are doing everything automatically, but they are still ending up with a piece of paper at their end or either an email in their inbox. It is a bit of dream to get everybody on board, their existing systems automatically generating orders, so orders are coming in automatically. That's the way things should be. But I think that is still long away. (Anon, B., personal communication, June 2005)

The company also notes that change management is a big issue in implementing e-procurement. It is not easy to change the mindsets of

Table 3. Classification of barriers

Hard Barriers	Soft Barriers
Technology Problems	Organizational Barriers Lack of Domain Knowledge

people who have been used to doing things in a particular style. People are interested, but they do not want to change and there is not much you can do about it. Without the explicit support of senior management, we feel that we are not in a position to change their mindset. The senior management, I think, if it does not really affect them, they will not be really interested. Most of the time, they do not bother about it, if they have to spend some time and money. From their point of view, as long as the material is procured and they are on time, it is "task accomplished," no matter which method is used. If they want to manufacture product X and the material is not there, then there is a problem, and if it is there, it is not a problem in their perspective.

Looking forward to the future, Company B's top priority is to develop a better and easy method of communicating electronically with their supplier base. Table 4 illustrates the barriers that were identified from the analysis of the above studies. Barriers could be broadly classified into *hard* and *soft*. Hard barriers are those which have to do with things and regulations. Soft barriers are the problems related to people.

Hard barriers could further be segregated into:

- Technical integration problems
- Technical infrastructure problems
- General problems

As can be inferred from the table, technical problems and integration problems dominate the barriers, followed by lack of knowledge and awareness about the benefits offered by e-procurement. Many studies have clearly demonstrated that cost is the primary focus of drivers, while technology and business partner integration are the main focus of barriers (Hawking & Stein, 2004).

Table 4. Summary of barriers

HARD BARRIERS			
Technical Integration Problems	**Technical Infrastructure Problems**	**General Problems**	**Soft Barriers**
Lack of robust technical standards that are needed to make IOIS adoption economical	Lack of adequate tools and systems	Inadequate e-procurement solutions	Company culture
Complexity in inter-organizational communication	Access to and availability of strategic e-business resources	Esoteric nomenclature usage in literature	Business processes
Infrastructure integration	High cost of technology implementation	The small number of suppliers accessible through many organizations e-procurement procurement systems	Cooperation of business-partners
Integration with existing technologies	Inadequate technical infrastructure of partners	Failure to invest sufficiently in catalog development	Poor value proposition for the supplier
Lack of integration with business partners	Inefficiencies in locating information and infrastructure	Insufficient return on investment	Upper management support
The lack of standards for e-commerce software development	Lack of technical expertise	Uncertainty surrounding the costs and benefits of e-business	Inadequate business processes to support e-procurement
Data exchange standards lacking	Lack of information and education	Regulatory and legal controls	
Security	Lack of technically-skilled staff	Lack of knowledge about e-procurement concepts and solutions	
	Immaturity of technology		

THE APPLICATION OF WEB SERVICES IN E-PROCUREMENT

Today, a typical organization consists of a range of diverse systems, each utilizing different protocols for communication and different formats for data representation. Previously, the need for communication among these heterogeneous systems was minimalist. But with the ubiquitous Internet, connecting to worldwide markets in search of new business partners or communicating with suppliers for better coordination of supply chain activities has become very affordable for even the small and medium enterprises. Business-to-business (B2B) e-commerce has arrived in big style and is now considered the future of businesses.

Collaboration has become the latest trend of doing business, and it is beneficial from both business and customer points of view. A new concept called *co-opetition* has emerged, replacing the concept of competition. Co-opetition is where competitors cooperate for the benefit of customers. Laura D'Andrea Tyson, (lawson, 2000) one of the world's most distinguished economists says that "it was innovate or die, but here are the days when it is co-operate or die." All companies, small, medium, and large can experience increased growth through tightly-integrated partnerships (Samtani & Sadhwani, 2003; Themistocleous & Chen, 2004).

For these collaborations to occur in real-time, all of the participant organizations systems (both intra- and inter-) need to be seamlessly integrated in real-time. This process involves opening up organizations' systems to the outside world which need to be highly compatible and at the same time non-comprising on the security front. Large corporations have the necessary resources to implement costly integration programs. Small and medium enterprises, which generally are limited by resources, are not able to fully exploit the benefits of collaborative commerce. The extraordinary benefits of this new digital age are being hampered owing to the lack of systems integration among the diverse and complex systems used by organizations. Thus, B2B integration has become the most important issue for SMEs. B2B integration can be defined to cover all business activities of an enterprise that have to do with electronic message exchange between it and one or more of its trading partners (Bussler, 2003).

In today's new global economy, it is data, information, and knowledge that have value. Any information technology solution that is designed needs to center on data and information, rather than the platform itself, that is, the solution must be platform-agnostic. The emergence of XML Web services standards attempts to solve this complex problem of integration in an affordable manner at reasonable costs. Web services are a set of XML standards-based technology which promises to provide solutions plaguing the current world of information technology through a simple and standards-based approach.

Web services represent a significant opportunity in tying together the various participants of the global supply chain puzzle in a very cost-effective manner. The key to the successes of Web services lies in its simplistic approach and the usage of industry-wide protocols like XML, HTTP, and TCP/IP. Web services leverage the ubiquitous Internet for application communication. Web services represent the fulfillment of an unprecedented cooperation among industry leaders. At no other instance in the history of Information Technology has there been such a wide industry support in the formation of standards. Old adversaries, Microsoft and IBM, have worked together with Ariba to develop simple object access protocol (SOAP), Web Services Description Language (WSDL), and universal discovery and description interface (UDDI) as cross-platform standards, in a spirit of community-oriented constructive engagement.

Web services are an evolution of the previous attempts by the industry like CORBA and DCOM. Primarily, the lack of universal acceptance of these two approaches could be attributed to the

Figure 5. Convergence of business, technology, and the Internet

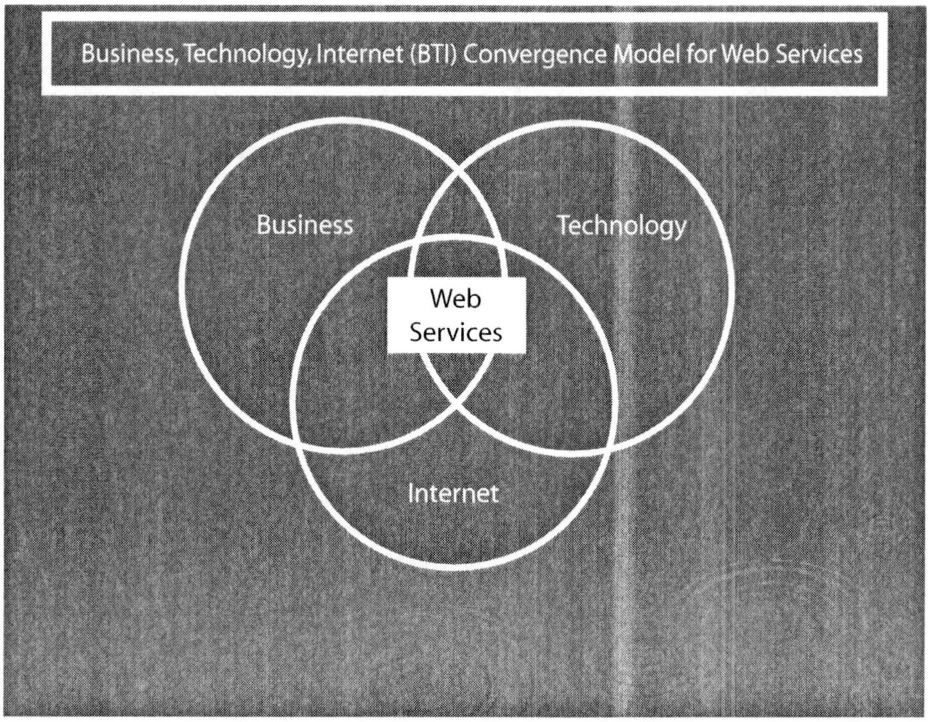

absence of a common network to share information and the lack of a common data format. The emergence of the Internet provided a common ubiquitous network, and the development of XML provided a universal data format. Web services are the killer applications of XML, and of the Internet protocols like HTTP and TCP/IP. This represents a huge leap forward in the way applications are built, communicated, and distributed.

The need for Web services arises owing to the demands for:

- The need for collaboration among different organizations of various sizes with the internet as the backbone
- The strategic importance being attributed to the supply chains as a way to be more competitive among organizations
- The need for real-time seamless communication among various tiers of the supply chain
- The expectation among CEOs of organizations for an instant return on investment.

Technical Definition

Web services are defined as "loosely coupled, reusable software components that semantically encapsulate discrete functionality and are distributed and programmatically accessible over standard Internet protocols" (Stencil, 2003).

Business Definition

Web services are an approach that helps the business connect with customers, partners, and employees in a seamless manner with standard open interfaces by leveraging the investments in existing IT infrastructure. The benefits offered by adopting and developing Web services are manifold in nature, both on the technical and business fronts. Let us look at a list of business benefits of Web services.

Benefits of Web Services

By enabling applications to share data across different hardware platforms and operating systems, Web services provide many benefits, including:

- Opening the door to new business opportunities by making it easy to connect with partners
- Delivering dramatically more personal, integrated experiences to users through the new breed of smart devices, including PCs
- Saving time and money by cutting development time
- Increasing revenue streams by enabling businesses to easily make their own Web services available to others (Microsoft, 2003)

Web services use three kinds of new technologies which are purely XML-based, which makes it even more easy to use because of its relative merits and also due to the widespread acceptance of XML. The use of XML standards is very important in the overall scheme of the Web services universe. XML is a data format that represents data in a serialized form that can be transported over the network from one endpoint to another. "XML is nearly as widely accepted as the TCP/IP protocols on which the Internet itself is built (Fu, 1999)." Web services using XML standards is a new paradigm in the way B2B collaborations are modeled. It provides a conceptual and architectural foundation which can be implemented using a variety of platforms and products.

Figure 6. The relationships among the core Web services components (Source: Gottschalk, Graham, Kreger, & Snell, 2002)

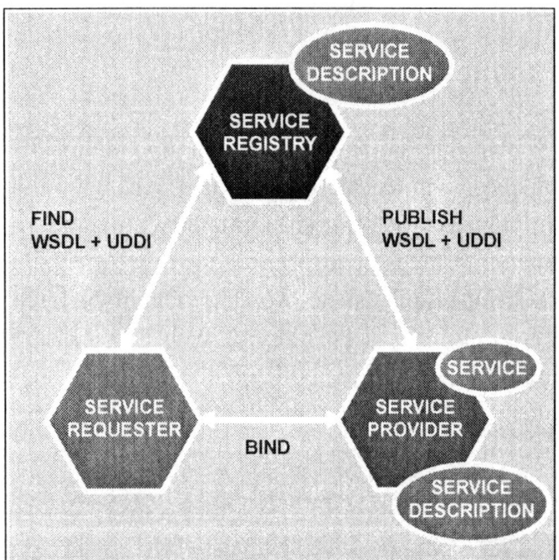

Put simply, a service provider deploys Web services. A service broker lists various services and arranges transactions, helping service providers and service requesters find each other. A service requester uses an application programming interface (API) to discover Web services, asking the service broker about the services it needs. When the service broker returns results, the service requester can then invoke those services it needs to create applications.

The whole process of how Web services work is explained below:

- Just build your system normally.
- Expose them as Web services.
- Any service requester wishing to use the Web services will send in a SOAP request to the application which is exposed as a Web service.
- If you intend to use third-party deployed Web services, look into the UDDI registry to locate the required Web service. Next, Web services Description Language (WSDL) associated with the particular Web service provides technical details about how Web service could be consumed by the required applications.

The following are the three standards on which Web services are based. We will take a closer look into these three XML-based standards:

1. **UDDI** (universal description, discovery, and integration)
2. **WSDL** (Web Services Description Language)
3. **SOAP** (simple object access protocol)

Universal Description, Discovery, and Integration (UDDI)

UDDI stands for universal description, discovery, and integration. Before a business partner can make any Web service request, it must first understand the technical details and perform some activities which include discovering the call interface and semantics, and writing or configuring their software to collaborate with the service. To enable this discovery, a platform is needed to publish these Web services. UDDI fulfils this requirement. UDDI registry is the central database which contains information on all Web services. It provides a platform for Web services requesters to discover or query for new services and to understand their technical details like the WSDL nature of Web services in a common XML format. The UDDI registry is organized into various categories to facilitate the easy discovery and invocation of the Web services. This categorization resembles the yellow pages which are commonly found in telephone directories. A white pages section provides business contact information, a yellow pages section categorizes businesses and services, and a green pages section provides technical information about the services that a business offers. Once a Web services requester validates the details found in the White pages and the Yellow pages section, the Green pages provides the necessary technical details necessary to invoke the services.

Web Services Description Language (WSDL)

Once a business discovers the service it wants to use from the UDDI registry, it needs to understand the call syntax and semantics prior to actually making a call which can be found in the green pages section of the UDDI registry. The WSDL specification is an XML document which describes the interface and semantics of a call to the Web service. It defines how service providers and requesters communicate with each other about Web services. This allows for simple services to be quickly and easily described and documented. Like XML, WSDL is extensible to allow the description of endpoints and their messages, regardless of what message formats or network protocols are used for communicating. WSDL can be used to design specifications to invoke and operate Web services on the Internet and to access and invoke remote applications and databases.

Simple Object Access Protocol (SOAP)

The simple object access protocol is the specification which leverages the power of XML and HTTP. It provides the specification for the exchange of structured information in a decentralized distributed environment. SOAP utilizes the XML for exchanging messages over a variety of underlying protocols, such as HTTP or SMTP. Also, XML is utilized owing to its massive industry support, language-neutrality, and extensibility. HTTP is utilized as any Web-enabled application communicates, using sockets, and it utilizes the Port 80, which makes HTTP traffic firewall-friendly. Simplicity is what makes SOAP powerful. The original specification of SOAP 1.1 was made in 1997. However, the original definition was limited in scope. However, the current version 1.2 has enhanced the specification to serve to a broader audience. SOAP is a "lightweight," very easy-to-understand technology, and it is also easy to implement. It has industry momentum and buy-in from all major e-business platform vendors. Zhao (2001) clarifies the meaning of "lightweight" and notes that "SOAP is an XML marshalling and unmarshalling mechanism and does not need heavy libraries like CORBA and DCOM. The main objective of SOAP is to achieve interoperability by using XML to interact with interoperable Web services."

Earlier protocols such as Internet inter-ORB protocol (IIOP) for CORBA or Java remote method protocol (JRMP) for Java remote method invocation (RMI) did not utilize the XML. This made it difficult to debug them, as binary streams tend to be more complex to read than simple XML structures. Also, sending information through text-based protocols like SOAP over the HTTP enhances the success rate of the information passing through firewalls as HTTP utilizes port 80, which is open to Internet traffic. However, there might be some performance penalties as text-based information requires more bandwidth than binary streams. But this slight inconvenience can be ignored when considering the bigger benefits related to interoperability that it provides. Once a potential partner who wishes to use the service looks at the WSDL using UDDI, he can make a request to one or more of the services offered in our Web service utilizing the simple object access protocol (SOAP).

Integration Made Easier

Sending and receiving invoices and purchase orders across corporate boundaries, with partners who often employ a complex jugglery of Information Technology solutions, is a daunting challenge. Web services enable these kinds of external communications by exposing internal functions as Web services which could be invoked by other applications. This can be achieved by wrapping the internal functionalities of the system with SOAP wrappers. Web services have been used to wrap a legacy system's functions to support application-to-application integration inside a firewall (Vecchio, 2001). Thus, not compromising the security of the systems and also reaching a wider audience with heterogeneous platforms. The deployment of Web services reduces the integration costs associated with achieving extended enterprise, as well as improves service levels that would otherwise not be achievable (Adams et al., 2003, Samtani & Sadhwani, 2003).

The Application of Web services in e-procurement is a very recent area of development. Very few researchers have concentrated on this area, and very little empirical data exists in this area (Chen & Meixell, 2003).

Many large organizations like Dell and Dollar One have successfully demonstrated how they could effectively use Web services in improving the agility of their supply chain operations without changing the existing infrastructure. This represents a significant opportunity for SMEs because they can participate in the new initiatives of large companies by making minimal investments and not foregoing their existing IT investments. E-procurement is a supplier-facing operation which involves integrating with suppliers' systems which are often asynchronous and located outside the corporate firewalls. Integration of systems becomes a very important aspect in this kind of scenario.

Neff (2001) clearly notes that e-procurement is still in its infancy because it involves integration with other systems. Integration is one of the most contentious issues facing the world of information technology. But fortunately, Web services with its standards-based approach attempts to provide solutions to integration issues by allowing communications among software applications in a neutral way. The widespread adoption of Web service standards in e-business will address that area of concern.

The key to the success of any supply chain is the ability to share information seamlessly. A study conducted jointly by Stanford University and Accenture (formerly Anderson Consulting), looked at 100 manufacturers and 100 retailers in the food and consumers products industry. The results were revealing; Companies that reported higher than average profits were the ones who were engaged in higher levels of information sharing (Lee & Whang, 2001).

Web services take a service and process-oriented approach in addressing integration issues in supply chain management. An application enabled with Web services can provide streamlined capabilities by consuming Web services from legacy systems (such as for checking inventory status) and external suppliers (such as requesting price quotes from suppliers). These Web services are composed transparently behind the scene in the application to give users access to more supply chain functions from a single application (Chen & Meixell, 2003).

Web Services and B2B Marketplaces

As emphasized earlier, B2B marketplaces are the preferred method for conducting external e-procurement. But of late, we have seen the demise of many marketplaces. One of the main reasons attributable for the closure of many marketplaces is the closed-systems approach followed by many of them. McKertich (2004) emphasizes that "the challenge of integrating quickly, easily, and still maintaining much of the functionality that is offered by e-marketplaces, has been exceptionally difficult." For the marketplace to be successful, there are various aspects on the technical front that needs to be addressed. The following are the IT requirements of a B2B marketplace as highlighted by Ganesh, Das, Chatterjee, Verma, Chawla, and Marwah (2004):

- Ability to integrate with buyer and seller systems
- Ability to integrate smoothly with other partners (e.g., credit card firms, courier companies, etc.)
- Ability to configure/reconfigure services
- Ability to match the information of the participants in a transaction

Previous generation information technologies did not provide much leeway in designing a loosely-coupled system. But, with the anvil of Web services, designing a loosely-coupled system, where heterogeneous systems could communicate using industry standards and open interfaces, has become a reality.

From the above scenarios, we can conclude that Web services can be applied in e-procurement in a variety of ways. This is primarily due to the excellent support for providing dynamic data from a plethora of platforms, which is the basic requirement of e-procurement as it is a supplier-facing operation.

PROCUREMENT TRANSFORMATION FRAMEWORK ENABLED BY WEB SERVICES

The need for an exhaustive framework detailing the complete procurement process, with the role played by information technology in enabling this process, is much desired. The procurement transformation framework enabled by Web services provides a comprehensive set of structured information on how information technology could aid in the procurement process, in particular how deploying Web services would simplify the task of integration, which is a prerequisite of the new digitally-networked economy.

Step 1: Procurement Process Reengineering (PPR)

Grouping procurement tasks into *strategic* and *transactional* allows SMEs to focus more on the strategic aspects and automate the transactional element. This reduces the cost of order generation and also provides ample time to the buyer who can focus more on the strategic aspects rather than the mundane operational ones. On the strategic side, the company should perform a review of expenditures, determine market complexity, de-

Figure 7. Procurement transformation framework enabled by Web services

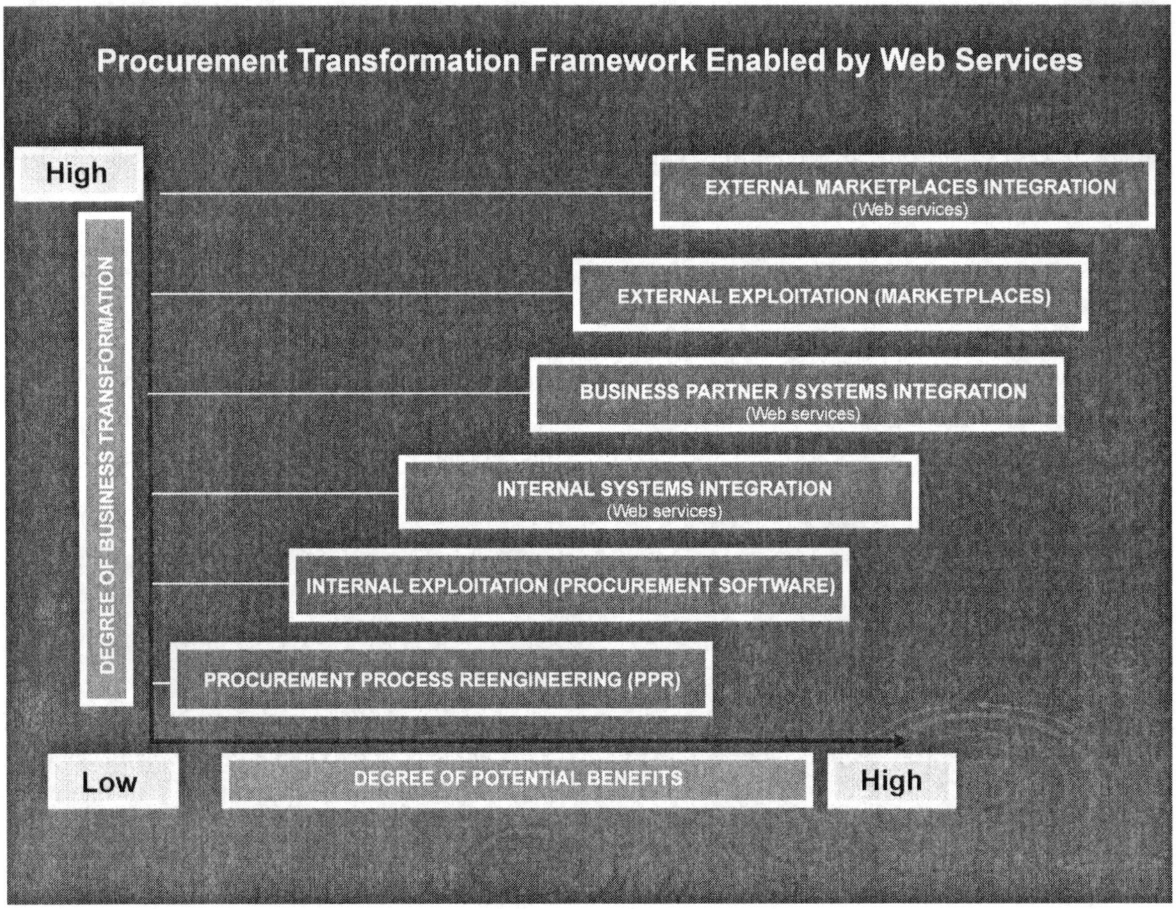

velop a sourcing strategy, and review the entire procure-to-pay cycle.

Step 2: Internal Exploitation (Procurement Software)

After clearly segregating the procurement tasks, focus should be shifted to the automation of the *internal procurement* tasks. Information technology should be exploited internally to aid in streamlining the internal procurement-related activities. This could be achieved by the utilization of an internal procurement software which could be either in the form of an added functionality to an ERP system, or in-house software.

Step 3: Internal Systems Integration (Web Services)

The automation of the internal part of the procurement process is followed by the integration of the procurement software with the financial and stock management or any other relevant software specific to the particular organization. This is very crucial as often procurement-related information provides valuable inputs for various other information systems. Web services, with its unique standards-based approach, enables SMEs to perform this internal integration tasks in a very cost-effective way and also leverages investments in existing IT systems.

Step 4: Business Partner Systems Integration (Web Services)

Procurement systems sit on the edge of the enterprise and are required to "talk" to a multitude of partners. These partners often employ a complex jugglery of information systems. Without integration with these partners, real-time seamless flow of information is hampered, which defeats the very purpose of having an integrated procurement system. Web services can be used to seamlessly integrate with partners' systems outside the corporate boundary without the problem of firewall. As Web services are built on open standards like XML, HTTP, TCP/IP, organizations do not run into the risk of being locked into proprietary data formats. Also, these kinds of communications do not warrant upfront commitment and significant investments, which makes them ideal for small and medium enterprises.

Step 5: External Exploitation

External exploitation is defined as looking at the possibility of external modes of procurement. This usually involves leveraging the potential of the Internet. E-marketplaces, e-auction, and e-bidding are the preferred way for SMEs to conduct e-procurement. These provide valuable services like aggregation of buyers and sellers, and are an economic way for SMEs to tap into more sourcing opportunities.

Step 6: External Integration with E-Marketplaces

Internal procurement software can contain a number of features and can host a catalogue service. E-marketplaces could be integrated with that of Internal Marketplaces of SMEs. This provides extraordinary benefits and a host of security-related features without any costly investment.

FUTURE TRENDS

We see that over the coming years the strong business value proposition offered by the Internet will impact the SME community in a tremendous way. We see the increased usage of the Internet by the SME community over and above the existing levels. At the heart of all this activity will be procurement and also the need for seamless loosely-coupled interactions among the various participants of the supply chain, who predominantly are SMEs. The concept of Web services will help SMEs tremendously in their ability to deal with the integration puzzle in a cost-effective way. With Web services crossing the chasm and gaining widespread acceptance over the next few years, we envision a world where a host of marketplaces and e-procurement solution vendors will be offering a suite of products based on Web services. McKertich (2004) emphasizes that "e-marketplace providers will be quick to see the opportunity, and modify their software technology to incorporate Web Services support so that they can continue to 'build the bridges' between buyers and sellers of disparate computing technology, and disparate business priorities."

Chen and Meixell (2003) asserts that companies may soon participate in dynamic e-business via collaborative XML-based Web services that provide remote access to programmable business services and use XML for data interchange.

CONCLUSION

The above discussions clearly indicate that supply chain integration and information sharing are the key factors which will determine the success of any organization in the future ahead. E-procurement, due to its potential for savings and also because of its high importance in the supply chain, is an important area of focus for SMEs.

Web services with its standards-based approach are clearly the path SMEs should take in the integration of supply chain activities. Soon, innovative business strategies and business models, as well as supply chain integration relying on Web service-based architecture, will become the driving force for XML and Web services adoption (Sullivan, 2002). The fact that Web services can be used internally to provide programmable interfaces to legacy systems, and to integrate Web-enabled applications directly with some legacy systems, make it an ideal choice for its adoption in supply chain context, especially in e-procurement which involves interaction with suppliers' systems and vice versa (Samtani & Sadhwani, 2003; Vecchio, 2001).

Apart from the solutions to barriers on the technical arena, for the widespread adoption of e-procurement among SMEs, a concerted effort needs to be made by the SME managers at the organizational level and by the regional and the national governments at the regional and the national levels, respectively. For example, in developed countries like the United Kingdom (UK), the national government has initiated an ambitious National E-Procurement Project (NEPP). As per the government mandate, all SMEs dealing with the local authorities should possess the ability to deal with them electronically by the end of 2005, and participation in an electronic marketplace would count as one of their criteria for evaluating a supplier. The challenges faced by SMEs in adopting e-procurement are more profound in developing countries. Therefore, the government in those countries needs to play an even more proactive role in enabling SMEs to harness the full potential of e-procurement. A noteworthy example in India is the state government of Andhra Pradesh. The government has been very proactive in the implementation of e-procurement technology. As of 1-1-2005, all departments of the state government have shifted towards e-procurement, which is an extraordinary achievement. This mandates that all suppliers to the government trade electronically. This kind of strong commitment on the part of government in embracing e-procurement goes a long way in providing fresh stimulus to SMEs in adopting e-procurement.

Also, the local and national governments should make a concerted effort in collaboration with the academic community in the dissemination of hype-free, unbiased information to the SME community, who are soaked in the unrealistic, hyped-up, biased information promoted and marketed by product vendors.

REFERENCES

Aberdeen Group. (2001). *Best practices in e-procurement, the abridged report.* White paper. Retrieved June 2, 2004, from http://www.ariba.com/com_plat/white_paper_form.cfm

ABI. (2003). *Are you e-ready? An initial assessment of e-procurement potential.* Research report. Retrieved July 30, 2004, from http://www.abi.co.uk

Adams, H., et al. (2003). *Custom extended enterprise exposed business services application pattern scenario.* Retrieved February 24, 2004, from http://www-106.ibm.com/developerworks/webservices/library/ws-best5/

Bakos, J. Y. (1991). A strategic analysis of electronic marketplaces. *MIS Quarterly, 15*(3), 295-310.

Bakos, J. Y. (1998). The emerging role of EM on the Internet. *Communications of the ACM, 41*(8), 35–42.

Benbasat, I., Goldstein, D. K., & Mead, M. (1987). *The case research strategy in Berkeley.* 1999.

Bhattacharaya, A. K., Coleman, J. L., & Brace, G. (1996). The structure conundrum in supply chain management. *International Journal of Logistics Management, 7*(2), 39-49.

Bigonline.org. (2005). *Report on the e-procurement benchmarking survey.* Research report. Retrieved July 30, 2005, from http://www.bigonline.org

Boston Consulting. (2001). *Report on the Canadian e-business opportunity roundtable.* Retrieved April 2002, from http://www.bcg.com/practice/022201_FINAL_Canada_Roundtable_English.pdf

Bradley III, D. B., & Peters, D. (1997, June). Electronic marketplaces: Collaborate if you want to compete. In *Proceedings of the 42nd World Conference International Council for Small Business*, San Francisco.

Bussler, C. (2003). *B2B integration concepts and architecture*. Springer-Verlag.

Cagliano, R., Caniato, F., & Spina, G. (2003). E-business strategy: How companies are shaping their supply chain through the Internet. *International Journal of Operations and Production Management, 23*(10), 1142-1162.

Cash, I. J., & Konsynski, B. R. (1985). IS redraws competitive boundaries. *Harvard Business Review, 63*(2), 134-142.

Chan, J. K. Y., & Lee, M. K. O. (2003). SME e-procurement adoption in Hong Kong: The roles of power, trust and value. In *Proceedings of the 36th Hawaii International Conference on System Sciences (HICSS'03).*

Chen, M., & Meixell, M. J. (2003). Web services-enabled procurement in the extended enterprise: An architectural design and implementation. *Journal of Electronic Commerce and Research, 58*(3), 259-279.

Christensen, E., Curbera, F., Meredith, G., & Weerawarana, S. (2001). *Web Services Description Language (WSDL) 1.1.* Retrieved February 19, 2004, from http://www.w3.org/TR/wsdl

Christopher, M. (1998). *Logistics and supply chain management* (2nd ed.).

Cuthbert, C., Hamzic, D., & Archer, N. (2003). *Barriers to SME e-procurement solutions in Canada: A survey.* Hamilton, Ontario: McMaster E-Business Research Centre (MeRC), DeGroote School of Business, McMaster University.

Dai, Q., & Kauffman, R. J. (2000, January). Business models for Internet-based e-procurement systems and B2B EM: An exploratory assessment. In *Proceedings of the 34th Hawaii International Conference on Systems Science*, Maui, HI.

Davila, A., Gupta, M., & Palmer, R. (2003). Moving procurement systems to the Internet: The adoption and use of e-procurement technology models. *European Management Journal, 21*(1), 11–23.

Day, G. S., Fein, A. J., & Ruppersberger, G. (2003). Shakeouts in digital markets: Lessons from B2B exchanges. *California Management Review, 45*(2), 131-150.

DTI. (2003, August 28). National statistics: Statistical press release. *Department of Trade and Industry, UK*, 03/92.

Eisenhardt, K. M. (1989). Building theories from case study research. *Academy of Management Review, 14*(4), 532–550.

Fu, S. (1999). A practical approach to Web-based Internet EDI. *IBM.* Retrieved from http://www.research.ibm.com/iac/papers/icdcsws99.pdf

Gallivan, M. (1997). Value in triangulation: A comparision of two approaches for combining qualitative and quantitative methods. In A. Lee, J. Liebenau, & J. DeGross (Eds.), *Information systems and qualitative research* (pp. 417-443). London: Chapman & Hall.

Ganesh, J., Das, A. S., Chatterjee, A. M., Verma, A., Chawla, M., & Marwah, A. (2003). Web services-based inter-organisational architectural framework for B2B marketplaces. *Infosys Technologies Ltd.* Retrieved February 19, 2005, from http://infolab.uvt.nl/~fjl/mikep/demos/3.pdf

Gebauer, J., Beam, C., & Segev, A. (1998). *Procurement in the Internet age—current practices and emerging trends*. Fisher Center for Management and Information Technology, Haas School of Business, University of California.

Gottschalk, K., Graham, Kreger, S. H., & Snell, J. (2002). Introduction to Web services architecture. *IBM Systems Journal, 41*(2), 168-177.

Grewal, R., Comer, J. M., & Mehta, R. (2001, July). An investigation into electronic markets. *Journal of Marketing, 65*, 17-33.

Hauser, E. (2000). *SMEs in Germany: Facts and figures* (Bonn: Institut fu¨r Mittelstandsforschung).

Hauser, H. -E. (2000). *SMEs in Germany. Facts and figures.* IfM Institut für Mittelstandsforschung Bonn. Retrieved from www.ifm-bonn.de/ergebnis/sme.zip

Hawking, P., & Stein, A. (2004). E-procurement: Is the ugly duckling actually a swan down under? *Asia Pacific Journal of Marketing and Logistics, 16*(1).

Henderson, D. R. (1984). Electronic marketing in principle and practice. *American Journal of Agriculture Economics, 66*(5), 848–853.

Heywood, B. J., Barton, M., & Heywood, C. C. (2002). *E-procurement managing successful e-procurement implementation.*

IBM. (1998). *Small and mid-sized business in the global networked economy.* White paper. Retrieved August 18, 1999, from http://www.ibm.com/ibm/publicaffairs/smbus1998

IMPAQ. (2004). *UKPLC not realizing full payback from e-procurement, reveals new study.* Retrieved November, 2004, from http://www.impaq.co.uk/press/news34.htm

Kalakota, R., & Robinson, M. (2000). *E-business: Roadmap for success.* Canada: Addison–Wesley.

Kaplan, S., & Sawhney, M. (2000). E-hubs: The new B2B marketplaces. *Harvard Business Review, 78*(3), 97–104.

Kaufmann, L. (1999). Purchasing and supply management: A conceptual framework. In L. Kaufmann & D. Hahn (Eds.), *Handbuch Industrielles Beschaffungsmanagement: Internationale Konzepte: Innovative Instrumente—Aktuelle Praxisbeispiele* (pp. 3-32). Wiesbaden, Germany: Gabler.

Kaufmann, R. J., & Mohtadi, H. (2004, Summer). Open vs. proprietary systems in B2B e-procurement: A risk-adjusted transaction cost perspective. Forthcoming in the *Journal of Management Information Systems.*

Knusden, D. (2003). *Improving procurement performance with e-business mechanisms.* Doctoral dissertation, Lund University, Sweden.

Lamming, R. (1995). *Strategic procurement management in the 1990's: Concepts and cases.* Stamford, CT: Earlsgate Press.

Lawson, D. (2000). *Home procurement.* Retrieved November, 2004, from http://specials.ft.com/eprocurement/FT33SC3ALFC.html

Lee, H. L., & Whang, S. (2001). E-business and supply chain integration. In *Proceedings of the Stanford Global Supply Chain Management Forum (SGSCMF-W2-2001)* (p. 20).

Leonard, S. R. (n.d.). *Electronic Procurement.* President EDS E.solutions EMEA 2813– 2837.

Levi, D. S., Kaminsky, P., & Levi, E. S. (2003). *Designing and managing the supply chain: Concepts, strategies, and case studies* (2nd ed.). New York: McGraw-Hill.

MacGregor, R. C., & Vrazalic, L. (2005). A basic model of electronic commerce adoption barriers: A study of regional small businesses in Sweden and Australia. *Journal of Small Business and Enterprise Development, 12*(4), 510-527.

Malone, T. W., Yates, J., & Benjamin, R. I. (1987). Electronic markets and electronic hierarchies. *Communications of the ACM, 30*(6), 484-497.

Markham, W. J., Morales, J. T., & Slaight, T. H. (2000). Creating supply advantage by leveraging the strategic nature of procurement. In J. Cavinato & R. Kauffman (Eds.), *The purchasing handbook* (6th ed.). New York: McGraw Hill Publishing.

McKertich., A. (2004). *What do SOAP, ebXML, UDDI, and OASIS all have in common?*

McMillan, J. (2002). *Reinventing the bazaar.* A natural history of markets. New York: W W Norton and Company Inc.

Microsoft (2003).*What is .NET?* Retrieved February 1, 2004, from http:// www.microsoft.com/net/basic.mspx

National e-Procurement Project. (2004). *Overarching guide to e-procurement.* Retrieved February 11, 2005, from http://www.idea.gov.uk/knowledge/eprocurement

Neef, D. (2001). *E-procurement: From strategy to implementation.* London: Prentice Hall/Financial Times.

NEPP. (2004). *Local e-gov national e-procurement project, overview of solutions.* Retrieved December 13, 2006 from http://www.localegovnp/default.asp?sID=1100774743609.

New, S., Meakin, T., & Southworth, R. (2002). *Understanding the e-marketspace: Making sense of B2B.* Retrieved June, 11, 2005, from http://www.achilles.com

New, S. J., & Payne, P. (1995). Research frameworks in logistics: Three models, seven dinners, and a survey. *International Journal of Physical Distribution and Logistics Management, 25*(10), 60-77.

Obrecht, J. (2000). Playing e-hub name game. *Netb2b.com, 3*(July, BtoB), 9. Retrieved from http://www.economist.com/editorial/free-forall/20000226/

OGC. (2002). *A guide to e-procurement for the public sector.* Office of Government Commerce, UK.

OGC. (2005). *E-procurement in action: A guide to e-procurement for the public sector.* Report. Retrieved February 30, 2005, from http://www.ogc.gov.uk/sdtoolkit/reference/ogc_library/procurement/bluefrog2.pdf

Presutti, W. D. (2002). Supply management and e-procurement: Creating value added in the supply chain. *Industrial Marketing Management, 32*(2003), 219-226

Price Waterhouse Coopers (PWC). (2002). Electronic business outlook: E-markets realism, not pessimism. *Price Waterhouse Coopers.* Retrieved May 15, 2002, from http://pwcglobal.com/ebusinessinsights.

Poon, S., & Swatman, P. (1998), A combined-method study of small business Internet commerce. *International Journal of Electronic Commerce, 2*(3), 31-46

Puschmann, T., & Alt, R. (2005). Successful use of e-procurement in supply chains. *Supply Chain Management: An International Journal, 10*(2), 122–133.

Samtani, G., & Sadhwani, D. (2002). Return on investment and Web services. In P. Fletcher & M. Waterhouse (Eds.), *Web services business strategies and architectures* (pp. 9-24). Birmingham, UK: Expert Press, Ltd.

Schmid, B. (1993). Elektronische Markte. *Wirtschaftsinformatik, 35*(5), 465-480.

Schmid, B. F., & Lindemann, M. A. (1998). Elements of a reference model for EM. In *Proceedings of the 31st Hawaii International Conference on System Sciences (HICCSS-31)*, HI (Vol. 4, pp. 193–201). IEEE Computer Society Press.

Scott, C., & Westbrook, R. (1991). New strategic tools for supply chain management. *International Journal of Physical Distribution and Logistics Management, 21*(1), 23–33.

Segev, A., Gebauer, J., & Faeber, F. (1999). Internet-based electronic markets. *EM—International Journal of Electronic Markets, 9*(3), 167-176.

Shimada, T. (2004). *The challenge of B2B exchange operators on Southeast Asia.* Unpublished manuscript.

Stencil Group. (2001). *Defining Web services.* Retrieved from http://www.stencilgroup.com/ideas_scope_ 200106wsdefined.pdf

Stevens, G. C. (1989). Integrating the supply chain. *International Journal of Physical Distribution & Materials Management, 19*(8), 3-8.

Stockdale, R., & Standing, M. (2004). Benefits and barriers of electronic marketplace participation: An SME perspective. *The Journal of Enterprise Information Management, 17*(4), 301-311.

Sullivan, T. (2002). *App dev on the Web services path.* Retrieved from http://www.infoworld.com/articles/fe/xml/02/06/10/020610feapp.dev.xml

Themistocleous, M., & Chen, H. (2004). Investigating the integration of SMEs' information systems: An exploratory case study. *International Journal of Information Technology and Management, 3*(2/3/4), 208–234.

UN-ECE (1997, November 13-14). *SMEs—their role in foreign trade.* Background paper prepared by the UN/ECE Secretariat for the BSEC Workshop, Kyiv, Ukraine.

Vecchio, D. (2001). Legacy software: Junkyard wars for Web services? In *Proceedings of the Gartner Symposium/ITxpo*, Orlando, FL.

Yin, R. K. (2003). *Case study research: Design and methods.* London: Sage.

Zhao, Y. (2001). *XML-based frameworks for Internet commerce and an implementation of B2B e-procurement* (SE-581 83). Linköping, Sweden: Linköpings Universitet.

Zheng, J., Caldwell, N. D., Harland, C. M., Powell, P., Woerndl, M., & Xu, S. (2004). Small firms and e-business: Cautiousness, contingency, and cost benefits. *Journal of Purchasing and Supply Management,* (Special Issue IPSERA 2003), *10*(1), 27-39.

This work was previously published in E-Procurement in Emerging Economies: Theory and Cases, edited by A. K. Pani & A. Agrahari, pp. 265-305, copyright 2007 by IGI Publishing, formerly known as Idea Group Publishing (an imprint of IGI Global).

Chapter XVI
E-Business Adoption in SMEs:
Some Preliminary Findings from Electronic Components Industry

Mark Xu
Portsmouth Business School, UK

Ravni Rohatgi
Southampton, UK

Yanqing Duan
University of Bedfordshire, UK

ABSTRACT

The lack of anticipated engagement in e-business by Small and Medium sized Enterprises (SMEs) is a rising concern to the UK government and service providers alike. This article is based on the e-adoption model to examine the current practice of e-business technology adoption in SMEs and the driving forces for and against the adoption. Through interviews with 40 owner managers in the electronic components industry, the article reveals that most of the small firms in this industry are at the lower level of the "e-adoption ladder"—predominantly using the Internet and e-mail. SMEs in this industry have not yet widely engaged in online transactions. The current level of adoption is driven by both internal and external factors, including operational benefits, industry common practice, and peer pressure. External forces such as a lack of push from suppliers and customers and a lack of strategic vision of using advanced e-business technology for competitive advantages have determinant effects on the level and scale of e-adoption in SME sector. The e-adoption ladder model is modified by incorporating the influential factors identified within this study. The findings have many implications for researchers, service providers, and policy makers.

INTRODUCTION

The Internet is described as the SME's gateway to global business and markets (Liikanen, 2001), and e-business technologies are expected to allow SMEs to gain capabilities that were once the preserve of their larger competitors. These new technologies offer the potential for creating entirely new ways of working, giving rise to a new breed of SMEs whose management and employees use a more flexible and more effective way of working. E-business is expected to become a key driver in the way companies across the globe conduct business. However, whether these new technologies are put to efficient use by SMEs and what driving forces that push SMEs up the adoption ladder remains a question that attracts considerable attention of researchers and policy makers (Fillis, Johannson, & Wagner, 2004; Parish, Kibblewhite, Woodley, & Richardson, 2002; Ramsey, Ibbotson, Bell, & Gary, 2003).

Studying e-business adoption in the SMEs sector is of particular importance. This is because SMEs are regarded as significantly important on a local, national, or even global basis and have a history of continual growth. SMEs play an important part in the UK economy with 3.7 million firms employing over 12 million people, which generates 55% of UK employment. These firms contribute approximately 51% to the UK GDP with an annual turnover of over one trillion pounds sterling (Dixon, Thompson, & McAllister, 2002). However, studying e-business adoption in SMEs is a challenge since SMEs are not miniature versions of large firms; they are unique in their own right (Barnett & Mackness, 1983). This includes a small management team, strong owner influence, multi-functional management, limited ability to obtain financing, and a lack of control over the business environment. In addition, SMEs rely on an environment in which structures and processes must remain simple, flexible, and adaptable (Carmichael, Turgoose, Older Gary, Todd, 2000). Firm and managerial factors are merged due to the high locus of control exerted by the key decision makers (Boone, De Brabander, & Hellemans, 2000). These unique characteristics affect Internet technologies adoption in SMEs. Research suggests that there is a correlation between the size of a business and the level of IT adoption (McDonagh & Prothero, 2000). The typical microenterprise exhibits much lower rates of e-business activities than larger firms when excluding smaller high-technology firms (Smyth & Ibbotson 2001). Large organizations are inclined to adopt the click and mortar model by integrating offline and online business or spin-off online operations. In contrast, small and medium-sized firms lack a general pattern on adoption of Internet technologies (Chavez, Leiter, & Kiely, 2000). The extent of adopting Internet technologies may vary widely among small and medium sized enterprises (Kula & Tatoglu, 2003). This creates great demands and challenges to construct a clear picture of the level of e-business adoption in the SME sector.

Research into the level of adoption of e-business technologies in the SMEs sector reported very contradictory results, which exacerbates the current situation of confusion. For example, Smyth and Ibbotson (2001) reported from a multiple industry survey that an extremely low adoption rate was found in Ireland and Northern Ireland. Daniel, Wilson, and Myers (2002) found 50% of e-business adoption in UK SMEs. The statistics of the European Observatory for SMEs show that most SMEs are not using the Internet and the World Wide Web (WWW) for commercial transactions despite the allure of e-business benefits (Ramsey et al. 2003). A multi-industry survey conducted in the North and South of Ireland by Ramsey et al. (2003) revealed that only 33% of the firms had a Web site, 10% of the firms used Web sites to generate online orders, and none of the Web sites could facilitate online payments. However, in a study of the adoption of e-commerce in the UK electronics industry (Parish et al., 2002), a relative high level of adoption of Internet technologies has been reported (i.e., 85% the firm (larger than 100 employees) buy online, and 43% of the firms sell online). The disparity of those empirical findings reflects a lack of consensus and the complexities in gaining a holistic view of e-business adoption in the SME sector.

In view of this, this study aims to reveal the current level of adopting e-business technologies by SMEs in a specific industry, rather than to construct a holistic picture of the whole SME sector cross multiple industry. Based on the E-Adoption Ladder (DTI, 2001) and the E-Adoption Staircases (Allcock, Webber, & Yeates, 1999), which are the theoretical underpinning of this study, this study examines the driving forces that put SMEs up the e-adoption ladder and the barriers that hold SMEs up in climbing up the ladder. Such a study is not a pioneer as far as the topic is concerned, but the novel method of this study will generate findings that are appropriate to construct an accurate picture of the level of e-business adoption in a particular industry, based on which practical solutions can be postulated to improve the effective usage of e-business technologies. The findings will be useful to verify the e-adoption models.

DEFINITIONS OF E-BUSINESS AND SME

The terms "e-business," "e-commerce," and "Internet commerce" are often used interchangeably. Fillis et al. (2004) define e-business as companies that utilize e-technology in their business operations, but exclude sending and receiving text-based e-mail messages. Stone (2003) states that e-business is not just the World Wide Web (www); it involves technology (e.g., intranets, portals, content management, middleware, mobile) to enhance profitability. The UK Department of Trade and Industry (DTI) specifies e-business as the integration of all the activities within the internal processes of a business through ICT (Information Communication Technology). The activities include full integration of information and communication technologies (ICTs) into a firm's operations and potentially include redesigning its business processes around ICT or completely reinventing its business model. In this article, e-business refers to the incorporation of Internet technologies into entire enterprise's operations and management.

The term SMEs is commonly referred to as Small- and Medium-sized Enterprises, but these firms can differ significantly in terms of employee numbers. The European Union's definition of SMEs suggests that a small business includes 10-99 employees, and that a medium sized business includes 100-250 employees. A microenterprise includes less than 10 employees (Ramsey et al., 2003). A study of Internet adoption in Turkey by Kula et al. (2003) defines SME as one that employs less than 100 persons. In this study SMEs refers to VAT (Value Added Tax) registered companies in the UK with employee numbers between 10 to 250. This is a working definition defined and used by the UK Department of Trade and Industry (DTI).

MODELS OF E-ADOPTION/GROWTH

With increasing attention to e-business application, a number of e-business growth / adoption models have been developed (e.g., DTI e-business adoption ladder (DTI 2001)); British library staircase of Internet engagement model (Allcock, 1999); The stage of growth for e-business maturity (SOGe) model (McKay, Prananto, & Marshall, 2000; Prananto, McKay, & Marshall, 2003); SMEs stages of adoption and use of e-commerce OUBS model (Gary, 2003); and the IBM model of stages and states of e-business (Stone, 2003). Gary (2003) suggests that ICT adoption is driven by two theories. One is social network theory where adoption is encouraged by the everyday influences that shape opinions, attitudes and behavior coming from individual expectations, peer pressure, and the business milieu in which firms operate. The second is technology determinist—a rational process where the benefits of simple ICT applications attract small firm owners. The owners move to another stage of business development and become aware of the benefits of more advanced ICT applications.

In this chapter, the e-adoption Ladder and the British Library Staircase models are used to inform the investigation, because the former focuses on the increasing e-business technology complexity along with incremental steps of adoption, which is related to the objective of revealing the level of usage of Internet technologies. The latter considers the driving forces that push firms up the adoption stairs or hold up their adoptions, which is related to the objective of examining the factors driving or inhibiting the adoption. The two models thus are reviewed next.

The "E-Adoption Ladder"

Martin and Matlay (2001) suggest that there are different levels of e-business in SMEs, known as "e-adoption." In the UK DTI benchmarking study report, e-adoption is defined as incremental tiers or steps and can be represented in the form of an "e-adoption ladder" with each stage increasing in level of sophistication as depicted in Figure 1. The first two stages involve acquiring basic ICT skills and technology to operate e-mail for messaging and simple brochure Web sites for online marketing. The e-commerce stage involves online interaction between a business and its customers, or a business and its suppliers, for the placement of an order and online payment processing. The e-business stage allows integration of the supply chain. The final stage enables open information sharing between customers, suppliers, and partners based on which existing business processes are radically transformed or new business models are formed. The adoption ladder emphasizes e-business technology adoption along with organizational change. The final three stages require advanced technology and a wide range of specialist business skills and expertise in areas such as management, strategy, and marketing. Criticism of the adoption ladder concentrates on the linear progression and

Figure 1. The e-adoption ladder (Adapted from Cisco led Information Age Partnership study on e-commerce in small business (DTI, 2001))

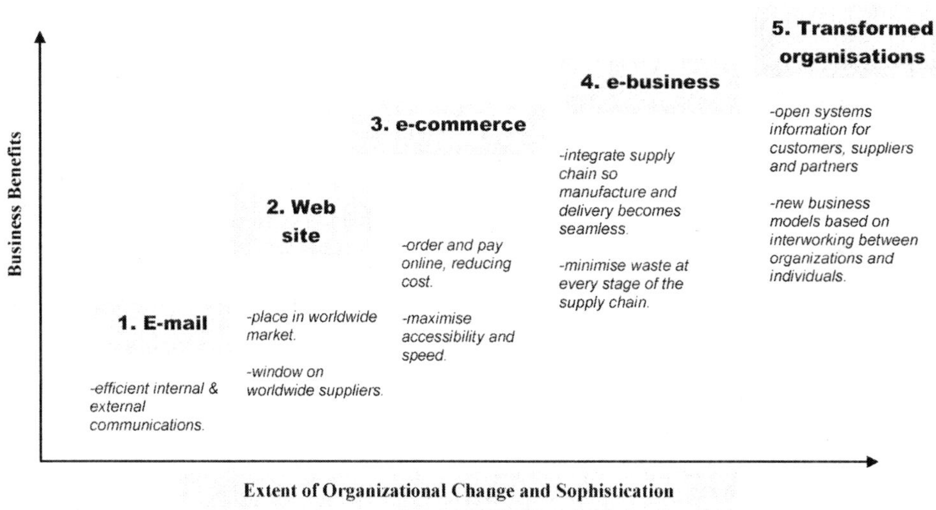

technology sophistication aspects. Gary (2003) commented that the adoption ladder is a simple technology stage model, which provides a useful sense of technological progression, but it is too linear to fully describe processes that are often non-linear and very complex. Ramsey et al. (2003) argued in line with Gary (2003) that the e-adoption ladder assumes a linear progression from being less mature to increased sophistication over time. Ideally, the organization will move through the stages of using e-commerce purely for informational purpose, then transactional, and ultimately progress to having a strategic e-focus. They speculate that the majority of SMEs may have very low-level requirements and/or follow a non-linear/discontinuous path. In reality, the diffusion and assimilation of Internet commerce by SMEs is likely to follow a "zig-zag" path based on a "trial and error" approach (Poon, 2002; Poon & Swatman, 1999).

The Staircase of Internet Engagement

Based on information needs rather than a technology push and considering SME sector characteristics, the British Library adopted a four stages staircase model (Allcock, et al. 1999), which is depicted in Figure 2.

The model shows four stages and technology sophistication, but it is different from the adoption ladder in that the model includes non-technology driving forces (e.g., external pressure, increased ICT skills, business driver). These forces may push SMEs up the stairs, but influential factors (e.g., lack of resource and skills, system changeover, etc.) may send the firm down the stairs. Gary (2003) positively commented that the British Library Staircase model takes the perspective of the SMEs owner-managers, linking technology evolution to their capability to learn, to manage

Figure 2. The staircase of internet engagement (Allcock, et al. 1999)

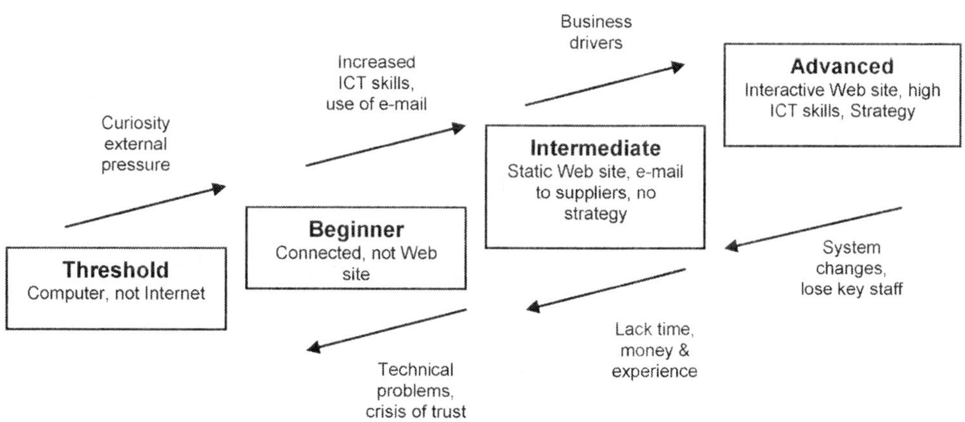

new ICT knowledge, and to introduce business changes. Related to this staircase model, Fillis, et al. (2004) developed a conceptual model of factors that impact on e-business adoption in small firms. The model consists of three tiers of influence factors including macro-factors (e.g., globalizations, competition, government policy, etc), industry/sectoral factors, and micro level firm/managerial factors. Fillis et al. (2003) argue that macro-level factors are the drivers behind technological change. They emphasize that specific industry and sectoral factors will influence SMEs demand for e-business. At the firm level, resource-based issues (i.e., e-business competencies, managers' attitudes and benefits are highlighted as the main factors driving e-business adoption). This model is useful in informing the research design of this study.

METHODOLOGY

This study chooses the electronic components manufacturer and supplier industry as the source for sampling. There are three reasons: firstly, according to Ramsey et al. (2003), this industry has been under researched relative to other industry sectors such as retail chain, services or the travel industry. For example, the highest Internet presence is in the hospitability/leisure sector and the lowest is in agriculture and transport sectors. Secondly, the aforementioned studies are primarily multiple industry-based and country-specific surveys, which lead to disparity in findings. The aggregated findings on the level of e-business adoption of multiple industries are inconclusive due to industry sectoral differences. This is evident from Fillis et al. (2004) who argue that specific industry and sector factors will influence the demand for e-business technologies in SMEs, and Internet usage will not be consistent across SMEs in every business sector. They explain that e-business is not appropriate for all firms across all industry sectors. Specific sectoral circumstances may mean that more traditional methods of securing business will still dominate. Thus, an accurate national or international picture of e-business adoption in SMEs is difficult to construct due to macro, industrial, firm and owner manager differences. An industry specific study can produce more accurate results showing the level of e-business adoption and the driving forces that are appropriate to that industry. Lastly, according to Executives from Business Link (a UK government enabled support agency providing business solutions to SMEs), specialist manufacturers are more likely to be pro-e-business, and would adopt future technologies if they have not already done so. The electronic components industry fits well into this category.

The approach for data collection conforms to both qualitative and quantitative techniques. The target population is small to medium sized enterprises in the electronic components manufacturers and suppliers industry. This is a typical SME manufacturing sector in the UK. With the help of the Southampton and Fareham Chamber of Commerce and Industry, which maintains close contacts with regional SMEs, 40 companies in the South of England have been contacted and chosen to participate in the study. The selection process assumed that there is no pre-knowledge as to the usage of Internet technologies within those firms, thus the sample is framed in random nature, although its size is relatively small.

The primary method is a structured interview with managing directors, which was conducted during April and May 2004. A questionnaire was used during the one to one interviews. In the case where managing directors were not available for an interview, a substitute such as sales director, IT director, or finance director was interviewed. Interviewing owner managers or directors for this topic is based on the consideration that investment in Internet technology is a major strategic decision of owner managers for small and medium firms. Ramsey et al. (2003) used a similar approach in their study. We echo their view that due to the dynamic nature, e-business decision-making is based largely on the intuitive competencies of the entrepreneurial owner/managers. Most of the interviews lasted approximately half an hour. A number of standard questions were asked at each interview, this is to ensure that minimum consensus can be tabulated in data analysis. The interviewees were invited to discuss the topics and their concerns relevant to the study without prompting them with directions or constraints. Each interview was recorded with the consent of the interviewee. Copies of the interview transcriptions were given to each interviewee shortly after the interview. Where appropriate, they could add any extra information as appropriate. Due to the qualitative nature of data and the small size of sample, statistical tests are not used to analyze the data.

RESULTS AND DISCUSSION

Profile of Sample Companies and Interviewees

To understand the context of the responses, the sample companies were broken down by the number of employees and the position of the interviewees. Table 1 shows the profile of the companies.

The table shows that the majority of interviews (62.5%) were conducted with companies with less than 50 employees, thus the sample may be biased towards small manufacturing firms. Seventy percent of interviewees are managing directors, and the rest are all at director level. Most of the companies were that established in the 1980s with a few new companies established in the 1990s.

Position in the Ladder: The Level of Adoption of E-Business Technology

The adoption of e-business technology in those SMEs is examined in light of the e-adoption ladder. Table 2 shows the extent of usage of these technologies in this industry.

The data shows that all the companies interviewed have access to the Internet. E-mail has been widely used by small and medium firms. Sixty-eight percent of the firms are using broadband, which enables fast access to the Internet and e-mail and 20% uses wireless access. One third of the companies used Intranets for internal communication and an Extranet to link to suppliers. However, using instant messaging, video conferencing, and other tools for business are low in these firms.

A further enquiry on the level of complexity of the firms' Web site and the primary purposes

Table 1. The profile of the sample

Number of Employees	Managing Director	Sales Director	Finance Director	IT Director	Production Director	Marketing Director	**Total (%)**
10-49	20	2	1	0	1	1	62.5%
50-99	5	3	0	0	0	0	20.0%
100-149	3	0	0	0	0	0	7.5%
150-199	0	0	0	2	0	0	5.0%
200-249	0	0	0	1	1	0	5.0%
Total (%)	70%	12.5%	2.5%	7.5%	5%	2.5%	100%

Table 2. Usage of e-business technology

e-business technology	Responses	% (N=40)
Internet	40	100%
E-mail	40	100%
Broadband Technology	27	67.5%
Intranets/Extranets	13	32.5%
Wireless Technology	8	20 %
EDI	7	17.5%
Instant Messaging	4	10 %
Video Conferencing	4	10 %
Other (Voice Operated Internet Protocol)	1	2.5%

of the Web site reveals that 88% of Web sites are static (i.e., displaying information about the company and products). Fifteen percent of the Web sites have only one Web page showing contact details. Only five companies (12%) enabled customers to buy products online, and those five companies are medium-sized companies with employees over 100. The primary purposes of using the Web site are discussed with the managers, which are summarized in Table 3. The data shows that the top four (over 70%) usages of Web sites are related to Internet marketing and information communication, which suggests that the Web sites are predominantly used as a marketing and communication tool. It is worth highlighting that only 12.5% of the Web sites offer an online buying or selling e-commerce function. This is in contrast to some of the findings mentioned earlier where higher level of e-business applications was reported (Daniel et al. 2002; Parish, et al. 2002; Stone, 2003). It also differs from Ramsey et al.'s (2003) finding that there was no indication (0%) of high-level functionality—the ability to buy and pay for service/product online.

The high-level usage of Web sites and e-mails confirms many findings reported in other similar studies. For example, Kula et al. (2003) report the ranking of Internet application usage from the highest to lowest level are: e-mail, browsing company homepages, and market and product searches. They suggest that Internet applications are principally concerned with external communications and gathering information for market and product research. Ramsey et al. (2003) reported that owner managers perceive e-mail as an important function for their business. Man-

Table 3. Purposes and functionality of the Web site

Purpose	No of Responses	% (n=40)
Display information on product or service	34	85.0%
Increase information exchanges and communication	33	82.5%
Improve marketing/advertising	31	77.5%
Reach wider audience	29	72.5%
Increase profits	17	42.5%
Because everybody else has one	12	30.0%
Sell products and services over the Web	5	12.5%
Create a 365/7 service	3	7.5%

agers interviewed in this study acknowledged that the reasons of high-level usage of Internet and e-mails are the great benefit as compared to other means (i.e., using the Internet and e-mail can increase the response rate of receiving and sending information, which in turn reduces the cost of postage). Other benefits include sharing information, improving marketing and communication, and access to a wide range of information. It needs to note that only four managers regard an additional benefit being increased profits through interactive Web sites, which enable customers to purchase components and parts over the Internet. Only five medium-sized companies actually sell products on the Web. This is in line with Lymer, Nayak, Johnson, and Spaul's (1998) findings that the main Internet tools identified as available for small business were a Web site, e-mail, access to online information, and networking. Even though one third of the firms acknowledged using intranet and/or extranet, the main benefit is enabling information communication and sharing, not online buying or selling. Referring to the e-adoption ladder, firms in this particular industry widely adopt the most common Internet technologies (e-mail and Internet) that constitute the first and the second levels of the ladder. This firmly positions the SMEs in this industry on the lower two ladders. The adoption of broadband (68%) and wireless technology (20%) shows the firms attempt to maximize accessibility and speed. Even though these technologies are used, there is little sign to show that the firms are moving up to the full e-commerce stage. This adds to criticism over the e-adoption model that technology complexity may not necessarily lead to a higher degree of e-commerce/or e-business adoption. In terms of the British Library Staircase, there are influential factors that can hold firms up on the adoption ladder. The next section will examine these factors.

PUSHING UP: THE DRIVING FORCES OF E-BUSINESS ADOPTION

Business Benefits

Business driver has been regarded as a main driving force for technology adoption as shown in the Staircase model. Levy, Powell, and Yetton (2002) suggest that SMEs tend to be driven by short-term efficiency and operational benefits to the detriment of strategic, long-term business benefits. Evidence shown in Table 4 confirms this assertion.

The data shows that the vast majority of the owner managers believe their firms gained immediate operational benefits from using Internet technologies, for example, cost reduction, sharing information, improved marketing, and communication. A few managers comment that the cost of postage and postal mail were significantly reduced due to the introduction of using e-mail. Another key benefit is faster responses to customers needs. Carmichael et al. (2000) suggest that the key driver for SMEs to innovate is competition and customer feedback. SMEs realized that they need to remain competitive in order to survive, thus responding to customer feedback is an important weapon of competition. One manager owes the benefits to increased profit due to their interactive Web site enabling customer to purchase components and parts over the Internet. These operational benefits and response to competition needs clearly constitute the main driving forces that push firms up the adoption ladder.

Industry Common Practice or Peer Pressure

Kula et al. (2003) suggest that most SMEs innovate only when they clearly perceive business opportunities for their firms, or because they are under pressure from suppliers and clients. It is interesting to note that one third of the companies

Table 4. Benefit of adopting e-business technologies

Main improvement / benefits	No of Responses	% (n=40)
Reduced cost	29	72.5
Faster response rate	28	70.0
Share and exchange information more effectively and quickly	28	70.0
Improved marketing and communication	23	57.5
Access to more information	18	45.0
Increased profit by enabling online purchasing	1	2.5

interviewed (30% in Table 3) don't have a clear idea about the reasons for having a Web site. Some managers said that it is common to have a company Web site in the industry, as everyone else has one. The reason "everyone else has one" shows the effect of benchmarking or peer pressure from the industry. The finding appears to suggest that peer pressure or industry standard is a main driving force to pushing firms up the ladder of adoption of e-business technologies. However, this could become an inhibitor to adopting new technologies if there is no industry leader or champion to innovate and to demonstrate the strategic advantages of using advanced e-business technologies.

Awareness of E-Business Function

Ramsey et al. (2003) argue that growing awareness and understanding of the benefits of e-commerce among SMEs can positively influence their desire and interest in adopting e-commerce. It is evident from this study that over 90% of the managers have some understanding of the e-business function and its potential, although the degree of understanding vary significantly. Table 5 presents the awareness level against e-adoption ladder. The four categories are based on the responses generated from the structured interviews.

The synthesized data shows that 25% of the managers can relate e-business to buying and selling over the Internet. A few managers are quoted as saying that:

e-business is buying and selling over the Internet, also including instant messaging, chatting to customers.

e-business is electronic business activities, for example internal and external communications, being able to e-mail customers—current and potential, to buy and sell products.

Conducting business through the Internet using Web Technology, using the Internet to extend business overseas.

Table 5. Managers' awareness of e-business function

e-business function awareness against adoption ladder	Responses	%
On e-business ladder: Doing business over the Internet involving procurement, supply chain	3	7.5
On e-commerce ladder: Doing business over the Internet including taking orders and selling	10	25.0
On Internet ladder: Using Web site for marketing, information gathering, or something to do with the Internet	20	50.0
Under the ladder: Do not know e-business function	7	17.5

Those remarks reflect managers' understanding/awareness of the "e-commerce" function—the third level of the e-business adoption ladder. Three managers can even relate e-business to supply chain for procurement, or to integrate with ERP (Enterprise Resource Planning) system. For example,

Using the Internet for information gathering. The ability to procure electronically. Using ERP systems, portals to place orders, appearing on industry wide Web sites, and placing orders via electronic means.

Using the Internet to process orders and communicate between companies. To make more contacts internationally and to ease the communication between suppliers and customers via digital technology, such as broadband.

Doing everything electronically—the next evolution from the 3rd party stage. Getting suppliers online and clients online and doing every bit of business online. The Web site has 4 stages: static, interactive, transactional, involves the whole Supply Chain.

This shows sufficient awareness of the higher level of e-business sophistication (i.e., the e-business ladder of the adoption model). However, none of the managers indicate that there will be a radical transformation of the way of doing business in the industry (further discussion is in Table 7).

It is interesting to note that the combination of the first two categories adds up to 32.5%, which shows that over one third of the managers are aware of the e-commerce/e-business functionality, but actual online selling is conducted within only five companies (12.5%). There must be factors that hold firms up from adopting technology to the level as managers perceived.

Table 5 also shows that half of the owner managers do not relate e-business to online buying, selling, and transforming business process, but regard e-business as the same as online marketing, information searching, a part of customer process, or simply something to do with the Internet. For example:

E-business complements other business channels but cannot replace it. Ten years ago, banks, shops etc. closed many of their physical premises, just to find they were not generating as much business because people were not familiar with using the Internet and were not comfortable. There is no point adopting something new where no one is going to use it. E-business is about making business processes a part of the customer process. It is a way of interacting more technically with the customer.

E-business is a marketing and advertising tool with the ability to promote products and services (e.g., using the WWW to have company information listed on search engines so people can see what you do on a global scale).

Seventeen and a half percent of the owner managers do not know e-business functionality and its potential opportunity. One manager even perceived e-business as

Doing business in Europe (!).

Overall, the findings are in contrast to some of the claims that a lack of understanding of the benefits (Goode, 2002) and the difficulties of evaluating them contribute to the low level of e-commerce adoption in SMEs (Stockdale & Standing, 2004). Our study reveals that the majority of managers' understanding of e-business tends to be consistent with the current level of e-business adoption in their firms.

Table 6. Barriers to implement e-business technology

Items as Barriers	Mean	Standard Deviation
Lack of resources to adopt	2.73	1.20
Lack of training to implement these technologies	2.75	1.26
Lack of customer demand	2.80	1.32
Unconvinced of the potential benefits	2.98	1.33
Lack of relevance to the business	3.08	1.35
Cost of enabling e-business technology	3.13	1.14
E-business seen as a greater threat than an opportunity	3.85	1.21
Bandwidth – connecting to the Internet	4.10	0.87

1-Hardest obstacle, 5- Not an obstacle

Holding UP: The Influential Forces For E-Business Non-Adoption

The barriers that hold companies back from adopting e-business technology are discussed with the directors through a structured question. The question adopted several measurements appeared in literature, and used 5 likart scale in order to identify the most influential inhibitors that hold-up firms in climbing up the adoption ladder. The results are summarized in Table 6.

Lack of Resources and Training

Limited resources (e.g., financial, time, management, training, personnel) are often highlighted as major factors impacting the decision to adopt e-business. Lawrence (2002) argues that resource limitations such as time and capital coupled with preferences for traditional mechanisms to do business, inhibited firms from gaining benefits from introducing e-commerce technology. In this study, lack of resources has been seen as a main obstacle to adopting e-business technologies. This refers to limited personnel, training, and expertise. Managers explained that being small companies, the employees have to train themselves on how to use the functions of the technologies that the company has adopted, i.e. how to use the Internet and how to access information and how to use search engines to obtain higher numbers of hits. As the usage of complex e-business technology is minimal in these firms, formal training is not required by the users, nor is such training provided by the firm.

SMEs have been seen as spending little on technology, therefore they do not use the optimum solutions for much of their business. As a result, they are unable to invest in new technology that could actually help put them on the fast track. However, this study shows that the cost of enabling e-business technology appears not to be a barrier to these firms as shown by the mean score (3.13). This support the arguments that financial resources do not affect the decision on whether or not to adopt Internet technologies (Mehrtens, Cragg, & Mills, 2001), and that cost is not a main concern when making e-business decisions (Ramsey et al. 2003).

The Industry Nature and Tradition

Some managers commented that e-business technologies are not relevant to the industry and there is no demand from customers for using these technologies. Managers explained that the nature of the industry requires regular face-to-face or telephone contact when describing electronic components. Another reason is that people are used to using traditional methods such as phone or fax. They feel more comfortable continuing to use these technologies, as opposed to investing in new technologies, which may require considerable training. This suggests that the nature of the industry, the common practice, and the traditional way of doing business impose a significant impact on the adoption of new technologies. Ramsey et al.'s (2003) addresses the unique nature of an industry in relation to utilization of Internet technology. They assert that each day the owner manager is more preoccupied with "fire-fighting" to realize and fulfill customer orders, where there is a heavy reliance on face-to-face contact. The service is highly tangible and is not really suited to the e-business environment. The high level of intangibility of the service/product mix can be viewed as one of the major impediments to future utilization of Internet commerce by this particular business.

Lack of Push from Supply Chain (Customer Demand)

Fillis et al. (2004) speculate that there may be a sense that business is dictated mainly by the end customer, supplier or distributor who does not want to embrace e-business technology, instead preferring conventional, traditional methods. The data in Table 6 shows that the SME managers in this industry feel there is a lack of demand from customers to use online selling and buying. This implies that the downstream supply chain (could also be from the upstream chain) demand has a notable impact on the level and scale of adopting advanced e-business technologies.

Lack of Vision and Industrial Champion

The vision and attitude of the owner managers towards IT adoption are identified as an influential factor by Chong, (2001) and Levy and Powell (2002). Successful companies that embrace IT and Internet technologies are often ones in which the visionary owner takes on the role as innovation champion of IT adoption. However, many managers of SMEs prefer the comfort of what they perceive as familiar over indulging into any new venture. They are reluctant to "think outside the box" in order to seek new business solutions (Cyert & March, 1992). In this study, some managers don't perceive (or are not convinced by) the potential strategic benefits of being the first to utilize new technologies. Some managers do not perceive the relevance of using new technologies to their business, although they understand the online buying and selling functions offered by the technologies. A lack of vision and risk taking may be speculated as the reason leading to the current situation. We echo Gary's (2003) argument that whether the adoption is driven by business demand or technology push, the owner managers need to be personally ready before moving on to the next stage and that the process involves learning and new knowledge.

In summary, a lack of resources, and a lack of vision of the potential benefits are influential factors that are internal to the SMEs, whereas the industry common practice and a lack of push from supply chain constitute external factors. These factors hamper SMEs in proactively adopting e-business technologies (i.e., holding up the firms on the adoption ladder/staircase). Other internal factors, such as Internet access, bandwidth, and cost appear not to be critical obstacles in adopting e-business technologies in those firms.

A Forward View of E-Adoption Pattern

Regarding the importance and the future of adopting e-business technology, 65% of the managers interviewed think e-business technology (predominantly Internet and e-mail) is important to their companies. Table 7 shows managers' perceptions of the future of adopting e-business technology within their firms.

Table 7. The future outlook of e-business

Views	Number	% (N=40)
"Use e-business technology together with conventional business methods"	31	77.5%
"Consider using minimal e-business technology in the future"	7	17.5%
"No intention to use e-business in the future"	2	5.0%
"Rely entirely on e-business technology and become a purely online business"	0	0.0%

The dominant view is to adopt e-business technology in conjunction with conventional methods of doing business (i.e., the "clicks and mortar" pattern. None of the firms interviewed are considering transforming into a purely online business. This has been emphasized by the managers that the industry requires regular face-to-face or telephone contact with customers and employees prefer to adhere to the traditional way of doing business. It is noted that 17.5% consider using e-business technology to a minimum level and 5% firms never intend to use e-business technologies. It appears that industry common practice has a strong influence on these SMEs. This situation may not change significantly in a short period of time, as 67.5% of the managers interviewed are satisfied with the e-business technology adopted, and less than a quarter (22.5%) of the managers expressed dissatisfaction, unless significant pressure and push from external stakeholders, particularly from suppliers and customers emerge.

MANAGERIAL IMPLEMENTATIONS

Although some of the findings tend to be common to all SMEs (e.g., lack of resources), some findings are unique in the context of this study. These distinct findings have implications in providing guidance on practical application of e-business technologies in SMEs and in developing e-adoption models. Firstly, industry common practice, peer pressure, and customer push need to be recognized as major external forces that influence the level of adoption of e-business technology in SMEs. Even though this study is not aimed to scientifically test whether external forces outweigh internal forces, its results indicate that external forces tend to be a strong influential factor in affecting the level and scale of e-technology adoption in this particular industry. The findings approve that most SMEs are followers in their sector in terms of adopting technology. It can be envisaged that an industry champion/or leader who demonstrates strategic benefits of adopting advanced technologies, together with a strong demand from suppliers or customers could influence many SMEs moving up to the higher level of the adoption ladder, although there are internal resource constraints. This implies that the pattern of adopting e-business technologies may not be linear as depicted in Figure 1 (i.e., SMEs may not necessarily move from Internet level to e-commerce level and then to e-business level). It is possible that many SMEs in the electronic components industry may engage in business process change based on an intranet-based supply chain infrastructure while conducting online buying and selling. This is a non-linear path of adopting e-business technology. Based on such speculation, the e-adoption model may need to be modified to include a non-linear path with consideration of the driving forces from a firm's internal and external environment. Figure 3 depicts such a model.

Secondly, owner managers need to develop a strategic vision, and the industry needs a champion to lead. As far as the SMEs in the electronics components industry is concerned, there needs to be an external push as well as an internal business

Figure 3. An e-adoption ladder with influential factors

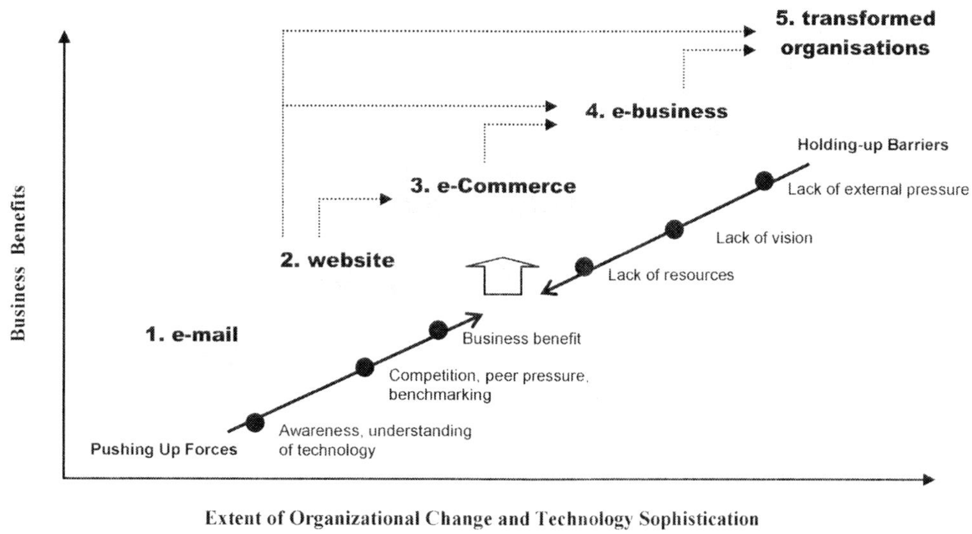

driver to make small firms proactively engage in adopting advanced e-business technologies. This could be achieved by inspiring owner managers with immediate benefits and strategic (competitive) advantages of using e-business technologies. The key to success is to provide a cost/time saving as well as flexible learning opportunity for the owner managers who are busy in managing daily business and seeking new business opportunities. Thirdly, the IT industry that provides e-business solutions needs to articulate explicitly the potential and added value of technologies to owner managers. The products and services need to be tailor-made to suit the unique needs of SMEs, and vendors' support and training should be prioritized to SMEs clients, due to the significant lack of expertise, specialist knowledge, and resources in the SME sector. Lastly, the e-business environment and infrastructure need to be continuously improved to facilitate e-business application in SMEs. This includes easy Internet/broadband access, government incentives for SMEs, secure order processing and payment systems, distribution infrastructure supporting online transactions, online taxation and legislation. These are generally uncontrollable factors to SME managers but they could pose direct impact on the level of adoption as external forces.

CONCLUSION

The findings of this study shed light on some of the issues concerning the engagement of e-business in SMEs. SMEs in the electronic components industry are at the lower ladder of adopting e-business technology. The technologies used are predominantly e-mail and Internet, and are used primarily as an additional marketing tool to display company's products and services information, rather than as an e-commerce platform to enable online transactions and organizational transformation. The problems underpinning the low adoption of sophisticated e-business technology lie not in Internet access, cost and managerial understanding, but in the external forces including industry/sector practice, lack of push from supply chain, as well as internal factors such as lack of resources, expertise and strategic vision to lead. Even though half of the owner managers are aware of e-business functions, awareness of e-business strategic benefits can be further improved. As far as this industry is concerned, a push from external forces could quickly change the picture of the level and the scale of e-business adoption. The findings also suggest that e-business adoption may not follow a linear path and the adoption pattern may be specific to each industry/sector.

The findings reported in this study need to be interpreted with caution due to the limitations of the unique industry selected and the small sample size. However, the findings are useful in raising the question as to whether there exists a general pattern or model of e-business adoption that can fit all SME sectors. It also opens a door to examine if external forces have more influence than internal forces in the SME sector. Aggregated findings on the level of e-business adoption from multiple industry-based studies neglected sector difference, and the results are not consistent to generate a common adoption pattern/model. Therefore, further study of a similar nature in specific industry needs to be conducted, so that the unique needs and problems related to that industries/sectors in adopting e-business technology can be appropriately addressed, and the findings generated from different industry/sector can be compared in the context of developing an e-business adoption model.

REFERENCES

Allcock, S. P. A., Webber, S., & Yeates, R. (1999). Business information and the Internet: Use of the Internet as an information resource for SME. *British Library Research and Information Report*. (136).

Barnett, R. R., & Mackness, J. R. (1983). An action research study of small firm management. *Management Journal of Applied Systems, 10*, 63-83.

Boone, C., De Brabander, B., & Hellemans, J. (2000) Research note: CEO locus of control and small firm performance. *Organization Studies, 21*(3), 641-646.

Carmichael, C., Turgoose, C., Gary, M.O., & Todd, C. (2000). Innovation and SMEs the case of Yorkshire, UK. *Journal of Industry and Higher Education, 14*(4) 244-248.

Chavez, R., Leiter, M., & Kiely, T. (2000). Should you spin off your Internet business? *Business Strategy Review, 11*(2), 19-31.

Chong, S. (2001). Electronic commerce adoption by small-medium sized enterprises in Australia and Singapore. *Working Paper*, School of Information Systems, Curtin University of Technology, Perth, Western Australia.

Cyert, R. M., & March, J. G. (1992). *A behavioral theory of the firm* (2nd ed.). Oxford: Blackwell.

Daniel, E., Wilson, H., & Myers, A. (2002). Adoption of e-commerce by SMEs in the UK. *International Small Business Journal, 20*(3), 253-270.

Dixon, T., Thompson, B., & McAllister, P. (2002). *The value of ICT for SMEs in the UK: A critical review of literature*. Report for the Small Business Service Research Programme.

DTI. (2001). *Business in the information age—international benchmarking study 2000*. (UK Department of Trade and Industry) Retrieved from www.ukonlineforbusiness.gov.uk

Fillis, I., Johannson, U., & Wagner, B. (2004). Factors impacting on adoption and development in the smaller firm. *International Journal of Enterpreneurial Behaviour & Research, 10*(3), 178-191.

Gary, C. (2003). A stage model of ICT adoption in small firms. *Workshop in Rimini—Firms and Consumers Facing E-Commerce: Strategies to Increase Its Adoption and Usage*. Open University Business School, UK

Goode, S. (2002). Management attitudes towards the World Wide Web in Australian small business. *Information Systems Management, 19*(1), 45-48.

Kula, V., & Tatoglu, E. (2003). An exploratory study of Internet adoption by SMEs in an emerging market economy. *European Business Review, 15*(5), 324-333.

Lawrence, K. (2002). Factors inhibiting the collaborative adoption of electronic-commerce among Australia SMEs. In S. Burgess (Ed.), *Managing information technology in small business: Challenges & solutions* (pp. 178-192). Hershey, PA: Idea Group Publishing.

Levy, M., & Powell, P. (2002). SME transformation: Modelling progressions. In S. Wrycza (Ed.), *Information systems and the future of the digital economy, Proceedings of the 10th European Conference on Information Systems*, Gdansk, Poland, June 2002.

Levy, M., Powell, P., & Yetton, P. (2002). The dynamics of SME information systems. *Small Business Economics, 19*(4), 341-354.

Liikanen, E. (2001). *eEurope and the role of SMEs.* Paper presented at the European Commission Go Digital Meeting, April 6.

Lymer, A., Nayak, A., Johnson, R., & Spaul, B. (1998). *UK business and the information superhighway: The impact of the Internet on SMEs.* ACCA Occasional Research Paper, No. 23: The Association of Chartered Certified Accountants.

Martin, L. M., & Matlay, H. (2001). Innovative use of the Internet in established small firms: The impact of knowledge management and organisational learning in accessing new opportunities. *Qualitative Market Research: An International Journal, 6*(1), 18-26.

McDonagh, P., & Prothero, A. (2000). Euroclicking and the Irish SME: Prepared for E-commerce and the single currency. *Irish Marketing Review, 13*(1), 21-33

McKay, J., Prananto, A., & Marshall, P. (2000). *E-business maturity: The SOGe model.* Paper presented at the Proceedings of the 11th Australasian Conference on Information Systems (ACIS), Dec, 6-8, Queensland University of Technology, Brisbane, Australia.

Mehrtens, J., Cragg, P. B., & Mills, A. M. (2001). A model of Internet adoption by SMEs. *Information & Management, 39*(3), 165-176.

Parish, A., Kibblewhite, G., Woodley, M., & Richardson, J. (2002). *The UK electronics industry e-commerce initiative—a study of the adoption of e-commerce.* Retrieved from www.intellectuk.org/publications/reports

Poon, S. (2000). Business environment and Internet commerce benefits—a small business perspective. *European Journal of Information Systems, 9*(2), 72-81.

Poon, S., & Swatman, P. M. C. (1999). An exploratory study of small business Internet commerce. *Information & Management, 35*(1), 9-18.

Prananto, A., McKay, J. A., & Marshall, P. (2003). A study of the progression of e-business maturity in Australian SMEs: Some evidence of the applicability of the stages of growth for e-business model. *Proceedings of the 7th Pacific Asia Conference on Information Systems (PACIS)*, July 10-13.

Ramsey, E., Ibbotson, P., Bell, J., & Gary, B. (2003). E-opportunities of service sector SMEs: An Irish cross-boarder study. *Journal of Small Business and Enterprise Development, 10*(3), 250-264.

Smyth, M., & Ibbotson, P. G. (2001). *Internet connectivity in Ireland.* Retrieved from www.bankofireland.co.uk

Stockdale, R., & Standing, C. (2004). Benefits and barriers of electronic marketplace participation:

An SME perspective. *The Journal of Enterprise Information Management*, *17*(4), 301-311.

Stone, M. (2003). SME e-business and supplier-customer relations. *Journal of Small Business and Enterprise Development*, *10*(3), 345-353.

This work was previously published in International Journal of E-Business Research, Vol. 3, Issue 1, edited by I. Lee, pp. 74-90, copyright 2007 by IGI Publishing, formerly known as Idea Group Publishing (an imprint of IGI Global).

Chapter XVII
How Can Internet Service Providers Tap into the Potentially -Lucrative Small Business Market?

Avinash Waikar
Southeastern Louisiana University, USA

Minh Q. Huynh
Southeastern Louisiana University, USA

ABSTRACT

Small businesses need Internet service to be competitive, and their spending on IT activities continues to grow. How can Internet Service Providers tap into this potentially lucrative market? This study attempts to identify Internet service features that are important to small businesses. Specifically, it used a survey method to explore the relationships between the importance of various features and organizational characteristics of small businesses, for example, size and type of business. The results show that the size of business affects the perceived importance placed on certain features, while the type of business does not. Implication of this finding for packaging Internet service is discussed.

INTRODUCTION

There is little doubt that the Internet is changing the way that many businesses are operating. According to Cottrill (1997), and Power and Sohal (2002), the Internet is the enabler that ultimately revolutionizes the way business is conducted in some industries. Research shows that the use of the Internet by businesses has led to improvement in lead times (Hauguel & Jackson, 2001; Power & Sohal, 2002), better communication and collaboration within and across organizations (Garcia-Dastugue & Lambert, 2003), and significant gain in achieving greater cost efficiencies (Barnes, Hinton, & Mieczkowska, 2003). Given these findings, it appears that the Internet may be assuming a pivotal role in achieving business objectives (Levenburg, 2005).

The Internet was also envisioned as a powerful tool enabling small businesses to "level the playing field" when competing with larger firms (Levenburg 2005). There is growing evidence that the Internet has indeed changed the way that many small businesses are conducting their operations (Barnes et al., 2003). Perhaps the use of the Internet has penetrated much deeper into the small business market. To gain competitiveness in producing and selling products or delivering services effectively and efficiently, small businesses must rely on the use of the Internet. This in turn shows a critical connection between small businesses and their Internet service providers. As we searched the literature, to our surprise, we found almost no academic study that examines any aspects of the relationship between small businesses and their Internet service providers. Yet the potential market of small businesses is quite promising, as more small businesses are spending more on information technology activities today than at any other times. According to the research firm AMI Partners, businesses with fewer than 100 employees spent more than $12 billion on network and telecom equipment in 2004. Furthermore, small businesses are expected to account for 24% of all IT hardware and software spending in 2006 (Hochmuth, 2005). The CEO of Vendio, Mr. Rodrigo Sales said, "We are entering a new era in e-commerce—one increasingly driven by smaller businesses and merchants" (Kooser, 2003). Therefore, a study of small businesses is important because these firms comprise a significant proportion, not only in the U.S., but also in most other countries' economic activity (McMillan & Woodruff, 2002).

How can Internet service providers (ISP) tap into the potentially-lucrative small business market? One of the keys to successfully exploiting this market, we believe, rests upon the Internet service providers' ability to understand the market needs and to fulfill these needs effectively. To achieve that, an ISP needs to provide features that are needed by small businesses to conduct their operations. This is essential because how effectively small businesses use the Internet would depend on "features of the Internet service". In this context, this study focuses on exploring what features of Internet service are important to small businesses and to ascertain whether these preferences are related to certain organizational characteristics such as "type of small business" and "size of small business". Specifically, this article looks for some insights into two aspects of the issue: (1) Is "size of small business" related to the perceived importance for various features of the Internet service? and (2) Do different "types of small businesses" have different levels of perceived importance for various features provided in the Internet service by ISPs? If so, what are the differences?

CONCEPTUAL BACKGROUND

Figure 1 shows a research diagram used to seek answers to the questions in this study. It consists of three major variables: "size of business", "type of business", and the "perceived importance of various Internet service features". In this section, we will discuss some of the justifications for these variables, including their descriptions and significance.

One of the challenges in our study is how to define the term "small businesses". According to the Small Business Administration (SBA) in the United States, businesses with less than 500 employees are considered small businesses. Taking the context beyond the U.S., the definition of small businesses becomes a little more complicated. Instead of using the term "small businesses", various descriptive terms such as micro-, small-, and medium-sized enterprises are used in Europe, and their interpretations may vary widely. For instance, the term MSE includes "micro-enterprises" and "small enterprises", and these enterprises are considered the smallest. However, most numerous businesses within

Figure 1. The association between "size" and "type" of business and the perceived importance of various Internet service features

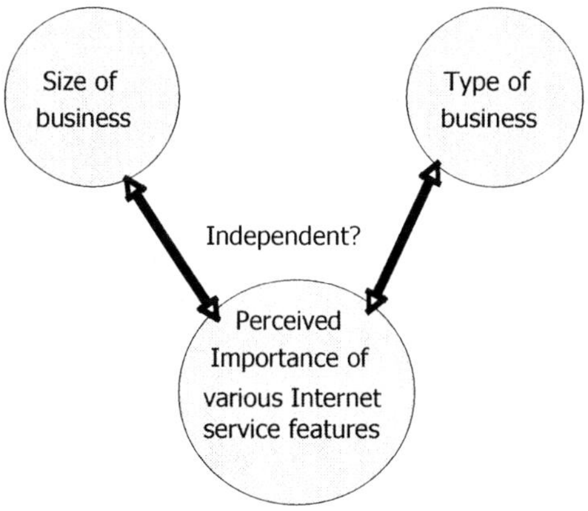

the larger group of enterprises are called SMEs (small- and medium-sized enterprises) (Donner, 2004). Not having one common term with a precise description is just one problem in research involving small businesses. Another difficulty is how to determine the threshold for the size. What size makes a business a small business? There is no agreement on an absolute number. While SBA set 500 employees as a drawing line, this arbitrary number is impractical because it has been found that a large number of U.S. small businesses have fewer than 20 employees (Zimmerer & Scarborough, 2003). Therefore, studies (such as Barua, Konana, Whinston, & Yin, 2001; Boyer & Olson, 2002; Zank & Vokurka, 2003) of "small businesses" that track firms with fewer than 100 employees may not fully capture the nuances in usage within very small businesses. This means that small business population is not homogeneous but diverse in terms of size. To account for the non-homogeneity, this study differentiates various small businesses based on the number of employees using four size groups: (a) 1-25 employees; (b) 26-50 employees; (c) 51-100 employees; and (d) more than 100 employees.

Our review of literature further reveals that most of the past studies on "the Internet use" focused on larger firms. Because of the inherent difference in structure and organization between large and small businesses, many of the known findings in the large business environment cannot be generalized to small business environment. For instance, Brynjlfsson and Hitt (2000) confirm the positive contribution of information technology (IT) on productivity by using company-level data. No firm size was taken into consideration, although it could be an important factor. Prior studies showed the relevance of the construct "size" to the firm's adoption and use of IT. For instance, the size of the firm, in particular, has been found to be related to adoption rates (DTI, 2000; Haynes, Becherer, & Helms, 1998; Riquelme, 2002) as well as the intensity and level of information and communication technology (ICT) activity (Fallon & Moran, 2000; Palvia & Palvia, 1999). In their literature review, Chen, Melinda, and Zapatero, (2006) reported that the size of business, along with age, education, and computer knowledge, are the most important variables related to information systems (IS) in small businesses. Furthermore, it is also reflected in Radovilsky and Hedge (2004)'s study of the variables influencing Web commerce implementation, in which they found that company size was positively correlated with the adoption of Web commerce as a business strategy. Our first research question is: "How does the size of the small business relate to the perceived importance of various Internet features?" There has been no previous study looking at the relationship between the size of the small business and factors related to Internet use, specifically the Internet features. This is why "size of business" was included as one of the major constructs in this study.

The use of the Internet may not be embraced by all firms (Daniel, Wilson, & Myers, 2002; Feindt, Jeffcoate, & Chappell, 2002). Past studies on small businesses tended to ignore subtle differences among various types of small businesses. For example, in many studies, all small businesses were considered as one homogeneous entity (Cragg & King, 1993; Magal & Lewis,

1995; Mirchandandi et al., 2001). However, in reality the small businesses are not uniform, but they include a wide range of business types such as construction, retailing, manufacturing, health care, services, and so forth. Based on their review of studies related to Information Communication Technologies (ICT), Barton and Bear (1999) found that not all enterprises have the same ICT needs, because not all microenterprises and small firms face similar challenges. We posit that different types of small businesses may have different needs in terms of Internet features. Hence, "type of business" was employed as one of the major constructs in this study. Our second research question is: "How does the perceived importance for various Internet features differ according to type of business?"

When considering different features/benefits offered by various ISPs in the Internet service, it may not be simple to identify a list/subset of the most important features. Almost two decades ago, simple capabilities such as file transfer, terminal emulation, and speed of the dial-up would be sufficient. Over the years, the choices of features have greatly expanded. They now range from ease of installation to connection reliability, and from quality of customer support to multi-protocol operability. Recently, security and privacy have also become important factors to consider. Because of such a wide scope of features and capabilities, it is necessary to categorize them with a broader notion. Our literature review revealed a very limited number of studies on ISPs regarding this aspect. As a result, there is no existing framework that we could adopt for our study.

Therefore, we developed a list of features and benefits of the Internet service that we believed are relevant and important to small businesses. This list was refined and modified after informally consulting a number of small business owners. The final list of features as shown in Table 1 was adopted and used in this study. To organize these features further, we classified them into three categories of technical capability, technical support, and non-technical features.

Table 1. List of categories, important features, and their descriptions

CATEGORY	FEATURE	DESCRIPTION
Technical Capability	Multiple User Capability	Permits multiple users to connect to network and share information at the same time without breakdowns
	Speed of Connection	Speed with which Internet data is transmitted over telephone lines; speed is dependent on the type of connection. Different connections work at different speeds, such as Dial up (56 Kbs), ISDN (64 Kbps-128 Kbps), DSL (128 Kbs - 768 Kbs), Satellite (400 Kbps), and Cable (200 Kbs - 2 Mbs).
	Remote Access Capability	Access through a terminal to a computer that is geographically-removed from the terminal
	Web Presence (also called Server Space)	File storage space that is available to anyone on the World Wide Web through ISPs; Web space is typically used for storing personal Web pages. Web hosting is a typical service provided by many Internet Service Providers to design Web sites for small businesses and help them maintain Internet presence on a continuous basis.
Technical Support	Repair/Quality of Service	Quality of after-sale and repair services offered by an Internet Service Provider
	Accessible Help Line	Telephone help line that can be easily/readily accessed 24 hours a day
	Ease of Installation/Set–up	Ease with which configuration of hardware and connectivity to the Internet is established
Non-technical	Company's Name Recognition	Reputation and standing of Internet Service Provider
	Small Business Incentives	Special incentives offered to small businesses
	Cost per Month of Service	Fee and other costs paid per month by user for Internet Services

RESEARCH QUESTIONS AND HYPOTHESES

In this study, we wanted to examine the relationship between the type and size of small businesses and their perceived importance of various features of Internet service provided by ISPs. Understanding how the perceived importance (reflecting preference) varies with type and size of small business and how important specific features are to different small business would be very beneficial to ISPs. Such knowledge would help in guiding their marketing campaign and also in developing appropriate packages of features to meet the needs of various small businesses. The importance of "size" and "type" variables was discussed earlier in the background section. Therefore, this study attempted to answer the following primary research questions related to "size" and "type" of business as independent variables. Because the focus of this study was not on the impact or the cause-effect relationship among variables, all of the hypotheses below were expressed as "null" hypotheses.

Question 1: *Is the perceived importance of different technical capability features of Internet service independent of the "size of business"? To answer this question, the following hypotheses were proposed and tested.*

Hypothesis 1: *Perceived importance of the feature "multiple user capability" is independent of the size of business.*

Hypothesis 2: *Perceived importance of the feature "speed of connection" is independent of the size of business.*

Hypothesis 3: *Perceived importance of the feature "remote access capability" is independent of the size of business.*

Hypothesis 4: *Perceived importance of the feature "Web space presence" is independent of the size of business.*

Question 2: *Is the perceived importance placed on different technical support features of Internet service independent of the "size of business"? To answer this question, the following hypotheses were proposed and tested.*

Hypothesis 5: *Perceived importance of the feature "repair/quality of service" is independent of the size of business.*

Hypothesis 6: *Perceived importance of the feature "accessible help line" is independent of the size of business.*

Hypothesis 7: *Perceived importance of the feature "ease of installation/setup" is independent of the size of business.*

Question 3: *Is the perceived importance of different features of Internet service in the non-technical category independent of the "size of business"? To answer this question, the following hypotheses were proposed and tested.*

Hypothesis 8: *Perceived importance of the feature "company's name recognition" is independent of the size of business.*

Hypothesis 9: *Perceived importance of the feature "small business incentives" is independent of the size of business.*

Hypothesis 10: *Perceived importance of the feature "cost per month of service" is independent of the size of business.*

Question 4: *Is the perceived importance of different technical capability features of Internet service independent of the "type of business"? To answer this question, the following hypotheses were proposed and tested.*

Hypothesis 11: *Perceived importance of the feature "multiple user capability" is independent of the type of business.*

Hypothesis 12: *Perceived importance of the feature "speed of connection" is independent of the type of business.*

Hypothesis 13: *Perceived importance of the feature "remote access capability" is independent of the type of business.*

Hypothesis 14: *Perceived importance of the feature "Web space presence" is independent of the type of business.*

Question 5: *Is the perceived importance placed on different technical support features of Internet service independent of the "type of business"? To answer this question, the following hypotheses were proposed and tested.*

Hypothesis 15: *Perceived importance of the feature "repair/quality of service" is independent of the type of business.*

Hypothesis 16: *Perceived importance of the feature "accessible help line" is independent of the type of business.*

Hypothesis 17: *Perceived importance of the feature "ease of installation/setup" is independent of the type of business.*

Question 6: *Is the perceived importance of different features of Internet service in the non-technical category independent of the "type of business"? To answer this question, the following hypotheses were proposed and tested.*

Hypothesis 18: *Perceived importance of the feature "company's name recognition" is independent of the type of business.*

Hypothesis 19: *Perceived importance of the feature "small business incentives" is independent of the type of business.*

Hypothesis 20: *Perceived importance of the feature "cost per month of service" is independent of the type of business.*

METHODOLOGY

Participants

To accomplish the objectives of the study, a mail survey research was used to collect the data. The population for the study consisted of small businesses from the region of Southeastern Louisiana. A convenience sample of 500 companies was selected from Southeastern Louisiana University's Small Business Development Center's client database. Five hundred questionnaires were sent out, and 120 questionnaires were completed and returned. The response rate was 24%. The participants (n=120) consisted of businesses from seven types of industries: retailing (R), services (S), real estate (RE), housing (H), construction (C), manufacturing (M), and others (O). They were categorized into four different groups based on the number of employees: (a) 1-25, (b) 26-50, (c) 51-100, and (d) more than 100 employees. All of the respondents included in the analysis indicated that they had subscribed to the Internet service. To ensure this, the questionnaire included the question: "How long has your company had an Internet service provider?" Respondents who did not have Internet service were eliminated from the analysis.

Instrument

A questionnaire was developed containing a list of features and benefits (see Table 1) that the small businesses would like to see in their Internet service. Our literature review indicated a very limited number of academic studies on this topic. Hence, no instrument was available for adoption in our study. Drawing from related trade journals, we developed a list of features and benefits of the Internet service that we believed was relevant and important to small businesses. The content validity of the initial list was evaluated by a number of small business owners. They were asked to judge each item and to comment on the relevance, as well as provide suggestions for improving the list. Their input allowed us to develop the final list of features, as shown in Table 1.

The questionnaire, along with a letter explaining the purpose of the study, was sent to the businesses in the selected sample. Participants completed the questionnaire, which requested them to provide demographic information and to respond to items related to the importance of various features of Internet service. The demographic questions included information on their type of industry, number of employees, years of existence, and the gender of the respondent; for instance: "What industry is your company in?" Possible responses included: construction, retail, real estate, manufacturing, healthcare, service, and other. Finally, a question asked participants to rate the importance of the features/benefits when selecting an Internet Service Provider. Ten features shown in Table 1 were presented to respondents for importance ratings. The importance ratings for reflecting preferences were to be based on Likert rating scale of 1 to 5, where 1 = Very Unimportant, 2 = Unimportant, 3 = Neutral, 4 = Important, and 5 = Very Important. The importance ratings reflected their preferences for each of the features/benefits.

Data Analysis

The research questions assess how the perceived importance of various features/benefits of Internet service is related to different types and sizes of small businesses. We employed the frequency analysis in this study. Specifically, we used Chi-square test of independence to examine the association between the type and size of small businesses and the perceived importance of various features on Internet service provided by ISPs. The questionnaire responses were analyzed using statistical software SPSS-Version 10. Although Chi-square analysis is a rather simple statistical technique, it is an appropriate tool for the purpose of our study, namely, to assess the association between variables rather than to determine the cause and effect relationship. Since Chi-square test is a common tool for frequency analysis, the data was coded and analyzed according to the standard practices outlined in the SPSS manual and statistical textbook such as Anderson, Sweeney, and Williams' Statistics for Business and Economics, 2005 edition. Past studies (Bennett, Sagas, & Dees, 2006; Harman & Koohang, 2005/2006; Mahony, Riemer, Breeding, & Hums, 2006) had used the same technique for similar purpose to examine the association between two variables. Thus, Chi-square test of independence was applied in this study because the data obtained from the survey were measured at ordinal levels. Contingency tables were used to examine the pattern between importance ratings for features offered by ISPs and organizational variables for significance. Categories were collapsed because, while computing χ^2 test statistics, it is necessary to ensure that none of the cells have expected frequencies of less than five. Categories were collapsed as necessary for computing χ^2 test statistics to ensure that none of the cells had expected frequencies of less than five. Figure 2a below is an example of a contingency table with collapsed categories for both factors: size of business (number of employees), and the importance rating. The initial five categories for importance ratings (Very Unimportant, Unimportant, Neutral, Important, and Very Important) were collapsed into two categories of Unimportant and Important. The initial four categories for size of business (1-25, 26-50, 50-100, more than 100) were collapsed into two categories (<50 and >50). Figure 2b also shows an example of a contingency table with collapsed categories for both factors: type of business, and the importance rating. Seven categories of business type were collapsed into two categories, as shown in Figure 2b. A high value of the Chi-square test statistic indicates that the observed frequencies significantly deviated from the expected frequencies, leading to the rejection of the "null" hypothesis. This implies dependence or association between the two factors. A low value indicates no significant deviation between the observed and expected frequencies, implying independence, that is, no relationship between the two factors.

Figure 2a. Example of a contingency table for importance rating and size of business used in Chi-square test

Importance rating for feature Multiple User Capability:

Size (# of emp.)	Unimportant	Important
< 50	**36 (observed freq.)** *31.12 (expected freq.)*	**59 (observed freq.)** *63.88 (expected freq.)*
> 50	**2 (observed freq.)** *6.88 (expected freq.)*	**19 (observed freq.)** *14.12 (expected freq.)*

The Chi-square test statistic = 6.28 with p-Value = 0.01

Figure 2b. Example of a contingency table for importance rating and type of business used in Chi-square test

Importance rating for feature Multiple User Capability:

Type of business	Unimportant	Important
C+M+RE+O	**13 (observed freq.)** *13.75 (expected freq.)*	**29 (observed freq.)** *28.25 (expected freq.)*
R+H+S	**24 (observed freq.)** *23.25 (expected freq.)*	**47 (observed freq.)** *47.75 (expected freq.)*

The Chi-square test statistic = 0.10 with p-Value = 0.76

Note: Retailing (R), services (S), real estate (RE), housing (H), construction (C), manufacturing (M) and others (O)

RESULTS

Demographic Analysis

Several demographic variables were explored in the study such as type of business, number of employees, years in existence, the respondent's position in the organization, and the respondent's gender. The respondents were requested to classify their business in one of the seven categories, as shown in Figure 3. Thus, the sample represented companies from seven different industries, namely, retailing (R), services (S), real estate (RE), housing (H), construction (C), manufacturing (M), and others (O). About 29% of the companies were from retailing, 27% were from services, 6% were from construction, 8% were from real estate, 4% were from manufacturing, 7% were from housing, and 19% were from other industries.

As seen in Figure 4, 68% of the companies in the sample had fewer than 25 employees, 15% had between 25 and 50 employees, 8% had between 51 and 100 employees, and only 9% had more than 100 employees.

"Null" Hypothesis Testing Results

The results for the hypotheses are summarized in Table 2 and 3 below. Table 2 shows various null hypotheses, along with the conclusion and the p-value grouped by the three research questions associated with the "size of business". Table 3 shows various null hypotheses, along with the conclusion and the p-value grouped by the three

Figure 3. Businesses in the sample belonging to different industries

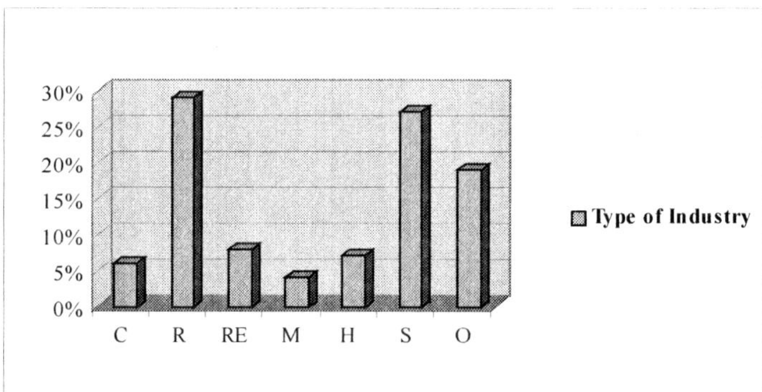

Figure 4. Proportion of industries in the sample by the number of employees

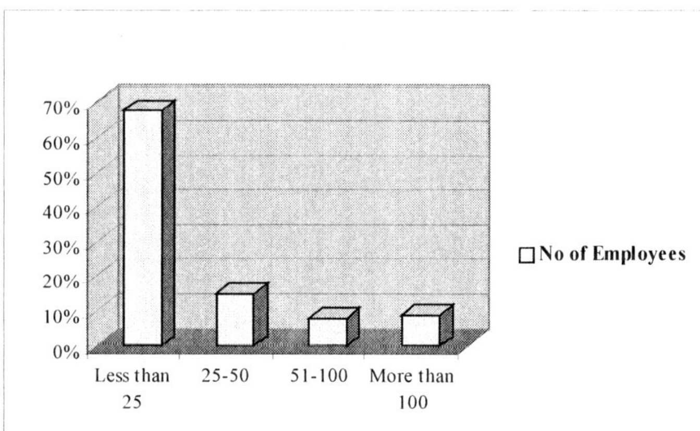

Table 2. Summary of all "null" hypothesis testing associated with the "size of business"

"Null" Hypotheses	Conclusion	χ^2	p-Value
"Null" Hypotheses related to technical capability features			
Hypothesis 1: Perceived importance of the technical feature "multiple user capability" is independent of the size of business.	Rejected	6.28	0.01
Hypothesis 2: Perceived importance of the technical feature "speed of connection" is independent of the size of business.	Rejected	3.37	0.07
Hypothesis 3: Perceived importance of the technical feature "remote access capability" is independent of the size of business.	Supported	2.17	0.14
Hypothesis 4: Perceived importance of the technical feature "Web space presence" is independent of the size of business.	Supported	0.82	0.36
"Null" Hypotheses related to technical support features			
Hypothesis 5: Perceived importance of the support feature "repair/ quality of service" is independent of the size of business.	Supported	2.58	0.11
Hypothesis 6: Perceived importance of the support feature "accessible help line" is independent of the size of business.	Rejected	2.99	0.08
Hypothesis 7: Perceived importance of the support feature "ease of installation/setup" is independent of the size of business.	Rejected	3.25	0.07
"Null" Hypotheses related to non-technical features			
Hypothesis 8: Perceived importance of the non-technical feature "company's name recognition" is independent of the size of business.	Rejected	2.73	0.10
Hypothesis 9: Perceived importance of the non-technical feature "small business incentives" is independent of the size of business.	Supported	0.03	0.86
Hypothesis 10: Perceived importance of the non-technical feature "cost per month of service" is independent of the size of business.	Supported	0.04	0.84

research questions associated with the "type of business". P-value for hypotheses that are supported was not shown in Table 2 since they were not relevant, when observed frequencies are very close to the expected frequencies, implying no association between factors.

Interpretation of Findings for the Research Questions #1, #2, and #3

The first research question explored whether there is a relationship between the perceived level of importance regarding various features provided by Internet service providers and the size of small business. Specifically, is the perceived importance of different technical capability features independent of the size of the business? Recall that size was measured in terms of the number of people that a business employs.

The finding for the research question #1 was that the "size of business" as a variable was found to be significantly related to some technical capability features. More specifically, these technical capability features are multiple-user capability ($p < 0.01$, hypothesis #1 was rejected) and speed of connection (with $p < 0.07$, hypothesis #2 was rejected).

This is expected because the more employees that a small business has, the more likely that it has to rely on a multi-user environment to support its operation rather than on a cluster of stand-alone systems. Then, network connection becomes the key to provide shared resources such as files, documents, printers, and database. With more users accessing the system via the network, the speed of connection also becomes critical. Hence, it is consistent that the result showed a relationship between the importance of both multiple-user

Table 3. Summary of all "null" hypothesis testing associated with the "type of business"

"Null" Hypotheses	Conclusion	χ^2	p-Value
"Null" Hypotheses related to technical capability features			
Hypothesis 11: Perceived importance of the technical feature "multiple user capability" is independent of the type of business.	Supported	0.10	**0.76**
Hypothesis 12: Perceived importance of the technical feature "speed of connection" is independent of the type of business.	Supported	0.01	**0.93**
Hypothesis 13: Perceived importance of the technical feature "remote access capability" is independent of the type of business.	Supported	0.88	**0.35**
Hypothesis 14: Perceived importance of the technical feature "Web space presence" is independent of the type of business.	Supported	0.24	**0.62**
"Null" Hypotheses related to technical support features			
Hypothesis 15: Perceived importance of the support feature "repair/quality of service" is independent of the type of business.	Supported	0.30	**0.59**
Hypothesis 16: Perceived importance of the support feature "accessible help line" is independent of the type of business.	Supported	0.22	**0.64**
Hypothesis 17: Perceived importance of the support feature "ease of installation/setup" is independent of the type of business.	Supported	1.64	**0.20**
"Null" Hypotheses related to non-technical features			
Hypothesis 18: Perceived importance of the non-technical feature "company's name recognition" is independent of the type of business.	Supported	0.24	**0.63**
Hypothesis 19: Perceived importance of the non-technical feature "small business incentives" is independent of the type of business.	Supported	0.02	**0.88**
Hypothesis 20: Perceived importance of the non-technical feature "cost per month of service" is independent of the type of business.	Supported	0.91	**0.34**

capability and speed of connection with the size of small business.

The relationships between the importance for remote access capability (hypothesis #3) and Web space presence (hypothesis #4) and the size of small business were found to be not statistically significant. This could be explained in terms of small businesses' scope of operations. Many small businesses tend to cater their products and services to local needs. Hence, their scope is local or regional. As a result, their employees are not scattered at many different locations, as in the case of large businesses. Furthermore, their reach is also limited to local rather than global community. These are perhaps reasons why remote access capability and Web space presence are perceived to be lower in the level of importance than other technical capability features.

Research question #2 focused on the relationship between the technical support features and the size of small business. Specifically, the question is whether the perceived importance placed on features related to technical support is independent of the size of small business. Again, it was found that two support features, accessible help line ($p < 0.08$) and ease of installation/set up ($p < 0.07$), significantly related to the size of business, with both hypotheses #6 and #7 rejected.

The increase in the number of employees does logically lead to an increase in the perceived importance of accessible help line and ease of installation/set up to ensure better productivity and efficiency of the workforce. These results are consistent with those of hypothesis #1. As the size of small businesses increases, so does the complexity, especially with the reliance on a multi-user environment. Most small businesses are generally not "tech-savvy". As a result, easy access to tech support and simple installation/set up become important. However, an unexpected finding is that the increase in the size of small businesses does not increase the preference for repair/quality of service (hypothesis #5). This may be explained in terms of service contract. To save costs, many small businesses do not maintain a service contract with their ISPs, as is the case with their counterpart large businesses. Consequently, for them, the level of importance for repair/quality of service may apparently be lower than other features.

The research question #3 addresses the relationship between the importance of non-technical features and the size of the small business. With regard to this question, only hypothesis #8 was weakly rejected, that is, only company's name recognition was found to be significantly related to the size of the small business ($p < 0.10$). As expected, the ISP's reputation is important in the selection of service by small businesses. This is perhaps related to the small businesses' lack of technical knowledge and limited exposure of various choices. They tend to pick services from those that they are familiar and recognize. What is interesting is that the small businesses placed a low level of importance on both small business incentives and cost (monthly service charge by ISPs). It is expected that most small businesses are generally cost-conscious. For them, discount incentive and low service charge were thought to be highly important. Yet, they were not. One possible explanation is that there are not enough incentives offered by ISPs to small businesses as well as various cost structures from which to choose. The lack of those incentives and one set of charges for all may have caused small businesses to perceive these features as less important.

Interpretation of Findings for Research Questions #4, #5, and #6

The next three research questions #4, #5, and #6 focused on whether there is a relationship between the perceived level of importance for various features provided by ISPs and the "type of small business". Type was specified according to the following categories: construction, retail, real estate, manufacturing, healthcare, service, and others.

The results show no statistically-significant relationship between various features and the type of small business. None of the hypotheses was rejected. Although the relationships between the type of industry and the importance of features in all three categories were found to be statistically insignificant, these results are interesting in a number of ways. Common wisdom suggests that different types of businesses would have different preferences regarding features, because of differences in their operations. Perhaps this is true in the case of larger businesses. Yet, unexpectedly for small businesses in this study, the "type of business" variable did not seem to play a significant role. The perceived importance level for features did not vary according to the type of small business. This could be taken as good news for ISPs. Instead of custom-creating packages for various types of small businesses, ISPs should pay attention to different needs based on the various sizes of small businesses. In other words, ISPs should offer a few packages with a subset of features that meet the preference of certain size groups. This could simplify greatly the design of Internet service packages for small businesses, given their characteristics of highly-fragmented market segment. Also, ISPs could concentrate on the size of small businesses and cater their services to meet the needs of small businesses based on their size rather than their type.

DISCUSSION

As seen, there is an ever-increasing competition between Internet service providers, largely because there are no restrictions to market entries. The gap between a local and a national player is waning, as all ISPs compete on the same platform and try to lure as many customers as they possibly can. They could possibly use the results of this study. Findings from this study suggests that the size rather the type of small business is a relevant variable in assessing what features in Internet service are perceived to be important by small businesses. Perhaps this is why more and more ISPs have recently begun to woo "smaller" businesses with tailor-made online services (Kooser, 2003). For instance, many new offerings include:

- Yahoo (http://smallbusiness.yahoo.com) with Web hosting, e-commerce solution, Web promotion, management tools, access to partners such as Cisco Systems, Inc, MasterCard International; others include financial news, stock reports and tools, and paid content services;
- AOL for small business (www.aolforsmallbusiness.com) with seven simultaneous log-ons under one account, priority technical support, Web site building, and business e-mail;
- Covad Communications Group, Inc. (www.covad.com) with focus on cost-effective e-mail and Web hosting solutions;
- Microsoft bcentral (www.bcentral.com) with e-mail marketing, targeted sales leads, Web hosting, e-commerce, Web collaboration, and live Web chats; and
- Vendio Services, Inc (www.vendio.com) with help for businesses to organize, manage, and automate the sales process across multiple channels, including auctions, e-commerce, and online stores (Kooser, 2003)

While common knowledge suggests that service charges such as cost per month of service should be perceived to be important, the result for this study shows the contrary. What does this mean? This should not be taken to mean that small businesses do not prefer low-cost Internet service. Rather, the result reveals the need for differentiated pricing structure. In an increasingly-significant segment of the Internet, the market is moving away from simple, cost-driven, undifferentiated commodity market into a market where there is a serious attempt to provide differentiation based on a specific feature of the delivered services.

The result of a low level of importance being placed on the non-technical feature "small business incentives" provides evidence for opportunity that ISPs could pursue. What this means is that ISPs should develop more differentiated incentives to attract their potential small business clients.

An observation that is most characterized of the challenges facing ISPs is the readily-available alternative for today's small business customers. For instance, small business customer awareness has increased manifolds over the years. Consumers have become much more demanding than before and make their choices after considering all relevant factors. Due to the availability of wide choice, switching from one provider to another is not overruled at any time. As per a report published by J.D. Power and Associates (AT&T Ranks, 2000), 14% of ISP subscribers are likely to change their provider in a single year, and another 22% consider making a change at some point in the future. The study also cited that connection speed is the most common reason for changing providers (79%).

Selection of a service provider is also affected by word of mouth. A bad experience of one customer may lead to a loss of another ten potential customers, thereby making it essential for Internet Service Providers to gauge customers' needs from time to time so as to provide them with competent and valuable services.

CONCLUSION

ISPs serve as an electronic gateway to the outside world. They play a critical role in the operation of many small businesses. Thus, the needs of the small businesses go beyond the level of technical expertise. It is important for ISPs to have what it takes to survive and thrive in the good as well as bad times. One of the critical success factors is that the ISPs must be reliable, service-oriented, and capable of offering packages that are relevant and desirable to specific sizes of small businesses. Today's typical offering for businesses may include the followings: A DSL fast access, dedicated access, and Web hosting solutions. The typical package may include static IP, 20 e-mail addresses, backup dial-up account, DNS hosting with customer's domain name, and 24-hour technical support. Other possible emerging features to be included are good pricing model for connectivity, disaster recovery services, single bill, single service and support standard, and single point of responsibility.

According to the research company AMI-Partners, small and midsize businesses in 2006 will spend $175 billion on IT (Pereira, 2005). Hence, the small businesses in part represent the most growth and a potential lucrative market for ISPs. A number of big online service providers have already taken a position in carving out this market. That is why companies such as AOL, Covad, Microsoft, Vendio, and Yahoo are actively wooing small businesses with many offerings designed specifically to meet their unique needs (Kooser, 2003). This is certainly an awakening call for many smaller ISPs. To survive, they need to right-set their strategy and engage small businesses to utilize their services. They have to be competitive and proactive in developing their own niche.

Practical Implications

All the respondents in the survey indicated that they have Internet service and reported it to be beneficial. This confirms the finding of Hochmuth (2005) and other researchers. Thus, one of the implications of this study is that small businesses are a potentially-lucrative market for ISPs. As indicated earlier, big companies such as AOL and Yahoo have started offering services targeted specifically to small business (Luhn, 2003). Despite such moves by a few big ISPs, many parts of the small business market opportunity remains untapped, especially for the smaller ISPs. The reason is the fragmented nature of the small business market itself that is made up of many disparate entities and companies. Hence, there are many potential niches that small ISPs could carve into this billion-dollar-a-year market. Another implication is that while there are many potential niches, the cost of capitalizing these niches might not be as high as many small ISPs believe. The reason is because different types of small businesses show little or no variation in perceived importance of various features packaged in the service, as shown in this study. Furthermore, most of today's small businesses do not want to confine themselves to traditional ways of doing business. An increasing number of them are relying on and using Internet technology for carrying their operations, and are demanding services specifically designed to satisfy their business needs. More and more firms realize that the use of Internet-based applications and platforms such as electronic mail and instant messaging helps promote improved communications among employees, customers, and partners, while reducing associated costs, and enables them to establish a national or even global presence without having to invest in physical infrastructure. What this means is a strong growing demand for good, reliable Internet service for small businesses. In turn, this demand will continue to drive the growth of ISPs in the years to come.

Another implication is the importance of adaptability. Like any other technology, the pace of changes in IT field is rapid. Any of the technological changes will likely impact small businesses and Internet Service Providers. For instance, one such study by ISP-Market LLC (Taking the Pulse, 2003) reported that wireless broadband and Web hosting are two new fast-growing business areas. The worldwide market for Web hosting services is expected to grow from some $10.3 billion in 2001 to more than $46.9 billion, and more than 40% of small businesses are expected to subscribe to broadband in 2006 (Pastore, 2002). What this means is that to be successful, today's ISPs must be flexible and adaptable to changes, so that they can respond to the small businesses' rapidly-changing preferences of Internet service features.

Research Limitations

The findings of this study should be interpreted in the context of the following limitations. The first major limitation of this study is the sample. It included small businesses from Southeastern Louisiana only. Any generalization should be done with caution. The second limitation is the rapid change of technology. It is difficult to include in an academic study the most up-to-date developments in the world of ISPs. What we did here is to provide a snapshot picture of the whole industry and point out some of the opportunities within the small business market segment. Another limitation is the list of Internet service features. We acknowledged that our list is quite narrow. Due to certain constraints, a number of features such as business log service, script support, data backup, scalability, virtual or independent server, security control, and so forth, could not be included although these are relevant to small businesses. The scope of future studies could be expanded to examine these features thoroughly. Finally, because of the lack of previous literature, we proposed and adopted variables and constructs that have not been tested before this. Furthermore, most of the measures in our survey were based on the input from a few small business owners and our synthesis from literature. An adoption of this survey for future study should be noted with this limitation.

Despite these limitations, this study is one of the few that has looked at an under-exposed area of research-related to ISPs and small businesses' needs. One contribution that it makes is to open up some issues and encourage many more future studies.

REFERENCES

Anderson, D., Sweeney, D., & Williams, T. (2005). *Statistics for business and economics, 9th ed.* Thomson South Western Publishers.

AT&T WorldNet Ranks Highest in Customer Satisfaction Among Largest National Subscription Internet Service Providers. (2000, September). J. D. Power and Associates Report. Retrieved from http://www.jdpa.com/pdf/2053.pdf.

Barnes, D., Hinton, M., & Mieczkowska, S. (2003). Competitive advantage through e-operations. *TQM & Business Excellence, 14*(6), 659–675.

Barton, C., & Bear, M. (1999, March). Information and communications technologies: Are they the key to viable business development services for micro and small enterprises? Retrieved from http://www.mip.org/pdfs/mbp/ict.pdf

Barua, A., Konana, P., Whinston, A. B., & Yin, F. (2001). Driving e-business excellence. *MIT Sloan Management Review, 43*(1), 36–44.

Bennett, G., Sagas, M., & Dees, W. (2006). Media preferences of action sports consumers: Differences between generation X and Y. *Sport Marketing Quarterly, 15*(1), 40-49.

Boyer, K. K., & Olson, J. R. (2002). Drivers of Internet purchasing success. *Production and Operations Management, 11*(4), 480–498.

Brynjolfsson, E., & Hitt, L. M. (2000). Beyond computation: Information technology, organizational transformation, and business performance. *Journal of Economic Perspectives, 14*(4), 23-48.

Chen, J., Melinda, H., & Zapatero, E. (2006, February). Understanding Web commerce adoption by very small businesses. *Proceedings of ASBBS, Las Vegas, NV: Vol. 13*(1), 268-277.

Cottrill, K. (1997). The supply chain of the future. *Distribution, 96*(11), 52-54.

Cragg, P. B., & King, M. (1993). Small-firm computing: Motivators and inhibitors. *MIS Quarterly, 7*(1), 47-60.

Daniel, E., Wilson, H., & Myers, A. (2002). Adoption of e-commerce by SMEs in the UK. *International Small Business Journal, 20*(3), 253–268.

Donner, J. (2004, Fall). Microentrepreneurs and mobiles: An exploration of the uses of mobile phones by small business owners in Rwanda. *Information Technologies & International Development, 2*(1), 1-21.

DTI (2000). International bench marking survey for ICT use by UK department of trade and industry. Retrieved from http://www.ukonline.gov.uk

Fallon, M., & Moran, P. (2000). Information communication technology (ICT) and manufacturing SMEs. *Proceedings of the 2000 Small Business and Enterprise Development Conference, Manchester University* (pp. 100-109).

Feindt, S., Jeffcoate, J., & Chappell, C. (2002). Identifying success factors for rapid growth in SME e-commerce. *Small Business Economics, 19*(1), 51–62.

Garcı́a-Dastugue, S. J., & Lambert, D. M. (2003). Internet enabled coordination in the supply chain. *Industrial Marketing Management, 32*(3), 251–263.

Harman, K., & Koohang, A. (2005/2006, Winter). Frequency of publication and topical emphasis of knowledge management books versus doctoral dissertations: 1983-2005. *Journal of Computer Information Systems, 46*(2), 64-68.

Hauguel, P., & Jackson, N. (2001). Outward-looking supply-chain strategy. *European Business Journal, 13*(3), 113–118.

Haynes, P. J., Becherer, R. C., & Helms, M. M. (1998). Small and mid-sized businesses and Internet use: Unrealized potential? *Internet Research, 8*(3), 229–235.

Hochmuth, P. (2005, November 11). Cisco service targets small business. *Network World, 22*(45), 8-9.

Kooser, A. (2003, November). They want you. *Entrepreneur, 31*(11), 34.

Levenburg, N. M. (2005, June). Does size matter? Small firms' use of e-business tools in the supply chain. *Electronic Markets, 15*(2), 94-105.

Luhn, R. (2003, June). CNET review. Retrieved from http://reviews.cnet.com/4520-6536_7-726606-2.html?tag=st.is.3762-8-%250920777559-1.arrow.3762-8-20777559-2

Magal, S. R., & Lewis, C. (1995, Spring). Determinants of information technology success in small businesses. *Journal of Computer Information Systems*, 75-83.

Mahony, D., Riemer, H., Breeding, J., & Hums, M. (2006, April). Organizational justice in sport organizations: Perceptions of college athletes and other college students. *Journal of Sport Management, 20*(2), 159-188.

McMillan, J., & Woodruff, C. (2002). The central role of entrepreneurs in transition economies. *Journal of Economic Perspectives, 16*(3), 153-170.

Mirchandandi, D. A., & Motwani, J. (2000, Spring). Understanding small business electronic commerce adoption: An empirical analysis. *Jour-*

nal of Computer Information Systems, 70-73.

Palvia, P., & Palvia, S. (1999). An examination of IT satisfaction of small-business users. *Information and Management, 35*(3), 127-137.

Pastore, M. (2002, January 30). The broadband and wireless revolution. Retrieved from http://ISP-Planet.com/research/2002/ne

Pereira, P. (2005, November 16). SMBs will lead channel. *eWeek, 22*(45A), 33.

Power, D. J., & Sohal, A. S. (2002). Implementation and usage of electronic commerce in managing the supply chain: A comparative study of ten Australian companies, benchmarking. *An International Journal, 9*(2), 190–208.

Radovilsky, Z., & Hedge, V. (2004, March). Factors influencing e-commerce implementation: Analysis of survey results. *Journal of Academy of Business and Economics, 4*(1), 29.

Riquelme, H. (2002). Commercial Internet adoption in China: Comparing the experience of small, medium and large businesses. *Internet Research, 12*(3), 276–286.

Taking the Pulse of the Internet Service Provider Industry: Evolutions and Revolutions driving the ISP Business in 2003. (2003). Retrieved from www.isp-market.com/reports/pulse03_summ.PDF

Zank, G. M., & Vokurka, R. J. (2003). The Internet: Motivations, deterrents, and impact on supply chain relationships. *SAM Advanced Management Journal, 68*(2), 33–40.

Zimmerer, T. W., & Scarborough, N. M. (2002). *Essentials of entrepreneurship and small business management, 3rd ed.* Upper Saddle River, NJ: Pearson Education, Inc.

This work was previously published in International Journal of E-Business Research, Vol. 4, Issue 1, edited by I. Lee, pp. 82-98, copyright 2008 by IGI Publishing, formerly known as Idea Group Publishing (an imprint of IGI Global).

Chapter XVIII
Process-Driven Business Integration Management for Collaboration Networks

Dominik Vanderhaeghen
Institute for Information Systems (IWi) at the German Research Center for Artificial Intelligence (DFKI), Germany

Anja Hofer
Institute for Information Systems (IWi) at the German Research Center for Artificial Intelligence (DFKI), Germany

Florian Kupsch
Institute for Information Systems (IWi) at the German Research Center for Artificial Intelligence (DFKI), Germany

ABSTRACT

In the chapter, a framework for cross-enterprise business integration management addressing the organizational and technical dimension is developed. Firstly, the authors identify basic characteristics of cross-organizational business processes whose complexity results in the need for an efficient and effective business integration management. Therefore, a holistic framework is focused, consisting of a view concept for knowledge management in collaboration networks, a three-tier architecture, and a process-oriented life-cycle model. The framework for business integration management offers the required methods to set up enterprise processes and ICT-support in collaboration networks. It proposes a management guideline for collaboration participants defining what, why, when, and how they might manage their business integration intra- and cross-organizationally.

BUSINESS INTEGRATION IN THE VALUE-ADDED CHAIN

Regarding the value-added chain of enterprises, a transition from an intra-organizational perspective, keeping value-creation within its own borders, towards a cross- or inter-organizational view, value-creation within a network of specialized firms, can be observed (Kanter, 1991). The growing importance of cooperation is a result of globalization in combination with the disappearance of political borders and, above all, technological advances caused mainly by the Internet (Scheer, Erbach, & Thomas, 2000; Scheer, Grieble, Hans & Zang, 2002). Thus, enterprises have to react to the raised innovation pressure and facilitate flexible collaboration on a global scale by aligning their business processes.

The borderless enterprise has been the subject of scientific discussion for years (Naisbitt, 1982; Picot, Wigand, & Reichwald, 1997). Current approaches addressing solutions to specific problems of dynamically interacting organizations are summarized under the term "*collaborative business (c-business)*" (Röhricht & Schlögel, 2001). It describes the Internet-based, interlinked collaboration of all participants in a value-added network, from the raw material supplier to the end-consumer (Scheer, Grieble, & Zang, 2003). Unlike former concepts regarding only small parts of the value chain, as for example, e-procurement, c-business incorporates all stages of added value (Scheer, Feld, & Zang, 2003).

The ability to network enterprises turns out to be a key success factor in c-business. As a consequence, *business integration* (Scheer et al., 2002) with a holistic view on networking solutions and their business value concerns both, economic-driven as well as information technology-driven aspects of collaboration networking. The link between evolving economic requirements towards the implementation with technology especially gains importance within collaborative environments with a growing heterogeneity of participating partners. Cross-organizational processes have to be designed, implemented, and managed sustainably. While, for example, the technological implementation (Linthicum, 2003) on the one hand, or the life cycle of cooperations (Liebhart, 2002) on the other hand, have already been intensively researched, too little consideration has been given to interconnecting, complexity-reducing management concepts. A rethinking from a pure technology-driven implementation or profit-driven business model discussion to an integrated view spanning from the conceptual level to the system blueprint is needed in order to reduce the inherent complexity and required efforts of business integration in cross-organizational business processes.

A management framework meeting these requirements provides a basis for a holistic and systematic Business Integration. This includes planning, design, and controlling of cross-organizational processes. A proposal for such a framework is being developed by the research projects "ArKoS—Architecture for Collaborative Scenarios" (Adam, Hofer, Zang, Hammer, Jerrentrup, & Levenbach, 2004) and "P2E2—Peer-to-Peer Enterprise Environment" (Kupsch & Werth, 2005). Existing business process management (BPM) methods and cooperation phase models are used as a foundation in the framework, regarding all necessary requirements for business integration from a business process-oriented view with state-of-the art implementation technology.

For a purpose-driven definition of requirements towards a process-oriented management of business integration, central objectives must be identified in order to specify efficient and effective management and implementation instruments. Due to its elementary importance in business networks, the *cross-organizational business process* may be seen as the initial point considering business integration issues. Hence, the authors exemplarily point out the basic characteristics of such processes motivating business integration management in the next section. The authors stress the need for appropriate management instruments on both an *organizational* as well as a *technical* dimension. The complexity which is emphasized by these upcoming examples, managing and implementing business integration through the management and implementation of cross-organizational processes, requires a business-driven reduction. The execution of business integration management activities has to be simplified within the scope of their intra- and cross-organizational application in an effective and efficient manner. Therefore, an appropriate framework which addresses the organizational as well as technical dimensions of business integration is developed in the following sections. The chapter ends with a conclusion and an outlook on future work.

CROSS-ENTERPRISE BUSINESS PROCESS INTEGRATION

As the most characterizing part of c-business resp. collaboration networks, processes among two or more enterprise departments, branches, and also business partners are integrated (Schmitt, 2000). However, only subprocesses have been supported by business process management (BPM) in the past. Single subprocesses of collaborating enterprises have to be integrated on different layers. Process characteristics indicating differences between ordinary, *intra-* and *inter*-organizational business processes mainly base on two pillars:

- **Interorganizational business process flows** as tangible objects describing static and dynamic process elements and characteristics on the one hand;
- **Security and trust** as a fuzzy necessity for collaboration network design, implementation, and controlling

Both classes of characteristics are coexisting interdependently and complementarily. They are explained in the following.

Characteristics of Interorganizational Business Processes

Business Process Flows

Business processes include different flows as continuous, directed movements of data or information; goods and services; or currency between process objects as well as a determination of an underlying processing logic. These flows remain inside an enterprise, for instance, as a data flow between departments (e.g., internal transfer of bills). But they also cross enterprise borders and address external stakeholders (Hirschmann, 1998; Leimstoll, 2003; Thaler, 2001). A complex mesh of connections among the flows of individual and distributed process steps characterizes those inter- or cross-organizational flows. From an organisation's perspective, internal process steps are initiated with well-defined *interfaces* by external process events. Thus, the authors will have a closer look at interfaces implying flowing objects between different sending and receiving participants of different organizations in a collaborative business process.

Decentralization leads to high coordination efforts of cross-enterprise business processes. The circumstance results in an increasing number of organizational and IT-related (process) interfaces (Schmitt, 2000). Interfaces interlink activity-executing process objects as application systems or databases, but also employees via, for instance, data exchange. Such interfaces may be identified both internally (intra-organizationally) and externally (interorganizationally, e.g., between one enterprise and its business partners or customers) (Schubert, 2003). These *process interfaces* cause friction losses. They result from long lead times caused by redundant work, high coordination efforts, and competence breaks (Thaler, 2001). In the following, the authors focus on external interfaces only. They are divided into two main interface classes: process interfaces on an *organizational, human layer,* and on a *technical, machine-oriented layer.*

Organizational Interfaces

Enterprise-spanning business processes are characterized by interfaces concerning the organizational units involved in process executions (Hirschmann, 1998). Depending on cooperation forms, value-adding partners, which participate in cooperation, have different roles: Central cooperation instances, as they exist, for example, in supply chain management, define *organizational requirements* for cross-enterprise process design and execution, whereas electronic markets grant equal roles and autonomy to their value-adding participants (Wölfle, 2003). The existence of organizational interfaces has numerous impacts on the type of process execution and on the involved organizational control instances. From an organizational point of view, explicit responsibilities concerning "power structures" and explicit "control instances" have to be defined in enterprise-spanning business processes. They ensure a smooth process flow even across the borders of a single enterprise (Scheer et al., 2002). However, this turns out to be particularly complicated in cross-enterprise processes as these responsibilities are mostly non-existent or even unintentional due to the kind of cooperation. A lack of organizational regulations leads to increasing coordination efforts concerning the process execution (Hirschmann, 1998).

Technical Interfaces

Cross-enterprise integration and optimization of business processes aim at a minimization of interruptions in process flows caused by information and communication technology (Wölfle, 2003). In a cooperation scenario, the compatibility of application or information systems is required for a smooth cross-enterprise data and information exchange (Hirschmann, 1998). The benefits concerning an increase in efficiency and effectiveness is only achieved with a vast implementation of processes over different application systems (Wölfle, 2003). Thus, the technical layer of process execution considering IT interfaces as relevant process interfaces are described in the following in detail:

- **Heterogeneous IT infrastructures** may be identified as one central problem causing ineffective and inefficient process hurdles: Predefined standards for IT interfaces have to ensure that IT systems used can be integrated (Scheer, Grieble, Hans, & Zang, 2002). As various application systems of different software engineers are applied in different enterprises for heterogeneous purposes, the complexity of the process integration increases as a result of the heterogeneity of IT landscapes. However, systems have to be interlinked through suitable mechanisms to reach business objectives (Wölfle, 2003). Integration of heterogeneous application systems is addressed within the field of enterprise application integration (EAI) (Linthicum, 2003) on a rather technical layer.
- The number of existing **format mismatches**, which describes the frequency of changed communication media for the transmission of relevant information, may be seen as one resulting problem of IT heterogeneity. The manual transfer of information from a fax document (an order, for instance) to an online form of an ERP system may serve as an example. In the context of interorganizational business process controlling, the number of format mismatches can be used as a value for the analysis of the process as a whole (Bullinger, Lebender, Otto, & Weisbecker, 2003).
- The **use of different standards** may be identified as another relevant technical aspect within interorganizational business processes. The integration of IT systems requires standardized methods for the connection of different communication end points and IT interfaces respectively. With interface heterogeneity, integration efforts

increase (Wölfle, 2003). Inefficiencies concerning the electronic exchange of data and information can be eliminated by the definition of central semantic and syntactic standards for exchange objects (for example, business documents) as well as transfer methods (e.g., transmission medium, or exchange protocols) (Müller-Lankenau, 2003). The complexity of a holistic process integration, caused by the multiplicity of potential business partners and IT systems to be integrated, is intensified by the existence of numerous specific and differently sophisticated standardization approaches (Wölfle, 2003). This has negative impacts on process integration efforts. Adequate measures reducing the complexity are required.

- Finally, **automation** of process steps is addressed with IT support as a primary objective in a cross-enterprise collaboration. A reduction of format mismatches is intended. With regard to process efficiency and effectiveness, improvements concerning process performance can be realized by the removal of manual process executions (Scheer Grieble, Hans, & Zang, 2002). Moreover, by defining automation as a valuable characteristic (key performance indicators) (Scheer & Jost, 2002), interorganizational processes can be analysed in a measurable manner (Bullinger, Lebender, Otto, & Weisbecker, 2003).

Security and Trust

Exchange of information between employees is complicated. Employees receive information willingly, but they only reveal them under individual circumstances (Wölfle, 2003). This aspect is even worse at a level of collaboration and interorganizational business processes. This information exchange is much more complicated due to cultural and mental aspects. Collaborations are characterized by insecurities during many phases of the collaboration life cycle (Wehner, 2001). With the Internet as the central medium for information exchange and transfer, the network economy turns out to be more impersonal and insecure in practice. The electronic exchange of information is a weak point for hacker attacks. A disturbance of interorganizational partner relationships may result. Hence, *security and trust* can be regarded as particularly critical for an interorganizational process integration. Trust has to be regarded as an essential basis for an effective and efficient information exchange. It enables communication between business partners. The aspects described have to be regarded as key success factors for the realization of collaborative networks (Ratnasingam, 2003).

Regarding the design of cross-enterprise processes, enterprises rely on negotiations for the coordination and the discussion or avoidance of potential partner conflicts. As the communication among partners plays a major role in this context, *cultural* and *social discrepancies* have to be taken into account as well (Hirschmann, 1998). Thereby, organizations are characterized considerably by cultural imprints because of organizational behavior patterns and values (Scholz, 1997). Within international cooperations, the problem to find common agreements due to cultural (e.g., language, terminology, and understanding barriers, mental imprinting, legal distinctions) and temporal barriers (different time zones) by cooperating with acceptable coordination efforts is even aggravated (Wölfle, 2003).

Impacts on Collaboration Networks

From a high number of interfaces and resulting efforts concerning process coordination, explicit and purpose-driven description instruments are derived. From a conceptual point of view, an adequate graphical and model-based visualization of problems, requirements, and possible solutions is required.

To derive appropriate and relevant information for the design of integrated but heterogeneous IT landscapes, business process models have to be extended considering IT-related information. The crucial information of which system covers which part of a subprocess has to be specified explicitly, similarly to the description of organizational responsibilities. Moreover, interfaces have to be described in detail with special attributes marking heterogeneous systems (e.g., syntactical description of exchange formats as individual XML structures or supported standards) (Lebender, Ondrusch, Otto, & Renner, 2003) or necessary associations to related detail descriptions as sequence specification with UML sequence diagrams (Jeckle, Rupp, Hahn, Zengler, & Quiens, 2004).

Modeling and model exchange aiming at partner coordination have to be applied with reasonable efforts. Existing knowledge, cast in models, should be reused in order to save former investments (Vanderhaeghen, Zang, & Scheer, 2005) of, for example, business process reengineering (BPR), or software engineering (SE)-tasks (Vanderhaeghen, Zang, & Scheer, 2005). Furthermore, global information sharing with process models requires model integration and security mechanisms. Any flexible exchange of process data with heterogeneous description formats needs support in business integration. Process information has to be secured, and mechanisms to hide critical information in models towards business partners are required (Vanderhaeghen, Zang, & Scheer, 2005). Finally, adaptation mechanisms for the translation of business process data should be provided regarding a low-effort implementation.

Thus, all possible weak points disturbing cross-organizational business process flows ought to be analyzed in the design phase of a process, monitored during its implementation, as well as measured during process execution of enterprise-spanning business processes. A framework for business integration management requires necessary measures and instruments for a holistic solution based on business processes.

FRAMEWORK FOR BUSINESS INTEGRATION MANAGEMENT

The presented framework, which is described in the following section, consists of three basic elements: a view concepts for knowledge management in collaboration networks, a three-tier architecture which defines the necessary instruments and tools for the management of business integration, and a dynamic life-cycle model for a process-oriented planning and implementation of business integration in collaboration networks.

Knowledge Views

As a foundation of the framework, existing business process management (BPM) methods and phase models are used. However, they have to be adapted to the specifications of collaborative scenarios. Especially because of its completeness of vision and its proven practicability, both in the scientific as well as the economic context, the *ARIS House* (Scheer, 1994) is accepted as a generic framework for business process management and serves as a basis for further considerations. The ARIS House describes a business process, assigning equal importance to the questions of organization, functionality, and the required documentation. First, it isolates these questions for separate treatment, in order to reduce the complexity of the field of description, but then all the relationships are restored using the control view introduced for this purpose.

The framework is based on the ARIS House. The approach divides it into a vertical axis of global knowledge of all collaboration partners and a horizontal axis of local knowledge of single participants (see Figure 1). The organization view and the output view are global knowledge, because a goal-oriented collaboration is impossible

Figure 1. Global and local knowledge in value-added networks

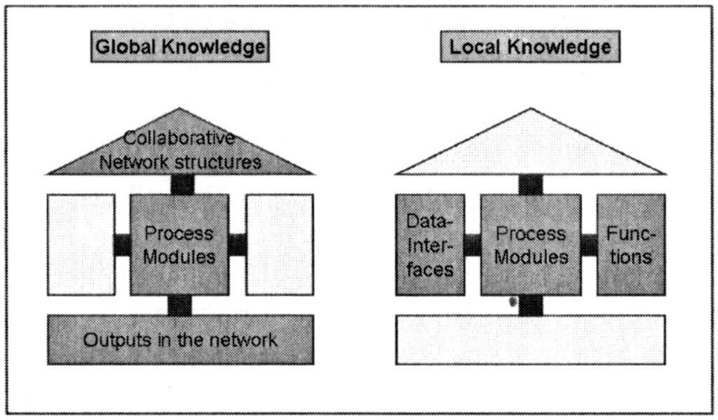

without them. At the time the interaction occurs between two partners, local knowledge is shared (bilaterally) in collaboration networks between the partners, that is, additional information, like data structures and semantics, are exchanged. Updates of the local knowledge do not influence the network, as network knowledge has to be available for all partners. This information is stored in the description of interfaces between the process modules of the partners (see further the following sections). Changes in the global network knowledge, and as a consequence, changes in the output and organization view have to be accessible to all partners immediately, for example, if a company leaves the network or if a product or service is no longer available within the network.

Global and local knowledge merge gradually in the step-by-step development of business integration process engineering. Following the distinction between global and local knowledge, a language is needed for the exchange of these knowledge fragments. Because the necessary detail functions and data schemes of the respective enterprise are determined in the data and the function view, these are treated from a micro perspective. They are characterized by an intensive internal interdependence, whereas externally a standardized encapsulation has to be provided. Interfaces of the data and function views to other network participants become visible in the process view in the form of attribute correlations to process modules, and concern the technological field of the cooperation during the realization much more intensely than the conceptual one.

This technique enables the generation of *public* (visible to network partners) and *private* (enterprise-internal) *views* and levels of detail for management, process owner, and IT-experts out of a c-business model.

Architecture for Business Integration Management

The three-tier architecture is composed of three levels affiliated with each other (see Figure 7):

1. **Business integration strategy:** On a first *business integration strategy* level, strategic management activities concerning business integration in collaboration networks are considered. The question of core enterprise competences is directly associated with the question, "Which process remains in the enterprise, and which is supposed to be assigned to partner enterprises?" (Jost & Scheer, 2002, p. 37). Hence, partner definitions must be specified on a strategic collaboration level. From here, the need for specific business integration solutions evolves for the first time. It characterizes the

Figure 2. Example of a c-business scenario

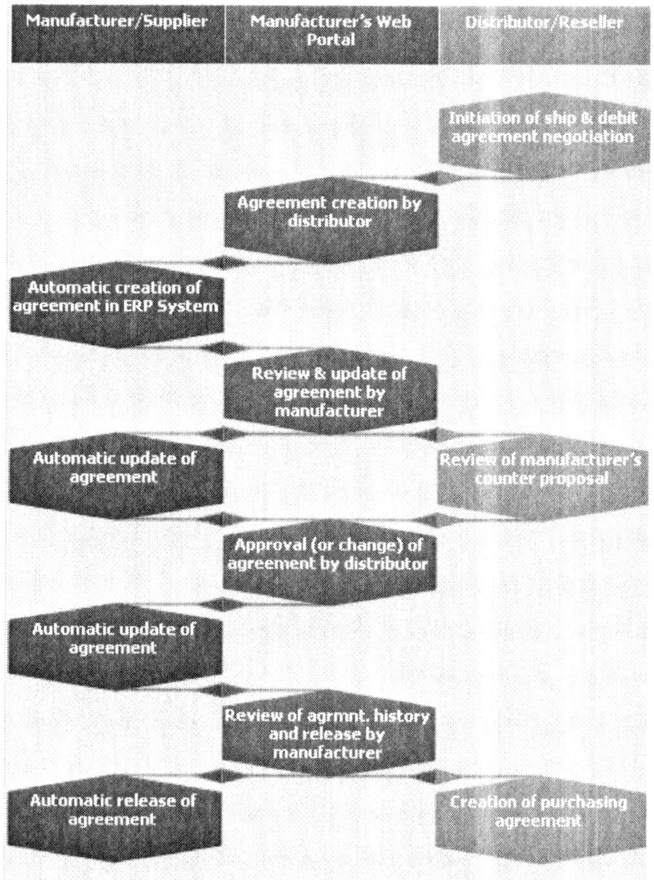

scope of business integration solutions sustainably: Collaborative business processes are not planned in detail at the strategic level, but are designed as concentrated, high-level process modules. They combine a public knowledge about the collaborative processes that is shared by all participants. As a basic instrument, business process models for collaborative scenarios at the strategic level no longer act on the assumption of a chronological view of the process exclusively. They rather rely on a more role-based view to discover new value-added potentials in collaboration networks. As an example of an instrument for the business integration strategy management, c-business scenario-diagrams used by SAP for the description of mySAP.com collaboration scenarios may be mentioned. This practical notation aims at the representation of a collaboration of different enterprises and participants by means of an easily understandable method and the documentation of the value-added potentials resulting from ICT (Hack, 2000). This method can be integrated into the ARIS concept and combined with methods of classical business process and data modeling. Individual, intra-corporate views and levels of detail for the management, different departments, and IT experts can thereby be derived from a c-business model.

2. **Business integration process engineering:** Detailed global and local processes have to be planned, designed, implemented, and controlled cross-organizationally on a second *business integration process engineering* level, considering the organizational and technical dimension. A global view on the collaborative process is generated in order to manage common processes and to reduce the complexity of integrating participating organizations into one virtual unit. In doing so, it is important that the partners provide access to all relevant information described as global knowledge, and at the same time are able to hide their business secrets. The so-called process module chain (PMC) (Grieble, Klein, & Scheer, 2002) facilitates appropriate modeling on a global, cross-organizational level, considering private business process definitions as, for example, event-driven process chain (EPC) or business process modeling notation (BPMN) models in the "back-end" of business integration management. The process module chain illustrates the whole global process over the complete cooperation, thus providing knowledge about the process to all organizational units involved in the process. Special importance should be attached to the editing and systematization of process information so that, on the one hand, only relevant data are extracted out of the mass of information and, on the other hand, private corporate data are hidden from other partners.

   Figure 3 exemplarily shows a process module chain which is used for the extended illustration of cross-organizational processes, according to Klein, Kupsch, and Scheer (2004).

   This process module chain at the highest abstraction level consists of individual process modules or building blocks, which again can contain deposited process module chains. Moreover, the single process modules are connected by magenta symbols which form the interfaces between the modules. They represent the output of the previous module and the input of the following module. The interface can thereby contain products/services or information/data which are necessary for the process continuation.

   The value-added chain diagram (VACD) serves as a representation of highly aggregated processes (Rosemann & Schwegmann, 2002). The value-added chain links illustrate the value-adding functions of an enterprise in a highly abstracted way. Furthermore, organizational units can be annotated to the links as executing subjects of the functions (McMichael, 2003). Both services and application systems can additionally be

Figure 3. Generic process module chain

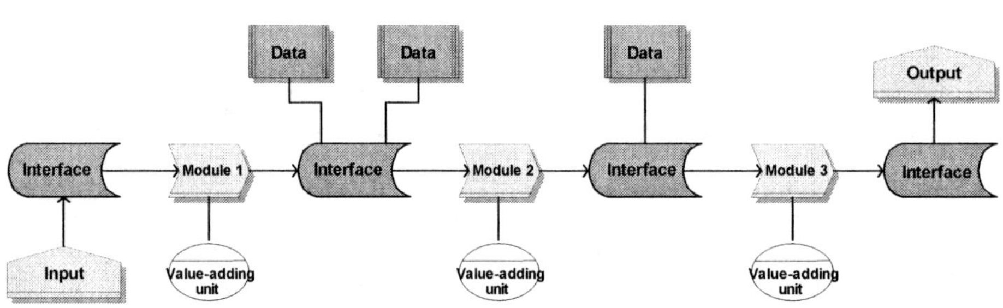

Figure 4. Value-added chain diagram at different hierarchy levels

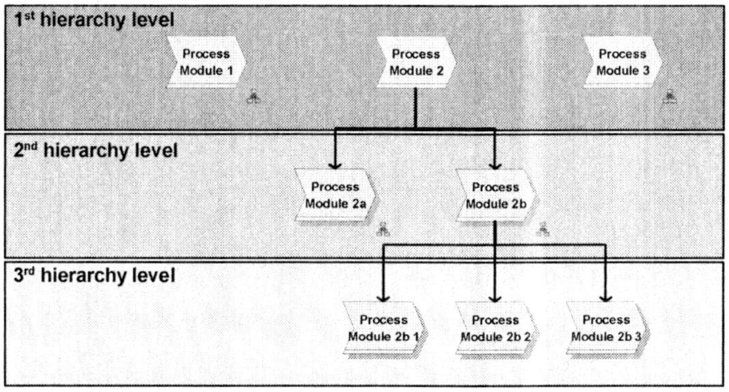

represented. The hierarchization of chain links and whole chains is symbolized by directed arrows.

Key performance-indicators are defined based on records, log files, time stamps, and so forth, which afterwards can be measured and analyzed by means of intelligent tools (Jost & Scheer, 2002) within the scope of business integration process engineering.

3. **Business integration execution:** Instead of closed systems which have been used so far in an entrepreneurial environment, business integration requires the integration of different applications in a business network with a business-oriented view to execute collaboration activities. Cross-organizational business process models serve as the elementary initial point to implement cross-enterprise ICT solutions. Such technology-driven issues are addressed at the last layer called *business integration execution.*

Component-based, process-driven architectures which rely on fully-developed standards and interfaces can be seen as a state-of-the-art approach to overcome integration problems (McMichael, 2003). The term *process-driven* emphasizes the importance of process models created on the preliminary layer as the foundation for implementation. In this context, approaches such as the model-driven architecture (MDA) (Object Management Group, 2003) of the Object Management Group (OMG) are developed. On the execution layer, process models are used, for example, for the orchestration of Web services. Orchestration describes the composition of business objects in a process flow. In detail, it defines the complex interaction between business objects, including the business logic and execution order of the interactions and the exchange of messages between them. Based on predefined processes of the second architecture layer, business process models have to be translated into corresponding, execution-driven workflow models. After the mapping of the business process layer onto workflow-dimensions, the final process execution can be performed. To ensure interoperability between heterogeneous application systems, different approaches have to be considered with their strengths and shortcomings: middleware architectures, enterprise application integration (EAI), as well as service-oriented architectures with Web services.

Depending on strategic arrangements, an explicit engineering of business processes is obtained aiming at a high-value business integration. So, on the one hand, the design and implementation of intra- and cross-organizational business processes closely depends on the design of a collaboration network. On the other hand, executable processes cast in ICT implementations determine business process engineering. As a consequence, the different dimensions of the architecture for business integration management are connected through control loops, expressing interdependencies.

An integration of the core IT-systems is essential to guarantee a frictionless handling of business processes. In an optimal scenario, the result would be a seamless IT infrastructure that is completely transparent for all participants: It appears as one single system, supporting a service-oriented interaction of all relevant business processes. So far, the efforts to manage this integration are pooled with the keyword enterprise application integration (EAI). They contain a set of technologies and concepts such as middleware; extract, transform, load (ETL)-tools; and EAI-software that focus on a central planning and control of business application data in real-time. In Figure 5, an example for embedding an EAI server into the enterprise architecture is shown.

In the scenario in Figure 5, a central EAI-server manages the coordination of both control and data flow between the attached systems. In this manner, the number of required interfaces can be reduced, as there is only one bidirectional connection from each system to the server.

Because of the central component (ordinarily called *information hub*), these approaches cause several problems that complicate a reliable integration of numerous systems. Major well-reported problems are the following:

- **Single point of failure:** The Information Hub is the central node between the different applications. In case of a breakdown,

Figure 5. Intra-enterprise-integration

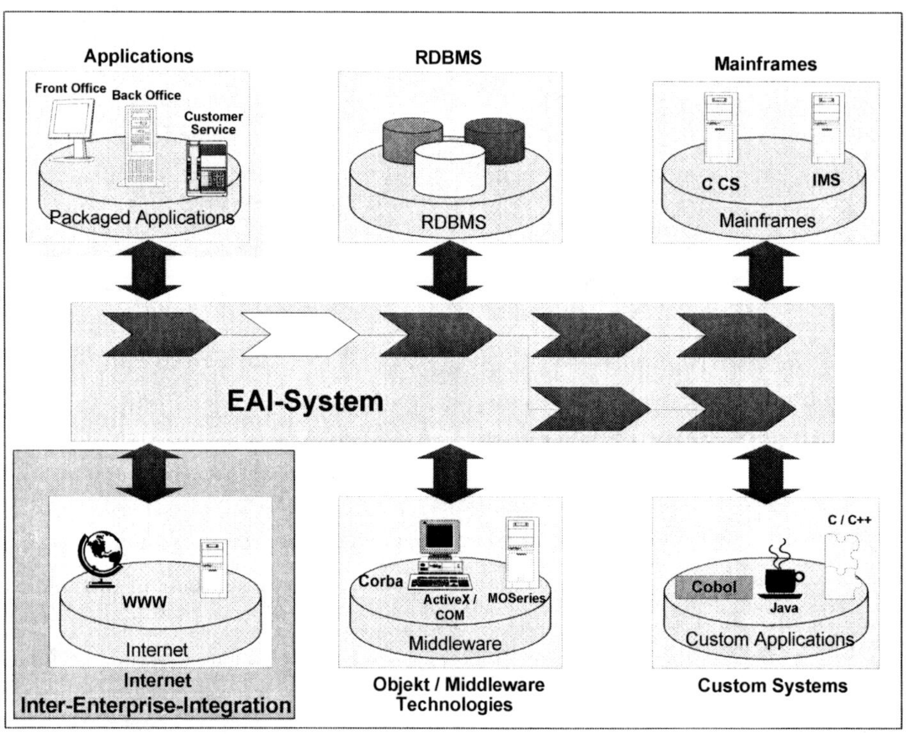

Figure 6. Peer-to-peer approach towards business integration execution

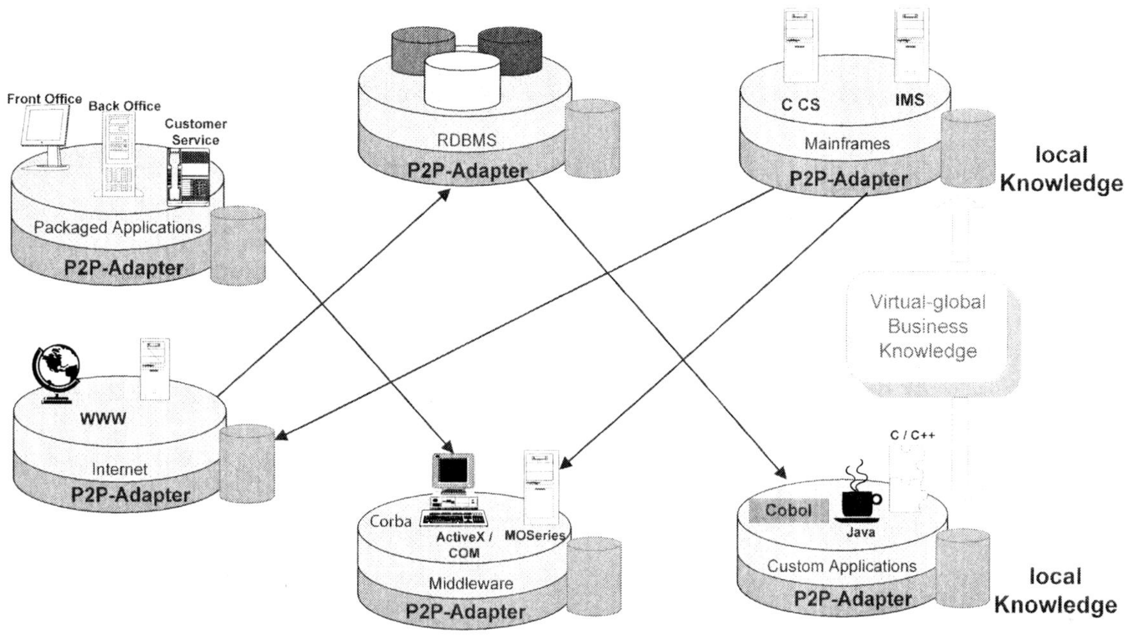

all business processes are affected, possibly even inoperable.

- **Bottleneck:** All network traffic has to be forwarded through the information hub. This results in an extremely high load of data that has to be handled. In a situation of peak load, the system performance will crash down dramatically.
- **Configuration icebergs:** The EAI application must contain all relevant business transactions: The distribution of information has to be represented by formal rules for transformation and routing. Because of its complexity, interdependencies, and lots of exceptions, the number of configuration rules increases exponentially. This may cause insufficient and fault-prone integration solutions.

We consider EAI systems as mission critical applications whose blackout is associated with a substantial business risk. In recent years, awareness of cost-intensive administration and insufficient management of complex business application systems by centralistic approaches has arisen. New fields of research such as *Autonomic Computing* gave thought-provoking impulses to find better alternatives for an efficient management of business integration.

Assigning the *peer-to-peer paradigm* to the context of business integration means that all systems and components of an enterprise work in a self-organizing manner. This allows a flexible and dynamic coupling of applications and processes. Thereby, administration and integration costs can be reduced (Leymann, 2003). A basis for this approach is the non-centralized architecture of a peer-to-peer system which offers the following advantages:

- **Non-central topology:** The complete IT-infrastructure is defined by a variable number of flat (non-hierarchical) peers. Every peer offers (and receives) at least one service (e.g., generate an order, create an invoice, check consistency of data, dispose payment, etc.), where several peers may contain the same services.

- **Reliability:** There is no central component that may cause problems. If a peer breaks down, another peer with similar functionality can replace the broken peer. If a peer with unique services crashes, only those business process instances are affected that require that service.
- **Scalable performance:** The performance of the network can be enhanced nearly unlimited by appending additional peers. Already existing components do not have to be replaced.
- **Easy configuration:** It is no longer necessary to customize the whole EAI system by central transformation rules. Every peer only contains the business knowledge it requires to accomplish its functionality. The configuration of the complete architecture results from the sum of the configuration of the single peers.
- **Adaptive self-configuration:** By implementing intelligent search mechanisms, a peer can find the next service in the process chain by a broadcast into the network. If another peer is able to offer the desired service, it responds. From now on, this peer is part of the process chain and can accept tasks from other peers as well as delegating services to any peers.

While the advantages mentioned above are mainly of a technical nature, these features will not be sufficient to manage the complete field of business integration execution. There is also a high demand of adequate logical representations of business processes to provide an essential process-oriented view that focuses also economical aspects. The vision of both, distributed business processes that are associated with distributed IT-systems, allows an optimization of business processes as well as improving IT applications without interacting each other. In the following Figure, a P2P scenario is shown that gives a first impression:

Every application system (AS) that participates in the whole business process is encapsulated by a P2P-adapter. Every adapter enhances the functionality offered by the single components with additional Web services (WS) that allow a composition of very complex services by a dynamic interaction of different adapters. A peer can initiate business processes, embed local processes in the application flow, and even get embedded by other peers. It only has its own *local business knowledge*, but can also acquire *global business knowledge* by interacting with other peers. In this way, a comprehensive management of meta-data can be achieved without requiring centralistic client/server architectures.

The problem faced above is complex and versatile. Therefore, a highly structured and planned proceeding will be necessary. In contrast to other approaches, we follow a *meet in the middle* strategy, analysing the problem space and creating solving concepts both from the business-oriented as well as from the IT-oriented direction. This ensures that the conceptual solutions are suitable for the business problems targeted and that they are realizable with today's state-of-the-art technologies.

The business-oriented approach will evaluate the requirements of enterprises within internal or collaborative business integration scenarios. The main reference object here is the abstract business process that has to be supported. Thus, the business-oriented conceptual solution has to provide mechanisms and techniques on how to interconnect independent business processes using the P2P paradigm. The main challenge is the lack of a central coordination instance. As a logical consequence, appropriate business process negotiation techniques have to be developed.

Looking at the system-oriented problems, the main question is how to find a mapping between heterogeneous application systems in conformity with the business processes and rules to be supported. This does not only mean to connect interfaces, but also requires to find *reasonable matches* within concrete contexts, as well as to handle a reliable control of the interaction.

Peer-to-peer technologies have been proven to be very flexible and robust. From the authors' point of view, they seem to be an appropriate approach. Hence, new methods and algorithms for a distributed interface and interaction management will be created using the P2P paradigm. The idea is to enable an auto-configuration of the interaction between two independent application systems that succeeds to predefined business processes and that is also compliant to existing, constraining business rules.

Finally, only developing the two solving concepts described above is not sufficient, as there are strong interdependencies between the business- and system-layer. The formation of business process chains within business integration use cases is always limited by the capabilities of the existing applications supporting the business processes. On the other hand, applications themselves can only be interconnected in a way that the combination of systems is realizing a predefined business process.

Hence, a relationship between the two partial solutions has to be found and specified. The combination of these three concepts will be a conceptual methodology for a dynamic binding of business processes to the behavior of the distributed environment via a semi-automatic reconfiguration in case of need. Figure 7 depicts the three-tier architecture for business integration management.

Life Cycle for Business Integration Management

The third element of the business integration management framework is addressed in a dynamic, time-centric perception. The life-cycle model serves as a manual for the process-oriented setting-up and operation of collaboration networks. Using a consistent phase model and standardized modeling methods increases transparency and structuring of collaborations and creates a basis for communication between participants,

Figure 7. Three-tier business integration management architecture

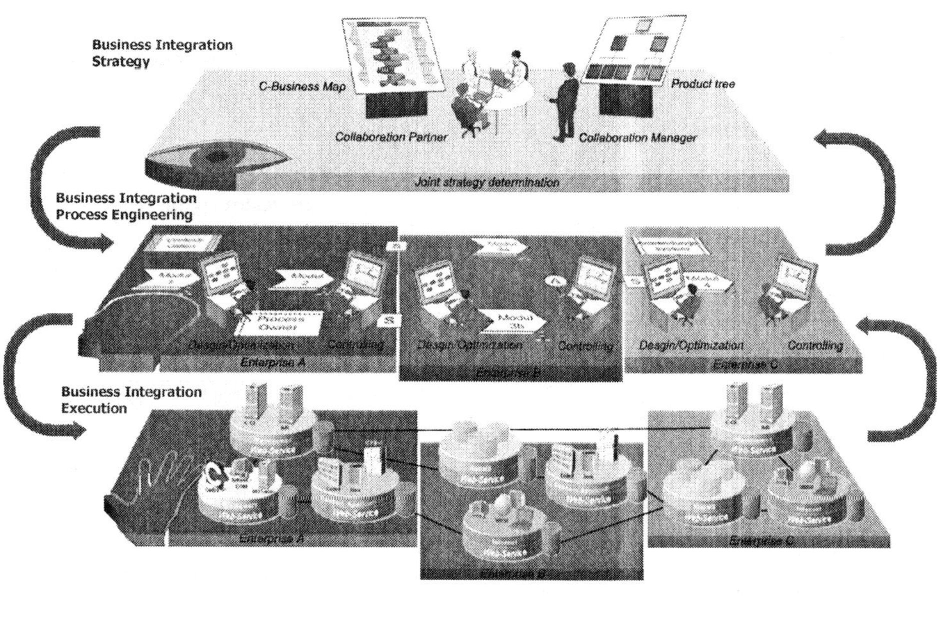

including management that lays down strategies, process-owners in the departments, and IT-experts that integrate the different application systems. Thus, the organizational and technical dimension of business integration is considered in one common life cycle. The model is a fusion of classic phase, models with life-cycle models of virtual enterprises (Mertens & Faisst, 1995). The resulting dynamic model is consistent with the structure-oriented business integration management architecture and represents a cyclical approach.

Prior to the use of the architecture is an *awareness* (pre-phase) of one or more enterprises that they can profit by collaboration with complementary core competence partners. *Exploring* partner competences and suitable collaboration compositions (pre-phase) precedes the first main phase *strategy partner analysis* or formation phase. This is also referred to as initiation and agreement of the enterprise network. The collaboration partners are determined by the shared goals of the collaboration and the aspired win-win situation of all partners. The joint aims of the collaboration have to be defined as synthesis of individual economic objectives. To facilitate a collaborative service or product delivery, graphical notations, like product models, are used in this stage for the determination of a common service or product bundle. Having completed the strategy finding, in the second main phase, *local to-be-concept*, an existing or a new local as-is model and the global to-be concepts of business processes are compared. According to predefined conditions about collective product creation, feasible cross-organizational business processes are derived. Each partner considers their part in the inter-enterprise process. Starting with process modeling and optimization over process controlling up to implementation, the processes involved are aligned with the requirements of the collaborative scenario agreed on in the former phase. In the third main phase *global to-be-concept*, coordinated public parts are allocated over the network, establishing a collective to-be concept. Every partner is able to connect their own private model with every other public process model. Every partner gains their partial view of the collaborative process or, in other words, a virtual process chain of the whole collaboration is designed. Global knowledge is described in a public interface, which can be provided by a standardized representation as, for instance, BPMN. The public processes as well as the message formats and contents can be formally defined by B2B protocols as RosettaNet or ebXML. Furthermore, the semantic combination of models of the different partners is necessary. The integrated collaborative business process model enables all partners to configure their application systems locally in a fourth main phase called *local implementation*. Reference systems for interfaces are provided by interface definitions of the collective to-be concept. Now every partner is prepared for the execution of interactions within the collaborative framework. That is the transition to the fifth main phase *collaboration execution*. Based on bilateral coordination, interacting information systems are able to communicate by using standardized protocols and interfaces. Transactions are arranged and executed. The aim of this phase is to support collaboration through the appropriate use of ICT. That requires primarily the configuration of interfaces and the implementation of cross-organizational workflows; at the same time, a permanent monitoring and adaption of the collaboration, based on business ratio defined in the conception phase, must be assured (Scheer, Grieble, & Zang, 2003). In order to automate cross-organizational processes the conceptual models are transformed into formal models applied as configuration data for the orchestration of business objects. The applications of the partners have to communicate bilaterally to negotiate the interface specifications based on the formal models (see Figure 8)

After the collaboration project ends, companies regroup or split and *reconfigurate* themselves. Hence, the life cycle returns to its starting position, *awareness* (pre-/post-phase).

Figure 8. Life-cycle model

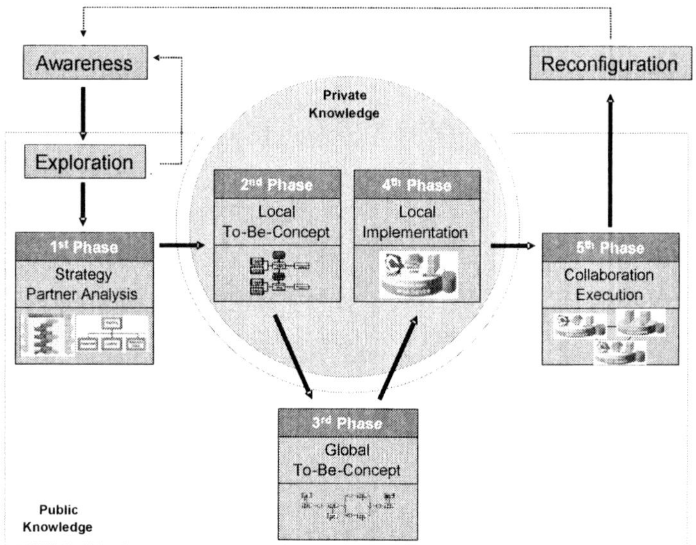

CONCLUSION

The outlined framework for business integration management offers the necessary instruments to set up enterprise processes and ICT-support in collaboration networks. It proposes a management guideline for collaborating enterprises defining *what, why, when,* and *how* they might manage their *business integration* in collaboration networks. With the different approaches, especially the static three-tier architecture and the dynamic life cycle, the authors aim at a holistic and sustainable treatment for managing business integration intra- and cross-organizationally. In the chapter, the authors have presented basic framework elements which are based on the characteristics of cross-organizational business processes. As a result of high complexity in handling such processes in collaboration networks, the need for business integration originally arises. Appropriate solutions are necessarily needed in order to address the properties of collaboration processes in an organizational and technical dimension. With the framework for business integration management, the authors address both, people and machines, acting operational as well as for planning purposes. A few basic examples emphasizing the scope of requirements and solutions were given throughout all sections.

The presented framework has been developed within the scope of the research projects *ArKoS* and *P2E2,* funded by the Federal Department for Education and Research (BMBF). The competence centre business integration (CCBI) at the Institute for Information Systems (IWi) at DFKI facilitates synergies concerning coherent research of different research projects. By clustering national and international research projects, current research problems are addressed in a holistic view on economical and IT-related topics. Accordingly, the outlined framework results from research merged from both projects aiming at a completeness of vision.

REFERENCES

Adam, O., Hofer, A., Zang, S., Hammer, C., Jerrentrup, M., & Leinenbach, S. (2004). *Architecture for collaborative business process management—enabling dynamic collaboration.* Paper presented at the European Conference on Product and Process Modeling (ECPPM 2004), Balkema, Istanbul, Turkey.

Bullinger, H. J., Lebender, M., Otto, B., & Weisbecker, A. (2003). Unternehmensübergreifende Prozessintegration für den elektronischen Geschäftsverkehr. In Kersten, W. (Ed.), *E-Collaboration—Prozessoptimierung in der Wertschöpfungsketten* (pp. 59-82, p. 61, pp. 66-78, p. 68). Wiesbaden: Dt. Univ.-Verl.

Grieble, O., Klein, R., & Scheer, A. -W. (2002). Modellbasiertes Dienstleistungsmanagement (p. 22). In A. –W. Scheer (Ed.), *Veröffentlichungen des Instituts für Wirtschaftsinformatik*, No. 171, Saarbrücken.

Hack, S. (2000). Collaborative business scenarios – Wertschöpfung in der Internetökonomie. In A. –W. Scheer (Ed.), *E-business—Wer geht? Wer bleibt? Wer kommt?* (pp. 85-100, p. 88 et seq.). 21. Saarbrücker Arbeitstagung für Industrie, Dienstleistung und Verwaltung. Heidelberg: Physica-Verlag.

Hirschmann, P. (1998). *Kooperative Gestaltung unternehmensübergreifender Geschäftsprozesse* (p. 39, p. 66, pp. 69-70, pp. 77-80). Wiesbaden: Gabler.

Jeckle, M., Rupp,C., Hahn, J., Zengler, B., & Queins, S. (2004). *UML 2 glasklar* (p. 323 et seq.). München: Hanser.

Jost, W., & Scheer, A. -W. (2002). Geschäftsprozessmanagement: Kernaufgabe einer jeden Unternehmensorganisation. In W. Jost & A. -W. Scheer (Eds.), *ARIS in der Praxis: Gestaltung, Implementierung und Optimierung von Geschäftsprozessen* (pp. 33-44). Berlin: Springer.

Kanter, R. M. (1991). Transcending business boundaries: 12,000 world managers view change. *Harvard Business Review, 69*(3), 151-164.

Klein, R., Kupsch, F., & Scheer, A. -W. (2004). Modellierung inter-organisationaler Prozesse mit Ereignisgesteuerten Prozessketten. In A. -W. Scheer (Ed.), *Veröffentlichungen des Instituts für Wirtschaftsinformatik*, No. 178, Saarbrücken.

Kupsch, F., & Werth, D. (2005). Integrating business processes with peer-to-peer technology. In *Proceedings of the First International Conference on Interoperability*, Geneva, Switzerland (pp. 277-289). London: Springer.

Lebender, M., Ondrusch, N., Otto, B., & Renner, T. (2003). *Business integration software: Werkzeuge Anbieter, Lösungen*. Fraunhofer-Institut für Arbeitswirtschaft und Organisation IAO (Ed.). Stuttgart: Fraunhofer IRB Verlag.

Leimstoll, U. (2003). Kaved AG (Informing AG)—Elektroindustrie. In P. Schubert, R. Wöfle, & W. Dettling (Eds.), *E-business integration: Fallstudien zur Optimierung elektronischer Geschäftsprozesse* (pp. 67-80, p. 73). München et al: Hanser.

Leymann, F. (2003). Web services: Distributed applications without limits. In G. Weikum, H. Schöning, & E. Rahm, (Eds.), *Proceedings of the 10th Conference of Databases for Business, Technology und Web (BTW 2003)* (LNI 26). Bonn: Gesellschaft für Informatik.

Liebhart, U. E. (2002). *Strategische Kooperationsnetzwerke: Entwicklung, Gestaltung und Steuerung.* Wiesbaden: Dt. Univ.-Verl.

Linthicum, D. S. (2003). *Enterprise application integration* (4th ed.). Boston: Addison-Wesley.

McMichael, C. (2003). Business process integration may eclipse EDI, EAI. *HP Chronicle, 17*(6), p. 1, p. 6.

Mertens, P., & Faisst, W. (1995). Virtuelle Unternehmen—eine Organisationsstruktur für die Zukunft? *Technologie & Mangement, 44*(2), pp. 61-68.

Müller-Lankenau, C. (2003). Interessengemeinschaft Datenverbund für die Haustechnik IGH. In P. Schubert, R. Wöfle, & W. Dettling (Eds.), *E-business integration: Fallstudien zur Optimierung elektronischer Geschäftsprozesse* (pp. 123-136, p. 128). München: Hanser.

Naisbitt, J. (1982). *Megatrends: Ten new directions transforming our lives* (6th ed.). New York: Warner Books.

Object Management Group. (2005). *OMG model driven architecture*. Retrieved December 12, 2005, from http://www.omg.org/mda/

Picot, A., Wigand, R., & Reichwald, R. (1997). *Information, organization, and management—expanding markets and corporate boundaries*. Chichester: Wiley.

Ratnasingam, P. (2003). *Inter-organizational trust for business-to-business e-commerce* (pp. 2-4, p. 3). Hershey: IBM Press.

Röhricht, J., & Schlögel, C. (2001). *C-business: Erfolgreiche Internetstrategien durch collaborative business am Beispiel mySAP.com*. München: Addison-Wesley.

Rosemann, M., & Schwegmann, A. (2002). Vorbereitung der Prozessmodellierung. In J. Becker, M. Kugeler, & M. Rosemann (Eds.), *Prozessmanagement: Ein Leitfaden zur prozessorientierten Organisationsgestaltung.* (3rd ed., pp. 47-94). Berlin: Springer.

Scheer, A. -W. (1994). *Business process engineering: Reference models for industrial enterprises* (2nd ed.). Berlin: Springer.

Scheer, A. -W., Grieble, O., Hans, S., & Zang, S. (2002). Geschäftsprozessmanagement—the 2nd wave. *IM Information Management & Consulting, 17*(special issue), pp. 9-15, p. 11, p. 12.

Scheer, A. -W., & Jost, W. (2002). Geschäftsprozessmanagement: Kernaufgabe einer jeden Unternehmensorganisation. In A. -W. Scheer & W. Jost (Eds.), *ARIS in der Praxis: Gestaltung, Implementierung und Optimierung von Geschäftsprozessen* (pp. 33-44, p. 43). Berlin: Springer.

Scheer, A. -W., Erbach, F., & Thomas, O. (2000). E-Business—Wer geht? Wer bleibt? Wer kommt? In A. -W. Scheer (Ed.), *E-business—Wer geht? Wer bleibt? Wer kommt?* (pp. 3-45). 21. Saarbrücker Arbeitstagung 2000 für Industrie, Dienstleistung und Verwaltung. Heidelberg: Physica-Verlag.

Scheer, A. -W., Feld, T., & Zang, S. (2003). Vitamin C für Unternehmen—Collaborative business. In K. Küting, & H. -C. Noack (Eds.), *Der große BWL-Führer: Die 50 wichtigsten Strategien und Instrumente zur Unternehmensführung*. Frankfurt am Main: Frankfurter Allg. Buch im FAZ-Inst.

Scheer, A. -W., Grieble, O., & Zang, S. (2003). Collaborative business management. In W. Kersten (Ed.), *E-collaboration—Prozessoptimierung in der Wertschöpfungskette* (p. 30 et seq.). Wiesbaden: Dt. Univ.-Verl.

Scheer, A. -W., Herrmann, K., & Klein, R. (2004). Modellgestütztes service engineering—Entwicklung und Design neuer Dienstleistungen. In M. Bruhn & B. Stauss (Eds.), *Dienstleistungsinnovationen: Dienstleistungsmanagement Jahrbuch 2004*. Wiesbaden: Gabler.

Schmitt, R. (2000). *Unternehmensübergreifender Engineering Workflow: Verteilte Produktentwicklung auf der Grundlage eines parameterbasierten Daten- und Prozessmanagements*. TU Clausthal.

Scholz, C. (1997). *Strategische Organisation: Prinzipien zur Vitalisierung und Virtualisierung* (pp. 225-229). Landsberg/Lech: Moderne Industrie.

Schubert, P. (2003). E-business integration. In P. Schubert, R. Wölfle, & W. Dettling (Eds.), *E-*

*business integration: Fallstudien zur Optimierung elektronischer Geschäftsprozesse (*pp. 1-22, p. 5, p. 7). München: Hanser.

Thaler, K. (2001). *Supply chain management: Prozessoptimierung in der logistischen Kette* (3rd ed., pp. 43-44, p. 46, p. 49, p. 76, p. 95, p. 117). Köln: Fortis Verlag.

Vanderhaeghen, D. et al. (2005). XML-based transformation of business process models—enabler for collaborative business process management. In M. Nüttgens & J. Mendling (Eds.), *XML4BPM 2005, Proceedings of the 2nd GI Workshop XML4BPM—XML for Business Process Management at 11th Conference Business, Technology, and Web (BTW 2005)* (pp. 81-94). Karlsruhe: SUN Site Central Europe (CEUR).

Vanderhaeghen, D., Zang, S., & Scheer, A. -W. (2005). Interorganisationales Geschäftsprozessmanagement durch Modelltransformation. In A. -W. Scheer (Ed.), *Veröffentlichungen des Instituts für Wirtschaftsinformatik*, Saarbrücken (Vol. 182, pp. 6-7).

Wehner, J. (2001). Projektnetzwerke—Neue Unternehmensstrukturen und neue Qualifizierungen. In M. Rohde, W. Rittenbruch, & V. Wulf (Eds.), *Auf dem Weg zur virtuellen Organisation: Fallstudien, Problembeschreibungen, Lösungskonzepte* (pp. 33-54, p. 41). Heidelberg: Physica-Verlag.

Wölfle, R. (2003). Stellenwert von E-Business-Integrationsprojekten in Unternehmen. In P. Schubert, R. Wölfle, & W. Dettling (Eds.), *E-business integration: Fallstudien zur Optimierung elektronischer Geschäftsprozesse* (pp. 22-38, p. 27, p. 29, p.34, p. 37). München: Hanser.

This work was previously published in Knowledge and Technology Management in Virtual Organizations: Issues, Trends, Opportunities and Solutions, edited by G. D. Putnik & M. M. Cunha, pp. 190-210, copyright 2007 by IGI Publishing, formerly known as Idea Group Publishing (an imprint of IGI Global).

Chapter XIX
Measurements in E-Business

Damon Aiken
Eastern Washington University, USA

ABSTRACT

This chapter is designed to answer two fundamental questions related to research on electronic surveys and measures. First, what are some of the major measures specifically related to e-business? Second, what makes Internet research methods different from off-line research methods? The chapter partly delineates what makes Internet research methods distinctive through its discussion and separation of the most common measures. This separation not only provides the framework for the chapter, but it distinguishes research for understanding the evolving e-consumer from measures related to the new paradigm for e-business strategy. In total, 17 different measures are discussed. The chapter concludes with a discussion of emerging issues in e-business metrics, and possibilities for future research.

INTRODUCTION

The Internet has emerged as the very foundation for business communications worldwide. Indeed, in the instant that it takes to read these words, millions of people are shopping on the Internet, checking the status of orders and shipments, investigating stock prices and mortgage rates, and browsing and bidding in a new realm of online auctions. The Internet has transformed the physical marketplace into a virtual marketspace (Varadarajan & Yadav, 2002); it has created a shift from reasonably well-informed buyers to worldly Web-enabled e-consumers (Bakos, 1997); and, it has accelerated business into an information age wherein issues of technological expertise, privacy, security, and control are now essential aspects of business (Glazer, 1991; Hoffman, Novak, & Peralta, 1999).

Marketing practitioners, strategists, and researchers cannot deny the critical changes that have occurred in the realm of global business communications. Most have come to realize that online retailing is distinctive and that it requires a great deal of new research. Interactive communications and transactions now occur together in a single virtual medium that has increased risks for online consumers, and has placed a heavy communications burden on sellers whose Web site effectiveness is affected by a multitude of design characteristics (Geissler, Zinkhan, &

Table 1. Summary of measures in e-business

Measurements for understanding e-consumers	Measurements for e-business strategy
Online trust	Exposures
Privacy	Impressions
Control of information	Hits
Cognitive effort	Visits
Information search	Clicks
Flow	Path analysis
	Conversion
	Frequency
	Recency
	Average time per visit
	Stickiness

Watson, 2001). Internet consumers are placed in a unique inference-making position in which information asymmetry abounds. The task at hand now, for researchers and practitioners alike, is to accurately measure, analyze, and interpret online behaviors.

The purpose of this chapter is to introduce the topic of e-business measurement, and delineate some of what makes Internet research methods different from off-line research methods. The chapter separates measures for understanding the evolving e-consumer from measures related to the new paradigm for e-business strategy (a separation derived from the work of Biswas and Krishnan, 2004). The measures discussed in this chapter are graphically displayed in Table 1. The chapter concludes with a discussion of emerging issues in e-business metrics, and possibilities for future research.

Internet technologies are like an arms race in which both sides develop increasingly powerful weapons. (Bakos, 1998, p. 41)

MEASUREMENTS FOR UNDERSTANDING E-CONSUMERS

Understanding how the Internet has influenced consumer psychology is a critical task for business people. Speaking of the transformative nature of the Internet, it appears that businesses and consumers alike are now "armed" with previously unthinkable advances in information acquisition, classification, evaluation, and storage. In the unusual context of the Internet, key traditional elements of business exchange are noticeably absent, such as personal, nonverbal cues, and physical contact with products (Keen, Wetzels, de Ruyter, & Feinberg, 2004). In an effort to understand the Internet consumer, business researchers have begun to study notions of online trust, privacy, issues of control of personal information, cognitive effort and information search, and flow. Many of these issues are interrelated and, given that we are still in the early stages of Internet research, the topics need further exploration and insightful analysis.

Online trust. Internet marketing researchers have reported that, regardless of the number of privacy policies or "high-tech" encryption systems, what Web consumers really want is "... another type of exchange—characterized by an explicit social contract executed in the context of a cooperative relationship built on trust" (Hoffman et al., 1999; p. 82). This finding is both a recognition of the uniqueness of the Internet as a computer-mediated business environment, and an allusion towards the critical importance of trust in any Internet relationship. A consumer wishing to shop or purchase over the Internet needs to trust the e-tailer, but also needs to trust the Internet itself as a mode of shopping.

A small but growing subset of the business and marketing literature has attempted to define and measure the concept of trust in a computer-mediated environment (CME) (Handy, 1995; Hine & Eve, 1998; Jarvenpaa & Tractinsky, 1999; McKnight & Chervany, 2002). New definitions of trust in the CME reflect particular concerns about risk, reliability, privacy, and control of information. Milne and Boza (1999) operationalize trust in terms of an affective privacy element as "the expectancy of a customer to rely upon database marketers to treat the consumer's personal information fairly" (p. 8). Through unique processes of interactive communication, consumers must achieve a level of trust that surpasses perceptions of personal vulnerability (Aiken, Liu, Mackoy, & Osland, 2004). Inasmuch as trust requires a cognitive and affective leap of faith (a movement beyond calculative prediction—see Williamson, 1993), trust in the Internet implies, to some extent, behaviorally overcoming a concern for privacy. To take action in the face of risk is to engage in trusting behavior. Thus, much of the research on trust seems to derive three primary dimensions: (1) the affective/emotional element, (2) the cognitive/rational element, and (3) the behavioral element.

Privacy. Recent research reveals that concern for privacy is the most important consumer issue facing the Internet, ahead of ease-of-use, spam, security, and cost (Benassi, 1999). In the off-line world, consumers think nothing of giving their phone numbers or home addresses to seemingly disinterested servers, cashiers, and sales clerks. However, Internet consumers worry about everything from excessive spam e-mails and intrusive cookie files, to costly credit card fraud and perilous identity theft.

Measuring perceptions of privacy, as well as the e-consumer's felt need for privacy, is a critical issue in e-business. Researchers have observed that privacy is a multidimensional concept, and plays a critical role in fear of purchasing online (Hine & Eve, 1998; Sheehan & Hoy, 2000). Much of the concern for privacy may stem from fear of the unknown (Hoffman et al., 1999). Online consumers often cite feelings of helplessness while shopping on the Internet (Hine & Eve, 1998).

Control of personal information. Issues of control further substantiate the unique nature of Internet business relationships. Degrees of interactivity between consumer and e-business become a communicative "tug-of-war" as consumers strive for varied levels of control just as businesses strive to gather more and more strategic information (Yadav & Varadarajan, 2005). User control over personal information, over the actions of a Web vendor, and over the Internet site itself all relate to issues of trust. Additionally, control over the actions of a Web vendor affects consumers' perceptions of privacy and security of the online environment (Bhatnagar & Ghose, 2004; Hoffman et al., 1999). Consumers often guard their personal information carefully. Hoffman and Novak (1998) note that "Virtually all Web users have declined to provide personal information to Web sites at some point, and close to half who have provided data have gone to the trouble of falsifying it" (p. 1). Consequently, perceptions and levels of control become key measures in e-business.

Cognitive effort and information search. Many researchers have noted that decision making is both task dependent (Bettman, Johnson, & Payne, 1990; Maule & Edland, 1997) and context dependent (Bettman, Luce, & Payne, 1998; Wright, 1974). Given that both the decision task and the decision context are different in a CME; new research has just begun to measure cognitive effort, search characteristics, and decision-making processes. Weiner et al. (Weiner, Deighton, Gupta, Johnson, Mellers, Morwitz, & O'Guinn,1997) note, "The ability of [Internet] consumers to sort on attributes and make reasoned decisions at home about which brands to choose ... has the potential to change decision processes and ultimately brand choice" (p. 291). These authors also reason that customization, searching, and sorting will drastically change decision making on the Internet. Within a decision context, cognitive effort relates to the mental resources required, as well as to the individual resources available. *Cognitive effort* can be thought of as information load that deals with how cognitive processes handle incoming stimuli (information), matching the cognitive resources required with the cognitive resources available. The experience, skill, and amount of resources a decision maker has are negatively correlated with the cognitive effort required in the decision task (Bakos 1997; Garbarino & Edell, 1997).

Cognitive effort, within the context of Internet decision making, can be seen from two perspectives. First, it seems logical that cognitive effort could be *reduced* within the CME. Certainly, consumer search costs have been drastically lowered with the assistance of the Internet (Bakos, 1997). This premise allows price and product information to be readily gathered, analyzed, and compared. Furthermore, one could argue that there is less noise when shopping on the Web compared to shopping in a crowded, information-packed retail outlet. Additionally, people can gain experience and skill in utilizing the Internet as a shopping tool. As experience and skill grow, less cognitive effort may be required to gather, sort, and analyze attributes of a choice set. However, a second perspective yields precisely the opposite conclusions: that, as a rule, cognitive effort is persistently *increased* for Internet decision makers. It seems reasonable that users are required, by necessity of the medium, to hold more information in working memory. More cognitive resources are needed to "surf" from Web page to Web page, recording, analyzing, and maintaining information in memory. Further, given the wealth of information available on the Web and the relative ease of searching for additional facts and advice, one could summarily argue that increases in cognitive effort are the norm. The sheer volume of Web advertising is a critical noise factor that would seem to rival the distractions of any retail environment. Internet consumers' may routinely have their decision processes clouded by information overload. Future research should strive to resolve this issue.

Flow. Flow is not only useful in describing general human-computer interactions (Csikszentmihalyi, 1990), it is also an important construct in the study of Internet navigations. Hoffman and Novak (1996) have ascribed the flow experience to Web behavior, measuring the loss of self-consciousness in an essentially blissful encounter. In this situation, *flow* can be defined as the state occurring during Web navigations characterized by (1) a seamless sequence of responses facilitated by interactivity, (2) an intrinsically enjoyable experience, (3) accompanied by a loss of self-consciousness that is (4) self-reinforcing (Novak,Hoffman, & Yung, 2000). Of course, flow is not only a difficult concept to identify, it is also a difficult concept to measure. E-business researchers have just begun to study the effects of consumers entering (and Web sites facilitating) the flow experience (Richard & Chandra, 2005).

Just as human experiences are evolving because of the Internet's influence, so too are the possibilities and methods of commerce evolving. (Parasuraman & Zinkhan, 2002, p. 294)

MEASUREMENTS FOR E-BUSINESS STRATEGY

The evolution of business and communications has transpired at lightning speed. The Internet has made the collection of data faster, easier, and less costly than ever before in the history of business. Consequently, a new paradigm is emerging in terms of e-business research strategy (see Hoffman & Novak, 1997) wherein the challenge is no longer in the painstaking meticulousness of data collection, but rather it emerges as researchers strive to "mine" truly meaningful information, insights, and predictions from figurative "mountains" of data. Over the last decade, e-business researchers have made valiant attempts to measure consumer actions in an effort to more strategically communicate with and influence Internet consumers. Studies have measured primary actions (i.e., initial exposures, impressions, hits, and visits), secondary actions (i.e., what happens next in terms of clicks and path analyses), transforming actions (i.e., consumer conversions), and "involving" actions (i.e., Web site stickiness). Measures of all types of consumer actions directly relate to strategic changes in site design as well as alterations to multiple elements of the marketing mix.

Exposures, impressions, hits, and visits. A wealth of strategic measures evaluate e-consumers' primary actions including exposures, impressions, hits, and visits. The simple essence of measuring exposures entails measuring frequency counts of Web traffic by page. This is an important matter for advertisers as they convert fees into cost per thousand (CPM), and partially evaluate advertising according to the number of people exposed. Page impressions deal with counting the number of Web pages requested by users' browsers (Bhat, Bevans, & Sengupta, 2002). Hits are essentially similar measures of user actions. Finally, put plainly, visits count the number of user-sessions at a Web site. This is an important measure because businesses can track trends, charge advertisers accordingly, modify their sites and servers, and so forth.

Clicks and path analysis. A second set of measures attempts to interpret the paths of Web consumers. Researchers note that the sheer number of clicks may be important as to time spent on a Web site, the length of time a user is exposed to an ad, and the overall level of interest expressed in average time per visit. Researchers have measured click-throughs and click-through rates for some time. Essentially, this is when a potential e-consumer clicks on an advertisement and is taken, via hyperlink, to another online location (i.e., another Web site, another e-tailer, etc.). Path analysis provides strategic insight into the popularity of various pages, the ease (or difficulty) of navigating a site, and general navigational trends. Often, this type of data is labeled *click-stream* data as it measures the series of links that a user goes through when steering through the Web (Rayport & Jaworski, 2002)

Conversion. A third topic of strategic measures relates to tracking *conversion rates*. Conversion basically implies the completion of some action by an e-consumer (Rayport & Jaworski, 2002). For example, conversion events include completing a membership form, requesting a newsletter, opting in to receive future e-mails and updates, filling out online forms, and so forth. A conversion rate measures the number of visitors who come to a Web site and take action relative to the total number of visitors to the site (Bhat et al., 2002). Conversion rates are of strategic importance because of their abilities to bring the customer closer to the business, converting and escalating a new and heightened level of involvement and perhaps loyalty.

Stickiness. A final topic of strategic Internet business measures is that of Web site *stickiness*. Web site stickiness relates the notion of user involvement to an evaluation of how attractive and memorable a site is (Gladwell, 2000). Stickiness can also be evaluated according to the frequency of site visits, the recency between visits, and the average time per visit (Bhat et al., 2002). The attractiveness of this metric is that it makes a good deal of intuitive sense, and that it encompasses multidimensional aspects of a site experience. However, there may be a misconception in simply evaluating length of time on the site as a measure of stickiness. In this case, researchers may be mislabeling time as stickiness, as opposed to patience spent searching through a complex and perhaps frustrating Web site.

Thus, operationaliztions, or measures, are the means by which we attempt to capture a moonbeam and hold it in our hands. (Straub, Hoffman, Weber, & Steinfield, 2002, p. 228)

EMERGING ISSUES IN E-BUSINESS MEASUREMENTS

Online interviewing and focus groups. Purely quantitative analyses of clickstream data and Internet survey research methods are limited in their abilities to enlighten us. Web surveys have notoriously low response rates, and are often suspect in their abilities to gather a representative sample (Dillman, 2000). Simple frequency counts of consumer actions yield very shallow data. Since technology has sped up the transmission of Internet content, and advances in software have dramatically enhanced Web design and graphics, researchers have expanded the use of online qualitative research. For instance, it is not uncommon to hold online focus groups wherein respondents can interactively participate in virtual forums. Participants can evaluate prototypes, respond to potential advertisements, and hold meaningful, insightful conversations about various aspects of e-business. Furthermore, online interviewing is growing in popularity. This is a way to effectively reach some very narrow groups of respondents and gather very rich, powerful data. Online interviews also allow for greater flexibility, follow-up questions, and provide greater depth of analysis. Qualitative Internet research is certainly an emerging field.

Content analysis. Again, as advances in technology, hardware, and software progress, researchers have begun to analyze Internet content more directly and more precisely (Boush & Kahle, 2004). The essence of content analysis is to measure words and phrases throughout a page, a site, a chatroom, a blog, and so forth. Researchers have detected meaningful patterns in the data, made fitting interpretations, and derived strategic insights for future actions. Researchers have even coined a new phrase to describe the word-of-mouth communication over the Internet. Dubbed word on-line (WOL), researchers have noted the powerful influence of the online community and the ever-expanding number of conversations (Granitz & Ward, 1996).

Continuing challenges in electronic survey research. As technological advances make electronic survey research easier, faster, and cheaper, a number of challenging issues arise. First, the issue of low response rates must be addressed. Surely a nonresponse bias must be affecting some research results. Second, asking the right questions and recording the right answers from the right respondents has become increasingly difficult. We cannot simply continue to make up in quantity of data what we knowingly lack in quality of data. We must strive to keep e-business research meaningful and strategically useful. Finally, we must develop a viable communications framework that encompasses the interactivity of e-business, the informational asymmetry that abounds, as well as the unique perspectives of Internet users and e-businesses. Within a sound framework, valid, reliable, and relevant metrics will emerge as the new standard.

Future research. The emergence of the Internet as the foundation for business communications worldwide has given rise to a wealth of truly spectacular measurement tools. Business researchers now have access to an abundance of data that, just a few years ago, might have been deemed unimaginable. Furthermore, they have the research tools to analyze and interpret mass quantities of information; thereby, giving valuable meaning to seemingly chaotic data. Researchers can now track consumer responses and measure psychological issues in a multitude of forms. Straub, et al. (2002) not only provide an expert synopsis of existing metrics, but also provide excellent foresight into numerous e-business metrics that require further exploration, examination, and validation. The likely "next step" in online business metrics will be the measurement of the Internet consumption experience. Some major research questions arise, including (1) What makes the Internet consumption experience so different? (2) Which off-line behavioral/communications/business theories apply to the online context and which need to be altered? (3) What information processing and decision-making theories apply to the CME? (4) Which metrics apply to the online business-to-business context?

REFERENCES

Aiken D., Liu, B., Mackoy, R., & Osland, G. (2004). Building Internet trust: Signaling through trustmarks. *International Journal of Internet Marketing and Advertising*, *1*(3), 1-17.

Bakos, Y. (1997). Reducing buyer search costs: Implications for electronic marketplaces. *Management Science*, *43*(12), 1676-1692.

Bakos, Y. (1998). The emerging role of electronic marketplaces on the Internet. *Communications of the ACM*, *41*(8), 35-42.

Benassi, P. (1999). TRUSTe: An online privacy seal program. *Communications of the ACM*, *42*(2), 56-59.

Bettman, J., Johnson, E., & Payne, J. (1990). A componential analysis of cognitive effort in choice. *Organizational Behavior & Human Decision Processes*, *45*, 111-139.

Bettman, J., Luce, M. F., & Payne, J. (1998, December). Constructive consumer choice processes. *Journal of Consumer Research*, *25*, 187-217.

Biswas, A., & Krishnan, R. (2004). The Internet's impact on marketing: Introduction to the JBR special issue on "Marketing on the Web - Behavioral, strategy and practices and public policy." *Journal of Business Research*, *57*, 681-684.

Bhat, S., Bevans, M., & Sengupta, S. (2002). Measuring users' Web activity to evaluate and enhance advertising effectiveness. *Journal of Advertising*, *31*(3), 97-106.

Bhatnagar A., & Ghose, S. (2004). Segmenting consumers based on the benefits and risks of Internet shopping. *Journal of Business Research*, *57*, 1352-1360.

Boush, D. M., & Kahle, L. (2004). What, and how, we can learn from online consumer discussion groups. In C. Haugtvedt, K. Machleit, & R. Yalch (Eds.), *Online consumer psychology: Understanding and influencing behavior in the virtual world* (pp. 101-121). Mahwah, NJ: Lawrence Erlbaum Associates.

Csikszentmihalyi, M. (1990). *Flow: The psychology of optimal experience.* New York: Harper and Row.

Dillman, D. (2000). *Mail and Internet surveys: The tailored design method.* New York: John Wiley and Sons.

Garbarino, E. C., & Edell, J. A. (1997). Cognitive effort, affect, and choice. *Journal of Consumer Research*, *24*, 147-158.

Geissler, G., Zinkhan, G., & Watson, R. T. (2001, April). Web home-page complexity and communication effectiveness. *Journal of the Association for Information Systems*, *2*, 1-46.

Glazer, R. (1991). Marketing in an information-intensive environment: Strategic implications of knowledge as an asset. *Journal of Marketing*, *55*(Oct.), 1-19.

Gladwell, M. (2000). *The tipping point.* New York: Little, Brown and Company.

Granitz, N. A., & Ward, J. C. (1996). Virtual community: A sociocognitive analysis. *Advances in Consumer Research*, *23*, 161-166.

Handy, C. (1995, May-June). Trust and the virtual organization. *Harvard Business Review*, *73*, 40-50.

Hine C., & Eve, J. 1998). Privacy in the marketplace. *The Information Society*, *14*(4), 253-262.

Hoffman, D., & Novak, T. (1996). Marketing in hypermedia computer-mediated environments: Conceptual foundations. *Journal of Marketing*, *60*, 50-68.

Hoffman, D., & Novak, T. (1997). A new marketing paradigm for electronic commerce. *The Information Society, 13*, 43-54.

Hoffman, D., & Novak, T. (1998). Trustbuilders vs. trustbusters. *The Industry Standard.* Retrieved Aug, 2003, from http://www.thestandard.com/articles/article_print/0,1454,235,000.html

Hoffman, D., Novak, T., & Peralta, M. (1999). Building consumer trust online. *Communications of the Association for Computing Machinery, 42*(4), 80-85.

Jarvenpaa, S. L., &Tractinsky, N. (1999). Consumer trust in an Internet store: A cross-cultural validation. *Journal of Computer-Mediated Communications, 15*(2), 1-35.

Keen C., Wetzels, M., de Ruyter, K., & Feinberg, R. (2004). E-tailers vs. retailers: Which factors determine consumer preferences. *Journal of Business Research, 57*, 685-695.

Kirmani, A., & Rao, A. R. (2000). No pain, no gain: A critical review of the literature on signaling unobservable product quality. *Journal of Marketing, 64*, 66-79.

Maule, J. A., & Edland, A. C. (1997). The effects of time pressure on human judgment and decision making. In R. Ranyard, W. R. Crozier, & O. Svenson (Eds.). *Decision making: Cognitive models and explanations* (pp. 189-204). London: Routledge.

McKnight, H. D., & Chervany, V (2002). What trust means in e-commerce customer relationships: An interdisciplinary conceptual typology. *International Journal of Electronic Commerce, 6*(2), 35-59.

Milne, G. R., &Boza, E. (1999). Trust and concern in consumers' perceptions of marketing information management practices. *Journal of Interactive Marketing, 13*(1), 5-24.

Novak, T., Hoffman, D., & Yung, Y. F. (2000). Modeling the flow construct in online environments: A structure modeling approach. *Marketing Science, 19*(1), 22-42.

Parasuraman, A., & Zinkhan, G. M. (2002). Marketing to and serving customers through the Internet: An overview and research agenda. *Journal of the Academy of Marketing Science, 30*(Fall), 286-295.

Rayport, J. F., & Jaworski, B. J. (2002). *Introduction to e-commerce*. Boston: McGraw-Hill.

Richard, M. O., & Chandra, R. (2005). A model of consumer Web navigational behavior: Conceptual development and application. *Journal of Business Research, 58*, 1019-1029.

Sharma A., & Sheth, J. N. (2004). Web-based marketing: The coming revolution in marketing thought and strategy. *Journal of Business Research, 57*, 696-702.

Sheehan, K. B., & Hoy, M. G. (2000). Dimensions of privacy concern among online consumers. *Journal of Public Policy and Marketing, 19*(1), 62-73.

Straub, D. W., Hoffman, D. L., Weber, B. W. , & Steinfield, C. (2002). Toward new metrics for net-enhanced organizations. *Information Systems Research, 13*(3), 227-238.

Varadarajan, P. R., & Yadav, M. S. (2002). Marketing strategy and the Internet: An organizing framework. *Journal of the Academy of Marketing Science, 30*(4), 296-312.

Weiner, R., Deighton, J., Gupta, S., Johnson, E., Mellers, B., Morwitz, V., et al. (1997). Choice in computer-mediated environments. *Marketing Letters, 8*(3), 287-296.

Williamson, O. E. (1993, April). Calculativeness, trust, and economic organization. *Journal of Law and Economics, 36*, 487-500.

Wright, P. (1974). The harassed decision maker: Time pressures, distractions, and the use of evidence. *Journal of Applied Psychology, 59*(5), 555-561.

Yadav, M. S., & Varadarajan, P. R. (2005). Interactivity in the electronic marketplace: An exposition and implications for research. *Journal of the Academy of Marketing Science, 33*(4), 585-604.

KEY TERMS

Click-Stream: The series of links that a user goes through when using the Internet (Rayport & Jaworski, 2002).

Cognitive Effort: Information load that deals with how cognitive processes handle incoming stimuli (information) (Bettman et al., 1990).

Conversion Rates: A frequency measurement of the completion of some action(s) by an e-consumer as a proportion of the total number of visitors to site (Bhat et al., 2002; Rayport & Jaworski, 2002).

Flow: The state during Web navigations characterized by (1) a seamless sequence of responses facilitated by interactivity, (2) an intrinsically enjoyable experience, (3) accompanied by a loss of self-consciousness that is (4) self-reinforcing (Novak, et al., 2000).

Stickiness: Sometimes a subjective/attitudinal measurement of how attractive and memorable a site is (Gladwell, 2000). Stickiness can also be evaluated according to the frequency of Web-site visits and the average time spent per visit (Bhat et al., 2002).

This work was previously published in Handbook of Research on Electronic Surveys and Measurements, edited by R. Reynolds, R. Woods, & J. Baker, copyright 2007 by Information Science Reference, formerly known as Idea Group Reference (an imprint of IGI Global).

Section V
Critical Issues

Chapter XX
E-Business in Developing Countries:
A Comparison of China and India

Peter V. Raven
Seattle University, USA

Xiaoqing Huang
Seattle University, USA

Ben B. Kim
Seattle University, USA

ABSTRACT

The Internet has changed the way many companies do business, but has also tended to increase the disparity between firms in developed countries and those in developing countries. As the digital divide seems to grow, the question becomes how will developing countries catch up? We examine two large developing countries, China and India, in an attempt to understand their approaches to developing e-business. While both countries had access to the technology at about the same time, each has taken a different path to utilizing it. These approaches are based on a number of factors, including government initiatives and focus, infrastructure building, experience and understanding of business operations, and culture, among others. China appears to be ahead of India in the mechanics and infrastructure, but India is ahead in e-readiness. Both countries are poised for rapidly increasing e-business, however, they have huge problems of poverty and inequality between urban and rural connectivity must be resolved to really take advantage of e-business.

INTRODUCTION

The personal computer and the Internet have changed the nature of business worldwide—in both developed and developing countries. People geographically isolated from each other are now able to communicate in real time. However, how has this ability to communicate affected global businesses, especially among developing nations? This is not a trivial question, as the notion of the "digital divide" appears to be expanding, rather than contracting, as businesses in developed countries are increasingly connected, while those in developing countries lag relatively farther behind. The promise of the Internet and efficiencies of e-business are not equally distributed.

In this study, we examine the adoption and use of Internet strategies in furthering e-business in two large developing nations—China and India. We will see that each country has chosen a different path to utilizing the Internet in business. This may be instructive for other developing countries as they increasingly adopt the Internet and utilize its efficiencies for business and development.

Industrialized countries have adopted the Internet for business purposes at different rates. The U.S., where the Internet first developed, appears to be farthest along in business usage and near the top at a consumer level, although many other countries have significantly increased their use of the Internet (see Table 1). The Internet penetration of China and India are shown in Table 2. Most U.S. firms have an Internet presence, but not all use the Internet in the same way or to the same extent. Increasingly, U.S. firms feel the need to have a Web presence to reach their customers and to serve them efficiently. Sometimes the result is a full-service, e-business exchange site, but for other firms the result is merely an informational site.For marketers in developing countries, though, the question may be to what extent can the Internet be used in marketing products both locally and globally? Firms from industrialized countries have successfully done this, but there is little information about developing countries using the Internet to market their products internally or externally. This study examines the commercial use of the Internet in China and India in an attempt to understand their approaches to e-business. We examine several key areas we think may explain the adoption of e-business in these developing countries: regulatory issues, infrastructure, policy, and culture.

Table 1. Growth of the Internet—World Wide (Note 1: % Pop. is the Penetration Rate, expressed as population percentage; Note 2: Internet Growth Percent is between December, 2000 and June, 2005; source: The Internet WorldStats News, No. 008, July 2005, http://www.internetworldstats.com/pr/edi008.htm, accessed August 6, 2005)

World Regions	Internet Users, 2000	Internet Users, 2005	Growth	% Population 2005
Northern America	108,096,800	223,392,807	106.7 %	68.0 %
Oceania	7,619,500	16,448,966	115.9 %	49.2 %
Europe	103,096,093	269,036,096	161.0 %	36.8 %
Latin America & Caribbean	18,068,919	68,130,804	277.0 %	12.5 %
Asia	114,303,000	323,756,956	183.2 %	8.9 %
Middle East	5,284,800	21,770,700	311.9 %	8.3 %
Africa	4,514,400	16,174,600	258.3 %	1.8 %
Total World	**360,983,512**	**938,710,929**	**160.0 %**	**14.6 %**

Table 2. Comparisons of China and India (Sources: iWatch: Wake up call for India, http://www.wake-upcall.org/china_india_comparision/china_india_chart.php, accessed 8/6/2005; Strauss, El-Ansary, and Frost [2006])

Economic or social factor	Unit of measurement	China	India
Electrical Generation Capacity	Megawatts	258,000	89,000
Electricity Generated	Billions of kilowatts	1,166	417
Telephone lines connected	Millions	240	43
Mobile/cellular phones	Millions	400	75
Internet connections	Millions	45	9
GDP	USD – billions	1121	460
Population	Millions	1260	1060
Population Increase per year	Millions	10	19
Birth Rate	Numbers per 1000	8.8	27
Per Capita Income	USD/year/person	1060	480
Internet Users (2004)	Millions	95.8	39.2
Internet Penetration (2004)	Percent	7.48	3.77

BACKGROUND AND LITERATURE REVIEW

Both China and India have large, growing populations and are frequently compared to each other because of this fact. However, they also have very different cultures and political traditions, which affect the dynamics of a direct comparison. While Internet usage is growing rapidly in both India and China, each country suffers from poverty, illiteracy, poor information, and communication technology (ICT) infrastructure. As these countries approach Internet business strategies differently, can we learn from their experiences? Are the strategies and metrics used in describing China and India of use for other developing countries—or to developed countries? We anticipate that an understanding of the ways in which the Internet is used in China and India, especially in business-to-business (B2B) transactions, will help firms in both developing and developed countries utilize better Internet strategies to compete globally. Although our focus is on B2B e-business, we will also discuss business-to-consumer (B2C) e-business where it is appropriate. While there are differences between the two in target customer, there are also many similarities and the lines between them are often blurred. Previous work has shown that B2B is primarily driven by global forces in more of a "push" mode, while B2C is more internally driven—"pulled" by consumer markets (Gibbs, Kraemer, & Dedrick, 2003).

Why compare China and India in this study? Both are developing rapidly in certain sectors and represent the largest of the emerging markets. China is the largest communist country with a population of 1.3 billion and India is the largest democracy with a population of 1.08 billion (CIA, 2006). Besides their respective sizes, each country has similar problems of disparate ethnicities, languages, and skewed distributions of wealth. Both China and India are developing economies, encountering many of the same problems of transition from traditional to developing to global economy. Both are now members of the global trading community, the World Trade Organization (WTO). They have approached their entry into the WTO, though, in different ways. India, probably because of its British-colonization heritage, has approached the world markets in a more market-driven fashion. China having no such market tradition, is still feeling its way into the world marketplace and seems to perceive a greater need to control the process. These approaches result in different paths to development and to e-business (Kshetri, 2005; Levinson, 2004).

Economic Development

The level of development of a country impacts its ability to trade with other countries, improve its standard of living, and prosper (Economist, 2006; Harrison, 1996). It should be no surprise that countries develop at different rates and in different ways. Each country has a different set of inherent resources—from natural resources to human resources—which have influenced their history, culture, and personality. Until recently, these phenomena, including wars, have had the greatest impacts on rates of development and development typically proceeded at a relatively slow and predictable pace. The industrialized countries of Europe and North America, for example, took about 200 years to become developed. Today, however, technology, especially the Internet, is seen as helping developing countries "leapfrog" the traditional stages of development (Levinson, 2004). In fact, developing countries are often too impatient to wait for the slow pace of traditional development processes, as they fall further and further behind developed countries.

There are many barriers to Internet and e-business adoption in developing countries. For example, incentives for the integration of the Internet in businesses may be low due to poverty and perceived low demand for goods and services. The infrastructure may be inadequate to sustain growing adoption of Internet business strategies and government policies may not support technology development. There may also be deep cultural problems acting as barriers, such as illiteracy and language issues, credit problems, and a limited tradition of entrepreneurship and innovation (Levinson, 2004).

Development is a complex process. Many developing countries do not have a tradition of a market economy and wrestle with the notion of privatization of public enterprises (Yoder, Borkholder, & Friesen, 1991). While developing countries open to international capital flows are likely to receive advanced technology through foreign investments, policy measures are more likely to be successful if directed towards stimulating the accumulation of location-specific assets, including ICT, rather than investment incentives to foreign investors (Nordas, 2002). Technology transfer is also affected by cultural and political differences (Al-Ghailani & Moor, 1995). Other indicators of a "chicken/egg" dilemma suggest that economic development precedes Internet development, thus contributing to the "digital divide" (Norris, 2000).

Outward-oriented countries are those that look elsewhere for growth. They seem to grow at a more rapid pace than more inward-oriented countries (CIA, 2006; Panagariya, 2004; Santos-Paulino, 2005; Young, Huang, & McDermott, 1996). Dollar (1992) cites the recent rapid growth of Asian developing economies compared to those of Africa and Latin America as support for an outward-orientation. An outward-orientation implies that trade liberalization, devaluation of the real exchange rate, and stabilized real exchange rates improve growth in developing countries.

With that, what is the role of technology, and specifically the Internet, in development planning? Akel (2001) suggests a four-step process she calls the "Internet Advantage," consisting of creating a technology intensive environment, offering services to create a unique community, encouraging a climate of entrepreneurship, and providing appropriate assistance. These steps were applied to development within the U.S., but can they also apply to developing countries? We explore on the applicability of this process in subsequent sections.

Because of its relative newness and the rapid rate of development of the industry, the theoretical literature on e-business in developing countries is relatively sparse. However, the literature provides a basis for modeling the diffusion of e-business, including some of the barriers facing early adopters (Travica, 2002). Limitations and/or barriers to e-business in developing countries include limited Internet accessibility, lack of competition in international telephone traffic (which increases the cost of a network), lack of intra-regional infrastructure, and disproportionate penetration of the telephone in urban areas. E-business depends on several layers: an infrastructure layer—transportation (roads, air, railroads, etc.); a telecommunications layer (pervasive, modern, secure, and affordable channels); a software industry to support e-business; the opportunity for e-payments; and a cultural layer—including a tradition of remote shopping, such as catalogs and mail-order, and standardized goods and services assuring consumers consistent quality leading to trust.

Development of Technology

Technology predictably enhances existing inequalities between economies. Scientists rely on information to be current, but much is available electronically today, so even if it is free, scientists in developing countries may not have access to it. Ninety-five percent of all computers are in developed nations. Ten nations, accounting for just 20% of world population, have three-quarters of the world's telephone lines (Arunachalam, 1999). The unequal availability of information in developing economies may also inhibit business knowledge and decision-making. Developing countries with better access to current information of their own and other markets, such as economic trends, consumer preferences, demand, currency exchange rates, and other business information, should be able to be more successful in business.

A number of factors affect the rates of adoption of technologies, including industrial organization, reliance on IT (Information Technology), local resources, management styles, political influence, regulatory requirements, etc. (Lanjouw & Mody, 1996). For example, stringent environmental requirements have encouraged adoption of pollution control and recycling technologies in Germany and Japan. Policies and economic incentives can retard or accelerate the rates of technology adoption by businesses (Chien & Salem, 2001; Colaco, 2003). In addition, cultural issues such as entrepreneurship and leveraging first mover advantage influence adoption of e-business (Gregorio, Kassicieh, & de Gouvea Neto, 2005).

Managers have control over organizational factors, but little control over broader environmental factors, such as increased competition, liberal government policies, and market stability—all of which have a positive impact on IT adoption (Dasgupta, Agarwal, Ionnidis, & Gopalakrishnan, 1999). There is also a strong correlation across countries between GDP/capita and Internet connectivity. While information technology is believed to be a new source for global economic growth (Friedman, 2005), there is also concern that the Internet may be a factor in widening the income differentials between countries. The regulatory environment's influence on competition also has an impact on Internet connectivity (Kiiski & Pohjola, 2002). These issues suggest the extremely complex phenomena of technology adoption and development in developing countries. Without efficient access to the Internet, e-business is likely to be retarded.

With the possible exception of China, India has been affected more by changes in IT than any other developing country, yet it remains very poor. India has lagged far behind many other Asian countries in the adoption of the Internet. In a population of one billion people, there are fewer than two million Internet subscribers, a figure that contrasts with India's closest comparator in size, China, which has more than three times as many telephone lines and four times as many Internet users. However, Internet users in India are estimated to be four times that of subscribers (Miller, 2001).

UN Secretary General Kofi Anan has warned of the dangers of excluding the world's poor from the Internet suggesting that being cut off from telecommunications services is a hardship almost as acute as other deprivations such as jobs, shelter, food, health care, and drinkable water. The fact there are absolute inequalities between rich and poor nations in the virtual world is hardly surprising given the substantial disparities in every other dimension of life from health care and nutrition to education and longevity. The more interesting question concerns relative inequality of opportunities. Relative opportunities may lay in equalizing technological resources, such as through distribution of computer hardware, skills training, and network connections (Norris, 2000). Thus, many developing countries see a way out of their never-ending cycle of poverty through technology, especially the Internet.

CHINA'S APPROACH TO E-BUSINESS

In this section, we examine the ways in which China has approached e-business. Chinese universities joined the Internet six years after those in India, but policy makers and politicians soon realized its potential (Press, Foster, Wolcott, & McHenry, 2002). China's leaders saw the impact of the Internet on Western and other Asian economies and understood its importance for China in the future (Hachigian, 2001). Chinese businesses are encouraged to embrace new technologies to be competitive in world markets and to be connected to the information needed through regulation and other initiatives.

China has taken to the Internet rapidly and has become the second largest Internet market in the world with around 8.5% of its population of 1.3 billion now connected. This translates to about 120 million users by the end of 2005 (Communications, 2006). More than half of China's Web users access it through broadband, attracting firms such as Amazon.com, eBay, and Google.

Regulatory Environment

The Chinese government has made a concerted effort to develop the infrastructure necessary to fully utilize the Internet. However, because of the vastness of this country, most infrastructure development has occurred in urban areas. Rural areas are largely untouched by the promise of the Internet and e-business (Chen, 2003). This disparity does not seem to be a big issue to central planners, as their focus is more on consumers than on business (CII, 2000).

Government regulations play a much more important role in China than in the U.S. (Xu, Zhu, & Gibbs, 2004). Other facilitators of e-business in China include technology competence, enterprise integration, and competition intensity. In China, firms lag in using e-business related technologies, especially inter-organizational technologies.

Infrastructure

China's development of the Internet was in two phases—1) First Phase (1987-1993)—when a few scientific research institutions were allowed access, 2) Second Phase (1994 to the present)—implementation of full services (Lu, Du, Zhang, Feicheng, & Le, 2002). By 1999, most government departments were connected and had their own sites. The Chinese government had hoped to have one million enterprises connected by 1999 and double that in the following few years. Five main Internet applications were approved: 1) electronic government; 2) electronic business, including the Golden Bridge, Golden Card, and Golden Gate projects; 3) distance education; 4) distance medical treatment; and 5) digital library. However, problems of slow speeds, high usage costs, poor information quality, ineffective management, incomplete policies, and unbalanced information flow remain.

China has improved its infrastructure and readiness for e-business considerably, but there is much room for further improvement. In order to take full advantage of the Internet in managing the supply chain, fast and accurate information is needed, along with the ability to adjust inventory, production, and transportation systems and react quickly to market changes (Daly & Cui, 2003).

Between 1999 and 2002, China added 106 million landlines, 163 million cell phone subscribers, and 36 million new cable television subscribers—considerably more than other countries (WEF, 2004). Currently, China is adding four million mobile subscribers a month and has the world's largest broadband Internet market with almost 25 million users, growing at more than a million per month (Economist, 2005). Clearly, China is building an infrastructure to sustain future growth.

Policy

For reasons of national pride and prestige in the world community, China seems to focus on increasing the number of people using the Internet. This strategy has long-term implications for development. In what might be called a pull strategy by emphasizing the consumer use of the Internet, China may be hoping that demand will eventually be filled by local businesses meeting the needs of local Internet consumers. Indeed, PC penetration has had rapid growth—from only 1600 in 1994, 80,000 in 1996, to 22.5 million in 2000. However, still only a small portion of the total population (<2%) has a PC (Harwit & Clark, 2001).

Culture

Culture plays a significant role in adoption of technology and use of the Internet (Bagchi, Hart, & Peterson, 2004; Levinson, 2004). For example, the Technology Adoption Model (TAM) helps explain IT adoption by suggesting that perceived ease of use and perceived usefulness of technology influence attitudes toward technology. Attitude toward technology in turn influences intentions and then behaviors, including adoption. The TAM has demonstrated its usefulness in several cultures, but notably not in Japan. An explanation for the differences in technology adoption is in cultural values (Bagchi et al., 2004). The Japanese tend to rank lower than many other cultures on Individualism and higher on Collectivism and Power Distance, the opposite of cultural values necessary for positive attitudes toward technology adoption. Culture, of course, does not act alone in technology adoption, as suggested by the technology transfer literature, which also indicates a role for income per capita, human capital, openness, type of government, and others (Bagchi et al., 2004).

The technology adoption model (extended version) has been tested in several industries in China, where it was supported (Di Benedetto, Calantone, & Zhang, 2003). In addition, the authors suggest that cultural factors such as cosmopolitanism and mobility may lead to diffusion patterns across countries.

Other Chinese cultural characteristics that influence technology adoption include a preference not to be in debt, a desire to touch and feel articles before buying them, a fear of a disappointing shopping experience, security issues with providing credit or debit card numbers to strangers, and the perils of an ineffective distribution system where purchased items may be lost or delayed in transit. Chesse (2001) also depicts the reliability and efficiency of distribution systems in China to be an issue in e-business acceptance. In addition, transparency is not universal among Chinese firms and many companies are reluctant to share operational and financial details, which could reduce the effectiveness of B2B e-business.

Interpersonal relationships in doing business are important to the Chinese. The Chinese tend to prefer face to face business negotiations and rely on long-term trust and family relationships in doing business (University, 2004). These cultural business characteristics may be difficult to facilitate through the Internet and may make Chinese business leaders more reluctant to accept e-business.

There is also a language barrier for Chinese Internet users (University, 2004). Although Chinese language Web sites are increasing, most business sites are still in English or other Western languages. To compensate, Chinese students are learning English and other Western languages in schools. In comparison to India, this may be facilitated by the considerably higher literacy rates in China—90.9% compared to 59.5% in India (CIA, 2006).

The literature suggests that technology could be at odds with traditional cultures—that "Western" technologies may negatively influence "non-Western" cultures (Shoib and Nandhakumar, 2003). While this may have some merit, the reverse could also be true—that "non-western" cultures may use "Western" technology in different ways that are innovative and mesh better with their non-Western culture. For example, collaborative Internet programs have been used by Navajo tribal elders in traditional consensus decision-making (Keating, et al., 2001).

The Internet has facilitated innovativeness and entrepreneurship in the developed countries, which adopted it early on. While China is not well known for producing entrepreneurs, adoption of the Internet in China is helping to develop a number of entrepreneurs who do not rely on official connections or government sinecures. These new Net entrepreneurs are becoming role models for a future generation of Chinese business owners (McCarthy, 2000). However, competition among Chinese B2B enterprises is still in its early stages, limited by a lack of trust in partners and a reluctance to share information (University, 2004).

Taken together, these factors of e-business adoption suggest that China is progressing rapidly toward integrated e-business, but still has a long way to go to reach the level of many developed countries.

E-Business

It is difficult to determine the exact nature and extent of e-business in China, as data varies widely by source, if it is even available. It does appear that B2B online transactions far surpass B2C, with one estimate suggesting 75% are B2B (E-Commerce, 2005a). It is estimated that about 18% of surfers in China buy online. Internet use has been especially rapid in online financial services.

China's potential for e-business is huge. With 100 million currently online and that number expected to pass that of the U.S. in a few years, e-business can only grow (Panlogic, 2006). In addition, the user profile lends itself to online buying—90% of users are under 40 and 2/3 of users are expected to buy online. However, e-business will be held back by low credit card usage and intellectual property issues. Most Web sites in China still do not support transactions.

The value of e-business in China is difficult to discern, as estimates vary greatly. One Chinese language report (CCID, 2005) indicates that the B2B market grew from 107.5 billion Yuan ($12.97 billion) in 2001 to 178.4 billion Yuan ($21.528 billion) in 2002 and to 346.4 billion Yuan ($41.803 billion) in 2003. The B2C market grew from 790 million Yuan ($95.33 million) in 2003 to 1.6 billion Yuan ($193.08 million) in 2004 (CCID, 2005). Another estimate for general e-commerce revenue suggests it is expected to reach USD 16 billion in 2006 (E-Commerce, 2005a). In any case, the various state and local governments continue to influence e-business, with Beijing, for example, wanting 80% of department stores in the capital to offer online shopping in 2005.

INDIA'S APPROACH TO E-BUSINESS

The Indian economy has been growing between 6.0 and 6.5% annually (James, 2002).

In a country well known for its role in outsourcing of IT and offshore call centers for industrialized countries; it is perhaps surprising that India has not progressed further in Internet penetration and e-business. Despite a large number of high-tech employees, only about 0.4% of the population was connected to the Internet in 2000 (Kiggen, 2001). However, current information suggests a combination of low broadband costs and inexpensive computers has increased Internet connectivity in India to about 38.5 million in 2005—and that is expected to increase to 100 million in 2007 (eMarketer, 2006). It is also interesting to note that the proportion of women Internet users will increase to about 40% of the user population.

Like China, India is a large and heterogeneous country with many dialects and cultures. It is still expensive to get online and the quality of the infrastructure needs improving, but India is moving rapidly towards greater Internet penetration.

One advantage India may have over China is widespread fluency in English, arguably the business language of the Internet. This is especially true in urban areas, where Internet connectivity is likely to be highest. Several issues that influence Internet use in India follow.

Regulatory Environment

The Indian government has strongly encouraged the development of the Internet and information technology through various incentives, including exempting the industry from burdensome regulations and controls (Miller, 2001). The government has followed up its encouragement by allocating 2-3% of its budget for IT and encouraging innovative uses of the Internet, such as using solar power and locating cyber-cafes near railway stations (Rao, 2002a). Unfortunately, while Internet backbone costs have been reduced, last mile costs are still high in India. In addition to more traditional uses, India anticipates that the Internet will empower poor, rural villagers to improve their lives (Quibria, Tschang, & Reyes-Macasaquit, 2002).

Infrastructure

The IDC expects India's ISP (Internet Service Provider) sector to grow by 27% in coming years and to reach 8.2 million subscribers by 2005 (Corp, 2003). As personal computer (PC) prices fall, increasing PC penetration will lead to greater Internet penetration. The IT sector, in fact, seems to be propelling the Indian economy forward. The Indian Government, through the Ministry of Information and Communication Technology, is developing infrastructure to support IT (Colaco, 2003), but there is considerable variation between states (Press et al., 2002). However, between 1999 and 2002, India added only 15 million landlines, while China added 106 million (WEF, 2004). In the race between India and China in infrastructure development, India is coming in at a distant second. India is adding mobile subscribers at one quarter the rate of China (one million/month) and has only 3 million broadband accounts to China's 25 million (Economist, 2005).

Indeed, the outsourcing of IT from western countries has stretched the infrastructure in many cities to its breaking point; resulting in power outages, increasing costs, and a shortage of qualified graduates, in what some refer to as the Bangalore Effect (Aspden, 2006).

Policy

Like China, India has a large rural population, much of which is not connected to the Internet. However, India has developed several initiatives to help connect rural villages (Rao, 2002c). The Indian model uses unique combinations of low-cost indigenous technology with low-cost delivery that utilizes the ability of the informal sector to respond and adapt to local needs (James, 2003). Examples of "pro-poor innovations" include small-scale rural telephone exchanges and very low cost computers that are accessible to poor, often illiterate users. The results suggest that sustainable Internet models for developing economies may look quite different from those in industrial countries.

As early as 1998, Prime Minister Vajpayee proclaimed that "IT is India's tomorrow," implying that the Internet is a key to this vision as an enabler of technology-based change (Wolcott & Goodman, 2003). Although the Indian government is still overly bureaucratic, its attitude toward regulation is beginning to change. Foreign investment in India has increased dramatically and the government has raised the levels of permitted foreign direct investment (FDI) in the oil and private banking industries (Walsh, 2004).

India provides an example of how fundamental, focused changes in policy and legislation can set free forces that accelerate Internet diffusion. While private sector initiatives expanded the Internet infrastructure and Internet services markets, government initiatives promoted the expansion of the Internet into parts of the country not well served by private ISPs (Wolcott et al., 2003).

Prakash (2005) considers the importance of ICT (Information and Communications Technology) in "leapfrogging" India into the knowledge era. Not everyone agrees, however, with the Indian Government's focus on ICT. Rather than acting to leapfrog India into the forefront of the global knowledge community, Mir and Mir (2005) suggest its role should be more of "catalysis." As such, ICT works better when integrated into existing institutional programs of growth and welfare. Catalysts have more of an accelerating or facilitating role, rather than a transforming one, and work upon activities already taking place.

Culture

As with China, the societal culture, as well as the organizational culture, influences the adoption rate of IT in India (Dasgupta et al., 1999). Poverty levels are high in India, but some of the best run software firms also exist (Cheung, 2001a). Only a fraction of the population can be considered a target for Internet use, but that part is well educated, media-savvy, and an early adopter of new technology. Indian users tend to be young, male, and members of the middle class and above. Indian users prefer e-mail and Web surfing, rather than online shopping. Their reluctance to use credit cards also reduces the rate of growth of B2C activities (Cheung, 2001b).

India has a relatively high capacity for entrepreneurship, especially necessity-based, rather than opportunity-based entrepreneurship (Rao, 2002b). Young, moderately educated and well-off men are more likely to be entrepreneurs, as social rigidities still reduce the chances for women. However, changes are occurring. Poverty stricken rural areas are being targeted in India for IT development (Rao, 2002c). Some of these initiatives encourage women entrepreneurs to develop Web based businesses. For example, an Indian Institute of Technology project put women in charge of running 80% of the fast-growing number of Internet cafes and kiosks in Madras (News, 2004).

Most IT commercial initiatives are focused on products for global markets, but there are also "pro-poor" initiatives that have been generated by Indian IT institutions in an attempt to narrow the digital divide (James, 2003). Some of these have included small-scale rural telephone exchanges and ultra-low cost computers to provide the rural poor with access to the Internet. For example, less than 1% of the Indian population has access to a computer and more than 40% are illiterate, but a government initiative has developed the SIMPUTER, an inexpensive, portable, battery-operated, hand held computer. The SIMPUTER has text to speech capabilities and voice mail, but no keyboard. It can break written words into sounds in English, Tamil, Hindi, and Kannada (Meall, 2002). One interesting application has been in the Bay of Bengal, where fishing villages now have access to U.S. Navy weather forecasts, helping to keep fisherman safe, as well as showing locations of fish and current market prices.

Other direct impacts of ICT on development in India include providing market and other information, acting as electronic marketplaces in poor communities, farm cooperative information, farm management tasks, and other applications in education, healthcare, and governance (Quibria et al., 2002).

Traditional farmers in remote Indian villages are now conducting e-business through ITC, one of India's largest agribusiness companies, which has created the e-choupal concept (Sawhney, 2002). Using ITC computers charged by solar panels and backed by batteries, e-choupals are like an integration of Internet kiosk, village gathering place, and e-business hub. Since their launch in June 2000, e-choupal services have reached 600,000 farmers in 6000 villages. Farmers gain by lower transaction costs and better prices and ITC benefits from better quality produce, higher prices in the international marketplace, and savings on procurement.

E-Business

Such data as exists indicates that e-business is limited in India, although it appears ready for rapid growth in the near future. Online consumer purchases were about USD 130 million in 2004/5 and are expected to increase to USD 550 million by 2006/7 (E-Commerce, 2005b). Low PC and Internet penetration, security issues, among others, are holding back e-business in India. E-mail is used by 98% of Internet users in India, while banking is used by 32%, online bill payment by 18%, and stock trading by 15% (eMarketer, 2006). This data suggests a slow, but steady increase in e-business.

DISCUSSION

While Internet usage is growing rapidly in both India and China, both countries suffer from poverty, illiteracy, and poor ICT infrastructure. Technology transfer is affected by cultural and political differences. Thus, we should see a difference in rate of technology adoption and direction of economic growth between China and India.

A number of observers see technology as enabling developing countries to "leapfrog" the development process (Miller, 2001). While technology can be an enabler, the development process is much more complex than technology alone can rectify (Quibria et al., 2002). Government policies and regulations must not restrict businesses excessively. Infrastructure development and educational levels need to increase to allow e-business to occur. Economic growth will rely on complex interactions between private firms, the public and private sectors, and within and between governments. Foreign Direct Investments (FDI) and exports are seen as key to continued growth of the China economy (Yao, 2006). However, IT is also expected to have an important role in the continued development of China (Lemon, 2005).

China appears to have several advantages over India in the race to economic development through ITC (Thiagarajan, 2002).

- The general infrastructure is superior to that of India, both in fixed-line subscribers and Internet penetration. China has invested about ten times as much in telecommunications as India and is spending about three times more than India on telecommunications, as a percentage of GDP.
- China attracts more foreign direct investment (FDI) – many times that of India. Much of this investment is going into the China IT industry, creating significant opportunities for employment.
- China policies allow for rapid clearances and approvals for technology businesses, especially those located in five economic zones and technology parks.

- China has a stronger domestic sector than does India, allowing it to absorb production that may not be exported.

In addition, the centrally planned policies of China have focused on developing infrastructure nation-wide and especially in rural markets, and are quite dispersed. On the other hand, India's market–oriented policies are not focused on the broad access to broadband, but rather on serving relatively few outsourcing companies serving the global community (Economist, 2005).

Yet, a number of obstacles stand in the way of adopting e-business. Wang (2002) lists ten obstacles he thinks most important. Among them are three critical issues for China that differ from obstacles in India: computer and English illiteracy among elderly business decision-makers; insufficient technical and legal protection; and incomplete understanding of the real sense of e-business.

Computer and English literacy are lower in China than in India. Colonization by the British in India required English as the *lingua franca* used for business and government communications. There has been no such systematic use of English in China. Computer literacy is probably also higher in India because of the huge software outsourcing business. Technical and legal protection in China is lacking. The legal system in India tries to protect intellectual property rights. Finally, an understanding of e-business has come late to China (Wang, 2002). E-business is not merely the use of e-mail and Web sites – it includes all the business processes that can be made more efficient through the Internet. India has substantial experience with software outsourcing to aid in their use of supply chain management, including the ordering, producing, marketing, paying, and delivering processes.

E-payment has been an obstacle to e-business in China, although Alibaba and its subsidiary auction site, Taobao, plan to use Taobao's online payment tool, AliPay, for Alibaba's B2B e-business site (Agency, 2005).

Also, China still has control issues, which it attempts to address by prohibition of certain activities. China is thought to have the most sophisticated Internet filtering regime in the world and uses it in various ways to prevent citizen access to political, religious, and other sensitive information (Bambauer et al., 2005). A recent example is the registering of bloggers and enlisting ISPs to help prohibit content that refers to democracy or political change (Chan, 2005). Even more recently, a controversy about Google, Yahoo!, and Microsoft's presence in China brings to light the issues of censorship, free markets, and Internet control (Elgin, 2006).

On the other hand, India has some advantages over China (Thiagarajan, 2002).

- India has a greater fluency in English, the language of the Web. This, and the training of a large number of skilled technology workers, has enabled India to capitalize on its offshore outsourcing initiatives. China will have a difficult time in catching up on outsourcing.
- The Indian government has also favored the software industry and encouraged it through tax incentives.
- India probably has the highest number of SEI-CMM (Software Engineering Institute – Capability Maturity Model) Level 5 engineers in the world. The combination of this certification of quality and good management systems and processes has allowed Indian software suppliers to perform projects with great efficiency.

The rapid growth of Indian software and outsourced IT services has been a catalyst for continuing technology-based change and integration into the global economy (Sarkar & El Sawy, 2003). It has not hurt, either, that this growth is primarily outward focused on providing the large economies of North America and Western Europe with software and back office services. China, on the other hand, has focused more on internal e-business and the production of electronic products (Xu et al., 2004).

The Indian experience of integration of Internet into business is an example of how fundamental, focused changes in governmental policy and regulations can accelerate Internet diffusion. While private sector initiatives expanded the infrastructure for the Internet, governmental initiatives promoted Internet expansion to parts of the country poorly served by ISPs (Wolcott et al., 2003). Like China, India still has problems of poverty and unequal distribution of wealth, as well as infrastructure problems to overcome.

China has promoted a strategy of competition among government-owned organizations, while India has set policy through publicly visible task forces. India's approach is relatively more transparent and market driven than China's (Press et al., 2002). It is unclear at this stage which approach will yield faster economic growth in e-business, although China seems to have the advantage currently.

By many measures, China is ahead of India in the ITC race and is likely to remain so at least in the near future (see Table 3). However, we see India as progressing rapidly in adoption of ITC especially in business applications. In fact, the Economist Intelligence Unit (Unit, 2005), in its 2005 e-readiness rankings, lists India at 49 out of 60 countries measured and China at 54 (Table 3). The e-readiness rankings are based on a number of items comprising six weighted categories: connectivity and technology infrastructure—25%; business environment—20%; consumer and business adoption—20%; legal and policy environment—15%; social and cultural environment—15%; and supporting e-services—5%.

Both countries dropped in ranking somewhat from the previous year. China's consumer and business adoption, legal and policy, social and cultural environments, and supporting e-services indices are lower than India's. China's lower level of entrepreneurial initiatives is also reflected in the rankings. China does do slightly better in connectivity and technology infrastructure and business environment. The drop from the previous year, and growth in the top ranked countries, should be of concern to both countries, though. The e-business rankings are interesting because they suggest that to succeed in e-business, a number of business and cultural factors must be in place, not just technological factors. Also, the rankings suggest that although e-business is growing rapidly in both countries, it is not yet large enough to transform large parts of their economies. However, both countries continue to attract foreign direct investment in technology.

The e-readiness rankings and other sources suggest that adoption of Internet and e-business technologies does not automatically result in increased e-business. Like other businesses, e-business requires good management, finance, marketing, and other business processes (Oyelaran-Oyeyinka & Lal, 2004). In order for any business, but especially e-business to succeed in

Table 3. E-business readiness rankings and scores: 2004-2005 (Source: Unit, 2005)

	2005		2004	
	Rank	**Score (of 10)**	**Rank**	**Score (of 10)**
Denmark	1	8.74	1	8.28
India	49	4.17	46	4.45
China	54	3.85	52	3.96

international markets, understanding these markets and their consumers, whether other businesses or final consumers, is critical. Export promotion councils set up by industry and government can help entrepreneurial e-businesses in both India and China market to appropriate markets. Governments and industry should not neglect this critical element.

CONCLUSION AND RECOMMENDATIONS

A number of studies have confirmed that China is generally ahead of India in Internet infrastructure development and e-business (Press et al., 1999, 2002), but others see it differently. Kshetri (2005), for example, argues that because India has a higher e-readiness rank (Table 3), it is actually better prepared for e-business than is China. The e-readiness rankings consider a number of factors and India has better "legal support for virtual transactions and digital signatures, well-developed private sector and entrepreneurship, the regulatory environment including taxation, and openness to trade and investment" (p. 11), among others. Improving IP protection and more consistent application of the rule of law will help China achieve greater development through the Internet and e-business.

While the adoption of technology to enable e-business in China is occurring rapidly, conducting e-business transactions is lagging, due to barriers in business, legal, and cultural perspectives that fail to adapt to the potential of the technology (Tan & Ouyang, 2004). The major differences between e-business in China and India are summarized in Table 4. While India will probably not overtake China in the ITC race anytime soon, we do see India attempting to uplift its poor rural areas through technology and also penetrate large foreign markets. Of course, there is a long way to go and as urban areas in both countries advance, the distances between urban and rural,

Table 4. Summary of e-business differences between China and India (Data from various sources indicated in text + or _ indicates the degree of difference)

Factor	China	India	Advantage
Regulatory Environment	+ focus on consumers	+ focus on business, but primarily offshoring	China
Infrastructure	+++ broadband high penetration +++ mobile	+ broadband - mobile	China
Policy	++ central policy is very focused on growth throughout China	+ less planning for growth – mostly focused on key offshoring centers	China
Culture	+ literacy >90% - English & computer (low literacy levels) - entrepreneurship - Poverty	- literacy < 60% + English and computer (higher literacy levels) ++ entrepreneurship - Poverty	India
Internet Users (2004)	95.8 million (2005 est. 100 million)	18.481 million	China
Internet Penetration (2004)	7.48%	3.77%	China
E-Readiness	54	49	India
Current e-business * (2004/5)	$41.99 billion (Chinese source)	$150 million	China
Expected e-business * (2006/7)	$16 billion (non-Chinese source)	$550 million	China

** As indicated in the text, estimates vary depending on source. These are reported values for both B2B and B2C. B2B is the largest portion in both China and India.*

as far as technology and development go, continue to widen. This disparity between urban and rural connectivity may have long range internal implications for both countries.

What should other countries, developing and developed, learn from the technology experiences of China and India? Can their experiences be a guide for development and utilization of the Internet and e-business? The answer is yes, with the caveat that what has worked for both countries will likely need localization and modification to work well in individual countries. With that caveat, we offer the following observations and suggestions:

- The Internet is a compelling communications system that, properly used, can inform and educate people in ways that have not been possible before. While urban areas benefit initially, rural areas can also benefit if the proper infrastructure is built.
- The Internet can change business models through e-business. E-business has the potential of unleashing innovative and entrepreneurial ways of thinking and doing business that will aid in economic development.
- Landline based Internet models are rapidly being overtaken by mobile Internet connections in developing countries. Mobile technology has the potential of allowing even more users access to the potential of the Internet and e-business.
- Developing countries can take advantage of the experiences of both developed countries and other developing countries as models for their own growth.
- Governmental policy is an influential driver of Internet usage and e-business. Countries with a focused policy of infrastructure development (e.g., China) will likely outpace those with confused and unfocused policies (e.g., India).
- Intellectual property protection and the rule of law must be enforced for sustained development, but has apparently not been critical in development during the initial stages (e.g., China).

REFERENCES

Agency, X. N. (2005). *Competition on China's e-commerce market intensifies*. Business CustomWire. Retrieved August 10, 2005, from http://home.businesswire.com

Akel, M. (2001). The Internet advantage: A process for integrating electronic commerce into economic development strategy. *Economic Development Review, 17*(3), 13-19.

Al-Ghailani, H. H., & Moor, W. C. (1995). Technology transfer to developing countries. *International Journal of Technology Management, 10*(7,8), 687-703.

Arunachalam, S. (1999). Information technology: What does it mean for scientists and scholars in the developing world? *American Society for Information Science, 25*(4), 21-24.

Aspden, R. (2006). The Bangalore Effect. *New Statesman, 135*(4777), 26-27.

Bagchi, K., Hart, P., & Peterson, M. (2004). National culture and information technology product adoption. *Journal of Global Information Technology Management, 7*(4), 29-46.

Bambauer, D., Diebert, R. J., Palfrey, J. G., Jr., Rohoziniski, R., Villeneuve, N., & Zittrain, J. (2005). Internet filtering in China 2004-2005: A country study. *Berkman Center for Internet & Society at Harvard Law School, Research Publication No. 2005-10.*

CCID. (2005). Report on the Status of EC in the World—April 2004. *Chinese Center for Information Industry.* (in Chinese).

Chan, K. (2005). *China tightens censorship of foreign broadcasters*. The Christian Post. Retrieved August 21, 2005, from www.christianpost.com

Chen, X. (2003). *Comparison of Internet development between China and Korea*. Retrieved August 10, 2005, from http://news.cinhuanet.com/newsmedia/2003-02/09/content_720249.htm

Chesse, J. P. (2001). Distribution: It's more than moving the goods. Retrieved June 6, 2005, from www.madeforchina.com

Cheung, E. (2001a, January 4). *Profiling Indian Internet users: Part 1*. Retrieved August 10, 2005, from www.mail-archive.com/gkd@phoenix.edc.org/msg00368.html

Cheung, E. (2001b). *Profiling Indian Internet users: Part 2*. Retrieved August 21, 2004, from www.mail-archive.com/gkd@phoenix.edc.org/msg00368.html

Chien, A., & Salem, E. (2001). *Building an e-business strategy for Mainland China*. Retrieved May 29, 2004, from http://www.cio.com/research/ec/edit/110501_china.html

CIA. (2006). *World Fact Book*. Retrieved February 10, 2006, from http://www.odci.gov/cia/publications/factbook/geos/ch.html

CII. (2000). *China e-commerce index report*. Retrieved May 29, 2004, from http://tech.sina.com.cn/internet/china/2000-08-08/33014.shtml

Colaco, S. (2003). *Internet potential in India*. Retrieved August 21, 2004, from http://www.stylusinc.com/internet_potential_india.htm

Communications, M. (2006). China's Web users increase 18% in 2005. *Telcomworldwide, 1*.

Daly, S. P., & Cui, L. X. (2003). E-logistics in China: Basic problems, manageable concerns, and intractable solutions. *Industrial Marketing Management, 32*, 235-242.

Dasgupta, S., Agarwal, D., Ionnidis, A., & Gopalakrishnan, S. (1999). Determinants of information technology adoption: An extension of existing models to firms in a developing country. *Journal of Global Information Management, 7*(3), 30-40.

Di Benedetto, C. A., Calantone, R. J., & Zhang, C. (2003). International technology transfer. *International Marketing Review, 20*(4), 446-462.

Dollar, D. (1992). Outward-oriented developing economies really do grow more rapidly: Evidence from 95 LDCs, 1976-1985. *Economic Development and Cultural Change, 40*(3), 523-544.

E-Commerce. (2005a). Country commerce: China. IIn *Country Commerce 2005*. Economist Intelligence Unit of Economist (www.eiu.com) (pp. 123-134).

E-Commerce. (2005b). Country commerce: India. In *Country Commerce 2005*. Economist Intelligence Unit of Economist (www.eiu.com) (pp. 93-99).

Economist. (2005). India vs. China. *Business China*, April 25, 4-5. Retrieved from http://www.businesschina.com

Economist. (2006). Exporting success. *Economist, 378*(8463), 69.

Elgin, B. (2006). *The Web and China: Not so simple*. Business Week Online. Retrieved February 15, 2006, from www.businessweek.com

eMarketer. (2006). *Indian Internet users to reach 100 million*. eMarketer.com. Retrieved February 13, 2006, from www.emarketer.com/Articles/Print.aspx?1003821

Friedman, T. L. (2005). *The world is flat: A brief history of the twenty-first century*. New York: Farrar, Strauss, and Giroux.

Gibbs, J., Kraemer, K. L., & Dedrick, J. (2003). Environment and policy factors shaping global e-commerce diffusion: A cross-country comparison. *Information Society, 19*(1), 5-20.

Gregorio, D. D., Kassicieh, S. K., & de Gouvea Neto, R. (2005). Drivers of k-business activity in developed and emerging markets. *IEEE Transactions on Engineering Management, 52*(2), 155-166.

Hachigian, N. (2001). China's cyber strategy. *Foreign Affairs*, 118-133.

Harrison, A. (1996). Openness and growth: A time-series, cross-country analysis for developing countries. *Journal of Development Economics, 48*(2), 419-447.

Harwit, E., & Clark, D. (2001). Shaping the Internet in China: Evolution of political control over network infrastructure and content. *Asian Survey, 41*(3), 377-408.

James, D. (2002). Dark clouds should part for international market. *Marketing News, 36*(1), 9, 13.

James, J. (2003). Sustainable Internet access for the rural poor? Elements of an emerging Indian model. *Futures, 35*, 461-472.

Keating, G., Ramussen, S., Raven, M., Tso, E., Cocq, J., & Dotson, P. (2001). *Use of Web-based consensus building and conflict clarification process for the Navajo Nation governmental efficiency evaluation*. Unpublished manuscript.

Kiggen, E. (2001, January 8). *Study: High-tech scores low in India*. Retrieved February 2, 2002, from www.newsfactor.com

Kiiski, S., & Pohjola, M. (2002). Cross-country diffusion of the Internet. *Information Economics and Policy, 14*(2), 297-310.

Kshetri, N. (2005). *What determines Internet diffusion loci in developing countries: Evidence from China and India*. Unpublished manuscript.

Lanjouw, J. O., & Mody, A. (1996). Innovation and the international diffusion of environmentally responsive technology. *Research Policy, 25*(4), 549-571.

Lemon, S. (2005). Chinese official calls for expanding IT use. *Computerworld, 39*(47), 12.

Levinson, N. S. (2004). Developing nations. In H. Bidgoli (Ed.), *The Internet encyclopedia* (Vol. 1, pp. 434-443). Hoboken, NJ: John Wiley & Sons, Inc.

Lu, W., Du, J., Zhang, J., Feicheng, M., & Le, T. (2002). Internet development in China. *Journal of Information Science, 28*(3), 207-223.

McCarthy, T. (2000). China's Internet gold rush. *Time, 155*(8), 50-51.

Meall, L. (2002). Eastern promise. *Accountancy*, 60-61.

Miller, R. R. (2001). *Leapfrogging? India's information technology industry and the Internet*. Retrieved May 10, 2002, from http://www.ifc.org/economics/pubs/dp42/dp42.pdf

Mir, R., & Mir, A. (2005). Catalysis, not leapfrog: An institutionalist argument for a limited role of ICTs in India's development. *Asian Business & Management, 4*(4), 411-429.

News, BBC. (2004). *Women lead rural India's Internet rush*. Retrieved August 21, 2004, from http://newsvote.bbc.co.uk/mpapps/pagetools/print/news.bbc.co.uk/2/hi/south_asia/3871529.stm

Nordas, H. K. (2002). Patterns of foreign direct investment in poor countries. *Journal of International Trade & Economic Development, 11*(3), 247-266.

Norris, P. (2000, August 1-6). *The global divide: Information poverty and Internet access worldwide*. Paper presented at the International Political Science World Congress, Quebec City.

Oyclaran-Oyeyinka, B., & Lal, K. (2004). Determinants of e-business adoption: Evidence from firms in India, Nigeria, Uganda. *INTECH Discussion Paper Series* (2004-14).

Panagariya, A. (2004). The miracles and debacles: In defence of trade openness. *World Economy, 27*(8), 1149-1171.

Panlogic. (2006). *Connecting with China.* Panlogic. Retrieved from www.panlogic.co.uk

Prakash, G. (2005). Leapfrogging into the knowledge era: Use of ICT for development. *IIMB Management Review, 17*(3), 47-56.

Press, L., Foster, W., & Goodman, S. (1999). *The Internet in India and China.* Retrieved February 12, 2004, from http://www.isoc.org/inet99/proceedings/3a/3a_3.htm

Press, L., Foster, W., Wolcott, P., & McHenry, W. (2002). The Internet in India and China. *First Monday, 7*(10). Retrieved from http://firstmonday.org/issues/issue_10/press/index.html.

Quibria, M. G., Tschang, T., & Reyes-Macasaquit, M. L. (2002). New information and communication technologies and poverty: Some evidence from developing Asia. *Journal of the Asia Pacific Economy, 7*(3), 285-310.

Rao, M. (2002a, January 25). *E-government services to create billion-dollar market in India.* Retrieved March 11, 2002, from http://kotakstreet.com/webapp/kotak/MarketMonitor/KotakByLanesID.jsp?id=63

Rao, M. (2002b, April 18). *New report highlights entrepreneurial drive in India, calls for better infrastructural and educational support.* Retrieved April 22, 2002, from www.indiainfoline.com/nevi/inwi/

Rao, M. (2002c, February 25). *Rural community networks: Growing social capital via interactive technologies.* Retrieved May 2, 2002, from www.indiainfonline.com

Santos-Paulino, A. (2005). Trade Liberalisation and economic performance: Theory and evidence for developing countries. *World Economy, 28*(6), 783-821.

Sarkar, M. E., & El Sawy, O. A. (2003). The four tigers of global e-business infrastructure: Strategies and implications for emerging economies. *Communications of the Association for Information Systems, 12*, 1-22.

Sawhney, M. (2002). Fields of online dreams; e-commerce can flourish anywhere if you build the right business model. *CIO*, 128-130.

Shoib, G., & Nandhakumar, J. (2003). Cross-cultural IS adoption in multinational corporations. *Information Technology for Development, 10*(4), 249-261.

Strauss, J., El-Ansary, A., & Frost, R. (2006). *E-Marketing* (Fourth ed.). Upper Saddle River, NJ: Pearson/Prentice Hall.

Tan, Z. A., & Ouyang, W. (2004). Diffusion and impacts of the Internet and e-commerce in China. *Electronic Markets, 14*(1), 25-35.

Thiagarajan, K. (2002, March 31). China: The hidden dragon. *Businessline*, March 31.Retrieved from http://www.thehindubusinessline.com/iw/2002/03/31/stories/2002033100341300.htm

Travica, B. (2002). Diffusion of electronic commerce in developing countries: The case of Costa Rica. *Journal of Global Information Technology Management, 5*(1), 4-24.

Unit, E. I. (2005). *The 2004 economist intelligence unit e-readiness rankings*, ebusinessforum.com. Retrieved August 29, 2005, from www.ebusinessforum.com

University, B. (2004). *B2B e-commerce: Is Chinese enterprise getting ready?* Retrieved May 29, 2004, from http://www.chinabyte.com/20010904/1416727.shtml

Walsh, J. K. (2004). India. *Global Markets Update,* March, International Banking Group, US Bank Publication.

Wang, G. (2002). On obstacles to e-business development in Mainland China. *Quarterly Journal of Electronic Commerce, 3*(4), 417-427.

WEF. (2004). *WEF Report: Developing countries lead in ICT access*. Economic Bureau of the World Economic Forum. Retrieved from www.domain-b.com/economy/general/200401jan-wef-report.html.

Wolcott, P., & Goodman, S. (2003). Global diffusion of the Internet I: India: Is the elephant learning to dance? *Communications of the Association for Information Systems, 11*, 560-646.

Xu, S., Zhu, K., & Gibbs, J. (2004). Global technology, local adoption: A cross-country investigation of internet adoption by companies in the United States and China. *Electronic Markets, 14*(1), 13-25.

Yao, S. (2006). On economic growth, FDI, and exports in China. *Applied Economics, 38*(3), 339-351.

Yoder, R. A., Borkholder, P. L., & Friesen, B. D. (1991). Privatization and development: The empirical evidence. *The Journal of Developing Areas, 25*, 425-434.

Young, S., Huang, C. H., & McDermott, M. (1996). Internationalization and competitive catch-up processes: Case study evidence on Chinese multinational enterprises. *Management International Review, 36*(4), 295-314.

This work was previously published in International Journal of E-Business Research, Vol. 3, Issue 1, edited by I. Lee, pp. 91-108, copyright 2007 by IGI Publishing, formerly known as Idea Group Publishing (an imprint of IGI Global).

Chapter XXI
A Model of Information Security Governance for E-Business

Dieter Fink
Edith Cowan University, Australia

Tobias Huegle
Edith Cowan University, Australia

Martin Dortschy
Institute of Electronic Business–University of Arts, Germany

ABSTRACT

This chapter identifies various levels of governance followed by a focus on the role of information technology (IT) governance with reference to information security for today's electronic business (e-business) environment. It outlines levels of enterprise, corporate, and business governance in relation to IT governance before integrating the latter with e-business security management. E-business has made organisations even more reliant on the application of IT while exploiting its capabilities for generating business advantages. The emergence of and dependence on new technologies, like the Internet, have increased exposure of businesses to technology-originated threats and have created new requirements for security management and governance. Previous IT governance frameworks, such as those provided by the IT Governance Institute, Standards Australia, and The National Cyber Security Partnership, have not given the connection between IT governance and e-business security sufficient attention. The proposed model achieves the necessary integration through risk management in which the tensions between threat reduction and value generation activities have to be balanced.

INTRODUCTION

Governance has gained increasing attention in recent years, primarily due to the failures of well-known corporations such as Enron®. The expectations for improved corporate governance have become very noticeable, especially in the

United States, where the Sarbanes-Oxley (SOX) Act of 2002 aims to restore investor confidence in U.S. markets by imposing codes of conduct on corporations. The concept of corporate governance is much quoted as "the system by which companies are directed and controlled" (Cadbury, 1992, p.15). The corporate governance structure, therefore, specifies the distribution of rights and responsibilities among different participants in the corporation, such as the board of directors and management. By doing this, it provides the structure by which the company objectives are set and the means of attaining those objectives and monitoring performance.

Corporate governance includes concerns for information technology governance because without effective information management, those charged with corporate responsibilities would not be able to perform effectively. *eWeek* (2004) make the case for IT professionals to take a leading role in corporate governance since they have control over the processes underpinning governance activities. They mention the example of the human resource database providing information about employees' compensation which, if the information is properly monitored, could provide an early indication of malpractice. This means that IT functions need to be secure so that "business data is not altered by unscrupulous hands" (*eWeek*, 2004, p. 40). With business increasingly utilising modern digital technology in a variety of ways, effective information security governance has, therefore, become a key part of corporate governance.

In this chapter, the role of corporate governance in relation to the security of information technology and *information and communications technology* (ICT) will be examined. Current developments and models such as those offered by the IT Governance Institute and Standards Australia will be outlined and the current lack of model development in extending the governance concept to information security in today's world of e-business will be identified and discussed. The purpose of the chapter is thus to develop a model that aligns IT governance with security management in an e-business environment through a review of existing approaches and synthesis of concepts and principles.

NEED FOR GOVERNANCE

The case of Enron® exemplifies the need for effective corporate governance. Enron®'s downfall was brought about, as described in broad terms by Zimmerman (2002) in USA TODAY®, by "over-aggressive strategies, combined with personal greed." He believes that there were two main causes for this failure: first, breakdowns caused by ignored or flawed ethics, and second, "Board of directors failed their governance." He recommends that in order to keep this from happening again, corporate governance should no longer be treated as "soft stuff," but rather as the "hard stuff" like product quality and customer service. He quotes *Business Week*® of August 19-26, 2002 when he concludes that "a company's viability now depends less on making the numbers at any cost and more on the integrity and trustworthiness of its practices." In other words, good corporate governance.

The term corporate governance is often used synonymously with the term enterprise governance since they are similar in scope as can be seen from the following definitions. They both apply to the role and responsibilities of management at the highest level in the organisation. An example of a framework for enterprise governance is one that is provided by the *Chartered Institute of Management Accountants* (CIMA) and the *International Federation of Accountants* (IFAC) (2004):

[Enterprise governance is] the set of responsibilities and practices exercised by the board and executive management with the goal of providing strategic direction, ensuring that objectives are achieved, ascertaining that risks are managed appropriately and verifying that the organization's resources are used responsibly.

The term corporate governance is used by the *Organisation for Economic Co-operation and Development* (OECD) (Brand & Boonen, 2003) and understood to be:

the system by which business corporations are directed and controlled. The corporate governance structure specifies the distribution of rights and responsibilities, among different participants in the corporation such as board, managers, shareholders and other stakeholders and spells out the rules and procedures for making decisions on corporate affairs. By doing this, it also provides the structure by which the company objectives are set and the means of attaining those objectives and monitoring performance. (pp. 15-16)

The above definitions not only reveal commonality but also emphasize two dimensions, namely, conformance and performance. Conformance focuses on structure such as the existence of the board and executive management, who in turn communicate their perceptions of corporate objectives. Performance, on the other hand, provides expectations about the achievement of corporate objectives and is associated with activities such as risk management, resource utilisation, and performance measurement. It could be argued that the former has a greater corporate orientation as it has a leadership role, unlike the latter that is linked to the execution of business activities and has more an operational orientation and could be termed business governance.

IT systems contribute to the performance dimension of the organisation as they support the organisational processes by delivering IT services. They are, therefore, most closely linked with the business governance component of the above dichotomy. However, as IT is increasingly becoming an integral part of business, the responsibility for IT becomes part of the responsibility of the board of directors, and thereby also very much part of the conformance aspects of governance. The latter is much broader in scope, implying greater strategic and diligence responsibilities on the part of the board and executive management.

Figure 1 shows how the enterprise governance framework extends to IT governance through the influences of corporate and business governance as outlined above. The two levels interact with IT governance as follows: the key role for corporate governance is to provide strategic objectives and their monitoring, while business governance provides control and assessment of the operational activities of IT. Both are required to make IT play its intended role for the organisation.

The following section provides a more detailed examination of IT governance by examining the perspectives of a professional, government, and research body. This will explain in more depth the interaction between IT governance with the higher levels of governance as well as the scope of IT governance itself. With regard to the latter, attention will be given to IT security within IT governance in line with the objectives of the chapter.

Figure 1. IT governance and enterprise governance

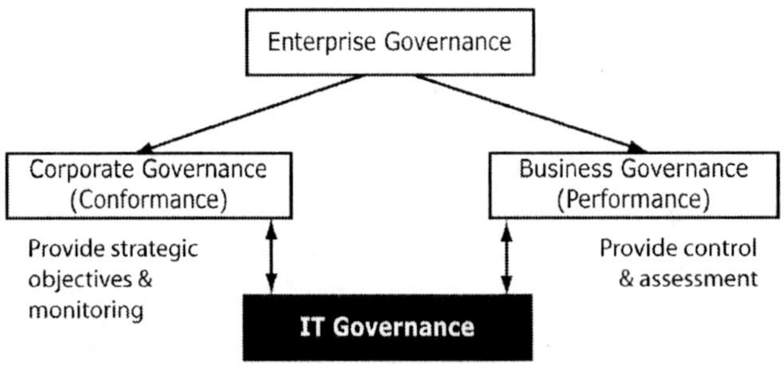

IT GOVERNANCE

Perspectives on IT governance from three significant institutions in this field are examined below: they are the IT Governance Institute, *Standards Australia* (SA), and National Cyber Security Partnership. The analysis focuses on the activities of IT governance and the integration of IT security in the respective frameworks in order to synthesis these views later into a model of information security governance.

ITGI® (2001) argued that executives are getting more and more dependent on information technology to run their businesses. Hence, IT governance is defined by the Institute (2003) as:

the responsibility of the board of directors and executive management. It is an integral part of enterprise governance and consists of the leadership and organisational structures and processes that ensure that the organization's IT sustains and extends the organization's strategies and objectives. (p.10)

According to ITGI®, IT governance has as its main purposes the achievement of strategic alignment, value delivery, risk management, and performance management. The question of IT security is addressed by providing emphasis to risk management, as it is realised that with IT's benefits and opportunities comes greater risk. Mechanisms, therefore, are required to exercise control over the use of IT in order to cope with these risks. Risk management is perceived as the appropriate management of threats relating to IT, addressing the safeguarding of IT assets, disaster recovery, and continuity of operations.

SA (2004), an Australian federal government department, recently developed a detailed approach for ICT governance to guide senior officeholders in evaluating, directing, and monitoring the operations of ICT systems. They defined the governance of ICT as:

the system by which the use of ICT is controlled. It involves evaluating and directing the plans for the use of ICT to support the organisation and monitoring this use to maintain that plan. It includes the strategy and policies for using ICT within an organisation. (p. 6)

SA identified seven key principles of ICT governance, namely establishing clearly understood responsibilities for ICT, planning ICT to best support the organisation, acquiring ICT in a cost-beneficial manner, ensuring ICT is of the required quality, performs when required, conforms with formal rules, and respects human factors.

The principle "ensure ICT is of the required quality" refers to different tasks that are part of IT security management, such as ensuring system availability and security from attack, theft, and misuse of crucial business data. This also includes the preparation of disaster recovery plans to ensure business continuity. Additionally, it is suggested that the organisation is able to monitor and report all security breaches, including attacks and fraud. Finally, accurate procedures for the measurement of the effectiveness of security measures have to be in place. SA advocates risk management methods for the identification of security risk, its evaluation, and mitigation. It is essential for the well-being and legal compliance of the organisation that upper management is informed about security risks and their implications while making decisions.

The Corporate Governance Task Force of the National Cyber Security Partnership (2004) argued that although information security is often considered a technical issue, it is also a governance challenge that involves risk management, reporting, and accountability and, therefore, requires the active engagement of executive management. The managerial aspect of security management is defined as *information security governance* (ISG), a subset of an organisation's overall governance program. Within ISG, risk management, reporting, and accountability are considered key policies.

The *National Cyber Security Partnership* (NCSP) made the topic of IT security contemporary by including cyber security for effective ISG. It made a number of recommendations for the adoption of ISG in the U.S. using the IDEAL framework (initiating, diagnosing, establishing, acting, and learning). Appendices of the NCSP report provide extensive information on functions and responsibilities, organisation and processes for implementation, and ISG assessment tools.

While the above approaches provide an overview of IT governance and an acknowledgment of its responsibilities with respect to information security, they do not go as far as providing prescriptions on how best to integrate security issues into governance. Guidance in this respect is desirable as IT security has become more complex with the emergence of the e-business phenomenon.

E-BUSINESS AND SECURITY

E-business has been defined by McKay and Marshall (2004) as:

a business that creatively and intelligently utilises and exploits the capabilities of IT and Internet technologies to create efficiencies, to achieve effectiveness gains such as flexibility and responsiveness, and to create strategic opportunities through competitive uses of IT to alter markets and industry structures. (p. 5)

This type of business is a development of e-commerce, a system that uses the Internet to provide a new channel to conduct trade with customers and suppliers. Further integration of ICT into the business itself enabled value chains to be developed with customers and suppliers. Inside the organisation, enterprise resource planning (ERP) software provided integration with new applications, such as supply chain management, and between existing applications, such as accounting and finance. With e-business, organisations have become even more dependent on the utilisation of ICT to create and maintain business advantages, albeit using technologies that are different from previous ones (e.g., the Internet).

The e-business environment can be contrasted from the traditional IT environment in three major ways (Fink, 2004). First, under the new approach, systems are open while previously they were considered closed. In other words, globally networked systems are more accessible and open to attack than systems kept strictly in-house without Internet access. Second, assets are now more virtual than tangible and more difficult to track as networks of cooperating organisations emerge. The assets of such organisations largely lie in intellectual property rather than in "bricks and mortar." Third, in the past, emphasis was placed on developing systems with the objective of meeting users' expectations, while now operations are critical since organisations are dependent on the continued functioning of their IT systems. For example, business is lost should the Web site on the Internet cease to function and customer may never return to the site.

The new environment has created new sets of technological risks. Technological risks, despite the name, are largely brought about by the actions of humans. They attract the greatest attention when brought about maliciously. Methods of attack are numerous and include viruses that can be introduced through data obtained from the Internet. The opportunity for hacker attacks is provided since the Internet enables others sharing the network to penetrate information systems in an unauthorised manner. Data and messages being forwarded on this network are potentially subject to interception and modification while being transmitted. Systems themselves can be brought down by denial-of-service attacks designed to prevent services requests to specific services such as accessing a Web application on the Internet.

In response to these concerns, e-business should implement a system of security measures.

These measures include those that ensure the availability of systems (to prevent system outages), integrity (so that data can be relied upon for decision making), confidentiality (to prevent unauthorised disclosure of information), and authenticity (verifying that users are who they claim to be). In addition, an organisation should implement broad security approaches, including the use of security policy, contingency planning, and disaster recovery. These will ensure that the e-business continues to operate efficiently and effectively.

MODEL FOR INFORMATION SECURITY GOVERNANCE

The preceding sections provided an overview of enterprise governance and highlighted the importance of IT governance at the corporate (conformance) and business (performance) levels. An overview was also provided of three perspectives on IT governance itself. The three approaches describe IT governance as an executive management task in which IT activities at the highest level are strategically managed in order to gain maximum alignment between IT and business. At a more operational level, the role of IT is perceived to be one of generating value for the organisation, ameliorated by the need to practice effective risk management in order to secure the organisation from new and complex technological and human threats.

This section proposes a model for information security governance, shown in Figure 2. It consists of two major components, namely, information security governance and e-business security management. Within the former are strategic high-level processes (e.g., setting objectives) as well as lower-level operational processes (e.g., IT value delivery) that were identified in previous discussions. However, it does not include risk management, which performs the special function of integrating the two major components as seen

Figure 2. Integration of IT governance and e-business security management

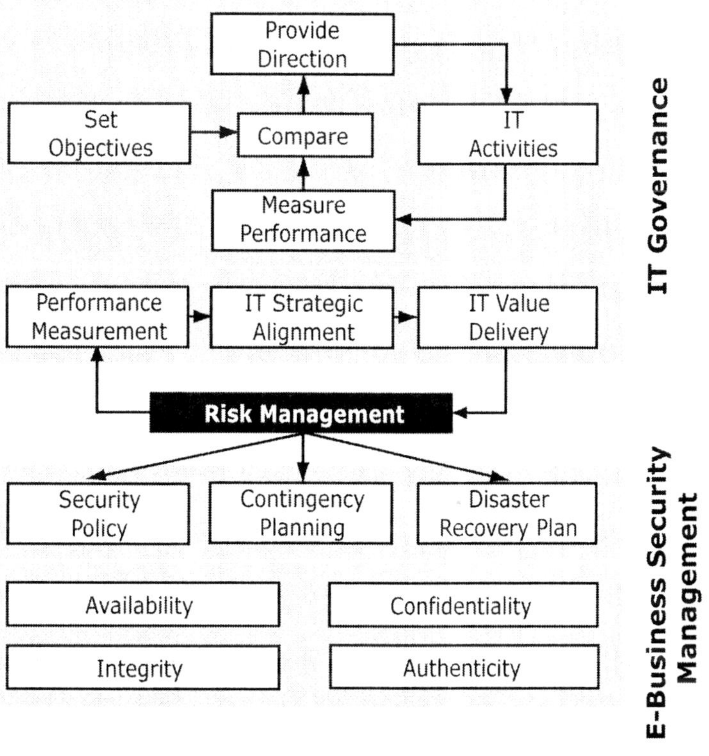

in Figure 2. The e-business security management component deals with security issues, again at a high level (e.g., developing a security policy) and at a lower level (e.g., implementing security to ensure system availability).

The approach adopted to develop the above model was a methodical and structured one since the objective was to achieve overall effective information security management as part of IT governance. The random introduction of security software, tools, and techniques is likely to be ineffective, as information can not be protected without considering all the activities that impinge on security. The holistic point of view that is required is within the broad objectives of IT governance, since "IT governance provides the processes to develop, direct, and control IT resources" (Korac-Kakabadse & Kakabadse, 2001, p. 1). Therefore, effective IT governance processes and mechanisms are seen as the enablers of a structured approach to IT management and thus are a precondition to effective information security governance for e-business.

IT Governance

At the highest level, IT governance does not differ from what would be expected to take place within enterprise governance. The governance process starts with setting objectives for the enterprise's IT, thereby providing the initial direction. From then on, a continuous loop is established for measuring IT performance, comparing outcomes to objectives, and providing redirection of activities where necessary and a change to objectives where appropriate. To be effective, an iterative process is most appropriate (ITGI®, 2003).

At the more detailed level, the key missions of IT need to be accomplished. The IT Governance Institute (2003) states that the purpose of IT governance is to direct IT endeavours and to ensure that IT's performance meets the following objectives: strategic alignment, value delivery, risk management, and performance measurement. Strategic alignment refers to the leveraging of IT into business activities, while value delivery is the exploitation of business opportunities and the maximization of benefits by the use of IT. The two activities are closely connected (ITGI®, 2003), since benefits will emerge if IT is successfully leveraged into business activities. The performance of IT has to be managed according the motto "What you can not measure, you can not manage," and hence a system of performance measurement metrics is required.

As discussed in a later section, risk management plays a significant integrating role in the proposed model, as shown in Figure 2. Basically, risk management integrates the management of security measures in the governance processes of an organisation, and consequently it can be seen as the connecting link between IT governance and e-business security management.

E-Business Security Management

To mitigate risk at the highest level requires the establishment of an information security policy, contingency planning, and the development of a disaster recovery plan (Hong, Chi, Chao, & Tang, 2003). The purpose of a security policy is to articulate management's expectations of good security throughout the organisation. Polices should be achievable and encourage employees to follow them rather than viewing them as another odious task to be performed. Contingency planning and the disaster recovery plan should prevent an IT disaster from becoming catastrophic. The latter ensures that there is an arrangement to resume normal operations within a defined period of time after a disaster has struck.

Underpinning the high-level management approach is a system of security measures that should ensure that the organisation's assets — particularly its information — are protected against loss, misuse, disclosure, or damage (ITGI®, 2001). More specifically, Braithwaite (2002) states:

E-business security represents an accumulation and consolidation of information processing threats that identify the need to protect the integrity and confidentiality of information and the need to secure the underlying support technologies used in the gathering, storage, processing, and delivery of that information. (p. 1)

Measures are required to assure high levels of availability, integrity, confidentiality and authenticity of business critical information (Halliday, Badenhorst, & v. Solms, 1996).

- **Availability**: this implies a number of requirements, such as ensuring continuing access to systems by users and the continued operation of the systems. The use of a firewall gateway will ensure that the internal, trusted systems are secured from attacks originating in outside, untrusted systems.
- **Integrity**: measures to ensure the completeness and unaltered form of data being processed in the organisation. Strong organisational controls, such as the hiring of competent staff and their supervision, and application controls, such as reconciling balances between different business applications as transactions are processed, are required.
- **Confidentiality**: this ensures that data can be read only by authorized people. In an e-business environment, all sensitive and confidential data should be encrypted while it is being transmitted over networks and as it is stored in the organisation's databases.
- **Authenticity**: e-business systems enable participants of the extended organisation (like suppliers, employees and customers) to be connected (Rodger, Yen, & Chou, 2002). User identification and authentication via digital signatures and certificates are therefore a specific requirement for this networked business environment (Wright, 2001).

When aligning governance with security, a number of issues emerge. They essentially focus on incorporating governance practices into security via effective risk management and reconciling the conflicting objectives of value delivery and security.

Risk Management

As observed in the preceding discussions, effective risk management is a key objective of IT governance (ITGI®, 2004; Standards Australia, 2004) and is required to minimise the IT risks associated with operating an e-business. In the proposed model, it can furthermore be seen as an integrating force, linking IT governance processes with e-business security management. It can also be viewed as a way of integrating security into the processes of an organisation — an important but also a very challenging task (McAdams, 2004).

Greenstein and Vasarhelyi (2002, p. 251) define risk as "the possibility of loss or injury" and risk management as a methodology, which assesses first "the potential of future events that can cause adverse affects," and second, the implementation of strategies that mitigate these risks in a cost-efficient way. Eloff, Labuschagne, and Badenhorst (1993) propose a risk management life cycle and define it as a process of risk identification, analysis, assessment, resolution, and monitoring.

The elements of the traditional risk management life cycle are important for e-business, but due to e-business' inherent needs for flexibility and responsiveness (e.g., to react to emerging customer demands), an ongoing and more dynamic risk management approach is required (Mann, 2004). This implies the capability to quickly adapt IT structures, including security, to business conditions while being able to adequately monitor the changing risk environment. Furthermore, Internet-based technologies are subject to rapid change in an increasingly complex threat landscape. This may require the deployment of a real-time risk management approach in which risks are identified and reported as transactions are processed in real-time (see Labuschagne & Eloff, 2000).

Fink (2004) reviewed existing risk management methodologies as to their suitability for the Internet environment and found significant shortcomings among some well-known products. He recommended that an effective methodology should be able to meet the following criteria:

- **Comprehensive**: the methodology must cover both the technological (e.g., Internet) and business (trading partners) scenarios of an e-business.
- **Inclusive**: the methodology must cover all types of assets (physical and virtual) and all types of vulnerabilities and threats that can be encountered in an e-business environment.
- **Flexible**: it must offer a variety of techniques (quantitative and qualitative) that can be applied across all types of e-business models (e.g., supply chain management, ERP).
- **Relevant**: the application of the methodology should lead to the identification and successful implementation of security measures relevant to e-business (e.g., digital signatures and certificates for trading partners).

A key aspect of risk management is making trade-offs. For example, the greater the desired level of security, the more administration and control are required and the greater the tendency to reduce the ability to access data and information. Consequently, more security comes along with an increased cost and a reduction in the initiatives that employees are allowed to use in creating opportunities for their organisation. Hence, e-business security might conflict with the objective of value delivery in IT governance.

Some, however, have argued that security can be seen as value itself. McAdams (2004, p. 38), for example, states that "an organization could embrace security as a core value much like customer service rather than merely as an adjunct support activity." Indeed, the previously discussed objectives of e-business security management (availability, confidentiality, integrity, and authenticity) are connected with positive outcomes for the organisation. However, the value resulting from security measures is finite, as eventually additional efforts for security are not rewarded with additional value for the business. Hence, it is important to determine the required level of security during risk management so as to ensure that costs of security are balanced by resultant benefits.

In practice, this task is difficult, as the cost of security is either unknown or difficult to measure. This problem is demonstrated by a recent study of Forrester Research (2004). The survey "How much security is enough" was conducted in August 2003 among 50 security executives at organisations with more than $1 billion in revenue. The results are illustrative of the problem: 40% of the respondents stated that their organisation's security spending was improperly focused, and 42% stated that it was inadequate for 2003. However, 60% of respondents said that they did not even know how much security incidents cost their businesses every year. Thus, determining the right level of security is difficult but crucial in order to achieve benefits from IT while adequately managing security.

GUIDELINES FOR IMPLEMENTATION

While the above discussions provide the theoretical background and rational for the proposed information security model, this section provides guidelines for the organisation on how such a model can best be implemented.

- A clear understanding needs to exist within the organisation on the responsibilities of governance at the enterprise level and how

IT governance integrates into this. The approach recommended for the information security model is two-pronged, namely, ensuring conformance via corporate governance and performance through business governance.

- For an e-business, information security has become an important consideration. The organisation has to understand the nature and significance of current and possible future threats and risks as well as the counter measures that are available to an e-business. Risk in this environment can be of a business nature (e.g., unresponsive trading partners) and technological nature (e.g., malicious attacks via the Internet). Risk is complex and specialist advice may be required from professionals such as IT security analysts and IT auditors.
- Risk management plays the key role in balancing what appears to be conflicting objectives when applying ICT, namely, value realisation and security. A suitable risk management methodology needs to be acquired that recognises these two competing functions of ICT and takes into account the characteristics of e-business. The criteria for such a methodology were outlined in an earlier section.
- A program of education to raise competence and awareness should be implemented across all levels of management to ensure that the requirements for effective information security governance are well understood. Such a program should be delivered in stages, as the concepts are complex, and regularly reviewed in response to changes in technology and the business environment. By being systematic and structured, organic management behaviour is encouraged.
- It is recommended that an adaptable and flexible attitude be adopted during implementation in that the model needs to integrate into the existing ICT, and organisational and management structures. Current organisational culture and resource constraints need to be taken into account to achieve the best fit possible and to manage any resistance to change successfully. For example, a new ethos in support of governance may have to emerge.
- Lastly, implementation progress should be reviewed and monitored on a regular basis applying the well accepted feedback loop. It is recommended that a project sponsor from senior management be identified to guide implementation and to ensure that the model receives strong commitment from executive management.

CONCLUSION

This chapter has shown the need for governance and suggested a concept for the integration of IT governance with enterprise governance. It then identified three major approaches to IT governance and their management of IT security. The latter was shown to be critical for the operation of an e-business. Hence, a framework was developed in which IT governance and e-business security operate together in an integrated, structured, yet holistic manner. The proposed model recognises that IT governance aims to optimise the value delivery of ICT while e-business security ensures that identified risks are controlled in an efficient manner. This model emphasizes the importance of risk management as the method that links IT governance and e-business security and thereby resolves the often conflicting objectives of security and value delivery.

REFERENCES

Braithwaite, T. (2002). *Securing e-business systems: A guide for managers and executives.* New York: John Wiley & Sons.

Brand, K., & Boonen, H. (2004). *IT governance - A pocket guide based on COBIT.* The Netherlands: Van Haren Publishing.

Cadbury, A. (1992). *Report of the committee on the financial aspects of corporate governance.* London: The Committee on the Financial Aspects of Corporate Governance.

CIMA/ IFAC. (2004). *Enterprise governance: Getting the balance right.* Retrieved January 3, 2005, from http://www.cimaglobal.com/downloads/enterprise_ governance.pdf

Eloff, J. H. P., Labuschagne, L., & Badenhorst, K. P. (1993). A comparative framework for risk analysis methods. *Computers & Security, 12*(6), 597-603.

eWeek (2004). The governance edge. *21*(42), 40.

Fink, D. (2004). Identifying and managing new forms of commerce risk and security. In M. Khosrow-Pour (Ed.), *E-commerce security advice from experts* (pp. 112-121). Hershey, PA: CyberTech Publishing.

Forrester Research. (2004). *How much security is enough.* Retrieved September 6, 2004, from http://www.forrester.com/

Greenstein, M., & Vasarhelyi, M. A. (2002). *Electronic commerce: Security, risk management, and control* (2nd ed.). Boston: McGraw-Hill.

Halliday, S., Badenhorst, K., & v. Solms, R. (1996). A business approach to effective information technology risk analysis and management. *Information Management & Computer Security, 4*(1), 19-31.

Hong, K.-S., Chi, Y.-P., Chao, L. R., & Tang, J.-H. (2003). An integrated system theory of information security management. *Information Management & Computer Security, 11*(5), 243-248.

ITGI® - IT Governance Institute. (2001). *Information security governance.* Retrieved September 6, 2004, from www.ITgovernance.org/resources.htm

ITGI® - IT Governance Institute. (2003). *Board briefing on IT governance.* Retrieved September 6, 2004, from www.ITgovernance.org/resources.htm

ITGI® - IT Governance Institute. (2004). *IT control objectives for Sarbanes-Oxley.* Retrieved September 6, 2004, from www.ITgovernance.org/resources.htm

Korac-Kakabadse, N., & Kakabadse, A. (2001). IS/IT governance: Need for an integrated model. *Corporate Governance, 1*(4), 9-11.

Labuschagne, L., & Eloff, J. H. P. (2000). Electronic commerce: The information-security challenge. *Information Management & Computer Security, 8*(3), 154-157.

Mann, D. (2004). *A life-cycle approach to risk management.* Retrieved October 10, 2004, from http://www.computerworld.com/securitytopics/security/

McAdams, A. (2004). Security and risk management: A fundamental business issue. *Information Management Journal, 38*(4), 36.

McKay, J., & Marshall, P. (2004). *Strategic management of eBusiness.* Milton, Queensland, AUS: John Wiley & Sons.

National Cyber Security Partnership (2004). *Information security governance - A call to action.* Retrieved October 26, 2004, from http://www.cyberpartnership.org/InfoSecGov4_04.pdf

Rodger, J., Yen, D., & Chou, D. (2002). Developing e-business: A strategic approach. *Information Management & Computer Security, 10*(4), 184-192.

Standards Australia. (2004). *Corporate governance of information and communication technology - Draft for public comment.* Retrieved April 20, 2004, from http://www.standards.com.au

Wright, A. (2001). Controlling risks of E-commerce Content. *Computers & Security, 20*(2), 147-154.

Zimmerman, J. W. (2002, November). Is your company at risk? Lessons from Enron®. *USA TODAY®*, 1, 27-29.

TRADEMARK NOTICE

- ITGI® is a registered trademark of Information Systems Audit and Control Association, Inc. / IT Governance Institute (ITGI).
- USA TODAY® is a registered trademark of Gannett Co. Inc.
- Business Week® is a registered trademark of the McGraw-Hill Companies, Inc.
- Enron® is a registered trademark of Enron Corp.

This work was previously published in Enterprise Information Systems Assurance and Systems Security: Managerial and Technical Issues, edited by M. Warkentin, pp. 1-15, copyright 2006 by IGI Publishing, formerly known as Idea Group Publishing (an imprint of IGI Global).

Chapter XXII
A Security Blueprint for E-Business Applications

Jun Du
Tianjin University, China

Yuan-Yuan Jiao
Nankai University, China

Jianxin (Roger) Jiao
Nanyang Technological University, Singapore

ABSTRACT

This chapter develops a security blueprint for an e-business environment taking advantage of the three-tiered e-business architecture. This security blueprint suggests best practices in general. It involves (1) security control by layers—from physical access, to network communication, to operating systems, to applications, and (2) different stages of the management process, including planning, deployment, administration, and auditing. Also reported is a case study of the implementation of the proposed security blueprint in a Singapore multinational corporation. Such issues as security control analysis, management process analysis, and cost-benefits analysis are discussed in detail.

INTRODUCTION

The Internet has created huge opportunities for new companies and new business for those established organizations formerly bound by a saturated market. E-business is defined as the conduction of business with the assistance of telecommunications and telecommunication-based tools, mainly over the Internet (Clarke 1999), including *business-to-business* (B2B), *business-to-customer* (B2C), and intra-organizational commerce (Siau & Davis, 2000). Security is essential and very critical to e-business applications. The importance of information privacy to e-business has been recognized for some time (Agre & Rotenberg, 1997; Bingi, Mir, & Khamalah, 2000; Lichtenstein & Swatman, 2001), with the Gartner

Group (2002) nominating information privacy as the greatest impediment to consumer-based e-business through 2006.

However, when building up a secure environment for e-business applications, there are no industry standards for people to follow on their design or implementation jobs. All that can be referred is from the security product manufacturers and system integrators. The truth is that security systems can only provide a certain level of protection to an e-business environment. Therefore, security protection must be in place at different layers, and the management process must be carried out at different stages. From the authors' viewpoint, security is not a by-product; it is a combination of managing technologies and security processes, rather than "put the firewall here, put the intrusion detection system there."

This chapter develops a security blueprint for a typical e-business environment based on the discussion of the major components in three-tiered e-business architecture. This security blueprint includes general security control layered from physical access, network communication, operating system, to application; and security management processes staged from planning, deployment, administration, to auditing.

TYPICAL E-BUSINESS ENVIRONMENT

Originally, business computing was carried out as a point task, without any real concept of a networked operation. All the business processes are run on a single platform or single tier. Later, many systems evolved to a two-tiered approach, also known as client/server architecture, where most of the business process runs on the server and the client is mainly concerned with presentation and only holds a limited amount of user-specific data. Today, more and more e-business applications are deployed as a three-tiered architecture owing to its increased performance, flexibility, maintainability, reusability, and scalability, while hiding the complexity of distributed processing from the user. After this, things get more complicated, with additional applications running in different tiers, which is so-called multi-tiered architecture. However, multi-tiered architectures have arisen not necessarily because great thought was given to this choice of architecture; in truth, they are more the result of trying to make the best of what was there.

This section will describe a typical three-tier e-business environment and identify the major components from system architecture perspectives.

Three-Tier E-Business Architecture

When it comes to an e-business environment, usually, these three tiers (layers) can be described as the *presentation* layer, *business* logic layer, and *data* layer. These tiers are logical, not physical. One machine can run several business tiers and tiers can be distributed across several machines. A typical three-tiered e-business architecture is shown in Figure. 1.

Major Components in an E-Business Environment

In the three-tiered e-business architecture, the major components can be identified as a Web browser, a Web server, an application server, a database server, an AAA/directory service, a corporate network, and the Internet, as illustrated in Figure 2.

A SECURITY BLUEPRINT

A secure e-business environment must prevent most attacks from successfully affecting valuable e-business resources. While being secure, the e-business environment must continue to provide critical services that users expect. Proper security and good functionality can be provided at the same

Figure 1. A typical e-business environment

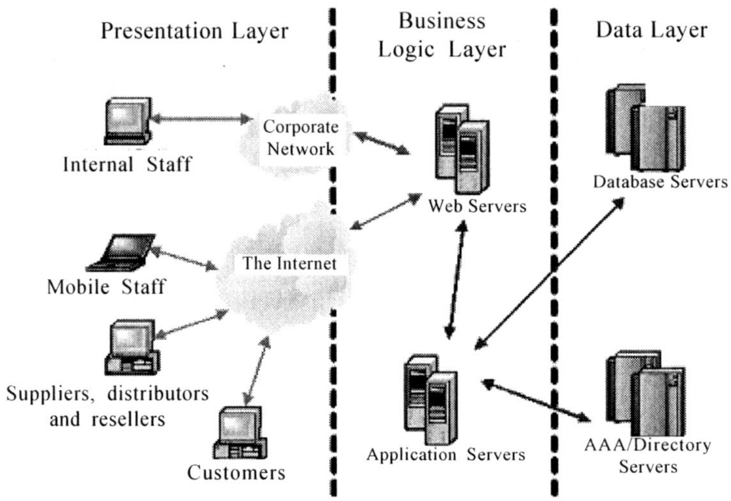

Figure 2. Major components in an e-business environment

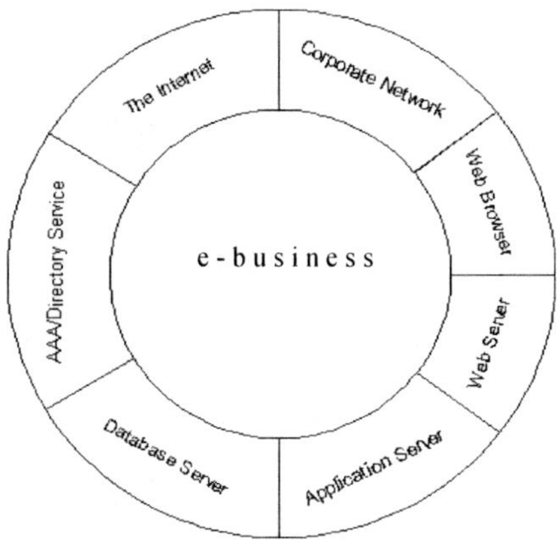

time. A secure e-business environment must also be resilient and scalable.

This section will develop a security blueprint for an e-business environment based on a three-tiered e-business architecture and major components described in the previous section.

Security Blueprint Overview

This security blueprint emulates as closely as possible the functional requirements of the typical e-business environment discussed in the previous section, which can help people to build or maintain a secure e-business environment for e-business applications.

As illustrated in Figure 3, this security blueprint consists of four security control layers, starting from physical access, network communication, operating system, to application. As part of this security blueprint, to maintain a secure e-business environment, the major security management processes included and staged are planning, deployment, administration, and auditing.

Figure 3. Security blueprint overview

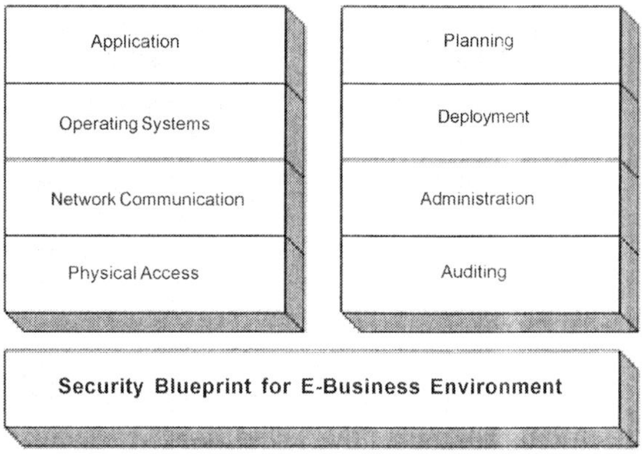

Security Control Layers

As part of the security blueprint for e-business environment, the security control layers cover all major components identified in a typical three-tiered e-business environment, including physical access, network communication, operating system, and application layer.

Physical Access Layer

The security control for physical access is an extremely important part of keeping all sensitive devices and data secure in an e-business environment. In the typical e-business environment discussed previously, all components of the business logic layer and data layer are considered as critical devices from a security perspective, as illustrated in the Table 1. It is necessary to put all critical devices into a separate space (data center, computer room, and even server racks) and maintain very strict control over who can enter it, then use card key or keypad systems, log books, and human security to limit unauthorized access.

Network Communication Layer

The corporate network and the Internet are the major components that fall into this layer, as illustrated in Table 1. These components perform specific roles in an e-business environment, and thus they have specific security requirements. Network attacks are among the most difficult attacks to deal with because they typically take advantage of an intrinsic characteristic of the way the corporate network operates. Hence, most

Table 1. Major components in security control layers

Layers \ Components	Web Browser	Web Server	Application Server	Database Server	AAA/Directory Service	Corporate Network	Internet
Physical Access Layer		✓	✓	✓	✓	✓	
Network Communication Layer						✓	✓
Operating System Layer	✓	✓	✓	✓	✓		
Application Layer	✓	✓	✓	✓	✓		

security technologies are applied at this layer to analyze the network traffic and eliminate malicious threats, including router access control, switch access control, firewall, intrusion detection system, virus detection system, virtual private network, and secure sockets layer.

Operating System Layer

As the most likely target during an attack, the operating system layer presents some of the most difficult challenges in an e-business environment from a security perspective. In a typical e-business environment, the major components, such as the Web browser, Web server, application server, database server, and AAA/directory service, are all running on top of various operating systems like Unix, Linux, Windows, and the like, as illustrated in the Table 1.

Meanwhile, for various reasons, these operating systems provide strong functionality to support different application services while numerous system holes or bugs remain. Because of this vulnerability, operating systems are the most frequently attacked components in an e-business environment.

To secure these operating systems, careful attention must be paid to each of the components in the e-business environment. Here are two important guidelines to reinforce operating system layer: (1) keep any operating system up-to-date with the latest patches, fixes, and so forth; and (2) lock down any operating system by disabling unwanted service.

Application Layer

Most components of a typical e-business environment, such as a Web browser, Web server, application server, database server, and AAA/directory service, fall into this layer, as illustrated in the Table 1.

As we know, applications are coded by human beings (mostly) and, as such, are subject to numerous errors. These errors can be benign (e.g., an error that causes a document to print incorrectly) or malignant (e.g., an error that makes the credit card numbers on a database server available via an anonymous FTP). It is the malignant problems, as well as other more general security vulnerabilities, that need careful attention. Similar to the operating system layer, care needs to be taken to ensure that all applications within an e-business environment are up-to-date with the latest security fixes.

Management Process Stages

To maintain a secure e-business environment, numerous security management processes of the daily operations of e-businesses are involved. As part of the security blueprint for an e-business environment, the management processes have been organized into four stages, planning, deployment, administration, and auditing.

Planning Stage

The most important stage of security management is planning. It is not possible to plan for security, unless a full risk assessment has been performed. Security planning involves three processes: *asset identification*, *risk assessment*, and *action planning*, as illustrated in Figure 4.

Asset identification is used to identify all the targets of the actual e-business environment. Risk assessment is used to analyze the risks for each asset and determine the category of the cause of the risk (natural disaster risk, intentional risk, or unintentional risk). Action planning is used to describe the security guidelines and present a security architecture using the enabling security technologies.

Deployment Stage

The deployment stage is relatively simpler than the planning stage. At this stage, the action plan

Figure 4. Processes at the planning stage

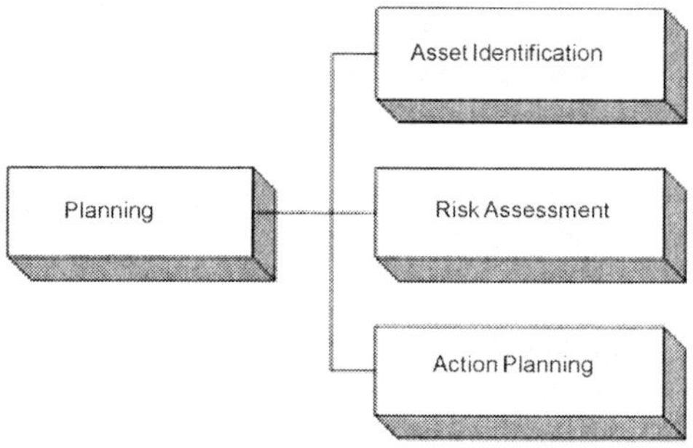

Figure 5. Processes at the deployment stage

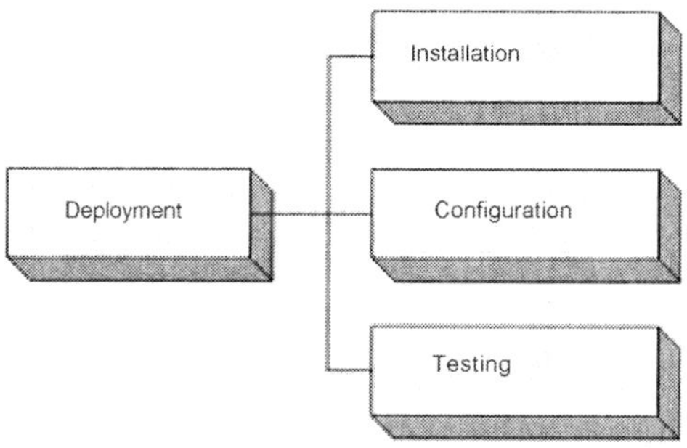

Figure 6. Processes at the administration stage

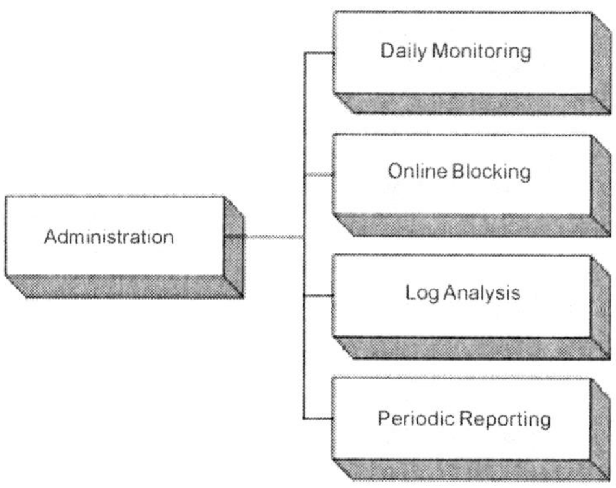

Figure 7. Processes at the auditing stage

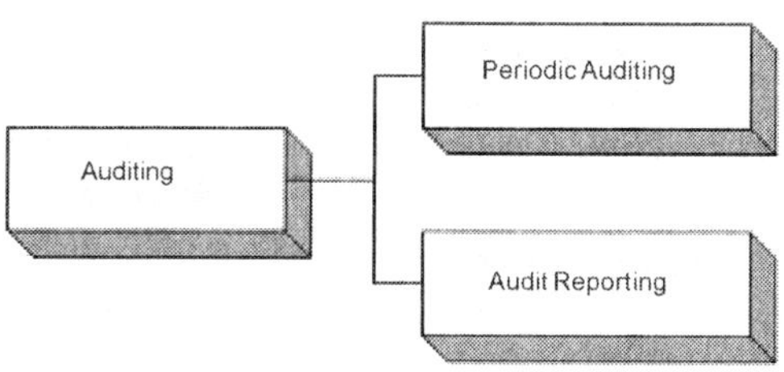

developed at planning stage will be implemented accordingly. This stage includes three key processes: *installation*, *configuration*, and *testing*, as illustrated in Figure 5.

Administration Stage

After the deployment stage, a "secure" e-business environment has been built. However, it is not really secure without a proper security administration. This is true because most assets need to be maintained daily to ensure that they have no proven vulnerabilities. In addition, security systems (such as firewall, IDS, antivirus) keep generating alerts, events, and logs that require adminito strators take necessary actions.

The administration layer consists of four major processes, including *daily monitoring*, *online blocking*, *log analysis*, and *periodic reporting*, as illustrated in Figure 6. These processes are not only applied to security systems, but also to other assets in the actual e-business environment.

Auditing Stage

The auditing stage provides the formal examination and review of the established e-business environment. This layer contains two major processes, *periodic auditing* and *audit reporting*, as illustrated in Figure 7. These processes can be carried on by either internal staff or external parties. In an e-business environment, an annual security audit conducted by external party is recommended.

CASE STUDY

Company XYZ, with its operational headquarters in Singapore and branch offices in the U.S., Japan, India, Thailand, Malaysia, and Hong Kong, is a telecommunications service provider that provides end-to-end networking and managed services to *multinational corporations* (MNC) and *small and medium enterprises* (SME) across Asia.

The company has *points-of-presence* (POP) located in 17 cities across 14 countries. Technical support is available 24 hours a day and 7 days a week. The company has built an *Internet data center* (iDC) in Singapore to provide e-business hosting services as part of its managed services. Of course, its own e-business applications, such as *customer portal system*, *billing system*, and *trouble ticketing system*, are running on this iDC as well.

This section will discuss the applicability of the developed security blueprint using the Singapore-based MNC company as a case study.

Established E-Business Environment

An Internet data center is defined as a service provider offering server outsourcing, hosting, and collocation services, as well as IP and broadband connectivity, *virtual private networks* (VPNs), and other network and transport services. It needs to be physically secure against physical intrusions and equipped with fire suppression, uninterrupted power supply, and disaster recovery systems.

As a telcom provider and managed services provider, the company's iDC has a complex architecture and multiple functions. However, the authors just intend to discuss the environment related to e-business hosting service in this chapter. The simplified e-business environment is shown in Figure 8. This established e-business environment is mainly made up of core routers (two Cisco 7513 routers), distribution switches (two Cisco Catalyst 6509 switches), firewalls, access switches, and other necessary devices. All those critical devices are configured as duplex to provide redundancy to ensure the continuous operations of e-business applications.

The corporate LAN of this company is connected into distribution switches, thus allowing internal staff to access the company's e-business applications such as the customer portal, billing system, and trouble ticketing system for daily jobs. Putting these e-business applications into iDC will take advantage of the established e-business environment while saving money on the security protection for the corporate network.

Security Control Analysis

Applying security control to the e-business environment is critical for building a trust relationship between e-business owners and the company.

Physical Access Layer

In order to prevent unauthorized people from getting into the company's iDC, which keeps all the network devices, application servers and important data, the company has implemented very strict physical access control systems, including biometrics HandKey II system, access card control system, lifetime CCTV recorder system, multi-level password restriction, centralized UPS system, and standby power generator. Besides these systems, the iDC is also monitored by on-shift engineers all the time. In addition, all equipment (network devices and hosts) are put into server racks and locked, while all network cables are put under the floating floor or within server racks. Authorized personnel must sign in and out at memo books to obtain the rack keys.

Additionally, to protect the data backup against fire, theft, and other natural risks, the company has an agreement with another managed service provider for off-site backup, which allows both companies to store data backup media for each other. The data backup media will be duplicated monthly.

Network Communication Layer

As most attacks come from the Internet and corporate network, the company has employed industry-standard security systems in place to eliminate risks at the network communication

Figure 8. A case study for security blueprint

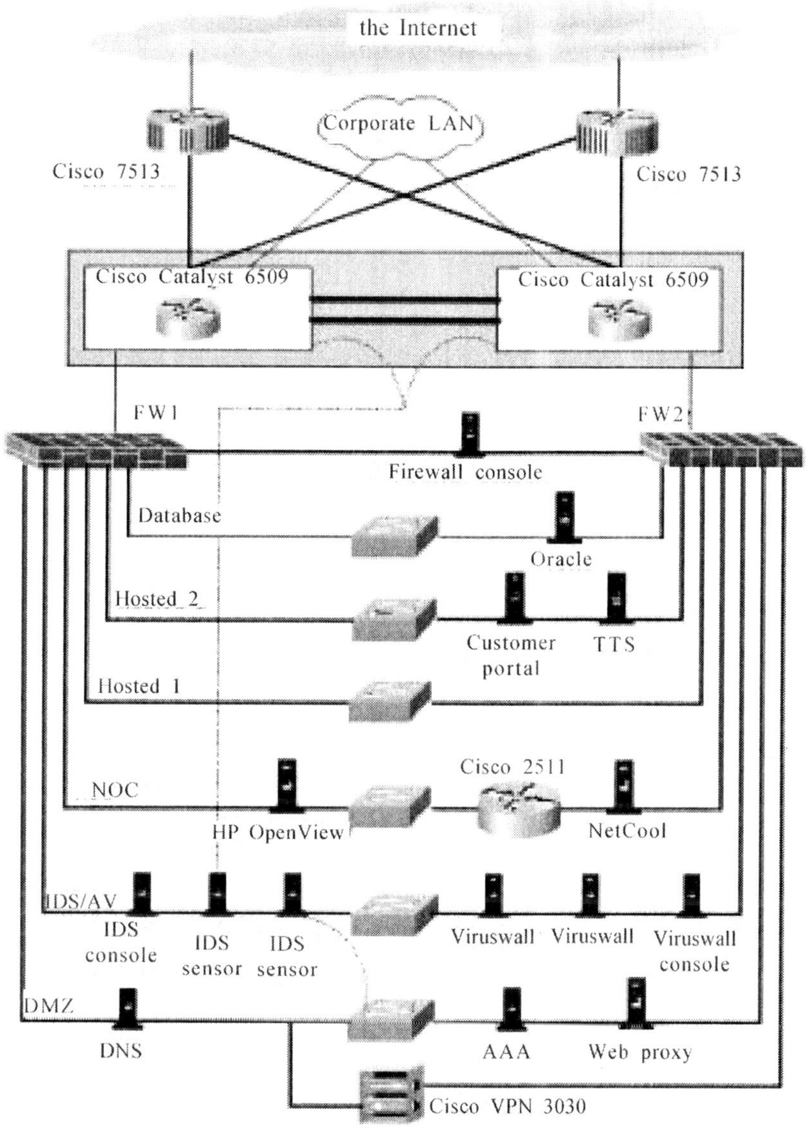

layer. These include firewall cluster, gateway antivirus cluster, *intrusion detection system* (IDS), AAA system, reverse Telnet access, and VPN access. In addition to the security systems, all network devices including routers and switches are locked down, and *access control list* (ACL) is applied for better security control.

All network devices and hosts are also configured to send *simple network management protocol* (SNMP) traps and logs to HP OpenView and NetCool systems for monitoring purpose. HP OpenView shows a graphic diagram of the health status of the e-business environment, while NetCool collects all logs and SNMP traps from network devices and hosts. On-shift engineers keep monitoring this information to ensure the network health and security protection is in place.

Operating System Layer

The company uses various operating systems to implement its services, such as SUN Solaris, HP-UX, and Windows NT/2000. As required by the corporate security policy, all operating systems must be hardened and kept updated with the latest security patches from their manufacturers.

Application Layer

The security control for this layer is mainly to keep security patches and service packs for commercial applications up-to-date (for example, CheckPoint Firewall-1 service pack 6, Radiator RADIUS patches, virus pattern for TrendMicro InterScan Viruswall, attack signature for RealSecure IDS, etc.).

For customized e-business applications, such as a customer portal system, billing system, and trouble ticketing system, the software development team is responsible to review program logics and coding to avoid any system holes and backdoors.

Management Processes Analysis

In addition to the four layers of security control implemented at iDC, the company has also installed security management processes to continuously maintain a secure e-business environment. A security team has been formed by the engineers from different departments (IT, network operations, network planning, and software development) and is led by a security specialist who reports directly to the *chief technology officer* (CTO).

This section discusses the related security management processes in the established e-business environment using a real e-business application—a Web-based *trouble ticketing system* (TTS).

The TTS enables customers to report fault and check status online, and allows engineers to enter the troubleshooting progress and sales to understand the troubleshooting procedure. It couples with the customer portal and billing system to provide a single-point solution to corporate customers. The TTS consists of one Web server, one application server, and one database server. Both the Web server and the application server are running at one physical server box, while the database server is running at another server box.

Planning Stage

Three processes are executed at this stage, including asset identification, risk assessment, and action planning.

When running the asset identification process, the major assets for TTS will be identified as follows: Web and application server, database server, and TTS data.

Following the risk assessment process, the major risks to those identified assets are listed as follows: physical attack to the server boxes and network devices; network attack to the operating systems, Web server, application server, database server, and TTS application; and attack or damage to the TTS data either physical or remotely.

Once the above asset and risks have been identified, the following actions are developed to eliminate those risks to the assets: (1) physically locate those server boxes and network devices into iDC and lock them to server racks; (2) deploy the Web and application server boxes according to the database segment; (3) utilize the firewall cluster to block most remote attacks with certain firewall policies; (4) utilize each IDS sensor located at distribution switches to monitor potential attacks and intruders; (5) utilize the gateway antivirus cluster to scan and clean viruses contained in HTTP traffic; (6) lock down the operating system for Web and application server boxes and allow only Web and application services to run; (7) lock down the operating system for the database server boxes and allow only database services to run; (8) examine the TTS program code to prevent any system holes and back doors.

Deployment Stage

Following the action planning, the installation process will be carried out to setup physically all server boxes and access switches if any, and install the operation system and software such as Web server, application server, oracle server, and TTS application. The configuration process will go through the lock-down procedures for operation system and application software, and tunes up parameters for better performance. Sometimes, since misconfiguration may cause more risks and even bring the server down and crash application services, the testing process will ensure that deployment is in compliance with the action plan.

Administration Stage

The security team coupled with the on-shift operation team carries out all processes defined at this stage at any time. Daily monitoring includes the following tasks: network diagram view from HP OpenView, SNMP traps from NetCool, firewall console, IDS console, antivirus console, and syslog window.

Online blocking will be carried out once a remote attack has been identified. The security team will do the log analysis every day and generate security reports every week and every month.

Auditing Stage

The security team will carry out an internal audit every half year to determine the effectiveness of existing security controls, watch for system misuse or abuse by users, verify compliance with corporate security policies, validate that documented procedures are followed, and so on. An audit report will be generated after the auditing and given to management for review and further action.

Cost-Benefit Analysis

The cost of building a secure e-business environment involves not only the one-time hardware/software/project expenses but also the recurring cost for users, operations, and ongoing changes. For the company's established e-business environment, the cost analysis can be done via four areas, including iDC features, security systems, network and communications, and maintenance staff.

The physical construction, including a floating floor, CCTV camera system, biometrics handkey system, server racks, UPS, and power generator, together form the iDC features.

Security systems consist of the firewall cluster, gateway antivirus cluster, IDS console and sensors, Cisco VPN concentrator, and various monitoring and logging systems.

Network and communication cost refers to the expense of the Cisco router 7513, Cisco switch 6509, network cabling, Internet bandwidth subscription, and access switches for individual network segments behind the firewall cluster.

Maintenance staff means internal skilled manpower needed to maintain this established e-business environment for fulfilling operation and security requirements. This mainly refers to the company's security team and on-shift operation engineer team.

In this study, the acquisition and implementation cost is a one-time charge and takes a very huge percentage (65%), while expenses for operation costs and ongoing changes and growth are estimated on an annual basis, assuming there are no big changes required on the e-business environment. Table 2 shows the summarized implementation cost and other estimated costs.

Although the cost may be high to SMEs, it is indeed cost-effective for large organizations and e-business providers, due to the great benefits obtained from the secure e-business environment. These benefits include shared bandwidth, shared security protection, scalability, reliability, and total ownership cost saving.

Table 2. Cost analysis for e-business environment

Cost (SG$)	Acquisition & implementation	Operation	Ongoing Changes & Growth	Total	% of Total
IDC Features	280K	12K	0	292K	18%
Security Systems	350K	36K	15K	401K	25%
Network & Communication	420K	168K	27K	615K	39%
Maintenance Staff	0	240K	50K	290K	18%
Total	1050K	456K	92K	1598K	-
% of Total	65%	29%	6%	-	100%

CONCLUSION

Building a secure e-business environment is very critical to e-business applications. The chapter develops a security blueprint for an e-business environment based on the analysis of a three-tiered architecture and provides general best practices for companies to secure their e-business environments. Also discussed is the applicability of this security blueprint based on the case study of a Singapore-based MNC. This case study shows that the security blueprint for e-business environment is suitable and cost-effective in particular for large companies like *multi-national corporations* (MNC).

REFERENCES

Agre, P. E., & Rotenberg, M. (1997). *Technology and privacy: The new landscape*. Cambridge, MA: MIT Press.

Bingi, P., Mir, A., & Khamalah, J. (2000). The challenges facing global e-commerce. *Information Systems Management, 17*(4), 26-34.

Clarke, R. (1999). *Electronic commerce definition*. Retrieved July 30, 2004, from http://www.anu.edu.au/people/Roger.Clarke/EC/ECDefns.html

Gartner Group (2002). Retrieved May 20, 2003, from http://www.zeroknowledge.com/business/default.asp

Lichtenstein, S., & Swatman, P. M. C. (2001, June 25-26). Effective management and policy in e-business security. In B. O'Keefe, C. Loebbecke, J. Gricar, A. Pucihar, & G. Lenart (Eds.), *Proceedings of Fourteenth International Bled Electronic Commerce Conference*, Bled, Slovenia. Kranj: Moderna organizacija.

Siau, K., & Davis, S. (2000). Electronic business curriculum-evolution and revolution @ the speed of innovation. *Journal of Informatics Education & Research, 2*(1), 21-28.

This work was previously published in Enterprise Information Systems Assurance and Systems Security: Managerial and Technical Issues, edited by M. Warkentin, pp. 80-94, copyright 2006 by IGI Publishing, formerly known as Idea Group Publishing (an imprint of IGI Global).

Chapter XXIII
E-Business Process Management and Intellectual Property: Issues and Implications

Kathleen Mykytyn
Southern Illinois University, USA

Peter Mykytyn
Southern Illinois University, USA

ABSTRACT

The emergence of e-business as a viable business model is unquestioned and global in its involvement and impact. Further, the value that intellectual property (IP) in the form of trademarks, copyrights, and patents plays in that medium of doing business impacts businesses, information technology (IT) professionals, academics responsible for IT coursework and programs, and, of course, the legal community. This chapter reviews these IP types with particular emphasis on their relationship and impact on e-business. Relevant legal cases are cited and discussed to provide additional foundation to the e-business community. The chapter also provides appropriate recommendations for e-business in light of these IP issues, and identifies some possible future trends and research issues.

E-BUSINESS PROCESS MANAGEMENT AND INTELLECTUAL PROPERTY: ISSUES AND IMPLICATIONS

The advent of the Information Age has brought about a different way of thinking about how information should be used in both the public and private domain. It has also challenged businesses to take advantage of information technology (IT) in conducting everyday tasks. The introduction of the Internet into the business model, that is, electronic commerce, has not only provided new opportunities and efficiencies for firms, but has also posed threats to them. In particular, firms are confronting numerous issues that today are impacting their intellectual property (IP) assets. All of this is truly a new, virtual frontier. However, computers and the Internet are presenting new and challenging legal questions that may take many years to become well-settled points of law.

One area of the law that has been dramatically affected by computer technology is in the field of IP, for example, trademarks, copyrights, and patents. Referring to intellectual property, Ghosh (2002, pp. 454-455) states that:

The field is hot, so to speak, and often eclipses other more compelling issues in the media and legal fora. Intellectual property issues are ubiquitous precisely because intellectual property is the final frontier. Market economies expand and thrive by conquest, and our world has expanded as much as it can geographically. Real property, or land-based systems, offer very few prospects for further exploitation. Personal property similarly offers few remaining challenges for entrepreneurial enterprise..... It is not hard to fathom the importance of intellectual property in commodifying the intangible inputs and outputs of an economy based on the selling of services, whether medical, legal, financial, or entertainment.

Caught in the middle of these emerging e-business issues are the IT professionals, for example, Webmasters, who create and/or maintain a company's Web site and e-commerce systems. They may feel that their technological expertise in developing and maintaining Web sites is their only responsibility, that is, any social, political, or legal issues are not their concern. Consequently, Webmasters not only have no noticeable knowledge regarding the applicable IP laws, they also have a large dose of disdain for them (Kamarck, 1999). They believe that their job is to drive users to a corporate Web site efficiently and effectively, and without any knowledge of, or belief in, IP laws, they can be creative and successful in their abilities to do so. Consequently, firms may have manipulated the technical aspects of Web-site development without regard for the IP rights of others (Kamarck, 1999).

Underscoring the important role played by IT professionals today is the nature and amount of e-business being conducted today. The U.S. Department of Commerce's Economics and Statistics Administration publishes an annual report about the digital economy. Its 2003 report, the latest available, indicates that retail e-business activity has shown a 28% increase over the second quarter of 2002, but that the B2B e-business arena has not shown as much improvement and has fallen short of expectations (Digital Economy, 2003). At the same time, as shown in Figure 1, the rise in e-commerce-related lawsuits from 1995 to 2005, comprising trademark, patent, and copyright litigation, attests to the apparent lack of knowledge of IP law by either firms or Webmasters. As shown, the number of Internet-related lawsuits is increasing dramatically, which should be a cause of concern for organizations and information technology (IT) researchers who are investigating various e-commerce issues today.

Figure 1. E-commerce-related IP lawsuits, 1994-2004

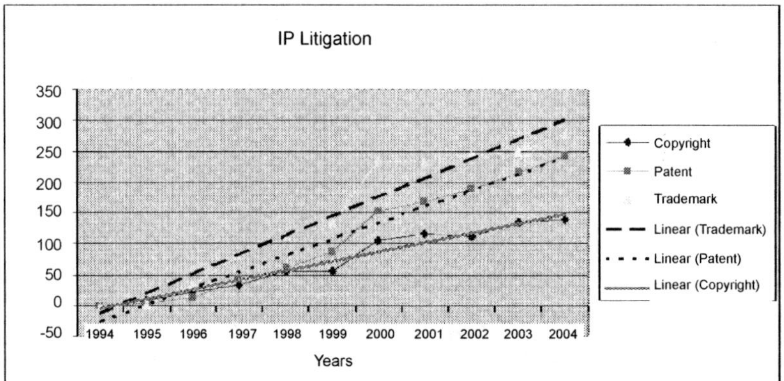

The overall purpose of this chapter is to provide an awareness of the relationship between e-business and IP for IT professionals and others, including business professionals. In doing so, we hope that many readers may have an increased awareness of the importance of these issues that impact business professionals, IT professionals, and many in the academic community. We will define the law dealing with the three areas of protection covered in the chapter–trademarks, copyrights, and patents. We will also integrate how these forms of IP relate to e-business. It is important to understand just why these forms of IP are an important area of consideration involving today's e-commerce. The chapter will conclude with areas of suggested research appropriate for academic researchers, and our assessment of some future trends involving IP and e-business. For further support, the chapter will cite relevant court cases involving IP and e-business.

INTELLECTUAL PROPERTY LAW: TRADEMARKS, COPYRIGHTS, AND PATENTS

Intellectual property is a broad area of the law related to protecting ideas, concepts, and products. For purposes of this chapter, the relevant topics addressed will be limited to trademarks, copyrights, and patents.

Trademarks

Today, trademarks are used by businesses to distinguish themselves from their competition. They are also used to protect commercial goodwill, and could be regarded as an intangible benefit. Intangible benefits may have direct organizational benefits, but cannot be easily measured in dollars or with certainty. The reputation of a firm is too valuable to risk misunderstanding what trademarks are and how to use them to preserve legal rights in them. The importance of trademarks to current business practice is undisputed. Perhaps Field said it best when he stated that, "Assuming that its owners are not the type to write their name in chalk on the company truck, no business is small enough that it can afford to ignore trademarks" (Field, 2000).

Trademark rights exist at common law and are recognized and enforced by most states. The U.S. Congress recognized these rights and extended them by way of federal statute; this source of trademark rights has become predominant in the U.S. (15 U.S.C. §§1051, 1988). This statute, commonly known as the Lanham Act, provides a national registry for trademarks that carries with it national protection for registered marks (15 U.S.C. §§1114, 1988). Once registered, the trademark is valid for 10 years and may be renewed for like periods as long as the mark is in constant use. Failure to use the mark can result in the loss of the rights in the mark.

The fundamental purpose for the trademark statute is to protect the public against misidentification of a product or service so that there is little likelihood of confusion as to the manufacturer of a product. The statute also protects a trademark owner, who generally has made a substantial investment in the promotion of the product or service being placed in the marketplace, from its misappropriation by competitors. Under this statute, trademark holders can sue for trademark infringement if they can show that they possess a protectable mark. Protectability is generally a function of the strength of a mark and the likelihood of confusion in the marketplace.

A trademark can be viewed as any word, phrase, symbol, design, sound, smell, color, or product structure that is adopted and used by a business to identify and distinguish its products and/or services (Guillot, 2000). Trademarks can be considered synonymous to brand names, and are determined to be important intellectual properties that distinguish one company's products or services from another's. In addition to trademarks, there are service marks; technically, a trademark is a symbol used to identify a specific source of goods, while a service mark is used to identify a service. Such "marks" are denoted as any symbol that can be legally used by only one organization or a group of legally related organizations. Whatever types of "marks" are used, they enable consumers to look for, or avoid, products or services that are marketed under those names or symbols (Field, 2000).

When consumers perceive a name, symbol, and so forth, to be associated with a product or service as indicative of its source, then that name, symbol, and so forth, is entitled to legal protection as a trademark. It would not serve consumer interests if businesses could duplicate a product or service but not identify it in a manner that the consumer would recognize. Field (2000) notes that consumers may even create a trademark or create a second trademark using a nickname; "Coke" was accorded legal protection before the company used it.

Trademark Applicability to E-Business

Until the Internet was developed, only companies that conducted business on a national or international level needed to be concerned about trademark law. If a business was local, there was little likelihood of customer confusion with other local businesses and, thus, little concern over trademark conflicts. Regarding e-commerce, however, there is no such thing as a local business, and the names of businesses, products, and/or services must be given attention to ensure that legal benefits are obtained and legal threats are avoided. When a company invests heavily in consumer goodwill, it needs to understand how to protect its investment. More succinctly, a company wishing to ensure the viability of its trademarks must ensure that its trademarks are not infringed upon by others.

One of the more important areas dealing with e-business and trademark infringement pertains to domain names. When doing business on the Internet, trademark law determines when the use of a domain name infringes someone else's trademark. In the recent past, trademark owners who desired to use their marks as domain names found that the name had already been taken. Further, trademark owners found that unauthorized parties were using their marks as domain names, many times in a deliberate attempt to free ride on the goodwill of the mark's owner (Dueker, 1996). Others have obtained domain names for the purpose of selling them back to a trademark owner. With the passing of the Anticybersquatting Consumer Protection Act (ACPA) in 1999, a domain name that is the same, or confusingly similar to an existing trademark anywhere in the U.S., cannot be used for the purpose of selling the name back to the mark's owner (ACPA, 2000). Two fundamental rules of trademark law and domain names are:

1. Names, logos, or domain names cannot be used if they can confuse consumers as to the source of goods or services:
   - If a domain name is in conflict with an existing mark and is likely to cause customer confusion, a court could force the infringer to relinquish the name. Further, if the infringement is deemed willful, compensation to the mark's owner for losses and statutory damages may be ordered.
2. Names, logos, or domain names cannot be used if they invoke a famous product or service, even if consumers would not be confused.

If a domain name is the same or similar to an existing known mark, the owner of the mark may file a suit preventing any further use of the domain name, even though there is little likelihood that consumers would be confused. For example, if a marriage counselor decided on the domain name withfidelity.com, fidelity.com, the domain name of Fidelity brokerage, would probably prohibit the use of the name simply because it causes fidelity.com to come to mind.

One example emphasizes the importance of this point. In September 1998, former Stanford University graduate students incorporated the search engine, Google, and registered its domain name a year later. In December 2000 and January 2001, Sergey Gridasov of St. Petersburg, Russia registered the domain names googkle.com, ghoogle.com, gfoogle.com and gooigle.com. The practice of deliberately misspelling registered domain names for the purpose of creating confusion has become known as "typosquatting." In May 2005, Google filed a complaint with The National Arbitration Forum, a legal alternate to litigating in court, complaining that Gridasov had engaged in this practice. Gridasov didn't respond to Google's complaint, meaning that the arbitrator could accept all reasonable allegations as true. The arbitrator endorsed Google's contention that the misspelled addresses were part of a sinister plot to infect computers with programs, known as "malware," that can lead to recurring system crashes, wipe out valuable data, or provide a window into highly sensitive information. As a result of this decision, the rights to the above referenced domain names were transferred to Google.com (National Arbitration Forum, 2005).

Trying to piggyback on the popularity of a heavily trafficked Web site like Google.com is not new. For instance, the address Whitehouse.com used to display ads for pornography was a surprise for Web surfers looking for Whitehouse.gov, the president's official online channel. Whitehouse.com now operates as a private Web site that sells access to public records.

Besides domain name issues, the selection of a trademark should involve serious consideration. Just because a business may acquire a domain name registration, that does not give it priority in obtaining a trademark on that name. The registration of a domain name on the Internet does not override long-established principles of trademark law. The utilization of a competitor's trademark in a domain name would likely confuse users as to its source or sponsorship, and this form of confusion is precisely what the trademark laws are designed to prevent.

It is also important to recognize that e-business encompasses many dimensions, dimensions that are broader than what is often labeled as e-commerce today. For example, in the case of Planned Parenthood Federation of America, Inc. vs. Bucci, (Planned Parenthood, 1997), the district court found that Bucci impeded Planned Parenthood's ability to use its service mark, Planned Parenthood. Bucci, a pro-life advocate, registered the domain name http://www.plannedparenthood.com and posted antiabortion literature on that site. Although Bucci did not promote a good or service on that site, the court found that Bucci was still engaging in a commercial use of the domain name based on the fact that Bucci affected Planned Parenthood's ability to offer its services over the Internet. This case illustrates quite emphatically the degree/breadth of infringing activities that can violate the ACPA.

Copyrights

Basically, copyrights in the U.S. are a collection of rights, defined by federal statute, that give the copyright owner the exclusive right to do or authorize others to do any of the following: (1) reproduce the copyrighted work; (2) prepare a derivative (adaptation) work based upon the copyrighted work; (3) distribute copies of the copyrighted work to the public by sale or other transfer of ownership or by rental, lease, or lending; (4) publicly perform the work, (5) publicly display the work, and (6) perform a sound recording publicly through digital transmission when the copyrighted work is a sound recording. See Lipson (2001) and Blaise (2005) for additional information regarding copyright history and characteristics.

Creations that can be copyrighted comprise: literary works; musical works; dramatic works; pantomimes and choreographic works; pictorial, graphic, and sculptural works; motion pictures; sound recordings; architectural works; and computer software. Copyright has generally been associated with the "arts" since it has been applied to most forms of artistic works, such as plays, paintings, novels, poetry, music, and so forth.

Copyrights do not exist in facts, ideas, procedures, processes, systems, methods of operation, and so forth, regardless of the form in which they are described or embodied. Copyright does not protect a blank form or commonplace phrases, images, or organizational choices. Essentially, it only protects expression–the way an author, artist, or performer expresses an idea or describes facts.

Over the years, much of IP, and copyright in particular, did not generate that much interest or enthusiasm by businesses and organizations. Rather, these entities were most likely concerned about other more physical assets such as buildings, plants, equipment, and the land upon which those assets rested (Hunter, 2005). In dealing specifically with copyright, that form of IP was considered most relevant to stop commercial reproduction of, say, a book, similar to the previous discussion. Focusing on copyright, in order to preserve the balance between property rights and the ability of the public to have appropriate access to copyrighted works, a copyright owner was never granted complete control over his/her work. Rather, the copyright holder's rights are limited to the six rights listed previously. With the commercialization of the Internet and the development of e-business, the older view of copyright and what businesses must be concerned with changed significantly.

COPYRIGHT AND THE EVOLUTION OF ELECTRONIC BUSINESS

What is often not addressed, at least from an IT research point of view, are some of the legal issues and ramifications encompassing e-business and copyrights that can affect organizations. Essentially, organizations need to be aware that some actions that they take may lead to infringing on others' copyrights. Likewise, those same organizations need to take appropriate measures to ensure that others do not infringe on the organization's copyrighted material.

Realistically, there are a countless number of issues involving copyright and copyright infringement that might arise in the course of e-business. For our purposes, we feel that the topics addressed next are very relevant today as they might impact businesses. These topics are the Digital Millennium Copyright Act (DMCA), digital rights management (DRM), the posting of copyrighted material on Web sites, appropriate and inappropriate linking to other Web sites, liability issues related to Internet service providers (ISPs), and steps that can be taken by organizations to protect their copyrighted material from being infringed by others.

In 1998, the Digital Millennium Copyright Act (DMCA) was enacted in direct response to what were seen as critical challenges from the Internet (Digital, 1998). The U.S. Congress was concerned about the ease with which exact copies of copyrighted materials could be made with hardly any loss of quality, possibly leading to the unauthorized distribution of perhaps millions of copies. The DMCA involved two basic changes to the copyright law. First, it directly prohibited the use of specific technologies: those that can be used to circumvent technological protection measures (Samuelson, 1999). In other words, the protection of expression is, for the first time, achieved through the regulation of devices (Merges 2000). Second, this regulation was attached to a new list of infringing activities focusing on the circumvention of technical protection schemes. In reality, the two sets of provisions–those regulating the deployment of devices, and those defining illicit acts of circumvention-are so distinct that the detailed exemptions to the latter provisions do not apply at all to the former (Samuelson, 1999).

The DMCA is not without its opponent. After 7 years since enactment of the DMCA, critics have stated that the act infringes on a person's free speech and allows copyright owners to override fair use (Fitzdam, 2005). Still others believe that the DMCA stifles competition and innovation and even serves as an impediment to accessing computer networks (Fitzdam, 2005). The Act has thus far withstood all constitutional challenges, and even though Congress has proposed some changes to the Act in order to quiet some of the more discordant critics, it appears to be here to stay.

An important part of copyright today relates to digital rights management (DRM), which is various technologies and methods that can control or restrict users' access to and use of digital media, for example, movies, music, computer games, on various devices, for example, personal computers, that have such technology installed (McCullagh & Homsi, 2005). Early applications of DRM dealt with security and encryption as a means of solving the issue of unauthorized copying. The second-generation of DRM covers the description, identification, trading, protection, monitoring, and tracking of all forms of rights usages over both tangible and intangible assets including management of rights holders' relationships (Iannella, 2001).

With the importance of all types of digital media as relates to e-business today, it is important that all parties involved are cognizant of DRM. Holders of copyrighted material, such as movies, music, photos, and other digital media, have the right to ensure that they receive appropriate rewards for the digital media that they have copyrighted, media that may easily find itself in the stream of e-commerce; these individuals or organizations would be classified as DRM proponents. On the other hand, opponents of DRM are fearful that inappropriate restrictions will be placed on consumers and others who use the Internet lawfully.

Suffice it to say that DRM is an evolving concept that has strong proponents and opponents. Hardware and software technologies are also evolving with regard to how best to implement DRM. Those engaged in e-business, whether they are businesses themselves or end users/consumers who are making purchases of digital media online, need to be aware of the issues so as to ensure that the rights of all parties are protected.

Notwithstanding the importance of the DMCA as discussed, another section of the DMCA has received considerable attention of late that is extremely important to e-business. That concerns the possible liability incurred by ISPs that post copyrighted material on others' Web sites.

ISPs run the risk of substantial liability for passively providing for the opportunity for their subscribers to commit acts that could lead to copyright infringement (Croman 2005). This has become one of the most contentious issues surrounding e-business and copyright, and is perhaps best represented as an issue in terms of the inappropriate, that is, illegal download of copyrighted music, videos, and even software. For the most part, however, the DMCA exempts ISPs from liability for monetary, injunctive, or other equitable relief regarding copyright infringement, even if the ISP transmits, routes, or even provides a connection for such material, including just temporarily storing the material (Albert, Sanders, & Mazzaro, 2005). The caveat for ISPs is that they must not have actual knowledge of the infringing activity, they cannot be aware of information indicating that the material is infringing, and does not receive financial benefit directly attributable to the infringing activity (Albert et al., 2005). These have often been referred to as the "safe harbor" provisions of the DMCA. However, even though the law does not require an ISP to monitor activity on its network or attempt to obtain information that might indicate that an infringing activity is occurring, the ISP must remove the material or disable access to it once the ISP becomes aware of the activity.

Although many of the references are directed toward ISPs, non-ISPs may find that they too may have committed copyright infringement. In the case of A&M Records vs. Napster, Inc. (A&M Records, 2000), Napster allowed uploading of music recordings for access by its customers who had allegedly acquired proper copies of the files. Napster claimed that it should be protected under the safe harbor provisions of the DMCA. The Court found otherwise, and also raised questions about whether Napster's copyright policies were adequate with regard to what the DMCA requires. Further appeals by Napster were denied, leading to significant business problems for Napster.

Another practice that may have negative impacts involving e-business is inappropriate linking of Web sites/Web pages; the practice is often referred to as deep linking. Essentially, deep linking occurs if Web site A links to pages within Web site B and in so doing bypasses the homepage of Web site B. On the one hand, given the relative free nature and free access to the Web, one might not even give such a technique a second thought. However, a number of court cases have led to injunctions against e-business companies that occurred as a result of inappropriate linking.

One of the first hyperlinking cases occurred in Scotland and involved the *Shetland Times* vs. *The Shetland News*. *The Shetland Times* (*Times*) was a well-established newspaper, and *The Shetland News* (*News*) was an electronic paper. The *News* used headlines of *Times* newspaper articles as captions for its hyperlinks, with the links connecting users to the *Times* Web site and the stories themselves, bypassing the *Times*' homepage. The *Times* claimed copyright infringement, while the *News* argued that the Internet in based on free access. The Court found that *News* violated the *Times* copyrights and circumvented the advertising on the *Times*' homepage. The case was eventually settled out of court. (*Shetland Times*, 1996).

In another case involving copyright infringement and hyperlinking, Intellectual Reserve, Inc. vs. Utah Lighthouse Ministry, Inc., the Court ruled in 1999 that the defendant, Utah Lighthouse Ministry, Inc., had engaged in copyright infringement. Its Web page contained copyrighted materials of Intellectual Reserve, Inc. as well as hyperlinks that linked users to three Web sites that they knew contained infringing copies of Intellectual Reserve's copyrighted material. The Court issued a preliminary injunction against Utah Lighthouse Ministry (Dockins, 2005) and made specific mention of the infringing activities associated with deep linking.

With regard to deep linking, some Courts have concluded that this activity does not constitute copyright infringement, for example, Ticketmaster Corp. vs. Tickets.com, Inc. (Ticketmaster, 2000). This uncertainty only serves to lead to confusion and doubt for those engaged in e-business activities. On the one hand, those engaged in e-business as well as most Internet users are accustomed to seeing and using hyperlinks constantly. It follows then that e-businesses should ensure that any linking from their sites to others' sites are appropriate and covered by hyperlinking agreements between the parties.

E-businesses should aggressively pursue those that may infringe on their copyrighted material, especially if the infringing activities could lead to financial harm. With the importance of the Internet and related commerce today, e-businesses should seriously consider securing appropriate legal counsel to protect their interests and also to keep them from infringing on others' copyrighted material. It would be unwise for e-businesses to rely solely on IT professionals, such as Webmasters and Web designers, who generally know very little about the legal issues involved and their ramifications (Mykytyn, Mykytyn, & Harrison, 2005).

The seriousness of copyright infringement was emphasized in the MP3.com case: a case that received much public attention. Judge Rakoff "sent a message" to would-be copyright infringers, stating that:

...while the difficult issue of general deterrence must always be approached with caution, there is no doubt in the Court's mind that the potential for huge profits in the rapidly expanding world of the Internet is the lure that tempted an otherwise generally responsible company like MP3.com to break the law and that will also tempt others to do so if too low a level is set for the statutory damages in this case. Some of the evidence in this case strongly suggests that some companies operating in the area of the Internet may have a misconception that, because their technology is somewhat novel, they are somehow immune from the ordinary applications of laws of the United States, including copyright law. They need to understand that the law's domain knows no such limits. (UMG, 2000, pp. 17-18)

Patents

The U.S. Constitution, dating back to the late 1700s, provides the basis for patent laws in the U.S. These laws are intended to advance science and industry by providing inventors, as well as their assignees, with financial incentives for their inventions for 20 years from the date that a patent application is filed (Voet, 1995). Inventors or assignees are also provided with exclusive rights to the invention during that same period. These rights include the right to exclude others from making, selling, or even using the invention. In addition, the patent holder is also provided with the right to license others to make, sell, or use an invention for a period of 20 years from the patent filing date.

One of the important aspects of patent protection is the rights afforded to the patent holder should someone engage in infringing activities against the patented invention. This makes perfect sense because of the time and/or money to develop the invention and obtain a patent on it. Essentially, patent infringement is defined as any activity by someone who makes, sells, or uses a patented product or process that is substantially the same as the invention even though there may be no knowledge of the existence of a patent on that product or process (Koffsky, 1995). When a patented product or process is copied exactly, infringement is fairly easy to prove. One example of this occurred in 1994 between Microsoft Corporation and Stac Electronics. Stac had received a patent for data compression software, which Microsoft wanted to license. When licensing negotiations broke down, Microsoft decided to use its own technology, which was essentially the same as Stac's. Stac then sued Microsoft for patent infringement. Not only did Microsoft lose the case, the jury awarded Stac $120 million in damages (Chin, 1994).

Based on the Doctrine of Equivalents, a product or process that is substantially the same can also infringe. This doctrine is founded on the theory that "*...if two devices do the same work in substantially the same way and accomplish substantially the same result, they are the same, even though they differ in name, form or shape*" (Graver, 1950, p. 605). Remedies for infringement can include injunctive relief; adequate compensation to the patent holder that, when appropriate, can be trebled and, under no circumstances, would be less than a reasonable royalty plus interest for the use of the invention by the infringer; and in exceptional cases—those cases where a defendant knowingly infringes–the awarding of attorneys' fees.

During the 1980s, actions were taken by the government to strengthen and revitalize the patent system. This revitalization has come with legislation—much of it intended to curb infringement—and, more significantly, with the creation of the Court of Appeals for the Federal Circuit (CAFC) in 1982, which has been granted exclusive jurisdiction over patent appeals (Merz & Pace, 1994). The impact the CAFC has had on patent prosecution through enforcement was studied by Merz and Pace (1994). Using data for the period from July 1971 through December 1991, they questioned whether patent litigation had also increased since the CAFC increased enforceability. Their results indicated that a significant increasing trend in litigation occurred some time after April, 1982. This may be due in part to the creation of the CAFC and a more patent friendly environment. Further, they theorize that the increase in enforceability and, thus, the value of patents, may explain the dynamic increase in patent application filings. Although the data presented in Figure 1 deals with Internet-related patent lawsuits only, there is ample evidence of the growing importance for businesses and IT researchers as well regarding the relationship between IP in general and e-business activities. We address this relationship next.

Patents and The Evolution of Electronic Business

With regard to e-business activities and computer software related thereto, some might raise the question as to whether software is even patentable. For a very long time, such was the case. That changed, however, in 1981, when the U.S. Supreme Court held that software could be patented (Diamond, 1981). The U.S. Supreme Court's decision to provide for the patentability of software in the Diamond vs. Diehr case is significant. The Court declared that a claim for an invention using a computer for one or more steps of a process was valid subject matter for patent protection. Since that time, the number of patents for computer software is measured in the thousands. For example, the following well-known companies have been assigned software-related patents (the number in parentheses is the number of software-related business method patents assigned through late August 2005): Electronic Data Systems – 46; Merrill Lynch – 24; MasterCard International – 15; Priceline.com – 14; Amazon.com – 24 (USPTO, 2005).

The software patents awarded to Priceline.com and Amazon.com are significant in that these organizations deal directly with e-business. In fact, their only method of doing business is based on the Internet. Thus, some of the patents that have been awarded for e-commerce are, in fact, patents for ways of doing business; these are often referred to as business method patents (Wiese, 2000).

Much of the impetus to secure business method patents rests with a now-famous case involving State Street Bank & Trust Co. vs. Signature Financial Group, Inc. Signature had developed and patented a program to calculate changes in the allocation of assets of mutual funds. State Street attempted to negotiate a license with Signature, but was unable to do so. Subsequently, State Street sued Signature, claiming that Signature's patent was invalid. A U.S. District Court in Massachusetts agreed with State Street, finding that the patent was for a business method, which, in its opinion, would invalidate the patent. The case ultimately reached the CAFC, which stated that even though the patented application involved an algorithm (algorithms by themselves are not patentable), the idea itself was applied in such a way as to produce a useful and practical application, which is patentable (State Street, 1998). The aftermath of this decision has seen a flood of business method patent applications being submitted to the U.S. Patent and Trademark Office (Cantzler, 2000), many, as stated, involving e-business initiatives.

As stated, business method patents are especially relevant to the e-business environment. Notwithstanding their importance, many have argued that this type of patent should, for the most part, not be granted because in many instances the method being patented is not a unique business process, or that it tends to stifle e-business. One of the requirements for an invention to be patented is that it not exist as "prior art;" rather, it must be novel and nonobvious. Interesting research by Allison and Tiller (2003) found results that support the position that business method patents are no more invalid than nonbusiness method patents. They found that patents, in general in the late 1990s, as compared with business method patents, are not any better in terms of their quality. More specifically, applications for business method patents spent more time with the USPTO than patents in general; for example, they received more scrutiny, and business method patent applications cited nonpatent prior art of a similar quality to that in the average patent (Allison & Tiller, 2003). These results tend to question the belief that business method patents should be eliminated.

Another interesting and highly relevant patent infringement case is currently being litigated and resides with the CAFC. The case, MercExchange vs. eBay, involves one of the better-known e-businesses, eBay, and a small one-man company called MercExchange owned by Tom Woolston. Woolston's three patents, one for a method and apparatus for Internet-worked auctions, one for using search agents to return a list of matched goods from a number of different sources, and a third patent dealing with the creation of a computerized market for goods for sale or auction. This lawsuit is considered very relevant not only to e-business in general, but also to eBay since the patents at issue allegedly covered significant parts of eBay's Web-based business. These parts include the auction activity, fixed price sales, and a search activity that links a buyer's interest to the database containing the merchandise (GuFN, 2005). The patent infringement issue dealing with the Internet worked auction patent was dismissed, but the issues involving the remaining two patents were adjudicated. In May 2003, the jury found that eBay and Half.com, a subsidiary company, had willfully infringed the two remaining patents and assessed damages in the amount of $35 million. Appellate proceedings before the CAFC are pending (GuFN, 2005).

The role of patents as they relate to computer software extends far beyond the e-business perspective. Some would suggest that patents are not appropriate for computer software because software innovation is a cumulative activity rather than something that is sequential in nature (Campbell-Kelly, 2005). There are other views. For instance, a number of IT researchers, for example, Mata, Fuerst, and Barney (1995) conclude that software patents are ineffective in protecting software because the patented software could easily be reverse engineered, thereby eliminating any value. What is not considered, however, is that reverse engineering of a patented protected invention, that is, computer software, is grounds for patent infringement if such reverse engineering activity leads in any way to the development of an invention that is based on what was learned through the reverse engineering process (Moffat, 2004). Yet, focusing on e-business in the global environment in which many businesses must compete today, the number of e-business-related software patents, that is, business method patents, continues to increase. This type of protection for software assets cannot be ignored by businesses or IT professionals.

Avoiding Patent Infringement

At first glance, one might suggest that it would be easy to avoid infringing on another's patented software application, especially since any application that is patented is readily available from the USPTO. In fact, a copy of any patent can be obtained from the USPTO and, in most cases, it is available at the USPTO's Web site (http://www.uspto.gov). In addition to the description of the patent, all diagrams and figures related to it, as well as all of the claims for what the application does, are also available. With all of this information available, it would seem that merely developing a different application that does not infringe on any of the claims included with the patented application would suffice. While that is true, it ignores the amount of time, effort, and money that would need to be invested to accomplish that task. Recall that the Doctrine of Equivalents can make it quite difficult to avoid infringing. And recall too that reverse engineering of patented inventions in order to develop follow-up processes to be patented that are based on the original patented process is not allowed. To avoid the time and expense associated with being accused of infringing, there are a number of things an organization can do.

- **Be aggressively vigilant:** Organizations should consider hiring or retaining attorneys who specialize in IP law, with special emphasis on software. These firms can conduct appropriate searches of existing patents, and they are well aware of what to look for. Organizations themselves can be alert by examining patents that have been awarded and comparing those patented applications with business methods they may be using or considering to use.
- **Consider licensing arrangements:** Rather than take the time to attempt to "invent around" another's existing patented application and to possibly risk infringing that way, organizations can attempt to develop licensing agreements with the patent holder. The patent holder may view this quite positively, especially if the firm attempting to arrange for the license has, itself, patents that it could license back. Cross-licensing agreements can benefit both parties.
- **Consider following a "defensive patenting" strategy:** This strategy essentially mirrors a first mover strategy in that an organization would engage the services of a patent attorney to submit a patent application in the hopes of being first. Such a strategy could also prove beneficial later on, in that another organization might wish to attempt to arrange for a licensing arrangement. There are possible strategic advantages that could follow from this action.

The Internet presents interesting and significant opportunities for e-businesses today. Many of these involve the development and use of patented software applications for use in those ventures. These include patented applications for online auctions, for example, patents awarded to Priceline.com and online credit card payments, for example, Open Market, Inc. and BroadVision, Inc. In addition, as of late August 2005, there were in excess of 23,000 patent applications pending in patent class 705, which is defined as Data Processing: Financial, Business Practice, Management, or Cost/Price Determination. Not surprisingly, nearly 2,800 of these pending applications are in class 705/26, which is defined as Electronic Shopping (USPTO, 2005). It is obvious that the protection of e-business-related software applications and the potential value made possible by patenting these processes is a critical segment of e-business today. Organizations engaged in e-commerce activities must rethink their business approaches and strategies if they are not only to be competitive, but also to survive!

MULTIPLE IP PITFALLS

In many instances involving both large and smaller businesses, the strategy of driving users to a Web site may not be reviewed by attorneys or even marketing personnel, but rather handed over to a Webmaster running the site. This may be especially true for some e-businesses that may be small and who may rely on an IT person for many critical aspects of the site. While these issues may appear to be applicable to only the U.S., they have also resonated globally. Of course, e-business today is a global enterprise. A number of issues addressed previously are relevant specifically to trademark, copyright, and patent infringement. Still other possible infringing activities can relate to more than just one of the types of IP. That is, some types of activity can infringe on a copyright as well as a trademark. Some examples of these activities, among others, that can lead to copyright and trademark infringement include:

- The **posting** of copyrighted material from one organization onto another's Web site. This technique involves the practice of obtaining images or literature, even if copyrighted, from selected Web sites on the Internet, and placing them on your Web site. This activity can infringe a copyright and, depending on what is downloaded and posted, it could also lead to trademark infringement.

- **Metatags:** Improper use of metatags to trick search engines by placing another's name or key word within the metatag, is a technique used by Web developers to attract visitors to a Web site. Many search engines rely on metatags in determining ranking, and is an invaluable technique for getting a Web site to the top of a search engine. A series of cases have found such usage impermissible under trademark and unfair competition theories.
- **Misspelling** of famous trademarks in defining domain names as noted earlier in the Google case. Since people often misspell trademark names, a common technique is to register domain names of misspelled trademarks. For example, the following sites were pornographic Web sites registered by Global Net 2000, Inc.: usaday.com, abcnewss.com, busnessweek.com, Playboyy.com and windos95.com. Courts have uniformly enjoined the use of misspelled trademarks as domain names, even characterizing them as a "misuse of the Internet."
- **Framing:** improper framing, which is viewing contents of one Web site that is framed in another site, may trigger a dispute under copyright and trademark law theories, because a framed site possibly alters the appearance of the content and creates the impression that its owner sanctions or voluntarily chooses to associate with the framer.

OTHER LEGAL ISSUES

One of the more contentious topics being addressed today is IT outsourcing. It is an issue that affects individual IT professionals, IT organizations, and client organizations that employ outsourcing vendors. Although IT researchers have invested considerable time in examining the issues, the relationship between outsourcing and IP is normally not addressed. Consider the following scenario. A client organization contracts with an outsourcing vendor to develop some type of software application that will be used by the client organization. Once the application has been developed, the client uses it throughout the term of the outsourcing contract. Unless the contract specifies otherwise, it is possible that the vendor could patent the application and essentially own it. At the end of the contract, the vendor could require the client to pay licensing revenue or even deny access and use of the application to the client, thereby causing considerable disruption to the client's business. Furthermore, the application could even be licensed to the client's competitors, and the client would have no say in the matter. With the continuing growth in the e-business economy today, it is conceivable that many organizations might consider outsourcing arrangements. It would behoove them to ensure that any legal contract is secure for them.

E-business today is global! There is no mistaking that fact. Emphasizing this importance, Biddinger (2001) indicated that globalization involving businesses has led to an increase in the awareness and importance of IP rights, especially involving patents. Along with IP issues today, defamation and jurisdiction are other legal issues worthy of mention that are looming on the horizon. A recent case between an Australian businessman and Dow Jones emphasizes this. The case involved Mr. Joseph Gutnick and an article that appeared in *Barron's*, which is a weekly financial magazine and a cousin of the *Wall Street Journal*. An October 2000 article, which appeared in print and on Dow

Jones's Internet site, claimed that Mr. Gutnick was "the biggest customer" of a convicted money launderer. Dow Jones was sued by Mr. Gutnick in the Australian state of Victoria, which has some very strict laws regarding defamation and libel. The case involved considerable legal wrangling in terms of jurisdiction, whether Australian law was applicable since Dow Jones is a U.S.-based company, and which specific Australian law was applicable. After an initial opinion against Dow Jones and two subsequent higher court appeals in favor of Mr. Gutnick, Dow Jones and other publishers engaged in global e-business activities have been left to wonder how future issues might impact them (Gutnick, 2004). Questions relate to existing court precedents and the issues they address. Are these precedents providing the basis for future legislation? And, of course, there is the ever-present matter of technology and its use always outpacing the law governing its use in general.

As if defamation actions involving civil litigation are not troubling enough, jurisdictional issues have also entailed criminal law as well. One of the most famous cases involved Yahoo and the sale of Nazi memorabilia on one of its auction Web sites. A French court ruled that such activity breached French law against the display of Nazi items. Yahoo took positive steps to remove and ban all such hate paraphernalia from its auction sites, but it has continued to fight jurisdiction of the French ruling in American courts. It did win its case in a U.S. federal court on 1st Amendment and free speech protections, but French civil rights supporters appealed to a U.S. federal appeals court (Sprigman, 2001).

There are other important issues relevant to how different countries address IP and other issues. For example, although Canada and the U.S. follow similar copyright schemes, Canada does not consider copying or downloading music from the Internet for personal noncommercial use to be copyright infringement. Thus, ISPs in Canada are not liable for contributory infringement (Kotlyarevskaya, 2005). On the other hand, laws in Germany, Japan, and the European Union contain provisions concerning ISP liability (Gervais, 2001). Some have suggested that a Canadian system is appropriate for the U.S., whereas others have indicated the opposite (Kotlyarevskaya, 2005).

Differences in trademark law exist as well. For example, the U.S. Congress enacted the "Controlling the Assault of Non-Solicited Pornography and Marketing Act of 2003," which is popularly known as the CAN_SPAM Act. This statute requires e-mail recipients to be able to "opt out" of receiving unwanted commercial e-mail, whereas in Europe commercial e-mailers must obtain consent before sending bulk e-mails, an obvious significant difference for those engaged in e-business.

There are differences in patent laws as well among countries. For example, in the U.S., patents are awarded to the person who invents, whereas in Europe the patent goes to the first to file. Moreover, in the U.S., an inventor is given a 1 year grace period following disclosure to file a patent application, whereas in Europe, no patent is possible if an invention were disclosed in that way prior to filing. Finally, business method patents, which have a strong relationship to e-business activity, have become very popular in the U.S., whereas in Europe the view is that the U.S. awards too many trivial patents (Bray, 2005).

In addition to IP differences among countries, those engaged in e-business must also be aware of the lax or nonexistent enforcement of IP laws in some countries, for example, lax or no enforcement of laws related to downloading digital content. Such an environment only serves to make matters difficult for e-business ventures and could even lead to some organizations refusing to engage in business activity because of that laxness.

RECOMMENDATIONS FOR E-BUSINESSES

The previous sections of this chapter have provided in depth discussion about trademark, copyright, and patent issues as they can and do relate to e-business. Table 1 also highlights some of the IP issues that we have addressed.

The changing business environment associated with e-commerce today is dynamic, to say the least. Organizations are faced with a myriad of decisions related to business practices, for example, brick and mortar, click and mortar, e-commerce only, and so forth. Confounding the problem is the lack of understanding, perhaps even ignorance, related to e-business and the array of IP laws that can affect those businesses. Indeed, the subject matter can be quite involved, can be replete with legal jargon, and can change as a result of new statutes or court-mandated decisions. This uncertainty suggests that e-businesses need to become fully cognizant of these issues and how best to deal with them. In this section, we offer some suggestions that will be helpful for e-businesses, and may go a long way toward ensuring the proper safeguard of a business' IP assets, while at the same time serving to protect them from infringing others. It should also be noted that the suggestions offered are representative of the issues that e-businesses face every day, and that to address all of them would require much more investigation than is possible in this chapter.

Establish a team to identify a firm's important intellectual capital. Skyrme (1997) suggests that management of intellectual capital to audit and manage intangible assets is important today. IP professionals in organizations must be able to work as part of this team to identify significant intellectual capital, protect it, and transform it into tangible corporate assets. Ultimately, the firm's national/international reputation and position could be safeguarded, and barriers to substitution could be created, thereby preventing imitation by competitors.

Secure the services of the right attorney. Most businesses, e-business or otherwise, realize the importance of appropriate legal counsel, so it is not unusual to find organizations, especially larger ones, with many on staff attorneys or attorneys on retainer as needed. Although these attorneys may

Table 1. IP issues and e-business

IP Type	Applicable Issues	Legal Cases Referenced
Trademark	Appropriate use of domain names	Sergy Gridasov vs. Google[a]
	Anticybersquatting Consumer Protection Act (ACPA)	Planned Parenthood Federation of America, Inc., vs. Bucci
	Registration of domain names	
	Infringing on others' rights	
Copyright	Digital Millennium Copyright Act (DCMA)	ACM Records vs. Napster, Inc.
	Digital rights media (DRM)	Shetland Times vs. The Shetland News
	Posting of copyrighted material on Web sites	Intellectual Reserve, Inc. vs. Utah Light Ministry, Inc.
	Appropriate and inappropriate linking	Ticketmaster Corp. vs. Tickets.com, Inc.
	ISP liability issues	
Patents	Patents applicable to software	Diamond vs. Diehr
	Business method patents	State Street Bank & Trust, Inc. vs. Signature Financial Group
	Effectiveness of software patents	MercExchange vs. eBay
	Reverse engineering	

Note: [a] Google did not file a lawsuit against Gridasov. Instead, Google filed a complaint with The National Arbitration Forum, a legal alternative to court litigation.

be highly appropriate for most corporate needs, they may lack the necessary background in IP law. If a business is considering the development of an e-business model, or is currently engaged in e-business, it is extremely necessary that attorneys with IP knowledge be consulted.

Be sure to include IP attorneys in all e-business discussions, design, and development efforts. The nature of e-business most often involves an organization's knowledge assets that are IP as well. These can take the form of copyrighted digital information, the organization's domain names, trademarks, and software and other patents. It is essential that IP attorneys be consulted regarding what others, such as competitors and customers, may do as a result of accessing an organization's IP information online. At the same time, these same attorneys will assist in determining just what actions this organization can do legally regarding others' similar assets.

Consider appropriate IP training for MIS professionals. Although most IP professionals involved with e-business activity, for example, programmers, Webmasters, and Web designers, are very good technically; they may lack any IP knowledge. Issues such as appropriate and inappropriate linking and use of metatags are common for these individuals, but they may have little to no knowledge about the legal aspects of employing these techniques. This type of training can be very fulfilling to the organization in that it could integrate into all of the organization's training activities, which are most likely tied to many internal processes of the organization.

Ensure the appropriateness of all legal contracts affecting e-business activities. Many e-businesses, especially perhaps smaller ones, may lack technical resources to design, develop, implement, and maintain e-business Web sites. Instead, they may find it much more effective to hire a consultant or an outsourcing vendor to do this work. It is imperative that all duties, responsibilities, and expectations as they pertain to IP assets be thoroughly defined. For example, it is theoretically possible for a company to hire a consultant to develop an e-business application with the expectation that the e-business will be able to use the application. This may be spelled out in the contractual language between the parties. However, unless otherwise specified, the consultant could patent that application and retain ownership of it. At the end of the contract, the e-business could find that it is no longer able to use that application unless it licenses it from the consultant.

Consider cross-licensing agreements with other patent holders. Many organizations, for example, IBM, have a patent family numbering in the thousands. In turn, these companies often consider arrangements with other organizations to allow those organizations to use IBM's patented products in exchange for rights to use or license that organization's patented products. In the end, it can be a win/win matter for both parties. However, it is imperative that any business recognizes the importance of appropriate legal counsel before entering into any such arrangement.

Clarify relationships with ISPs. Many e-businesses will enter relationships with ISPs or other Web-hosting organizations. It is important to recognize that ISPs are, for the most part, shielded from any liability regarding possible copyright infringement that may result from posting of copyrighted material on Web sites or related to e-business activity.

CONCLUSIONS, RESEARCH ISSUES, AND TRENDS

The relationship between e-business activity and IP is strong and very much a vibrant issue today. While corporate attorneys may be very knowledgeable about traditional business-related issues such as contracts, they may be less aware of the potential issues and problems arising from the use and misuse of IP assets of their own organizations and that of others as well. Except for isolated examples, IT researchers have generally ignored these topics too. Unfortunately, the role of trademarks, copyrights, and patents as related to e-business activity is too important to ignore anymore.

This chapter has discussed important issues related to the conduct of e-business and the relationship that IP issues, specifically trademarks, copyrights, and patents, play today in this approach to doing business. Generic subject matter relevant to these three forms of IP was discussed, along with specific points relevant to e-business activity today. We have also provided some important recommendations for e-business organizations.

From the standpoint of importance, although all of the issues discussed are significant and relevant to e-business success today, we believe two things may not be considered by e-business organizations, but which are crucial for their success. The first is the nature of appropriate legal advice. The domain of IP law is unique, certainly much different from traditional contract and business law that may be familiar to most corporate attorneys. Therefore, identifying legal counsel knowledgeable in e-business aspects of IP law is crucial. Second is the matter of appropriate training for IT professionals. Although this group is very knowledgeable about the technical aspects of Web design and development, they are often less aware, if aware at all, of the IP issues confronting these IT areas. It is important that they receive appropriate training so as to minimize, if not eliminate, the threats of lawsuits being levied against e-businesses.

The role that IP plays today involving e-business activities is not what many would call mainstream IT research. As an example, many IT researchers have dismissed the importance of software patents for more than 2 decades, even though the business community continues to invest heavily in this for of IP protection (e.g., see Mykytyn & Mykytyn, 2002, for a review of this issue). At the same time, more recent research (Mykytyn et al., 2005) reports that IT academics/faculty are much more amenable to incorporating IP issues into there IT coursework; in fact, that research included follow-up contact with a number of IT academics who participated in the initial phase of the study. Many reported that they had begun to incorporate some IP aspects into their coursework. Notwithstanding this bit of encouraging news, we believe that more is needed by IT researchers today.

This issue of software ownership is an important topic for IT researchers that may or may not be considered. If the issue of software patents is considered part of the equation, it is probable that most IT researchers may not have considered such elements. They have the opportunity to do so.

Another research question concerns economic gains achieved by e-businesses as a result of protecting IP. Are there specific gains that can be attributed to taking protective measures? These gains could come in the form of increased market share, greater number of customers, or more satisfied customers. Related to possible direct financial gains are indirect gains. Should an e-business protect assets through copyright, trademark, and/or patents, what is the indirect effect on the business' competition? The competition could be forced into playing catch-up or even worse. This is a rich research question that could be grounded in organizational theory and behavior, economics, and, of course, IP law.

IT researchers should find the relationship between e-businesses, Web content, and other countries' laws and requirements not only interesting, but critical for research if businesses are going to be able to protect themselves and their IP assets. This is especially relevant in terms of content posted on e-business sites. Here again, IT researchers should find abundant research opportunities with regard to what actions e-businesses take, if any, to deal with these issues and protect themselves.

Additional research should examine IT curricula to see if any additional progress has been made following the work by Mykytyn et al. (2005). It is true that graduates from most IT programs receive considerable coursework in Web development, JAVA, Web design, and the like. It is less certain, however, whether these graduates know anything about the potential legal effects and impacts that their work may have on their organizations.

Along with the proposed research agenda, we believe there are a number of issues that should be categorized as trends. First, the international aspects of e-business will continue to heighten. Today, for example, the U.S. patent laws regarding computer software differ from those of the European Union. In fact, patent law in general between the U.S. and most other countries differs. As noted, the U.S. follows a "first to invent" policy, whereby the first person to invent an invention is awarded a patent. Most other countries follow a "first to file" policy, whereby a person who discloses his/her invention to the public and gains protection is awarded the patent. Issues surrounding which countries' courts have jurisdiction in lawsuits will most likely increase as the overall breadth of this approach to doing business increases. These types of international issues will most likely lead to significant challenges to businesses to identify legal counsel that is knowledgeable of the international environment (Bray, 2005).

We also believe that undergraduate and graduate IT curricula will need to be reexamined for its lack of depth and attention to the legal issues surrounding e-business. Many textbooks on e-business and e-commerce devote little to no detail about IP issues other than perhaps some discussion about how it can be illegal to download music. As we have shown in this chapter, the depth of issues involving trademarks, copyrights, and patents is much greater than that. Model curricula for IT majors will hopefully provide greater attention to these issues in e-business courses such as Web programming, Web development, and e-commerce/e-business.

The creation of laws seems to follow the advancement of technology, that is, the law lags. In particular, with the growing dependence involving e-business, greater attention may be forthcoming in terms of how tort laws may impact this environment. One such tort is defamation, which was addressed briefly. In general, contracts between business-to-business (B2B) partners can address the legal environment involving their relationships. Unfortunately, innocent third parties may be hurt.

Finally, we believe e-business activity throughout the world will continue to increase. With that increase, we see nothing to indicate that the IP environment will diminish in terms of its importance and its impact on businesses, consumers, and governmental bodies.

REFERENCES

A & M Records, Inc. vs. Napster, Inc., 54 U.S.P.Q.2d 1746 (ND Cal. 2000)

Albert, S. N., Sanders, J. A., & Mazzaro, J. M. (2005). Twentieth survey of white collar crime: Article: Intellectual property crimes. *American Criminal Law Review, 42*, 632-676.

Allison, J. R., & Tiller, E. H. (2003). The business method patent myth. *Berkeley Technology Law Journal, 18*, 987-1084.

Anticybersquatting Consumer Protection Act, 15 U.S.C. 1114(2)(D) (2000).

Biddinger, B. P. (2001). Limiting the business method patent: A comparison and proposed alignment of European, Japanese, and United States patent law. *Fordham Law Review, 69*, 2523-2554.

Blaise, F. (2005). Comment: Game over: Issues arising when copyrighted work is licensed to video game manufacturers. *Albany Law Journal of Science & Technology, 15*, 518-542.

Bray, R. (2005). The European Union software patents directive: What is it? Why is it? Where are we now? *Duke Law & Technology Review, 11.*

Campbell-Kelly, M. (2005). Not all bad: An historical perspective on software patents. *Michigan Telecommunications and Technology Law Review, 11*, 191-248.

Cantzler, C. S. (2000). Comment: State Street: Leading the way to consistency for patentability of computer software. *Colorado Law Review, 71*, 423-461.

Chin, D. (1994). MS, Stac battle it out. (Microsoft Corp.; Stac Electronics). *Computer Dealer News.* Retrieved June 29, 1994, from http://www.findarticles.com/p/articles/mi_m3563/is_n13_v10/ai_16146374

Croman, S. (2005). Note & comment: Where the Netcom yardstick comes up short: Courts should not apply the facts of Netcom as an example of intermediate and transient storage under § 512(a) of the DMCA. *Washington Law Review, 80*, 417-445.

Diamond vs. Diehr, 450 US 175 (1981).

Digital Economy 2003. (2003). Washington, DC: US Department of Commerce, Economics and Statistics Administration. Retrieved October 25, 2005, from https://www.csa.doc.gov/2003.cfm

Digital Millennium Copyright Act, Pub. L. No. 105-304, 112 Stat. 2860 (1998).

Dockins, M. (2005). Comment: internet links: The good, the bad, the tortuous, and a two-part test. *Toledo Law Review, 36*, 367-402.

Dueker, K. S. (1996). Trademark law lost in cyberspace: Trademark protection for internet addresses. *Harvard Journal of Law & Technology, 9*, 483-512.

Field, T. G., Jr. (2000). *Trademarks & business goodwill.* Retrieved September 9, 2005, from http://www.fplc.edu/tfield/trademk.htm

Fitzdam, J. D. (2005). Note: Private enforcement of the digital millennium copyright act: Effective without government intervention. *Cornell Law Review, 90*, 1085-1117.

Gervais, D. (2001). Transmissions of music on the internet: An analysis of the copyright laws of Canada, France, Germany, Japan, the United Kingdom, and the United States. *Vanderbilt Journal of Transnational Law, 34*, 1363-1416.

Ghosh, S., (2002). The merits of ownership; or, how I learned to stop worrying and love intellectual property review essay of Lawrence Lessig, the future of ideas, and Siva Vaidhyanathan, copyrights and copywrongs. *Harvard Journal of Law & Technology, 15,* 454-496.

Graver Tank & Mfg. Co. Vs. Linde Air Prods. Co., 339 U.S. 605 (1950).

Guillot, G. H. (2000) *A guide to proper trademark use, all about trademarks.* Retrieved March 30, 2000, from http://www.ggmark.com/guide.html

GuFN, Z. (2005). MercExchange vs. e-Bay: Should newsgroup postings be considered printed publications as a matter of law in patent litigation? *Golden State University Law Review, 35*, 225-258.

Gutnick vs. Dow Jones. Retrieved September 7, 2005, http://www.fact-index.com/g/gu/gutnick_v__dow_jones.html

Hunter, D. (2005). Culture war. *Texas Law Review, 83*, 1105-1136.

Iannella, R. (2001). Digital rights management (DRM) architectures. *D-Lib Magazine*, 7. Retrieved October 26, 2005. from http://www.dlib.org/dlib/june01/iannella/06iannella.html

Kamarck, M. D. (1999). Detours, misdirections and false starts on the information super highway: The hidden dangers in marketing your Web site. *E-Commerce Law Reports.* Retrieved September 7, 2005.from http://www.rmslaw.com/articles/art89.htm

Koffsky, M. I. (1995). Patent preemption of computer software contracts restricting reverse engineering: The last stand? *Columbia Law Review, 95*, 1160-1187.

Kotlyarevskaya, O. (2005). Annual review 2005: Part II: Entertainment law and new media: XI. Foreign & international law: A note: BMG Canada, Inc. vs. Doe & Society of Composers, Authors & Music Publishers of Canada vs. Canadian Ass'n of Internet Providers: Why the Canadian music compensation system may not work in the United States. *Berkeley Technology Law Journal, 20*, 953-973.

Lipson, J. C. (2001). Financing information technologies: Fairness and function. *Wisconsin Law Review, 2001*(4), 1067-1157.

Mata, F. J., Fuerst, W. L., & Barney, J. B. (1995). Information technology and sustained competitive advantage: A resource-based analysis. *MIS Quarterly, 19*, 487-505.

McCullagh, D., & Homsi, M. (2005, Spring). Leave DRM along: A survey of legislative proposals relating to digital rights management technology and their problems. *Michigan State Law Review*, 317-327.

Merges, R. P. (2000). One hundred years of solicitude: Intellectual property law, 1900-2000. *California Law Review, 88*, 2187-2240.

Merz, J. F., & Pace, N. M. (1994). Trends in patent litigation: The apparent influence of strengthened patents attributable to the Court of Appeals for the Federal Circuit. *Journal of the Patent and Trademark Office Society, 76*, 579-590.

Moffat, V. (2004). Mutant copyrights and backdoor patents: The problem of overlapping intellectual property protection. *Berkeley Technology Law Journal, 19*, 1473-1532.

Mykytyn, P. P. Jr., & Mykytyn K. (2002). Computer software patents: A dilemma in competitive advantage IT research. *Communications of the Association for Information Systems, 8*, 109-130. Retrieved September 7, 2005. from http://cais.isworld.org/articles/8-7/default.asp?View=Journal&x=31&y=5

Mykytyn, P., Mykytyn, K., & Harrison, D. (2005). Integrating intellectual property concepts into IS training: An empirical assessment of relevance-rigor disconnections. *Decision Sciences Journal of Innovative Education, 3*, 1-27.

National Arbitration Forum. (2005). Retrieved August 13, 2005, from http://www.arb-forum.com/domains/decisions/474816.htm

Planned Parenthood Federation of America vs. Bucci, No. 97 Civ. 0629 (KMW), 1997 WL 133313, at 1 (S.D.N.Y. Mar. 24, 1997), aff'd, 152 F.3d 920 (2d Cir. 1998).

Samuelson, P. (1999). Intellectual property and the digital economy: Why the anti-circumvention regulations need to be revised. *Berkeley Technology Law Journal, 14*, (pp. 519-566).

Shetland Times vs. Shetland News. 1997 S.L.T. 669 (Sess. Cas. 1996).

Skyrme, D. J. (1997). *From information management to knowledge management: Are you prepared?* Retrieved December 12, 2005, from http://www.skyrme.com/pubs/on97full.htm

Sprigman, C. (2001). *Why the Hague convention on jurisdiction threatens to strangle e-commerce and internet free speech*. Retrieved August 31, 2005, from http://writ.corporate.findlaw.com/commentary/20010927_sprigman.html

State Street Bank & Trust Co. vs. Signature Financial Group, Inc. 149 F.3d 1368 (Fed. Cir. 1998), cert. denied, 525 U.S. 1093 (1999).

Ticketmaster Corp. vs. Tickets.com, Inc., No. CV99-7654 HLH, 2000 U.S. Dist. LEXIS 4553, at 1 (C.D. Cal. Mar. 27, 2000), 54 U.S.P.Q.2d (BNA) 1344 (C.D. Cal. 2000).

UMG RECORDINGS, INC., et al., Plaintiffs, vs. MP3.COM, INC, 00 Civ. 472 JSR, U.S. District Court for the Southern District of New York, September 6, 2000.

USPTO, United States Patent and Trademark Office, http://www.uspto.gov

15 U.S.C. §§ 1051-1127 (1988 & Supp. IV 1992).

15 U.S.C. §§ 1114(1), 1125(a) (1988 & Supp. IV 1992).

Voet, M. A. (1995). Patent practitioners—don't let GATT get you. *Managing Intellectual Property, 47*, 20-25.

Wiese, W. D. (2000). Death of a myth: The patenting of internet business models after State Street Bank. *Marquette Intellectual Property Law Review, 4*, 17-47.

This work was previously published in E-Business Process Management: Technologies and Solutions, edited by J. Sounderpandan and T. Sinha, pp. 45-67, copyright 2007 by IGI Publishing, formerly known as Idea Group Publishing (an imprint of IGI Global).

Chapter XXIV
E-Business Risk Management in Firms

Ganesh Vaidyanathan
Indiana University South Bend, USA

ABSTRACT

In order to understand the different types of e-business risks, this chapter uses a framework focusing on five dimensions of e-businesses. This chapter examines e-business risk management in a broader context by integrating various functions within firms. Primary consideration is given to characteristics of the integrated supply chain functionalities of a firm and their associations with information technology (IT), business models of firms, business processes that have become important to e-business, services that have been interlocked into e-business, the relative importance of partnerships, trust, and the necessity of adaptation in managing the supply chain in order to attain competitive advantage. The purpose of this chapter is to understand how to identify and manage various online risks.

INTRODUCTION

E-business has paved a path for new growth potential for many businesses around the globe. E-business is emerging as the medium of choice in trade, and is replacing traditional commerce. Some of the brick-and-mortar companies have made e-business the solution of the future. Corporations can now trade goods and services, ranging from steel to medical equipment, with potential unknown buyers and sellers using online technology. These trading hubs might be further enhanced in the future to deliver substantial value to their members, including greater liquidity, better pricing, better quality, better delivery time, efficient transactions, and better quality assurance. Why is it that the many e-businesses have not performed as expected? Despite very optimistic projections for business-to-business e-commerce, businesses have been very cautious to embrace the technology as well as using e-business to their maximum advantage. Is this due to perceived risks inherent or associated with e-business? The perceived risks are multi-faceted and includes security and privacy (Mercuri, 2005), privacy assurance (Moores, 2005), credibility and information asymmetry (Ba & Pavlou, 2002), reliability, damage and loss of systems (Dillon & Pate-Cornell, 2005; Straub & Welke, 1998), supply chain (Spekman & Davis, 2004), decision-making processes (Pathak, 2004), poor business models (Grover & Saeed, 2004), and online services (Lange, Davis, Jaye, Erwin, Mullarney, Clarke, & Loesch, 2000; Orr, 2005). These risks have played a role in impeding the growth and acceptance of e-business.

Risk may be defined as a factor, thing, element, or course involving uncertain danger in a firm, while challenge is a test of a firm's abilities or resources in a demanding but stimulating undertaking. In this study, we focus on risks. Risk has been defined by various scholars in many ways. Cox and Rich (1964) refer to perceived risk as the overall amount of uncertainty perceived by a consumer in a particular purchase situation. Cunningham (1967) recognized the risk resulting from poor performance, danger, health hazards, and costs. Jacoby and Kaplan (1972) classified consumers' perceived risk into the following five types of risk: physical, psychological, social, financial, and performance. Murphy and Enis (1986) define perceived risk as customer's subjective assessment of the consequence of making a purchasing mistake. Ahn, Park, and Lee (2001) define perceived risk as the overall amount of uncertainty or anxiety perceived by a consumer in a particular product/service when the consumer purchases online. Using these definitions, risk is identified in the five dimensions that include technology, process, business models, services, and fulfillment in this study.

One of the critical factors playing a major role is the risk associated with online commerce in general. The purpose of this chapter is to provide an analysis of e-business risk management in a broader context that examines the integration of the functions within firms in the context of suppliers and customers at a firm level. A conceptual insight to e-business risk management will be developed with an understanding of the strategic aspects of business philosophy. Primary consideration is given to characteristics of the integrated supply chain functionalities of a firm and their associations with information technology (IT), business models of firms, the business processes that have become important to e-business, services that have been interlocked into e-business, and the relative importance of partnerships, trust, and the necessity of adaptation in managing the supply chain in order to attain competitive advantage. A review of the literature and an analysis of the characteristics and implications of the e-business risks in the context of changing global markets emphasize the importance of strategically managing the e-business initiatives of the firm. The remaining sections in this study are arranged as follows. The next section discusses how traditional businesses have transformed themselves to online businesses. The third section conceptualizes a framework of risks in e-businesses. The following sections expand each one of these risks. The final section discusses the management of risks and presents a summary of the five risk dimensions.

BACKGROUND

This section briefly describes both the traditional and online business models. The differences between these two models convey how e-business risk is really different from traditional risks. The traditional buy and sell business can be established as a process, as illustrated in Figure 1 (adapted from Vaidyanathan & Devaraj, 2003). The buyer approves a vendor using certain criteria, seller approves a customer using credit feed from credit bureaus and other selection criteria, buyer orders

Figure 1. Traditional buy/sell process

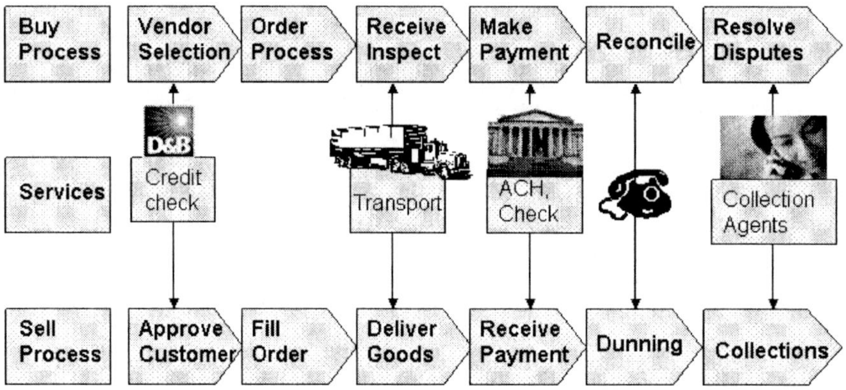

goods and services through purchase order, seller accepts the purchase order, both parties guarantee payment and receipt of goods using a letter of credit, seller sends an invoice and the buyer accepts the invoice, seller initiates the order by shipping the goods using a logistics provider, buyer accepts the goods/services, buyer verifies goods and services for quality, buyer approves payment, gets financed if needed, makes payments using financial institutions, and seller accepts payments. In some cases, disputes are resolved after dunning, and payments are collected using external legal and collection agency services.

This process works well regardless of whether the supply chain and backend computer services are connected or not. The performance and efficiency of the process depends on the presence or absence of connectivity. If the supply chain and back-end services function efficiently, the traditional process will perform very well (Vaidyanathan & Devaraj, 2003). In the traditional process, there are four different players: buyers, sellers, suppliers, and service providers. As we can see in Figure 1, the financial institutions and other service providers, such as logistic providers, collection agents, and legal firms, constitute the service providers. Financial institutions offer services such as financing the buyer and financing the seller, as well as being the intermediary for payment processing that traditional checks, wire transfer, credit cards, smart cards, and electronic fund transfer. On the consumer side of the buy/sell process, the financial institutions are also involved in credit and debit payment networks. Service providers offer logistics, warehousing, global transportation, inventory management, and all other fulfillment needs. The suppliers are material suppliers, contract manufacturers, and computer hardware, infrastructure, and software providers who support the traditional sellers. The balanced traditional model has certain risks like credit-card fraud and identification thefts. The service providers such as financial institutions, logistics providers, credit bureaus, insurance companies, banks providing letter of credits, have mitigated most of these risks. In the traditional model, the service providers charge the buyers, sellers, and suppliers to mitigate their business risks (Vaidyanathan & Devaraj, 2003). The evaluation of the risks of technology and enhancing the technologies to new, emerging technologies may mitigate certain technology risks.

Online business or e-business has transformed this traditional buy/sell process as seen in Figure 2 (adapted from Vaidyanathan & Devaraj, 2003). The fundamental buy/sell process does not change significantly online; however, new risks have been introduced (Vaidyanathan & Devaraj, 2003). There is perception that online businesses are faster, and this has changed the

Figure 2. Online buy/sell process

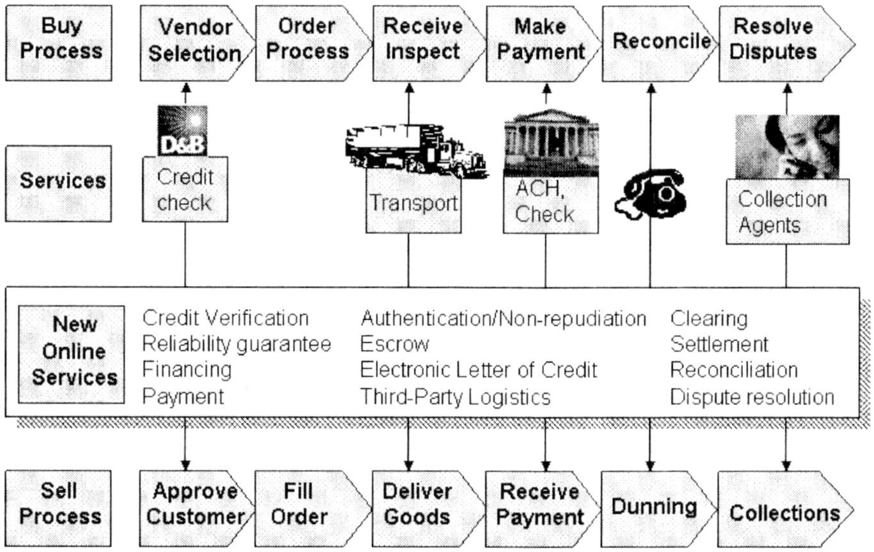

relationship between suppliers and sellers. Buyers expect faster fulfillment and suppliers have to work in maximum synchronization with the buyers. As with the traditional model, this online transformation of buy/sell process works very well when the supply chain and backend services are integrated and work together seamlessly. The performance and efficiency of the online process depends on the presence of this connectivity. If the supply chain and back-end services function well, the online process will be efficient and will perform as expected for the online community of buyers and sellers. In this new online buy/sell process, there is now an extra player who plays a critical role, as shown in Figure 2. This is the required online service provider. These service providers are essential in bringing together the online buyers and sellers. These new online service providers offer credit verification services, digital authorization and authentication services, online financing, online payments, online business intermediations, Internet hosting, and Internet collaborative tools to buyers, sellers, and suppliers. There are also other new service providers such as online financial transaction companies, online insurance companies, and online logistics providers who have newer business models and new business processes. The traditional service providers of insurance, finance, and logistics have also set up these new online services. Therefore, the online scene has the traditional buyers, sellers, traditional service providers, suppliers, and the new online service providers (Vaidyanathan & Devaraj, 2003). In addition, some of these new online service providers have collaborated with traditional service providers to form intermediaries. E-marketplaces that provide online buy/sell transactions are examples of these new online service providers.

Some of the new online service providers have established their new processes, new technology, new fulfillment needs, and new business models. The traditional buyers, sellers, suppliers, and the service providers have also changed their business models to suit the new online method of doing business. Moreover, they have modified their processes, introduced new processes, and introduced new technology to do online business. By introducing these new processes, new business models, new fulfillment requirements, new online services, and new technologies, the buyers, sellers, suppliers, customers, and traditional and online service providers have been introduced to new risks.

Throughout the supply chain network, there are substantial risks. There is risk that goods will be stolen or damaged. There is risk that they arrive in time but with inferior quality. There is risk that the warehouse burns down or is destroyed by natural disasters. In 1995, an earthquake hit the port town of Kobe in Japan. This earthquake destroyed hundreds of buildings and shut down Japan's largest port for more than 2 years. This disaster forced thousands of firms to change their production and distribution strategies just to survive. Automotive plants had to halt production, as parts were unavailable for a period of time. Furthermore, labor strikes, machine breakdowns, political instability, and customer changes also contribute to supply-chain failure (Kilgore, 2004). Supply-chain problems have more impact on stock price (Singhal, 2000). Some of the concerns of buyers and sellers in a supply-chain network are illustrated in Figure 3. The concerns reside in technology, process, business models, services, and fulfillment needs. The next section introduces a framework of these new risks.

CONCEPTUAL FRAMEWORK

Electronic business has paved a path for new growth potential to many businesses around the globe. Electronic business is emerging as the medium of choice in trade, and is replacing traditional commerce. The rise and then the fall of B2B vertical and horizontal exchanges within the electronic marketplace have been well documented. Current B2B models have three fundamental flaws (Wise & Morrison, 2000): (1) Economics, not quality, is being pursued by the current models; (2) sellers are being pressurized by price wars, profitability, and customers; and (3) customer priorities have not been considered. However, these are not the only fundamental flaws of e-business.

Although we have encountered the positive effects of B2B business, some studies have drawn attention to certain aspects of risk. Some of the

Figure 3. Concerns of a global trader

Seller	Buyer
Does the buyer have buying power?	Will the seller keep his promise?
Does the buyer have authority?	Does the seller have authority?
Will I get paid?	Will I receive the goods in good condition?
Is the product up to expectations?	Is the product up to expectations?
How can I maximize the price?	How can I minimize cost?
Will the sale go through?	Will the sale go through?
Will I retain loyalty?	Will the quality be maintained?
What are the regulations and rules?	What are the regulations and rules?
Are there "rogue" buyers?	Are there "rogue" sellers?
Alternative buyers?	Alternative sellers?
What is buyer's reputation?	What is seller's reputation?
How good is the security?	How good is the security?
Is the contract good in that country?	Is the contract good in that country?
How good is the Letter of Credit?	How good is the Inspection report?
How can we avoid litigation?	How can we avoid litigation?
Will the payment be on time?	Will the delivery be on time?
What are my total exposures?	What are my total exposures?

risks associated with e- business are due to weak procedures in software development process, deficiencies in electronic business protocols and other technology-related problems (Muiznieks, 1995). There are hosts of other electronic business risks that must be addressed, such as accidental or erroneous processing of business transactions (Ratnasingham, 1998).

A study illustrated that there are administrative threats in the form of risks, such as password sniffing, data modification, spoofing, and repudiation (Bhimani, 1996). Risks associated with fraud are due to the rapid growth of electronic business companies in general, as well as the rapid growth of electronic business lacking internal controls and good business sense (Baker, 1999). Many studies point electronic business risks toward information technology (IT) and/or security (Kolluru & Meredith, 2001; Salisbury, Pearson, Pearson, & Miller, 2001).

A model of traditional and electronic business to build trust in electronic business environments has been established (Papadopoulou, Andreou, Kanellis, & Martakos, 2001). A model, using global electronic business processes, has been presented by Caelli (1997). This latter model includes integrated schemes by financial institutions and consumers, open standardization, international standards for security and technology, and international agreements on legal, social, and economic systems. However, these models have not explicitly considered the elements of risk. A framework for trust requirements in electronic business was developed (Jones, Wilikens, Morris, & Masera, 2000). Although the framework does not view trust with respect to risk, it does identify complexities in the world of electronic business. The complexities that are identified relate to technology, process, and services. These complexities may be extended to business models and fulfillment needs as well. The literature regarding measurement of risk attitude of management concluded that decision makers can be simultaneously risk seeking and risk averse in different domains, that is, context-specific (Shapira, 1995).

Since there is an established perception that online businesses are faster, the relationship between suppliers and sellers has changed. Buyers expect faster fulfillment and suppliers have to work in maximum synchronization with the sellers. As with the traditional model, this online transformation of buy/sell process works very well when the supply chain and back-end services are connected and work together. The performance and efficiency of the online process depends on the presence of this connectivity. If the supply chain and back-end services function well, the online process will be efficient and will perform as expected by the online community of buyers and sellers.

Some of the brick and mortar companies have made electronic business the solution of the future. Corporations can now trade goods and services, ranging from plastics to medical equipment, with potential unknown buyers and sellers using online technology. These trading hubs might be further enhanced in the future to deliver substantial value to their members, including greater liquidity, better pricing, good quality and better delivery time, faster transactions, and better quality assurance. By creating these trading hubs, electronic marketplaces are initially focusing on gaining a critical mass of buyers and sellers in order to establish themselves as the leader in their particular core competencies. The electronic marketplaces are currently preoccupied with experimenting with different types of business models such as sell-side auctions, buy-side auctions, and pure exchange formats. In the B2B exchange market segment, the ability to be the first in the business, that is, gain the first mover advantage, is the paramount goal.

The new online risks have been either partially mitigated or not mitigated at all. Firms that face these risks need to address both their internal and external environments. For instance, one such external environment factors are the standards.

Much of the impetus for standard setting comes from the threat to B2B network posed by hackers and foreign governments (Vijayan, 2001). The global expansion of Internet use, combined with the global threats of increasing presence of hacker tools and the decreasing difficulty of use, argues for a permanence of constant risk. Organizations need to take responsibility for their protection of data and intellectual property. They need to achieve cooperation with other parties involved. They need to understand the weaknesses of the e-business systems that they are dependent on (McCrohan, 2003). The involvement of senior managers in risk awareness and risk assessment initiatives is required to mitigate the risks (McCrohan, 2003).

Many primary services crucial to the success of e-business have entered the scene. These services include guaranteed transaction services, financing services, quality assurance, integrated shipping, foreign exchange, and international fund transfers. Traditional service providers and new entrants have taken the reins to offer these primary services online. Internet consulting firms believe in potential growth despite recent setbacks. New business models are evolving. New buy and sell processes will make an impact on electronic business and some of them may fail. New technologies are paving a road for growth and some of them will be questionable. New fulfillment needs will arise and some of them will go unanswered. With the advent of these online services, new technologies, new processes, new business models and new fulfillment needs, new online risks, have surfaced, and these risks have accounted for some of the uncertainty associated with electronic business.

A framework for evaluating online risks is needed to analyze the impact of electronic business in the business-to-business (B2B) world. The traditional processes of buying and selling can be viewed as a model with conventional risk mitigation instruments including escrow, insurance, and contracts. As global B2B trade progresses using the electronic business as its medium of choice, an array of new business models, new processes, new fulfillment needs, new services, and new technology have emerged, resulting in a new set of online risks. These new online risks have created an imbalance in the traditional buying and selling process. A framework for examining the various risks in the online B2B buy and sell process was presented (Vaidyanathan & Devaraj, 2002). This chapter will expand that basic framework with the new insights, and include the entire major research that several scholars have provided in recent years. This study will include the risk environment with an analysis of how these firms can understand the risks and mitigate them. The next section expands on these five dimensions of risks.

FIVE DIMENSIONS OF NEW ONLINE RISKS

The new online risks may be attributed to the following five dimensions that have emerged for online B2B business: new services, new business models, new processes, new technologies, and new fulfillment needs. These five dimensions play an important role in this framework and, in fact, may be used to define the role of online B2B business. Figure 4 (adapted from Vaidyanathan & Devaraj, 2003) illustrates the five dimensions of this framework. These dimensions, consisting of services, business models, processes, technologies, and fulfillment needs, are offshoots of their traditional roles. They have been transformed to accommodate the online business scene. In each one of the dimensions, there are a number of types of risks. These types of risks are illustrated as a summary in Table 1. The next sections define each one of the types of risk in detail.

New Services

The rise of the e-business has changed the way that many organizations function and exist. E-

Figure 4. Conceptual framework

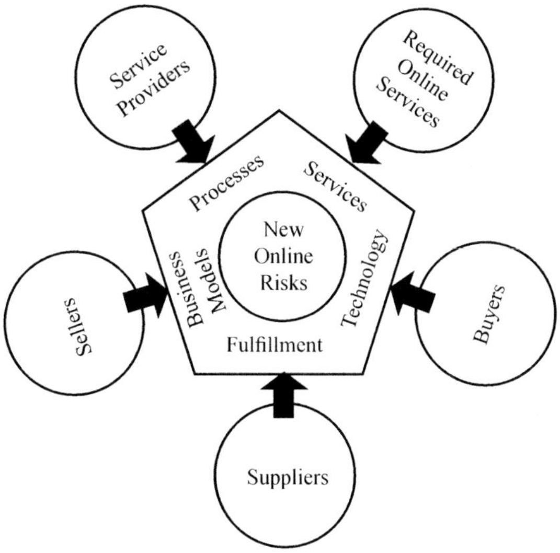

Table 1. Risk types in dimensions

Risk Dimension	Risk Type
Services	Service failure risks
	Service-specific security risks
	New jurisdiction risks
	Intangible property risks
	Obsolete assumption risks
	Online fraud
	Poaching
	Third-party liability risk
Business Models	Performance risks
	Financial risks
	Financial transaction risks
	Lack of trust
Technology	Security
	System failure risk (availability, reliability)
	Data integrity risks
Processes	Risks due to misfit between new processes and existing organizational processes and organizational structure
	Product quality risks
	Process Integration risks
Fulfillment	Order fulfillment risks
	Other supply chain management risks

services need to be included in the e-business models to make the business models robust. E-services, as compared to offline services, have grown rapidly, and the Internet has provided tremendous opportunities for service companies to offer quality services (Surjadjaja, Ghosh, & Antony, 2003). These services that have been offered by the service providers are often disparate and companies have to invest in integration of the services and systems. An example of an e-service is the experience of buying a ticket on the Internet. As seen in Figure 2, these new online services are conceptually the traditional services like banking, shipping, insurance, logistics, credit services, and so forth. During an e-service encounter, the customers are restricted to hearing and viewing whereas, in traditional service, customers can experience the service using all senses. However, traditional service is restricted by distance and opening hours, whereas e-service has substantially removed these barriers (Surjadjaja et al., 2003).

Empirical studies demonstrate that buyers perceive services to be riskier than products (Mitchell & Greatorex, 1993). Disparate services increase risk exposure. Furthermore, these services are threatened by internal factors including lack of standards, lack of regulations and rules, and lack of support systems. This contrasts with traditional service industries that have deep-rooted support systems, rules, regulations, and standards. The external factors that threaten the new online services are volatile online political sanctions, natural hazards, legal issues, environmental issues, and other political instabilities.

Several risks arise from these online services that include service failure risks, service-specific security risks, new jurisdiction risks, intangible property risks, and obsolete assumption risks. Jurisdiction on Internet sales is still ambiguous and sellers may find themselves in expensive litigation in distant forums (Lange et al., 2000). The intangible property rights create new risks both in the nature of uncertainty regarding existing transactions and in attempting to control risk of future transactions (Lange et al., 2000). Courts will have to determine whether the risks created by the use of new technology should be borne by the party who puts the technology into use, or whether the interest in innovation has for the potential benefit to third parties supports denial of liability (Lange et al., 2000). In the event of failure in the e-service, service recovery redresses loss to customers. Customers who experience a service failure can become more demanding and lose confidence with the firm that is offering the services or the firm who uses a third-party service. However, if service recovery is carried out satisfactorily, it can turn dissatisfied customers into satisfied customers (Ahmad, 2002), with a consequent decrease in negative word of mouth (Sparks & Bradley, 1997). In contrast, unsuccessful service recovery leads to a decline in customers' confidence, lost customers, negative word of mouth, negative publicity, and the direct cost of having to reperform the service (Berry & Parasuraman, 1992).

In banking, online fraud is a real problem (Streeter, 2005). The U.S. is a hotbed of online fraud, according to a report just published by the FBI and the National White Collar Crime Center (NWCCC). The same report claims a staggering 94.1% of all online fraud complaints reported to the Internet Fraud Complaint Center. These frauds include bogus invoices, cramming, slamming, loan scams, phishing, and so forth. According to a new survey, high fraud rates continue to plague electronic commerce Web sites, with criminals expected to steal $2.6 billion from online merchants. Suspicious merchants are now rejecting a far higher percentage of orders, meaning a steep increase in lost sales due to accidental rejection of legitimate orders (Sullivan, 2004).

Poaching is a contractual relationship risk where information that is transferred between parties for purposes specified in the contract is deliberately used by the receiving party for purposes outside the contract, to its own economic benefit, and to the detriment of the party that provided the information (Clemens & Hitt, 2004). This is a form of transactional risk and is one component of opportunistic behavior and abuse of power, when a client cannot monitor performance and when a client has become dependent upon a vendor's services. The rise of outsourcing and of interfirm activities that entail the transfer of intellectual property increases the risk of poaching (Clemens & Hitt, 2004).

Third-party liability exposure seems to be theoretical but can become a reality (Sclafane, 2000). The services risks are particular to Internet service provider (ISP) or application service provider (ASP). If interrupted, these services pose a problem to other businesses as well. For example, if AOL goes down, there is a significant business interruption to Amazon or eBay. Web-based storage services allow business users to store their documents and other digital files on third-party servers. Since most of these service users are small and medium enterprises (SME), data protection is absolutely critical in these instances for their survival (Aber, 2004). Web-based storage services ensure businesses to focus on their core business, and operate even if crises, outages, or disasters occur in their main offices. They also offer real-time collaboration and file sharing between SME and their partners in supply chain (Aber, 2004).

As firms expose applications to internal and external users, it is critical that these exposed interfaces are well defined, easy to use, and meaningful to the service consumer. This means that they must more closely reflect business concepts and requirements (documents, processes) rather than low-level technical concepts (APIs, data types, and platforms). Interfaces exposed in this way are referred to as business services. These e-services consist of three layers. The first layer consists of software standards and protocols that include Extensible Markup Language (XML) and simple object access protocol (SOAP) that allow information to be exchanged easily among Web applications. The second layer builds upon the protocols and standards, and forms a service grid managed by third parties that facilitate transport of messages and identify available services and assuring reliability and consistency as well. The third level comprises of a diverse area of application services, from credit card processing to production scheduling, that automate individual business functions (Hagel, 2002). Web services-specific security is still in rudimentary stage. Standards bodies like the W3C and OASIS are working diligently toward a solution, but Web services on the Internet today are completely defenseless against cyberterrorists and hackers. This level of exposure is far too risky for most IT executives. We will discuss the risks of business models in the next section.

New Business Models

New business models have emerged on the online scene. Portal models, such as dynamic pricing, free products and services, demand-sensitive pricing, and so on, may add further risks. Products and services have made their way to the e-business to be sold by original manufacturers, certified resellers, and sometimes noncertified resellers as well. The original manufacturer or service provider may find it attractive to channel their marketing and sales efforts using e-marketplaces or exchanges, only to find that the owners of the e-marketplaces or exchanges have different business models than their conventional marketing and sales practices. When the business models of the original manufacturer are not aligned with the certified resellers or noncertified resellers, the original manufacturers will be exposed to various new risks. The business models are threatened by internal factors, like loss of revenue, due to the cost of poor image, and so forth. In this case, these business models are threatened by socio-psychological external factors including trust, privacy, confidence, and other such factors. Businesses going global online have new exposures that are different from traditional ones. There are new regulatory exposures that they never thought about before.

The complexity of the business and the complex nature of risk itself is one of the concerns of the risk industry (Kaiser, 2002). The high consolidation levels within industries has translated into big channel conflicts and led to cannibalization of their own business (Kaiser, 2002). In many parts of the world, as in Latin America, sellers are in a much better position than buyers, and unless there is a steep rise in competition among sellers, the buyers will be at a disadvantage (Sinha, 1999). The most significant aspect of e-business is the transfer of power from the supplier to the buyer (Kaiser, 2002). There are risks associated with the seller credibility due to the availability of an overwhelming number of retailers, which is partially due to the perceived low entry and set-up costs business models (Biswas & Biswas, 2004; Peterson, Balasubramanian, & Bronnenberg, 1997). It becomes difficult for the customer to distinguish between "fly-by-night operators" and regular "honest" suppliers in e-business (Biswas & Biswas, 2004). This higher level of uncertainty would, in turn, increase the overall perceived risks (Biswas & Biswas, 2004). Some companies, like Fingerhut, abandoned strategic positioning for some of their new customers due to new business models and failed. The management also failed to adequately analyze their ability to sustain competitive advantages of the many online businesses in which they invested (Phan, Chen, & Ahmad, 2005).

Performance risk and financial risks have received strong attention (Grewal, Gotlieb, & Marmorstein, 1994) in growing markets. Performance risk is the uncertainty and consequence of a product not functioning at some expected level (Shimp & Bearden, 1982). Performance risks are likely to be higher in e-business since customers are unable to physically inspect the product before purchase (Biswas & Biswas, 2004; Lal & Sarvary, 1999). Financial risks are the uncertainty and monetary loss one perceives to be incurring if a product does not function at a certain expected level (Grewal et al., 1994). There exists transaction risks, which is the uncertainty associated with giving information such as credit card number to the seller during the course of a transaction. Consumers have higher levels of perceived performance, financial, and transaction risks in e-business (Biswas & Biswas, 2004). Retailer reputation, perceived advertising expense, and warranty have been shown as consumer risk perception signals in e-business conditions for products (Biswas & Biswas, 2004).

The strong ties associated between the high levels of trust and the banking industry have not yet been translated to its full potential (Yousafzai, Pallister, & Foxall, 2005). Trust has been identified as the key enabler to e-business (Keen, Balance, Chan, & Schrump, 2000). Lack of trust and privacy are risks and uncertainties that exist in e-business (So & Sculli, 2002). Customers are reluctant to adopt e-business, especially in online banking applications, because of trust (Lee & Turban, 2001). Trust has been looked upon as the major obstacle in e-business models (Gefan et al., 2003). Another risk is perceived reputation of a firm. Until executives actively manage the perceptions of their company with as much rigor as they apply to managing financial, operational, or technology risk, a company's most important intangible asset—its reputation—will be at risk (Resnick, 2004). The blemish in reputation may be due to any number of reasons, one of them being loss of confidence and trust due to online business models of the firm.

Privacy is infringement by online retailers by sharing or selling or renting personal information to other companies, contacting without consent, and tracking habits and purchases. System security includes concerns about potentially malicious individuals who breach firms' systems to acquire personal, financial, or transactional information. Frauds are concerns regarding any fraudulent behavior by either customer or supplier, including nondelivery or misrepresentation of ordered goods (Miyazaki & Fernandez, 2001). Trust is crucial to e-business, but e-businesses are failing to support ways of assuring it (Moores, 2005). Privacy seals, like TRUSTe, CPA Webtrust, and BBBOnline, are Web assurance seals to persuade buyers that the particular Web site can be trusted. The result in a recent study points out that many do not fully comprehend the form and function of the privacy seals and deciding to trust the site with the privacy seal (Moores, 2005). The results suggest that the seals have failed to play their intended role, and the buyers have to be educated with the process and assurance of these seals.

Technology can be the stimulus for the growth of e-business. Technology alone cannot be the stimulus. The transformation to online business is a complex social, technological, political understanding (Davison, Vogel, & Harris, 2005). However, technology has its own risks, as presented in the next section.

New Technology

E-business uses emerging technologies. Most of these technology applications may not have been tested for scalability, security, and availability. The integration with other software products has also been a challenge. Integration of various systems and software has exposed the integrated system's vulnerabilities. These vulnerabilities may highlight unique risks caused specifically by integration. Furthermore, security risks have been well documented in the literature (Kolluru & Meredith, 2001; Salisbury et al., 2001). The internal factors that threaten new technologies are complexity of systems and integration of systems, while the external factor that threatens the technologies is security.

Security refers to the technical safety of the network against fraud or hackers (Surjadjaja et al., 2003). Recent information thefts have left a mark on the risks of third-party data. About 145,000 consumers nationwide were placed at risk by a recent data theft at the database giant ChoicePoint. Personal information on 310,000 people nationwide has been stolen from LexisNexis, which compiles and sells personal and financial data on U.S. consumers. This is not a technology problem and is a legal problem (Schneier, 2005). These frauds and thefts would not have been public if it were not for the California law mandating public disclosure of such events (Schenier, 2005). Hacker attacks and rapidly spreading viruses, worms, and Trojans impact an organization causing anything from loss of productivity to loss of reputation (Nyanchama, 2005).

In addition, increased networking, mobility, and telecommuting have introduced serious technical issues and potential security problems (Dillon & Pate-Cornell, 2005). Fundamentally, the Internet and its infrastructure, system access, security, open standards, information access, reliance, integrity of data and information, complexity, interdependence, and interconnectivity, all lead to exposures.

New technologies have created new products, for example, capturing procurement habits of customer database. These technologies have led to intangible property rights and contracts. Unclear or overreaching agreements are risk exposures to these new products (Lange et al., 2000). IT has enhanced product marketing and distribution. If the experiences of Web site marketing simulations do not match the real experiences of the buyer, this new media way of marketing can create risks (Lange et al., 2000). Technology failure risks include lack of system functionality, system unavailability, loss of data integrity, loss of data confidentiality, and security of systems in general. IT systems crash when large waves of orders overload processing capacity. Business interruptions lead to financial risk as well as market share risk (Phan et al., 2005). Furthermore, standardization in exchange of data is lacking in industry (Kaiser, 2002), raising risks in integrity of data.

Other risks include antiquated network backbone, development of "spaghetti" code, poor configuration control, expensive conversion of data, noncompliance with embraced methodologies, no or lack of standards, poorly articulated requirements, and incompatible development tools. Most companies are focusing on how to use new technology by improving processes in order to increase productivity, reduce cost, and seek reliable partnerships in order to compete in e-business (Zhang, 2005). The new processes have been exposed to risks as well, and are illustrated in the next section.

New Processes

Businesses generally engage in three main processes (Klamm & Weidenmier, 2004): (a) acquiring and paying for resources, (b) converting resources into goods/services, and (c) acquiring customers, delivering goods and services, and collecting revenues. New e-business processes to enhance these three main processes have surfaced to fill a real business need. Companies that have emerged onto the online scene have changed the old processes to build new business models. Integration of external partner process with internal process has created new reengineered processes. These new processes may expose new risks. The creation of real-time process for e-business may also expose new risks. New outsourcing processes may also create risks for the business. In response to perceived risks, many existing businesses redesigned their processes for e-business conditions. Some emerged successfully, while many others failed (Phan et al., 2005). Some of these new processes are threatened by internal factors such as stringent product specifications for specific market needs. The processes are also threatened by external factors such as perceived quality of products and services.

The new processes in e-business include routine activities automated by computers for higher speed and reliability; business processes and services to extend across different organizations; the agility in business processes to be able to quickly adapt to customers needs and market conditions; and business functions desired to be readily shareable at a small granularity level (Zhang, 2005).

A new trend in e-business is to enable a business to dynamically connect arbitrarily complex e-services provided by different vendors in order to create a new service (Zhang, 2005). It is difficult to implement this process because it requires complicated coordination among various vendors based on exchange of data and process information (Zhang, 2005). In order to enable interoperability, it is important that vendors agree on basic common standards, and there is a lack of these standards. These process integrations give rise to new e-business risks. The return process is an essential criterion in any e-business operation (Curtis, 2000; Strauss & Hill, 2001). This is especially true if buyers need to see, touch, smell, and test a product before deciding whether to retain or return it (Surjadjaja et al., 2003). New audit and internal control procedures have given rise to new exposures (Yu, Yu, & Chou, 2000).

New technology leads to implementing new, better, improved, and standardized internal business processes (Barnes et al., 2003). These new levels of technically complex processes lead to contextual risk in e-business environment (Pathak, 2004). Streamlining approvals through electronic processes may remove existing internal controls and potentially increase the risk (Pathak, 2004). As issues of fulfillment and the need for new technology to be integrated increased in e-businesses, risks in integrating e-business capabilities into existing business processes increased (Krell & Gale, 2005). This is because of the misfit between new processes and existing organizational processes and organizational structure (Krell & Gale, 2005). Integrating complex systems in firms have caused firms to abandon projects either in the middle of the project or after a futile attempt (Cliffe, 1999). The objective of complex ERP implementation is to integrate information systems across all functional areas and to pursue a long-term sustainable competitive advantage. Failing to integrate the processes into ERP systems can lead to failure of ERP implementation and thus connectivity to e-business.

These new business models, new processes, new online services, and new technologies have created exposure to businesses. In the next section, fulfillment risks are explored.

New Fulfillment

The perception of online fulfillment has changed. Products and services are needed almost in real time in this online world. E-business may bring in sales from many new channels of marketing. The integration of these real-time sales orders with the existing supply-chain management and order fulfillment may increase risks. Inefficient fulfillment integration with external distribution providers may also expose risks. The internal factor that threatens the new fulfillment needs is supply-chain management. The external factor that threatens the fulfillment is the real-time demand for products and services.

Fulfillment refers to the delivery of products and services on time and, as specified, within a service level agreement (Surjadjaja et al., 2003). Order fulfillment risks, such as lost orders, shipment delays, and shipments of incomplete orders, can be detrimental to business health (Phan et al., 2005). Orders may take long to assemble, and Web partners have to pay for express shipments (Phan et al., 2005). Experience in order fulfillment and ample warehouse capacity do not automatically translate into success in e-business (Phan et al., 2005). Because e-business requires linkages between front-office and back-office operations with the supply chain, lack of integrated fulfillment systems create risks (Phan et al., 2005).

Factors of fulfillment can be viewed in the logistics framework proposed by Vaidyanathan (2005). The framework includes global servicing, global transportation, global warehousing, global inventory management, logistics, and information sharing. Fulfillment also includes inventory management, warehousing, and "e-fulfillment centers" (Reynolds, 2000), and coping with seasonal variations in demand (Ridley, 2002). The challenges are in delivering digital products and services where issues such as copyrights and data protection need to be addressed and resolved before delivering digital products and services. Of course, the delivery of physical products has its own challenges. Due to all these challenges, online businesses without strong financial resources and networks can experience difficulties in managing the fulfillment needs (Surjadjaja et al., 2003).

Risk in a supply chain is the potential occurrence of an incidence associated with inbound supply in which the result is the inability of the purchasing firm to meet customer demand (Zsidisin, 2000). Spekman and Davis (2004) illustrated a six-factor risk framework for supply chain. The first factor is the obsolete or unwanted inventory that can rise due to lack of communication with the supply-chain partners. An example would be of Cisco's inventory dilemma when the firm wrote off $2.5 billion in inventory. The second factor is associated with the flow of information. The third factor is with the supply chain's flow of money, and relates risks associated with stable pricing, hedging, letters of credit, timely payment of bills, and so forth. These three factors affect both inbound and outbound flows of the supply chain including risks on quality, product design, production, supplier development, supplier stability, logistics, and any other physical activity that affects supply chain's ability to meet its objectives. The fourth factor is the security of the firm's internal IT and the risks relating to who has access to the information and sharing of information. The fifth factor is associated with the relationships forged among supply chain partners, and the tendency of the partners to act in their self-interest. The sixth factor of risk relates to the supply-chain members' reputation and corporate social responsibility.

Moreover, supplier capacity constraints, process changes in production and design, inability to reduce costs, unanticipated delays, and supply disruptions (Zsidisin, Panelli, & Upton, 2000) can become a part of the risks in the six-factor risk framework. Many e-marketplaces have failed to deliver on promises that were made (Murtaza et al., 2004). There is a general concern of security ad standards in the supply-chain management. There are no common supplier qualification criteria, no consistent item coding schemes, and no technology integration guidelines (Murtaza et al., 2004). Furthermore, integration of systems to provide efficient supply chain is of concern as well (Murtaza, 2004). Antitrust laws are another major challenge, since highly successful e-marketplaces can run the risk of limiting competition unfairly, even though the laws improve efficiencies (Murtaza, 2004).

RISK MANAGEMENT

The risks of e-business are generally very similar to the risks of doing traditional business. The primary difference is that risks from e-business arises from and relates to novel contractual exchanges. Mitigating and management of e-business risks essentially start with identifying all the associated risks. Once all the risks are identified, then the risks need to be quantified using frequency and severity of risks. Once the e-business risks are quantified, the next task is to mitigate the risks by effective means. Then the risk management needs to be made into a process within the company. This is accomplished by adopting and using contract management policies. As with any process, the contract management needs to be monitored continuously. We will explore this four-step process in this section.

Identifying Risks

Risk analysis begins with the identification of assets and all possible threats to the identified assets (Jung, Han, & Suh, 1999). The firm needs to understand the requirements of the business processes, as well as to include concerns over financial loss, damage to reputation, loss of intellectual property, devaluation of goods, and regulatory requirements, among other business-specific risks.

The process of searching for risks may be iterative. A list of risks associated with each objective, key parameter, major deliverable, or principal activity may be prepared. It is essential that every aspect of the five dimensions is analyzed. This list preparation should be from first principles without the use of checklists or prompts, to avoid constraining the process of discovery. After this, the exercise should be repeated with the help of the risk matrix and other prompt aids. A brainstorming session to review the risks previously identified and to flush out further risks needs to be undertaken. Having identified all the risks, the identified risks need to be classified and grouped for further evaluation.

Quantifying Risks

Firms must understand their internal and external failure modes, including knowledge of how specific system compromises or failures can affect a business process and its relative risk. Usage of tools such as failure mode and effects analysis (FMEA) can be used to identify and quantify risks (Bongiorno, 2001; Carbone & Tippett, 2004; Chrysler Corp., Ford Motor Co., & General Motors Corp., 1995). Many firms have used FMEA in process development and product development. Usually, input is solicited from many experts across the organization. The input can be sought from customers and suppliers to understand the risks of supply chain. The FMEA is then used for troubleshooting and corrective action. The standard FMEA evaluates failure modes for occurrence, severity, and detection (Chrysler Corp., Ford Motor Co., & General Motors Corp., 1995). The experts, in their opinion, give input to the occurrences, severity, and detection of risks. The risk priority number (RPN) is then calculated as product of occurrences, severity, and detection.

Mitigating Risks

The quantified risks need to be aligned with the goals of the company. The quantified risks need to be mitigated using correcting measures if plausible, by developing compensating controls, by insuring the risk, and, in most cases, by developing a detection method for these failure modes.

E-services will be successful if more factual product service information is provided; shopping convenience, product value, and customer relations are emphasized; and customer needs, such as better purchasing experience, are understood (Verma, Iqbal, & Plaschka, 2004). In one instance, the government of Singapore initiated their e-business using e-services that allow the different government agencies to share components such as payment gateways, electronic data exchange, authentication, and other security features in the development of e-services. This reduced both the incremental cost for implementation of new e-services as well as the time needed for design and development. It also retains the flexibility to change business requirements in services easily, and offers services via multiple concurrent channels. Singapore citizens and businesses can obtain faster, more convenient access to government services as compared to waiting in line. This fast, efficient, and cost-effective implementation of e-services Singapore recognized as "Innovative Leaders," along with Canada and United States in recent report on global e-government. They used Sun Microsystems's Public Services Infrastructure (PHI), which allows the different government agencies to share components such as payment gateways, electronic data exchange, authentication, and other security features in the development of e-services (Sun Microsystems, 2001).

Structural assurance and situational normality mechanisms both have an impact on customers' trustworthiness perceptions, suggesting that firms need to use a portfolio of strategies to build customers' trust (Yousafzai et al., 2005). To improve the customers' confidence and to mitigate psychological risks associated with security, more Web sites are advertising a secure transaction sign (for example, VeriSign). VeriSign is effectively selling confidence, facilitated by the strong market reputation of Microsoft. In addition to VeriSign, many Web sites use the symbols of various accreditation bodies (such as ATOL, IATA and ABTA, BBBOnline). Firms can always secure Web services to a partner through existing network security technologies such as Virtual Private Networks (VPNs), Public Key Infrastructure (PKI), and digital certificates. Among various remedies to promote trust and reduce online fraud, online escrow services have been implemented as a trusted third party to protect online transactions and Internet fraud (Hu, Lin, Whinston, & Zhang, 2004). Courts need to recognize that in the information age, virtual privacy and physical privacy have no same boundaries (Schneier, 2005).

Data-mining capabilities are crucial for e-business. For example, Toys-R-Us has established affiliations with Amazon.com, leveraged from data collected from online customers with a company with a trusted brand (Phan et al., 2005). Being a component of information security management, vulnerability management is effective when defined with a risk management approach. To be effective, vulnerability management must incorporate key elements of effective processes such as policies, accountabilities, communication, and continuous improvement (Nyanchama, 2005).

Buyers can buffer against supply risks by developing multiple sources of supply and carrying safety stock (Giunipero & Eltantawy, 2004). In order to manage risk effectively, purchasers are moving to adopt closer relationships with key suppliers and expect the suppliers to provide solutions and compliment or enhance the buying firm's core competencies (Giunipero & Eltantawy, 2004). Joint buyer-supplier efforts may reduce risks in the supply process, and this type of collaborative supply management effort increases product reliability and reduces risks in product introduction (Giunipero & Eltantawy, 2004). For example, Chrysler minimized supply-chain risks by implementing long-term trading agreements and sharing the benefits of mutual involvement in design and development of products that Chrysler purchases (Viehland, 2002).

Firms need to develop policies regarding use of forms and conditions in which standard clauses may be negotiated. They have to monitor sales and distribution channels to determine that appropriate forms are being used and that contract policies are followed. In addition, the firms have to develop and administer policies on early dispute mitigation and alternate dispute resolution (Lange et al., 2000).

Managing Risks

A recent survey by nCircle, a provider of enterprise-class vulnerability and risk-management solutions, polled 1,700 CIOs, CSOs, and security directors for the Vulnerability and Risk Management Trend survey (Government Technology, 2005). The survey results indicate that many businesses still lack the information they need to determine the effectiveness of their security ecosystem:

- Sixty percent of respondents were unable to determine whether their network security risk was decreasing or increasing over time.
- Fifty-eight percent of respondents stated they are unable to generate reports about applications or vulnerabilities on their network by region business unit or business owner.

- Fifty-two percent of respondents stated they have no way to verify and manage compliance with their own internal security policies.

The prime objective of risk management is to minimize the impact and probability of occurrence of risks in firms. Firms must put in place detective controls and operational monitoring so that, when a failure mode occurs, it is detected without delay and the appropriate response is enacted. Effective institutionalization of e-risk management requires five additional factors (Lange et al., 2000):

- Implement an initial review and risk assessment of a firm's e-business risk exposures to include legal, network security, human resources, management personnel, and others, and make sure that the company's policies and procedures are followed.
- Establishing clear lines of authority for contract administration, a firm can best control the assumption of unintended business risks, and by implementing periodic reviews by outside control, bring multiple perspectives and best practices.
- Fine-tune contracts and substantially revise to reflect the technology and services relevant to e-business.
- Cover insurances with all the possible exposures due to e-business.
- Keep current with legal, technological, and market developments.

To have successful e-commerce ventures, firms need to show strength in four areas. These four areas revolve around their business models—their external environments and their corporate strategies, structures, systems, and resources. Based on the evaluation of these inputs, they must develop proper e-business leadership, strategies, structures, and systems (Epstein, 2005). A framework that helps a decision maker consider security issues early in the project has been developed by Dillon and Pate-Cornell (2005). This framework has a proactive approach, as it allows planning for contingency and setting priorities in resource allocation considering the system life cycle. Another methodology using case-based reasoning (CBR) was introduced to analyze IT risks (Jung et al., 1999). The learning component enables the software to update the case base dynamically in a fast-changing e-business environment.

CONCLUSION AND FUTURE RESEARCH

Even the insurance firms are in their rudimentary stage in enterprise risk management (ERM) (Oliva, 2005). A few firms have hired or appointed chief risk officers (CROs) and are embracing strategies and technologies to manage risk companywide, but most insurers are behind the curve. ERM needs to be embraced as a competitive strategy and linked to allocation of capital and growth goals. Critical success factors going forward will include (Oliva, 2005):

- Identifying, measuring, monitoring, mitigating, and financing all aspects of risk
- Instituting procedures for handling risk
- Computing and allocating capital based on risk tolerances

The framework presented in this article can help us understand the various risks involved in B2B commerce. The conceptual framework presented examines risk from five critical dimensions—services, business models, technology, fulfillment, and processes. Online businesses can benefit from a careful consideration and analyses of these five factors that are primary sources of risk. Such a planned risk analysis exercise can provide insights to practitioners of e-business, procurement managers, marketing managers, IT managers, as well as academicians. It remains to be seen if understanding and mitigating risk will indeed be the turning point for B2B commerce. E-business may be the most important value-creating activity for many businesses. The key is in its implementation (Epstein, 2005) and how these companies mitigate risks as well.

REFERENCES

Aber, R. (2004, July 12). Managing risks with online storage. *Entrepreneur.*

Ahmad, S. (2002). Service failures and customer defection: A closer look at online shopping experiences. *Managing Service Quality, 12*(1), 19-29.

Ahn, J., Park, J., & Lee, D. (2001). *Risk focused e-commerce adoption model—a cross-country study.* Working paper, last revised June 2001.

Ba, S., & Paulou, P. A. (2002). Evidence of the effect of trust in electronic markets: Price premiums and buyer behavior. *MIS Quarterly, 26*(3), 243-266.

Baker, C. R. (1999). An analysis of fraud on the electronic business. *Electronic Business Research: Electronic Networking Applications and Policy, 9*(5), 349-359.

Barnes, D., Hinton, M., & Mecgkowska, S. (2003). Focusing failures in competitive environments: Explaining decision errors in the Monty Hall game, the acquiring of a company problem, and multiparty ultimatums. *Journal of Behavioral Decision Making, 16*(5), 353.

Berry, L. L., & Parasuraman, A. (1992). Prescriptions for a service quality revolution in America. *Organizational Dynamics, 20*(4), 5-15.

Bhimani, A. (1996). Securing the commercial electronic business. *Communications of the ACM, 39*(6), 29-35.

Biswas, D., & Biswas, A. (2004). The diagnostic role of signals in the context of perceived risks in online shopping: Do signals matter more on the web? *Journal of Interactive Marketing, 18*(3), 30-45.

Bongiorno, J. (2001). Use FMEAs to improve your product development process. *Project Management Network, 15*(5), 47-51.

Caelli, W. J. (1997). Information security in electronic business. In *PACIS'97—The Pacific Asia Conference on Information Systems,* Brisbane, Australia (pp. 1-5).

Carbone, T. A., & Tippett, D. D. (2004). Project risk management using the project risk FMEA. *Engineering Management Journal, 16*(4), 28-35.

Chrysler Corp., Ford Motor Co., and General Motors Corp. (1995). *Potential failure mode and effects analysis (FMEA) reference manual* (2nd ed.), equivalent to SAE J-1739.

Clemons, E. K., & Hitt, L. M. (2004). Poaching and the misappropriation of information: Transaction risks of information exchange. *Journal of Management Information Systems, 21*(2), 87-107.

Cliffe, S. (1999) ERP implementation. *Harvard Business Review, 77,*16-17.

Cox, D. F., & Rich, S. U. (1964). Perceived risk and consumer decision making—the case of telephone shopping. *Journal of Marketing Research, 1*(4), 32-39.

Cunningham, S. M. (1967). The major dimensions of perceived risk. In D. F. Cox (Ed.), *Risk taking and information handling in consumer behavior* (pp. 82-108). Boston: Graduate School of Business Administration, Harvard University.

Curtis, J. (2000, February). Next generation customer service. *E-business,* 62-67.

Davison, R. M., Vogel, D. R., & Harris, R. W. (2005). The e-transformation of western China. *Communications of the ACM, 48*(4), 62-66.

Dillon, R. L., & Pate-Cornell, M. E. (2005). Including technical and security risks in the management of information systems: A programmatic risk management model. *Systems Engineering, 8*(1), 15-28.

Epstein, M. J. (2005, March). Implementing successful e-commerce initiatives. *Strategic Finance*, 23-29.

Gefan, D., Karahanna, E., & Straub, D. (2003). Trust and TAM in online shopping: An integrated model. *MIS Quarterly, 27*(1), 51-90.

Government Technology News. (2005). Retrieved from http://www.govtech.net/magazine/ channel_story.php/94696

Grewal, D., Gotlieb, J., & Marmorstein, H. (1994). The moderating effects of message framing and source credibility on the price-perceived risk relationship. *Journal of Consumer Research, 21*(7), 145-153.

Grover, V., & Saeed, K. A. (2004). Strategic orientation and performance of Internet-based businesses. *Information Systems Journal, 14*(1), 23-42.

Guinipero, L. C., & Eltantawy, R. A. (2004). Securing the upstream supply chain: A risk management approach. *International Journal of Physical Distribution & Logisitics Management, 34*(9), 698-713.

Hagel, J. (2002, November). Web services: Technology as a catalyst for strategic thinking. *Harvard Management Update*, 3-4.

Hu, X., Lin, Z., Whinston, A. B., & Zhang, H. (2004). Hope or hype: On the viability of escrow services as trusted theirs parties in online auction environments. *Information Systems Research, 15*(3), 236-249.

Jacoby, J., & Kaplan, L. B. (1972). The components of perceived risk. In *Proceedings of the 3rd Annual Conference of the Association for Consumer Research* (pp. 382-393). Association for Consumer Research.

Jones, S., Wilikens, M., Morris, P., & Masera, M. (2000). Trust requirements in e-business. *Communications of the ACM, 43*(12), 81-87.

Jung, C., Han, I., & Suh, B. (1999). Risk analysis for electronic commerce using case-based reasoning. *International Journal of Intelligent Systems in Accounting, Finance & Management, 8*, 61-73.

Kaiser, T. (2002). The customer shall lead: E-business solutions for the new insurance industry. *The Geneva Papers on Risk and Insurance, 27*(1), 134-145.

Keen, P., Balance, C., Chan, S., & Schrump, S. (2000). *Electronic commerce relationships: Trust by design.* Upper Saddle River, NJ: Prentice Hall.

Kilgore, J. M. (2004, April). *Mitigating supply chain risks.* Presented at the 89th Annual International Supply Chain Conference.

Klamm, B. K., & Weidenmier, M. L. (2004). Linking business processes and transaction cycles. *Journal of Information Systems, 18*(2), 113-125.

Kolluru, R., & Meredith, P. (2001). Security and trust management in supply chains. *Information Management and Computer Security, 9*(5), 233-236.

Krell, T., & Gale, J. (2005). E-business migration: A process model. *Journal of Organizational Change Management, 18*(2), 117-131.

Lal, R., & Sarvary, M. (1999). When and how is the Internet likely to decrease price competition? *Marketing Science, 18*(4), 485-503.

Lange, S. K., Davis, J. K., Jaye, D., Erwin, D., Mullarney, J. X., Clarke, L. L., & Loesch, M. C. (2000). *E-Risk: Liabilities in a wired world.* Cincinnati: The National Underwriter Co.

Lee, M., & Turban, E. (2001). A trust model for consumer Internet shopping. *International Journal of Electronic Commerce, 6,* 75-91.

McCrohan, K. F. (2003). Facing the threats of electronic commerce. *The Journal of Business and Industrial Marketing, 18*(2), 133-145.

Mercuri, R. T. (2005). Trusting in transparency. *Communication of the ACM, 48*(5), 15-19.

Mitchell, V. W., & Greatorex, M. (1993). Risk perception and reduction in the purchase of consumer services. *The Services Industries Journal, 13*, 179-200.

Miyazaki, A. D., & Fernandez, A. (2001). Consumer perceptions of privacy and security risks for online shopping. *The Journal of Consumer Affairs, 35*(1), 27-44.

Moores, T. (2005). Do consumers understand the role of privacy seals in e-commerce? *Communications of the ACM, 48*(3), 86-91.

Muiznieks, V. (1995, November). The electronic business and EDI. *Telecommunications*, 45-48.

Murphy, P. E., & Enis. B. M. (1986). Classifying products strategically. *Journal of Marketing, 50*(3), 24-42.

Murtaza, M. B., Gupta, V., & Carroll, R. C. (2004). E-Marketplaces and the future of supply chain management: Opportunities and challenges. *Business Process Management Journal, 10*(3), 325-335.

Nyanchama, M. (2005, July/August). Enterprise vulnerability management and its role in information security management. *Information Security Management*, 29-56.

Oliva, V. (2005, March). Predictions 2005: Insurance industry force-fed transformation. *Gartner Report*, 1-10.

Orr, B. (2005). Identify fraud, round two. *ABA Banking Journal, 97*(6), 64-65.

Papadopoulou P., Andreou A., Kanellis P., & Martakos, A. (2001). Trust and relationship building in electronic business. *Electronic Business Research: Electronic Networking Applications and Policy, 11*(4), 322-332.

Pathak, J. (2004). A conceptual risk framework for internal auditing in e-commerce. *Management Auditing Journal, 19*(4), 556-564.

Peterson, R. A., Balasubramanian, S., & Bronnenberg, B. J. (1997). Exploring the implications of the Internet for consumer marketing. *Journal of Academy of Marketing Science, 25*(4), 329-346.

Phan, D. D., Chen, J. Q., & Ahmad, S. (2005, Summer). Lessons leaned from an initial e-commerce failure by a catalog retailer. *Information Systems Management*, 7-13.

Ratnasingham, P. (1998). The importance of trust in electronic business. *Electronic Business Research: Electronic Networking Applications and Policy, 8*(4), 313-321.

Resnick, J. (2004). Corporate reputation: Managing corporate reputation - Applying rigorous measures to a key asset. *Journal of Business Strategy, 25*(6), 30-38.

Reynolds, J. (2000). eCommerce: A critical review. *International Journal of Retail and Distribution Management, 28*(10), 417-44.

Ridley, H. (2002, January). The ghost of e-christmas past. *e-Business*, 12-13.

Salisbury, W. D., Pearson, R. A., Pearson, A. W., & Miller, D. W. (2001). Perceived security and World Wide Web purchase intention. *Industrial Management and Data Systems, 101*(4), 165-176.

Schneier, B. (2005). Risks of third-party data. *Communications of the ACM, 48*(5), 136.

Sclafane, S. (2000, March). Emerging third-party risks lurk online. *Property & Casualty Risk & Benefits Management*, 15.

Shapira, Z., (1995). *Risk taking: A managerial perspective.* New York: Russell Sage.

Shimp, T. A., & Bearden, W. O. (1982). Warranty and other extrinsic cue effects on consumers' risk perceptions. *Journal of Consumer Research, 9*(7), 38-46.

Singhal, V. (2000, December). Putting price on supply chain problems: Study links supply chain glitches with falling stock prices. *Georgia Tech Research News.*

Sinha, T. (1999, December). The Internet, insurance, and Latin America. *Texas Business Review*, 4-5.

So, M. W. C., & Sculli, D. (2002). The role of trust, quality, value and risk in conducting e-business. *Industrial Management & Data Systems, 102*(3), 503-512.

Sparks, B. A., & Bradley, G. L. (1997). Antecedents and consequences of perceived service providers effort in the hospitality industry. *Hospitality Research Journal, 20*(3), 17-34.

Spekman, R. E., & Davis, E. W. (2004). Risky business: Expanding the discussion on risk and the extended enterprise. *International Journal of Physical Distribution & Logistics Management, 34*(5), 414-433.

Straub, D., & Welke, R. J. (1998). Coping with systems risk: Security planning models for management decision making. *MIS Quarterly, 22*(4), 441-469.

Strauss, J., & Hill, D. J. (2001). Consumer complaints by e-mail: An exploratory investigation of corporate responses and customer reactions. *Journal of Interactive Marketing 15*(1), 63-73.

Streeter, W. W. (2005, April). Call me paranoid. *ABA Banking Journal*, 4.

Sullivan, B. (2004, November 11). Online fraud costs $2.6 billion this year. *MSNBC*, 2004.

Sun Microsystems. (2001). *Singapore government public eServices infrastructure delivers one-stop services on demand, based on Sun ONE.* Sun Success Story. Retrieved from http://www.sun.com/br/government/PSi_final.pdf

Surjadjaja, H., Ghosh, S., & Antony, J. (2003). Determining and assessing the determinants of e-service operations. *Managing Service Quality, 13*(1), 39-53.

Vaidyanathan, G. (2005). A framework for evaluating third-party logistics. *Communications of the ACM, 48*(1), 89-94.

Vaidyanathan, G., & Devaraj, S. (2003). A five factor framework for analyzing online risks in E-business. *Communications of the ACM, 46*(12), 354-361.

Verma, R., Iqbal, Z., & Plaschka, G. (2004). Understanding customer choices in e-financial services. *California Review Management, 46*(4), 42-67.

Viehland, D. W. (2002, May). Risk e-business: Assessing risk in electronic commerce. *Decision Line,* 9-11.

Vijayan, J. (2001, September 25). Group pushes for B2B standards. *Computer World.* Retrieved from http://www.computerworld.com/governmenttopics/ government/legalissues/story/0,10801,51191,00.html

Wise, R., & Morrison. D. (2000). Beyond the exchange: The future of B2B. *Harvard Business Review,* 86-96.

Yousafzai, S. Y., Pallister, J. G., & Foxall, G. R. (2005). Strategies for building and communicating trust in electronic banking: A field experiment. *Psychology & Marketing, 22*(2), 181-201.

Yu, C., Yu, H., Chou, C. (2000). The impacts of electronic commerce on auditing practices: An auditing process model for evidence collection and validation. *International Journal of Intelligent Systems in Accounting, Finance & Management, 9*, 195-216.

Zhang, D. (2005). Web services composition for process management in e-business. *Journal of Computer Information Systems, 45*(2), 83-91.

Zsidisin, G. A., Panelli, A., & Upton, R. (2000). Purchasing organization involvement in risk assessments, contingency plans, and risk management: an exploratory study. *Supply Chain Management: An International Journal, 5*(4), 187-197.

This work was previously published in E-Business Process Management: Technologies and Solutions, edited by J. Sounderpandan & T. Sinha, pp. 267-291, copyright 2007 by IGI Publishing, formerly known as Idea Group Publishing (an imprint of IGI Global).

Section VI
Emerging Trends

Chapter XXV
Evaluating E-Business Leadership and its Links to Firm Performance

Jing Quan
Salisbury University, USA

ABSTRACT

Electronic business (e-business) has been popularly lauded as "new economy." As a result, firms are prompted to invest heavily in e-business related activities such as supplier/procurement and online exchanges. Whether the investments have actually paid off for the firms remain largely unknown. Using the data on the top 100 e-business leaders compiled by InternetWeek, the leaders are compared with their comparable counterparts in terms of profitability and cost in both the short-run and long-run. It is found that while the leaders have superior performance based on most of the profitability measurements, such superiority is not observed when cost measurements are used. Based on the findings, managerial implications are offered accordingly.

INTRODUCTION

The rapid expansion of e-business witnessed in the late 1990s was nothing short of a spectacle. It seemed that almost everyone was talking about it, and every firm was eager to invest in it, hoping to take away a slice of the pie. Andy Grove, chairman of Intel Corp, stated in 1998: "Within 5 years, all companies will be Internet companies or they would not be companies" (Intel, 2000). Merely mentioning of the "e" word could mean multi-million dollars. The case at hand was Zapata Corp., a fish oil processing company, co-founded by former U.S. President George H. W. Bush. The company announced on December 23, 1998 that it would transform itself into an Internet portal to compete with Yahoo!, Lycos, and alike. Immediately following the announcement, Zapata's stock price skyrocketed nearly 100% from 7.19 to 14.25 with trading volume at more than 2,000% higher than normal, according to Yahoo! Finance. Academic researchers rushed in and concluded that "a new economy was born."

The potential benefits of e-business are well documented by academic researchers and practitioners alike (InternetWeek, 2000/2001; Phan, 2003). Organizations that integrate e-business applications, such as shared online database and Internet-based reporting in their business processes, can lead to reduced cost, increased efficiency and profitability, and better customer relationship management. Perhaps one of the most significant contributions of e-business applications is its abilities to directly bring sellers and buyers together with little middleman's interventions.

Although the advantages of e-business exist in theory, little empirical work has been done to confirm them. Some study actually showed an inconclusive link between e-business and sustainable development (Digital Europe, 2003):

Our survey showed no conclusive evidence for companies that use a lot of e-business actually performing better than other companies on sustainable development, simply by virtue of their e-business use. There may be a relationship here—which could become more obvious as e-business applications are more fully integrated into companies' operations—but more research would be needed to prove a link.

Answering this call, researchers have attempted to build theoretical frameworks to pinpoint how e-business creates value. Using the technology-organization-environment (TOE) framework Zhu, Kraemer, Xu, and Dedrick (2004) found that technology readiness, firm size, global scope, financial resources, competition intensity, and regulatory environment may affect e-business value creation. Amit and Zott (2001) integrated several theoretical perspectives on entrepreneurship and strategic management to identify four interdependent dimensions: efficiency, complementarities, lock-in, and novelty as sources of value creation.

Despite the recent advancement of research in this area, the fundamental question regarding e-business remains unanswered, that is, whether e-business creates value. This article attempts to fill this vacuum by establishing a theoretical foundation to evaluating the linkage between e-business investments and firm performance in terms of profitability and cost savings. Confirmation or disconfirmation of the effectiveness of firms' investments in e-business will contribute to the knowledge accumulation in this area. It can also provide an insight for future investments.

The article begins by presenting the research framework grounded in the resource-based view (Barney, 1986; Barney, 1991; Conner, 1991; Rumelt, 1984). Resource-based view argues that firm-specific skills and resources that are rare and difficult to imitate or substitute are the main drivers of firm performance. How e-business initiatives create unique skills and resources for firms is shown. The hypotheses are then formulated, the data set and methodology discussed, and estimation results presented. Finally, discussion of the results and suggestions for future research are provided.

RESEARCH FRAMEWORK: THE RESOURCE-BASED VIEW

Broadly speaking, e-business value is a subset of the business value of IT. The business value of IT investments in general has been long debated, which led to the birth of the famous term "productivity paradox." Some studies provide positive support for the business value of computer investments (Brynjolfsson, 1993; Brynjolfsson & Hitt, 1996; Hitt & Brynjolfsson, 1996; Bharadwaj, 2000; Stratopoulos & Dehning, 2000). On the other hand, Strassmann (1997) argues that IT investments have no discernible effects on firm profitability measured in return on assets (ROA), return on equity (ROE), and economic value added (EVA).

In an attempt to explain the inconclusiveness, some researchers propose several theoretical models that examine the entire process needed for IT investments to make an impact on business value (Lucas, 1993; Markus & Soh, 1993). One of the dominate views is the resource-based view (RBV). Based on this view, IT investment itself does not provide any sustainable value because competitors can easily duplicate the investment by purchasing the same hardware and software. Rather, competitive advantages are derived from the manner in which firms deploy IT to generate a unique set of resources and skills that are difficult to duplicate (Clemons, 1986, 1991; Clemons & Row, 1991; Mata, Fuerst, & Barney, 1995). This type of resources is firm specific, rare, imperfectly imitable, and not strategically substitutable by others create competitive advantages for firms (Barney, 1991). Grant (1991) extends the RBV by linking resources to organizational capabilities. Firms generate organizational capabilities by optimally assembling their resources. When these capacities are embedded in organizational processes, it makes firms deploy resources more effectively and efficiently than its competitors. In turn, competitive advantages are created.

Adopting this RBV, one can see that IT investments themselves do not necessarily generate sustained value because competitors can easily duplicate the action by investing in the same or equivalent hardware and software. In order to achieve competitive advantages of IT investments, firms must leverage their investments (resources) to create unique capacities that impact their overall effectiveness.

E-BUSINESS AND COMPETITIVE ADVANTAGE

Information systems researchers have classified key IT-based resources into three categories: (1) the physical IT infrastructure (the tangible resources), (2) the technical and managerial IT skills (the human resources), and (3) the intangible resources such as knowledge base, customer relations, and synergy (Bharadwaj, 2000; Grant, 1995). To be successful, e-business based firms need to invest in a new type of IT infrastructure that can provide real time responses 24/7 to customer inquiries. Some emerging infrastructures include XML, server farms, and dynamic storage. In addition, to protect the infrastructures and ensure the integrity of information, firms need to heavily invest in security. All these require IT and management staff to possess necessary skills for managing the new working environment. This allows the firms to acquire unique, rare and firm specific technical and managerial skills. With the infrastructure and management skills in place, the firms can manage their knowledge base better and create synergies between different working units. In the process, they can become truly customer oriented. Therefore, from the resource-based perspective, e-business initiatives help firms to obtain competitive advantage in the marketplace.

In this article, competitive advantages in terms of either higher profit or lower cost are measured. As a result, the following hypotheses are proposed:

H_1: *The average profit ratios of the e-business leader firms are higher than those of the non-leaders.*

H_2: *The average cost ratios of the e-business leader firms are lower than those of the non-leaders.*

METHODOLOGY

The "matched sample comparison group" method, which has been extensively used in previous research (Bharadwaj, 2000; Stratopoulos & Dehning, 2000) is adopted. In this methodology, there are two samples: the first sample is a treatment group and the second is a carefully selected control group that is matched to the treatment group by size and type. Then the levels of interest variables of these two samples are compared. In this case, the treatment group consists of the firms identified by the industry as e-business leaders while the control group consists of the matched firms in terms of size and type.

Dataset

In 2000 and 2001 InternetWeek published a special issue, InternetWeek 100, in which 100 e-business leaders were identified for their effectiveness in using the Internet to achieve tangible business benefits (InternetWeek, 2000/2001). They were evaluated based on their e-business participation in customer-oriented activities, supplier/procurement activities, electronic marketplace, integration of front- and back-end systems, revenue growth, and cost cutting efforts.

In order to obtain a consistent sample, the selection of the companies that were identified as leaders in both years was restricted. In addition, firms must have complete financial data on Compustat for the period of 1999 to 2002. This process led to 46 companies in the treatment sample.

For the control sample, it was first specified that a matching firm must be in the same industry as the leader based on the 4-digit primary SIC. Second, the average sales of the matching firm must be within 70% to 130% of the leader firm's. When there were multiple matches, the firm with 5 year average sales closest to that of the leader firm was selected. If a match could not be identified in this fashion, then the 4-digit SIC matching rule was relaxed to three- or two-digit SIC. This procedure has been used by previous studies such as Bharadwaj (2000) and Barber and Lyon (1996). Firms in both groups are listed in the Appendix.

Table 1. Descriptive statistics

1999	E-Business Leaders		Control Sample		Difference of Means
	Mean	Median	Mean	Median	T
Sales (billion $)	20.84	11.27	18.56	10.28	1.326
Assets (billion $)	45.61	16.54	35.72	12.74	1.103
Number of Employees	82348	45504	120931	54450	-0.859

2000	E-Business Leaders		Control Sample		Difference of Means
	Mean	Median	Mean	Median	T
Sales (billion $)	23.05	12.26	20.78	11.42	1.207
Assets (billion $)	57.17	20.49	41.96	13.02	1.474
Number of Employees	89888	44000	121425	46546	-0.900

2001	E-Business Leaders		Control Sample		Difference of Means
	Mean	Median	Mean	Median	T
Sales (billion $)	21.69	12.81	20.72	11.33	0.531
Assets (billion $)	56.52	20.25	44.80	13.71	1.115
Number of Employees	85435	46800	121199	62175	-1.175

2002	E-Business Leaders		Control Sample		Difference of Means
	Mean	Median	Mean	Median	T
Sales (billion $)	21.66	11.92	20.38	11.45	0.605
Assets (billion $)	59.08	19.50	48.47	13.79	0.922
Number of Employees	83961	47480	101336	44323	-1.315

Table 1 provides the descriptive statistics for the two groups. The t-test does not reveal any systematical differences between them in terms of size measures such as sales, total assets, and number of employees.

Two categories of variables are collected for both treatment and control samples to test the aforementioned two hypotheses related to profit and cost. Five profit ratios include return on assets (ROA), return on sales (ROS), operating income to assets (OI/A), operating income to sales (OI/S), and operating income to employee (OI/E). Three cost ratios are total operating expenses to sales (OEXP/S), cost of goods sold to sales (COGS/S), and selling and general administrative expenses to sales (SG&A/S). Total operating expenses are defined as the sum of COGS and SG&A. The rational for those variables can be found in Bharadwaj (2000).

Statistical Tests and Outliers

The primary interest is to test the hypotheses that the mean levels of operational performance variables of e-business leaders are better than those of non-leader firms. Traditional standard t-test would be used for this purpose. However, since the distributions of financial ratios, such as the variables defined, tend to be non-normal, skewed and fat tailed, non-parametric test is preferred (Bharadwaj, 2000; Stratopoulos & Dehning, 2000). In this article, the Wilcoxon signed rank test is used.

Another characteristic of financial data is that there are a significant number of outliers. As a data treatment, a methodology suggested by Stratopoulos and Dehning (2000) was followed by removing those data points that fall more than 1.5 times the interquartile range above the third quartile or below the first.

RESULTS AND DISCUSSION

Table 2 provides the one-sided Wilcoxon signed rank results for the aforementioned profitability related variables between e-business leaders and control sample from 1999 and 2002. E-business leaders performed better in terms of all measures but one (OIE) in 1999, the year before they were

Table 2. E-business and profitability

	1999			2000			2001			2002		
	Mean	Median	Pr>Z	Mean	Median	Pr>Z	Mean	Median	Pr>Z	Mean	Median	Pr>Z
ROA-leaders	5.145	4.508	0.06[c]	5.327	3.810	0.31	2.789	1.659	0.22	3.126	2.892	0.02[b]
ROA-control	3.876	2.726		4.067	3.457		1.452	1.513		1.384	2.031	
ROS-leaders	0.076	0.067	0.01[a]	0.066	0.070	0.04[b]	0.052	0.043	0.10[c]	0.029	0.032	0.49
ROS-control	0.051	0.045		0.052	0.049		0.020	0.032		0.021	0.032	
OIA-leaders	0.112	0.092	0.02[b]	0.097	0.089	0.02[b]	0.076	0.064	0.12	0.068	0.069	0.02[b]
OIA-control	0.085	0.068		0.067	0.064		0.059	0.049		0.045	0.046	
OIS-leaders	0.136	0.121	0.01[b]	0.132	0.121	0.01[a]	0.088	0.079	0.32	0.096	0.104	0.05[b]
OIS-control	0.104	0.089		0.095	0.085		0.092	0.068		0.074	0.069	
OIE-leaders	0.033	0.025	0.18	0.042	0.032	0.01[a]	0.028	0.023	0.21	0.027	0.021	0.33
OIE-control	0.027	0.018		0.024	0.016		0.023	0.011		0.021	0.014	

Notes:
[a]1% level, [b] 5% level, [c] 10% level
ROA—return on assets; ROS—return on sales; OIA—operating income to assets; OIS—operating income to sales; OIE—operating income to employees.

identified as e-business leaders. This indicates that financial performance was one of the considerations for their selections. Most of the advantages were maintained in 2000, except for ROA, while the leaders now performed better based on the OIE measurement. In 2001, however, there were no significant differences between the leaders and matched firms in all financial variables. In the last year of the sample, e-business leaders performed better than the control sample in terms of three out of five financial ratios. Based on the discussion, it can be concluded that overall, the hypothesis #1 is partially supported.

Table 3 provides the one-sided Wilcoxon signed rank test results for the aforementioned cost related variables between the e-business leaders and the control sample from 1999 and 2002. Throughout all these years there were no significant differences between the leaders and the matched firms. This finding is largely consistent with other studies such as Bharadwaj (2000) and Mitra and Chaya (1996). Based on the results, it is concluded that the hypothesis #2 is not supported.

CONCLUSION

As businesses rushed to invest in the "new" economy, pressured by either the thinking of a paradigm swift or peers during the Internet boom, the payoff of such investments was not as important as making the move or taking action. Now that the bubble has burst, companies are forced to focus once again to justifying their IT investment decisions. This study aims to provide an assessment whether the investments made in e-business during the boom period had actually paid off in terms of profitability and cost in both short- and long-runs. Using the e-business leaders identified by InternetWeek, a control sample that matched the leaders based on industry type and size was created. The performances, measured in profit and cost, of these two groups were compared using the Wilcoxon signed rank non-parameter test. The results indicate that in terms of profitability, e-business leaders performed better than the control sample in the long-run but the superior performance fluctuated in the short-run. In terms of cost, there were no significant differences between the leaders and the control sample in both the short- and long-runs. The combination of leaders' higher profitability than and the same cost measures as the firms in the control sample is consistent with the observation by Bharadwaj (2000) that "IT leaders do not necessarily have a cost focus, but tend to exploit IT for generating superior revenues."

Based on the findings in this study, it is suggested that management should be very clear about the time horizon of the e-business, or IT in general, investments. The findings of this study demonstrate that the consistent superior financial

Table 3. E-business and cost

	1999			2000			2001			2002		
	Mean	Median	Pr>Z	Mean	Median	Pr>Z	Mean	Median	Pr>Z	Mean	Median	Pr>Z
COG/S-leaders	0.650	0.699	0.49	0.638	0.683	0.42	0.690	0.708	0.80	0.656	0.659	0.46
COG/S-control	0.653	0.669		0.644	0.650		0.670	0.683		0.679	0.683	
SGA/S-leaders	0.230	0.228	0.37	0.236	0.233	0.49	0.245	0.232	0.59	0.240	0.224	0.32
SGA/S-control	0.237	0.214		0.236	0.238		0.243	0.237		0.254	0.230	
OPEXP/S-leaders	1.086	0.788	0.13	1.227	0.952	0.33	1.208	0.956	0.25	1.263	1.238	0.22
OPEXP/S-control	1.223	1.301		1.175	1.234		1.229	1.316		0.909	1.315	

Notes:
COG/S—cost of goods sold to sales; SGA/S—selling and general administration expense to sales; OPEXP/S—operating expenses to sales.

performances of the e-business leaders are only observed in the long-run. In reality, management often fails to see the long-run benefits from new IT investments due to the cost concerns of new IT in the short-run. Dehning, Richardson, and Stratopoulos (2005) suggest that management should take a long-term view because IT might allow a firm to form relationships with its customers and suppliers and reduce variability in cash flows and earning. The combined effect of such interactions between the other variables may easily make up for the temporary increase in cost and decline in competitive advantage.

This type of research using a third party ranking suffers a few limitations, such as causality, indirectness of measurements, inherent biases of leader firms, and the selection of the control sample, as suggested by Bharadwaj (2000) and Stratopoulos and Dehning (2000). Those limitations may serve as the directions for future research.

Santhanam and Hartono (2003) suggest a different way of selecting the control sample. Instead of choosing a single benchmark firm for each e-business leader, one can consider all the firms in that industry for comparison. They argue that this method is more consistent with the procedure of selecting leaders, robust and general. Future research can consider adopting this approach of sample selection. Another logical follow-up study would be to extend the period beyond 2002 to examine the impact of e-business investment in the long term.

REFERENCES

Amit, R., & Zott, C. (2001). Value creation in e-business. *Strategic Management Journal, 22*, 493-520.

Barber, B. M., & Lyon, J. D. (1996). Detecting abnormal operating performance: the empirical power and specification of test statistics. *Journal of Financial Economics, 41*, 359-399.

Barney, J. B. (1986). Strategic factor markets: expectations, luck, and business strategy. *Management Science, 32*, 1231-1241.

Barney, J. B. (1991). Firm resources and sustained competitive advantage. *Journal of Management, 17*, 99-120.

Barua, A., Kriebel, C. H., & Mukhopadhyay, (1995). Information technologies and business value: an empirical investigation. *Information Systems Research, 6*(1), 3-23.

Bharadwaj, A. S. (2000). A resourced-based perspective on information technology capability and firm performance: an empirical investigation. *MIS Quarterly, 24*(1), 169-96.

Brynjolfsson, E. (1993). The productivity paradox of information technology. *Communications of ACM, 36*(12), 67-77.

Brynjolfsson, E., & Hitt, L. (1996) Paradox lost? Firm-level evidence on the return to information systems spending. *Management Science, 42*(4), 541-558.

Clemons, E. K. (1986). Information systems for sustainable competitive advantage. *Information & Management, 11*(3), 131-136.

Clemons, E. K. (1991). Corporate strategy for information technology: a resource-based approach. *Computer, 24*(11), 23-32.

Clemons, E. K., & Row, M. C. (1991). Sustaining IT advantage: the role of structural differences. *MIS Quarterly, 15*(3), 275-294.

Conner, K. R. (1991). A historical comparison of the resource-based theory and five schools of thought within industrial organization economics: do I have a new theory of the firm? *Journal of Management, 17*(1), 121-54.

Dehning, B., Richardson, V. J., & Stratopoulos, T. (2005). Information technology investments and firm value. *Information & Management, 42*(7), 989-1008.

Digital Europe. (2003). Is ebusiness good business? Survey key findings, May, DEESD IST-2000-28606.

Grant, R. M. (1991). The resource-based theory of competitive advantage. *California Management Review, 33*(3), 114-35.

Grant, R. M. (1995). *Contemporary strategy analysis*. Oxford, UK: Blackwell Publishers, Inc.

Hitt, L. M., & Brynjofsson, E. (1996). Productivity, business profitability, and consumer surplus: three different measures of information technology value. *MIS Quarterly, 20*(2), 121-142.

InternetWeek. (2000, June 8). InternetWeek 100 [Special Issue]. Retrieved on February 18, 2004. from http://internetweek.cmp.com/100/100-00.htm

InternetWeek. (2001, June 11). InternetWeek 100 [Special Issue]. Retrieved on February 18, 2004, from http://internetweek.cmp.com/100/100-01.htm

Lucas, H. C. (1993). The business value of information technology: a historical perspective and thoughts for future research. In R. Banker, R. Kauffman, & M. A. Mahmood (Eds.), *Strategic information technology management: perspectives on organizational growth and competitive advantage*. Hershey, PA: IGI Publishing.

Markus, M. L., & Soh, C. (1993). Banking on information technology: converting it spending into firm performance. In R. Banker, R. Kauffman, & M. A. Mahmood (Eds.), *Strategic information technology management: perspectives on organizational growth and competitive advantage*. Hershey, PA: IGI Publishing.

Mata, F. J., Fuerst, W. L., & Barney, J. B. (1995). Information technology and sustained competitive advantage: a resource-based analysis. *MIS Quarterly, 19*(4), 487-505.

Mitra, S., & Chaya, A. K. (1996). Analyzing cost effectiveness of organizations: the impact of information technology spending. *Journal of Management Information Systems, 13*(2), 29-57.

Phan, D. D. (2003). E-business development for competitive advantages: a case study. *Information & Management, 40*(6), 581-590.

Rumelt, R. P. (1984). Toward a strategic theory of the firm. In R. Lamb (Ed.), *Competitive strategic management* (pp. 556-570). Englewood Cliffs, NJ: Prentice-Hall.

Santhanam, R., & Hartono, E. (2003). Issues in linking information technology capability to firm performance. *MIS Quarterly, 27*(1), 125-153.

Strassmann, P. A. (1997) Computers have yet to make companies more productive. *ComputerWorld*, September 15, 1997.

Stratopoulos, T., & Dehning, B. (2000). Does successful investment in information technology solve the productivity paradox? *Information & Management, 38*(2), 103-117.

Zhu, K., Kraemer, K. L., Xu, S., & Dedrick, J. (2004). Information technology payoff in e-business environment: an international perspective on value creation of e-business in the financial service industry. *Journal of Management Information Systems, 21*(1), 17-54.

APPENDIX: E-BUSINESS LEADER FIRMS AND MATCHED SAMPLE

E-Business Leaders	SIC	Control Sample	SIC
ANHEUSER-BUSCH COS. INC.	2082	KIRIN BREWERY LTD -ADR	2082
MILLER (HERMAN) INC.	2520	HON INDUSTRIES	2522
KIMBERLY-CLARK CORP.	2621	3M CO.	2670
KNIGHT-RIDDER INC.	2711	AMERICAN GREETINGS -CL A	2771
AIR PRODUCTS & CHEMICALS INC.	2810	ROHM & HAAS CO.	2821
DU PONT (E I) DE NEMOURS	2820	BAYER A G -SPON ADR	2800
DOW CHEMICAL	2821	AVENTIS SA -ADR	2834
EASTMAN CHEMICAL CO.	2821	PRAXAIR INC.	2810
BRISTOL MYERS SQUIBB	2834	ABBOTT LABORATORIES	2834
AVON PRODUCTS	2844	LAUDER ESTEE COS INC -CL A	2844
PPG INDUSTRIES INC.	2851	COLGATE-PALMOLIVE CO.	2844
GILLETTE CO.	3420	CROWN HOLDINGS INC.	3411
CISCO SYSTEMS INC.	3576	SUN MICROSYSTEMS INC.	3571
EMERSON ELECTRIC CO.	3600	ELECTROLUX AB -ADR	3630
AMERICAN PWR CNVRSION	3620	ALTERA CORP.	3674
WHIRLPOOL CORP.	3630	KYOCERA CORP -ADR	3663
NORTEL NETWORKS CORP..	3661	ERICSSON (L M) TEL -ADR	3663
INTEL CORP.	3674	MOTOROLA INC.	3663
DAIMLERCHRYSLER AG	3711	FORD MOTOR CO.	3711
RAYTHEON CO.	3812	NORTHROP GRUMMAN CORP.	3812
CSX CORP.	4011	NORFOLK SOUTHERN CORP.	4011
UNION PACIFIC CORP.	4011	BURLINGTON NORTHERN SANTA FE	4011
UNITED PARCEL SERVICE INC.	4210	UNITED STATES POSTAL SERVICE	4210
CONSOLIDATED FREIGHTWAYS CP	4213	YELLOW CORP.	4213
ALASKA AIR GROUP INC	4512	AMERICA WEST HLDG CP -CL B	4512
AMR CORP/DE	4512	BRITISH AIRWAYS PLC -ADR	4512
DELTA AIR LINES INC.	4512	NORTHWEST AIRLINES CORP.	4512
AT&T CORP.	4813	DEUTSCHE TELEKOM AG -SP ADR	4813
COX COMMUNICATIONS -CL A	4841	BRITISH SKY BRDCSTG GP -ADR	4833
ARROW ELECTRONICS INC.	5065	GENUINE PARTS CO.	5013
AVNET INC.	5065	TECH DATA CORP.	5045
PENNEY (J C) CO.	5311	TARGET CORP.	5331
SEARS ROEBUCK & CO.	5311	KMART HOLDING CORP.	5331
OFFICE DEPOT INC.	5940	TOYS R US INC.	5945
STAPLES INC.	5940	RITE AID CORP.	5912
J P MORGAN CHASE & CO.	6020	CITICORP	6020
MELLON FINANCIAL CORP.	6020	BANCO COMERCIAL PORTGE -ADR	6020
SCHWAB (CHARLES) CORP.	6211	BEAR STEARNS COMPANIES INC	6211
HARTFORD FINL SVCS GRP INC.	6331	MILLEA HOLDINGS INC. -ADR	6331

continued on following page

E-Business Leaders	SIC	Control Sample	SIC
HILTON HOTELS CORP.	7011	STARWOOD HOTELS & RESORTS WLD	7011
MARRIOTT INTL INC.	7011	INTERCONTINENTAL HOTELS-ADR	7011
INTL BUSINESS MACHINES CORP	7370	FUJITSU LTD -SPON ADR	7373
COMPUTER ASSOCIATES INTL INC.	7372	KELLY SERVICES INC -CL A	7363
MICROSOFT CORP.	7372	ADECCO S A -SPON ADR	7363
GENERAL ELECTRIC CO.	9997	SIEMENS A G -SPON ADR	9997

This work was previously published in Journal of Global Information Management, 16(2), edited by F. Tan, pp. 81-90, copyright 2008 by IGI Publishing, formerly known as Idea Group Publishing (an imprint of IGI Global).

Chapter XXVI
Business Networking:
The Technological Infrastructure Support

Claudia-Melania Chituc
Faculty of Engineering of the University of Porto (FEUP), INESC Porto, Portugal

Américo Lopes Azevedo
Faculty of Engineering of the University of Porto (FEUP), INESC Porto, Portugal

ABSTRACT

The rapid evolution of information and communication technologies, the changing client's demands, and market conditions impelled enterprises to adapt their way of undertaking business, from traditional practices to e-business, and to participate in new forms of collaboration, such as networked organizations. In this context, standards, frameworks, technologies, and infrastructures supporting collaborative business, in a networked environment, become key factors in achieving environments with a desired high level of collaboration and inter- and intra-organization business processes alignment. The aim of this chapter is to underline the main issues, trends, and opportunities related to business integration from a technological perspective, analyzing and discussing the most relevant (existing and still under development) business integration reference models, frameworks, standards, technologies, and supporting infrastructures, and to briefly present relevant research projects in the area of business networking. A special emphasis is made on frameworks such as ebXML and RosettaNet, and the importance of papiNet, BPLE4WS, and freebXML is underlined. Challenges regarding self-forming networked organizations are also advanced.

INTRODUCTION

Current business trends and information and communication technology (ICT) developments determined enterprises to change their way of undertaking business, from vertically-integrated companies towards flexible collaborative networked organizations (CNOs). In this context, enterprise integration and interoperability emerge as key elements supporting real-time information flow and exchange, and intra- and interorganization business processes integration and alignment. CNOs represent a valuable and effective approach to achieve strategic objectives in a time-response and cost-effective manner, with a high level of quality of delivery and customer's satisfaction, while generating value to stakeholders.

CNOs represent a collection of heterogeneous organizations with different competences, but symbiotic interests that join, efficiently combining the most suitable set of skills and resources (e.g., knowledge, capital, assets) for a period of time in order to achieve a common objective, and make use of ICT to coordinate, develop, and support their activities. The term CNO is used in this chapter, in a broad sense, for other emerging business collaborative forms with similar proprieties, such as virtual enterprises (VE), virtual organizations (VO), or extended enterprises.

The aim of this chapter is to underline the main issues, trends and opportunities related to business integration, from a technological perspective, analyzing and discussing the most relevant (existing and still under development) business integration reference models, frameworks, standards, technologies, and supporting infrastructures, and to briefly present relevant research projects in the area of business networking in Europe and the USA. A special emphasis is made on frameworks such as ebXML and Rosetta Net, and the importance of papiNet, BPLE4WS, and freebXML is underlined.

The main research questions which motivated the present work are:

- **Question 1:** Which are the main benefits for technology integration, in a business collaborative environment formed by heterogeneous organizations with different goals, strategies, and technologies, but symbiotic interests?
- **Question 2:** Which are the main (existing or still under development) standards, technologies, and frameworks supporting business integration and interoperability?
- **Question 3:** Which are the most relevant developments/research projects in the area of business networking?

The remains of this chapter are organized as follows. The following section presents the main issues (e.g., benefits), opportunities and trends related to business integration and interoperability, from a technological perspective. The most relevant reference models, standards, frameworks, technologies, and supporting infrastructures for enterprise integration will be then analyzed, exemplifying with research projects developed in EU and the USA. A special emphasis will be made on ebXML, BPLE4WS, papiNet, freebXML, and Rosetta Net. The last section addresses the needs for further research and concludes this chapter.

NEEDS FOR ENTERPRISE INTEGRATION AND INTEROPERABILITY IN A COLLABORATIVE BUSINESS NETWORKED ENVIRONMENT

CNOs represent a powerful mechanism to achieve competitiveness and agility in today's turbulent market conditions by comprising various entities with complementary competences, but symbiotic interests. They include geographically-distributed organizations, having different cultures, working methods, or supporting technologies. Although CNO partners aim at achieving a common business goal and following a common business strategy, each member organization has its own goal and strategy, which makes CNO coordination and management assume a critical role.

CNO have several advantages, the most relevant ones being summarized in Camarinha-Matos and Afsarmanesh (2003): agility, complementary roles, achieving dimension, competitiveness, resource optimization, and innovation.

However, the formation, development, and operation of any CNO, and its success, depends on some base commonality among its members, such as common goals, common or interoperable ICT infrastructures and supporting services, real-time information sharing and flow among

CNO members, and common standards or common views in a number of areas (e.g., describing and orchestrating business process flows across multiple systems, trust, common system of values and common way to perform business processes) (Camarinha-Matos & Afsarmanesh, 2003). Adequate reference models, supporting infrastructures, and proper managerial and technological alignment of inter- and intra-organization business processes are required to achieve these common challenges.

Enterprise integration and interoperability aim at developing computer-based tools that facilitate coordination of work and information flow across organizational boundaries. While enterprise integration focuses on intra-enterprise distributed business processes (e.g., orchestration, communication) and flows, enterprise interoperability is focusing on inter-enterprise distributed business processes and flows. According to Vernadat (1996), enterprise integration (EI) refers to facilitating information, control, and material flows across organizational boundaries by connecting all the necessary functions and heterogeneous functional entities. It aims at improving communication, cooperation, and coordination in an enterprise. As a consequence, the enterprise behaves as an integrated whole, enhancing its overall productivity, flexibility, and capacity for the management of change. EI does not represent a new issue; evolving from physical integration to application and later business integration, EI has been a challenge for both information technology and manufacturing industries for several decades. IEEE (1990) provides a definition for interoperability, focusing on information exchanged and its use.

Major motivations for EI are mentioned in Vernadat (1996), and can be summarized as follows:

- The need for real information sharing
- The need for interoperability (e.g., the need to harmonize the operational networked environment)
- The need to improve task coordination or inter-working between organization units, individuals, and systems in interaction within an enterprise

In order to be competitive in a collaborative business networked environment, organizations should adopt a bipolar approach which allows them to fully benefit from the specific competences of each partner of a CNO (Chituc & Azevedo, 2005b):

- To develop a compatible organizational infrastructure allowing CNO members to join their competences while supporting the operations and functions to be performed
- To build up new management methodologies based on the most recent ICT developments, assuring high performance of the business activities with a minimum of human interaction

ENTERPRISE NETWORKING: RELEVANT INITIATIVES IN EUROPE AND THE USA

Several initiatives are currently being developed in the area of business networking in Europe and the USA, and also in Australia, Mexico, Canada, and more recently in Japan. As pointed out by Camarinha-Matos and Afsarmanesh (2003), the area of networked organizations/ enterprises is particularly active in Europe, and this can be somehow explained by the process of European integration. The European Union (EU), especially with the 6th Framework, supports a large range of research projects in the area of enterprise networking. Figure 1 illustrates the main "clusters" or targeted research initiatives in this field, as defined in VE-Forum (http://www.ve-forum.org):

- **Business networking cluster:** aiming at designing and developing reference models and technologies supporting organizations and

Figure 1. EU targeted research clusters for enterprise networking (Adapted after VE-Forum http://www.fe-forum.org—The European Research Clusters for Enterprise Networking)

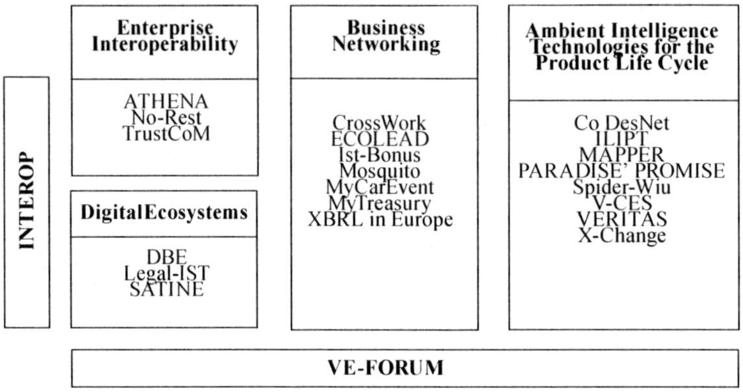

professionals, enhancing their collaboration and agility, and at fostering the development of suitable VO breeding environments; relevant research projects in this area are: ECOLEAD (European COLlaborative networked organizations LEADership initiative, http://www.ecolead.org), CROSSWORK (Developing Cross-Organizational Workflow Formation and Enactment, http://www.crosswork.info), VE-Forum (the European forum for virtual organizations domains, http://www.ve-forum.org).

- **Enterprise interoperability:** aiming at developing open and secure technologies to connect system and enterprises. Enterprise interoperability is addressed at different levels: physical integration, syntactic application integration, semantic application integration, business process integration, inter-enterprise coordination. ATHENA (Advanced Technologies for interoperability of Heterogeneous Enterprise Networks and their Applications, http://www.athena-ip.org) and INTEROP (Interoperability Research for Networked Enterprises Applications and Software, http://www.interop-noe.org) are relevant research projects in this area.
- **The ambient intelligence technologies for the product life-cycle cluster:** aiming at enabling organizations, in a networked business environment, to deliver better products to the market, in a more efficient way and faster, by enhancing the product and the product life-cycle processes using ambient intelligence technologies; CO-DESNET (Collaborative Demand and Supply NETworks, http://codesnet.polito.it) is a relevant research project in this area.
- **Digital ecosystems:** aiming at providing to small and micro-systems ICT applications and services which improve their efficiency and business integration within EU regions; SATINE (Semantic-based Interoperability Infrastructure for Integrating Web Service Platforms to Peer-to-Peer Networks, http://www.srdc.metu.edu.tr) is a relevant project in this area.

Reference Models, Standards, Frameworks, and Technologies Supporting Enterprise Integration and Interoperability

Several reference models, frameworks, and standards have been developed aiming at supporting enterprise integration and interoperability. This section concisely presents some integration reference models, frameworks, and standards referring to B2B domain, and relevant infrastructures and technologies supporting enterprise integration and interoperability. According to Vernadat (1996), a reference model represents a partial model, which can be used as a basis for certain model developments or evaluations. The term "framework" refers to a collection of elements (e.g., principles, methods, tools) put together for a certain purpose, and relevant for a given domain of application. Standards can be regarded as objects (e.g., hardware, software), which are accepted and shared within a community (i.e., business unit, value chain) (Crargill, 1989).

A. Reference Models, Architectures, and Frameworks

Purdue Enterprise Reference Architecture (PERA) provides the reference model of physical and informational interactions in enterprises (Li & Williams, 2000). An extension of the model is presented in Li and Williams (2003), which aims at enhancing the functionality of PERA as reference model for a distributed enterprises environment (e.g., VE), where the business processes in a group of enterprises are synchronously and simultaneously executed via information exchange.

Generalized Enterprise Reference Architecture and Methodology (GERAM) (IFAC/IFIP, 2000) defines a tool-kit of concepts for designing and maintaining enterprises for their entire life history. GERAM refers to the methods, models, and tools, which are needed to build and maintain the integrated enterprise, a single enterprise or a network of enterprises. GERAM encapsulates and orders previous architectures (e.g., CIMOSA, PERA, GRAI/GIM), providing an overall structure to use those methods and modeling techniques. GERAM is not a reference architecture; it is aimed at organizing enterprises' existing integration knowledge, and its framework has the potential for application to all types of enterprises by describing the components needed in all enterprises' engineering and integration processes. Generalized Enterprise Reference Architecture (GERA) is GERAM's most important component. It identifies basic concepts to be used in enterprise engineering and integration.

Supply chain operations reference model (SCOR) (http://www.supply-chain.org) is a process reference model developed by the Supply-Chain Council as a cross-industry standard for supply-chain management used to describe, measure, and evaluate supply-chain configurations. The SCOR model is organized around five primary management processes: plan, source, make, deliver, and return. It is composed by a hierarchic architecture of four level details: top level (process types), configuration level (process categories), process element level (decompose processes), and implementation level (decompose process elements).

Zachman's framework for enterprise architecture (Zachman, 1987) describes a holistic model of an enterprise information infrastructure from six perspectives: planner, owner, designer, builder, subcontractor, and working system. Its focus is to ensure that all aspects of an enterprise are well-organized and exhibit clear relationships that will ensure a complete system regardless of the order in which they are established.

Workflow reference model (Workflow Management Coalition, 1999) provides the general architectural framework that identifies interfaces and covers broadly five areas of functionality between a workflow management system (WfMS) and its environment: process definitions import and export; interaction with client applications and work-list handler software; software tools or applications invocation; interoperability between different WfMSs; and administration and monitoring functions.

B. Business-to-Business Integration Standards

In a broad sense, the term business-to-business (B2B) integration refers to electronic message exchange among trading partners. It includes issues such as product catalogs, classification systems, B2B protocol standards, synchronous/asynchronous communication, or back-end integration. According to Bussler (2003), B2B integration is the enabling technology and the necessary infrastructure to perform different operations: for example, automated supply chain integration, to send XML-formatted messages over the Internet, or to send messages in a peer-to-peer (P2P) pattern to trading partners.

According to SWWS (2003), B2B standards' scope can be roughly separated into catalogue and classification standards, document exchange, collaboration, and business processes, as follows:

- **Catalogue systems and classification standards** include: BMEcat (http://www.bmecat.org), eCX (Electronic Catalog XML, http://www.ecx-xml.org), OCP (Open Catalog Protocol, http://www.martsoft.com/ocp) as catalogue systems, and eCl@ss (http://www.eclass-online.com) or UNSPSC (United Nations Standard Products and Services Code, http://www.unspsc.org) as classification standards.
- **Document exchange** comprises electronic data interchange (EDI), electronic data interchange for administration, commerce and transport (EDIFACT), eXtensible Markup Language (XML, http://www.xml.org), XML common business library (xCBL, http://www.xcbl.org), Commerce eXtensible Markup Language (cXML, http://www.cxml.org), Open Applications Group Integration Specification (OAGIS, http://www.openapplications.org), RosettaNet implementation framework (RNIF, http://www.rosettanet.org), and Society For World-wide Interbank Financial Telecommunications (SWIFT) standard modeling (http://www.swift.com).
- **Collaboration** includes Electronic Business XML Initiative (ebXML, http://www.ebxml.org), Universal Business Language (UBL, http://docs.oasis-open.org/ubl), and RosettaNet (http://www.rosettanet.org)
- **Business processes** refer to executable business processes, ebXML business collaborations (http://www.ebxml.org), business process activities, or workflows. Business Process Modeling Language (BPML)/ Business Process Query Language (BPQL), Web Services Flow Language (WSFL), Business Process Execution Language for Web Services (BPEL4WS), XML Processing Description Language (XPDL), Unified Modeling Language, (UML, http://www.uml.org), and Process Specification Language (PSL, http://www.nist.gov.psl) are only some of the modeling languages dealing with business processes.

Other relevant developments for enterprise integration are: Open Buying on the Internet (OBI), Bolero.net, eCo framework, business transaction protocol (BTP), Transaction Authority Markup Language (XAML), and Microsoft BizTalk.

CNO require advanced infrastructures providing capabilities such as: multi-level support for interoperability, security, reconfiguration, and recovery mechanisms. The following section presents some relevant platforms and technologies for CNOs.

C. Infrastructures and Technologies

An overview of the current approaches and trends towards the establishment of flexible and configurable infrastructures for VE is presented in Camarinha-Matos and Afsarmanesh (2003). Emerging technologies for flexible VE infrastructures are grouped as follows:

- Open inter-operable underlying network protocols (e.g., TCP/IP, CORBA-IIOP, HTTP, RMI, SOAP)
- Open distributed object-oriented middleware services (e.g., J2EE Framework, CORBA Framework, Active X Framework)
- Information/object exchange mechanisms and tools (e.g., XML, ebXML, WSDL)
- Standardized modeling of business components, processes, and objects (e.g., EJBs)
- Business process modeling tools and languages (e.g., UML, UEML, WfMC XML-based Business Language, PSL)
- Open and standard business process automation and workflow management system (e.g., WfMC, OMG-JointFlow)
- Standard interfacing to federated multi-databases (e.g., JDBC)
- Intelligent mobile agents (e.g., FIPA, OMG-MASIF, Mobile Objects)
- Open and standard distributed messaging middleware systems (e.g., JMS, MS-message server, MQSeries, FIPA-ACC)
- XML-based e-commerce protocols (e.g., BizTalk, RosettaNet, OBI, WIDL)
- Web integration technologies (e.g., Servlets, JSP, MS-ASP, XSL)

Concerning infrastructures to support VE, Camarinha-Matos and Afsarmanesh (2003) illustrate two of the main approaches (from the software engineering perspective): transaction-oriented layer (TOL) based frameworks, and agent-based infrastructures (ABI).

TOL infrastructures add a cooperation layer to the existing IT platforms of the enterprises, and inter-enterprise communication is performed through layers interaction (e.g., transaction-oriented). Examples of projects developing such infrastructures are: National Industrial Information Infrastructure Protocols (NIIP, http://www.niiip.org), Production Planning and Management in an Extended Enterprise (PRODNET II, http://www.uninova.pt/~prodnet), and Virtual Enterprises using Groupware tools and distributed Architectures (VEGA) (Zarli & Poyet, 2001), which aimed at designing open platforms to support the basic information exchange and cooperation needs in industrial VE.

For ABI, enterprises are represented as agents, and the interactions in a distributed multi-agent system determine inter-enterprise cooperation. Multi-agent Manufacturing Agile Scheduling Systems for Virtual Enterprises (MASSYVE, http://www.cordis.lu/esprit/src/962219.htm) and Dynamic Forecast for Master Production Planning with stock and capacity constraints (DAMASCUS, http://www.damascos.com) are examples of projects developing such infrastructures.

Table 1 presents infrastructure characteristics of PRODNET II, NIIIP, DAMASCUS, and VEGA projects.

A more in-depth analysis concerning trends in VE support infrastructures is available in Camarinha-Matos and Afsarmanesh (2003). The authors present also limitations for current VE/VO infrastructures and collaborative frameworks. The main problems identified concern the lack of effective approach to interoperability (e.g., software inter-operation, information exchange/integration), and the lack of standard definitions and mechanisms. As pointed out by Camarinha-Matos and Afsarmanesh (2003), most of the technologies supporting integration and interoperability in a networked environment are at their beginnings, and they require considerable effort to implement and configure reliable infrastructures supporting CNO creation and development.

Several research projects are currently being pursued in the area of grid technology. Grids facilitate the sharing, selection, and aggregation of geographically-distributed resources (e.g., supercomputers, storage systems), which can cross single or multiple organizations, aiming at solving large-scale computational and data-intensive problems in science, engineering, and commerce (http://www.gridcomputing.com). Unlike other approaches (e.g., clusters, where the resources'

Table 1. Examples of infrastructure characteristics and typical services offered

Project	Project's aim	Infrastructure Characteristics	Supporting Technologies	Typical services offered by the platform/ architecture developed	Industry sector
PRODNET II	Design and develop an open platform and adequate information technology (IT) protocols and mechanisms to support virtual industrial enterprises	TOL	STEP, EDIFACT, Web and Internet technologies, Java	• exchange of commercial data via EDIFACT messages • exchange of technical product data using STEP • federated/ distributed information management • coordination module managing all cooperation-related events • monitoring of orders and production status • extended ERP/ PPC system adapted to interact with a VE environment • safe communications	SMEs in general
NIIIP	Solve incompatibility issues within VE, allowing organizations to collaborate with each other regardless of data structures or computing environments	TOL	STEP, OMG technologies (e.g., IDL, CORBA), workflow	• synthesizes collections of resources and technologies into a production system • control and flow of information • trap ORB (Object Request Broker) requests • inspect and validate the request NIIIP context • route requests to other components • dispatch rules and constraint-checking process associated with the request	Shipbuilding (with application in other sectors)
VEGA	Establish an information infrastructure which supports technical activities and business operations for VE	TOL	STEP, CORBA, SGML, EDI/ EDIFACT, Web technologies	• **Conceptual level:** STEP EXPRESS product data models supporting SGML documentary models and EDIFACT messages models • **Implementation level:** dedicated converters supporting the back and forth translation of SGML documents and EDIFACT messages towards STEP format, providing remote access to any kind of information for all actors involved in a construction project	Architecture construction and engineering
DAMASCOS	Design and develop an open platform providing adequate IT modules and mechanisms to manage customized supply networks in a multi-enterprise scenario	ABI	Workflow, Java	• enables customer relationship management at the sales level • supply chain management (inventory, production, logistics issues) and forecasting • interface between existing ERP systems	SMEs in general

allocation is performed by a centralized resource manager and all nodes cooperatively work together as a single unified resource), in the case of grids, each node has its own resource manager.

In the USA, large projects developed in the area of networked enterprises focus on middleware and grid technology. Started in 2001, National Science Foundation Middleware Initiative (NMI, http://www.nsf-middleware.org) aims at designing, developing, deploying, and supporting a set of reusable, expandable set of middleware functions and services that benefit applications in a networked environment. Two system integration projects started in Fall of 2003: Grid Research Integration Deployment and Support (GRIDS Center, http://www.grids-center.org) and Enterprise and Desktop Integration Technologies (EDIT, http://www.nmi-edit.org). GRIDS Center develops, tests, deploys, and supports standard tools for authentication, authorization and policy, resource discovery and directory services, and remote access to computers, data, and instruments. EDIT consortium developed a set of core middleware tools in the areas of identity and access management architectures, standards for deployments, elated directories, schemas, and tools.

In Europe, the European Commission has been financing grid research since early 2000, when the first EU grid-related projects were launched under the 5th research Framework Program (FP5) (CORDIS, 2005, http://www.cordis.lu/ist/grids). Grid research projects under FP5 were focused on technology development and application pilots, and results of these research projects are now deployed in grid-enabled research infrastructures made available by FP6 projects (e.g., EGEE, DEISA).

The approach for grid research being pursued in FP6 (2002-2006) refers to CORDIS (2005):

- **Technology push:** aims at developing the underlying technologies and tackling issues such as integration, open standards and interoperability.
- **Application pull:** aims at developing the enabling technologies for real-world applications, such as modeling, simulation, data-mining, and collaboration.

According to CORDIS (2005), the most relevant current EU grid initiatives are:

- **GRIDCOORD:** (http://www.gridcoord.org)
- **InteliGrid:** (http://www.inteliGrid.com)—interoperability of virtual organizations on a complex semantic grid
- **OntoGrid:** (http://www.ontogrid.net)—paving the way for knowledgeable grid services and systems;
- **Data Mining Grid:** (http://www.datamining-grid.org)—data mining tools and services for Grid computing environments;
- **Provenance:** (http://www.gridprovenance.org)—enabling and supporting provenance in Grids for complex problems;
- **K-WF Grid:** (http://www.kwfgrid.net)—knowledge-based workflow system for Grid applications;
- **UniGrids:** (http://www.unigrids.org)—uniform interface to grid services;
- **HPC4U:** (http://www.hpc4u.org)—highly predictable clusters for Internet Grids;
- **SIMDAT:** (http://www.scai.fraunhofer.de/simdat.html)—data grids for process and product development using numerical simulation and knowledge discovery;
- **NextGrid:** (http://www.nextgrid.org)—architecture for next generation grids;
- **Akogrimo:** (http://www.mobilegrids.org)—access to knowledge through the grid in a mobile world; and
- **CoreGRID:** (http://www.coregrid.net)—European research network on foundations, software infrastructures, and applications for large-scale distributed grid and peer-to-peer technologies.

Despite the existence of a significant number of computer-based tools aiming at enterprise integration and interoperability, and the scientific developments in the business networking area, it is generally accepted that more work needs to be done since available solutions are usually cumbersome and lack in flexibility to respond to the most recent technological outcomes, very often focusing on very specific aspects. The scientific community agrees that questions related to formalization, conceptual development, and semantic integration (namely, concerning the formal description of the domain or ontology) need to be urgently developed (Camarinha-Matos, 2003).

RELEVANT APPROACHES

Relevant initiatives, such as papiNet, ebXML, freebXML, and RosettaNet are discussed more in detail in the fallowing paragraphs.

papiNET

papiNET (http://www.papinet.org) is an international paper and forest products industry e-business initiative. It is a set of standard electronic documents which facilitates the flow of information among parties engaged in buying, selling, and distribution of paper and forest products. The papiNet Standards Group has the vision of enterprises of any size and in any geographical location meeting and conducting the business of paper, printing, and publishing with each other through the exchange of XML-based messages.

papiNet aims at increasing efficiency in transaction and marketplace activities through documented business processes with supporting standard XML messages and consistent data definitions, common terminology and formats, real-time exchange of information through the Internet, in order to ensure standards' interoperability among trading partners (in the paper and forest products industry, or in other industries). papiNet standard is a set of common electronic formats and terminology for the paper and forest products industry, designed to facilitate application-to-application information exchange. Its interoperability guidelines are based on ebXML message service specification. Messages have a very uniform structure with common definitions contained in the file that is shared among all the message schema files. The most prevalently implemented message is delivery message, followed by the purchase order, order confirmation, and invoice (http://www.papinet.org).

papiNet has formally accepted from ebXML the message service and collaboration (CPPA) aspects. The internal integration information is used to determine how ebXML envelope (which acts as a common interface between systems) is used, when received, and how it is going to be created the ebXML envelope when sending. Figure

Figure 2. papiNet: Interoperability standard approach (Adapted after papiNet, 2004)

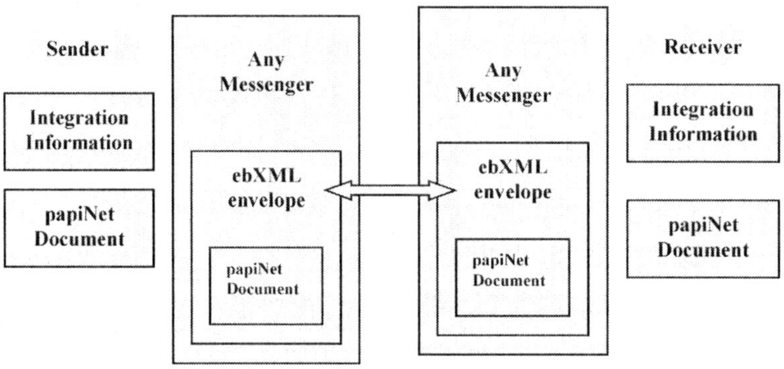

2 illustrates the papiNet interoperability approach. It is intended that any trading partner can open a message (payload) sent to them, regardless of the messaging service which was used.

ebXML and freebXML

eXtensible Markup Language (ebXML, http://www.ebxml.org) is a set of specifications that together enable a modular electronic business framework. ebXML vision is to enable a global electronic marketplace where enterprises of any size and in any geographical location can meet and conduct business with each other through the exchange of XML-based messages. Several industries endorse ebXML (e.g, computer/technology companies, banking, shipping).

One of the core values of ebXML is its vision of ubiquity from a technology perspective (Dournaee, 2004). ebXML is built around XML, SOAP, HTTP, and SMTP—all open standards.

ebXML provides a complete framework for business interactions, all delivered as a set of vendor-neutral specifications, and the concrete set of ebXML specifications refers to the following concepts:

- **Centralized shared registry:** Registry information model (ebRIM), registry service specifications (ebRS)
- **Business processes and collaboration:** Business processes specification schema (ebBPSS), collaboration-protocol profile and agreement specification (ebCPPA)
- **Messaging:** Message service specification (ebMS).

ebXML registry is similar to a database, being able to represent a large range of objects (e.g., XML schemas, business process descriptions, ebXML core components, UML models, generic trading partner information). ebXML registry architecture is defined in terms of registry service and registry client. The first one provides two interfaces, defined using Web Service Description Language (WSDL):

- **Life-cycle management interface:** used to manage the life cycle of the objects
- **Query management interface:** used to make queries against a registry

ebRIM is defining and managing interoperable registries and repositories. The core information model used by ebXML registry is a tree-based classification scheme, and the information (e.g., information referring to business partners, industries) is arranged in a hierarchy.

ebBPSS is used to define the business processes (BPs) and business documents (BDs) involved. BPs and BDs are designed and documented prior to their use. They are usually composed from existing components and processes. Both of them are documented using ebBPSS, and stored in an ebXML registry so that they can be referred from other structures (e.g., PPs, CPAs).

ebBPSS is used to specify public business processes. It provides an XML schema to specify binary collaborations among parties. A binary collaboration may consist of multiple business transactions, each one of them being specified in terms of business envelopes, business documents, and business signals which are communicated among parties.

A collaboration protocol profile (CPP) provides the information needed to do business with a specific trading partner (e.g., business processes, document formats). When two parties trade for the first time, their CPPs are combined into a collaboration protocol agreement (CPA), which serves as the basis for the interaction. ebCPPA specifies the XML schema for CPP and CPA, and includes guidelines to form a CPA from two CPPs. CPP defines the technical capabilities of a partner engaged in electronic business collaborations with other partners by exchanging electronic messages. It includes elements such as: party's information (e.g., contact name), transport protocol, transport security protocol, messaging protocol. CPA is a special business agreement tied to a specific transaction, and makes explicit requirements derived from the intersection of the various CPP instances published by each of the trading partners.

In order to assure the communication among applications and business processes from different business partners, it is necessary to capture critical information upon which organizations must agree. An electronic trading partner agreement (TPA) registers such information. A TPA is an XML document that records specific technology parameters for conducting electronic business (e.g., partner identification, communication protocol, security for message exchanges).

ebMS specification defines the ebXML message service protocol, and it is designed to enable a secure and reliable exchange of business messages between trading partners. The specification for the message-based service invocation focuses on defining a communication protocol neutral method for exchanging electronic business messages, defining specific enveloping constructs for a secure and reliable exchange of messages, and a specific enveloping technique, allowing messages to contain payloads of any format type.

ebXML is designed to meet enterprises' needs to conduct electronic business, by providing: an *infrastructure* which ensures data communication interoperability (e.g., standard message transport mechanism, business service interface); a *semantic framework* supporting business interoperability (e.g., meta-model for defining business processes and information models, set of reusable core components); and a *discovery mechanism* enabling enterprises to discover each other, to reach an agreement and to conduct business (e.g., shared repository network) (Campbell, 2001).

A high-level presentation on how an ebXML interaction occurs can be framed in terms of ebXML's three functional phases defined by the ebXML technical architecture. Each functional phase defines its own security requirements and processes: implementation phase, discovery and retrieval phase, and run-time phase (Dournaee, 2004).

The implementation phase starts when a trading partner makes an active decision to do business using ebXML framework. During this phase, the trading partner will analyze its business processes and will publish them into a registry. An actual ebXML implementation is made then, aiming at attaining a working ebXML framework, and includes a set of published business processes, the CPP, and interfaces.

During discovery and retrieval phase, trading partners use the registry to discover business

Figure 3. ebXML run-time phase (Adapted after Dournaee, 2004)

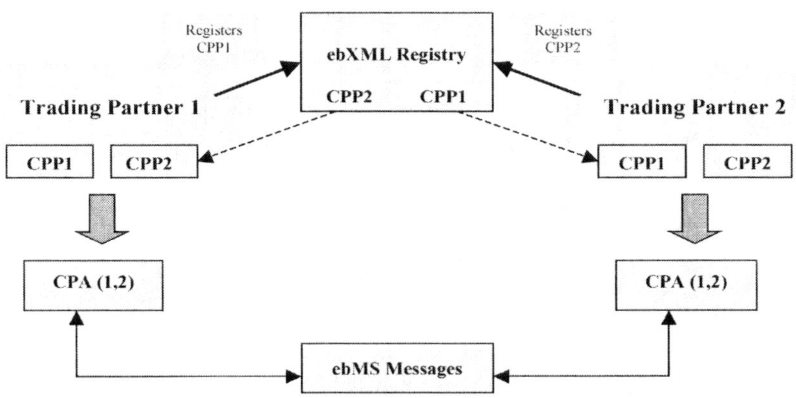

processes and interfaces published by other trading partners (e.g., the CPP for a specific partner is exchanged).

The run-time phase is concerned with the actual business transactions and choreography of messages exchanged between trading partners. Typically, there is no run-time access to the registry during this phase. Firstly, each trading partner is responsible for obtaining the necessary CPP document for a potential business partner. Usually, CPP is retrieved from an ebXML registry. Secondly, each partner derives the CPA, and finally the trading partners can start performing business transactions. Figure 3 illustrates run-time phase.

ebXML aims at creating a generic meta-model for business processes which allows it to model each business process in a machine-readable way. This can enable companies to deploy software that automatically adapts to specific business processes of different trading partners (SWWS, 2003).

ebXML specifications have matured rapidly over the past years, and its relevance for enterprise integration and interoperability in a collaborative business environment is emphasized by the augmenting number of research projects and technology infrastructures based on ebXML standard. Both OASIS and UN/CEFEACT pursued several standards developments, in real-world projects, combining ebXML with other technologies (e.g., Web services) in key industry sectors and government (ebXML, 2003). Examples of such projects are: JXTA Project, in the USA; COMOS Project (Cluster Of Systems of Metadata for Official Statistics), in Europe; and Kasumi B2B integration project in Japan. There is also underway a relevant project between RosettaNet (http://www.rosettanet.org) and ebXML, making use of ebXML BPSS, Registry, and ebMS. RosettaNet has adopted BPSS as they pursue the next evolution of the PIPs, and it is operating private registry with their technical dictionary content loaded. A more complete list of research projects focusing on ebXML is available in ebXML (2003).

Very few analytical comparisons are available concerning EI standards and technologies, based on different criteria. For instance, related to B2B standards, an interesting approach for the comparison of ebXML and RosettaNet was made by Pusnik, Juric, Rozman, and Sumak (2000), and Nurmilaakso and Kotinurmi (2004) compares XML-based B2B integration frameworks.

Comparing ebXML and Web Services, both of them use SOAP for message transport. XML Web services have a loosely coupled wire stack that consists of separate specifications for reliable transport and security, while ebXML rolls all this functionality into its messaging standard (ebMS), making use of different technologies. For the description of the discovery stacks, XML Web services use Web Services Description Language, (WSDL, http://www.w3.org/TR/wsdl) and universal description, discovery and integration protocol, (UDDI, http://www.uddi.org), while for ebXML these description and discovery mechanisms are part of ebXML registry. ebXML includes additional specifications for business process and collaboration. In fact, ebXML is a self-contained set of specifications, and does not rely on emerging standards and specifications (Dournaee, 2004).

freebXML (http://www.freebxml.org) is an initiative aiming at fostering the development and adoption of ebXML and related technologies through software and experience sharing. Its objectives are to create a centralized site for the sharing of "free" ebXML code and applications, and to promote ebXML as an e-commerce enabling technology. Relevant research projects have been developed, aiming at achieving these objectives (e.g., Hermes Message Service Handler, ebMail).

Messaging service is a key component of ebXML technical architecture. ebMS utilizes SOAP, Internet transport protocols, and other security standards, aiming at providing enterprises with a standardized, reliable, and secure infrastructure for the exchange of business documents.

Hermes B2B messaging server provides enterprises a standardized, reliable and secure infrastructure to exchange business data over the Internet. It supports secure messaging functions through security technologies such as XML signature, secure socket layer (SSL), and secure multipurpose internet mail extensions (S/MIME). Aiming at supporting different requirements from enterprises of all sizes, it implements reliable messaging, message packaging, message ordering, error handling, security, synchronous reply, message status service, and supports transport protocols, such as HTTP and SMTP. Hermes also supports the concept of "quality of service" by respecting in-force agreements, which are expressed as CPA.

ebMail is a GUI system. It makes use of open standards (ebXML), underlying GUI, in order to communicate with business partners. Business messages are composed and read in GUI form, so that enterprises do not need back-end integration. The project is platform-neutral; it is developed by using Java, and the GUI part is using Java Swing. For ebXML Messaging Service, ebMail makes use of Hermes project.

RosettaNet

RosettaNet (http://www.rosettanet.org) is a self-funded non-profit organization around a consortium of major IT, electronic components, and semiconductor manufacturing companies aiming at aligning business processes between partners in a given supply chain: Partners agree on partner interface processes (PIPs) to use, and are then ready to start a business scenario. RosettaNet implementation framework (RNIF) provides exchange protocols for quick and efficient implementation of PIPs. RNIF defines the overall RosettaNet business message format for business documents exchange, with elements to support authentication, authorization, encryption, and non-repudiation; details of the bindings for the transfer protocols (e.g., HTTP); and the specification for a reliable exchange of messages between business partners.

RosettaNet aims at aligning business processes of supply chain partners, a goal which is achieved by the creation of PIPs. Each PIP defines how two specific processes (running in two different partner organizations) will be standardized and interfaced across the entire supply chain. PIPs include all business logic, message flow, and message contents to enable alignment of the two processes. The purpose of each PIP is to provide common business/data models and documents enabling system developers to implement RosettaNet eBusiness interfaces. Each PIP includes: partner role descriptions (individuals/organizations); business data involved (and corresponding XML documents); and business process activities, a validation tool and implementation guide (http://www.rosettanet.org).

RosettaNet's standardization efforts refer to:

- **PIPs:** defining business processes between trading partners
- **PIP directory:** providing faster access to PIPs' information
- **Dictionaries:** which provide a common set of properties for PIPs. (e.g., **RosettaNet** Business Dictionary**:** designates the properties used in basic business activities, and Technical Dictionary provides proprieties for defining products)
- **RNIF:** providing specifications for packaging, routing, and transport of all PIP messages and business signals
- **Product and partner code:** which expedites the alignment of business processes between trading partners

RosettaNet does not provide a model for supply chain arrangements as a whole, but a model for linking supply chain members' information flows in a uniform manner, within specific

business processes. The RosettaNet model describes several business activities that can be mapped to RosettaNet XML-framework. These activities are collected inside PIPs.

Web Services and BPEL4WS

Web services (http://www.w3.org/2002/ws) aim at achieving universal interoperability among applications by using Web standards. They use loosely-coupled integration model to allow flexible integration of heterogeneous systems in a variety of domains, including B2B, B2C, and enterprise integration and interoperability. Specifications derived from Web services include: SOAP, WSDL, and UDDI. SOAP (http://www.w3.org/TR/soap) defines an XML messaging protocol for basic service interoperability. WSDL (http://www.w3.org/TR/wsdl) introduces a common grammar for describing services, and UDDI (http://www.uddi.org) provides the infrastructure required to publish and discover services in a systematic way. All these specifications allow applications to find each other and interact following a loosely-coupled platform-independent model. However, system integration requires much more than the ability to conduct simple interactions by using standard protocols. According to Andrews, Curbea, Dholakia, Goland, Klein, Leymann, Liu, Roller, Smith, and Thatte (2003), the full potential of Web services as an integrated platform will be achieved only when applications and business processes will be able to integrate their complex interactions by making use of a standard process integration model.

Business Process Execution Language for Web Services (BPEL4WS, http://xml.coverpages.org/bpel4ws.html) provides an XML-based process definition language that enables the formal description of business processes and interaction protocols (Andrews, et al., 2003). BPEL4WS defines an interoperable integration model that facilitates the expansion of automated process integration in both intra-enterprise and B2B integration.

BPEL4WS is meant to model the behavior of executable business processes (which are modeling the actual behavior of a participant in a business interaction), and abstract business processes (which are process descriptions for business protocols). In this way, BPEL4W extends Web services' interaction model and enables it to support business transactions.

BPEL4WS depends on the following XML-based specifications: WSDL 1.1, XML Schema 1.0, XPath 1.0, and WS-Addressing. Among these, WSDL has the most influence on BPEL4WS: P2P interaction between services, described in WSDL, is at the core of BPEL4WS process model, and both the process and its partners are modeled as WSDL services. The definition of business processes also follows the WSDL model of separation between the abstract message contents used by the business process and deployment information.

CONCLUSION AND FURTHER RESEARCH

Current market conditions and information and communication technology (ICT) developments determined enterprises to adopt new ways of undertaking business. As a consequence, new forms of collaboration emerged, such as collaborative networked organizations (CNO). In this context, the need to support enterprise integration and interoperability is increasing. Several conceptual frameworks, integration standards, technologies, and supporting infrastructures are being developed. Despite the relevant developments in the area of enterprise integration and interoperability, and the numerous scientific results in the business networking area, it is generally accepted that more work needs to be done, mainly concerning CNO creation or setting-up, support, and implementations (Camarinha-Matos & Afsarmanesh, 2003). Most of the technologies and infrastructures supporting CNO currently available are at their beginnings, and require considerable implementation and configuration efforts. In general, there is a lack of an effective approach to interoperability (mainly concerning software inter-operation and information exchange integration), and a lack of standard definitions and mechanisms.

Since it is very difficult (not to say impossible) to find a standard which is valid or easily configurable, supporting a wide range of services and operations concerning enterprise integration and interoperability, a convenient approach is to develop standards for specific industry sectors (e.g., papiNet for paper and forest industry), considering also the fact that a single process and document standard for communicating business transactions is critical to companies buying and selling products from the same industry. RosettaNet and papiNET are examples of successful standards developments supporting integration and interoperability for a specific industry sector: high-tech industry and paper industry, respectively.

Although several standards (e.g., ebXML) provide support for different requirements regarding enterprise integration and interoperability, in a networked environment, it would be naïve to consider that it is possible to convert everybody to a single platform (e.g., ebXML). Each technology or standard has its advantages and disadvantages. No true technology or standard can work as an isolated island; different technologies are combined or adapted to specific needs. It is therefore challenging to observe the rapid evolution of different technologies, standards, frameworks, and the development of emerging projects aiming at combining these standards and technologies (e.g., the development of research projects combining both ebXML and RosettaNet frameworks).

The questions that guided this work were answered. Major benefits for enterprise integration were identified. The most relevant standards, frameworks, technologies, and supporting infrastructures aiming at enterprise integration and interoperability were analyzed, and relevant research projects in the area of enterprise networking were briefly presented. Further research will be pursued to define criteria to be used to compare the available standards and frameworks. However, in the context of CNO, as mentioned by Bussler (2003), the grander challenge will be: how to achieve self-forming collaborative networked organizations (SFCNO)—that is CNO where the detection of service provider, as well as their contracting, is automated.

ACKNOWLEDGMENT

The author, Claudia-Melania Chituc, would like to acknowledge Fundação para a Ciencia e a Tecnologia for PhD grant SFRH/BD/19751/2004.

REFERENCES

Andrews, T., Cubera, F., Dholakia, H., Goland, Y., Klein, J., Leymann, F., Liu, K., Roller, D., Smith, D., & Thatte, S. (2003). *Business Process Execution Language for Web Services—Version 1.1.* White paper. Retrieved September 10, 2005, from http://ifr.sap.com/bpel4ws/BPEL%20V1-1%20May%205%202003%20Final.pdf

BPEL4WS. (2005). *Business Process Execution Language for Web Services Version 1.1.* Retrieved September 10, 2005, from http://www-128.ibm.com/developerworks/library/specification/ws-bpel/

Bussler, C. (2003). *B2B integration—concepts and architectures.* Springer.

Camarinha-Matos, L. M. (2003). *New collaborative organizations and their research needs in process and foundations for virtual organizations.* Kluwer Academy Publishers.

Camarinha-Matos, L. M., & Afsarmanesh, H. (2003). Elements of a base VE infrastructure. *Computers in Industry, 51*(2) 139-163.

Campbell, S. (2001). ebXML—the global standard for electronic business. Retrieved March 17, 2006, from http://www.gca.org/papers/xmleurope2001/papers/pdf/s03-2.pdf

Chituc, C. M., & Azevedo, A. L. (2005a) (in press). Enablers and technologies supporting self-forming networked organizations. *International Workshop on Enterprise Integration, Interoperability and Networking (EI2N),* Geneva, Switzerland. Hermes Publishing.

Chituc, C. M., & Azevedo, A. L. (2005b, September). Multi-perspective challenges on collaborative networks business environment. In L. Camarinha-Matos, H. Afsarmanesh, & A. Ortiz (Eds.), *Collaborative networks and breeding environments: Proceedings of the 6th IFIP Working Conference on Virtual Enterprises,* Spain (Vol. 186, pp. 25-32). Boston: Springer.

CORDIS. (2005). Building grids for Europe—a crucial technology for science and industry. Retrieved September 10, 2005, from http://www.cordis.lu/ist/grids

Crargil, C. F. (1989). *Information technology standardization: Theory, process, and organization.* Bedford: Digital Press.

Dournaee, B. (2004). *Introduction to ebXML.* White paper. Retrieved September 10, 2005, from http://dev2dev.bea.com/pub/a/2004/12/ebXML.html

ebXML. (2003). *ebXML adoptation update.* Retrieved from http://www.ebxml.org

European Commission. (2005). *Strengthening competitiveness through production networks—a perspective from European ICT research projects in the field of enterprise networking.*

IEEE. (1990). *IEEE standard computer dictionary: A compilation of IEEE standard computer glossaries.* New York: Institute of Electrical and Electronics Engineers.

IFAC/IFIP. (2000). GERAM: Generalized enterprise reference architecture and methodology. *IFAC/IFIP Task Force on Architectures for Enterprise Integration.*

Li, H., & Williams, T. J. (2000). The interconnected chain of enterprises as presented by the Purdue enterprise reference architecture. *Computers in Industry, 42,* 265-274.

Li, H., & Williams, T. J. (2003). Interface design for the Purdue enterprise reference architecture (PERA) and methodology in e-work. *Production Planning & Control, 14*(8), 704-719.

Nurmilaakso, J. M., & Kotinurmi, P. (2004). A review of XML-based supply-chain integration. *Production Planning & Control, 15*(6), 608-621

papiNet. (2004). *papiNet from top to bottom—an introduction to papiNet.* Retrieved September 10, 2005, from http://www.papinet.org/presentations.asp

Pusnik, M., Juric, M. B., Rozman, I., & Sumak, B. (2000). *A comparison of ebXML and RosettaNet.* White paper. Retrieved September 10, 2005, from http://www.ebpml.org/articles.htm

SCOR—Supply Chain Operations Reference Model. (n.d.). Retrieved from http://www.supply-chain.org

SWWS—Semantic Web-Enabled Web Services. (2003). *Analysis of B2B Standards and Systems: Deliverable D1.1 SWWS Project.* Retrieved from http://swws.semanticweb.org

Vernadat, F. (1996). *Enterprise modeling and integration—principles and applications.* Chapman & Hall.

Webber, D. (2004). The benefits of ebXML for e-business. In *XML 2004 Conference.* Retrieved September 10, 2005, from http://www.idealliance.org/proceedings/xml04/papers/44/webber.pdf

Workflow Management Coalition. (1999). *The workflow management coalition specifications: Terminology and glossary.* Retrieved from http://www.wfmc.org

Zachman, J. A. (1987). A framework for information systems architecture. *IBM Systems Journal, 26*(3), 276-292.

Zarli, A, & Poyet, P. (2001). A framework for distributed information management in the virtual enterprise: The VEGA project. In L. M. Camarinha-Matos & H. Afsarmanesh (Eds.), *Infrastructures for virtual enterprises—networking industrial enterprises* (1st ed.), (pp. 293-306). Boston: Kluwer Academic Publishers.

This work was previously published in Knowledge and Technology Management in Virtual Organizations: Issues, Trends, Opportunities and Solutions, edited by G. D. Putnik & M. M. Cunha, pp. 334-353, copyright 2007 by IGI Publishing, formerly known as Idea Group Publishing (an imprint of IGI Global).

Chapter XXVII
Outsourcing Non-Core Business Processes:
An Exploratory Study

Adriana Romaniello
Universidad Rey Juan Carlos, Spain

B. Dawn Medlin
Appalachian State University, USA

ABSTRACT

This study examines corporate performance effects when banks outsource noncore business processes. Additionally, the article proposes that knowledge management process plays a significant role in determining the outcomes of outsourcing. Drawing from resource theory and knowledge management literature, the authors develop the concept of managerial outsourcing competence and then propose a conceptual model. Also presented is an exploratory study of members of the North Carolina Bankers Association to assist in identifying the business processes they are currently outsourcing and their principal reasons for outsourcing.

INTRODUCTION

Outsourcing has been defined as a results-oriented relationship in which a business organization transfers ownership of a business process to an external service provider rather than perform the activity in house (Halvey & Melby, 2000). For some, the hint of outsourcing may be found as early as 1776, when, in *The Wealth of Nations,* Adam Smith wrote the following: "If a foreign country can supply us with a commodity cheaper than we can ourselves make it..." (Adam Smith Institute, 2007). This may have been one of the hints of the forthcoming principles related to outsourcing and later building on Adam Smith's ideas was British economist David Ricardo and his principle of comparative advantage, where he hypothesized that each nation should specialize in what it does best and trade with others in order to best meet their needs (Ricardo, 2004).

Certainly, the issues of competitive pressures, customer demands, cost efficiency, and the ability to gain access to world-class capabilities are considerations that have all manifested themselves in the increased use of outsourced functions. When the choice is made to outsource, and the move involves a vendor located in a different nation, outsourcing then becomes offshoring.

Business process outsourcing is another type of outsoucing that also relates to the investment of physical resources while still attempting to maintain internal effectiveness. In fact, one of the most commonly cited reasons for outsourcing is that management expects that they can gain cost advantages by hiring outsiders to perform certain services and produce certain products (Loh & Venkatraman, 1992). Banking activities that are not inherently or typically part of a bank's core functions are therefore logical processes thought generally suitable by management for outsourcing. Additionally, the implementations of such activities in-house can be prohibitively costly to smaller institutions.

For years, the financial industry has relied on the outsourcing of services where banks could seek advanced technologies and greater economies of scale while still lowering costs. It should be expected that the use of outsourcing will only increase as banks expand their product lines (e.g., Check 21 processing). Check 21 was specifically designed to foster innovation in the payments system and to enhance its efficiency by reducing some of the legal impediments to check truncation. More specifically, the Check 21 law that was created in 2004 introduced the notion of a substitute check, which permitted banks to process check information electronically.

Other methods of electronic processing have also been introduced to handle electronic check transfers. As an example, Amar Gupta and a team of MIT researchers have developed a fully electronic check transfer that can read handwritten infomation in order to increase check processing efficiency and accuracy, which may be of interest to countries outside of the U.S., where powerful banks are in a position to better control their overall check processes ("Gupta Eyes," 2007). Within the current process, check processing is an expensive prospect for banks due to the high cost of the technology required, and thus makes Check 21 processing a logical process to be outsourced by community banks.

In his March 17th, 2004, satellite address before the Independent Community Bankers of America Convention, Alan Greenspan stated, "Over the past 5 years, for every four bank mergers that have been approved, three de novo bank charters have been granted" ("Technology Outsourcing," 2005). Additionally, he added that 90% of all start-up banks will choose to outsource and that, overall, it is expected that all banks will use some type of outsourced services.

Financial institutions have been outsourcing technology projects for more than 30 years in their desire to reduce costs, focus on their core business, obtain knowledge, and increase efficiency and productivity. In particular, and within the past 10 years, the competition for customers and the consolidation of banks has brought these aforementioned issues to the forefront, as well as the need to outsource, both on and offshore, these activities in order to achieve the desired results.

Starting in the 1970s, the outsourcing trend began mainly with banks outsourcing software development and maintenance (http://www.financetech.com/showArticle.jhtml?articleID=17500105). Projects ranged from straightforward tasks such as application maintenance to complex long-term projects. Today, outsourcing large, complex technology projects is making a comeback, as evinced by J. P. Morgan Chase's recent decision to outsource their technology infrastructure to IBM.

In the 1990s, banks began to outsource business processes as well as technology projects. In the banking industry, the first forays into business processing outsourcing traditionally involved offshore call centers and credit card transaction processing. As an example, offshore call center outsourcing agencies in the Philippines have been quickly increasing their share of the global call center market resulting in more than 100 centers in different locations in the Philippines (http://www.piton-global.com/resource13.html).

In March 2007, Deloitte Research reported that financial institutions worldwide were increasingly interested in sending their IT work to lower cost countries such as India and China. The research group surveyed 27 global financial institutions around the world and indicated that 33% of the respondents had already sent IT work offshore; 75% said they will have work going to offshore companies within the next 2 years ("Deloite," 2006).

By 2015, it is estimated that there will be more than 472,632 jobs in the information technology field that are expected to move offshore to countries like Russia, China, India, and the Philippines, according to a November 2002 report by the Forrester Research Group Inc. Banking firms such as Bank of America (BofA) will send about one third of their systems programming jobs to India, where work costs approximately $100.00 U.S. vs. $20.00 U.S. an hour.

In additon, Bank of America cut 3,700 of its 25,000 technical and back-office jobs in 2002 with an estimated 1,100 jobs being lost in 2003 ("Banking & Securities," 2003). A majority of these positions will be sent to IT companies in India, where new technology parks are being built by companies partnering with U.S. firms such as Infosys Technologies Ltd. ("Banking & Securities," 2003).

In Europe, global cost competition forces financial companies such as ABN, AMRO Bank, and Deutsche Bank to bring their cost base in line with that of competitors from the U.S., such as American Express and Citigroup, which have already made aggressive use of cheaper offshore operations and services. Forrester's 2004 research into offshore services spending by European firms' shows what they call "two speed Europe" because of the differences between the United Kindom and other continental countries. Europe, along with the 16 countries they considered in their sample, will lose a cumulative 1.2 million jobs to offshore locations by 2015 (65% from UK), with financial firms being the largest and most aggressive of the offshoring participants. During the same period in the U.S. (2004-2015), they found a cumulative figure of 3.3 million jobs moving offshore, which has a smaller population overall than the 16 European countries studied (Parker, 2004).

While India is still the first choice of many companies' favorite outsourcing destinations, especially the UK, other countries within Central and Eastern European (CEE) are the favorite sites for Western European countries to develop near-shoring activities. Near-shoring outsourcing is generally defined as the outsourcing of work to companies with the economic benefits of an offshore location, but a closer cultural, linguistic, and geographic fit with the employing organisation. Also, from the total European jobs moving offshore forecasted by 2015, 13% are IT jobs, 34% are clerical jobs, 29% are business and management jobs, 20% are science and engineering jobs, and 4% are others type of jobs (Parker, 2004).

Thus, despite the differences in the outsourcing process, both U. S. and European companies must essentially become involved within this type of process because of two reasons: (1) they are in a global marketplace with global competition, and (2) they must bring their cost base in line with their competitors. The process of offshoring, as stated earlier, is a must, and the development of managerial outsourcing competence is part of the process companies must participante in to remain competitive. Nevertheless, this is not enough to be competitive, because there are a large number of vendors offering excellent managerial outsourcing services. Because of this, we believe that the outsourcing process will impact on a company's profit margin if they seize this opportunity to focalize on their core competences through a knowledge management process.

OBJECTIVES

Although recent studies have examined the relationship between outsourcing and firm performance, this research stream continues to be hampered by the lack of a widely accepted conceptualization of managerial outsourcing competence (MOC). The resulting body of research still continues to be contradictory and rely on differing conceptualizations, levels of analysis, and OC-related measures.

During the outsourcing process, organizations improve their knowledge about themselves and are learning and acquiring skills and new competences. Ex-ante outsourcing decision making includes two basic components of outsourcing capabilities: leadership in order to motivate the members of the organization and to resolve political and economic conflicts intra- and interorganizational, and an adequate organizational structure that can respond with flexibility to the requirement of strategic changes. Ex-post outsource decision making involves the managing of relationships with the vendors that necessitates the signing of good contracts, monitoring them, and building long-term and trusting relationships, because of the impracticality that all possible contingencies could be included within the contracts. During this process the organization has been developing a deeper knowledge about itself, and a new strategic vision about the resources and capabilities which allows for the possibility of still maintaining a competitive advantage in the market. Therefore, we suggest that the organization develops new competencies as a result of the outsourcing decision-making process and that these competencies will spill over throughout the knowledge management process (KMP).

Accordingly, the first objective of this article is to develop a conceptualization of managerial outsourcing competence in a form that will address these issues. As discussed in the next section, we propose the notion of outsourcing competences consisting of a construct of three components: (a) modular organizational design, (b) strategic outsourcing leadership, and (c) outsourcing relationship management.

The second objective of this article is to develop a better understanding of how outsourcing competences impact a firm's performance. It is not clear how outsourcing competences affects the specific organizational processes that contribute to improve firm performance.

The basic contention of this article is that the outsourcing decision may not necessarily improve firm productivity or profitability; it is the generation of additional competencies that is more important to achieve this aim. By developing managerial outsourcing competence and using it to leverage knowledge management processes, firms are in a better position to enhance their performance.

In the sections that follow, we begin with a conceptual background, and then we provide an overview of the resource-based approach that forms the theoretical basis for our work. We then discuss the concepts of managerial outsourcing competence and knowledge management process. Following this, we develop a conceptual model with three propositions representing the relationships between managerial outsourcing competencies, knowledge management process, and performance. We propose to test our hypothesis with the structural modeling technique in future work and we present in this article a statistical exploratory test supported by a survey administrated to bankers who are members of the North Carolina Bankers Association.

CONCEPTUAL BACKGROUND

Embedded in the general stream of research that seeks to understand how firm resources and capabilities are combined to produce some form of competitive advantage, the study of how outsourcing capabilities affects the strategic management of organizations continues to demand considerable attention. Prior to 1990, most of the literature focused on the importance of outsourcing and its potential to alter a whole range of strategic and industry structure variables, including cost positions. More recently, the focus of the literature has shifted to the relationship between outsourcing and specific components of the firm strategy, such as competitive advantage (Aranha & Wheelwright, 2007; Goo et al., 2000; Krebsbach, 2004), and organizational performance (Gilley & Rasheed, 2000).

A review of this literature reveals that most of the earlier conceptual work tends to favor the notion that outsourcing can be used favorably to create a competitive advantage and sustain firm performance. However, emerging empirical evidence has shown that outsourcing does not necessarily create a competitive advantage and that there is no significant direct connection between outsourcing and performance (Barthélemy & Quélin, 2006; Gilley & Rasheed, 2000). To provide a possible explanation for this discussion, we draw on the resource-based view (RBV).

Resource-Based View

Grounded in evolutionary economics and the work of Penrose (1959), the RBV has gained considerable attention during the last decade (Barney et al., 2001). In RBV, the firm is seen as a bundle of tangible and intangible resources and tacit know-how that must be identified, selected, developed, and deployed to generate superior success (Penrose 1959, Wernerfelt 1984).

Competitive advantage originates from firm heterogeneity in resources and capabilities through barriers to imitation by investing in inimitable idiosyncratic capabilities (Lippman & Rumelt, 1982) and leveraging these firm-core-specific assets for competitive advantage. Firms can achieve sustained competitive advantage by accumulating resources which produce economic value, are relatively scarce, and can sustain attempts at imitation, acquisition, or substitution (Barney, 1991).

According to the RBV, managerial outsourcing competence (MOC) per se may not generate a sustainable advantage, because it can be replicated. We see the most important vendors in the world are offering their expertise in financial services consulting, technology, and outsourcing. For example, Accenture Ltd has a 10-year contract with Caixa de Catalunya, Spain's third largest savings bank. Accenture is providing outsourcing for Caixa's technology infrastructure, as well as system integration, application maintenance and technical help service. The work is completed through ITC, a company jointly owned by Caixa and Accenture that also provides services to other Spanish firms (SharedExpertiseForums, 2005).

However, the advantages of outsourcing capabilities can be protected by embedding it in an organization through complementarities and cospecialization. Complementarities is said to exist when the value of one resource is enhanced by the presence of another. For example, the complementary use of information technology and human resources leads to superior firm performance (Powell & Dent-Micallef, 1997). Resources rarely act alone in creating or sustaining competitive advantage (Wade & Hulland, 2004). They play an interdependent role with other firm resources (Keen, 1993). This is particularly true in managerial outsourcing capabilities that act with other firm resources to provide strategic benefits. Thus, in banking environments, while managerial outsourcing competence may be essential to compete, it in itself conveys no particular sustainable advantage of one bank over another. The value of managerial outsourcing competence is enhanced when banks use it to develop the concentrating resources process, focusing on its core competences. Consequently, in this article, we focus on the role that knowledge management plays in enhancing the value of managerial outsourcing competence.

Cospecialization is said to exist if one resource has little or no value without another (Clemons & Row, 1991). We suggest that managerial outsourcing competence should not be examined as a stand-alone resource. In our article, we examine how managerial outsourcing competence as a resource can be embedded in an organization and protected through cospecialization. For example, a firm possessing a modular organizational design will realize very little advantage if it does not have the necessary outsourcing leadership to drive it successfully.

In the next section, we describe the concept of managerial outsourcing competence and suggest that it consists of three cospecialized resources: modular organizational design, strategic outsourcing leadership, and outsourcing relationship management. We then follow with a discussion of the components of knowledge management processes and examine the link between managerial-outsourcing competence and knowledge-management processes in order to determine how they might interact to enhance firm performance.

Managerial Outsourcing Competence

Modular Organizational Design

Modular organization design refers to the need of structuring the organization in business processes-ECT (electronic communication technologies) enabled. Banks operate in dynamic environments and must be continuously innovative in order to create and sustain a competitive advantage. This need brings into focus the importance of the flexibility of the organization through modular business processes in order to enable organizational adaptation. Business processes are activities structured and organized according to a predefined flow that allow an organization to carry out its business. Many of the business processes require process interdependencies and system dependencies that are established through integration of the business processes (Moitra & Ganesh, 2005).

Because communication is integral to organizational form, advances in communication capabilities through electronic technologies are implicated in a wide variety of changes in forms. ECTs are enablers of changed forms by offering capabilities to overcome constraints on time and distance, key barriers around which organizational forms have traditionally been designed. Electronic communication systems are also configurations that may be shaped as organizations evolve and change (Fulk & DeSantis, 1995).

Following Orlikowski, Yates, Okamura and Fujimoto (1995), electronic technologies can be viewed as an opportunity for structuring. In this view, communication technologies offer users opportunities to manipulate both the communication technologies themselves as well the organizational contexts in which they are embedded.

When a hierarchical organization such as a bank elects to outsource with other firms, their value chain becomes fundamentally altered. New forms of coupling may be developed through communication technology, in what has been termed the electronic integration effect (Zaheer & Venkatraman, 1994). Defining and implementing flexible business processes supported by flexible ECT systems is of significance to organizations because this allows them to collaborate with partners in new ways which can result in inimitability of the processes, and in turn allow them to adapt to the changing environment.

The modular design of organizations through business processes allows them to be prepared to outsource some of their functions, as seen in Table 1. We can see in this table the business processes which are most frequently being offshored.

Table 1. Most frequently outsourced business processes

	Spain	*Germany*	*Holland*	*USA*
Finance/Acc.	22%	29%	12%	29%
HR	15%	9%	5%	12%
IT	54%	65%	44%	54%
Contact centers	44%	36%	9%	34%
Freight & logistics	15%	25%	14%	14%
R+D	17%	29%	19%	22%
Product design	20%	20%	14%	11%
Others	17%	n/a	2%	8%

Note. From "El offshoring en España: Causas y consecuencias de la deslocalización de servicios," by J. E. Ricart & P.Agnese, 2006, Centro Anselmo Rubiralta de Globalización y Estrategia.

In their sample, Ricart and Agnese (2006) are considering firms from different sectors such as manufacturing, financial services, telecom, media and technology. As is also seen in their information, most countries are involved in some offshore outsourcing that may include the low-added-value activities such as IT and contact centers. These results are supported by a 2006 survey conducted by the Gartner Research Group. According with that, IT outsourcing in Western Europe will continue to increase over the next 2 years. The survey of 300 firms found that the proportion of companies with moderate or high levels of outsourcing will grow from 67% to 81% by 2008 (SharedExpertiseForums, 2005).

Outsourcing Leadership

Outsourcing decisions can be both rational and political in nature. Although most of the literature gives the illusion that the process is essentially rational, including legitimate goals such as cost efficiency and effectiveness (senior management evaluating the alternatives, apply a low cost criterion, and then select the most efficient option; Allison, 1971), we need to consider the political aspects of this subject, which are present not only during the outsourcing decision but during the entire life of the relationship. In this situation, we are referring to the politics, conflicts, and compromises involved during the development of this relationship.

During the outsourcing process managers improve their skills and acquire key competencies. One of those key competencies is the ability to coordinate the web of transactions that have to be undertaken effectively within the network that the outsourcing company establishes with its contractors. In addition, this situation requires establishing precise, measurable objectives for the outsourcing. Dun & Bradstreet suggest establishing a scorecard that quantifies each objective the outsourcing is supposed to accomplish and setting up periodic reviews with relevant internal staff and the outsourcing partner to assess how things are going and whether objectives are being met.

In this moment, in which the offshoring of production activities has given way to moving higher-added-valued services to emerging countries in order to be more competitive, Spanish companies are a good example of a gap in outsourcing leadership. As we see in Table 2, cultural differences with the host country (49%) and corporate resistance (44%) are the two main risks that Spanish business leaders have pinpointed when offshoring (Ricart & Agnese, 2006).

Table 2. Risks taken into account when offshoring an activity (percentage of companies surveyed)

	Spain	*Germany*	*Holland*	*USA*
Customer acceptance	43%	21%	24%	46%
Loss of control	42%	33%	44%	48%
Corporate resistance	44%	n.d.	32%	36%
Cultural differences *	49%	33%	36%	28%
Security of data	29%	14%	24%	55%
Quality of service	40%	28%	52%	68%
Recovery from disasters	28%	18%	n.d.	n.d.
Operational efficiency	32%	39%	46%	55%
Staff rotation	33%	26%	25%	40%
Loss of intellectual property	19%	20%	38%	40%
Political consequences	18%	22%	4%	22%
Staff lack of motivation	16%	31%	n.d.	n.d.
Political instability *	24%	14%	21%	22%
Instability *	26%	13%	n.d.	n.d.

Note. From "El offshoring en España: Causas y consecuencias de la deslocalización de servicios," by J. E. Ricart & P. Agnese, 2006, Centro Anselmo Rubiralta de Globalización y Estrategia.
** host country*

Relationship Outsourcing Management

The costs of outsourcing can be substantial if the vendor behaves opportunistically. Opportunism extends the notion that people act in their own self-interest with guile (Williamson, 1975). Williamson also suggests that opportunism is only a threat when there are a small number of vendors available to provide service.

Williamson found that markets with a large number of suppliers minimize opportunism because "rivalry among larger numbers of bidders will render opportunistic inclinations ineffectual" (Williamson, 1975, p. 27). Companies may still wish to buy transactions from a market with few suppliers, but they are admonished to reduce the threat of opportunism by signing appropriate contracts. Williamson recognizes that conditions change during contract execution. Thus, when banks first enter a market to outsource a business process, there may be a large number of suppliers to choose from. No one supplier may have a substantial advantage over the others, since each is assumed to have minimal knowledge about the idiosyncrasies of the bank's business. The outsourcing bank may select a supplier based on who provides the required service for the lowest cost. During this initial selection stage, opportunism is not a serious threat. However, once a supplier is selected, it gains valuable knowledge about the customer's organization during the contract period. At the end of the first contractual period, the supplier has an advantage over the other vendors in the marketplace. Renegotiation with the original supplier will be the most attractive alternative, but results in a situation called "small numbers bargaining", where the supplier may have opportunistically (Pisano, 1990; Williamson, 1975).

In spite of the contract, the outsourcing organization must continuously monitor the process during its execution because the vendor may impose excess charges or may not perform the duties as agreed upon. The contract monitoring capability involves holding suppliers accountable for both existing service contracts and the development of performance standards.

When companies are choosing outsourcing destination countries, the relationship of outsourcing management is a very important factor. Companies are more attractive not only for location cost advantages and abundant resources, but also for their cultural affinity. Aspects such as language skills, physical proximity, and cultural similarities are relevant when companies are choosing destination countriess to outsource because of their abilities to facilitate the management of the outsourcing relationships (Kearney, 2007).

Knowledge Management Process

This framework is grounded in the sociology of knowledge (Berger & Luckman, 1967) and is based on the view that organizations are social collectives and "knowledge systems". According to this framework, organizations as knowledge systems consist of four sets of socially-enacted "knowledge processes": 1) creation, 2) storage/retrieval, 3) transfer, and 4) application (Hozner & Marx, 1979). This view of an organization as knowledge systems represents both the cognitive and social nature of organizational knowledge and its embodiment is the individual's cognition and practices as well as the organization's collective practice and culture (Alavi & Leidner, 2001).

Knowledge Creation

Organizational knowledge creation involves developing new content or replacing existing content within the organization's tacit and explicit knowledge (Pentland, 1995). Through social and collaborative processes as well as an individual's cognitive processes (e.g., reflection), knowledge is created, shared, amplified, enlarged, and justified in organizational settings (Nonaka, 1994).

Knowledge Storage/Retrieval

Empirical studies have shown that while organizations create knowledge and learn, they also forget (Argote, Beckman, & Epple, 1990). Thus, the storage and retrieval of organizational knowledge, also referred to as organizational memory (Stein & Zwass, 1995) is a very important component of effective organizational knowledge management. Organizational memory covers aspects which go beyond the individual memory to include other components such as organizational culture, transformation (production processes and work procedures), structure, ecology and information archives (Walsh & Ungson, 1991).

Knowledge Transfer

Transfer occurs at various levels: transfer of knowledge between individuals, from individuals to explicit sources, from individuals to groups, between groups, across groups, and from the group to the organization. Gupta and Govindarajan (2000) have conceptualized knowledge flows in terms of five elements: (1) perceived value of the source unit's knowledge; (2) motivational disposition of the source; (3) existence and richness of transmission channels; (4) motivational disposition of the receiving unit; and (5) the absorptive capacity of the receiving unit, defined as the ability not only to acquire and assimilate but also to use knowledge (Cohen & Levinthal, 1990).

Knowledge Application

An important aspect of the knowledge-based theory of the firm is that the source of competitive advantage resides in the application of the knowledge rather than in the knowledge itself. Following Grant (1996), we can identify three primary mechanisms for the integration of knowledge to create organizational capability: directives, organizational routines, and self-contained task teams.

PROPOSITIONS

Below we present our three propositions. In addition, Figure 1 includes our conceptual model.

Managerial Outsourcing Competence and Firm Performance

Historically, banks outsourced repetitive tasks such as facilities management or logistics but currently have begun to outsourcing more visible and sensitive functions such as customer service and R&D. Moreover, this trend is expected to continue and grow in the foreseeable future.

As previously mentioned, up until now banks have been outsourcing fairly repetitive tasks, but outsourcing capabilities by themselves are ineffective at providing a basis for sustainable competitive advantage because they are easy to imitate. Thus, we expect that the impact of managerial outsourcing competence on a firm's performance cannot be measured directly, but can only be quantified by examining the indirect effect on some intervening capability (e.g. knowledge management process).

Therefore, the following proposition is set forth:

Proposition 1: *The relationship between managerial outsourcing competence and firm performance is mediated by organizational knowledge management processes.*

Managerial Outsourcing Competence and Knowledge Management Process

During the outsourcing relationship firms develop new managerial capabilities and improve upon those that already exist. We argue that outsourcing noncore activities is an interactive way to learn not just the objective and observable aspects of the other firm but also the more tacit aspects as well. This relationship represents a good opportunity of learning and improving the managerial knowl-

Figure 1. Conceptual model

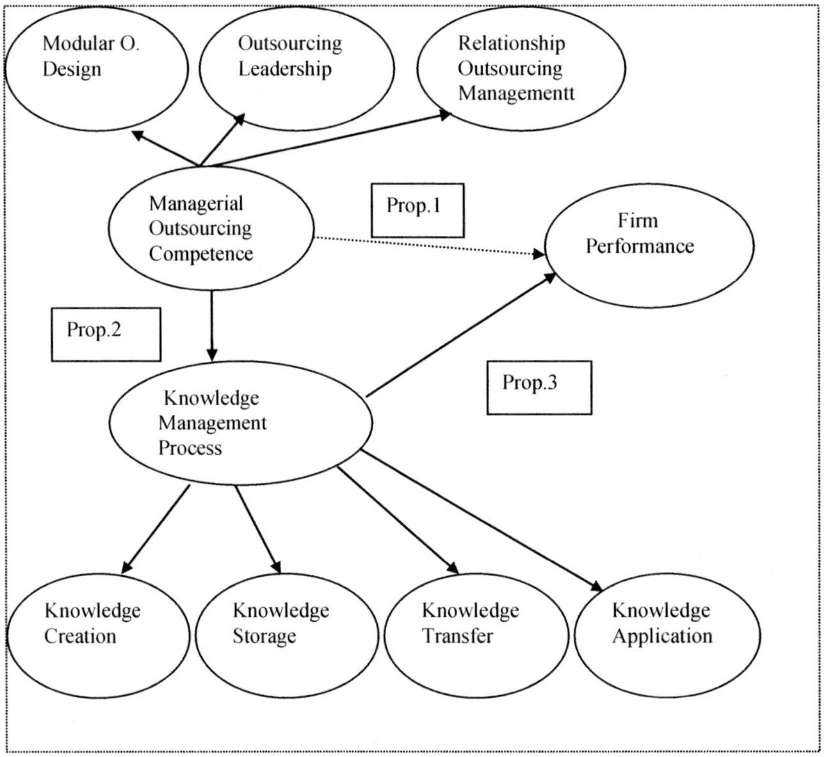

edge of the firm. Important sources of managerial capabilities are development from the relationship between the firm and the contractor. The firms spend substantial time and effort in identifying alliance partners, determining goals of outsourcing, negotiations terms, making agreements, choosing appropriate governance structures, building social and relational capital, and managing the alliances (Ireland, Hitt, & Vaidyanath, 2002).

Other sources of managerial capabilities streams from analyzing its current organizational structure, its processes, and its activities. The outsourcing firm knows more about its needs, routines, procedures, directives, and about its self-contained task teams because the process also implies asking itself about its current organizational structure, processes and activities.

Then, the managerial outsourcing needs trigger an organizational reflection process which enables knowledge creation. We can find here the four modes of knowledge creation: socialization, externalization, internalization, and combination (Nonaka, 1994). Each mode relies on, contributes to, and benefits from other modes. For example, the socialization mode can result in creation when the outsourcing firm obtains a new insight (internalization) which is triggered by an interaction with the other firm. On the other hand, the socialization mode may involve transferring existing tacit knowledge from one member to the other through a discussion of ideas (Alavi & Leidner, 2001). We are suggesting that knowledge creation can be enhanced through the outsourcing process.

In addition, the outsourcing process enlarges the organizational memory, in both semantic and episodic memory. For example, as semantic memory refers to general, explicit and articulate knowledge, we can refer to all documentation, reports, and charts generated by the outsourcing process. As episodic memory refers to context-specific and situated knowledge, outsourcing process generates a flow of organizational decisions and their outcomes.

During the outsourcing process, individuals and groups transfer knowledge through formal and informal channels. One important aspect of transferring knowledge is the absorptive capacity of the outsourcing firm, defined as the ability not only to acquire and assimilate but also to use knowledge (Cohen & Levinthal, 1990).

Thus, given the potential impact that managerial outsourcing competence has on knowledge process, the following proposition is set forth:

Proposition 2: *Managerial outsourcing competence is positively related to knowledge management process.*

Knowledge Management Process and Firm Performance

Competition is increasingly knowledge-based as firms strive to learn and to develop capabilities earlier than their rivals (D'Aveni, 1994; Teece & Pisano, 1994). In turbulent markets, the strategic value to a firm will naturally erode over time as substitutes appear and new competitive problems emerge. When firm's capabilities build on tacit knowledge and are rare, imperfectly tradable, and costly to imitate, these are the basis of superior performance (Barney, 1991, 1995; Spender, 1996). The fact of outsourcing noncore activities enables the firm to think strategically and critically on its core business processes of knowledge creation and transfer. Further, this process enables firms to focalize on what they do best, the converging of resources on a few clearly defined and consistent goals; focusing the effort of each group, department, and business unit in a sequential fashion; and targeting those activities that have the biggest impact on customers' perceived value (Yang & Peterson, 2004). Creating and sustaining competitive advantage is the core of strategic management (Barney, 1991). The following proposition is set forth:

Proposition 3: *There is a positive relationship between knowledge management process and firm performance.*

EXPLORATORY RESEARCH METHODOLOGY

As a first approach to the outsourcing problem within the community banking industry, we prepared an electronic survey with data gathered from participating executives of the North Carolina Bankers Association for the purpose of identifying the business processes that they are currently outsourcing, believe they will outsource in the future or that they will never outsource. We explain the composition of the sample and data collection, and then we analyze the results of the test.

Sample and Data Collection

The data set consisted of 132 possible respondents from the North Carolina Bankers Association, with 31 responses, thus providing a response rate of approximately 24%. Completing the research instrument was either the chief executive officer or the chief information officer of the organization. Other data collected included demographic information (location of the bank and its assets). The instrument was pilot tested using banking officials comparable to those used in the study to eliminate any ambiguity as well as to ensure a complete understanding of the questions and the survey instrument. These individuals were not included as sampling units in the actual survey.

A 5-point Likert-type scale was used to measure respondents' propensity to use onshore outsourcing methods (1 = *Currently Outsourcing* and 5 = *Never Outsource*). Additionally, the reason for outsourcing was measured on a scale of 1 to 5, with 1 being *Extremely Important* and 5 being *Unimportant*. The survey instrument did require that the bankers reveal their identity for tracking purposes, but individual responses remained confidential. Various statistical methodologies such as the stepwise and *t*-test procedures were applied using SPSS (2005).

Delivery of the survey was administered online. Electronic surveys provide a faster reaction time than traditional mail surveys, with many studies reporting that most e-mail responses arrive within 2 to 3 days following the initial e-mail contact (Bachmann & Elfrink, 1996). In addition, bankers received two e-mails, with the first asking for their assistance in the online survey. Two weeks after the initial e-mail, a second reminder e-mail was sent to those individuals who had not yet participated. Participants were given appropriate instructions in each of the e-mails on how to complete the online survey instrument. The internal validity of the survey was conducted using Cronbach's alpha and was found to be .886.

ANALYSIS AND RESULTS

In Table 3, the stepwise regression procedure identified three onshore variables at a significance level of 0.10, which influenced the respondent's views related to cost. The stepwise procedure identified the following significant variables: payroll services, which would include third-party preparation of payroll reports to promotes confidentiality of payroll information and complying with relevant regulations; ALM (Asset/Liability Management) modeling, or the measurement and management of asset and liability maturities or repayments in order to reduce interest rate risk; and, Check 21 imaging, or the federal requirement that banks accept images rather than hard-copy cancelled checks. Relationships are revealed in terms of cost. As indicated by the results in Table 3, the higher the importance of cost, the more payroll services will be outsourced onshore. This is also the case with ALM modeling. Additionally, the more important cost, the more likely banks were to outsource Check 21 imaging onshore.

Table 3. Results of stepwise procedure and cost

Dependent Variable	Independent Variables	Beta Coefficient	*t* statistic	*p* value
Cost	Payroll Services	0.763	8.97	0.000
	ALM Modeling	0.290	5.92	0.000
	Check 21 Imaging	–0.117	–2.35	0.033

In Table 4, the stepwise procedure identified the significant independent variable of fixed assets in relationship to the dependent variable of focusing on the banks' core function. Fixed Assets are nonearning assets such as buildings, fixtures and equipment. Software may also be included in fixed assets, as it has a depreciable life of five years. The more important this independent variable, the more likely the banks would outsource in the near future. The independent variable of human resources was found that the more important this variable the more likely offshore outsourcing would occur. Human resources would include those functions that allow the management of people, such as benefits, employee assessment and regulatory compliance.

Addressing the variable of gaining access to world-class capabilities in Table 5, it was found that the more important banking executives thought the dependent variable of gaining access to world-class capabilities, the more the banks outsourced the management of their fixed assets. This was also the case with the independent variables of ALM Modeling and Check 21 imaging.

CONCLUSION

Firms are increasingly relying on knowledge acquired from other firms to facilitate the development of their own capabilities. This study examines the role that outsourcing noncore business process plays in the success of a firm mediated by a knowledge management process.

We present managerial outsourcing competence (MOC) as a construct that is jointly determined by three resources of the outsourcing firm and we argue the impact of MOC over the performance is mediated by a knowledge management process. The MOC, which has been developed during the outsourcing process, is not enough to generate sustainable competitive advantage because is easy to replicate. The firm could

Table 4. Results of stepwise procedure and focus on core functions

Dependent Variable	Independent Variables	Beta Coefficient	*t* statistic	*p* value
Focus on Core Functions	Fixed Assets	0.443	3.95	0.001
	Human Resources	1.206	2.54	0.019

Table 5. Results of stepwise procedure world-class capabilities

Dependent Variable	Independent Variables	Beta Coefficient	*t* statistic	*p* value
Gain Access to World-Class Capabilities	Fixed Assets	0.913	23.073	0.000
	ALM Modeling	0.097	4.631	0.001
	Check 21 Imaging	0.100	2.056	0.070

obtain a desirable competitive position within an industry if it could utilize MOC to leverage other firm-specific capabilities. Outsourcing noncore business processes has no direct effect on a firm's performance. In this article we are enhancing the complementarities and cospecialization between MOC and a knowledge management process.

From one side, through a knowledge management process the outsourcer banks achieve a stronger awareness of its outsourcing "know how," which is embedded in routines, procedures, directives and in self-contained tasks. We argue that the more firms outsource noncore activities the more efficient they will become at using their outsourcing know-how. As we see in our exploratory, test banks always outsource more than one business process, and this suggests that banks could be achieving scope economies through the application of outsourcing know-how in the many different noncore business processes.

Another side, of the knowledge management process enables firms to focalize on what they do best, concentrating resources through the processes of converging resources on a few clearly defined and consistent goals, building core competences and understanding strategic know-how. We reinforce this theoretical aspect after analyzing the results of the test because in our survey banks reasons for outsourcing are majority strategic ones such as cost, focus on core functions and gain access to world-class knowledge A knowledge-based approach to strategy formulation effectively matches the opportunities and corporate capabilities of the banks and may generate economically feasible strategic alternatives.

Limitations

The model presented in this article is primarily conceptual in nature, and thus needs to be validated with other specific empirical studies which are adequate to the conceptual model we are proposing. In spite of this, the survey and the statistical tests we are showing in this article have been a very useful empirical tool that addresses the approach to the outsourcing problem within the banking industry. Anyway, we are aware that the following step of our work is to test our model with structural equations methodologies.

Data collected in the survey reflects information exclusively collected from North Carolina banks and, more specifically, only those banks that held memberships within the North Carolina Banking Association at the time the survey was distributed. By limiting this survey only to those members of the North Carolina Banking Association, we cannot generalize our findings to all community banking institutions and their outsourcing decisions.

Further Research

Several kinds of follow-up research studies could be done. In the case of outsourcing business process functions, banks can neither transfer risk nor share risk with the outside vendor. Therefore, the informal network appears as a very interesting alternative for community banks which need to manage their risks in a very efficient way. We think it could be particularly interesting in this industry to see the outsourcing decision as an agency problem and study problems that may result as lack of current information and knowledge for the institution.

Another interesting research area and related questions could address exactly what the banks have gained (economically and quality of service improvements) by outsourcing the various (Payroll Services...Fixed Asset) processes. Is the gain more evident in some of the processes over others?

REFERENCES

Adam Smith Institute. (2007). *The wisdom of Adam Smith (1723-1790).* Retrieved July 29, 2007, from http://www.adamsmith.org/smith/quotes.htm

Alavi, M., & Leidner, D. E. (2001). Review: Knowledge management and knowledge management systems: Conceptual foundations and research issues. *MIS Quarterly, 25*(1), 107-136.

Allison, G. (1971). *Essence of decision.* Boston: Little, Brown.

Ang, S., & Straub, D. (1998). Production and transaction economies and information systems outsourcing: A study of the U.S. banking industry. *MIS Quarterly, 22*(4), 535-552.

Aranha, H., & Wheelwright, S. (2007). Transition from business process outsourcing to knowledge process outsourcing. *Biopharm International, 20*(5), 58.

Arellano, N. E. (2007). *North American companies "can't find" qualified IT talent.* Retrieved May 19, 2007, from http://www.cio.com/article/108054/North_American_Companies_Can_t_Find_Qualified_IT_Talent/2

Argote, L., Beckman, S., & Epple, D. (1990). The persistence and transfer of learning in industrial settings. *Management Science, 36,* 140-154.

Bachmann, D., & Elfrink, J. (1996). Tracking the progress of e-mail versus snail-mail. *Marketing Research, 8*(2), 31-35.

Banking & securities: Still tightening those belts. (2003). Retrieved June 23, 2007, from http://www.businessweek.com/magazine/content/02_02/b3765651.htm?chan=search

Barney, J. (1991). Firm resources and sustained competitive advantage. *Journal of Management, 17*(1), 99-120.

Barney, J. (1995). Looking inside for competitive advantage. *Academy of Management Executive, 9,* 49-61.

Barthélemy, J., & Quélin, B. V. (2006). Complexity of outsourcing contracts and ex post transaction costs: An empirical investigation. *Journal of Management Studies, 43*(8), 1775-1797.

Berger, P. L., & Luckmann, T. (1966). *The social construction of reality.* Harmondsworth, England: Penguin.

Cohen, W. M., & Levinthal, D. A. (1990). Absorptive capacity: A new perspective on learning and innovation. *Administrative Science Quarterly, 35*(1), 128-52.

D'Aveni, R. A. (1994). *Hypercompetition: Managing the dynamics of strategic maneuvering.* New York: Free Press.

Deloitte 2006 security search. (2006). Retrieved June 1, 2007, from http://www.deloitte.com/dtt/cda/doc/content/us_fsi_150606globalsecurity-survey(1).pdf

Fulk, J., & DeSantis, G. (1995). Electronic communication and changing organizational forms. *Organization Science, 6*(4).

Gilley, M., & Rasheed, A. (2000). Making more by doing less: An analysis of outsourcing and its effects on firm performance. *Journal of Management, 26*(4), 763-790.

Gillis, A. (2005). *The future of outsourcing.* Retrieved June 9, 2007, from http://www.ababj.com/futureoutsourcing.html

Grant, R. M. (1996). Toward a knowledge-based theory of the firm. *Strategic Management Journal, 17,* 109-122.

Grover, V., Cheon, M., & Teng, J. (1996). The effect of service quality and partnership on the outsourcing of information systems functions. *Journal of Management Information Systems, 12*(4), 89-116.

Gupta, A. K., & Govindarajan, V. (2000). Knowledge flows within multinational corporations. *Strategic Management Journal, 21,* 473-496.

Gupta eyes paperless check clearance. Retrieved June 22, 2007, from http://mitsloan.mit.edu/newsroom/2002-gupta.php

Gupta, U. G., & Gupta, A. (1992). Outsourcing the IS function: Is it necessary for your organization? *Information Systems Management, 9*(3), 44-50.

Ireland, R., Hitt, M., & Vaidyanath, D. (2002). Alliance management as a source of competitive advantage. *Journal of Management, 28,* 413-446.

Kavan, C., Saunders, C., & Nelson, R. (1993). The information systems outsourcing bandwagon. *Sloan Management Review*, 73-86.

Kearney, A. T. (2007). *Destination Latin America: A Near-shore alternative.* Retrieved June 1, 2007, from http://www.atkearney.com

Kern, T., Kreijger, J., & Willcocks, L. (2002). Exploring ASP as sourcing strategy: Theoretical perspective, propositions for practice. *Journal of Strategic Information System, 11,* 153-177.

Krebsbach, K. (2004). Outsourcing dominates as banks seek savings. *Bank Technology News, 17*(9), 16.

Lacity, M. C., & Hirschheim, R. (1993). The information systems outsourcing bandwagon. *Sloan Management Review, 35,* 73-86.

Lacity, M. C., Hirschheim, R., & Willcocks, L. (1994). Realizing outsourcing expectations: Incredible expectations, credible outcomes. *Information Systems Management, 11*(4), 7-18.

Lacity, M. C., & Willcocks, L. P. (1998). An empirical investigation of information technology sourcing practices: Lessons from experience. *MIS Quarterly, 22*(3), 363-408.

Lacity, M. C., Willcocks, L. P. & Feeny, D. F. (1996). The value of selective IT outsourcing. *Sloan Management Review, 37,* 13-25.

Loh, L., & Venkatraman, N. (1992). Determinants of IT outsourcing: A cross-sectional analysis. 9, 7-24.

McAdam, R., & McCormack, D. (2001). Integrating business processed for global alignment and supply chain management. *Business Process Management Journal, 7*(2), 19-23.

McFarlan, F. W., & Nolan, R. L. (1995). How to manage an IT outsourcing alliance. *Sloan Management Review, 36,* 9-22.

McLaughlin, T. (2004). *The shape of banks to come.* Retrieved August 9, 2005, from http://www.gtnews.com

Moitra, D., & Ganesh, J. (2005). Web services and flexible business processes: Towards the adaptive influence of a learning culture on it investments. *Information and Management, 42,* 921-933.

Nonaka, I. (1994). A dynamic theory of organizational knowledge creation. 5(1), 14-37.

Orlikowski, W., Yates, J., Okamura, K., & Fujimoto, M. (1995). Shaping electronic communication: The metastructuring of technology in the context of use. *Organization Science, 6*(4), 423-444.

Parker, A. (2004). *Two-speed Europe: Why 1 million jobs will move offshore.* Retrieved June 12, 2007, from http://www.forrester.com

Penrose, E. (1959). *The theory of the growth of the firm.* London: Basil Blackwell.

Pentland, B. T. (1995). Read me what it says on your screen: The interpretative problem in technical service work. *Technology Studies, 2*(1), 50-79.

Pisano, G. P. (1990). The R&D boundaries of the firm: An empirical analysis. *Administrative Science Quarterly, 35,* 153-176.

Powell, T. C., & Dent-Micallef, A. (1997). Information technology as competitive advantage: The role of human, business, and technology resources. *Strategic Management Journal, 18*(5), 375-405.

Quinn, J. B. (1999). Strategic outsourcing: Leveraging knowledge capabilities. *Sloan Management Review*, 9-21.

Raysman, R., & Brown, P. (2005). Computer law: Sarbanes-Oxley's 404 and business process outsourcing. *New York Law Journal, 233*(34), 23-35.

Ricardo, D. (2004). *Exporting jobs is not free trade.* Retrieved January 15, 2007, from http://www.iht.com/articles/123898.html

Ricart, J., & Agnese, P. (2006). El offshoring en España. Causas y consecuencias de la deslocalización de servicios. *Centro Anselmo Rubiralta de Globalización y Estrategia.* Retrieved June 12, 2007, from http://www.iese.edu/en/ad/Anselmo-Rubiralta/Apuntes/EneroAbril2007/Espanades-localizacionconreservas.asp

Saunders, C., Gebelt, M., & Hu, Q. (1997). Achieving success in information systems outsourcing. *California Management Review, 39*(2), 63-79.

SharedXpertiseForums, SBPOA. (2005). Accenture gets $290M deal from Caixa. Retrieved November 14, 2007, from http://www.sharedxpertise.com/file/2314/accenture-gets-290m-deal-from-caixa.html

Spender, J. C. (1996). Competitive advantage from tacit knowledge? Unpacking the concept and its strategic implications. In B. Moingeon & A. Edmondson (Eds.), *Organizational learning and competitive advantage.* London: Sage.

Stein, E., & Zwass, V. (1995). Actualizing organizational memory with information systems. *ISR, 6*(2), 85-117.

Technology outsourcing: Trends to watch for in your due diligence. (2005). Retrieved May 15, 2005, from http://www.cunatechnologycouncil.org/news/204.html

Teece, D., & Pisano, G. (1994). The dynamic capabilities of firms: An Introduction. *Industrial and Corporate Change, 3*(3), 537-556.

Wade, M., & Hulland, J. (2004). Review: The resource-based view and information systems research: Review, extension and suggestions for future research. *MIS Quarterly, 28*(1).

Walsh, J., & Ungson, G. (1991). Organizational memory. *The Academy of Management Review, 16*(1), 57-91.

Wernerfelt, B. (1984). A resource-based view of the firm. *Strategic Management Journal, 5*(2), 171-180.

Willcocks, L., Hindle, J., Feeny, D., & Lacity, M. (2004). IT and business process outsourcing: The knowledge potential. *Information Systems Management, 21*(3), 7-15.

Willcocks, L., & Lacity, M. (1998). *Strategic sourcing of information systems: Perspectives and practices.* New York: Wiley.

Willcocks, L. P., Lacity, M., & Kern, T. (1999). Risk mitigation in IT outsourcing strategy revisited: Longitudinal case research at LISA. *Journal of Strategic Information Systems, 8*(3), 285-341.

Williamson, O. E. (1975). *Markets and hierarchies.* New York: Free Press.

Yang, Z., & Peterson, R. (2004). Customer perceived value, satisfaction, and loyalty: The role of switching costs. *Psychology and Marketing, 21*(10), 799-822.

Zaheer, A., & Venkatraman, N. (1994). Determinants of electronic integration in the insurance industry: An empirical test. *Management Science, 40*(5), 549-566.

This work was previously published in Journal of Information Technology Research, Vol. 1, Issue 2, edited by M. Khosrow-Pour, pp. 21-37, copyright 2008 by IGI Publishing, formerly known as Idea Group Publishing (an imprint of IGI Global).

Chapter XXVIII
Delivering the 'Whole Product': Business Model Impacts and Agility Challenges in a Network of Open Source Firms

Joseph Feller
University College Cork, Ireland

Patrick Finnegan
University College Cork, Ireland

Jeremy Hayes
University College Cork, Ireland

ABSTRACT

It has been argued that competitive necessities will increasingly require OSS companies to participate in cooperative business networks in order to offer the complete product/service (whole product) demanded by customers. It is envisaged that these business networks will enhance the business models of participant firms by supplementing their value-adding activities and increasing responsiveness to customers. However, while such propositions have intuitive appeal, there is a lack of empirical research on such networks. This article examines Zea Partners, a network of small open source companies cooperating to deliver the 'whole product' in the area of content management systems (CMSs). It investigates how participation in the network augments the business models of participant companies and identifies the business agility challenges faced by the network. The article concludes that reconciling the coordination needs of OSS networks with the operational practices of participant firms is a critical issue if such networks are to achieve adaptive efficiency to deliver whole products in a 'bazaar-friendly' manner.

INTRODUCTION

Researchers (Agerfalk, Finnegan, Hayes, Lundell, & Ostling, 2006; Feller, Finnegan, Hayes, & Lundell, 2006a; Fitzgerald, 2006) have recently argued that open source software firms should adopt a 'whole product' approach (cf. Moore, 1999) by forming a network/ecosystem of partners with complementary capabilities "to offer a professional product and service in an agile, bazaar-friendly manner" (Fitzgerald, 2006, p. 294). This 'whole product' approach is consistent with the challenges of "productizing OSS" discussed by Woods and Guliani (2005), as well as developments in the production and use of other complex product/service offerings as discussed by Davidow and Malone (1992). This approach is regarded as appropriate when there is a need for firms to quickly deliver a variety of customized products, and when the nature of the product development process means that individual organizations do not have sufficient competencies to deal with all parts of product design (Davidow & Malone, 1992; Huang, 2001). In such circumstances, market forces require organizations with similar goals to align themselves in IT-mediated partner networks in order to meet customer requirements (Stafford, 2002).

Moore (1999) popularized the concept of the 'whole product' as the cornerstone of market-driven, rather than product-driven, businesses. However, the concept resonates with the dynamics of the open source software phenomenon, which, due to the licensing structure, emphasizes services and meta-services surrounding the artifact. Indeed, Woods and Guliani (2005) describe as the challenge of 'productizing' open source software as the need to offer support, implementation, modification, and related services. Thus, networks of cooperating, small, open source software organizations may represent what Clemons and Row (1992) term a "move-to-the middle," where networks of organizations interact in order to deliver value (in the form of the whole product) to the end consumer.

This article examines Zea Partners, a business network of firms developing content management systems and selling related services, all based around the Zope application server. It investigates how participation in the network augments the business models of participant firms in order to adopt a 'whole product' approach, and identifies the challenges faced by the network in trying to ensure the business agility necessary to offer the 'whole product'. The article begins by discussing the theoretical foundation for the study. Next, the research objective and research methods are discussed. The case environment is then outlined and the findings presented. The article illustrates that participation in the network allows firms to share business model components within a centrally managed network, and to engage in agile competitive practices by making network-level changes in response to changes in the external environment. The need to address adaptability and alignment issues in addition to business agility is highlighted, however. Consequently, the article concludes that reconciling the coordination needs of OSS networks with the operational practices of participant firms is a critical issue if such networks are to achieve adaptive efficiency to deliver whole products in a bazaar-friendly manner.

THEORETICAL FOUNDATION

OSS has been investigated from a variety of disciplinary and theoretical perspectives. The two dominant research themes, however, have been: (1) OSS software engineering tools and techniques and (2) the socio-cultural analysis of OSS communities. Commercial organizations are under-represented in the research, not just in terms of quantity, but more importantly in terms of depth of research. In particular, the understanding of economic and business model issues surrounding OSS is limited (Feller, Finnegan, Kelly, & MacNamara, 2006b). In this section, we draw on the wider literature on business models and business networks to develop the theoretical grounding for our study. In particular, we examine how extant research on business models and networks can improve our understanding of the issues facing firms seeking to form the type of agile business ecosystems envisaged by Fitzgerald (2006).

In keeping with the increasing commercialization of OSS, researchers such as Krishnamurthy (2005), Weber (2004), Spiller and Wichmann (2002), Raymond (2001), and Hecker (2000) have documented a series of OSS business models. However, much of this work concentrates on the source of the revenue stream and neglects other aspects of the business models. This is not surprising, as the terms 'business model' and 'revenue model' are frequently, and incorrectly, used interchangeably. Looking outside the OSS literature, it is evident from the work of Timmers (1999), Mahadevan (2000), and Osterwalder and Pigneur (2002) that business models must examine value-adding activities in the context of a supply chain or business network. Osterwalder and Pigneur (2002) propose a comprehensive approach, and detail an ontology that focuses on four aspects of the organization: product innovation, infrastructure management, customer relationship, and financials. Mahadevan (2000) defines a business model as a blend of three streams: value, revenue, and logistics. The value stream is concerned with the value proposition for buyers, sellers, and market makers. The revenue stream identifies how the organizations will earn revenue, and the logistics stream involves detailing how supply chain issues will affect the organizations involved. Timmers (1999) argued that architectures for business models can be identified through the deconstruction and reconstruction of a value chain. Value chain elements are identified, as are the possible ways that information can be integrated both within the value chain and between the respective value chains of interacting parties. Furthermore, Evans and Wurster (2000) argue that as more advanced information standards are introduced, levels of collaboration between organizations can be achieved that were previously only possible within a vertically integrated hierarchical intra-organizational structure. Thus, many economic entities have recognized the importance of the composition of the supply chain (or business network) to the overall performance of the firm (Christiaanse, 2005).

The benefits of cooperative business relationships have been advocated for decades (Kaufman, 1966; Van de Ven, 1976; Cash & Konsynski, 1985; Henderson, 1990; Finnegan, Galliers, & Powell, 2003). These relationships have been described as business webs (Tapscott, Ticoll, & Lowy, 2000), partnerships (Henderson, 1990), networks (Nelson, 1988; Joynt, 1991; Finnegan et al., 2003), strategic alliances (Joynt, 1991; Bronder & Pritzl, 1992; Lei & Slocum, 1992), virtual organizations (Davidow & Malone, 1992; Goldman, Nagel, & Preiss, 1995), joint ventures (Kanter, 1989; Oliver, 1990; Campell, Hollingsworth, & Lindberg, 1991), service consortia and stakeholder or value-chain partnerships (Kanter, 1989), promotional and obligation networks (Campell et al., 1991), agency federations, trade associations, social service joint programs, corporate-financial interlocks, and agency-sponsor linkages (Oliver, 1990).

The reasons for such business cooperation include: resource procurement and allocation (Galaskiewicz, 1985; Clemons & Row, 1992; Alter & Hage, 1993), political advantages (Galaskiewicz, 1985), risk sharing and acquiring expertise (Alter & Hage, 1993), stability (Oliver, 1990), legitimacy (Galaskiewicz, 1985; Oliver, 1990), efficiency (Oliver, 1990; Clemons & Row, 1992), and innovating (Ticoll, Lowy, & Kalakota, 1998). Participants in business networks believe that collaboration will result in adaptive efficiency—the ability to change rapidly while providing customized services or products at a low cost (Alter & Hage, 1993). Thus, the ability to quickly assess new business opportunities, to identify suitable trading partners, and to effectively coordinate delivery of products and services across the business network is important (Sadeh, Hildum,

& Kjenstad, 2003). Following this logic, agility is seen as an important characteristic of business networks.

Agility is a business-wide capability that includes organizational structures, information systems, logistics processes, and mindsets (Christopher, 2000). The term agility has created significant interest in the business world (Lo, 1998) and is recognized as a prerequisite for success in dynamic or turbulent environments (Christopher, 2000; Camarinha-Matos, Afsarmanesh, & Rabelo, 2003). Fingar (2000) believes that "the ability to change is now more important than the ability to create…Change becomes a first class design goal and requires business and technology architectures whose components can be added, modified, replaced and configured" (p. 66). Sharifi and Zhang (1999) argue that the concept of agility has two main attributes: responding to change promptly and appropriately, and capitalizing on the opportunities that are created by change. In a business network, agility is highly dependent not only on the skills of the individual firms, but also on the flexibility of the supporting infrastructure (Camarinha-Matos et al., 2003). Infrastructure flexibility has been identified as an important characteristic of the agile organization (Christopher, 2000), and is dependent on both internal and external factors (Thomke & Reinertsen, 1998). External factors include changes in the needs of the end customer, while internal factors include changes in the development process. Thomke and Reinertsen (1998) argue that design flexibility can be brought about by: (1) following a development strategy that can endure a higher probability of design changes, (2) having the ability to produce late changes to the product design in order to better integrate it with the technology and the needs of the customer, and (3) preventing late changes to the product design by making design commitments at a very late stage in the development process.

To conclude, agile business networks designed to meet customer demands for customized products are reasonably well understood outside the OSS domain. Within the OSS field, recent work by Woods and Guliani (2005) and Fitzgerald (2006) has drawn attention to the importance of agile networks to OSS business models. However, small OSS firms have emerged from various OSS communities and thus cannot be considered to be the same as the type of firms that have been the subject of research on business networks to date. Therefore, there is a need for further research on the development of agile bazaar-friendly business ecosystems to deliver whole products in the OSS domain.

RESEARCH OBJECTIVE AND METHOD

The objective of this study is to explore the emerging phenomenon of a business network of OSS firms cooperating to deliver the 'whole product'. Two research questions were formulated to support this objective:

RQ1: *How does an OSS network affect the business models of participant organizations?*

RQ2: *What challenges are faced in ensuring that the network is agile?*

Case studies are regarded as the most commonly used qualitative research method in IS and are especially useful for studying organizational aspects of IS (Benbasat, Goldstein, & Mead, 1987). Cases are most appropriate when the objective involves studying contemporary events, without the need to control variables or subject behavior (Yin, 1994). The single case study method is considered to be a potentially rich and valuable source of data, while suited to exploring relationships between variables in their given context (Yin, 1994; Benbasat et al., 1987). We thus adopted a "soft positivist" epistemology as discussed by Kirsch (2004), and our method follows in the tradition of Eisenhardt (1989) and Madill, Jordan, and Shirley (2000); it is designed to reveal preexisting, relatively stable, and objectively extant phenomena and the relationships among them in a manner that is not limited to examining only pre-identified constructs.

The subject of the case study (Zea Partners) was chosen as it represented an interesting case in the area of open source business practice in that it is one of a small number of such networks aiming to deliver the 'whole product' in an OSS environment. The researchers first conducted a thorough archival search to determine the existence of public domain material on the network and participant companies. As a result of this preliminary analysis, the researchers prepared a case study protocol (cf. Yin, 1994). Based on this protocol, 16 interviews took place with key personnel from participant firms over a 17-month period from November 2004 to April 2006. In addition, the researchers had five separate interviews with the network founder (elite interviewing, cf. Marshall & Rossman, 1989) and also participated in four intensive workshops with network members during this time which facilitated member checking. The choice of interviewees was based on a number of factors. These were:

1. **Willingness to cooperate:** In order to obtain useful material, it was necessary for a potential interviewee to be interested in the study and willing to cooperate.
2. **History of network involvement:** Interviewees had to have been involved in ongoing network planning and/or project activity over a period of time. A consequence of this selection criterion was that the views of recent members were not studied.
3. **Seniority:** In order to get contextual material on business strategy and experience with network activities, it was necessary to speak with senior staff within each partner firm. A consequence of this selection criterion was that the views of junior staff were not studied.

Interviews, conducted using an interview guide (cf. Patton, 1980) were generally of one- to two-hour duration, with follow-up telephone interviews used to clarify and refine issues that emerged during transcription. Interviews were complemented by comprehensive reviews of documents and presentations at the workshops. The content analysis was conducted using Osterwalder and Pigneur's (2002) business model framework as well as Aitken et al.'s (2002) and Lee's (2004) agility frameworks. This is in line with Lee and Baskerville (2003), who, in addressing the issue of generalization, describe the process of generalizing from theory to empirical description (whereby the research seeks to apply findings confirmed in one setting to another one).

Case Environment

Zea Partners was founded in 2003 as the Zope Europe Association (ZEA) and changed its name to Zea Partners in 2006. Headquartered in Belgium, Zea Partners operates as an international network of businesses that build software and deliver services around the application server technology called Zope, which is widely used for developing content management systems, intranets, portals, and related applications. Zea Partners consists of 19 firms, with three managing partners and 16 associate partners located in The Netherlands, Italy, Norway, Belgium, Germany, the United Kingdom, Lithuania, the United States, Spain, France, and South Africa. The management team seeks project contracts on behalf of network members and performs network management activities such as marketing and project management. The team also develops the network's business strategy in conjunction with the managing partners.

The partner companies are typically small (10 people or less). These companies have recognized that their size limits the contract (deal) sizes for which they could effectively compete, as well as their geographic range. One of the benefits of the network is, thus, that a number of companies can pool their resources to compete for larger contracts on a global scale. More importantly, in the context of competing on the basis of a whole product, the network allows partners to offer a full range of value chain activities, rather than concentrating exclusively on their own specialties (e.g., development, consultancy, training, etc.). The network is currently working on ensuring that all partners can conduct marketing under the one brand.

According to the network's founder, the goal is:

...to say that we have the whole product. We are going to group together all the people who need a whole product made but can't invest the resources to do it, and then take that whole product and make it offerable by anyone in the network. It has so many benefits on profitability it's just amazing. It's really the only way to impact profitability.

He sees this as being the value proposition of the network, and acknowledges that, through partnering, the network can compete for larger deal sizes without competing directly with the large international consulting companies. In comparing the Zea Partners network with such consulting companies, he notes the increased flexibility offered to customers. In particular, he argues that:

Instead of having a cathedral[1] model of Accenture, or something like that, we want to have multiple players in multiple countries. We can move things around as new trends emerge, new specialties emerge, stuff like that."

He also highlights the importance of the fact that:

The people in the network are the people that created Silva, the creators of Plone, the creators of Workflow, the creators of Multilingual, the creators of each one of these things. And we want to explain to customers that it's in their interests to have a relationship that rewards these people. It's in their interests, first, because the guy who wrote it can get the job done at a pretty effective rate.

However, due to the early stage of development at which the network finds itself, coordination amongst partners is still on a person-to-person basis. There is an acknowledged need amongst members to evolve the organization of the network towards the use of quotas, geographical regions, and so forth. To date, coordination has meant observing trademark and domain rules, as well as some network terms and conditions to ensure that products/services delivered by partners meet the expectations of the customer. Finally, he acknowledges that it is critical to build trust amongst partners so that invoices are paid on time and other responsibilities are met.

Findings

The Osterwalder and Pigneur business model ontology was used as a lens to investigate how the presence of the Zea Partners network affects the business models of the member firms. The results are summarized in Table 1, classified as per the pillars of the Osterwalder and Pigneur (2002) framework, and are discussed below.

Zea Partners enhances the value that member firms can offer to a specific *target customer segment* (*value proposition*) by allowing smaller organizations to group together to deliver the whole product as part of a consortium. The fact that the network spans many geographic territories with multiple languages and specialized local knowledge means that a consortium made up of small organizations can compete with the larger consultancy firms. This cooperation increases the range of projects in which members can become involved. Zea Partners covers 12 different countries which, from a geographical spread, makes it comparable with a large company. In terms of targeting customers, the Zea Partners brand is purposefully designed to be a mark that

Table 1. Effects of Zea Partners network on participants' business models

Business Model Pillar		Effect of Zea Partners on Members' Business Models
Product Innovation	Target Customer Segment	Enhances reputation and branding of participants by providing a single 'market leader' brand
	Value Proposition	Extends geographic coverage, supports the ability to offer specialized expertise, products and services in many languages, and leveraging local knowledge
	Capabilities	Enhances existing capabilities by providing a broader range of business capabilities, especially project management and customer relationship management
Customer Relationship	Information Strategy	Aims to provide lead referrals and to contribute to the sharing of experiences and knowledge
	Feel and Serve	Facilitates profile building through common branding
	Trust and Loyalty	Leverages access to expertise of software originators to build customer trust
Infrastructure Management	Resources	Lowers friction when building teams, through information sharing, common methodology, tracking results, reporting bugs, and so forth
	Activity Configuration	Enables members to act as a "value shop" configuration; network reduces the information asymmetry between client and consultant resulting in customers 'joining' the community
	Partner Network	Network means that members do not have to outsource to partners outside the network
Financials	Revenue Model	Increases deal size for members by creating "whole product" consortia
	Cost Structure	Enables cost-sharing amongst members
	Profit/Loss	Increases revenue and lowers expenses through sharing among members, leading to bigger profits

distinguishes participants in the network as being leaders in the market. Thus, organizations must already have a good reputation before they can join the network. The Zea Partners network also enhances the business model of participants by adding to the range of *capabilities* that underpin their value propositions. Many of the Zea Partners members are small start-ups that consist of two to four people with mostly specialized technical expertise. A major benefit of Zea Partners membership has, thus, been the ability to access Zea Partners' expertise in areas such as project management, customer relationship management, requirements management, tendering, and sales to complement technical expertise. According to the founder of one of the participant companies (Infrae), the development of *capabilities* within Zea Partners is vital to delivering a professional service. In relation to the production of documentation, he noted that "over time we gradually removed all dependencies on the community, because it was completely unpredictable."

With regard to *information strategy,* Zea Partners' stated aim is to "learn together, share experiences and refer leads to each other." However, as yet, resource problems have limited Zea Partners' ability to meet their ideal in terms of information strategy. Nevertheless, Zea Partners are proving very successful in enhancing the manner in which a participant firm reaches its customers (*feel and serve*). The market for Zope and Plone is characterized by customers approaching firms in the network with whom they want to do business. A key value added by Zea Partners is that the profile-building activities of the network results in 'leads' for member firms. In some countries where the demand for Plone services exceeds supply, Zea Partners can partner with member firms in that country by co-signing the deal but leaving the local participant with ownership of the customer. Furthermore, a key aspect of customer relationships amongst open source firms is that *trust and loyalty* can be enhanced by providing access to the originator of the software. Thus,

Zea Partners aims to assemble project teams that contain relevant software originators from participant firms.

The OSS network model necessitates the inter-organizational management of business infrastructure. A key challenge has been integrating different participants in a seamless manner to deliver the 'whole product' to customers. Zea Partners aims to lower friction in inter-organizational teams by establishing a common approach through the use of *resources*, for example: standing contracts, having customer references on file, having a common methodology or a common way of thinking about a problem, assigning work, tracking results, and reporting bugs. This is summed up by the Zea Partners founder as being the:

...big difference between a rabble and an army. You can take a thousand people that speak different languages, that never worked together and they can get defeated by 50 people that are well trained.

This approach is also evident in the Zea Partners approach to the *configuration of activities* and processes at the level of individual firms and at the network level. The Zea Partners network allows members to act as a 'value shop' (cf. Stabell & Fjelstad, 1998) or service provider and carry out the phases of this configuration (problem finding and acquisition, problem solving, choice, execution, control, and evaluation) as if they were one integrated organization. One of the areas where Zea Partners differs from the "value shop" concept (as per Stabell & Fjeldstad, 1998) is that in the traditional "value shop" model, the information asymmetry between the client and the service provider (in this case a consultancy firm) is one of the main value drivers and results in high prices. This is not seen as desirable by Zea Partners. Instead the network endeavors to reduce this asymmetry so that the customer, instead of being a recipient of content management, becomes a participant in the OSS community:

There are certain people that need support contracts. There has not been a need for it in any of the projects we have been involved in. I'm a big believer in teaching the people to know enough about the solution to mostly fix it themselves. (Chief Architect, Plone Solutions)

Finally, in relation to infrastructure management, the *partner network* aspect of the business model is a service that Zea Partners completely operates on behalf of its members. Thus they do not need to outsource activities to non-member organizations.

Enhancing the *financial aspects* of the business models of participants is a key objective of the Zea Partners network. Zea Partners aims to increase the 'deal size' that members can tender for leading to increased profit margin. A key aspect of the Zea Partners' approach is, thus, the sharing of resources and common expenses. Thus participants can focus on key value-adding activities of their business models, while sharing the resources, costs, and risks of secondary value activities. An interesting revenue model arising in relation to OSS companies providing consulting services is an effort to move away from a 'bill-by-the hour' model to fixed price. This move is occurring as the constant innovation with OSS results in the need for much less customization and thus shorter development times. However, fixed-price billing creates challenges for network-based project management as time overruns cut into the profit margins of the participant providing the service.

The discussion of Table 1 above refers to the effects of the Zea Partners network on the business models of the network participants, and not the business model(s) of Zea Partners itself. However, the various effects, taken as whole, result in the Zea Partners network operating as an entity in its own right, and engaging in agile competitive practices. Aitken et al. (2002) present a framework for understanding agility in the context of internal activities such as marketing, production, design, organization, management, and people. This framework is utilized in the present study as a tool for describing the agile characteristics of Zea Partners, as summarized in Table 2 and discussed below.

The members of Zea Partners are already independently able to utilize recognition of the Zope and Plone brands as a marketing tool, but this is only relevant to client firms already aware of Zope/Plone. The unified brand image of Zea Partners promotes agile marketing in several ways, such as simplifying brand management (one brand vs. many) and allowing the network to devote resources to unified brand building, reducing the burden on individual members (e.g., in order to increase brand awareness of Zea Partners and its member organizations, the founder is active in giving interviews, attending conferences, etc.). The long-term goal of Zea Partners is to build up sufficient resources so that the network can project a professional image on behalf of the member organizations that simply would not possess the resources to do this individually.

The most important characteristic of Zea Partners vis-à-vis production is its ability to leverage the large amount of diverse skills possessed by the member organizations. According to the chief architect of Plone Solutions:

The thing that will make the network strong is that there is no single point of failure; you can swap out components or companies. If one company does not have the domain knowledge we normally have another company...It's very agile and very flexible.

Thus, the network allows delivery of the 'whole product', which would not be possible for the smaller members to do as a stand-alone provider. Likewise, many design issues associated with delivering the whole product are addressed through leveraging common experience with a common set of tools, working practices, communication norms, and cultures that serve to harmonize and integrate the practices of individual firms.

In terms of organizational activity, while the network facilitates matching member competency with customer need, Zea Partners does not currently use explicit coordination processes to schedule work. Previous attempts to do so have had negative results—for example, an incident in which a member firm was advised not to accept new work for a certain time period based on a client's intention, only to find that the client organization was unable to sign the contracts in the agreed timeframe, thus trapping the member firm into a period of non-productivity. However, by not having explicit scheduling mechanisms in place, Zea Partners believes that it is more agile than traditional consulting firms, as the network is able to allocate resources more dynamically and effectively and thus to smooth out the peaks

Table 2. Agile characteristics of Zea Partners

Activity Area	Key Characteristics
Marketing	Network provides and maintains unified Zope and Zea Partners brand
Production	Network provides harmonized and integrated collection of diverse production processes and capabilities to deliver the whole product
Design	Network provides harmonized and integrated collection of diverse design processes and capabilities to deliver the whole product
Organization	Network serves as competency rallying mechanism to deliver multi-lingual, whole product services across a wide geographic area
Management	Network distributes responsibility and revenue through simple, decentralized, and transparent network governance structures
People	Network provides customers with access to original software authors and/or experts with unique competencies

and valleys that are a characteristic of technology consulting and development work.

From a management perspective, the goal of Zea Partners is to ensure that network management and governance does not impede realizing the potential benefits associated with the fact that open source software is by nature highly decentralized. The founder of Zea Partners believes that this fact results in "a higher velocity of innovation," and that firms in the open source space are thus better equipped to adapt to the very specific needs of clients. For example, while a larger proprietary software development firm may decide not to support a particular language because the market is not big enough to sustain it, open source firms can leverage the work of individual developers and smaller groups who wish to support that language. Having a decentralized governance/management structure and a decentralized approach to consulting means that if a need is encountered for an unanticipated skill set, it is less of a problem to meet the need than it would be in the traditional consulting model. Finally, in relation to people, Zea Partners leverages the availability of access to the original author(s) and/or core maintainer(s) of the software products to respond to customer demand in an agile fashion.

Zea Partners is made up of a number of autonomous organizations, each having different philosophies, operating in different countries, and meeting the needs of a diverse group of clients—meaning that it can draw from a wider variety of experiences. The chief architect of Plone noted that there are consequential social and management challenges:

You will, of course, get the complexity that comes from coordinating different companies with different working styles, and the whole chemistry thing where not all people have worked with the other people all the time.

The business agility challenges that are faced by the network were analyzed using the work of Lee (2004) as a lens. He expands on the concept of internal agility by also considering the adaptability of a supply chain as well as the alignment of players within that supply chain. Lee's work is used to frame the content analysis of agility-related challenges facing Zea Partners and is summarized in Table 3. The categorization of challenges according to this classification reveals that the challenges extend beyond agility to matters of adaptability and alignment. Consequently, while Zea Partners has been able to engage in agile competitive practices, the challenges that management has articulated indicate the need to move beyond short-term agile practices to consider structural and technological changes in OSS markets, and create performance incentives.

CONCLUSION

This article has responded to the need to expand our understanding of economic and business aspects of the OSS phenomenon (cf. Feller et al., 2006b) by exploring the business model and agility aspects of participation by open source companies in a business network designed to deliver the 'whole product' (cf. Fitzgerald, 2006). This participation is seen by those studied as a business imperative in order for small OSS firms to compete for large 'deal sizes' with traditional integrated companies. The study indicates that participation in the network allows small firms to, in effect, outsource some elements of their business model to the network. This is particularly evident in the division of responsibility for customer-facing activities between participants and the central network. It is this division of responsibility that results in the network being able to engage in agile competitive practices, as network-level changes can be made rapidly in response to changes in the external environment. Thus, the challenges that the network faces in ensuring that the multitude of reciprocal interdependencies necessary for the delivery of a whole product do not adversely

Table 3. Key challenges for Zea Partners

AGILITY	
Objectives: To respond to short-term changes in demand or supply quickly and to handle external disruptions smoothly	**Key Challenges:** • Coordinate information flow amongst network participants to 'smooth out peaks and valleys' associated with traditional work • Foster collaborative relationships with partners based on the need for particular competencies • Develop network-level competencies (e.g., project management) to complement the core activities of participants
ADAPTABILITY	
Objectives: To adjust the network's design to meet structural shifts in markets; to modify supply network to strategies, products, and technologies	**Key Challenges:** • Leverage partner expertise in different geographical regions to understand the market for the total product • Plan for the introduction of new members into the network to meet requirements for particular competencies; also, ensure an adequate evaluation of potential members • Create an understanding of the needs of different types of customers (typically niche markets that traditional competitors do not serve) • Effectively manage the expertise of network partners to ensure that the competencies of the network evolve in response to changes in the product technologies that originate outside the network
ALIGNMENT	
Objectives: To create incentives for better performance	**Key Challenges:** • Exchange information and knowledge freely amongst network partners • Manage partner responsibilities in delivering the whole product in a manner that allows partners to focus on their core competencies • Effectively provide non-core competencies in a manner that participants can confidently delegate important business model components to the network • Equitably share risks, costs, and gains of initiatives • Enable customers to understand the business value of engaging with and contributing to the OSS community

affect the agility of the network. Nevertheless, it is clear that agile practices are only the first step for the network in competing in the software and consulting sector. It is evident that further work is necessary to address adaptability and alignment issues.

The need for agility, adaptability, and alignment is a problem in all business networks. However, Zea Partners is not typical of other business networks, which rely on formal coordination mechanisms and legal agreements. Rather we observe that the relatively informal characteristics, found in the Zea Partners network, reflects the informal structures characteristic of the online communities of OSS developers from which the firms emerged. Reconciling these two approaches to the coordination issue is a critical issue for future research if OSS networks are to achieve adaptive efficiency (cf. Alter & Hage, 1993) and to deliver whole products in a 'bazaar-friendly' manner (Fitzgerald, 2006).

Overall, our study contributes to the understanding of the commercialization of open source software. Previous studies of commercial firms have been dominated by studies of single firms, whether OSS start-ups such as RedHat and JBoss (e.g., Krishnamurthy, 2005; Watson, Wynn, & Boudreau, 2005) or very large multi-nationals like Apple, IBM, and Sun (e.g., West, 2003). Our study examines the perspective of small/micro firms engaged in a cooperative business network in a manner that takes more complete consideration of the business model concept than has been done to date in the OSS domain. Nevertheless, the methodology utilized for the study was exploratory, and thus the findings need further investigation. This study should be duplicated as part of the process of validating its findings in a context that is not just exploratory. In particular, further research is needed to replicate the study by assessing the results in a wider variety of networks.

ACKNOWLEDGMENT

The present work was funded by the European Commission (via IST Project 004337) and by the Irish Research Council for the Humanities and Social Sciences (via the O3C Business Models project).

REFERENCES

Agerfalk, P., Finnegan, P., Hayes, J., Lundell, B., & Ostling, M. (2006, June). 12 (not so) easy pieces: Grand challenges for open source software. *Proceedings of the 14th European Conference on Information Systems,* Gotenburg, Sweden.

Alter, C., & Hage, J. (1993). *Organisations working together.* London: Sage.

Benbasat, I., Goldstein, D.K., & Mead, M. (1987). The case research strategy in studies of information systems. *MIS Quarterly, 11*(3), 369–386.

Bronder, C., & Pritzl, R. (1992). Developing strategic alliances: A conceptual framework for successful co-operation. *European Management Journal, 10*(4), 412–421.

Camarinha-Matos, L.M., Afsarmanesh, H., & Rabelo, R.J. (2003). Infrastructure developments for agile virtual enterprises. *International Journal of Computer Integrated Manufacturing, 16*(4–5), 235–254.

Campell, J.L., Hollingsworth, J.R., & Lindberg, L.N. (Eds.). (1991). *The governance of the American economy.* New York: Cambridge University Press.

Cash, J.I., & Konsynski, B.R. (1985). IS redraws competitive boundaries. *Harvard Business Review, 63*(2), 131–142.

Christiaanse, E. (2005). Performance benefits through integration hubs. *Communications of the ACM, 48*(4), 95–100.

Christopher, M. (2000). The agile supply chain—competing in volatile markets. *Industrial Marketing Management, 29*(1), 37–44.

Clemons, E.K., & Row, M.C. (1992). Information technology and industrial cooperation: The role of changing transaction costs. *Journal of Management Information Systems, 9*(2), 9–28.

Davidow, W.H., & Malone, M.S. (1992). *The virtual corporation.* New York: HarperCollins.

Eisenhardt, K.M. (1989). Building theories from case study research. *Academy of Management Review, 14*(4), 532–550.

Evans, P., & Wurster, T.S. (2000). *Blown to bits: How the new economics of information transforms strategy.* Boston: Harvard Business School Press.

Feller, J., Finnegan, P., Hayes, J., & Lundell, B. (2006a, June 8–10). Business models for open source software: Towards a mature understanding of the concept and its implications for practice. *Proceedings of the IFIP 2.13 Conference on Open Source Software,* Genoa, Italy.

Feller, J., Finnegan, P., Kelly, D., & MacNamara, M. (2006b, July 12–15). Developing open source software: A community-based analysis of research. *Proceedings of the IFIP 8.2 Working Conference on Social Exclusion—Societal and Organisational Implications for Information Systems,* Limerick, Ireland.

Fingar, P. (2000). Component-based frameworks for e-commerce. *Communications of the ACM, 43*(10), 61–66.

Finnegan, P., Galliers, R.D., & Powell, P. (2003). Applying triple loop learning to planning electronic trading systems. *Information Technology and People, 16*(4), 461–483.

Fitzgerald, B. (2006). The transformation of open source software. *MIS Quarterly, 30*(3), 587–598.

Galaskiewicz, J. (1985). Interorganisational relations. *Annual Review of Sociology, 11,* 281–304.

Goldman, S.L., Nagel, R.N., & Preiss, K. (1995). *Agile competitors and virtual organizations: Strategies for enriching the customer.* New York: Van Nostrand Reinhold.

Hecker, F. (2000). *Setting up shop: The business of open-source software.* Retrieved from *http://www.hecker.org/writings/setting-up-shop*

Henderson, J.C. (1990). Plugging into strategic partnerships: The critical IS connection. *Sloan Management Review, 30*(3), 7–18.

Huang, C. (2001). Using intelligent agents to manage fuzzy business processes. *IEEE Transactions on Systems, Man, and Cybernetics—Part A: Systems and Humans, 31*(6), 508–523.

Joynt, P. (1991). International dimensions of managing technology. *Journal of General Management, 16*(3), 73–84.

Kanter, R.M. (1989). The future of bureaucracy and hierarchy in organizational theory: A report from the field. In P. Bourdieu & J. Coleman (Eds.), *Social theory for a changing society.* Boulder, CO: Westview.

Kaufman, F. (1966). Data systems that cross company boundaries. *Harvard Business Review, 44*(1), 141–155.

Kirsch, L.J. (2004). Deploying common systems globally: The dynamics of control. *Information Systems Research, 15*(4), 375–395.

Krishnamurthy, S. (2005). An analysis of open source business models. In J. Feller, B. Fitzgerald, S. Hissam, & K. Lakhani (Eds.), *Perspectives on free and open source software.* Cambridge, MA: MIT Press.

Lee, A.S., & Baskerville, R.L. (2003). Generalizing generalizability in information systems research. *Information Systems Research, 14*(3), 221–243.

Lee, H. (2004). The triple-a supply chain. *Harvard Business Review, 82*(10), 102–112.

Lei, D., & Slocum, J.W. (1992). Global strategy, competence-building and strategic alliances. *California Management Review, 35*(1), 81–97.

Lo, W.K. (1998). Agility, job satisfaction and organizational excellence: Their factors and relationships. *Third Proceedings of ISO 9000 and Total Quality Management* (pp. 330–336).

Madill, A., Jordan, A., & Shirley, C. (2000). Objectivity and reliability in qualitative analysis: Realist, contextualist and radical constructionist epistemologies. *British Journal of Psychology, 91*(1), 1–20.

Mahadevan, B. (2000). Business models for Internet-based e-commerce: An anatomy. *California Management Review, 42*(4), 55–69.

Marshall, C., & Rossman, B.G. (1989). *Designing qualitative research.* Thousand Oaks, CA: Sage.

Moore, G. (1999). *Crossing the chasm.* New York: Harper-Perennial.

Nelson, R.E. (1988). Social network analysis as intervention tool. *Group and Organisation Studies, 13*(1), 139–158.

Oliver, C. (1990). Determinants of interorganisational relationships: Integration and future directions. *Academy of Management Review, 15*(2), 241–265.

Osterwalder, A., & Pigneur, Y. (2002, June 17–19). An e-business model ontology for modelling e-business. *Proceedings of the 15th Bled eCommerce Conference,* Bled, Slovenia.

Osterwalder, A., Ben Lagha, S., & Pigneur, Y. (2002, July 3–7). An ontology for developing e-business models. *Proceedings of IFIP DSIAge 2002,* Cork, Ireland.

Patton, M.Q. (1980). *Qualitative evaluation and research methods.* Newbury Park, CA: Sage.

Raymond, E.S. (2001). *The cathedral and the bazaar* (2nd ed.). Sebastopol, CA: O'Reilly.

Sadeh, N.M., Hildum D.W., & Kjenstad, D. (2003). Agent-based e-supply chain decision support. *Journal of Organizational Computing and Electronic Commerce, 13*(3–4), 225–241.

Sharifi, H., & Zhang, Z. (1999). A methodology for achieving agility in manufacturing organisations: An introduction. *International Journal of Production Economics, 62*(1–2), 7–22.

Spiller, D., & Wichmann, T. (2002). *Basics of open source software markets and business models. FLOSS final report—part 3.* Berlin: Berlecon Research.

Stabell, C.B., & Fjeldstad, O.D. (1998). Configuring value for competitive advantage: On chains, shops, and networks. *Strategic Management Journal, 19*(5), 413–437.

Stafford, T. (2002). Trust, transactions, and relational exchange: Virtual integration and agile supply chain management. *Proceedings of the 8th Americas Conference on Information Systems* (AMCIS '02).

Tapscott, D., Ticoll, D., & Lowy, A. (2000). *Digital capital: Harnessing the power of business webs.* Cambridge, MA: Harvard Business School Press.

Thomke, E., & Reinertsen, D.G. (1998). Agile product development: Managing development flexibility in uncertain environments. *California Management Review, 41*(1), 8–30.

Ticoll, D., Lowy, A., & Kalakota, R. (1998). Joined at the bit: The emergence of the e-business community. In D. Tapscott (Ed.), *Blueprint to the digital economy: Creating wealth in the era of e-business.* New York: McGraw-Hill.

Timmers, P. (1999). *Electronic commerce: Strategies and models for business-to-business trading.* Chichester: John Wiley & Sons.

Van de Ven, A.H. (1976). On the nature, formation and maintenance of relations among organisations. *Academy of Management Review, 1*(4), 24–36.

Watson, R.T., Wynn, D., & Boudreau, M. (2005). Jboss: The evolution of professional open source software. *MIS Quarterly Executive, 4*(3), 329–341.

Weber, S. (2004). *The success of open source.* Cambridge, MA: Harvard University Press.

West, J. (2003). How open is open enough? Melding proprietary and open source platform strategies. *Research Policy, 32*(7), 1259–1285.

Woods, D., & Guliani, G. (2005). *Open source for the enterprise.* Sebastopol, CA: O'Reilly.

Yin, R.K. (1994). *Case study research, design and methods.* Newbury Park, CA: Sage.

ENDNOTE

[1] Raymond (2001) first articulated the much cited contrast between the hierarchical cathedral model characterizing proprietary software and the distributed model of the open source bazaar.

This work was previously published in Journal of Database Management, Vol. 19, Issue 2, edited by K. Siau, pp. 95-108, copyright 2008 by IGI Publishing, formerly known as Idea Group Publishing (an imprint of IGI Global).

Index

A

B

Q

R

S